Microsoft® Excel 2002

Illustrated Complete

Elizabeth Eisner Reding
Lynn Wermers

Australia • Canada • Mexico • Singapore • Spain • United Kingdom • United States

Microsoft Excel 2002 - Illustrated Complete

Elizabeth Eisner Reding
Lynn Wermers

Managing Editor:
Nicole Jones Pinard

Production Editor:
Karen Jacot

QA Manuscript Reviewers:
John Freitas, Ashlee Welz, Alex White, Harris Bierhoff, Serge Palladino, Holly Schabowski, Jeff Schwartz, Marianne Broughey

Product Manager:
Emily Heberlein

Developmental Editor:
Barbara Clemens

Text Designer:
Joseph Lee, Black Fish Design

Associate Product Manager:
Emeline Elliott

Editorial Assistant:
Christina Kling Garrett

Composition House:
GEX Publishing Services

Printed in the United States of America

5 6 7 8 9 BM 05 04 03

For more information, contact Course Technology, 25 Thomson Place, Boston, Massachusetts, 02210.

Or you can visit us on the World Wide Web at www.course.com

ISBN 0-619-04505-1

The Illustrated Series Vision

Teaching and writing about computer applications can be extremely rewarding and challenging. How do we engage students and keep their interest? How do we teach them skills that they can easily apply on the job? As we set out to write this book, our goals were to develop a textbook that:

- works for a beginning student
- provides varied, flexible and meaningful exercises and projects to reinforce the skills
- serves as a reference tool
- makes your job as an educator easier, by providing resources above and beyond the textbook to help you teach your course

Our popular, streamlined format is based on advice from instructional designers and customers. This flexible design presents each lesson on a two-page spread, with step-by-step instructions on the left, and screen illustrations on the right. This signature style, coupled with high-caliber content, provides a comprehensive yet manageable introduction to Microsoft Excel 2002—it is a teaching package for the instructor and a learning experience for the student.

ACKNOWLEDGMENTS

Thanks to the reviewers who provided invaluable feedback and ideas to us, especially Judy Irvine and Glenn Rogers (Western Nevada Community College).

Elizabeth Eisner Reding
Creating a book of this magnitude is a team effort: I would like to thank my husband, Michael, for putting up with my ridiculous mood swings, Emily Heberlein, the project manager, and my development editors, Barbara Clemens and Kitty Pinard, for their insightful suggestions and corrections. I would also like to thank the production and editorial staff for all their hard work that made this project a reality.

Lynn Wermers
Thanks to my editor, Barbara Clemens, for her helpful suggestions and encouragement.

Preface

Welcome to *Microsoft Excel 2002–Illustrated Complete*. Each lesson in the book contains elements pictured to the right in the sample two-page spread.

► How is the book organized?

Two units on Microsoft Windows 2000 introduce students to basic operating system skills. The book is then organized into sixteen units on Excel, covering basic skills from creating, editing and formatting worksheets, through advanced skills.

► What kinds of assignments are included in the book? At what level of difficulty?

The lesson assignments use MediaLoft, a fictional chain of bookstore cafés, as the case study. The assignments on the blue pages at the end of each unit increase in difficulty. Project files and case studies, with many international examples, provide a great variety of interesting and relevant business applications for skills. Assignments include:

- **Concepts Reviews** include multiple choice, matching, and screen identification questions.
- **Skills Reviews** provide additional hands-on, step-by-step reinforcement.
- **Independent Challenges** are case projects requiring critical thinking and application of the skills learned in the unit. The Independent Challenges increase in difficulty, with the first Independent Challenge in each unit being the easiest (most step-by-step with detailed instructions). Independent Challenges 2 and 3 become increasingly open-ended, requiring more independent thinking and problem solving.
- **E-Quest Independent Challenges** are case projects with a Web focus. E-Quests require the use of the World Wide Web to conduct research to complete the project.
- **Visual Workshops** show a completed file and require that the file be created without any step-by-step guidance, involving problem solving and an independent application of the unit skills.

Each 2-page spread focuses on a single skill.

Concise text that introduces the basic principles in the lesson and integrates the brief case study (indicated by the paintbrush icon).

Excel 2002

Changing Attributes and Alignment

Attributes are styling formats such as bold, italics, and underlining that you can apply to affect the way text and numbers look in a worksheet. You can also change the alignment of labels and values in cells to be left, right, or center. You can apply attributes and alignment options from the Formatting toolbar or from the Alignment tab of the Format Cells dialog box. See Table C-2 for a list and description of the available attribute and alignment toolbar buttons. Now that you have applied new fonts and font sizes to his worksheet labels, Jim wants you to further enhance the worksheet's appearance by adding bold and underline formatting and centering some of the labels.

Steps

1. Press [Ctrl][Home] to move to cell A1, then click the **Bold button** on the Formatting toolbar
   The title appears in bold.
2. Select the range A3:J3, then click the **Underline button** on the Formatting toolbar
   Excel underlines the text in the column headings in the selected range.
3. Click cell A3, click the **Italics button** on the Formatting toolbar, then click
   The word "Type" appears in boldface italic type. Notice that the Bold, Italics, and Underline buttons are selected.
4. Click
   Excel removes italics from cell A3 but the bold and underline formatting attributes remain.
5. Select the range B3:J3, then click
   Bold formatting is added to the rest of the labels in the column headings. The title would look better if it were centered over the data columns.
6. Select the range A1:J1, then click the **Merge and Center button** on the Formatting toolbar
   The Merge and Center button creates one cell out of the 10 cells across the row, then centers the text in that newly created large cell. The title "MediaLoft NYC Advertising Expenses" is centered across the 10 columns you selected. You can change the alignment within individual cells using toolbar buttons; you can split merged cells into their original components by selecting the merged cells, then clicking .
7. Select the range A3:J3, then click the **Center button** on the Formatting toolbar
   Compare your screen to Figure C-7. Although they may be difficult to read, notice that all the headings are centered within their cells.
8. Click the **Save button** on the Standard toolbar

QuickTip
Overuse of any attribute can be distracting and make a workbook less readable. Be consistent, adding emphasis the same way throughout.

QuickTip
Use formatting shortcuts on any selected range: [Ctrl][B] to bold, [Ctrl][I] to italicize, and [Ctrl][U] to underline.

QuickTip
To clear all formatting, click Edit on the menu bar, point to Clear, then click Formats.

Rotating and indenting cell entries

In addition to applying fonts and formatting attributes, you can rotate or indent cell data within a cell to further change its appearance. You can rotate text within a cell by altering its alignment. To change alignment, select the cells you want to modify, click Format on the menu bar, click Cells, then click the Alignment tab. Click a position in the Orientation box, or type a number in the degrees text box to change from the default horizontal alignment, then click OK. You can indent cell contents using the Increase Indent button on the Formatting toolbar, which moves cell contents to the right one space, or the Decrease Indent button , which moves cell contents to the left one space.

► EXCEL C-6 FORMATTING A WORKSHEET

Hints as well as troubleshooting advice, right where you need it – next to the step itself.

Clues to Use boxes provide concise information that either expands on the major lesson skill or describes an independent task that in some way relates to the major lesson skill.

Quickly accessible summaries of key terms, toolbar buttons, or keyboard alternatives connected with the lesson material. Students can refer easily to this information when working on their own projects at a later time.

Every lesson features large, full-color representations of what the screen should look like as students complete the numbered steps.

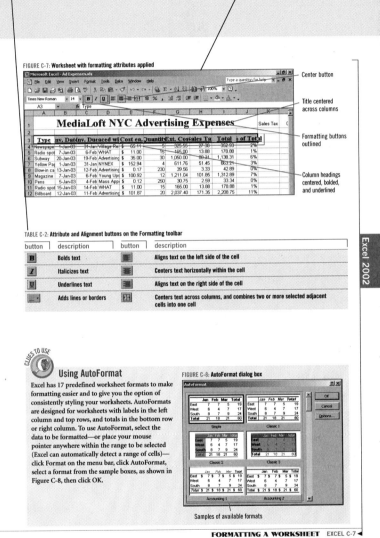

FIGURE C-7: **Worksheet with formatting attributes applied**

Center button

Title centered across columns

Formatting buttons outlined

Column headings centered, bolded, and underlined

TABLE C-2: **Attribute and Alignment buttons on the Formatting toolbar**

button	description	button	description
B	**Bolds text**		**Aligns text on the left side of the cell**
I	**Italicizes text**		**Centers text horizontally within the cell**
U	**Underlines text**		**Aligns text on the right side of the cell**
	Adds lines or borders		**Centers text across columns, and combines two or more selected adjacent cells into one cell**

CLUES TO USE

Using AutoFormat

Excel has 17 predefined worksheet formats to make formatting easier and to give you the option of consistently styling your worksheets. AutoFormats are designed for worksheets with labels in the left column and top rows, and totals in the bottom row or right column. To use AutoFormat, select the data to be formatted—or place your mouse pointer anywhere within the range to be selected (Excel can automatically detect a range of cells)—click Format on the menu bar, click AutoFormat, select a format from the sample boxes, as shown in Figure C-8, then click OK.

FIGURE C-8: **AutoFormat dialog box**

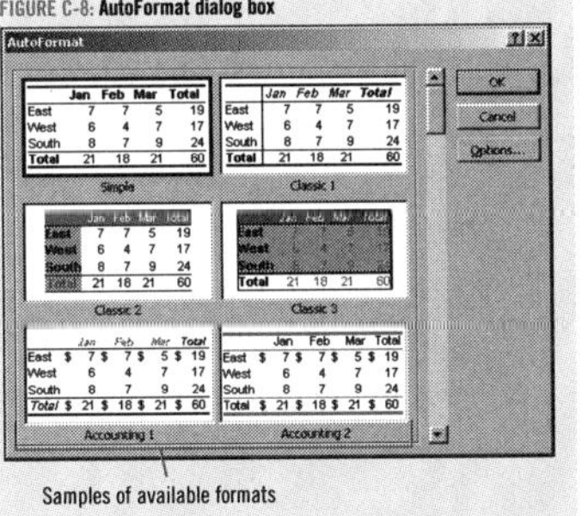

Samples of available formats

FORMATTING A WORKSHEET EXCEL C-7

The pages are numbered according to unit. C indicates the unit, 7 indicates the page.

Excel 2002

▶ Is this book MOUS Certified?

Microsoft Excel 2002 – Illustrated Complete covers the Core and Expert objectives for Excel and has received certification approval as courseware for the MOUS program. See the inside front cover for more information on other Illustrated titles meeting MOUS certification.

The first page of each unit includes MOUS symbols to indicate which skills covered in the unit are MOUS skills. A grid in the back of the book lists all the exam objectives and cross-references them with the lessons and exercises.

▶ What online content solutions are available to accompany this book?

MyCourse.com

Need a quick, simple tool to help you manage your course? Try MyCourse.com, the easiest to use, most flexible syllabus and content management tool available. MyCourse.com offers you brand new content, including Topic Reviews, Extra Case Projects, and Quizzes, to accompany this book.

WebCT

Course Technology and WebCT have partnered to provide you with the highest quality online resources and Web-based tools for your class. Course Technology offers content for this book to help you create your WebCT class, such as a suggested Syllabus, Lecture Notes, Practice Test questions, and more.

Blackboard

Course Technology and Blackboard have also partnered to provide you with the highest quality online resources and Web-based tools for your class. Course Technology offers content for this book to help you create your Blackboard class, such as a suggested Syllabus, Lecture Notes, Practice Test questions, and more.

Instructor Resources

The Instructor's Resource Kit (IRK) CD is Course Technology's way of putting the resources and information needed to teach and learn effectively into your hands. All the components are available on the IRK, (pictured below), and many of the resources can be downloaded from www.course.com.

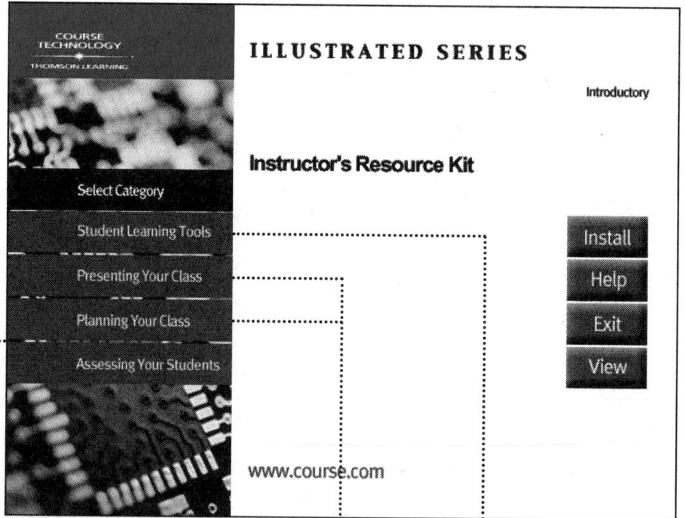

ASSESSING YOUR STUDENTS

Solution Files

Solution Files are Project Files completed with comprehensive sample answers. Use these files to evaluate your students' work. Or, distribute them electronically or in hard copy so students can verify their own work.

ExamView

ExamView is a powerful testing software package that allows you to create and administer printed, computer (LAN-based), and Internet exams. ExamView includes hundreds of questions that correspond to the topics covered in this text, enabling students to generate detailed study guides that include page references for further review. The computer-based and Internet testing components allow students to take exams at their computers, and also save you time by grading each exam automatically.

PRESENTING YOUR CLASS

Figure Files

Figure Files contain all the figures from the book in .jpg format. Use the figure files to create transparency masters or in a PowerPoint presentation.

STUDENT TOOLS

Project Files and Project Files List

To complete most of the units in this book, your students will need **Project Files**. Put them on a file server for students to copy. The Project Files are available on the Instructor's Resource Kit CD-ROM, the Review Pack, and can also be downloaded from www.course.com.

Instruct students to use the **Project Files List** at the end of the book. This list gives instructions on copying and organizing files.

PLANNING YOUR CLASS

Instructor's Manual

Available as an electronic file, the Instructor's Manual is quality-assurance tested and includes unit overviews, detailed lecture topics for each unit with teaching tips, comprehensive sample solutions to all lessons and end-of-unit material, and extra Independent Challenges. The Instructor's Manual is available on the Instructor's Resource Kit CD-ROM, or you can download it from www.course.com.

Sample Syllabus

Prepare and customize your course easily using this sample course outline (available on the Instructor's Resource Kit CD-ROM).

SAM, Skills Assessment Manager for Microsoft Office XP

SAM is the most powerful Office XP assessment and reporting tool that will help you gain a true understanding of your students' proficiency in Microsoft Word, Excel, Access, and PowerPoint 2002. (Available separately from the IRK CD.)

TOM, Training Online Manager for Microsoft Office XP

TOM is Course Technology's MOUS-approved training tool for Microsoft Office XP. Available via the World Wide Web and CD-ROM, TOM allows students to actively learn Office XP concepts and skills by delivering realistic practice through both guided and self-directed simulated instruction.

Brief Contents

Contents

Windows 2000

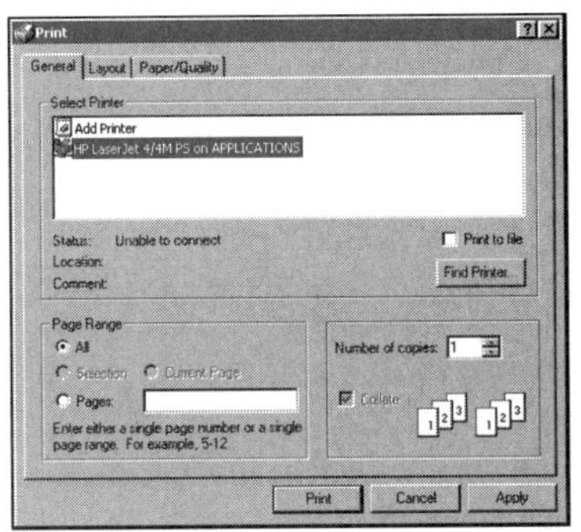

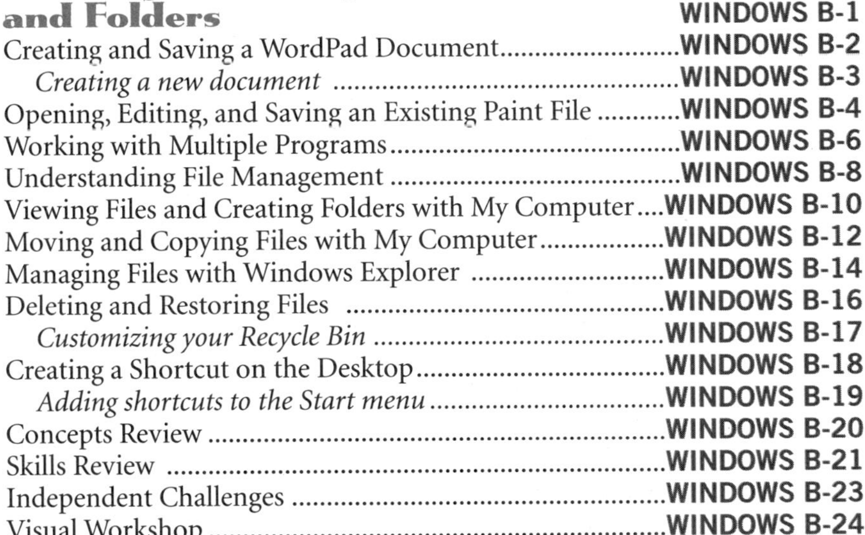

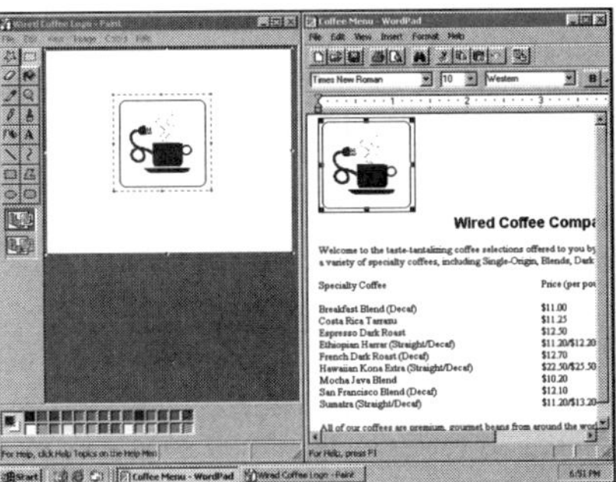

Contents

Excel 2002

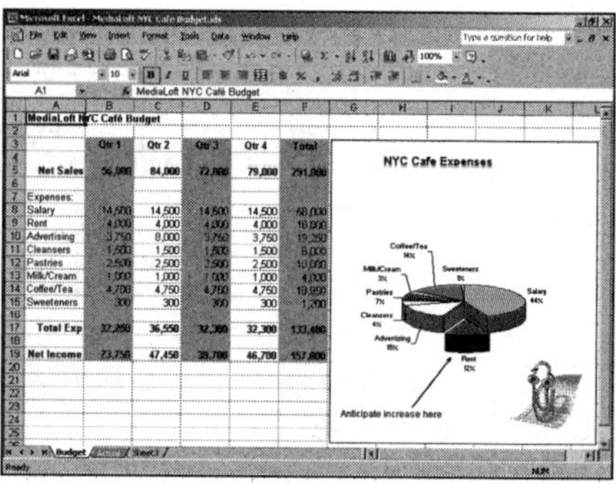

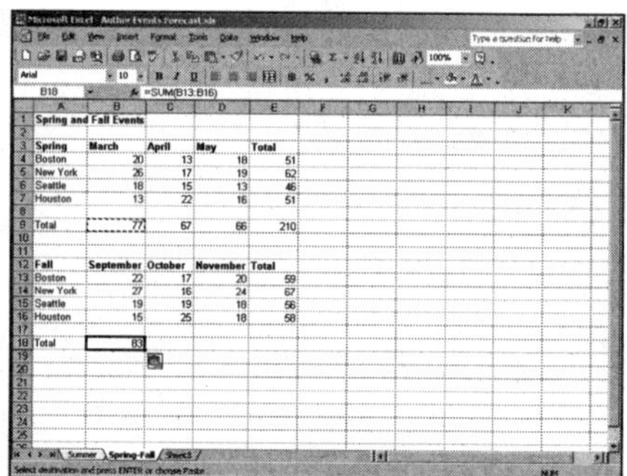

MediaLoft NYC Advertising Expenses

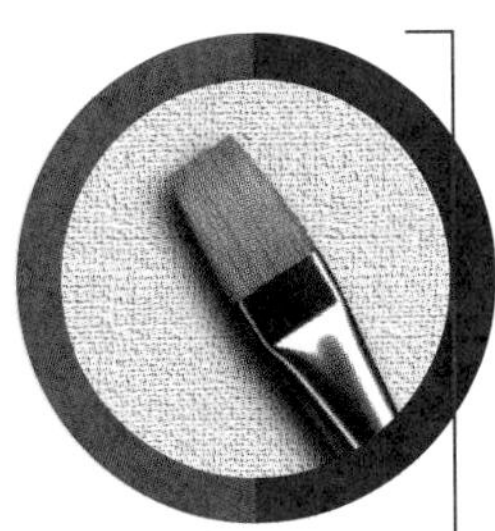

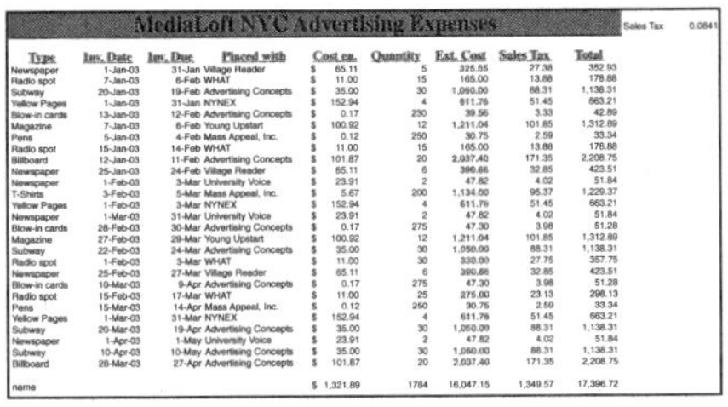

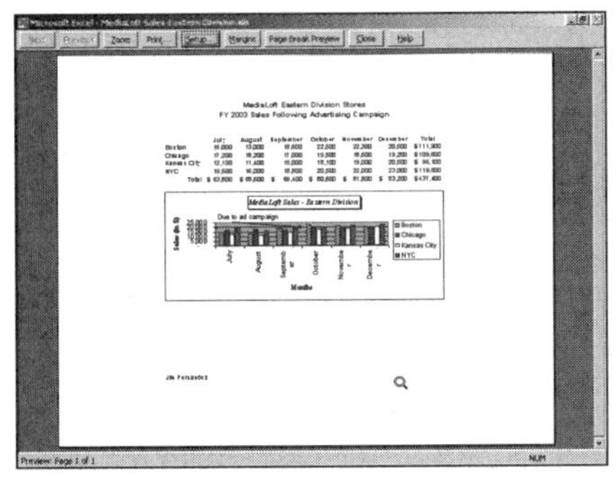

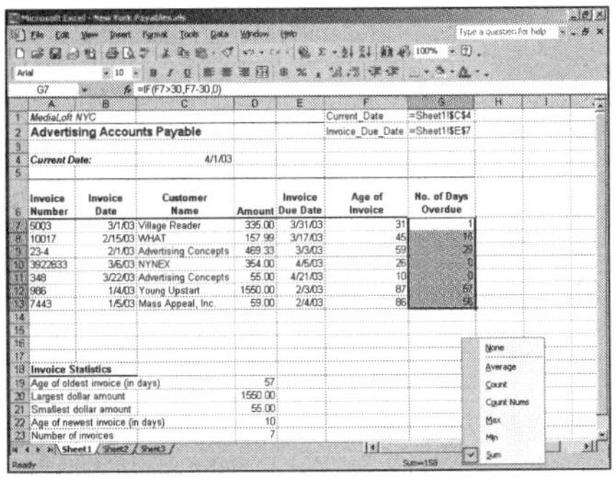

Contents

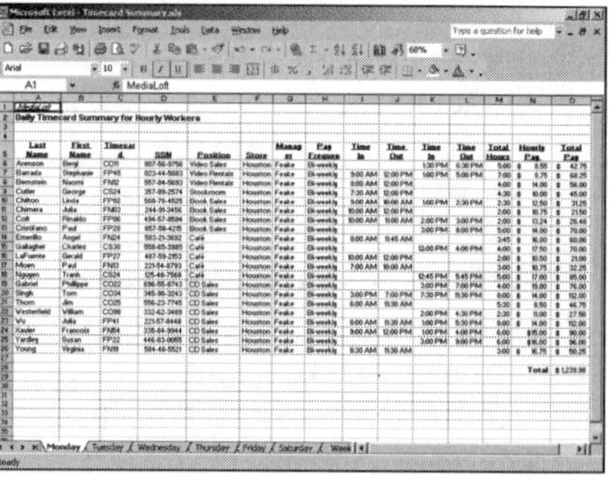

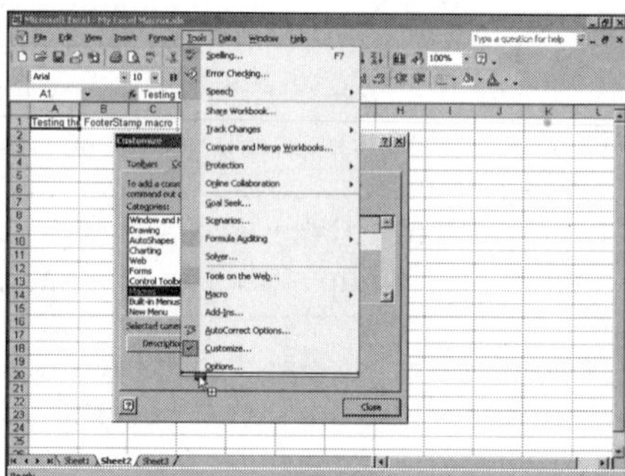

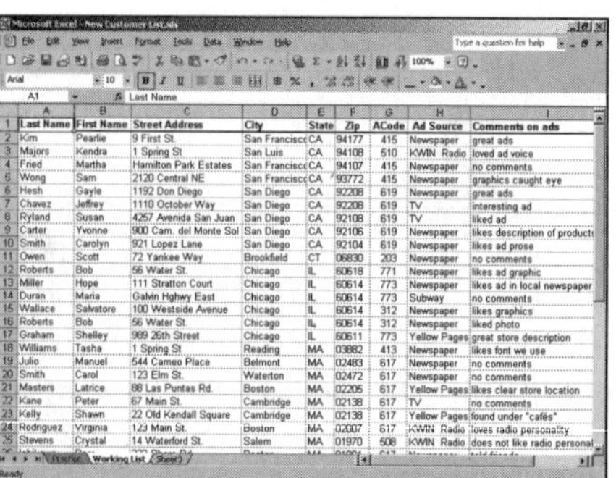

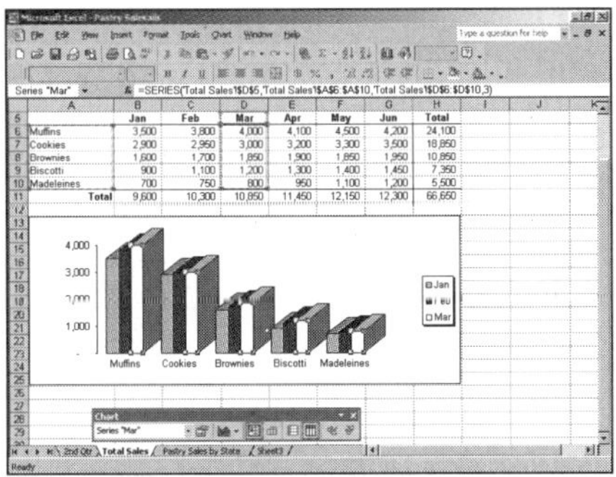

Contents

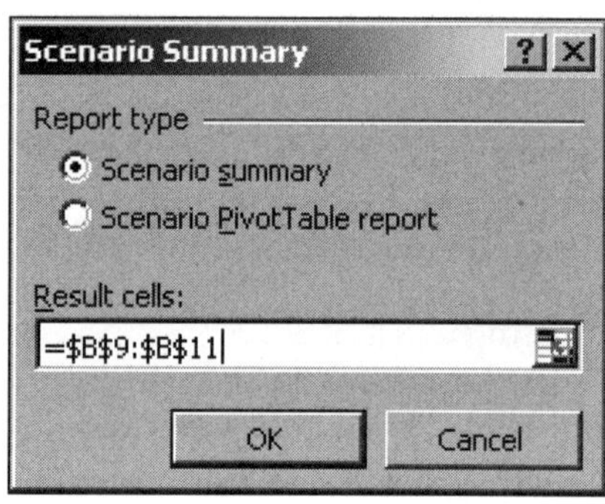

Scenario Summary
Report type
Scenario summary
Scenario PivotTable report
Result cells:
=$B$9:$B$11
OK
Cancel

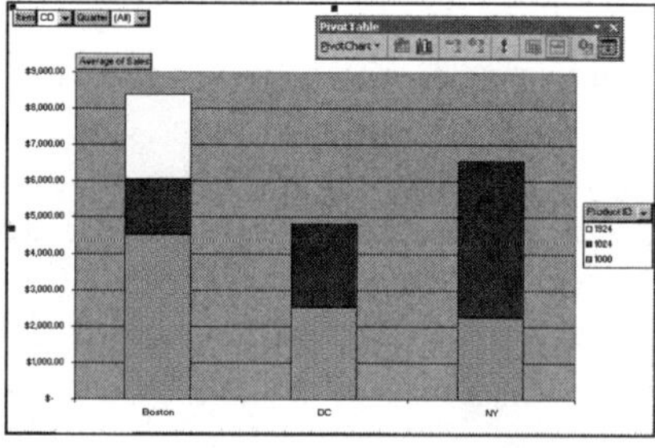

Boston
DC
NY

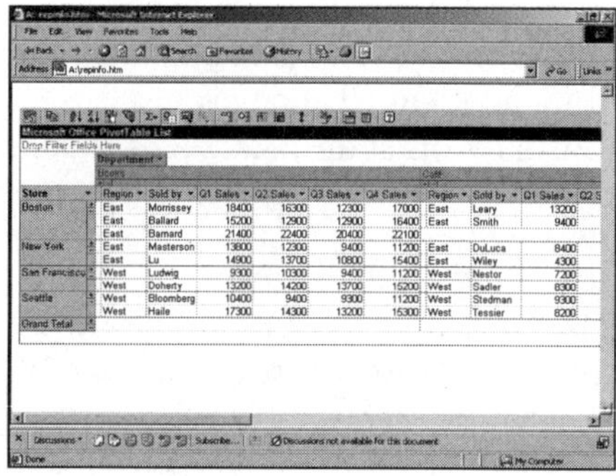

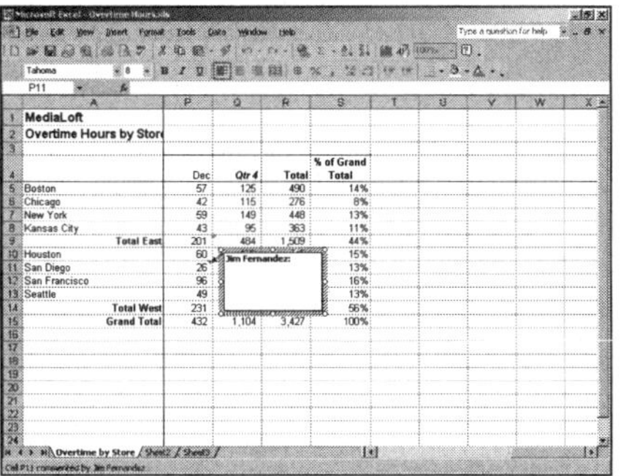

MediaLoft

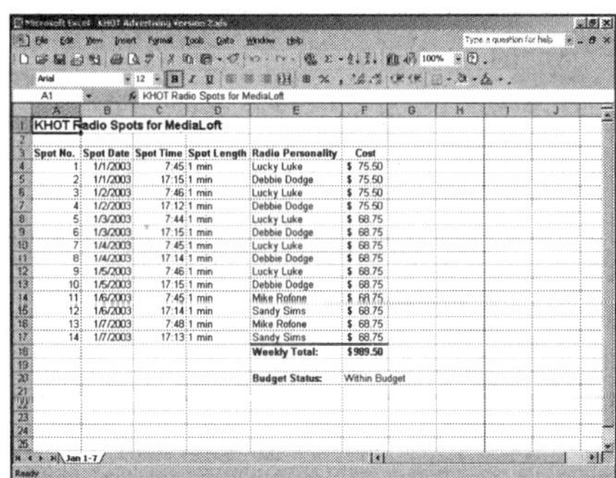

KHOT Radio Spots for MediaLoft

Read This Before You Begin

Software Information and Required Installation

This book was written and tested using Microsoft Office XP - Professional Edition, with a typical installation on Microsoft Windows 2000, with Internet Explorer 5.0 or higher. There are several instances where, in order to cover a software feature clearly, an additional feature not part of the typical installation is referenced. To insure that all the steps and exercises can be completed as written, make sure the following features are available before beginning these units:

- Unit A discusses Excel templates (not required for the lesson)
- Unit K requires the Solver Add-In
- Unit M assumes that students have Word, Access, and PowerPoint installed
- Unit O requires an Internet connection to get templates from www.microsoft.com

In units that require students to insert graphics from the Clip Gallery, this book assumes that students have a "live" Internet connection, which will automatically connect them to the Microsoft clip art collection. For those with dial-up connections to the Internet, they will see a reduced number of graphics, and can use any available graphic.

What are Project Files?

To complete many of the units in this book, you need to use Project Files. You use a Project File, which contains a partially completed document used in an exercise, so you don't have to type in all the information you need in the document. Your instructor will either provide you with a copy of the Project Files or ask you to make your own copy. Detailed instructions on how to organize you files, as well as a complete listing of all the files you'll need and will create, can be found in the back of the book (look for the yellow pages) in the Project Files List.

Why is my screen different from the book?

1. Your Desktop components and some dialog box options might be different if you are using an operating system other than Windows 2000
2. Depending on your computer hardware capabilities and the Windows Display settings on your computer, you may notice the following differences:
   - Your screen may look larger or smaller because of your screen resolution (the height and width of your screen)
   - The colors of the title bar in your screen may be a solid blue, and the cells in Excel may appear different from the purple and gray because of your color settings
3. Depending on your Office settings, your toolbars may display on a single row and your menus may display with a shortened list of frequently used commands. Office menus and toolbars can modify themselves to your working style by displaying only the most frequently used buttons and menu commands.

Toolbars on one row

To view buttons not currently displayed, click a Toolbar Options button at the end of either the Standard or Formatting toolbar. To view the full list of menu commands, click the double arrow at the bottom of the menu.

In order to have your toolbars display on two rows, showing all buttons, and to have the full menus display, you must turn off the personalized menus and toolbars feature. Click Tools on the menu bar, click Customize, select the show Standard and Formatting toolbars on two rows and Always show full menus check boxes on the Options tab, then click Close. This book assumes you are displaying toolbars on two rows and full menus.

Toolbars on two rows

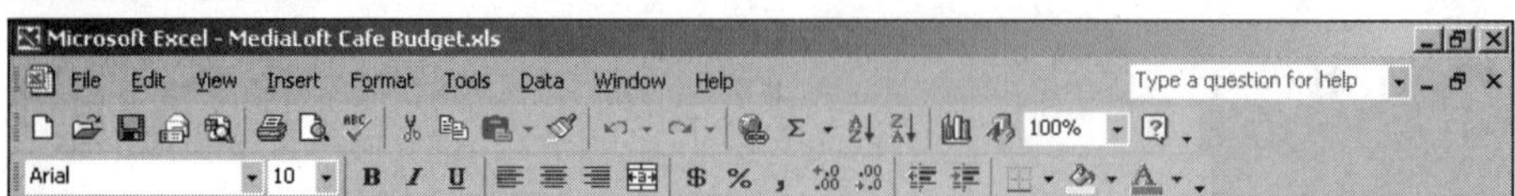

Getting Started with Windows 2000

Objectives

- Start Windows and view the Active Desktop
- Use the mouse
- Start a program
- Move and resize windows
- Use menus, keyboard shortcuts, and toolbars
- Use dialog boxes
- Use scroll bars
- Use Windows Help
- Close a program and shut down Windows

Microsoft Windows 2000 is an **operating system**, a computer **program**, or set of instructions, that controls how the computer carries out basic tasks such as displaying information on your computer screen and running programs. Windows 2000 helps you save and organize the results of your work as **files**, which are electronic collections of data. Windows 2000 also coordinates the flow of information among the programs, printers, storage devices, and other components of your computer system, as well as among other computers on a network. When you work with Windows 2000, you will notice many **icons**, small pictures intended to be meaningful symbols of the items they represent. You will also notice rectangular-shaped work areas known as **windows**, thus the name of the operating system. These icons, windows, and various other words and symbols create what is referred to as a **graphical user interface** (**GUI**, pronounced "gooey"), through which you interact with the computer. This unit introduces you to basic skills that you can use in all Windows programs.

Windows 2000

Starting Windows and Viewing the Active Desktop

When you turn on your computer, Windows 2000 automatically starts and the Active Desktop appears. The **Active Desktop**, shown in Figure A-1, is where you organize all the information and tools you need to accomplish your computer tasks. You can access, store, share, and explore information seamlessly, whether it resides on your computer, a network, or the **Internet**, a worldwide collection of over 40 million computers linked together to share information. The desktop is called "active" because it offers an interactive link between your computer and the Internet, so that Internet content displayed on your desktop, such as stock prices or weather information, is always up to date. When you start Windows for the first time, the desktop appears with the **default** settings, those preset by the operating system. For example, the default color of the desktop is blue. If any of the default settings have been changed on your computer, your desktop will look different than the one in the figures, but you should be able to locate all the items you need. The bar at the bottom of your screen is called the **taskbar**, which shows what programs are currently running. You use the Start menu, accessed by clicking the **Start button** at the left end of the taskbar, to perform such tasks as starting programs, finding and opening files, and accessing Windows Help. The **Quick Launch toolbar** is next to the Start button; it contains several buttons you can click to start Internet-related programs quickly, and another that you can click to show the desktop when it is not currently visible. Table A-1 identifies the icons and other elements you see on your desktop. If Windows 2000 is not currently running, follow the steps below to start it now.

Trouble?

If you don't know your password, see your instructor or technical support person.

1. **Turn on your computer and monitor**
   You might see a "Please select the operating system to start" prompt. Don't worry about selecting one of the options; Microsoft Windows 2000 Professional automatically starts after 30 seconds. When Windows starts and the desktop appears, you may see a Log On to Windows dialog box. If so, continue to Step 2. If not, view Figure A-1, then continue on to the next lesson.

Trouble?

If the Getting Started with Windows 2000 dialog box opens, move your mouse pointer over the Exit button in the lower-right corner of the dialog box and press the left mouse button once to close the dialog box.

2. **Enter the correct user name, type your password, then press [Enter]**
   Once the password is accepted, the Windows desktop appears on your screen. See Figure A-1.

Accessing the Internet from the Active Desktop

Windows 2000 provides a seamless connection between your desktop and the Internet with Internet Explorer. Internet Explorer is an example of a **browser,** a program designed to access the **World Wide Web** (also known as the **WWW**, or simply the **Web**). Internet Explorer is integrated with the Windows 2000 operating system. You can access it by clicking its icon on the desktop or on the Quick Launch toolbar. You can access Web pages, and place Web content such as weather or stock updates on the desktop for instant viewing. This information is updated automatically whenever you connect to the Internet, making your desktop truly active. You can also communicate electronically with other Internet users, using the Windows e-mail and newsreader program, Outlook Express.

FIGURE A-1: Windows Active Desktop

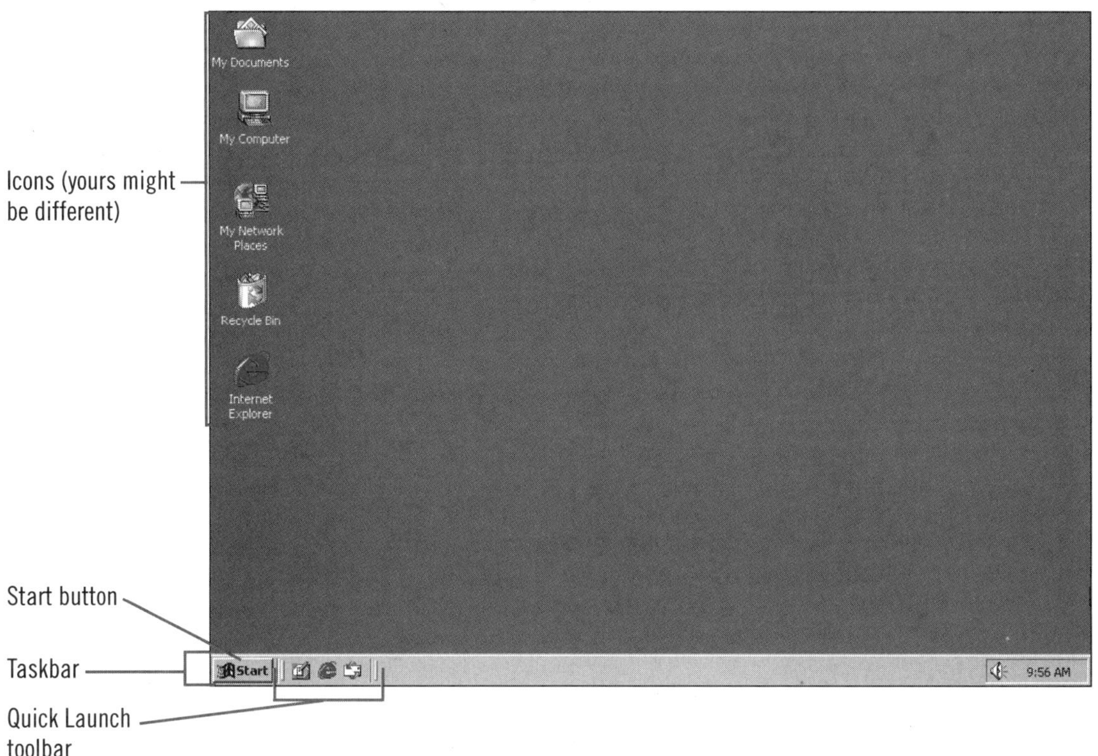

TABLE A-1: Elements of the Windows desktop

desktop element	icon	allows you to
My Documents folder		Store programs, documents, graphics, or other files
My Computer		Work with different disk drives and printers on your computer
My Network Places		Open files and folders on other computers and install network printers
Recycle Bin		Delete and restore files
Internet Explorer		Start Internet Explorer to access the Internet
Connect to the Internet		Set up Internet access
Start button	Start	Start programs, open documents, search for files, and more
Taskbar		Start programs and switch among open programs
Quick Launch toolbar		Start Internet Explorer, start Outlook Express, and display the desktop

Windows 2000

Using the Mouse

A **mouse** is a hand-held **input or pointing device** that you use to interact with your computer. Input or pointing devices come in many shapes and sizes; some, like a mouse, are directly attached to your computer with a cable; others function like a TV remote control and allow you to access your computer without being right next to it. Figure A-2 shows examples of common pointing devices. Because the most common pointing device is a mouse, this book uses that term. If you are using a different pointing device, substitute that device whenever you see the term "mouse." When you move the mouse, the **mouse pointer** on the screen moves in the same direction. The **mouse buttons** are used to select icons and commands, which is how you communicate with the computer. Table A-2 shows some common mouse pointer shapes that indicate different activities. Table A-3 lists the five basic mouse actions. Begin by experimenting with the mouse now.

Steps

1. **Locate the mouse pointer on the desktop, then move the mouse across your desk or mousepad**
   Watch how the mouse pointer moves on the desktop in response to your movements; practice moving the mouse pointer in circles, then back and forth in straight lines.
2. **Position the mouse pointer over the My Computer icon**
   Positioning the mouse pointer over an item is called **pointing**.
3. **With the pointer over the My Computer icon, press and release the left mouse button**
   Pressing and releasing the left mouse button is called **clicking** (or single-clicking, to distinguish it from double-clicking, which you'll do in Step 7). When you position the mouse pointer over an icon or any item and click, you select that item. When an item is **selected**, it is **highlighted** (shaded differently from other items), and the next action you take will be performed on that item.
4. **With the My computer icon selected, press and hold down the left mouse button, then move the mouse down and to the right and release the mouse button**
   The icon becomes dimmed and moves with the mouse pointer; this is called **dragging**, which you do to move icons and other Windows elements. When you release the mouse button, the item is positioned at the new location.
5. **Position the mouse pointer over the My Computer icon, then press and release the right mouse button**
   Clicking the right mouse button is known as **right-clicking**. Right-clicking an item on the desktop produces a **pop-up menu**, as shown in Figure A-3. This menu lists the commands most commonly used for the item you have clicked. A **command** is a directive that provides access to a program's features.
6. **Click anywhere outside the menu to close the pop-up menu**
7. **Position the mouse pointer over the My Computer icon, then quickly press and release the left mouse button twice**
   Clicking the mouse button twice quickly is known as **double-clicking**, which, in this case, opens the My Computer window. The **My Computer** window contains additional icons that represent the drives and system components that are installed on your computer.
8. **Click the Close button ☒ in the upper-right corner of the My Computer window**

Trouble?

If the My Computer window opens during this step, your mouse isn't set with the Windows 2000 default mouse settings. See your instructor or technical support person for assistance. This book assumes your computer is set to all Windows 2000 default settings.

QuickTip

When a step tells you to "click," use the left mouse button. If it says "right-click," use the right mouse button.

TABLE A-2: Common mouse pointer shapes

shape	used to
↖	Select items, choose commands, start programs, and work in programs
I	Position mouse pointer for editing or inserting text; called the insertion point
⧗	Indicate Windows is busy processing a command
↔	Change the size of a window; appears when mouse pointer is on the border of a window
☝	Select and open Web-based data

FIGURE A-2: Common pointing devices

FIGURE A-3: Displaying a pop-up menu

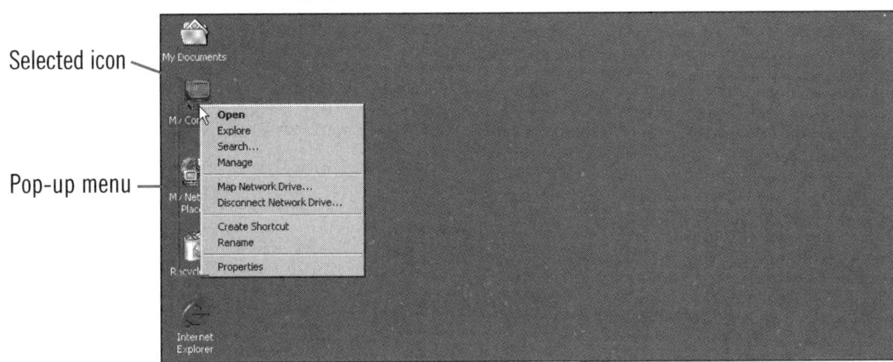

CLUES TO USE

More about the mouse: Classic style and Internet style

Because Windows 2000 integrates the use of the Internet with its other functions, it allows you to extend the way you click in a Web browser program on the Internet to the way you click in other computer programs. With the default Windows 2000 settings, you click an item to select it and double-click an item to open it. In a Web browser program, however, you point to an item to select it and single-click to open it. Windows 2000 gives you two choices for clicking: with the **Classic style**, you double-click to open items, and with the **Internet style**, you single-click to open items. To switch between styles, double-click the My Computer Icon (or click if you are currently using the Internet style), click Tools on the menu bar, click Folder Options, click the General tab if necessary, click the Single-click to Open an Item option or the Double-click to Open an Item option in the Click items as follows section, and then click OK.

TABLE A-3: Basic mouse techniques

technique	what to do
Pointing	Move the mouse to position the mouse pointer over an item on the desktop
Clicking	Press and release the left mouse button
Double-clicking	Press and release the left mouse button twice quickly
Dragging	Point to an item, press and hold the left mouse button, move the mouse to a new location, then release the mouse button
Right-clicking	Point to an item, then press and release the right mouse button

Starting a Program

Clicking the Start button on the taskbar opens the Start menu, which lists submenus for a variety of tasks described in Table A-4. As you become familiar with Windows, you might want to customize the Start menu to include additional items that you use most often. Windows 2000 comes with several built-in programs, called **accessories**. Although not as feature-rich as many programs sold separately, Windows accessories are useful for completing basic tasks. In this lesson, you start a Windows accessory called **WordPad**, which is a word-processing program you can use to create and edit simple documents.

Steps

1. Click the **Start button** on the taskbar
   The Start menu opens.
2. Point to **Programs**
   The Programs submenu opens, listing the programs and categories for programs installed on your computer. WordPad is in the category called Accessories.
3. Point to **Accessories**
   The Accessories menu, shown in Figure A-4, contains several programs to help you complete common tasks. You want to start WordPad. If you do not see WordPad, rest the mouse pointer over the double arrows at the bottom of Programs submenu and wait. The full menu will open after a few seconds.
4. Click **WordPad**
   WordPad opens with a blank document window open, as shown in Figure A-5. Don't worry if your window does not fill the screen; you'll learn how to maximize it in the next lesson. Note that a **program button** appears on the taskbar and is highlighted, indicating that WordPad is open.

QuickTip

Windows 2000 features personalized menus, which list only the commands you've most recently used. Whenever you want to view other commands available on the menu, rest the mouse pointer over the double arrows at the bottom of the menu.

TABLE A-4: Start menu categories

category	description
Windows Update	Connects to a Microsoft Web site and updates your Windows 2000 files as necessary
Programs	Displays a menu of programs included on the Start menu
Documents	Displays a menu of the most recently opened and recently saved documents
Settings	Displays a menu of tools for selecting settings for your system
Search	Locates programs, files, folders, people, or computers on your computer network, or finds information and people on the Internet
Help	Provides Windows Help information by topic, alphabetical index, or search criteria
Run	Opens a program or file based on a location and filename that you type or select
Shut Down	Provides options to log off, shut down, or restart the computer

FIGURE A-4: Cascading menus

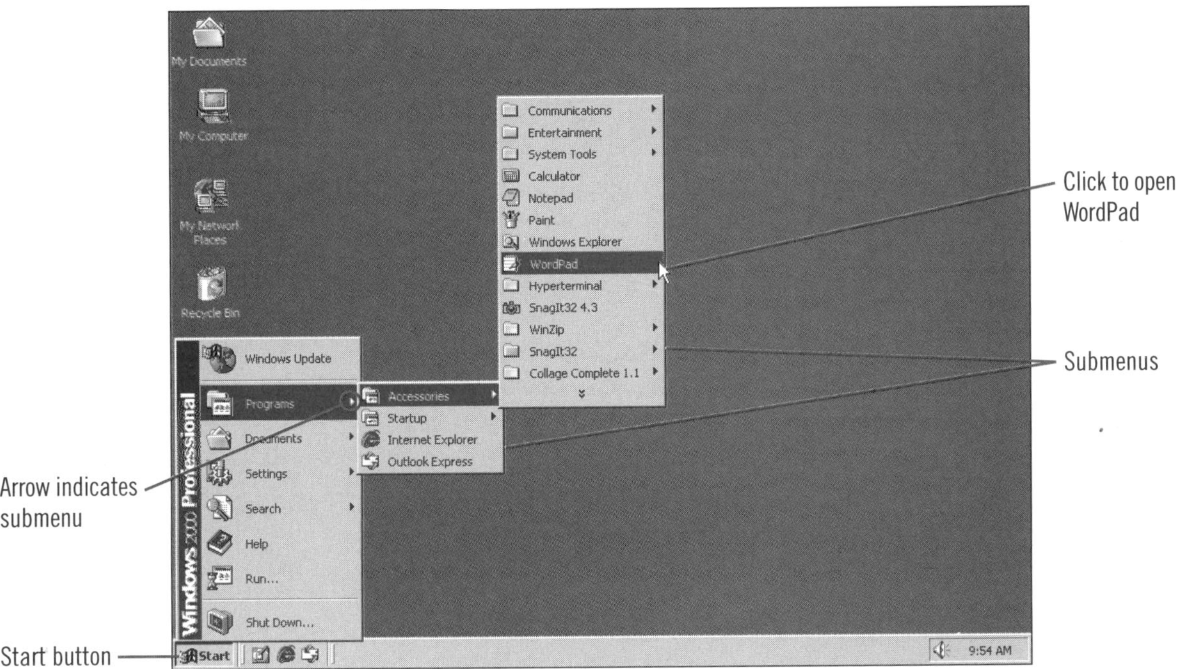

FIGURE A-5: WordPad program window

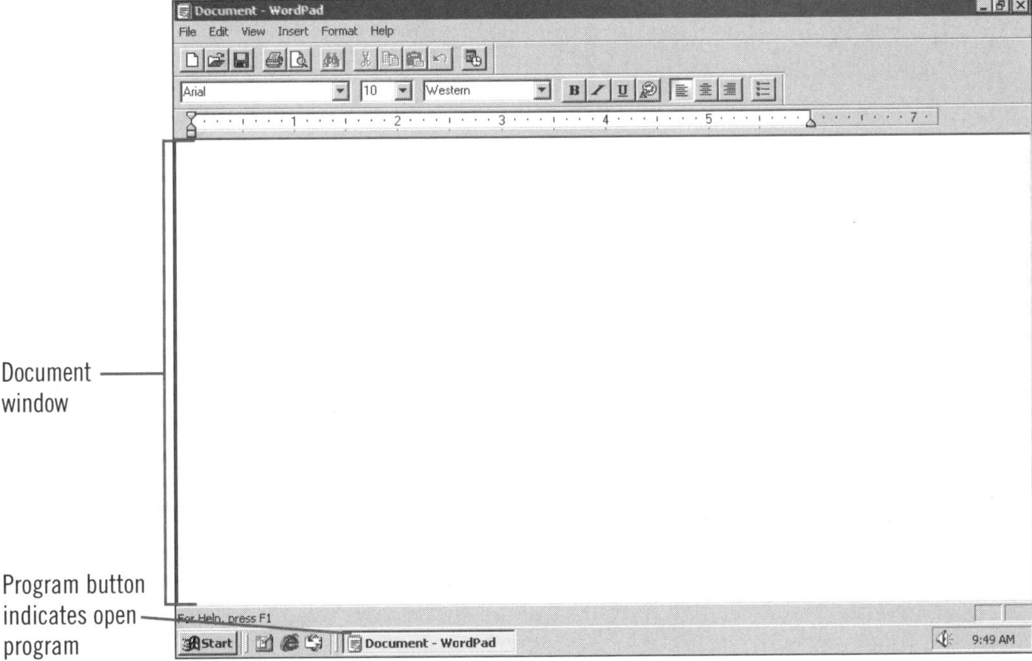

The Startup Folder

You can specify one or more programs to open each time you start Windows 2000 by placing shortcuts in the Startup Folder. This might be useful if you know you will be working in the same programs first thing every day. To place a program in the Startup Folder, click the Start button, point to Settings, then click Taskbar & Start Menu. Click the Advanced tab of the Taskbar and Start Menu Properties dialog box, click Advanced, and then, in the Start Menu folder, locate the shortcut to the program you want to specify, and drag it to the Startup folder.

Windows 2000

Moving and Resizing Windows

One of the powerful features of Windows is the ability to open more than one window or program at once. This means, however, that the desktop can get cluttered with the various programs and files you are using. You can keep your desktop organized by changing the size of a window or moving it. You can do this by clicking the sizing buttons in the upper-right corner of any window and dragging a corner or border of any window that does not completely fill the screen. Practice sizing and moving the WordPad window now.

Steps

1. **If the WordPad window does not already fill the screen, click the Maximize button in the WordPad window**
   When a window is **maximized**, it takes up the whole screen.
2. **Click the Restore button in the WordPad window**
   To **restore** a window is to return it to its previous size, as shown in Figure A-6. The Restore button only appears when a window is maximized.
3. **Position the pointer on the right edge of the WordPad window until the pointer changes to ↔, then drag the border to the right**
   The width of the window increases. You can size the height or width of a window by dragging any of the four sides individually.

QuickTip

You can resize windows by dragging any corner. You can also drag any border to make the window taller, shorter, wider, or narrower.

4. **Position the pointer in the lower-right corner of the WordPad window until the pointer changes to ↘, as shown in Figure A-6, then drag down and to the right**
   The height and width of the window increase proportionally when you drag a corner instead of a side. You can also position a restored window wherever you wish on the desktop by dragging its title bar. The **title bar** is the area along the top of the window that displays the file name and program used to create it.
5. **Drag the title bar on the WordPad window up and to the left, as shown in Figure A-6**
   The window is repositioned on the desktop. At times, you might wish to close a program window, yet keep the program running and easily accessible. You can accomplish this by minimizing a window.

QuickTip

If you have more than one window open and you want to quickly access something on the desktop, you can click the Show Desktop button on the Quick Launch toolbar. All open windows are minimized so the desktop is visible.

6. **In the WordPad window, click the Minimize button**
   When you **minimize** a window, it shrinks to a program button on the taskbar, as shown in Figure A-7. WordPad is still running, but it is out of your way.
7. **Click the WordPad program button on the taskbar to reopen the window**
   The WordPad program window reopens.
8. **Click the Maximize button in the upper-right corner of the WordPad window**
   The window fills the screen.

FIGURE A-6: Restored program window

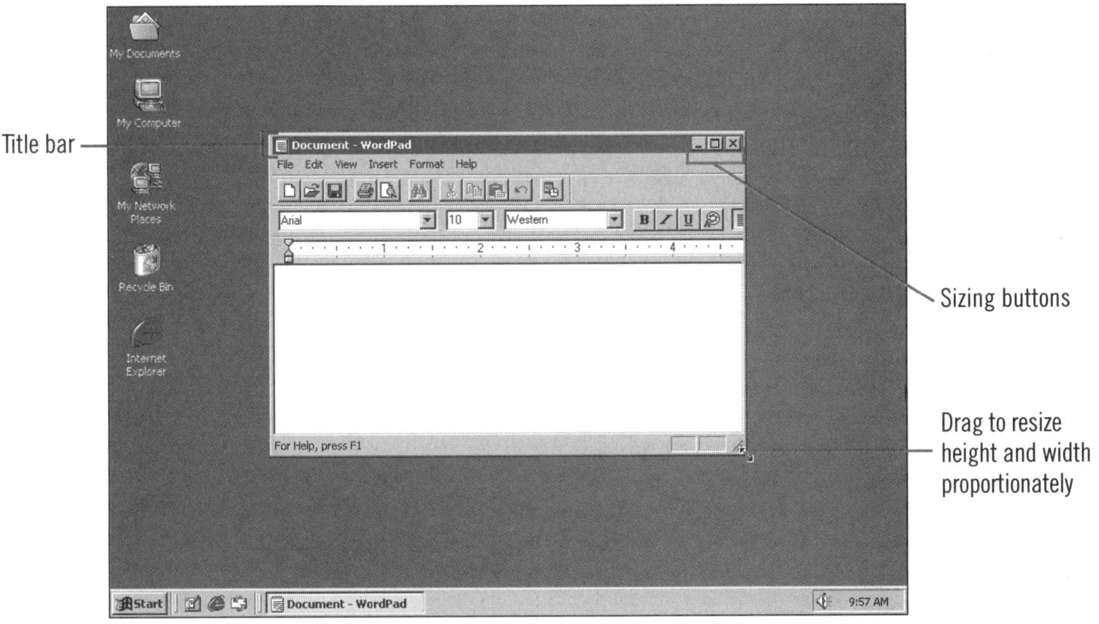

FIGURE A-7: Minimized program window

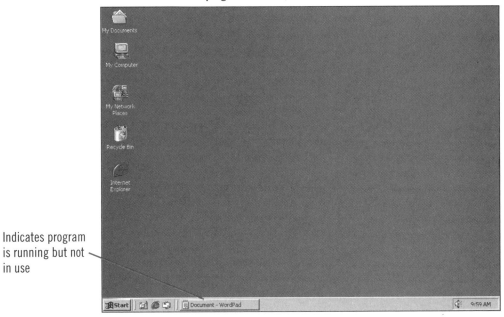

CLUES TO USE

More about sizing windows

Keep in mind that many programs contain two sets of sizing buttons: one that controls the program window itself and another that controls the window for the file with which you are working. The program sizing buttons are located in the title bar and the file sizing buttons are located below them. See Figure A-8. When you minimize a file window within a program, the file window is reduced to an icon in the lower-left corner of the program window, but the size of the program window remains intact.

FIGURE A-8: Program and file sizing buttons

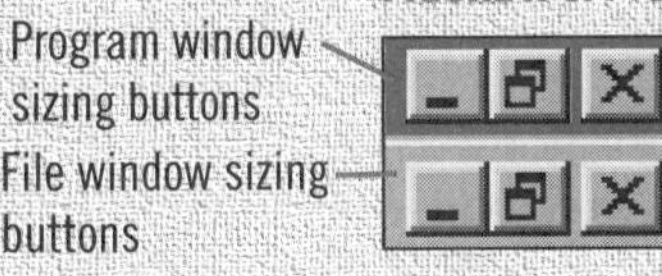

Windows 2000

Using Menus, Keyboard Shortcuts, and Toolbars

A **menu** is a list of commands that you use to accomplish certain tasks. You've already used the Start menu to start WordPad. Each Windows program also has its own set of menus, which are located on the **menu bar** under the title bar. The menus organize commands into groups of related operations. See Table A-5 for a description of items on a typical menu. **Toolbar buttons** offer another method for executing menu commands; instead of clicking the menu and then the menu command, you simply click the button for the command. A **toolbar** is a set of buttons usually positioned below the menu bar in a Windows program. In Windows 2000, you can customize a toolbar by adding buttons to or removing buttons from toolbars to suit your preferences. You will open the Control Panel, then use a menu and toolbar button to change how the contents of the window appear, and then add and remove a toolbar button.

Steps

QuickTip

You now have two windows open: WordPad and the Control Panel. The Control Panel is the active window (or active program) because it is the one with which you are currently working. WordPad is inactive because it is open but you are not working with it. Working with more than one window at a time is called multitasking.

1. Click the **Start button** on the taskbar, point to **Settings**, then click **Control Panel**
   The Control Panel window opens over the WordPad window. The **Control Panel** contains icons for various programs that allow you to specify how your computer looks and performs.
2. Click **View** on the menu bar
   The View menu appears, listing the View commands, as shown in Figure A-9. On a menu, a **check mark** identifies a feature that is currently enabled or "on." To disable or turn "off" the feature, you click the command again to remove the check mark. A **bullet mark** can also indicate that an option is enabled. To disable a bulleted option, you must select another option in its place.
3. Click **Small Icons**
   The icons are now smaller than they were before, taking up less room in the window.
4. Press **[Alt][V]** to open the View menu, then press **[T]** to execute the Toolbars command
   The View menu appears again, and then the Toolbars submenu appears, with checkmarks next to the commands that are currently selected. You opened these menus using the keyboard. Notice that a letter in each command on the View menu is underlined. These are **keyboard navigation indicators**, indicating that you can press the underlined letter, known as a **keyboard shortcut**, instead of clicking to execute the command.
5. Press **[C]** to execute the Customize command
   The Customize Toolbar dialog box opens. A dialog box is a window in which you make specifications for how you want a task performed; you'll learn more about working in a dialog box shortly. In the Customize Toolbar dialog box, you can add toolbar buttons to the current toolbar, or remove buttons already on the toolbar. The list on the right shows which buttons are currently on the toolbar, and the list on the left shows which buttons are available to add.
6. Click the **Favorites button** in the Available toolbar buttons section, then click the **Add button**
   As shown in Figure A-10, the Favorites button is added to the Standard toolbar of the Control Panel window.
7. Click **Favorites** in the Current toolbar buttons section, click the **Remove button**, then click **Close** on the Customize Toolbar dialog box
   The Favorites button disappears from the Standard toolbar, and the Customize Toolbar dialog box closes.
8. On the Control Panel toolbar, click the **Views button list arrow**
   Some toolbar buttons have an arrow, which indicates the button contains several choices. Clicking the button shows the choices.
9. In the list of View choices, click **Details**
   The Details view includes a description of each program in the Control Panel.

QuickTip

When you rest the pointer over a button without clicking, a Screentip appears, telling you the name of the button.

FIGURE A-9: Opening a menu

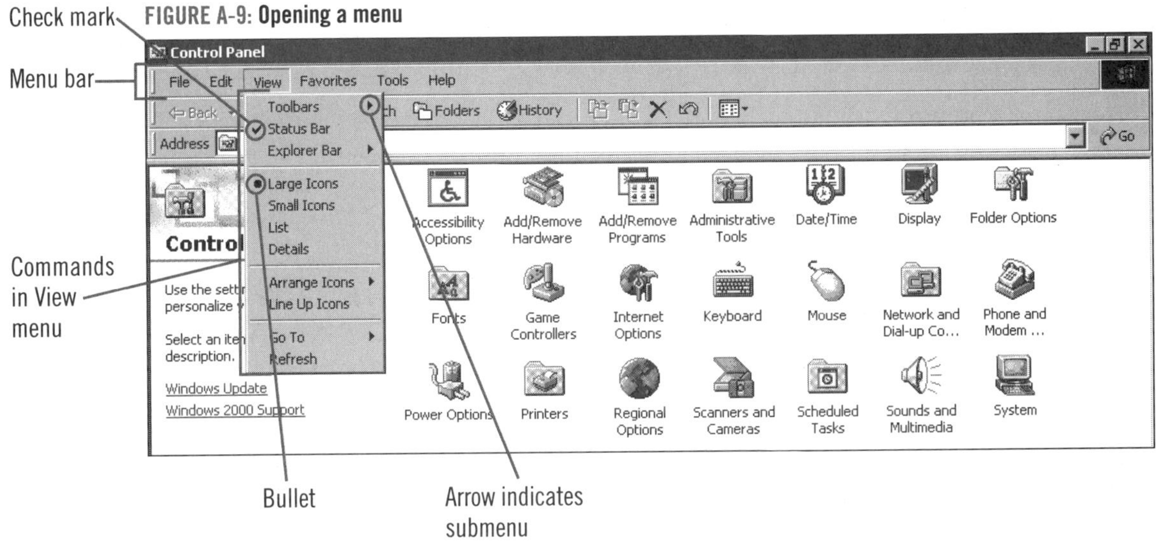

FIGURE A-10: Customize Toolbar dialog box

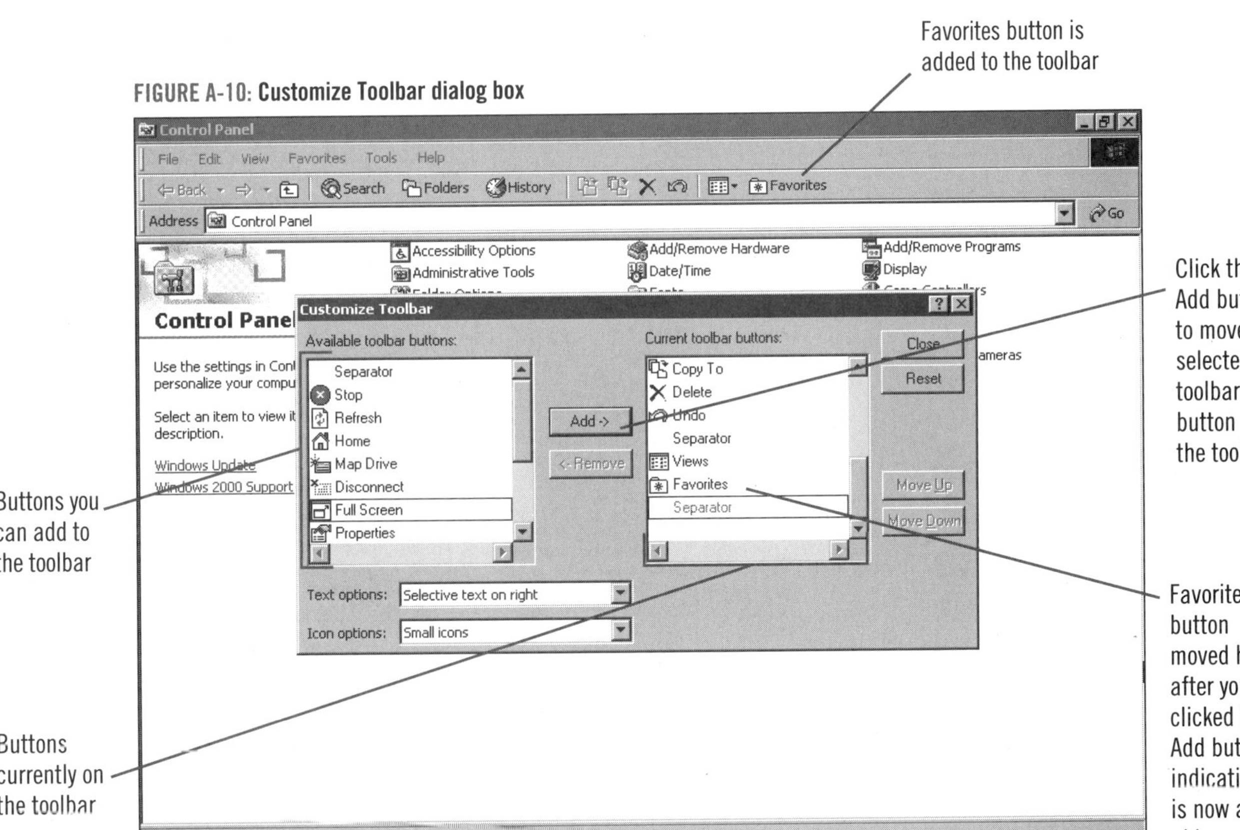

TABLE A-5: Typical items on a menu

item	description	example
Dimmed command	Indicates the menu command is not currently available	Undo Ctrl+Z
Ellipsis	Opens a dialog box that allows you to select different or additional options	Save As...
Triangle	Opens a cascading menu containing an additional list of commands	Zoom ▸
Keyboard shortcut	Executes a command using the keyboard instead of the mouse	Paste Ctrl+V
Underlined letter	Indicates the letter to press for the keyboard shortcut	Print Preview

Windows 2000

Using Dialog Boxes

A **dialog box** is a window that opens when you choose a menu command that is followed by an ellipsis (…), or any command that needs more information before the program can carry out the command you selected. Dialog boxes open in other situations as well, such as when you open a program in the Control Panel. See Figure A-11 and Table A-6 for some of the typical elements of a dialog box. Practice using a dialog box to control your mouse settings.

Trouble?

If you can't see the Mouse icon, resize the Control Panel window.

1. **In the Control Panel window, double-click the Mouse icon**
   The Mouse Properties dialog box opens, as shown in Figure A-12. **Properties** are characteristics of a specific computer element (in this case, the mouse) that you can customize. The options in this dialog box allow you to control the way the mouse buttons are configured, select the types of pointers that appear, choose the speed of the mouse movement on the screen, and specify what type of mouse you are using. **Tabs** at the top of the dialog box separate these options into related categories.

2. **Click the Motion tab if necessary to make it the front-most tab**
   This tab contains three options for controlling the way your mouse moves. Under Speed, you can set how fast the pointer moves on the screen in relation to how you move the mouse. You drag a **slider** to specify how fast the pointer moves. Under Acceleration, you can click an **option button** to adjust how much your pointer accelerates as you move it faster. When choosing among option buttons, you can select only one at a time. Under Snap to default, there is a **check box**, which is a toggle for turning a feature on or off—in this case, for setting whether or not you want your mouse pointer to move to the default button in dialog boxes.

3. **Under Speed, drag the slider all the way to the left for Slow, then move the mouse pointer across your screen**
   Notice how slowly the mouse pointer moves. After you select the options you want in a dialog box, you need to select a **command button**, which carries out the options you've selected. The two most common command buttons are OK and Cancel. Clicking OK accepts your changes and closes the dialog box; clicking Cancel leaves the original settings intact and closes the dialog box. The third command button in this dialog box is Apply. Clicking the Apply button accepts the changes you've made and keeps the dialog box open so that you can select additional options. Because you might share this computer with others, it's important to return the dialog box options back to the original settings.

QuickTip

You can also use the keyboard to carry out commands in a dialog box. Pressing [Enter] is the same as clicking OK; pressing [Esc] is the same as clicking Cancel.

4. **Click Cancel**
   The original settings remain intact and the dialog box closes.

FIGURE A-11: Elements of a typical dialog box

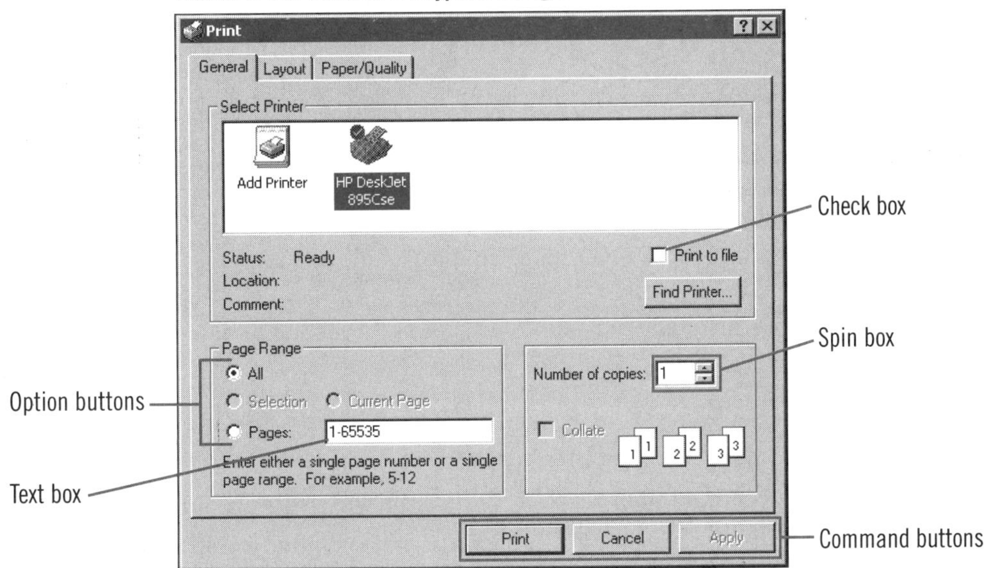

FIGURE A-12: Mouse Properties dialog box

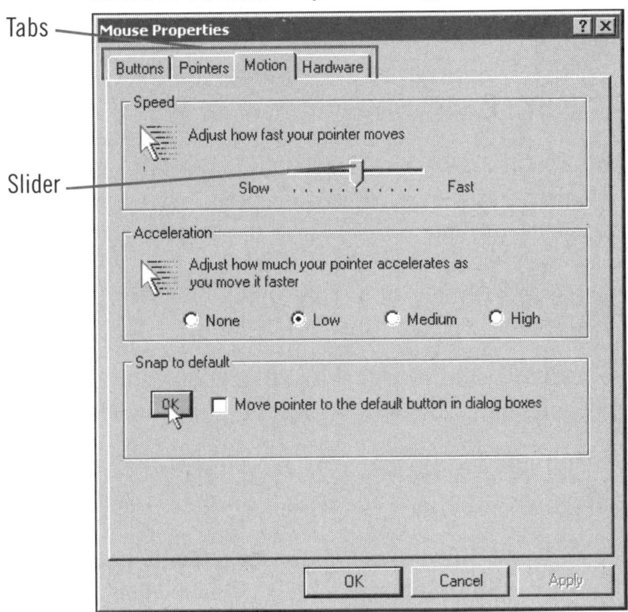

TABLE A-6: Typical items in a dialog box

item	description	item	description
Check box	A box that turns an option on (when the box is checked) and off (when it is unchecked)	**List box**	A box containing a list of items; to choose an item, click the list arrow, then click the desired item
Text box	A box in which you type text	**Spin box**	A box with two arrows and a text box; allows you to scroll in numerical increments or type a number
Option button	A small circle that you click to select a single dialog box option; you cannot check more than one option button in a list	**Slider**	A shape that you drag to set the degree to which an option is in effect
Command button	A rectangular button in a dialog box with the name of the command on it	**Tab**	A place in a dialog box where related commands and options are organized

Windows 2000

Using Scroll Bars

When you cannot see all of the items available in a window, scroll bars appear on the right and/or bottom edges of the window. **Scroll bars** allow you to view the additional contents of the window. There are several ways you can scroll in a window. When you need to scroll only a short distance, you can use the scroll arrows. To scroll the window in larger increments, click in the scroll bar above or below the scroll box. Dragging the scroll box moves you quickly to a new part of the window. See Table A-7 for a summary of the different ways to use scroll bars. With the Control Panel window in Details view, you can use the scroll bars to view all of the items in this window.

Steps 1 2 3 4

1. **In the Control Panel window, drag the lower-right corner of the dialog box up toward the upper-left corner until the scroll bars appear, as shown in Figure A-13**
   Scroll bars appear only when the window is not large enough to include all the information. After you resize the dialog box, they appear along the bottom and right side of the dialog box. You may have to size your window smaller than the one in the figure for your scroll bars to appear.
2. **Click the down scroll arrow, as shown in Figure A-13**
   Clicking this arrow moves the view down one line.
3. **Click the up scroll arrow in the vertical scroll bar**
   Clicking this arrow moves the view up one line.
4. **Click anywhere in the area below the scroll box in the vertical scroll bar**
   The view moves down one window's height. Similarly, you can click in the scroll bar above the scroll box to move up one window's height.
5. **Drag the scroll box all the way down to the bottom of the vertical scrollbar**
   The view now includes the items that appear at the very bottom of the window.
6. **Drag the scroll box all the way up to the top of the vertical scroll bar**
   This view shows the items that appear at the top of the window.
7. **Click the area to the right of the scroll box in the horizontal scroll bar**
   The far right edge of the window comes into view. The horizontal scroll bar works the same as the vertical scroll bar.
8. **Click the area to the left of the scroll box in the horizontal scroll bar**
   You should return the Control Panel to its original settings.
9. **Maximize the Control Panel window, click the Views button list arrow on the Control Panel toolbar, then click Large Icons**

QuickTip

The size of the scroll box changes to reflect how much information does not fit in the window. A larger scroll box indicates that a relatively small amount of the window's contents is not currently visible; you need to scroll only a short distance to see the remaining items. A smaller scroll box indicates that a relatively large amount of information is currently not visible.

FIGURE A-13: Scroll bars

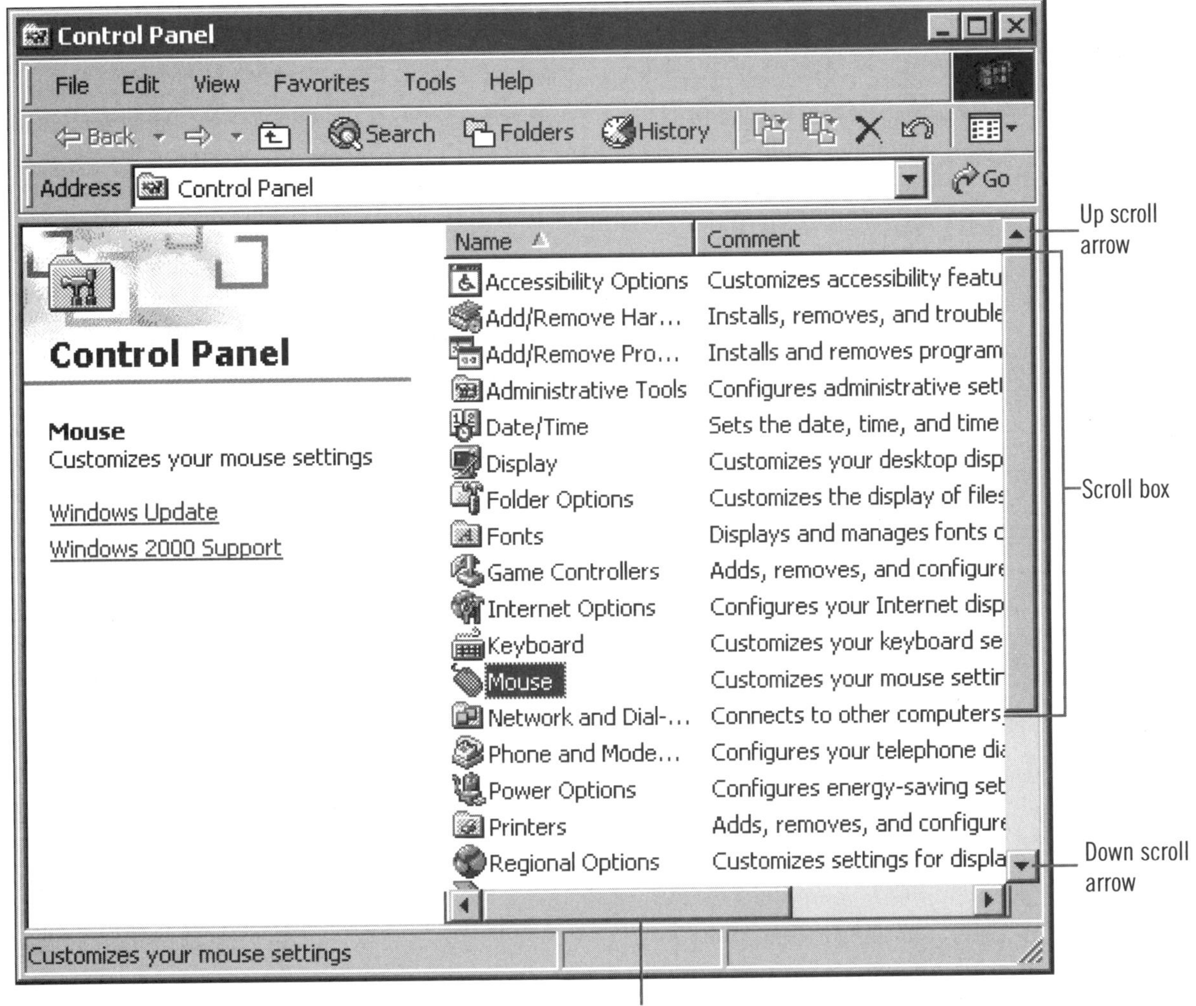

TABLE A-7: Using scroll bars in a window

to	do this
Move down one line	Click the down arrow at the bottom of the vertical scroll bar
Move up one line	Click the up arrow at the top of the vertical scroll bar
Move down one window height	Click in the area below the scroll box in the vertical scroll bar
Move up one window height	Click in the area above the scroll box in the vertical scroll bar
Move up a large distance in the window	Drag the scroll box up in the vertical scroll bar
Move down a large distance in the window	Drag the scroll box down in the vertical scroll bar
Move a short distance side-to-side in a window	Click the left or right arrows in the horizontal scroll bar
Move to the right one window width	Click in the area to the right of the scroll box in the horizontal scroll bar
Move to the left one window width	Click in the area to the left of the scroll box in the horizontal scroll bar
Move left or right a large distance in the window	Drag the scroll box in the horizontal scroll bar

Windows 2000

Using Windows Help

When you have a question about how to do something in Windows 2000, you can usually find the answer with a few clicks of your mouse. **Windows Help** works like a book stored on your computer, with a table of contents and an index to make finding information easier. Help provides guidance on many Windows features, including detailed steps for completing procedures, definitions of terms, lists of related topics, and search capabilities. You can browse or search for information in the Help window, or you can connect to a Microsoft Web site on the Internet for the latest technical support on Windows 2000. You can also access **context-sensitive help**, help specifically related to what you are doing, using a variety of methods such as right-clicking an object or using the question mark button in a dialog box. In this lesson, you get Help on starting a program. You also get information on the taskbar.

Steps 1 2 3 4

1. **Click the Start button on the taskbar, then click Help**
   The Windows Help window opens with the Contents tab in front, as shown in Figure A-14. The Contents tab provides you with a list of Help categories. Each category contains two or more topics that you can see by clicking the book or the category next to it.

QuickTip

Click the Glossary category on the Contents tab to access definitions for hundreds of computer terms.

2. **Click the Contents tab if it isn't the front-most tab, click Working with Programs, then view the Help categories that are displayed**
   The Help window contains a selection of topics related to working with programs.
3. **Click Start a Program**
   Help information for this topic appears in the right pane, as shown in Figure A-15. **Panes** divide a window into two or more sections. At the bottom of the text in the right pane, you can click Related Topics to view a list of topics that may also be of interest to you. Some Help topics also allow you to view additional information about important words; these words are underlined, indicating that you can click them to display a pop-up window with the additional information.
4. **Click the underlined word taskbar, read the definition, then press [Enter] or click anywhere outside the pop-up window to close it**
5. **In the left pane, click the Index tab**
   The Index tab provides an alphabetical list of all the available Help topics, like an index at the end of a book. You can type a topic in the text box at the top of the pane. As you type, the list of topics automatically scrolls to try to match the word or phrase you type. You can also scroll down to the topic. In either case, the topic appears in the right pane.
6. **In the left pane, click the Search tab**
   You can use the Search tab to locate a Help topic using keywords. You enter a word or phrase in the text box and click List Topics; a list of matching topics appears below the text box. To view a topic, double-click it or select the topic, then click Display.
7. **In the left pane, click the Favorites tab**
   You can add the To Start a Program topic, or any other displayed topic, to the Favorites tab of the Help window by simply clicking the Favorites tab, then clicking the Add button.
8. **Click the Web Help button on the toolbar**
   Information on the Web site for Windows 2000 Help appears in the right pane (a **Web site** is a document or related documents that contain highlighted words, phrases, and graphics that link to other sites on the Internet). To access online support or information, click one of the available options.

QuickTip

To get help on a specific Windows program, click Help on the program's menu bar.

9. **Click the Close button in the upper-right corner of the Windows Help window**
   The Help window closes.

FIGURE A-14: Windows Help window

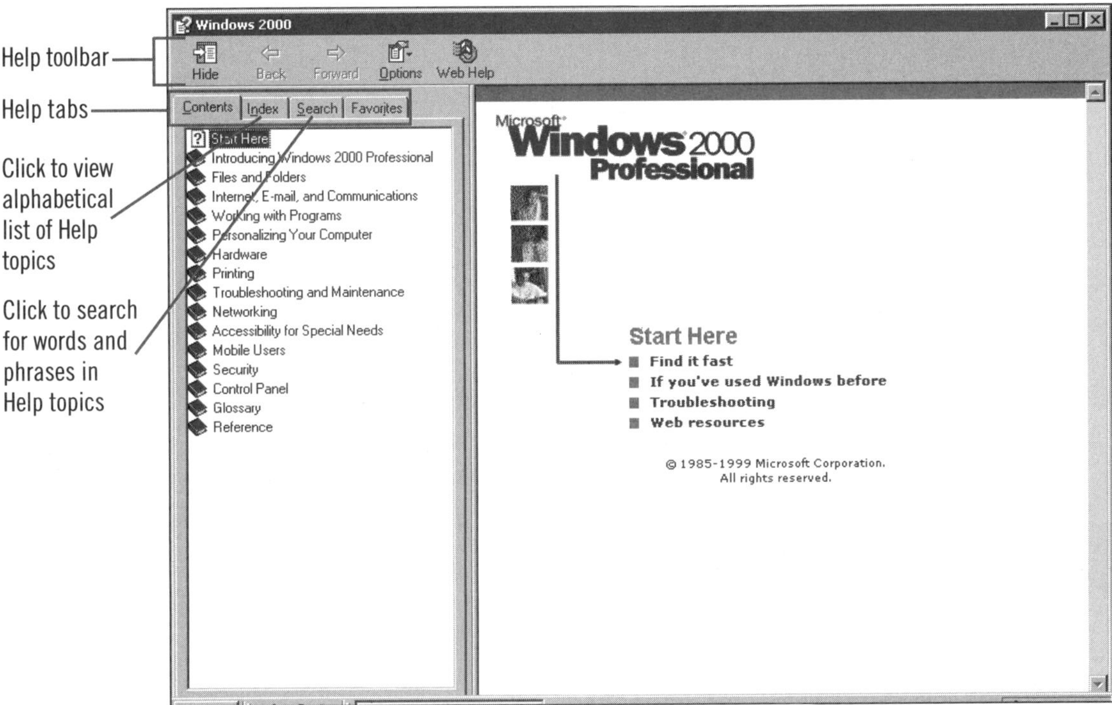

FIGURE A-15: Viewing a Help topic

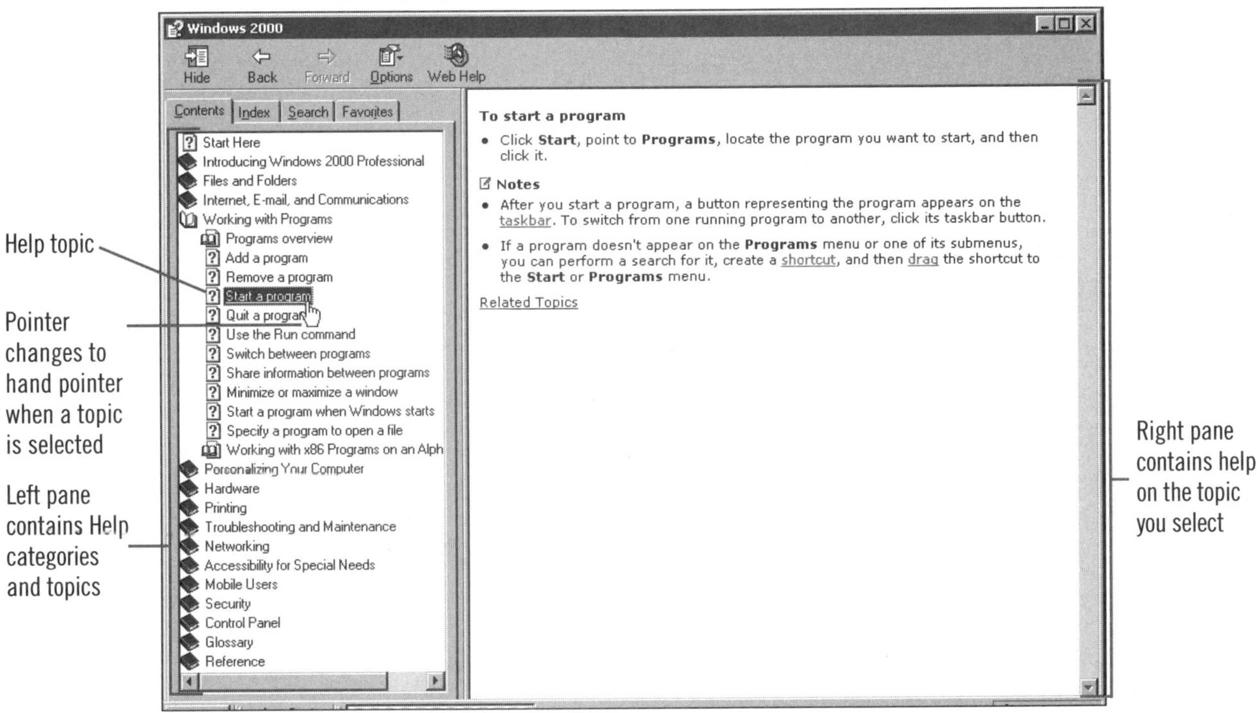

Context-sensitive help

To receive help in a dialog box, click the Help button in the upper-right corner of the dialog box; the mouse pointer changes to ?. Click the Help pointer on the item for which you need additional information. A pop-up window provides a brief explanation of the selected feature. You can also right-click the button on an item in a dialog box, then click the What's This? button to view the Help explanation.

Windows 2000

Closing a Program and Shutting Down Windows

When you are finished working on your computer, you need to make sure you shut it down properly. This involves several steps: saving and closing all open files, closing all the open programs and windows, shutting down Windows, and finally, turning off the computer. If you turn off the computer while Windows is running, you could lose important data. To **close** programs, you can click the Close button in the window's upper-right corner or click File on the menu bar and choose either Close or Exit. To shut down Windows after all your files and programs are closed, click Shut Down from the Start menu, then select the desired option from the Shut Down dialog box, shown in Figure A-16. See Table A-8 for a description of shut down options.

Close all your open files, windows, and programs, then exit Windows.

Steps

1. In the Control Panel window, click the **Close button** in the upper-right corner of the window
   The Control Panel window closes.
2. Click **File** on the WordPad menu bar, then click **Exit**
   If you have made any changes to the open file, you will be prompted to save your changes before the program quits. Some programs also give you the option of choosing the Close command on the File menu in order to close the active file but leave the program open, so you can continue to work in it with a different file. Also, if there is a second set of sizing buttons in the window, the Close button on the menu bar will close the active file only, leaving the program open for continued use.
3. If you see a message asking you to save changes to the document, click **No**
   WordPad closes and you return to the desktop.
4. Click the **Start Button** on the taskbar, then click **Shut Down**
   The Shut Down Windows dialog box opens, as shown in Figure A-16. In this dialog box, you have the option to log off, shut down the computer, or restart the computer.
5. Click the **What do you want the computer to do? list arrow**
6. If you are working in a lab, click the **list arrow** again and click **Cancel** to leave the computer running; if you are working on your own machine or if your instructor told you to shut down Windows, click **Shut down**, then click **OK**
7. If you see the message "It is now safe to turn off your computer," turn off your computer and monitor
   On some computers, the power shuts off automatically, so you may not see this message.

QuickTip

Complete the remaining steps to shut down Windows and your computer only if you have been told to do so by your instructor or technical support person.

FIGURE A-16: Shut Down Windows dialog box

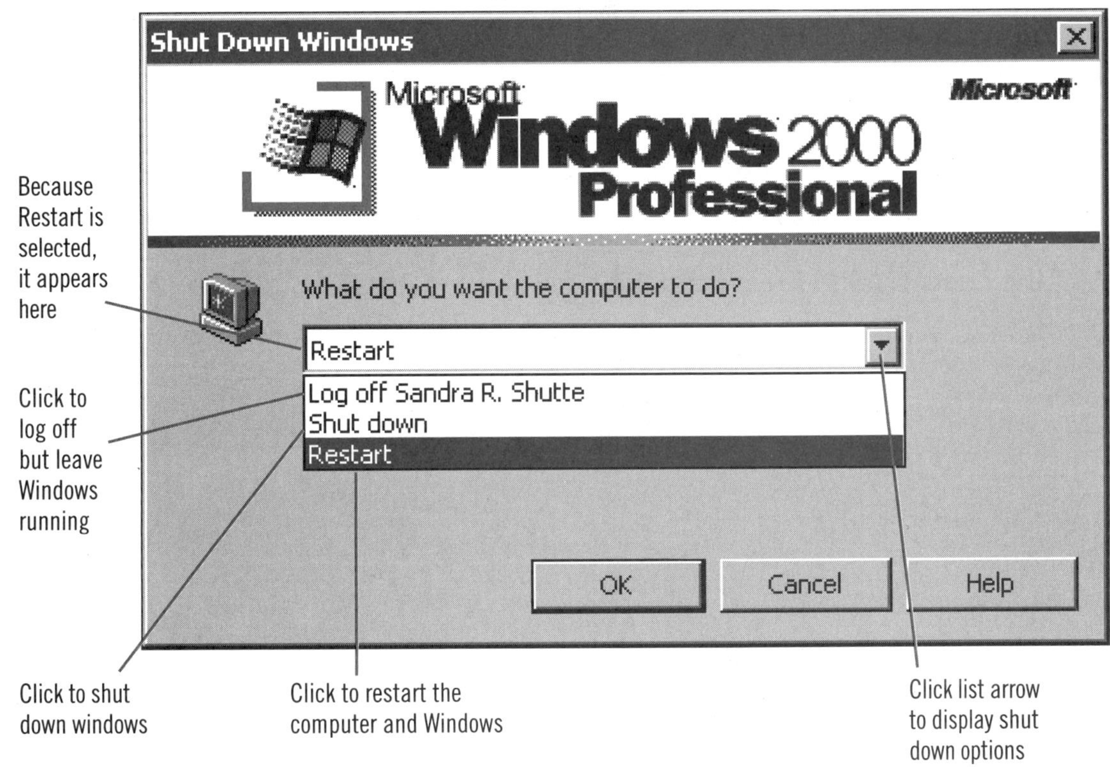

The Log Off command

To change users on the same computer quickly, you can choose the Log Off command from the Shut Down Windows dialog box. When you choose this command, the current user is logged off and Windows 2000 shuts down and automatically restarts, stopping at the point where you need to enter a password. When the new user enters a user name and password, Windows restarts and the desktop appears as usual.

TABLE A-8: Shut down options

shut down option	function	when to use it
Shut down	Prepares the computer to be turned off	When you are finished working with Windows and you want to shut off your computer
Restart	Restarts the computer and reloads Windows	When you want to restart the computer and begin working with Windows again (your programs might have frozen or stopped working)
Log off	Ends your session, then reloads Windows for another user	When you want to end your session but leave the computer running for another user

Practice

► Concepts Review

Identify each of the items labeled in Figure A-17.

FIGURE A-17

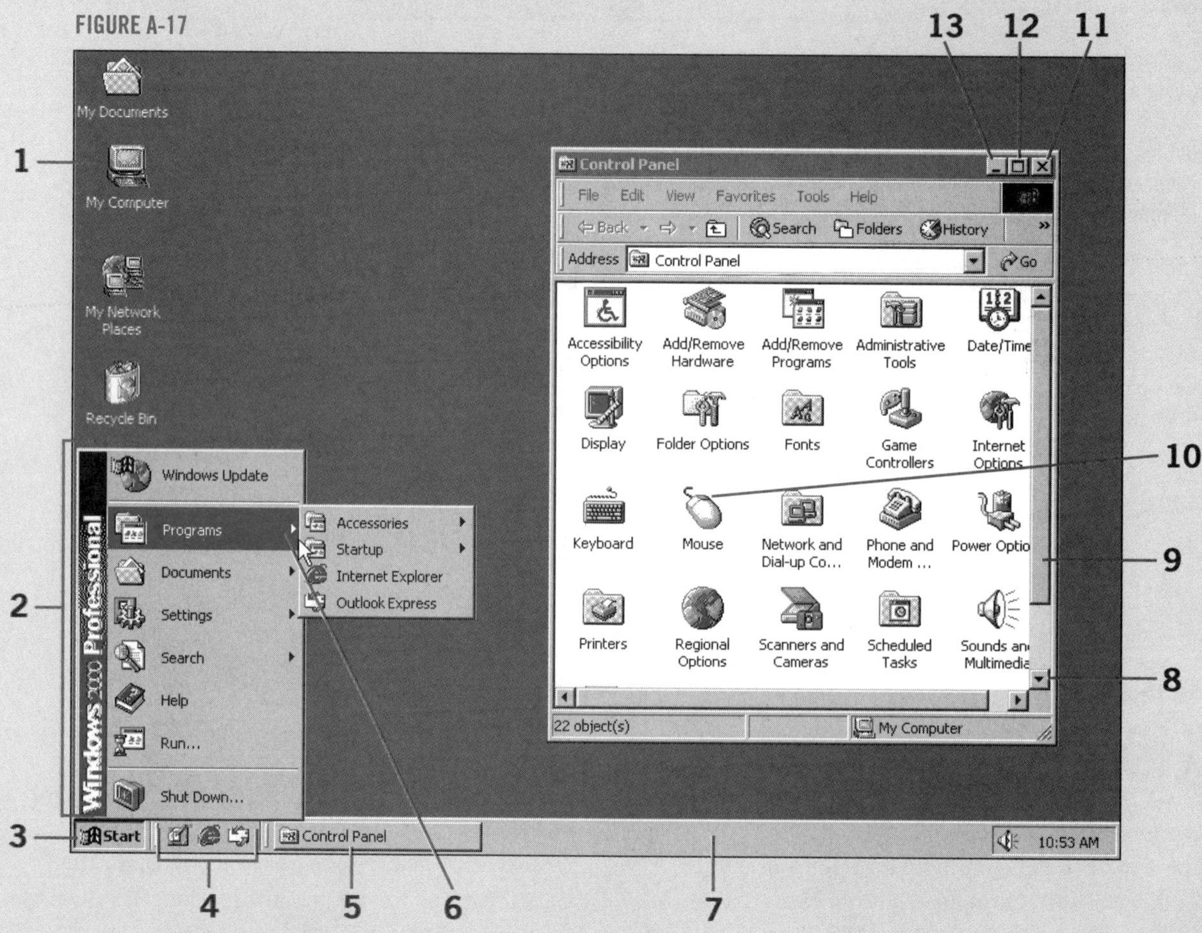

Match each of the statements with the term it describes.

14. Shrinks a window to a button on the taskbar
15. Shows the name of the window or program
16. The taskbar item you first click to start a program
17. Requests more information that you supply before carrying out command
18. Shows the Start button, Quick Launch toolbar, and any currently open programs
19. An input device that lets you point to and make selections
20. Graphic representation of program

a. Taskbar
b. Dialog box
c. Start button
d. Mouse
e. Title bar
f. Minimize button
g. Icon

Select the best answer from the list of choices.

21. The acronym GUI stands for
    a. Grayed user information.
    b. Group user icons.
    c. Graphical user interface.
    d. Group user interconnect.

22. Which of the following is NOT provided by Windows 2000?
- **a.** The ability to organize files
- **b.** Instructions to coordinate the flow of information among the programs, files, printers, storage devices, and other components of your computer system
- **c.** Programs that allow you to specify the operation of the mouse
- **d.** Spell checker for your documents

23. All of the following are examples of using a mouse, EXCEPT
- **a.** clicking the Maximize button.
- **b.** pressing [Enter].
- **c.** double-clicking to start a program.
- **d.** dragging the My Computer icon.

24. The term for moving an item to a new location on the desktop is
- **a.** pointing.
- **b.** clicking.
- **c.** dragging.
- **d.** restoring.

25. The Maximize button is used to
- **a.** return a window to its previous size.
- **b.** expand a window to fill the computer screen.
- **c.** scroll slowly through a window.
- **d.** run programs from the Start menu.

26. What appears if a window contains more information than can be viewed in the window?
- **a.** Program icon
- **b.** Cascading menu
- **c.** Scroll bars
- **d.** Check boxes

27. A window is active when
- **a.** you can only see its program button on the taskbar.
- **b.** its title bar is dimmed.
- **c.** it is open and you are currently using it.
- **d.** it is listed in the Programs submenu.

28. You can exit Windows by
- **a.** double-clicking the Control Panel application.
- **b.** double-clicking the Program Manager control menu box.
- **c.** clicking File, then clicking Exit.
- **d.** selecting the Shut Down command from the Start menu.

Skills Review

1. Start Windows and view the Active Desktop.
- **a.** Turn on the computer, if necessary.
- **b.** After Windows starts, identify as many items on the desktop as you can, without referring to the lesson material.
- **c.** Compare your results to Figure A-1.

2. Use the mouse.
- **a.** Double-click the Recycle Bin icon.
- **b.** Drag the Recycle Bin window to the upper-right corner of the desktop.
- **c.** Right-click the title bar of the Recycle Bin, then click Close.

3. Start a program.
- **a.** Click the Start button on the taskbar, then point to Programs.
- **b.** Point to Accessories, then click Calculator (rest your pointer on the double arrows to display more menu commands if necessary).
- **c.** Minimize the Calculator window.

4. Move and resize windows.
- **a.** Drag the Recycle Bin icon to the bottom of the desktop.
- **b.** Double-click the My Computer icon to open the My Computer window.
- **c.** Maximize the window, if it is not already maximized.

  d. Restore the window to its previous size.
  e. Resize the window until you see the vertical scroll bar.
  f. Minimize the My Computer window.
  g. Drag the Recycle Bin back to the top of the desktop.

5. **Use menus, keyboard shortcuts, and toolbars.**
  a. Click the Start button on the taskbar, point to Settings, then click Control Panel.
  b. Click View on the menu bar, point to Toolbars, then click Standard Buttons to deselect the option and hide the toolbar.
  c. Redisplay the toolbar.
  d. Press [Alt][V] to display the View menu, then press [L] to view the Control Panel as a list.
  e. Note the change, then use keyboard shortcuts to change the view back.
  f. Click the Up One Level button to view My Computer.
  g. Click the Back button to return to the Control Panel.
  h. Click View, click Toolbars, then click Customize.
  i. Add a button to the toolbar, remove it, then close the Customize the Toolbar dialog box.
  j. Click the Restore button on the Control panel window.

6. **Use dialog boxes.**
  a. Double-click the Display icon, then click the Screen Saver tab.
  b. Click the Screen Saver list arrow, click any screen saver in the list, then view it in the Preview box above the list.
  c. Click the Effects tab.
  d. In the Visual effects section, click the Use large icons check box to select it, then click Apply.
  e. Note the change in the icons on the desktop and in the Control Panel window.
  f. Click the Use large icons check box to deselect it, click the Screen Saver tab, return the screen saver to its original setting, then click Apply.
  g. Click the Close button in the Display Properties dialog box, but leave the Control Panel open.

7. **Use scroll bars.**
  a. Click View on the Control Panel toolbar, then click Details.
  b. Resize the Control Panel window, if necessary, so that both scroll bars are visible.
  c. Drag the vertical scroll box down all the way.
  d. Click anywhere in the area above the vertical scroll box.
  e. Click the down scroll arrow until the scroll box is back at the bottom of the scroll bar.
  f. Drag the horizontal scroll box so you can read the descriptions for the icons.

8. **Get Help.**
  a. Click the Start button on the taskbar, then click Help.
  b. Click the Contents tab, then click Introducing Windows 2000 Professional.
  c. Click Tips for New Users, click the Use the Personalized Menus feature, then click Overview of Personalized Menus.
  d. Read the topic contents, then click Related Topics.

9. **Close a program and shut down Windows.**
  a. Click the Close button to close the Help topic window.
  b. Click File on the menu bar, then click Close to close the Control Panel window.
  c. Click the Calculator program button on the taskbar to restore the window.
  d. Click the Close button in the Calculator window to close the Calculator program.
  e. Click the My Computer program button on the taskbar, then click the Close button to close the window.
  f. If you are instructed to do so, shut down your computer.

Independent Challenges

1. Windows 2000 has an extensive help system. In this independent challenge, you will use Help to learn about more Windows 2000 features and explore the help that's available on the Internet.

a. Open Windows Help and locate help topics on adjusting the double-click speed of your mouse and displaying Web content on your desktop.

If you have a printer, print a Help topic for each subject. If you do not have a printer, write a summary of each topic.

b. Follow these steps below to access help on the Internet. If you don't have Internet access, you can't do this step.

i. Click the Web Help button on the toolbar.

ii. Click the link Windows 2000 home page. A browser opens and prompts you to connect to the Internet if you are not already connected.

iii. Write a summary of what you find.

iv. Click the Close button in the title bar of your browser, then disconnect from the Internet and close Windows Help.

2. You may need to change the format of the clock and date on your computer. For example, if you work with international clients it might be easier to show the time in military (24-hour) time and the date with the day before the month. You can also change the actual time and date on your computer, to accomodate such things as time zone changes.

a. Open the Control Panel window, then double-click the Regional Options icon.

b. Click the Time tab to change the time to show a 24-hour clock rather than a 12-hour clock.

c. Click the Date tab to change the Short date format to show the date, followed by the month, followed by the year (e.g., 30/3/01).

d. Change the time to one hour later using the Date/Time icon in the Control Panel window.

e. Return the settings to the original time and format, then close all open windows.

3. Calculator is a Windows program on the Accessories menu that you can use for calculations you need to perform while using the computer. Follow these guidelines to explore the Calculator and the Help that comes with it:

a. Start the Calculator from the Accessories menu.

b. Click Help on the menu bar, then click Help Topics. The Calculator Help window opens, showing several help topics.

c. View the help topic on how to perform simple calculations, then print it if you have a printer connected.

d. Open the Perform a scientific calculation category, then view the definition of a number system.

e. Determine how many months you have to work to earn an additional week of vacation if you work for a company that provides one additional day of paid vacation for every 560 hours you work. (*Hint:* Divide 560 by the number of hours you work per month.)

f. Close all open windows.

4. You can customize many Windows features to suit your needs and preferences. One way you do this is to change the appearance of the taskbar on the desktop. In this challenge, try the guidelines described to explore the different ways you can customize the appearance of the taskbar.

a. Position the pointer over the top border of the taskbar. When the pointer changes shape, drag up an inch.

b. Resize the taskbar back to its original size.

c. Click the Start button on the taskbar, point to Settings, then click Taskbar & Start Menu.

d. In the upper-right corner of the General tab, click the Help button, then click the first check box to view the pop-up window describing it. Repeat this for each check box.

e. Click each check box and observe the effect in the preview area. (*Note:* Do not click OK.)

f. Click Cancel.

► Visual Workshop

Use the skills you have learned in this unit to customize your desktop so it looks like the one in Figure A-18. Make sure you include the following:

- Calculator program minimized
- Vertical scroll bar in Control Panel window
- Large icons view in Control Panel window
- Rearranged icons on desktop; your icons may be different (*Hint:* If the icons *snap* back to where they were, they are set to be automatically arranged. Right-click a blank area of the desktop, point to Arrange Icons, then click Auto Arrange to deselect this option.)

Use the Print Screen key to make a copy of the screen, then print it from the Paint program. (To print from the Paint program, click the Start button on the taskbar, point to Programs, point to Accessories, then click Paint; in the Paint program window, click Edit on the menu bar, then click Paste; click Yes to fit the image on the bitmap, click the Print button on the toolbar, then click Print in the Print dialog box. See your instructor or technical support person for assistance.)

When you have completed this exercise, be sure to return your settings and desktop back to their original arrangement.

FIGURE A-18

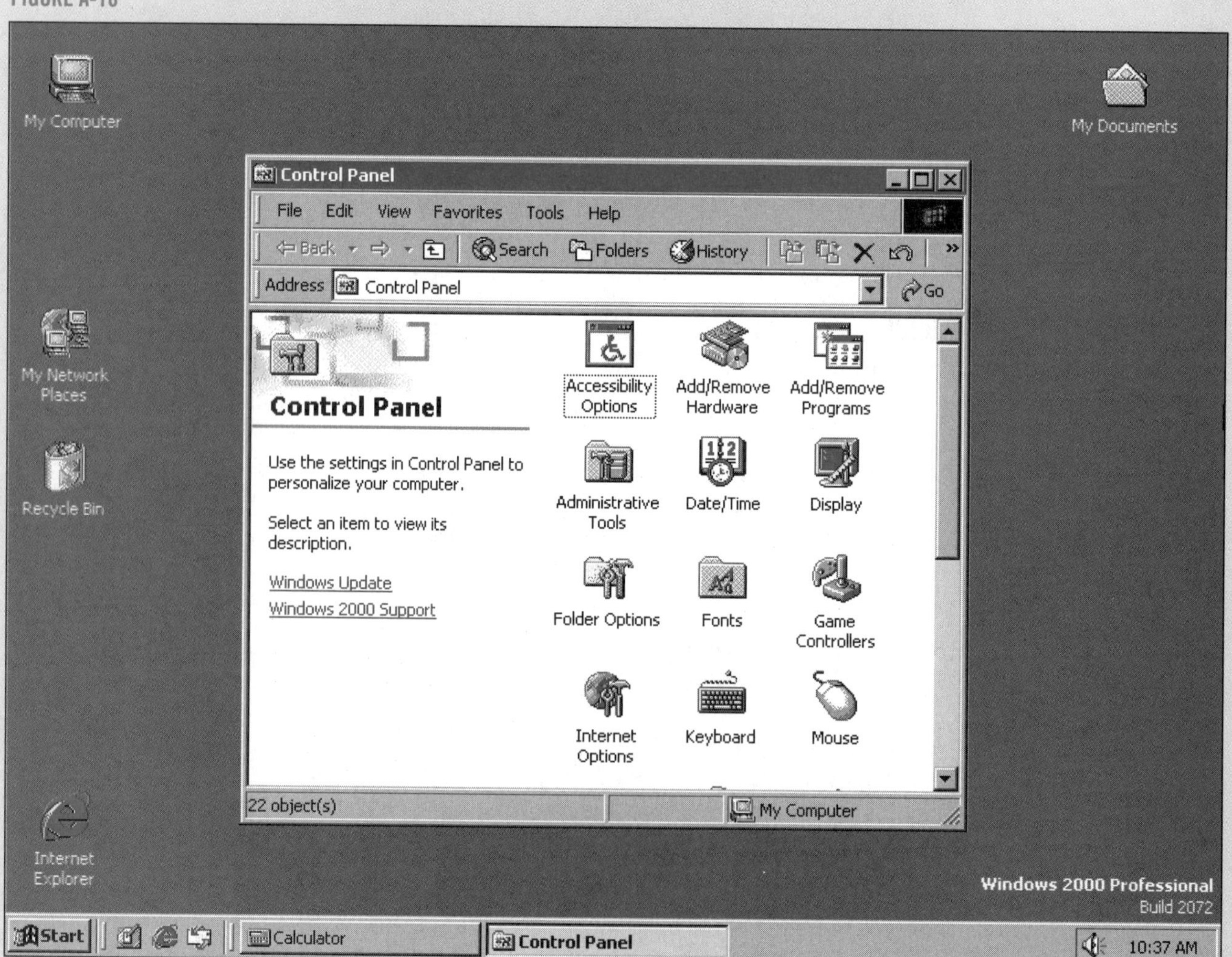

Windows 2000

Working with Programs, Files, and Folders

Objectives

- Create and save a WordPad document
- Open, edit, and save an existing Paint file
- Work with multiple programs
- Understand file management
- View files and create folders with My Computer
- Move and copy files with My Computer
- Manage files with Windows Explorer
- Delete and restore files
- Create a shortcut on the desktop

Most of your work on a computer involves using programs to create files. For example, you might use WordPad to create a resumé or Microsoft Excel to create a budget. The resumé and the budget are examples of **files**, electronic collections of data that you create and save on a disk. In this unit, you learn how to work with files and the programs you use to create them. You create new files, open and edit an existing file, and use the Clipboard to copy and paste data from one file to another. You also explore the file management features of Windows 2000, using My Computer and Windows Explorer. Finally, you learn how to work more efficiently by managing files directly on your desktop.

Windows 2000

Creating and Saving a WordPad Document

As with most programs, when you start WordPad a new, blank **document** (or file) opens. To create a new file, such as a memo, you simply begin typing. Your work is automatically stored in your computer's **random access memory (RAM)** until you turn off your computer, at which point anything stored in the computer's RAM is erased. To store your work permanently, you must save your work as a file on a disk. You can save files either on an internal **hard disk**, which is built into your computer, usually the C: drive, or on a removable 3.5" or 5.25" **floppy disk**, which you insert into a drive on your computer, usually the A: or B: drive. Before you can save a file on a floppy disk, the disk must be formatted. (See the Appendix, "Formatting a Disk," or your instructor or technical support person for more information.) When you name a file, you can use up to 255 characters including spaces and punctuation in the File Name box, using either upper- or lowercase letters. In this lesson, you start WordPad and create a file that contains the text shown in Figure B-1. Then you save the file to Project Disk 1.

Steps

1. **Click the Start button on the taskbar, point to Programs, point to Accessories, click WordPad, then click the Maximize button if the window does not fill your screen**
   The WordPad program window opens with a new, blank document in the document window. The blinking **insertion point** indicates where the text you type will appear.
2. **Type Memo, then press [Enter]**
   Pressing [Enter] inserts a new line and moves the insertion point to the next line.
3. **Press [Enter] again, then type the remaining text shown in Figure B-1, pressing [Enter] at the end of each line**
   Now that the text is entered, you can format it. **Formatting** changes the appearance of text to make it more readable or attractive.
4. **Click to the left of the word Memo, drag the mouse to the right to highlight the word, then release the mouse button**
   The text is now **selected** and any action you make will be performed on the text.
5. **Click the Center button on the Formatting toolbar, then click the Bold button on the Formatting toolbar**
   The text is centered and bold.
6. **Click the Font Size list arrow, then click 16 in the list**
   A **font** is a particular shape and size of type. The text is enlarged to 16 point. One **point** is 1/72 of an inch in height. Now that your memo is complete, you are ready to save it to your Project Disk.
7. **Click File on the menu bar, then click Save As**
   The Save As dialog box opens, as shown in Figure B-2. In this dialog box, you specify where you want your file saved and also give your document a name.
8. **Click the Save in list arrow, and then click 3½ Floppy (A:), or whichever drive contains your Project Disk 1**
   The drive containing your Project Disk is now active, meaning that any files currently on the disk appear in the list of folders and files and that the file you save now will be saved on the disk in this drive.
9. **Click the text in the File name text box, type Memo, then click Save**
   Your memo is now saved as a WordPad file with the name "Memo" on your Project Disk. Notice that the WordPad title bar contains the name of the file.

Trouble?

If you make a mistake, press [Backspace] to delete the character to the left of the insertion point.

QuickTip

Double-click to select a word or triple-click to select a paragraph.

Trouble?

This unit assumes that the Project Disk is in the A: drive. If not, substitute the correct drive any time you are instructed to use the 3½ Floppy (A:) drive. See your instructor or technical support person for help.

FIGURE B-1: Text to enter in WordPad

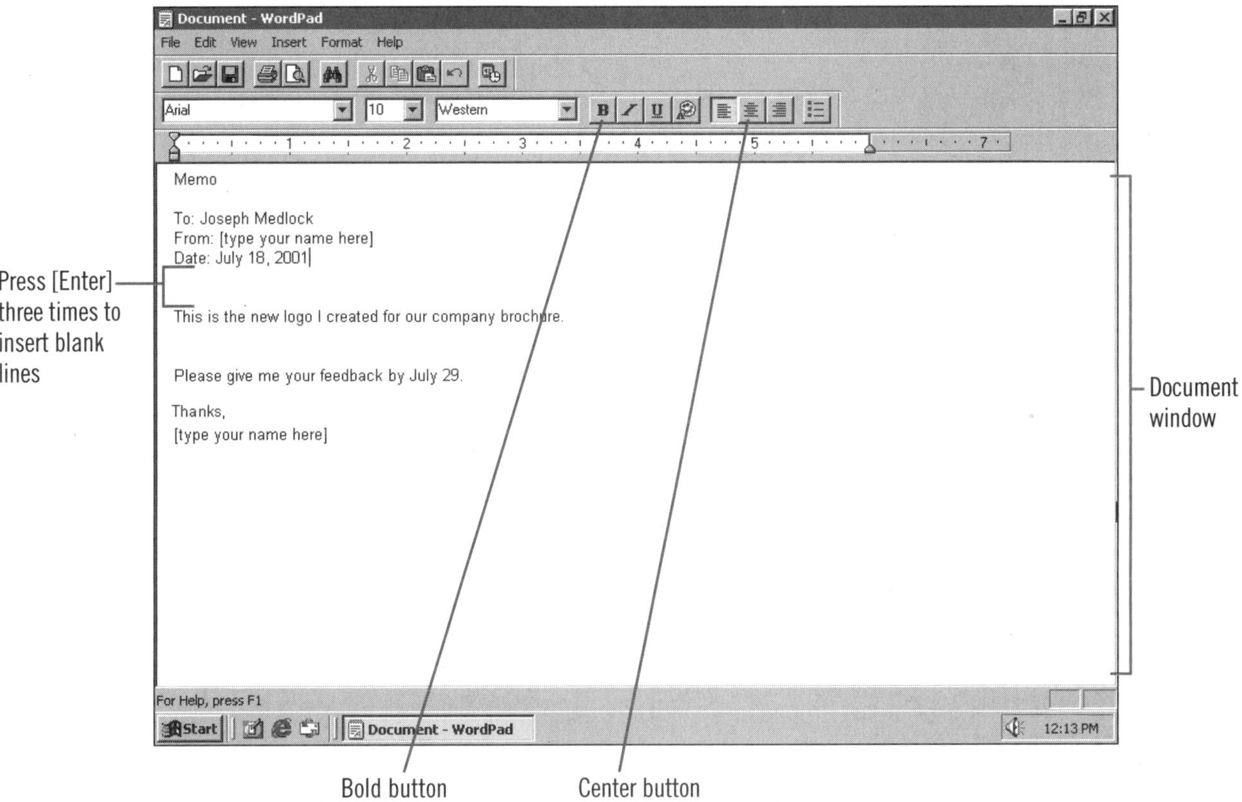

FIGURE B-2: Save As dialog box

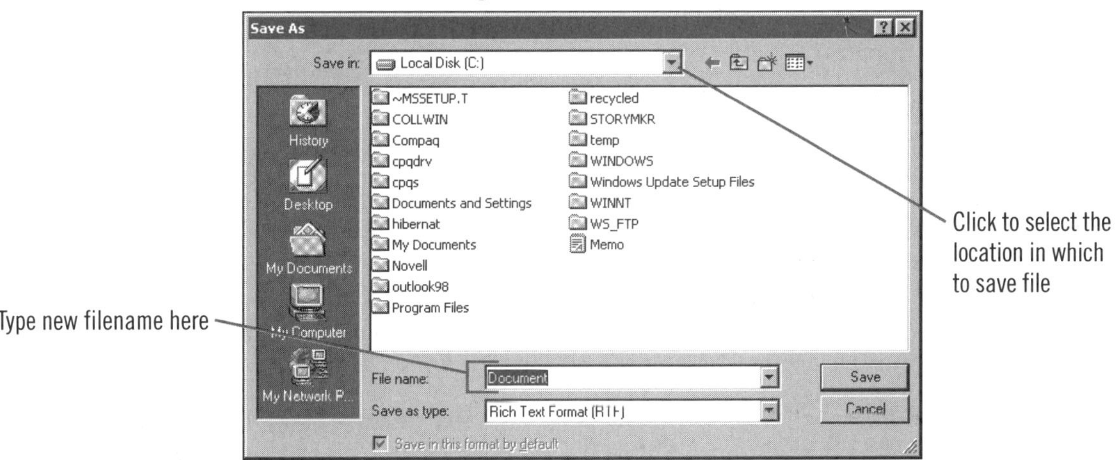

Creating a new document

When you want to create a new document in WordPad once the program is already open and another document is active, you can click the New button on the Standard toolbar. A dialog box opens from which you can choose to create a new Rich Text, Word 6, Text, or Unicode Text document. **Rich Text** documents, the WordPad default document format, can include text formatting and tabs, and be available for use in a variety of other word-processing programs; **Word 6** documents can be opened, edited, and enhanced in Microsoft Word version 6.0 or later without conversion; **Text** documents can be used in numerous other programs because they contain no formatting; and **Unicode Text** documents can contain text from any of the world's writing systems, such as Roman, Greek, and Chinese. You select one of the options by clicking it, and then clicking OK.

Windows 2000

Opening, Editing, and Saving an Existing Paint File

Sometimes you create files from scratch, but often you may want to use a file you or someone else has already created; to do so, you need to **open** the file. Once you open a file, you can **edit** it, or make changes to it, such as adding or deleting text. After editing a file, you can save it with the same filename, which means that you no longer will have the file in its original form, or you can save it with a different filename, so that the original file remains unchanged. In this lesson, you use **Paint**, a drawing program that comes with Windows 2000, to open a file, edit it by changing a color, then save the file with a new filename to leave the original file unchanged.

1. Click the **Start button** on the taskbar, point to **Programs**, point to **Accessories**, click **Paint**, then click the **Maximize button** if the window doesn't fill the screen
   The Paint program opens with a blank work area. If you wanted to create a file from scratch, you would begin working now.
2. Click **File** on the menu bar, then click **Open**
   The Open dialog box works similarly to the Save As dialog box.
3. Click the **Look in list arrow**, then click **3½ Floppy (A:)**
   The Paint files on your Project Disk 1 are listed in the Open dialog box, as shown in Figure B-3.
4. Click **Win B-1** in the list of files, and then click **Open**
   The Open dialog box closes and the file named Win B-1 opens. Before you make any changes to a file, you should save it with a new filename, so that the original file is unchanged.
5. Click **File** on the menu bar, then click **Save As**
6. Make sure **3½ Floppy (A:)** appears in the Save in text box, select the text **Win B-1** in the File name text box if necessary, type **Logo**, then click **Save**
   The Logo file appears in the Paint window, as shown in Figure B-4. Because you saved the file with a new name, you can edit it without changing the original file. You will now use buttons in the **Tool Box**, a toolbar of illustration tools available in Windows Paint, and the **Color Box**, a palette of colors from which you can choose, to modify the graphic.
7. Click the **Fill With Color button** in the Tool Box, then click the **Blue color box**, which is the fourth from the right in the first row
   Notice how clicking a button in the Tool Box changes the mouse pointer. Now when you click an area in the image, it will be filled with the color you selected in the Color Box. See Table B-1 for a description of the tools in the Tool Box.
8. Move the pointer into the **white area that represents the sky** until the pointer changes to , then click
   The sky is now blue.
9. Click **File** on the menu bar, then click **Save**
   The change you made is saved to disk.

QuickTip

You can also open a file by double-clicking it in the Open dialog box.

FIGURE B-3: Open dialog box

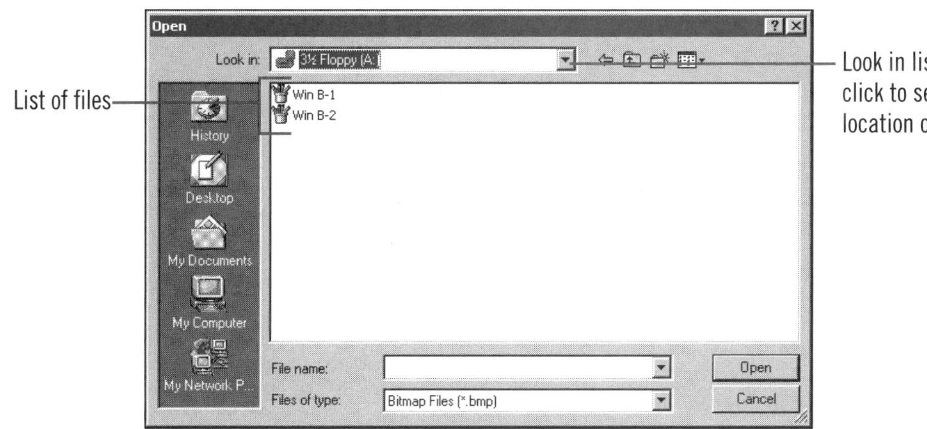

FIGURE B-4: Paint file saved with new filename

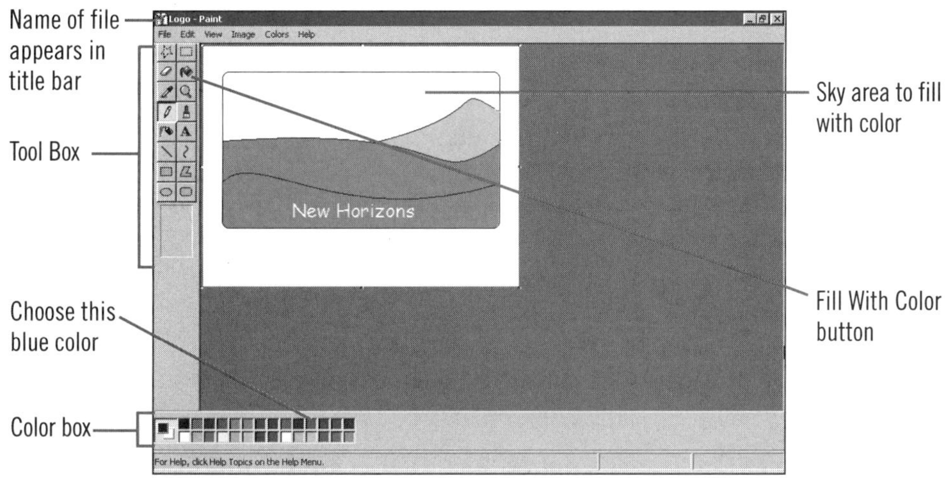

TABLE B-1: Paint Tool Box buttons

tool	description	tool	description
Free-Form Select button	Selects a free-form section of the picture to move, copy, or edit	**Airbrush button**	Produces a circular spray of dots
Select button	Selects a rectangular section of the picture to move, copy, or edit	**Text button**	Inserts text into the picture
Eraser button	Erases a portion of the picture using the selected eraser size and foreground color	**Line button**	Draws a straight line with the selected width and foreground color
Fill With Color button	Fills closed shape or area with the current drawing color	**Curve button**	Draws a wavy line with the selected width and foreground color
Pick Color button	Picks up a color off the picture to use for drawing	**Rectangle button**	Draws a rectangle with the selected fill style; also used to draw squares by holding down [Shift] while drawing
Magnifier button	Changes the magnification; lists magnifications under the toolbar	**Polygon button**	Draws polygons from connected straight-line segments
Pencil button	Draws a free-form line one pixel wide	**Ellipse button**	Draws an ellipse with the selected fill style; also used to draw circles by holding down [Shift] while drawing
Brush button	Draws using a brush with the selected shape and size	**Rounded Rectangle button**	Draws rectangles with rounded corners using the selected fill style; also used to draw rounded squares by holding down [Shift] while drawing

Windows 2000

Working with Multiple Programs

A powerful feature of Windows is its capability to run more than one program at a time. For example, you might be working with a document in WordPad and want to search the Internet to find the answer to a question. You can start your browser, a program designed to access information on the Internet, without closing WordPad. When you find the information, you can leave your browser open and switch back to WordPad. Each open program is represented by a program button on the taskbar that you click to switch between programs. You can also copy data from one file to another, (whether the files were created with the same Windows program or not), using the **Clipboard**, a temporary area in your computer's memory, and the Cut, Copy, and Paste commands. See Table B-2 for a description of these commands. In this lesson, you copy the logo graphic you worked with in the previous lesson into the memo you created in WordPad.

Trouble?

If some parts of the image or text are outside the dotted rectangle, click anywhere outside the image, then select the image again, making sure you include everything.

1. Click the **Select button** on the Tool Box, and then drag a rectangle around the entire **graphic**
   When you release the mouse button, the dotted rectangle surrounds the selected area, as shown in Figure B-5. Make sure the entire image is inside the rectangle. The next action you take affects the entire selection.
2. Click **Edit** on the menu bar, and then click **Copy**
   The logo is copied to the Clipboard. When you **copy** an object onto the Clipboard, the object remains in its original location and is also available to be pasted into another location.

QuickTip

To switch between programs using the keyboard, press and hold down [Alt], press [Tab] until the program you want is selected, then release [Alt].

3. Click the **WordPad program button** on the taskbar
   WordPad becomes the active program.
4. Click in the **first line below the line that ends "for our company brochure."**
   The insertion point indicates where the logo will be pasted.
5. Click the **Paste button** on the WordPad toolbar
   The contents of the Clipboard, in this case the logo, are pasted into the WordPad file, as shown in Figure B-6.
6. Click the **Save button** on the toolbar
   The Memo file is saved with the logo inserted.
7. Click the WordPad **Close button**
   Your WordPad document and the WordPad program close. Paint is now the active program.
8. Click the Paint **Close button**; if you are prompted to save changes, click **Yes**
   Your Paint document and the Paint program close. You return to the desktop.

TABLE B-2: Overview of cutting, copying and pasting

Toolbar button	function	keyboard shortcut
Cut	Removes selected information from a file and places it on the Clipboard	[Ctrl][X]
Copy	Places a copy of selected information on the Clipboard, leaving the file intact	[Ctrl][C]
Paste	Inserts whatever is currently on the Clipboard into another location within the same file, or in a different file	[Ctrl][V]

FIGURE B-5: Selecting the logo to copy and paste into the Memo file

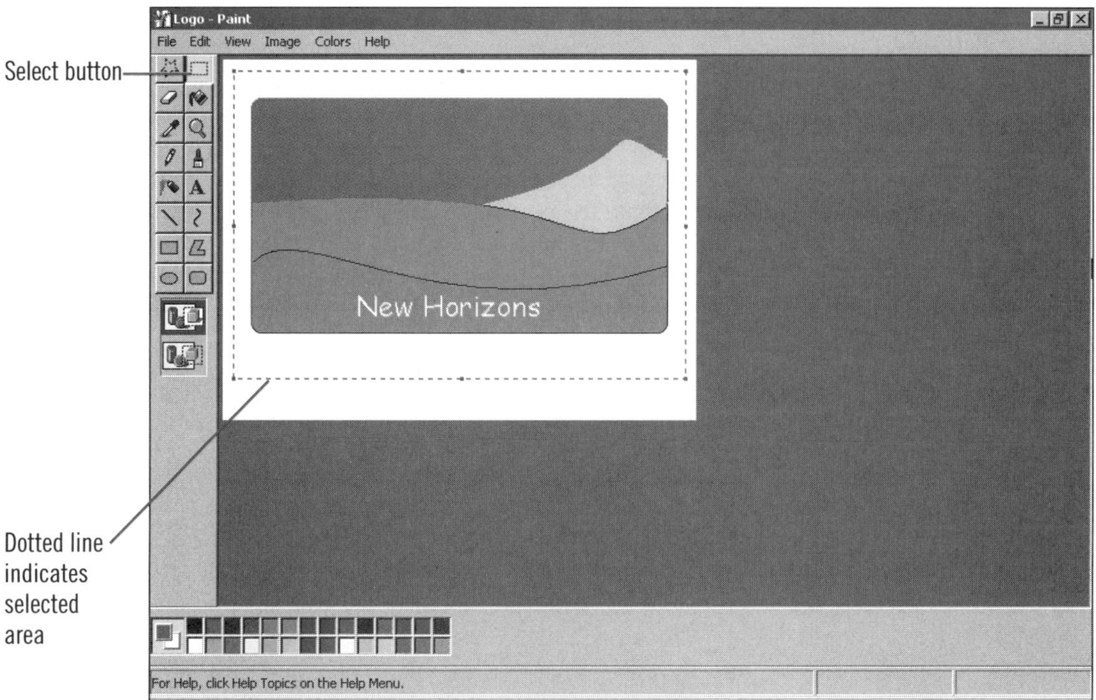

FIGURE B-6: Memo with pasted logo

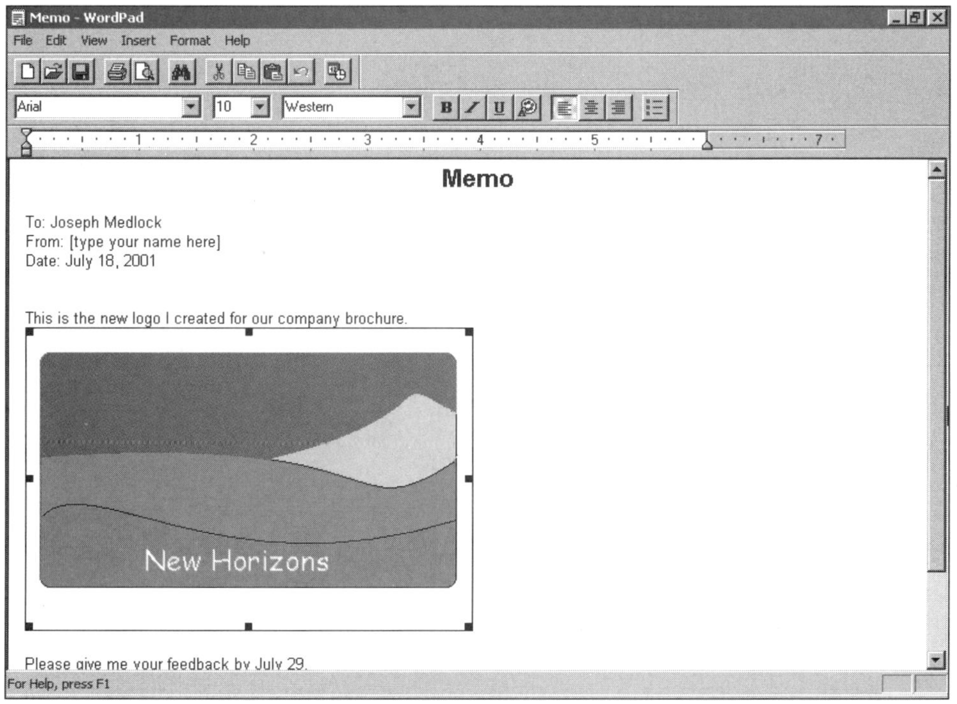

Windows 2000

Understanding File Management

After you have created and saved numerous files using various programs, **file management**, the process of organizing and keeping track of all of your files, can be a challenge. Fortunately, Windows 2000 provides tools to keep everything organized so you can easily locate the files you need, move files to new locations, and delete files you no longer need. There are two main tools for managing your files: My Computer and Windows Explorer. In this lesson, you preview the ways you can use My Computer and Windows Explorer to manage your files.

Details

Windows 2000 gives you the ability to:

Create folders in which you can save your files

Folders are areas on a floppy disk or hard disk in which you can store files. For example, you might create a folder for your documents and another folder for your graphic files. Folders can also contain additional folders, which creates a more complex structure of folders and files, called a **file hierarchy**. See Figure B-7 for an example of how files can be organized.

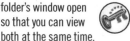

Examine and organize the hierarchy of files and folders

You can use either My Computer or Windows Explorer to see the overall structure of your files and folders. By examining your file hierarchy with these tools, you can better organize the contents of your computer and adjust the hierarchy to meet your needs. Figures B-8 and B-9 illustrate how My Computer and Windows Explorer list folders and files.

Copy, move, and rename files and folders

If you decide that a file belongs in a different folder, you can move it to another folder. You can also rename a file if you decide a different name is more descriptive. If you want to keep a copy of a file in more than one folder, you can copy it to new folders.

Delete files and folders you no longer need, as well as restore files you delete accidentally

Deleting files and folders you are sure you don't need frees up disk space and keeps your file hierarchy more organized. The **Recycle Bin**, a space on your computer's hard disk that stores deleted files, allows you to restore files you deleted by accident. To free up disk space, you should occasionally empty the Recycle Bin by deleting the files permanently from your hard drive.

Locate files quickly with the Windows 2000 Search feature

As you create more files and folders, you may forget where you placed a certain file or you may forget what name you used when you saved a file. With Search, you can locate files by providing only partial names or other factors, such as the file type (for example, a WordPad document or a Paint graphic) or the date the file was created or modified.

Use shortcuts

If a file or folder you use often is located several levels down in your file hierarchy (in a folder within a folder, within a folder), it might take you several steps to access it. To save time accessing the files and programs you use frequently, you can create shortcuts to them. A **shortcut** is a link that gives you quick access to a particular file, folder, or program.

QuickTip

To browse My Computer using multiple windows, click Tools on the menu bar, and then click Folder Options. In the Folder Options dialog box, click the General tab, and then under Browse Folders, click the Open each folder in its own window option button. Each time you open a new folder, a new window opens, leaving the previous folder's window open so that you can view both at the same time.

FIGURE B-7: Sample file hierarchy

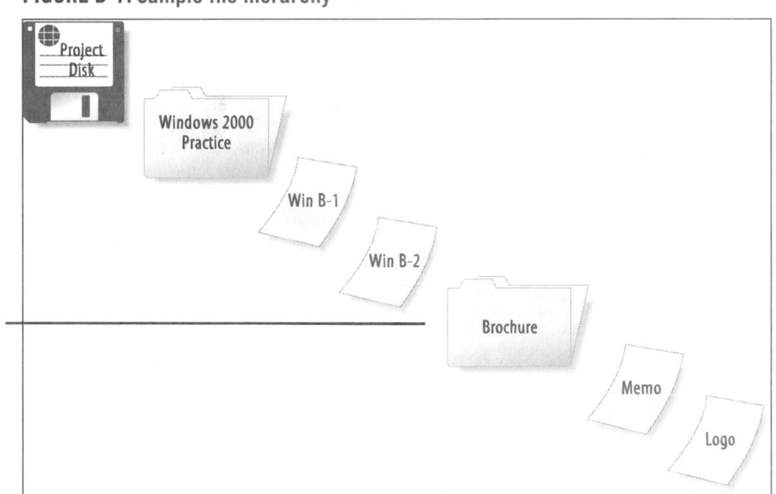

In this hierarchy, Brochure folder is a subfolder of Windows 2000 Practice folder

FIGURE B-8: Brochure folder shown in My Computer

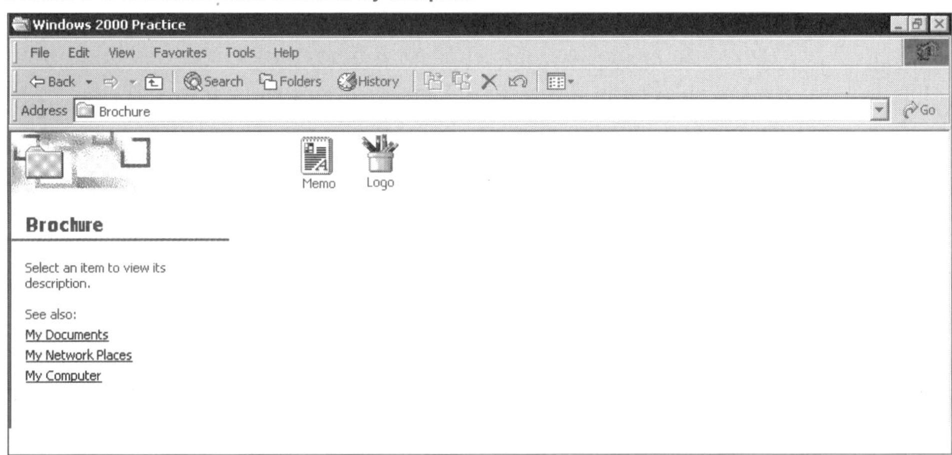

FIGURE B-9: Brochure folder shown in Windows Explorer

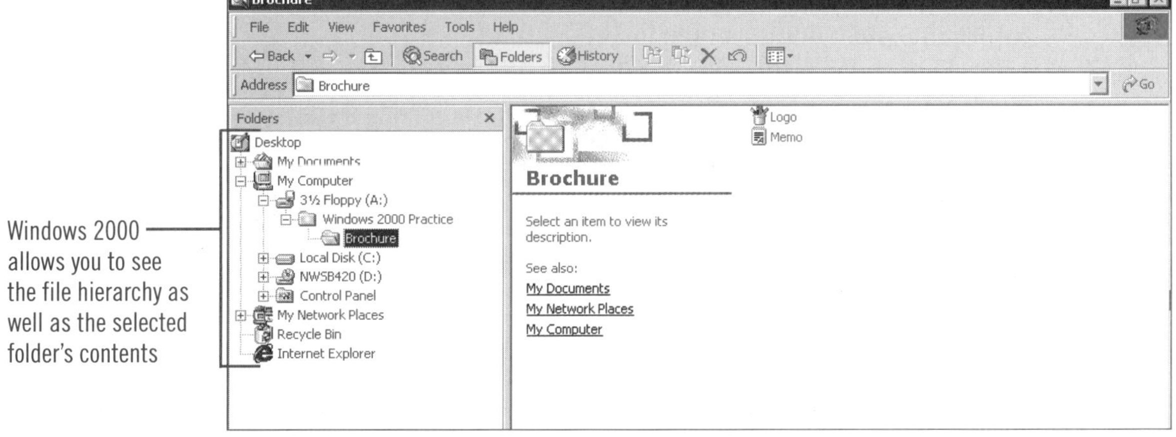

Windows 2000 allows you to see the file hierarchy as well as the selected folder's contents

Windows 2000

Viewing Files and Creating Folders with My Computer

My Computer shows the contents of your computer, including files, folders, programs, disk drives, and printers. You can click the icons representing these various parts of your computer to view their contents or properties. You can manage your files using the My Computer menu bar and toolbar. See Table B-3 for a description of the toolbar buttons. In this lesson, you begin by using My Computer to move around in your computer's file hierarchy, then you create two new folders on your Project Disk 1 for the files you created.

Steps

Trouble?

If you do not see the toolbar, click View on the menu bar, point to Toolbars, and then click Standard Buttons. If you do not see the Address Bar, click View, point to Toolbar, and then click Address Bar.

Trouble?

This book assumes that your hard drive is the C: drive. If yours differs, substitute the appropriate drive for the C: drive wherever it is referenced. See your instructor or technical support person for assistance.

QuickTip

To rename a folder, click the folder to select it, click the folder name so it is surrounded by a rectangle, type the new folder name, then press [Enter].

1. Double-click the **My Computer icon** on your desktop, then click the **Maximize button** if the My Computer window does not fill the screen
   My Computer opens and displays the contents of your computer, as shown in Figure B-10. Your window may contain icons for different folders, drives, and printers.
2. Make sure your Project Disk 1 is in the floppy disk drive, then double-click the **3½ Floppy (A:) icon**
   The contents of your Project Disk 1 appear in the window. These are the project files and the files you created using WordPad and Paint. Each file is represented by an icon, which indicates the program that was used to create the file. If Microsoft Word is installed on your computer, the Word icon appears for the WordPad files; if not, the WordPad icon appears.
3. Click the **Address list arrow** on the Address Bar, as shown in Figure B-10, then click **Local Disk (C:)** or the letter for the main hard drive on your computer
   The window changes to show the contents of your hard drive. The **Address Bar** allows you to open and view a drive, folder, or even a Web page. You can also type in the Address Bar to go to a different drive, folder, or Web page. For example, typing "C:\" will display drive C:; typing "E:\Personal Letters" will display the Personal Letters folder on the E: drive, and typing "http://www.microsoft.com" opens Microsoft's Web site if your computer is connected to the Internet.
4. Click the **Back button** on the toolbar
   The Back button displays the previous location, in this case, your Project Disk.
5. Click the **Views button** on the toolbar, then click **Details**
   Details view shows not only the files and folders, but also the sizes of the files, the types of files, folders, or drives and the date the files were last modified.
6. Click , then click **Thumbnails**
   This view offers less information but provides a preview of graphics and a clear view of the contents of the disk.
7. Click **File** on the menu bar, point to **New**, then click **Folder**
   A new folder is created on your Project Disk 1, as shown in Figure B-11. The folder is called "New Folder" by default. It is selected and ready to be renamed. You can also create a new folder by right-clicking in the blank area of the My Computer window, clicking New, then clicking Folder.
8. Type **Windows 2000 Practice**, then press **[Enter]**
   Choosing descriptive names for your folders helps you remember their contents.
9. Double-click the **Windows 2000 Practice folder**, repeat Step 7 to create a new folder in the Windows 2000 Practice folder, type **Brochure** for the folder name, then press **[Enter]**
10. Click the **Up button** to return to your Project Disk 1

FIGURE B-10: My Computer window

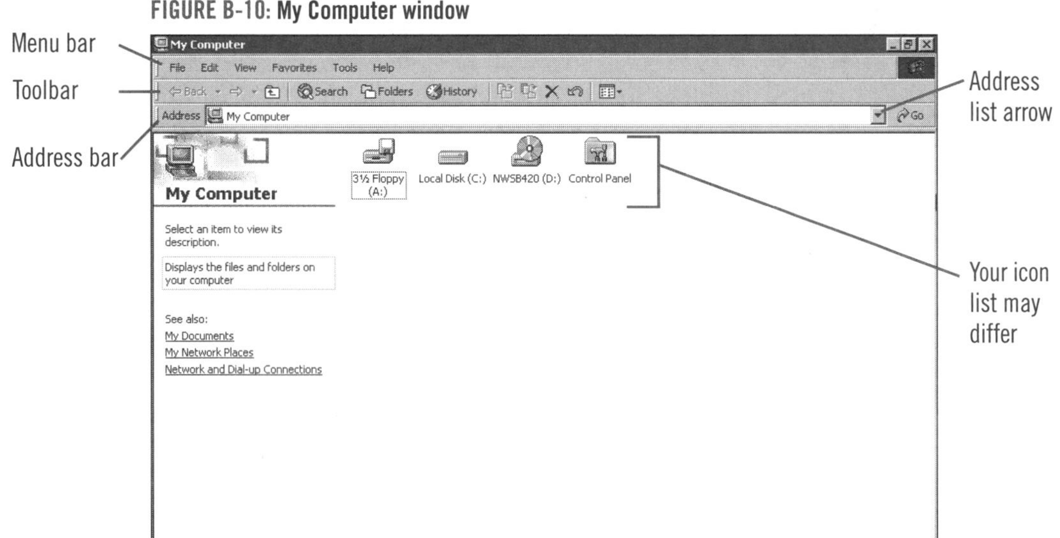

FIGURE B-11: Creating a new folder

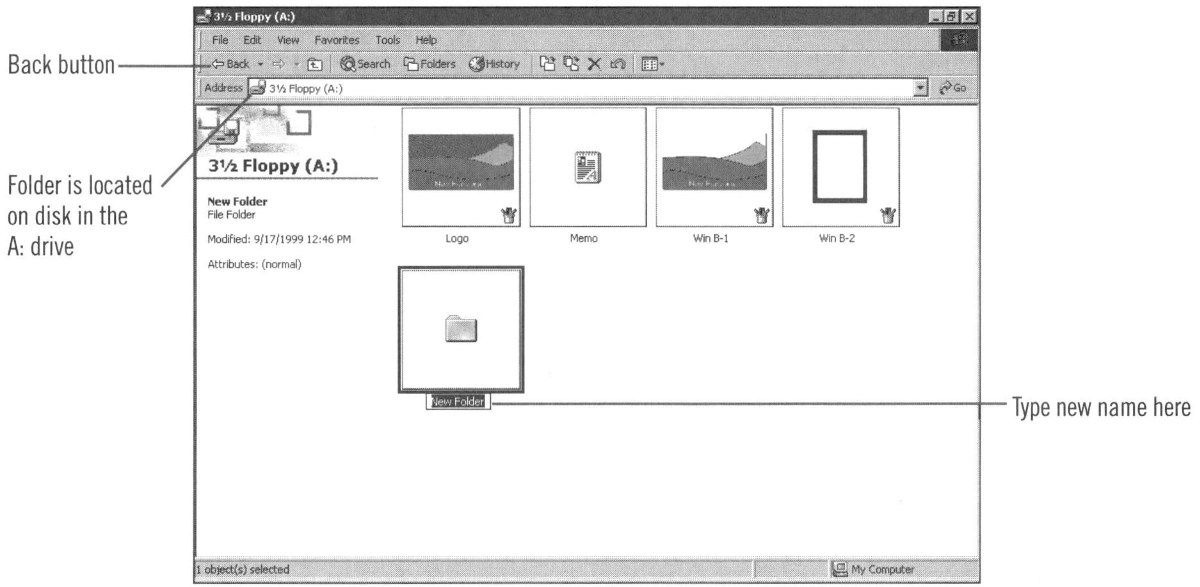

TABLE B-3: Buttons on the My Computer toolbar

button	function
[Back]	Moves back to the previous location you have already visited
[Forward]	Moves forward to the previous location you have already visited
[Up]	Moves up one level in the file hierarchy
[Move To]	Opens the Browse For Folder dialog box, to move the selected file to a new location
[Copy To]	Opens the Browse For Folder dialog box, to copy the selected file to a new location
[Undo]	Undoes the most recent My Computer operation
[Delete]	Deletes a folder or file permanently
[Views]	Lists the contents of My Computer using different views

Windows 2000

Moving and Copying Files with My Computer

You can move a file or folder from one location to another using a variety of methods in My Computer or Windows Explorer. If the file or folder and the location to which you want to move it are both visible on the desktop, you can simply drag the item from one location to the other. You can also use the cut, copy, and paste commands on the Edit menu or the corresponding buttons on the toolbar. Finally you can right-click the file or folder and choose the Send to command to "send" it to another location—most often a floppy disk for **backing up** files. Backup copies are made in case you have computer trouble, which may cause you to lose files. In this lesson, you move your files into the folder you created in the last lesson.

Steps

1. Click **View**, point to **Arrange Icons**, then click **by Name**
   In this view, folders are listed first in alphabetical order, followed by files, also in alphabetical order.
2. Click the **Win B-1 file**, hold down the mouse button and drag the file onto the **Windows 2000 Practice folder**, as shown in Figure B-12, then release the mouse button
   Win B-1 is moved into the Windows 2000 Practice folder.
3. Double-click the **Windows 2000 Practice folder** and confirm that it contains the Win B-1 file as well as the Brochure folder
4. Click the **Up button** on the My Computer toolbar, as shown in Figure B-12
   You return to your Project Disk. The Up button shows the next level up in the folder hierarchy.
5. Click the **Logo file**, press and hold down **[Shift]**, then click the **Memo file**
   Both files are selected. Table B-4 describes methods for selecting multiple objects.
6. Click the **Move To button** on the 3½ Floppy (A:) toolbar
   The filenames turn gray, and the Browse For Folder dialog box opens, as shown in Figure B-13.
7. Click the **plus sign** next to My Computer if you do not see 3½ Floppy (A:) listed, double-click the **3½ Floppy (A:) drive**, double-click the **Windows 2000 Practice folder**, double-click the **Brochure folder**, then click **OK**
   The two files are moved to the Brochure folder. Only the Windows 2000 Practice folder and the Win B-2 file remain.
8. Click the **Close button** in the 3½ Floppy (A:) window

QuickTip

It is easy to confuse the Back button with the Up button. The Back button returns you to the last location you visited, no matter where it is in your folder hierarchy. The Up button displays the next level up in the folder hierarchy, no matter where you last visited.

FIGURE B-12: Dragging a file from one folder to another

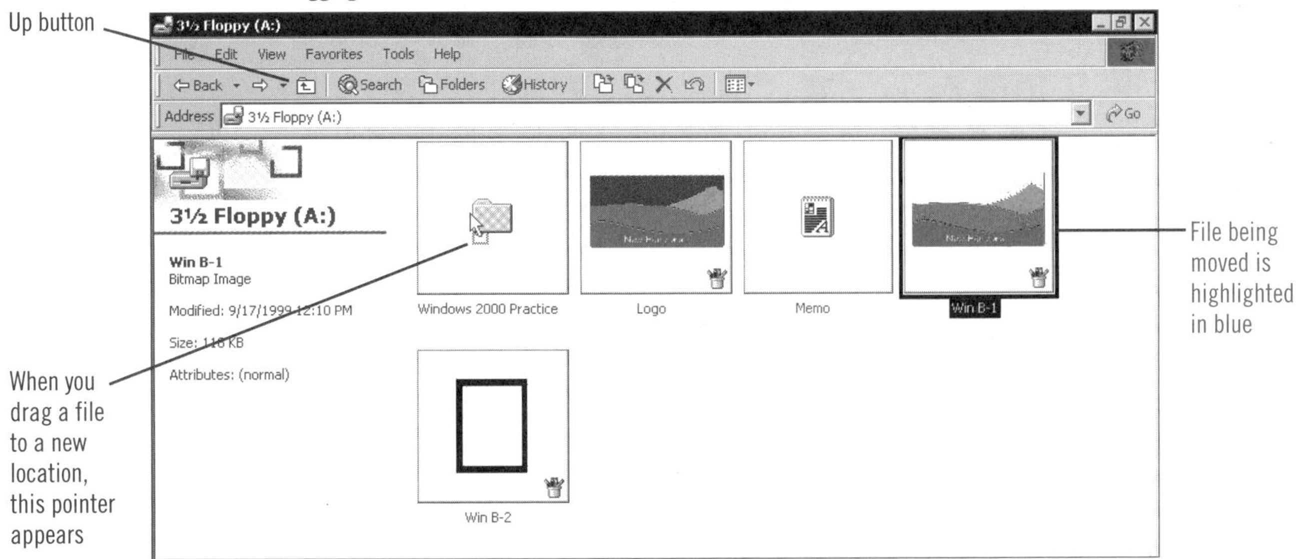

FIGURE B-13: Moving files

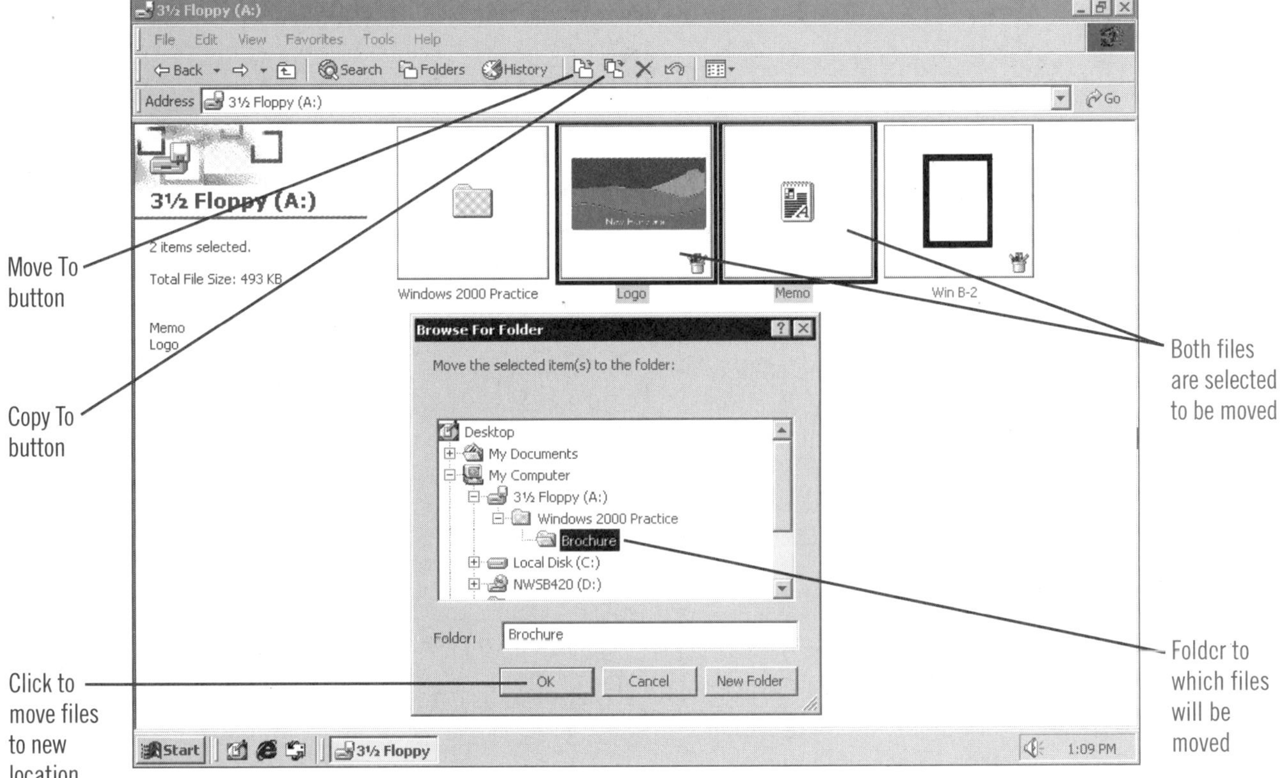

TABLE B-4: Techniques for selecting multiple files and folders

to select	do this
Individual objects not grouped together	Click the first object you want to select, then press and hold down [Ctrl] as you click each additional object you want to add to the selection
Objects grouped together	Click the first object you want to select, then press and hold down [Shift] as you click the last object in the list of objects you want to select; all the objects listed between the first and last objects are selected

Managing Files with Windows Explorer

As with My Computer, you can use Windows Explorer to copy, move, delete, and rename files and folders. However, **Windows Explorer** is more powerful than My Computer: it allows you to see the overall structure of the contents of your computer or network, (the file hierarchy), while you work with individual files and folders within that structure. This means you can work with more than one computer, folder, or file at once. In this lesson, you copy a folder from your Project Disk 1 onto the hard drive and then rename the folder.

Steps

Trouble?

If you do not see the toolbar, click View on the menu bar, point to Toolbars, then click Standard Buttons. If you do not see the Address Bar, click View, point to Toolbars, then click Address Bar.

1. Click the **Start button**, point to **Programs**, point to **Accessories**, click **Windows Explorer**, then click the **Maximize button** if the Windows Explorer window doesn't already fill the screen
   Windows Explorer opens, as shown in Figure B-14. The window is divided into two areas called **panes.** The left pane, called the **Explorer Bar**, displays the drives and folders on your computer in a hierarchy. The right pane displays the contents of whatever drive or folder is currently selected in the left pane. Each pane has its own set of scroll bars, so that changing what you can see in one pane won't affect what you can see in the other. Like My Computer, Windows Explorer has a menu bar, toolbar, and Address Bar.
2. Click **View** on the menu bar, then click **Details** if it is not already selected
   Remember that a bullet point next to a command on the menu bar indicates that it's selected.

Trouble?

If you cannot see the A: drive, you may have to click the plus sign (+) next to My Computer to view the available drives on your computer.

QuickTip

When neither a + nor a – appears next to an icon, it means that the item does not have any folders in it, although it may have files, which you can see listed in the right pane by clicking the icon.

3. In the left pane, scroll to and click **3½ Floppy (A:)**
   The contents of your Project Disk 1 appear in the right pane.
4. In the left pane, click the **plus sign (+)** next to 3½ Floppy (A:)
   You can click the plus sign (+) or minus sign (-) next to any item in the left pane to show or hide the different levels of the file hierarchy, so that you don't always have to look at the entire structure of your computer or network. A plus sign (+) next to a computer, drive, or folder indicates there are additional folders within that object. A minus sign (-) indicates that all the folders of the next level of hierarchy are shown. Clicking the + displays (or "expands") the next level; clicking the – hides (or "collapses") them.
5. In the left pane, double-click the **Windows 2000 Practice folder**
   The contents of the Windows 2000 Practice folder appear in the right pane of Windows Explorer, as shown in Figure B-15. Double-clicking an item in the left pane that has a + next to it displays its contents in the right pane and also expands the next level in the hierarchy in the left pane.

Trouble?

If you are working in a lab setting, you may not be able to add items to your hard drive. Skip Steps 6, 7, and 8 if you are unable to complete them.

6. In the left pane, drag the **Windows 2000 Practice folder** on top of the **C: drive icon**, then release the mouse button
   When you drag files or folders to a different drive, they are copied rather than moved. The Windows 2000 Practice folder and the files in it are copied to the hard disk.
7. In the left pane, click the **C: drive icon**
   The Windows 2000 Practice folder should now appear in the list of folders in the right pane. You may have to scroll to see it. Now you should rename the folder so you can distinguish the original folder from the copy.

QuickTip

You can also rename a selected file by pressing [F2], or using the Rename command on the File menu.

8. Right-click the **Windows 2000 Practice folder** in the right pane, click **Rename** in the pop-up menu, type **Practice Copy**, then press **[Enter]**

FIGURE B-14: Windows Explorer window

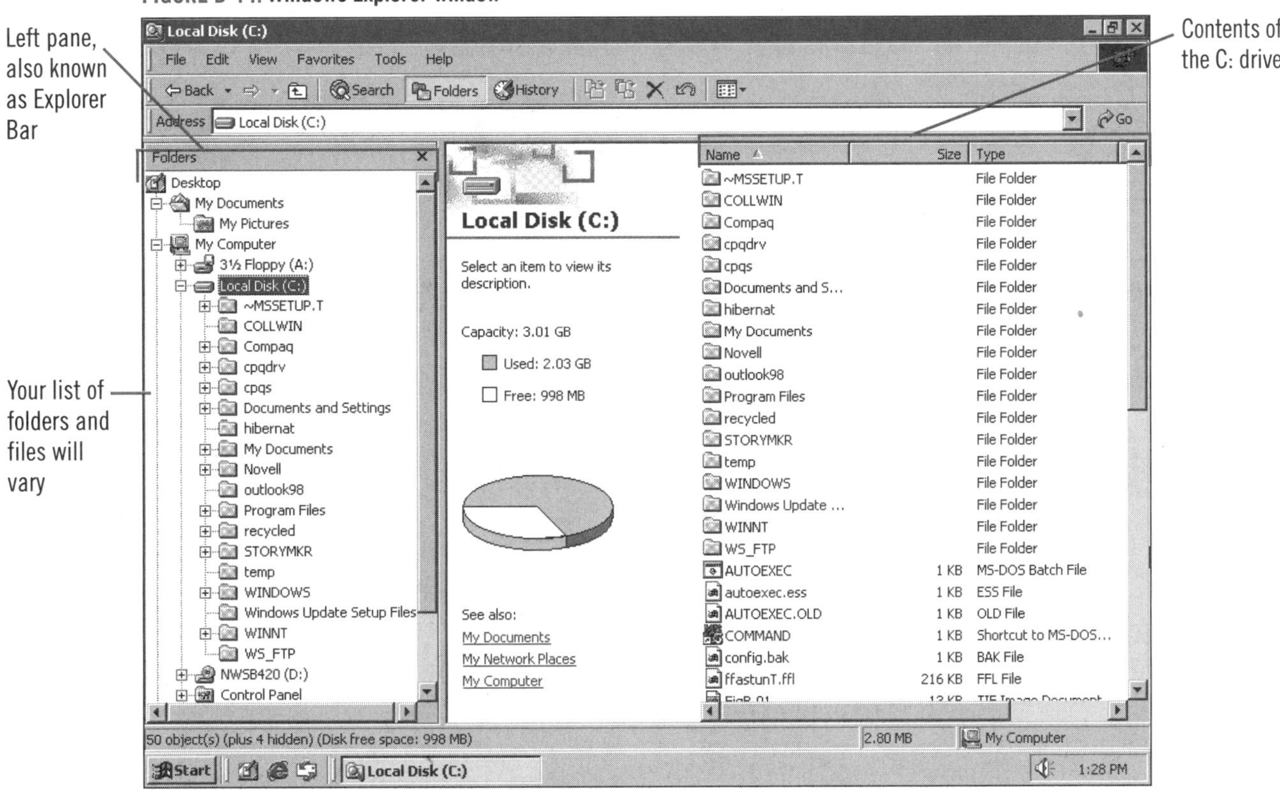

FIGURE B-15: Contents of Windows 2000 Practice folder

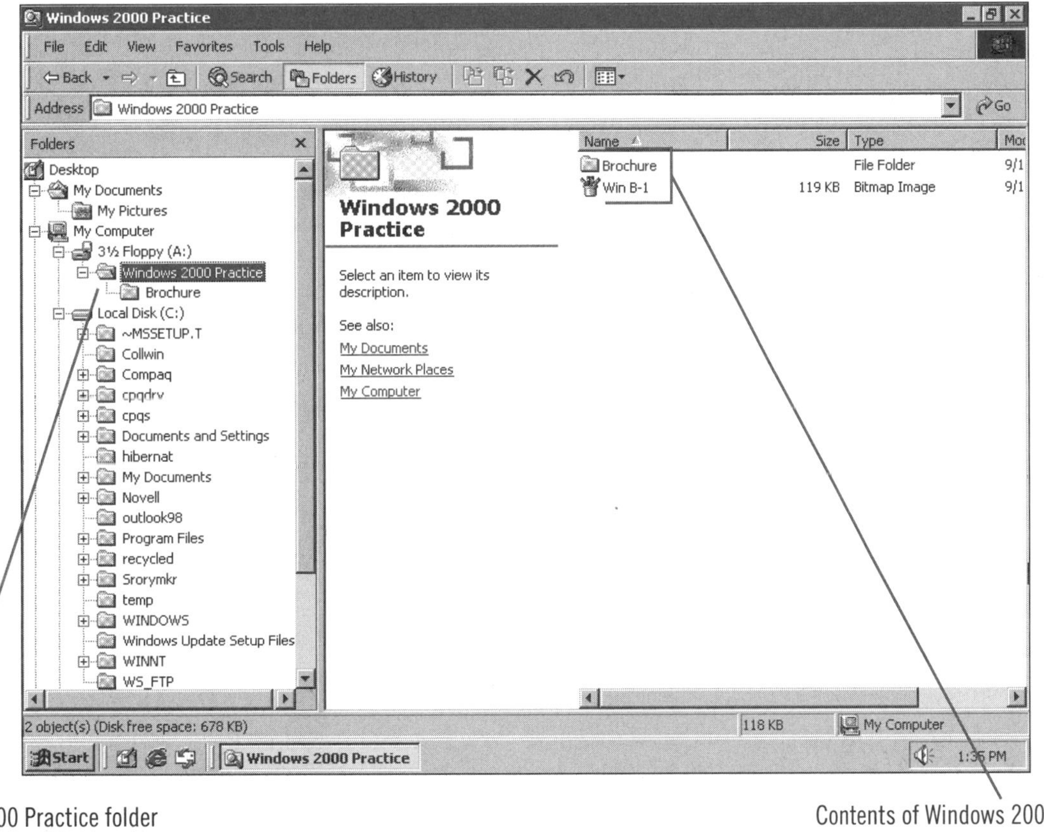

Windows 2000

Deleting and Restoring Files

To save disk space and manage your files more effectively, you should **delete** (or remove) files you no longer need. Because files deleted from your hard drive are stored in the Recycle Bin until you remove them permanently by emptying the Recycle Bin, you can restore any files you might have deleted accidentally. However, if you delete a file from your floppy disk it will not be stored in the Recycle Bin—it will be permanently deleted. See Table B-5 for an overview of deleting and restoring files. There are many ways to delete files and folders from the My Computer and Windows Explorer windows, as well as from the Windows 2000 desktop. In this lesson, you delete a file by dragging it to the Recycle Bin, restore it, and delete a folder by using the Delete command in Windows Explorer.

Steps

1. Click the **Restore button** on the Windows Explorer title bar
   You should be able to see the Recycle Bin icon on your desktop. If you can't see it, resize or move the Windows Explorer window until it is visible. See Figure B-16.
2. If necessary, scroll until you see the Practice Copy folder in the right pane of Windows Explorer
3. Drag the **Practice Copy folder** from the right pane to the **Recycle Bin** on the desktop, as shown in Figure B-16, then click **Yes** to confirm the deletion if necessary
   The folder no longer appears in Windows Explorer because you have moved it to the Recycle Bin.
4. Double-click the **Recycle Bin icon** on the desktop
   The Recycle Bin window opens, as shown in Figure B-17. Depending on the number of files already deleted on your computer, your window might look different. Use the scroll bar if you can't see the files.
5. Click **Edit** on the Recycle Bin menu bar, then click **Undo Delete**
   The Practice Copy folder is restored and should now appear in the Windows Explorer window. You might need to minimize your Recycle Bin window if it blocks your view of Windows Explorer, and you might need to scroll to the bottom of the right pane to find the restored folder.
6. Click the **Practice Copy folder** in the right pane, click the **Delete button** on the Windows Explorer toolbar (resize the window as necessary to see the button), then click **Yes**
   When you are sure you no longer need files you've moved into the Recycle Bin, you can empty the Recycle Bin. You won't do this now, in case you are working on a computer that you share with other people. But, when you're working on your own machine, simply right-click the Recycle Bin icon, then click Empty Recycle Bin in the pop-up menu.
7. Close the Recycle Bin
   If you minimized the Recycle Bin in Step 4, click its program button to open the Recycle Bin window, and then click the Close button.

QuickTip

If you are unable to delete the file, it might be because your Recycle Bin is full, or too small, or the properties have been changed so that files are not stored in the Recycle Bin but are deleted instead. See your instructor or technical support person for assistance.

FIGURE B-16: Dragging a folder to delete it

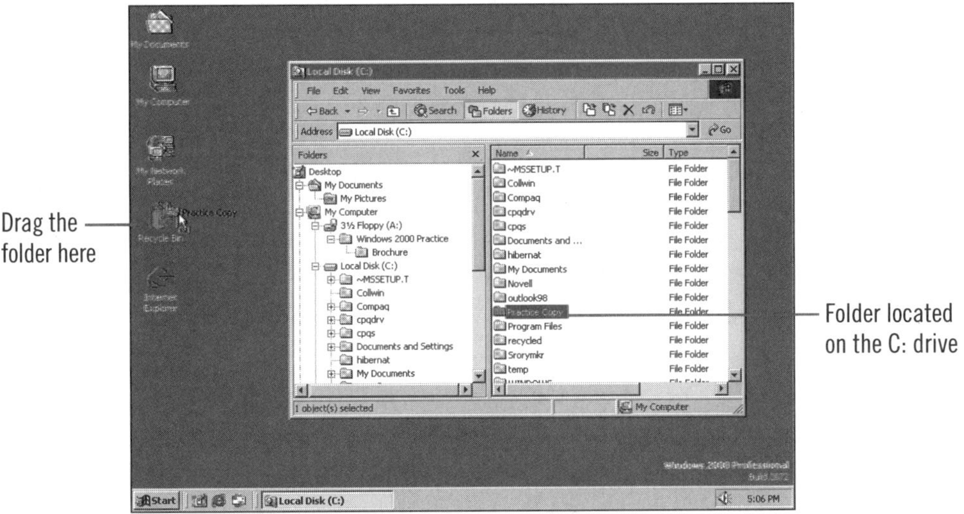

FIGURE B-17: Recycle Bin window

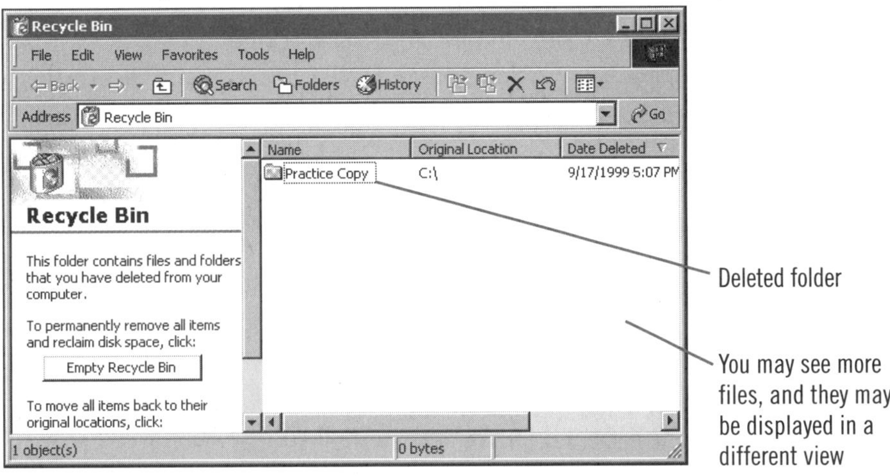

TABLE B-5: Methods for deleting and restoring files

ways to delete a file	ways to restore a file from the Recycle Bin
Select the file, then click the Delete button on the toolbar	Click the Undo button on the toolbar
Select the file, then press [Delete]	Select the file, click File, then click Restore
Right-click the file, then click Delete on the pop-up menu	Right-click the file, then click Restore
Drag the file to the Recycle Bin	Drag the file from the Recycle Bin to any other location

Customizing your Recycle Bin

You can set your Recycle Bin according to how you like to delete and restore files. For example, if you do not want files to go to the Recycle Bin but rather want them to be immediately and permanently deleted, right-click the Recycle Bin, click Properties, then click the Do Not Move Files to the Recycle Bin check box. If you find that the Recycle Bin fills up too fast and you are not ready to delete the files permanently, you can increase the amount of disk space devoted to the Recycle Bin by moving the Maximum Size of Recycle Bin slider to the right. This, of course, reduces the amount of disk space you have available for other things. Also, you can choose not to have the Confirm File Delete dialog box open when you send files to the Recycle Bin. See your instructor or technical support person before changing any of the Recycle Bin settings.

Windows 2000

Creating a Shortcut on the Desktop

When you frequently use a file, folder, or program that is located several levels down in the file hierarchy, you may want to create a shortcut to the object. You can place the shortcut on the desktop or in any other location, such as a folder, that you find convenient. To open the file, folder, or program using the shortcut, double-click the icon. In this lesson, you use Windows Explorer to create a shortcut on your desktop to the Memo file.

Steps

1. In the left pane of the Windows Explorer window, click the **Brochure folder**
   The contents of the Brochure folder appear in the right pane.
2. In the right pane, right-click the **Memo file**
   A pop-up menu appears, as shown in Figure B-18.
3. Click **Create Shortcut** in the pop-up menu
   The file named Shortcut to Memo file appears in the right pane. Now you need to move it to the desktop so that it will be accessible whenever you need it.
4. Click the **Shortcut to Memo file** with the right-mouse button, then drag the **shortcut** to an empty area of the desktop
   Dragging an icon using the left mouse button copies it. Dragging an icon using the right mouse button gives you the option to copy it, move it, or create a shortcut to it. When you release the mouse button a pop-up menu appears.
5. Click **Move Here** in the pop-up menu
   A shortcut to the Memo file now appears on the desktop, as shown in Figure B-19. You might have to move or resize the Windows Explorer window to see it.
6. Double-click the **Shortcut to Memo file icon**
   WordPad starts and the Memo file opens (if you have Microsoft Word installed on your computer, it will start and open the file instead). Using a shortcut eliminates the many steps involved in starting a program and locating and opening a file.
7. Click the **Close button** in the WordPad or Word title bar
   Now you should delete the shortcut icon in case you are working in a lab and share the computer with others.
8. On the desktop, click the **Shortcut to Memo file**, press **[Delete]**, then click **Yes** to confirm the deletion
   The shortcut is removed from the desktop and is now in the Recycle Bin.
9. Close all windows, then shut down Windows

Trouble?

Make sure to use the right mouse button in Step 4. If you used the left mouse button by accident, right-click the Shortcut to Memo file in the right pane of Windows Explorer, click Delete, and repeat Step 4.

QuickTip

Deleting a shortcut deletes only the link; it does not delete the original file or folder to which it points.

FIGURE B-18: Creating a shortcut

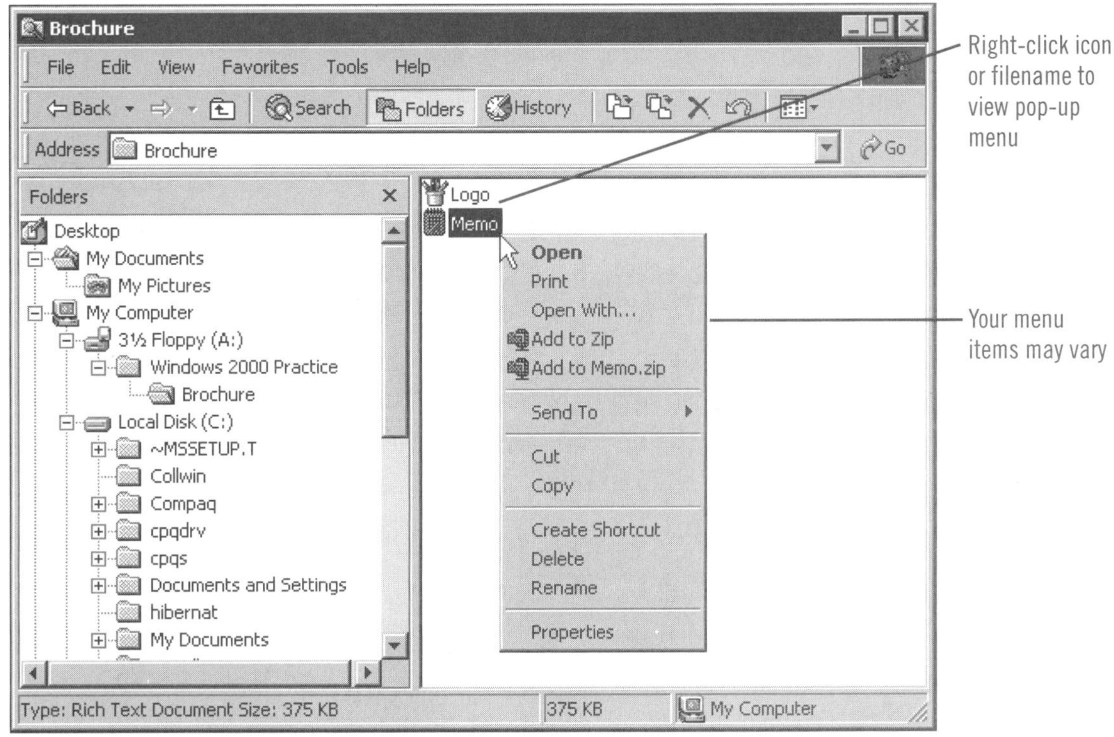

FIGURE B-19: Shortcut on desktop

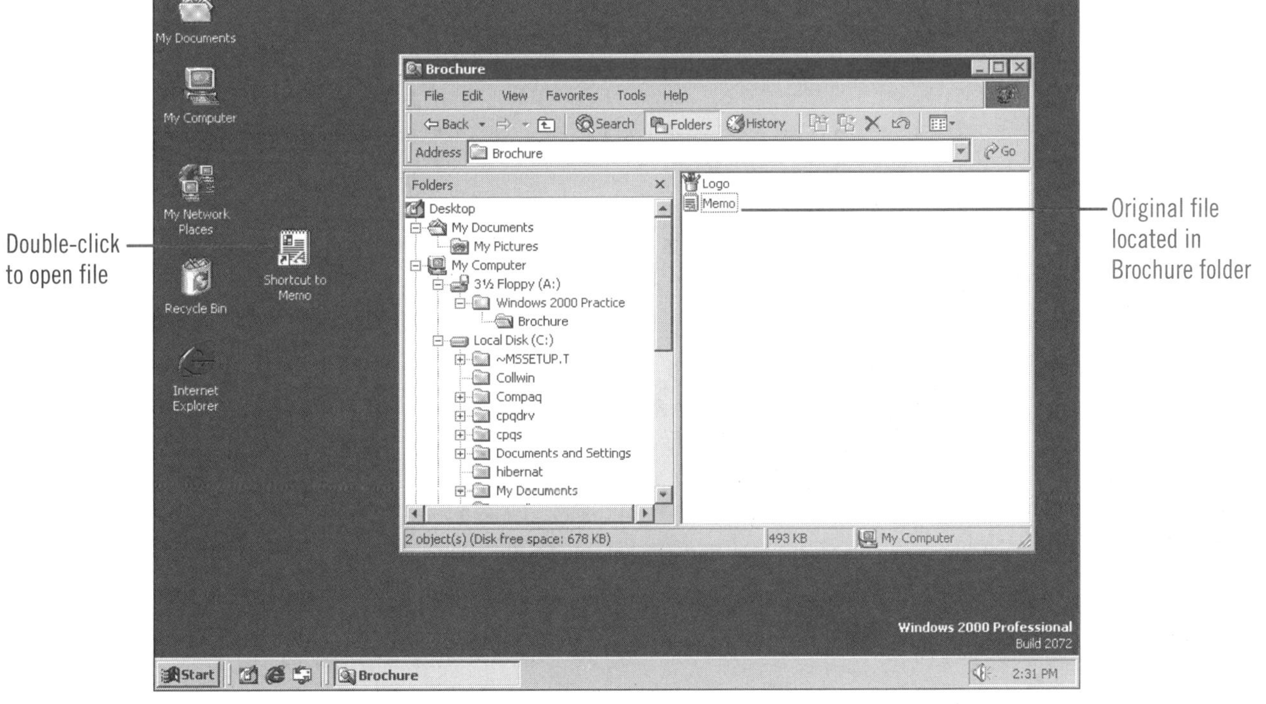

Adding shortcuts to the Start menu

If you do not want your desktop to get cluttered with icons but you would still like easy access to certain files, programs, and folders, you can create a shortcut on the Start menu. Drag the file, program, or folder that you want to add to the Start menu from the Windows Explorer window to the Start button. The file, program, or folder will appear on the first level of the Start menu.

Practice

► Concepts Review

Label each of the elements of the Windows Explorer window shown in Figure B-20.

FIGURE B-20

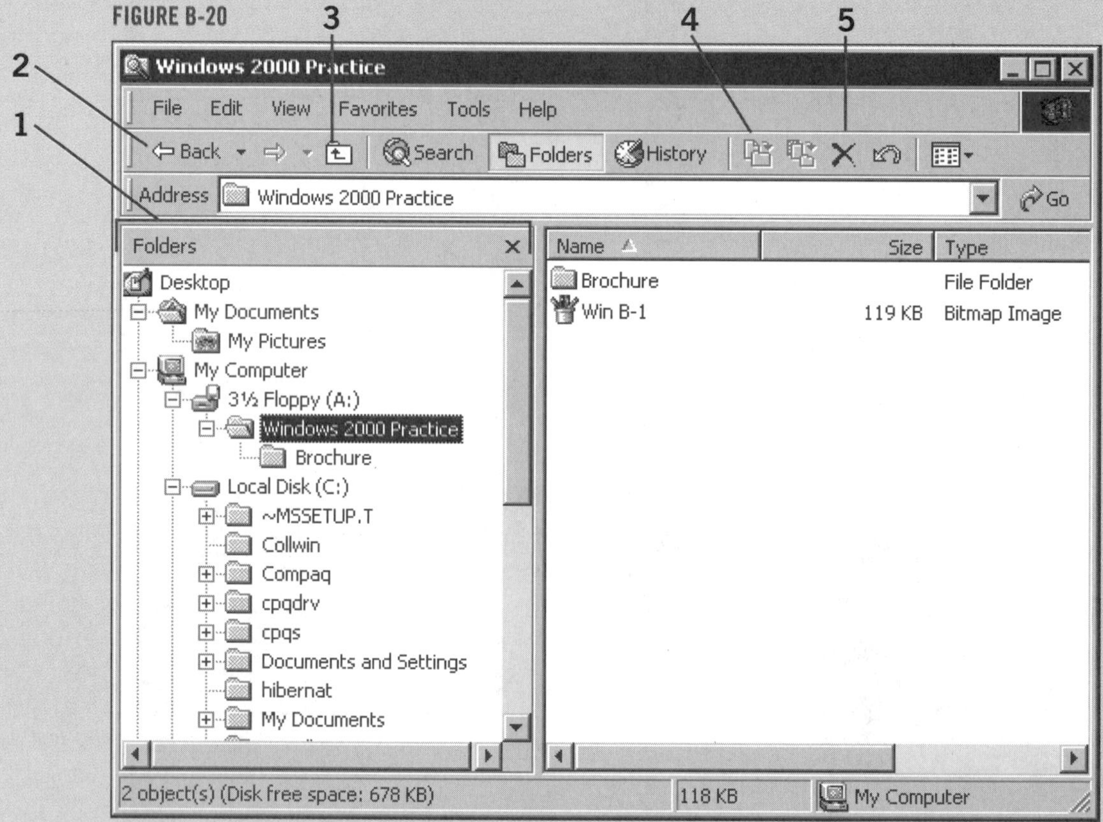

Match each of the statements with the term it describes.

6. Electronic collections of data
7. Your computer's temporary storage area
8. Temporary location of information you wish to paste into another program
9. Storage areas on your hard drive for files, folders, and programs
10. Structure of files and folders

a. RAM
b. Folders
c. Files
d. File hierarchy
e. Clipboard

Select the best answer from the list of choices.

11. To prepare a floppy disk to save your files, you must first do which of the following?
- **a.** Copy work files to the disk
- **b.** Format the disk
- **c.** Erase all the files that might be on the disk
- **d.** Place the files on the Clipboard

12. You can use My Computer to
- **a.** create a drawing of your computer.
- **b.** view the contents of a folder.
- **c.** change the appearance of your desktop.
- **d.** add text to a WordPad file.

13. Which of the following best describes WordPad?
- **a.** A program for organizing files
- **b.** A program for performing financial analysis
- **c.** A program for creating basic text documents
- **d.** A program for creating graphics

14. Which of the following is NOT a way to move files from one folder to another?

a. Open the file and use the Save As command to save the file in a new location

b. In My Computer or the Windows Explorer, drag the selected file to the new folder

c. Use the Move To button on the Standard toolbar in the My Computer or the Windows Explorer window

d. Use the [Ctrl][X] and [Ctrl][V] keyboard shortcuts while in the My Computer or the Windows Explorer window

15. In which of the following can you view the hierarchy of drives, folders, and files in a split pane window?

a. Windows Explorer

b. Programs

c. My Computer

d. WordPad

16. To restore files that you have sent to the Recycle Bin,

a. click File, then click Empty Recycle Bin.

b. click Edit, then click Undo Delete.

c. click File, then click Undo.

d. You cannot retrieve files sent to the Recycle Bin.

17. To select files that are not grouped together, select the first file, then

a. press [Shift] while selecting the second file.

b. press [Alt] while selecting the second file.

c. press [Ctrl] while selecting the second file.

d. click on the second file.

18. Pressing [Backspace]

a. deletes the character to the right of the cursor.

b. deletes the character to the left of the cursor.

c. moves the insertion point one character to the right.

d. deletes all text to the left of the cursor.

19. The size of a font is measured in

a. centimeters.

b. points.

c. places.

d. millimeters.

20. The Back button on the My Computer toolbar

a. starts the last program you used.

b. displays the next level of the file hierarchy.

c. backs up the currently selected file.

d. displays the last location you visited.

Skills Review

Use Project Disk 2 to complete the exercises in this section.

1. Create and save a WordPad file.

a. Start Windows, then start WordPad.

b. Type **My Drawing Ability**.

c. Press [Enter] three times.

d. Save the document as *Drawing Ability* to your Project Disk 2.

2. Open, edit, and save an existing Paint file.

a. Start Paint and open the file Win B-2 on your Project Disk 2.

b. Inside the picture frame, use the ellipses tool to create a circle filled with purple and then use the rectangle tool to place a square filled with yellow inside the circle.

c. Save the picture as *First Unique Art* to your Project Disk 2.

3. Work with multiple programs.

a. Select the entire graphic and copy it to the Clipboard, then switch to WordPad.

b. Place the insertion point in the last blank line, paste the graphic into your document, then deselect the graphic.

c. Save the changes to your WordPad document.

d. Switch to Paint.

e. Using the Fill With Color button, change the color of a filled area of your graphic.

f. Save the revised graphic with the new name *Second Unique Art* to Project Disk 2.

g. Select the entire graphic and copy it to the Clipboard.

h. Switch to WordPad, move the insertion point to the line below the graphic by clicking below the graphic and press [Enter], type **This is another version of my graphic.** below the first picture, then press [Enter].

i. Paste the second graphic under the text you just typed.
j. Save the changed WordPad document as *Two Drawing Examples* to your Project Disk 2.
k. Exit Paint and WordPad.

4. View files and create folders with My Computer.
a. Open My Computer.
b. Double-click the drive that contains your Project Disk 2.
c. Create a new folder on your Project Disk 2 by clicking File, New, then Folder, and name the new folder *Review*.
d. Open the folder to display its contents (it is empty).
e. Use the Address Bar to view your hard drive, usually (C:).
f. Create a folder on the hard drive called *Temporary*, then use the Back button to view the Review folder.
g. Create two new folders in it, one named *Documents* and the other named *Artwork*.
h. Click the Forward button as many times as necessary to move up in the file hierarchy and view the contents of the hard drive.
i. Change the view to Details.

5. Move and copy files with My Computer.
a. Use the Address Bar to view your Project Disk 2.
b. Use the [Shift] key to select *First Unique Art* and *Second Unique Art*, then cut and paste them into the Artwork folder.
c. Use the Back button as many times as necessary to view the contents of Project Disk 2.
d. Select the two WordPad files, *Drawing Ability* and *Two Drawing Examples*, then move them into the Review folder.
e. Open the Review folder, select the two WordPad files again, then drag them into the Documents folder.

6. Manage files with Windows Explorer.
a. Open Windows Explorer and view the contents of the Artwork folder in the right pane.
b. Select the two Paint files.
c. Drag the two Paint files from the Artwork folder to the Temporary folder on the hard drive to copy them.
d. View the contents of the Documents folder in the right pane.
e. Select the two WordPad files.
f. Repeat Step c to copy the files to the Temporary folder on the hard drive.
g. View the contents of the Temporary folder in the right pane to verify that the four files are there.

7. Delete and restore files and folders.
a. Resize the Windows Explorer window so you can see the Recycle Bin icon on the desktop, then scroll in Windows Explorer so you can see the Temporary folder in the left pane.
b. Delete the Temporary folder from the hard drive by dragging it to the Recycle Bin.
c. Click Yes if necessary to confirm the deletion.
d. Open the Recycle Bin, restore the Temporary folder and its files to your hard disk, and then close the Recycle Bin. (*Note:* If your Recycle Bin is empty, your computer is set to automatically delete items in the Recycle Bin.)
e. Delete the Temporary folder again by pressing [Delete]. Click Yes if necessary to confirm the deletion.

8. Create a shortcut on the desktop.
a. Use the left pane of Windows Explorer to locate the Windows folder on your hard drive. Select the folder to view its contents in the right pane. (*Note:* If you are in a lab setting, you may not have access to the Windows folder.)
b. In the right pane, scroll through the list of objects until you see a file called Explorer.
c. Drag the Explorer file with the right mouse button to the desktop to create a shortcut.
d. Close Windows Explorer.
e. Double-click the new shortcut to make sure it starts Windows Explorer. Then close Windows Explorer again.
f. Delete the shortcut for Windows Explorer and exit Windows.

► Independent Challenges

If you are doing all of the Independent Challenges, you may need to use additional floppy disks. Label the first new disk Project Disk 3, and the next Project Disk 4.

1. You have decided to start a bakery business and you want to use Windows 2000 to organize the files for the business.

   a. Create two new folders on your Project Disk 3, one named *Advertising* and one named *Customers*.

   b. Use WordPad to create a letter inviting new customers to the open house for the new bakery, then save it as *Open House Letter* and place it in the Customers folder.

   c. Use WordPad to create a list of five tasks that need to get done before the business opens (such as purchasing equipment, decorating the interior, and ordering supplies), then save it as *Business Plan* to your Project Disk 3, but don't place it in a folder.

   d. Use Paint to create a simple logo for the bakery, save it as *Bakery Logo*, and then place it in the Advertising folder.

   e. Print the file Bakery Logo, then delete it from your Project Disk 3.

FIGURE B-21

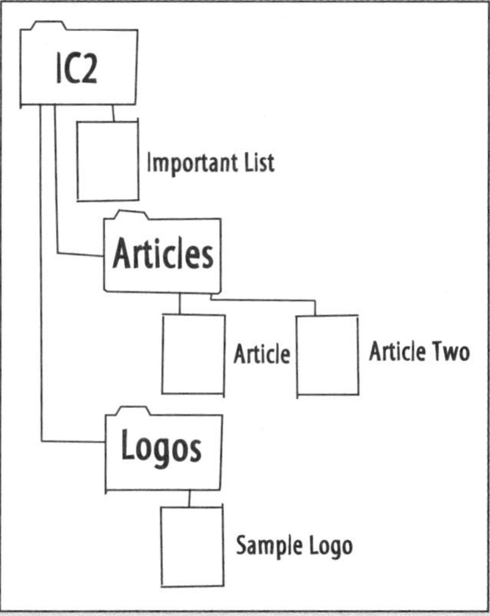

2. On your computer's hard drive, create a folder called *IC2*. Follow the guidelines listed here to create the file hierarchy shown in Figure B-21.

   a. Start WordPad, create a new file that contains a list. Save the file as *To Do List* to your Project Disk 3 (Project Disk 4 if you are out of space on Project Disk 3).

   b. Start My Computer and copy the Open House Letter file on your Project Disk 3 to the IC2 folder. Rename the file *Article*.

   c. Copy the Memo file again to the IC2 folder on your hard drive and rename the second copy of the file *Article Two*.

   d. Use My Computer to copy any Paint file to the IC2 folder and rename the file *Sample Logo*, then delete the Sample Logo file.

   e. Copy the To Do List from your Project Disk 3 to the IC2 folder and rename the file *Important List*.

   f. Move the files into the folders shown in Figure B-21.

   g. Copy the IC2 folder to your Project Disk 3. Then delete the IC2 folder on your hard drive. Using the Recycle Bin, restore the file called IC2. To remove all your work on the hard drive, delete this folder again.

3. With Windows 2000, you can access the Web from My Computer and Windows Explorer, allowing you to search for information located not only on your computer or network, but also on any computer on the Internet.

   a. Start Windows Explorer, then click in the Address Bar so the current location (probably your hard drive) is selected, type **www.microsoft.com**, then press [Enter].

   b. Connect to the Internet if necessary. The Microsoft Web page appears in the right pane of Windows Explorer.

   c. Click in the Address Bar, then type **www.course.com**, press [Enter], and then wait a moment while the Course Technology Web page opens.

   d. Make sure your Project Disk is in the floppy disk drive, then click 3½ Floppy (A:) in the left pane.

   e. Click the Back button list arrow, then click Welcome to Microsoft's Homepage.

   f. Capture a picture of your desktop by pressing [Print Screen] located on the upper-right side of your keyboard. (This stores the picture on the Clipboard.) Open the Paint program, paste the contents of the Clipboard into the drawing window, then print it.

   g. Close Paint without saving your changes.

   h. Close Windows Explorer and disconnect from the Internet.

4. Create a shortcut to the drive that contains your Project Disk 3. Then capture a picture of your desktop showing the new shortcut by pressing [Print Screen], located on the upper-right side of your keyboard. The picture is stored temporarily on the Clipboard. Then open the Paint program and paste the contents of the Clipboard into the drawing window. Click No when asked to enlarge the Bitmap. Print the screen, close Paint without saving your changes, then delete the shortcut when you are finished.

► Visual Workshop

Recreate the screen shown in Figure B-22, which contains the Brochure window in My Computer, two shortcuts on the desktop, and two open files. Press [Print Screen] to make a copy of the screen, (a copy of the screen is placed on the Clipboard), open Paint, click Paste to paste the screen picture into Paint, then print the Paint file.

FIGURE B-22

Excel 2002

Unit A

Getting
Started with Excel 2002

Objectives

- Define spreadsheet software
- Start Excel 2002
- View the Excel window
- MOUS Open and save a workbook
- MOUS Enter labels and values
- MOUS Name and move a sheet
- MOUS Preview and print a worksheet
- Get Help
- Close a workbook and exit Excel

In this unit, you will learn how to start Microsoft Excel 2002 and identify elements in the Excel window. You will also learn how to open and save existing files, enter data in a worksheet, manipulate worksheets, and use the extensive Help system. Jim Fernandez is the office manager at MediaLoft, a nationwide chain of bookstore cafés selling books, CDs, DVDs, and videos. MediaLoft cafés sell coffee and pastries. Jim wants you to help him use Excel to analyze a worksheet summarizing budget information for the MediaLoft Café in the New York City store.

Excel 2002

Defining Spreadsheet Software

Microsoft Excel is an electronic spreadsheet program that runs on Windows computers. You use an **electronic spreadsheet** to produce professional-looking documents that perform numeric calculations rapidly and accurately. These calculations are updated automatically so that accurate information is always available. See Table A-1 for common ways spreadsheets are used in business. The electronic spreadsheet that you produce when using Excel is also referred to as a **worksheet**. Individual worksheets are stored within a **workbook**, which is a file with the .xls file extension. Each new workbook contains three worksheets. Jim uses Excel extensively to track MediaLoft finances. Figure A-1 shows a budget worksheet that Jim created using pencil and paper, while Figure A-2 shows the same worksheet Jim created using Excel.

The advantages of using Excel include:

- **Enter data quickly and accurately**
  With Excel, you can enter information faster and more accurately than with pencil and paper. For example, in the MediaLoft NYC Café budget, certain expenses, such as rent, cleaning supplies, and products supplied on a yearly contract (coffee, creamers, sweeteners), remain constant for the year. You can copy the expenses that don't change from quarter to quarter, and then use Excel to calculate Total Expenses and Net Income for each quarter by supplying the data and formulas.

- **Recalculate data easily**
  Fixing typing errors or updating data using Excel is easy, and the results of a changed entry are recalculated automatically. For example, if you receive updated expense figures for Quarter 4, you enter the new numbers and Excel recalculates the worksheet.

- **Perform a what-if analysis**
  The Excel ability to change data and let you quickly view the recalculated results makes it a powerful decision-making tool. For instance, if the salary budget per quarter is increased to $14,500, you can enter the new figure into the worksheet and immediately see the impact on the overall budget. Any time you use a worksheet to ask the question "what if?" you are performing a **what-if analysis.**

- **Change the appearance of information**
  Excel provides powerful features for making information visually appealing and easy to understand. For example, you can use boldface type and colored or shaded text headings or numbers to emphasize important worksheet data and trends.

- **Create charts**
  Excel makes it easy to create charts based on worksheet information. Charts are updated automatically as data changes. The worksheet in Figure A-2 includes a 3-D pie chart that shows the distribution of the budget expenses for the MediaLoft NYC Café.

- **Share information with other users**
  Because everyone at MediaLoft is now using Microsoft Office, it's easy for them to share worksheet data. For example, you can complete the MediaLoft budget that your manager started creating in Excel. Simply access the files you need or want to share through the network or from a disk, or through the use of online collaboration tools (such as intranets and the Internet), and then make any changes or additions.

- **Create new worksheets from existing ones quickly**
  It's easy to take an existing Excel worksheet and quickly modify it to create a new one. When you are ready to create next year's budget, you can open the file for this year's budget, save it with a new filename, and use the existing data as a starting point. An Excel file can also be created using a special format called a **template**, which lets you open a new file based on an existing workbook's design and/or content. Office comes with many prepared templates you can use.

FIGURE A-1: Traditional paper worksheet

MediaLoft NYC Café Budget

	Qtr 1	Qtr 2	Qtr 3	Qtr 4	Total
Net Sales	56,000	84,000	72,000	79,000	291,000
Expenses					
Salary	14,500	14,500	14,500	14,500	58,000
Rent	4,000	4,000	4,000	4,000	16,000
Advertising	3,750	8,000	3,750	3,750	19,250
Cleansers	1,500	1,500	1,500	1,500	6,000
Pastries	2,500	2,500	2,500	2,500	10,000
Milk/Cream	1,000	1,000	1,000	1,000	4,000
Coffee/Tea	4,700	4,750	4,750	4,750	18,950
Sweeteners	300	300	300	300	1,200
Total Expenses	32,250	36,550	32,300	32,300	133,400
Net Income	23,750	47,450	39,700	46,700	157,600

FIGURE A-2: Excel worksheet

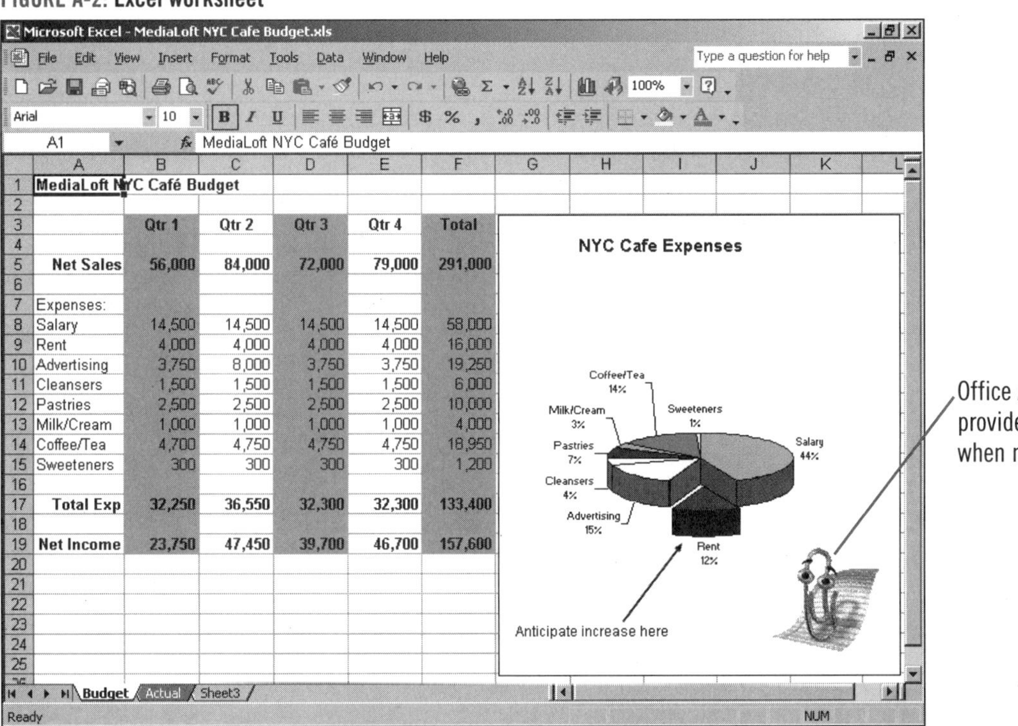

TABLE A-1: Common business uses for electronic spreadsheets

spreadsheets are used to	by
Maintain values	Calculating numbers
Represent values graphically	Creating charts based on worksheet figures
Create consecutively numbered pages using multiple workbook sheets	Printing reports containing workbook sheets
Organize data	Sorting data in ascending or descending order
Analyze data	Creating data summaries and short-lists using PivotTables or AutoFilters
Create what-if data scenarios	Using variable values to investigate and sample different outcomes

Excel 2002

Starting Excel 2002

To start any Windows program, you use the Start button on the taskbar. A slightly different procedure might be required for computers on a network and those that use Windows-enhancing utilities. If you need assistance, ask your instructor or technical support person. Jim is ready to begin work on the budget for the MediaLoft Café in New York City. He begins by starting Excel.

Steps

1. **Point to the Start button on the taskbar**
   The Start button is on the left side of the taskbar. You use it to start programs on your computer.
2. **Click Start**
   Microsoft Excel is located in the Programs folder, which is at the top of the Start menu, as shown in Figure A-3.
3. **Point to Programs**
   The Programs menu opens. All the programs on your computer, including Microsoft Excel, are listed on this menu. See Figure A-4. Your program menu might look different, depending on the programs installed on your computer.
4. **Click the Microsoft Excel program icon on the Programs menu**
   Excel opens and a blank worksheet appears. In the next lesson, you will learn about the elements of the Excel worksheet window.
5. **If necessary, click the Maximize button on the title bar**

Trouble?

If you don't see the Microsoft Excel icon, see your instructor or technical support person.

FIGURE A-3: **Start menu**

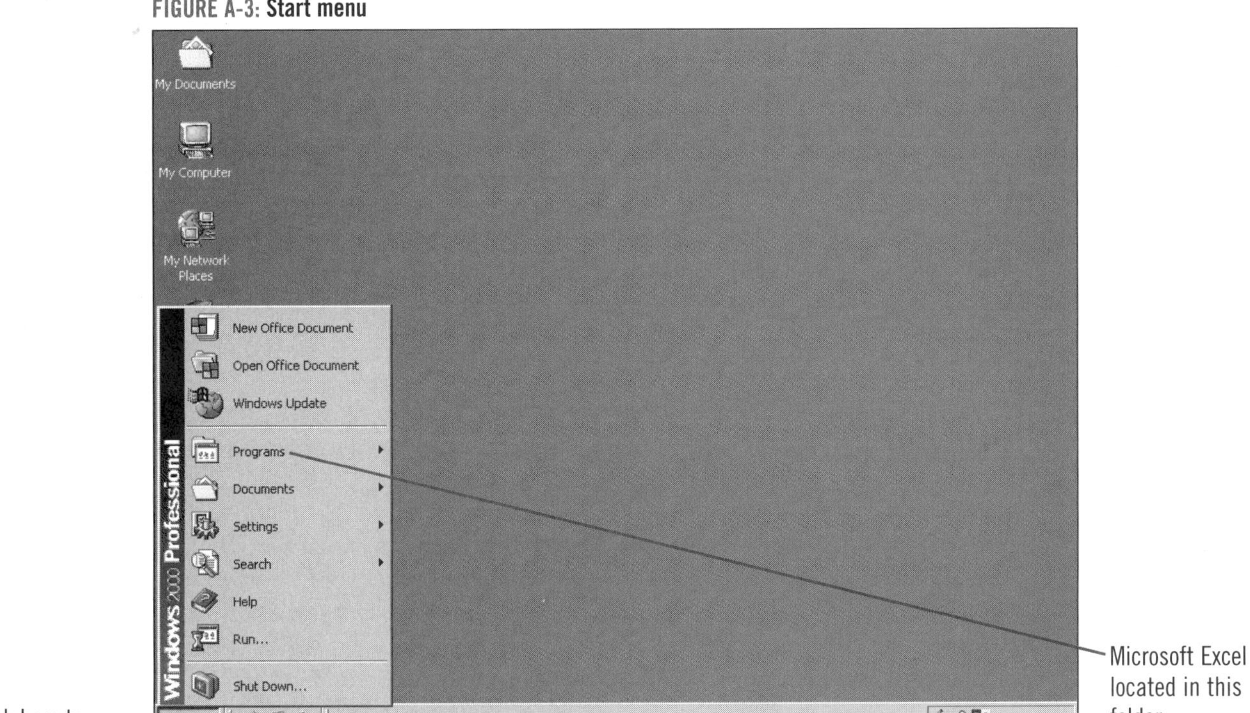

FIGURE A-4: **Programs list**

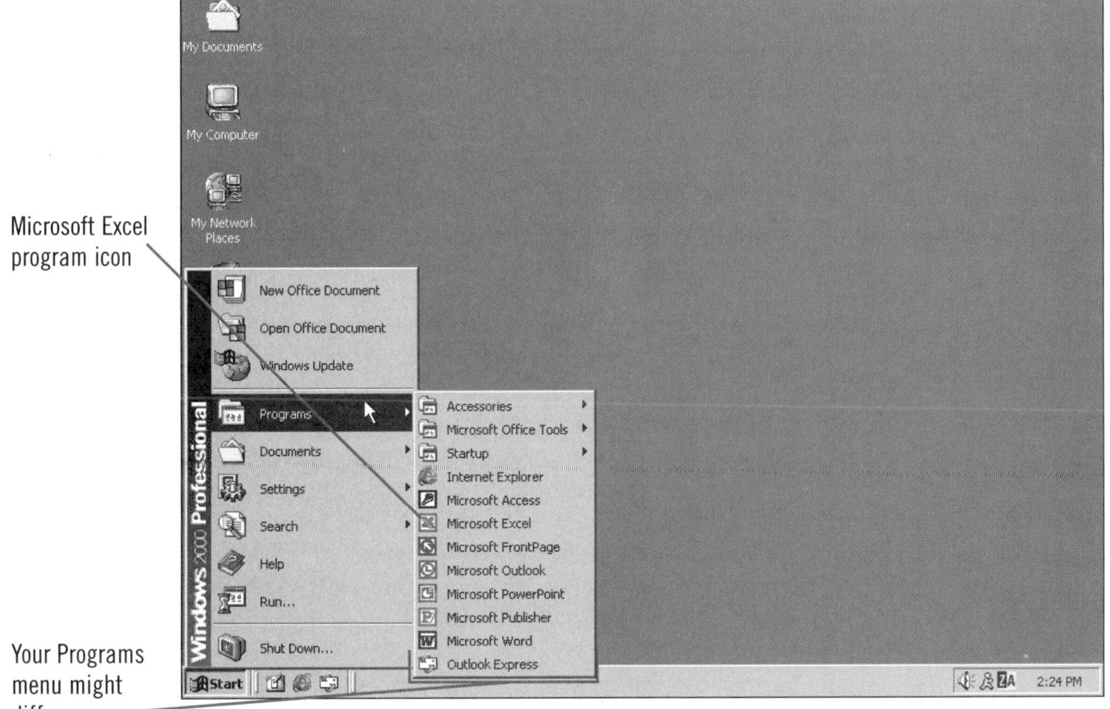

Excel 2002

Excel 2002

Viewing the Excel Window

When you start Excel, the **worksheet window** appears on your screen. The worksheet window includes the tools that enable you to create and work with worksheets. Jim needs to familiarize himself with the Excel worksheet window and its elements before he starts working with the budget worksheet. Compare the descriptions below to the elements shown in Figure A-5.

Details

- The **worksheet window** contains a grid of columns and rows. Columns are labeled alphabetically (A, B, C, etc.) and rows are labeled numerically (1, 2, 3, etc.). The worksheet window displays only a small fraction of the whole worksheet, which has a total of 256 columns and 65,536 rows. The intersection of a column and a row is called a **cell**. Cells can contain text, numbers, formulas, or a combination of all three. Every cell has its own unique location or **cell address**, which is identified by the coordinates of the intersecting column and row. For example, the cell address of the cell in the upper-left corner of a worksheet is A1. The **new workbook pane** appears to the right of the worksheet window and lets you quickly open new or existing workbooks. The **Task pane list arrow** lets you display other panes.

Trouble?

If your screen does not display cells in purple and gray as shown in the figure, ask your technical support person to check your Windows color settings.

- The **cell pointer** is a dark rectangle that outlines the cell you are working in. This cell is called the **active cell**. In Figure A-5, the cell pointer is located at A1, so A1 is the active cell. The column and row headings for the active cell are purple; inactive column and row headings are gray. To activate a different cell, just click any other cell or press the arrow keys on your keyboard to move the cell pointer elsewhere.
- The **title bar** displays the program name (Microsoft Excel) and the filename of the open worksheet (in this case the default filename, Book1). As shown in Figure A-5, the title bar also contains a control menu box, a Close button, and resizing buttons, which are common to all Windows programs.
- The **menu bar** contains menus from which you choose Excel commands. As with all Windows programs, you can choose a menu command by clicking it with the mouse pointer or by pressing [Alt] plus the underlined letter in the menu command name. When you click a menu, only a short list of commonly used commands may appear at first; you can wait or click the double arrows at the bottom of the menu to see expanded menus with more commands.
- The **name box** displays the active cell address. In Figure A-5, "A1" appears in the name box, indicating that A1 is the active cell.
- The **formula bar** allows you to enter or edit data in the worksheet.
- The **toolbars** contain buttons for frequently used Excel commands. The **Standard toolbar** is located just below the menu bar and contains buttons that perform actions within the worksheet. The **Formatting toolbar**—beneath the Standard toolbar—contains buttons that change the worksheet's appearance. Each button contains an image representing its function. For instance, the Print button contains an image of a printer. To choose any button, click it with the left mouse button.
- **Sheet tabs** below the worksheet grid let you keep your work in a collection called a **workbook**. Each workbook contains three worksheets by default and can contain a maximum of 255 sheets. Sheet tabs allow you to name your worksheets with meaningful names. **Sheet tab scrolling buttons** help you display hidden worksheets.
- The **status bar** is located at the bottom of the Excel window. The left side of the status bar provides a brief description of the active command or task in progress. The right side of the status bar shows the status of important keys such as [Caps Lock] and [Num Lock].

FIGURE A-5: Excel worksheet window elements

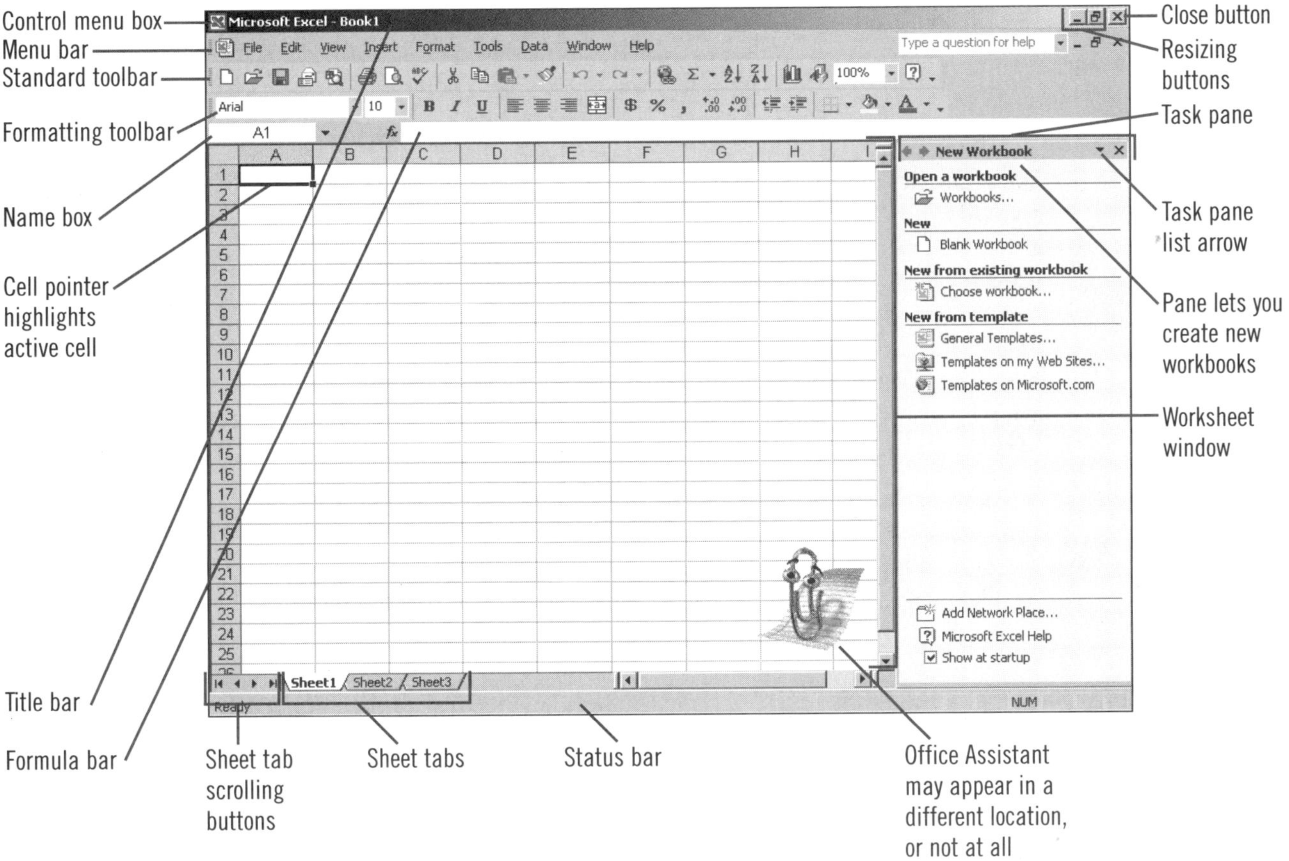

Control menu box
Menu bar
Standard toolbar
Formatting toolbar
Name box
Cell pointer highlights active cell
Title bar
Formula bar
Sheet tab scrolling buttons
Sheet tabs
Status bar
Office Assistant may appear in a different location, or not at all
Close button
Resizing buttons
Task pane
Task pane list arrow
Pane lets you create new workbooks
Worksheet window

Excel 2002

Working with toolbars and menus in Excel 2002

Although you can configure Excel so that your toolbars and menus modify themselves to conform to your working style, the lessons in this book assume you have turned off personalized menus and toolbars and are working with all menu commands and toolbar buttons displayed. When you use personalized toolbars, the Standard and Formatting toolbars appear on the same row and display only the most frequently used buttons, as shown in Figure A-6. To use a button that is not visible on a toolbar, you click the Toolbar Options button at the end of the toolbar, then click the button on the Toolbar Options list. As you work, Excel adds the buttons you use to the visible toolbars and drops the buttons you don't often use to the Toolbar Options list. Similarly, Excel menus adjust to your work habits, so that the commands you use most often appear on shortened menus. You can see all the menu commands by clicking the double arrows at the bottom of a menu. It is often easier to work with full toolbars and menus displayed. To turn off personalized toolbars and menus, click Tools on the menu bar, click Customize, on the Options tab select the Show Standard and Formatting toolbars on two rows and Always show full menus check boxes, and then click Close. The Standard and Formatting toolbars appear on separate rows and display all the buttons, and the menus display the complete list of menu commands. (You can quickly display the toolbars on two rows by clicking a Toolbar Options button and then clicking Show Buttons on Two Rows.)

FIGURE A-6: Toolbars in one row

Excel 2002

Opening and Saving a Workbook

Sometimes it's more efficient to create a new worksheet by modifying one that already exists. This saves you from having to retype information from previous work. Throughout this book, you will create new workbooks by opening a file from the location where your Project Files are stored, using the Save As command to create a copy of the file with a new name, and then modifying the new file by following the lesson steps. Use the Save command to store changes made to an existing file. It is a good idea to save your work every 10 or 15 minutes and before printing. Saving the files with new names keeps your original Project Files intact, in case you have to start the unit over again or you wish to repeat an exercise. Jim wants you to complete the New York City MediaLoft Café budget that a member of the accounting staff has been working on.

Steps

QuickTip
You can also click the Open button on the Standard toolbar.

QuickTip
If you don't see the three-letter extension .xls on the filenames in the Open dialog box, don't worry. Windows can be set up to display or not to display the file extensions.

QuickTip
You can create a new folder from within the Save As dialog box by clicking on the dialog box toolbar, typing a name in the Name text box, then clicking OK. To open a file from a folder you create, double-click folders or use the Look in list arrow in the Open dialog box to open the folder, click the filename, then click Open.

1. Click **More Workbooks** in the New Workbook task pane
   The Open dialog box opens. See Figure A-7. If no workbooks have been opened on your computer, the command will read "Workbooks."

2. Click the **Look in list arrow**, then click the drive and folder where your Project Files are located
   The Look in list arrow lets you navigate to folders and disk drives on your computer. A list of your Project Files appears in the Open dialog box.

3. Click the file **EX A-1**, then click **Open**
   The workbook file EX A-1 opens. The new workbook pane no longer appears.

4. Click **File** on the menu bar, then click **Save As**
   The Save As dialog box opens, displaying the drive where your Project Files are stored.

5. In the File name text box, select the current filename (if necessary), type **MediaLoft Cafe Budget**, as shown in Figure A-8, then click **Save**
   Both the Save As dialog box and the file EX A-1 close, and a duplicate file named MediaLoft Cafe Budget opens, as shown in Figure A-9. The Office Assistant may or may not appear on your screen.

Creating a new workbook

You can create your own worksheets from scratch by opening a new workbook. To create a new workbook, click the New button on the Standard toolbar. You can also use the New Workbook pane (located on the right side of the screen) to open a new file. Click the Blank Workbook button in the New Workbook pane, and a new workbook will open. Each new workbook automatically contains 3 sheets, although you can insert as many as you need.

FIGURE A-7: **Open dialog box**

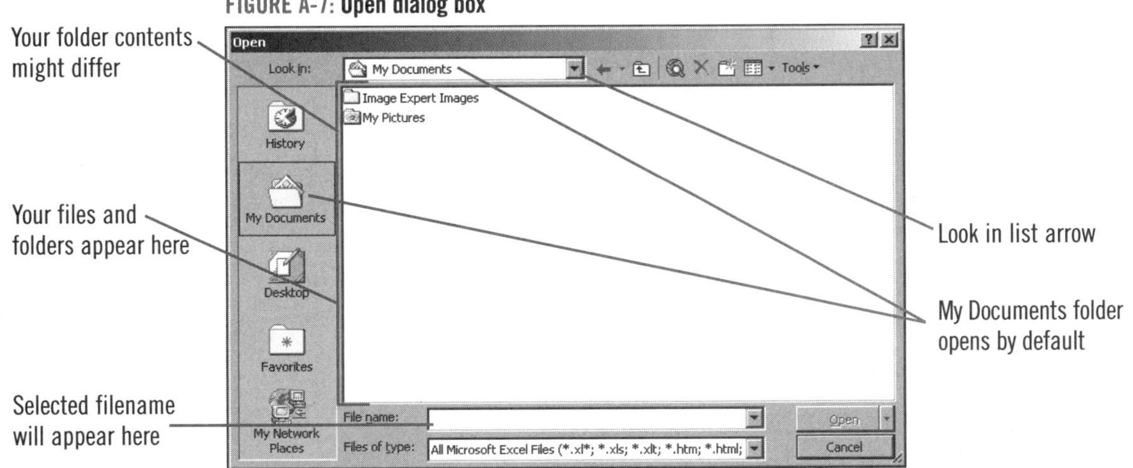

FIGURE A-8: **Save As dialog box**

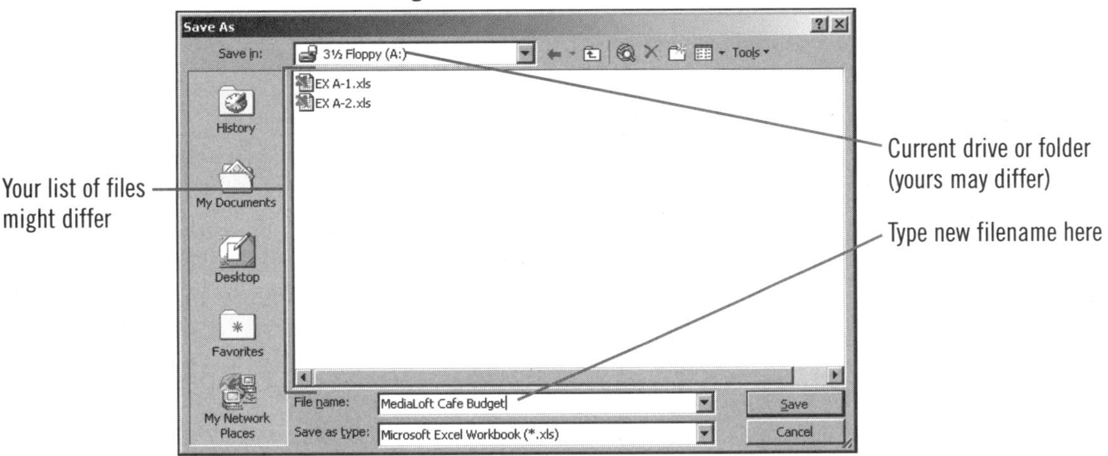

FIGURE A-9: **MediaLoft Café Budget workbook**

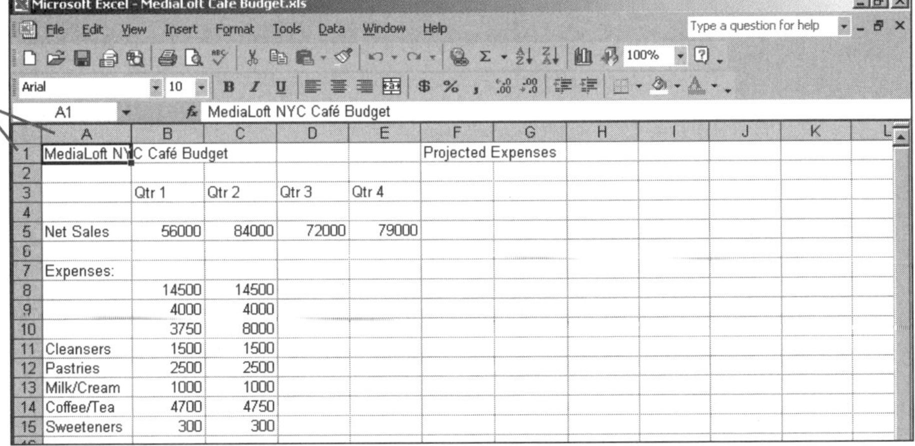

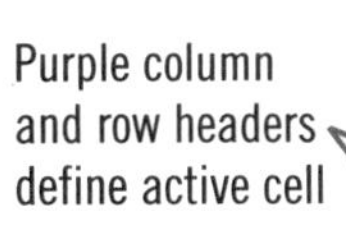

Opening a workbook using a template

You can create a workbook by entering data and formats into a blank workbook, or you can use predesigned workbooks called templates that are included with Excel. Templates let you automatically create workbooks such as balance sheets, expense statements, loan amortizations, sales invoices, or timecards. Templates save you time because they contain labels, values, formulas, and formatting. To open a new document based on a template, click General Templates from the New Workbook task pane, save it under a new name, then add your own information. You may need to have the Office CD available to install the templates.

Excel 2002

Entering Labels and Values

Labels help you identify the data in worksheet rows and columns, making your worksheet more readable and understandable. Try to enter all labels in your worksheet before entering the data. Labels can contain text and numerical information not used in calculations, such as dates, times, or addresses. Labels are left-aligned by default. **Values**, which include numbers, formulas, and functions, are used in calculations. Excel recognizes an entry as a value when it is a number or begins with special symbols: +, -, =, @, #, or $. Because Excel treats labels and values differently, you can have a label such as '2003 Sales' without affecting values used in a totals column. All values are right-aligned by default. When a cell contains both text and numbers it is not a valid formula; Excel recognizes the entry as a label. Jim wants you to enter labels identifying the rest of the expense categories, and the values for Qtr 3 and Qtr 4 into the MediaLoft Café Budget worksheet.

Trouble?

If you notice a mistake in a cell entry after entering it, double-click the cell, use [Backspace] or [Delete], make your corrections, then press [Enter]. You can also click Edit on the menu bar, point to Clear, then click Contents to remove a cell's contents.

QuickTip

To enter a number that will not be used as part of a calculation, such as a telephone number, type an apostrophe (') before the number.

1. Click cell **A8** to make it the active cell
   Notice that the cell address A8 appears in the name box. As you work, the mouse pointer takes on a variety of appearances, depending on where it is and what Excel is doing. Table A-2 lists and identifies some mouse pointers. The labels in cells A8:A15 identify the expenses.
2. Type **Salary**, as shown in Figure A-10, then click the **Enter button** on the formula bar
   As you type, the word "Enter" appears in the status bar. Clicking the Enter button indicates that you are finished typing or changing your entry, and the word "Ready" appears in the status bar. Because the cell is still selected, its contents still appear in the formula bar. You can also confirm a cell entry by pressing [Enter], [Tab], or one of the keyboard arrow keys. These three methods also select an adjacent cell. To confirm an entry and leave the same cell selected, you can press [Ctrl][Enter]. If a label does not fit in a cell, Excel displays the remaining characters in the next cell to the right, as long as it is empty. Otherwise, the label is **truncated**, or cut off.
3. Click cell **A9**, type **Rent**, press **[Enter]** to confirm the entry and move the cell pointer to cell A10, type **Advertising** in cell A10, then press **[Enter]**
   The remaining expense values have to be added to the worksheet.
4. Click cell **D8**, press and hold down the left mouse button, drag to cell **E8** then down to cell **E15**, then release the mouse button
   You have selected a **range**, which is two or more adjacent cells. The active cell is still cell D8, and the cells in the range are shaded in purple.
5. Type **14500**, press **[Enter]**, type **4000** in cell D9, press **[Enter]**, type **3750** in cell D10, press **[Enter]**, type **1500** in cell D11, press **[Enter]**, type **2500** in cell D12, press **[Enter]**, type **1000** in cell D13, press **[Enter]**, type **4750** in cell D14, press **[Enter]**, type **300** in cell D15, then press **[Enter]**
   You will often enter data in multiple columns and rows; selecting a range makes working with data entry easier because pressing [Enter] makes the next cell in the range active. You have entered all the values in the Qtr 3 column, as shown in Figure A-11. The cell pointer is now in cell E8.
6. Using Figure A-11 as a guide, type the remaining values for cells E8 through E15
   Before confirming a cell entry, you can click the Cancel button on the formula bar or press [Esc] to cancel or delete the entry. Notice that the AutoCalculate area in the status bar displays "Sum=64550," which is the sum of the figures in the selected range. This sum changes if you change any of the numbers in the selected range.
7. Click cell **D8**, type **14550**, press **[Enter]**, then select cells **D8:E15**
   Notice that the AutoCalculate area in the status bar now says "Sum=64600".
8. Press **[Ctrl][Home]** to return to cell A1
9. Click the **Save button** on the Standard toolbar
   You can also press [Ctrl][S] to save a worksheet.

FIGURE A-10: Worksheet with first label entered

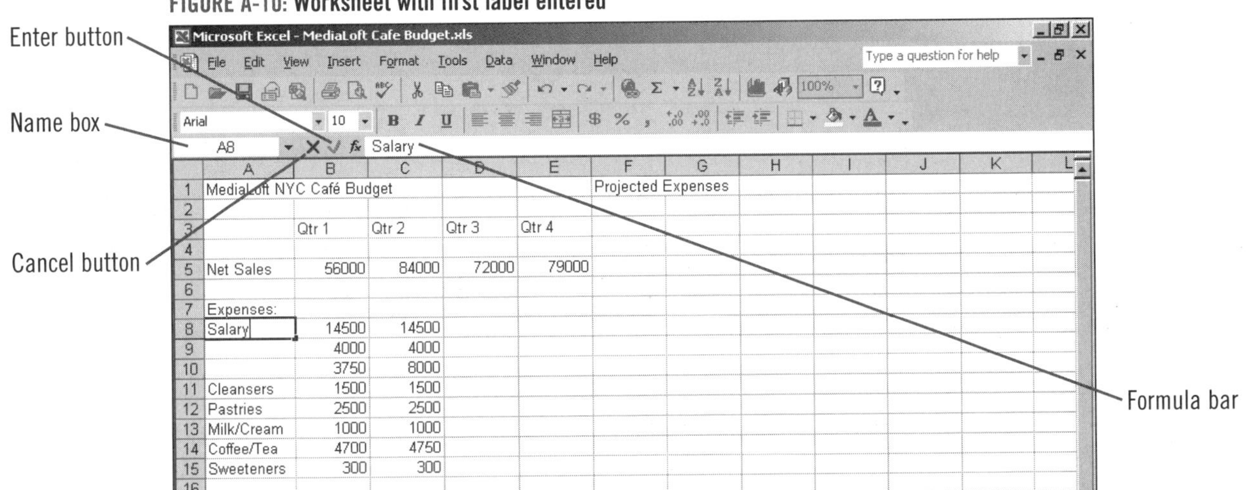

FIGURE A-11: Worksheet with new labels and values

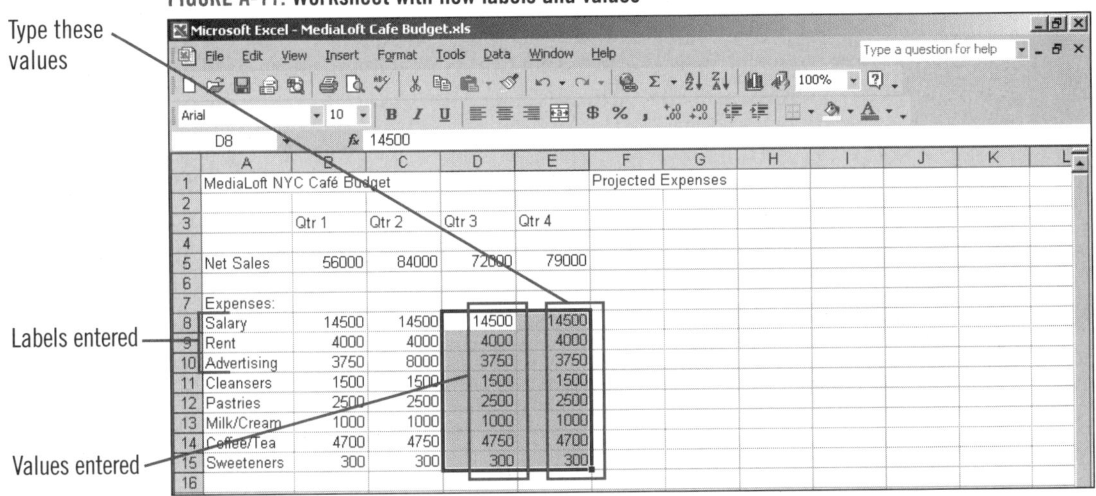

TABLE A-2: Commonly used pointers

name	pointer	use to
Normal	✚	Select a cell or range; indicates Ready mode
Copy	↖+	Create a duplicate of the selected cell(s)
Fill handle	+	Create an alphanumeric series in a range
I-beam	I	Edit contents of formula bar
Move	✥	Change the location of the selected cell(s)

Navigating a worksheet

With over a million cells available to you, it is important to know how to move around, or **navigate**, a worksheet. You can use the arrow keys on the keyboard ([↑] [↓] [←] or [→]) to move a cell or two at a time, or use [Page Up] or [Page Down] to move a screenful at a time. To move a screen to the left press [Alt][Page Up]; to move a screen to the right press [Alt][Page Down]. You can also use the mouse pointer to click the desired cell. If the desired cell is not visible in the worksheet window, use the scroll bars or the Go To command on the Edit menu to move the location into view. To return to the first active cell in a worksheet, click cell A1, or press [Ctrl][Home].

Excel 2002

Naming and Moving a Sheet

Each workbook initially contains three worksheets, named Sheet1, Sheet2, and Sheet3. When you open a workbook, the first worksheet is the active sheet. To move from sheet to sheet, you can click any sheet tab at the bottom of the worksheet window. The sheet tab scrolling buttons, located to the left of the sheet tabs, allow you to display hidden sheet tabs. To make it easier to identify the sheets in a workbook, you can rename each sheet, add color to the tabs, and then organize them in a logical way. The sheet name appears on the sheet tab. For instance, to better track performance goals, you could name each workbook sheet for an individual salesperson; then you could move the sheets so they appeared in alphabetical order. Jim wants to be able to easily identify the actual expenses and the projected expenses. He wants you to name two sheets in his workbook, add color to distinguish them, then change their order.

Steps

1. Click the **Sheet2 tab**
   Sheet2 becomes active; this is the worksheet that contains the actual quarterly expenses. Its tab moves to the front, and Sheet1 moves to the background.

2. Click the **Sheet1 tab**
   Sheet1, which contains the projected expenses, becomes active again. Once you have confirmed which sheet is which, you can assign them each a name that you can easily remember.

QuickTip

You can also rename a sheet by right-clicking the tab, clicking Rename, typing the new name, then pressing [Enter].

3. Double-click the **Sheet2 tab**
   Sheet 2 becomes the active sheet with the default sheet name ("Sheet2") selected.

4. Type **Actual**, then press **[Enter]**
   The new name automatically replaces the default name in the tab. Worksheet names can have up to 31 characters, including spaces and punctuation.

5. Right-click the **Actual tab**, then click **Tab Color**
   The Format Tab Color dialog box appears, as shown in Figure A-12.

QuickTip

To delete a worksheet, select the worksheet you want to delete, click Edit on the menu bar, then click Delete sheet. To insert a worksheet, click Insert on the menu bar, then click Worksheet.

6. Click the color **red** (first column, third row), click **OK**, double-click the **Sheet1 tab**, type **Projected**, then press **[Enter]**
   Notice that when you renamed Sheet1, the color of the entire Actual tab changed to red. Jim decides to rearrange the order of the sheets, so that Actual comes before Projected.

7. Click the **Actual sheet tab** and hold down the mouse button, then drag it to the left of the **Projected sheet tab**
   As you drag, the pointer changes to the sheet relocation pointer, and a small, black triangle shows its position. See Figure A-13. The first sheet in the workbook is now the Actual sheet. When you have more worksheets than can appear at once, click the leftmost tab scrolling button to display the first sheet tab; click the rightmost navigation button to display the last sheet tab. The left and right buttons move one sheet in their respective directions.

8. Click the **Projected sheet tab**, enter your name in cell **A20**, then press **[Ctrl][Home]**
   Your name identifies your worksheet as yours, which is helpful if you are sharing a printer.

9. Click the **Save button** on the Standard toolbar

FIGURE A-12: Format Tab Color dialog box

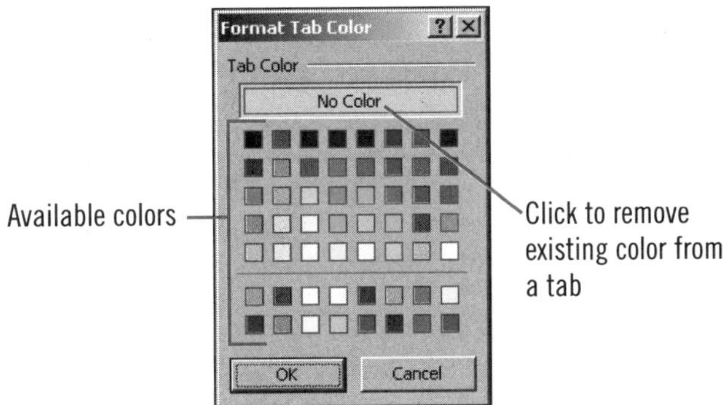

FIGURE A-13: Moving Actual sheet before Projected sheet

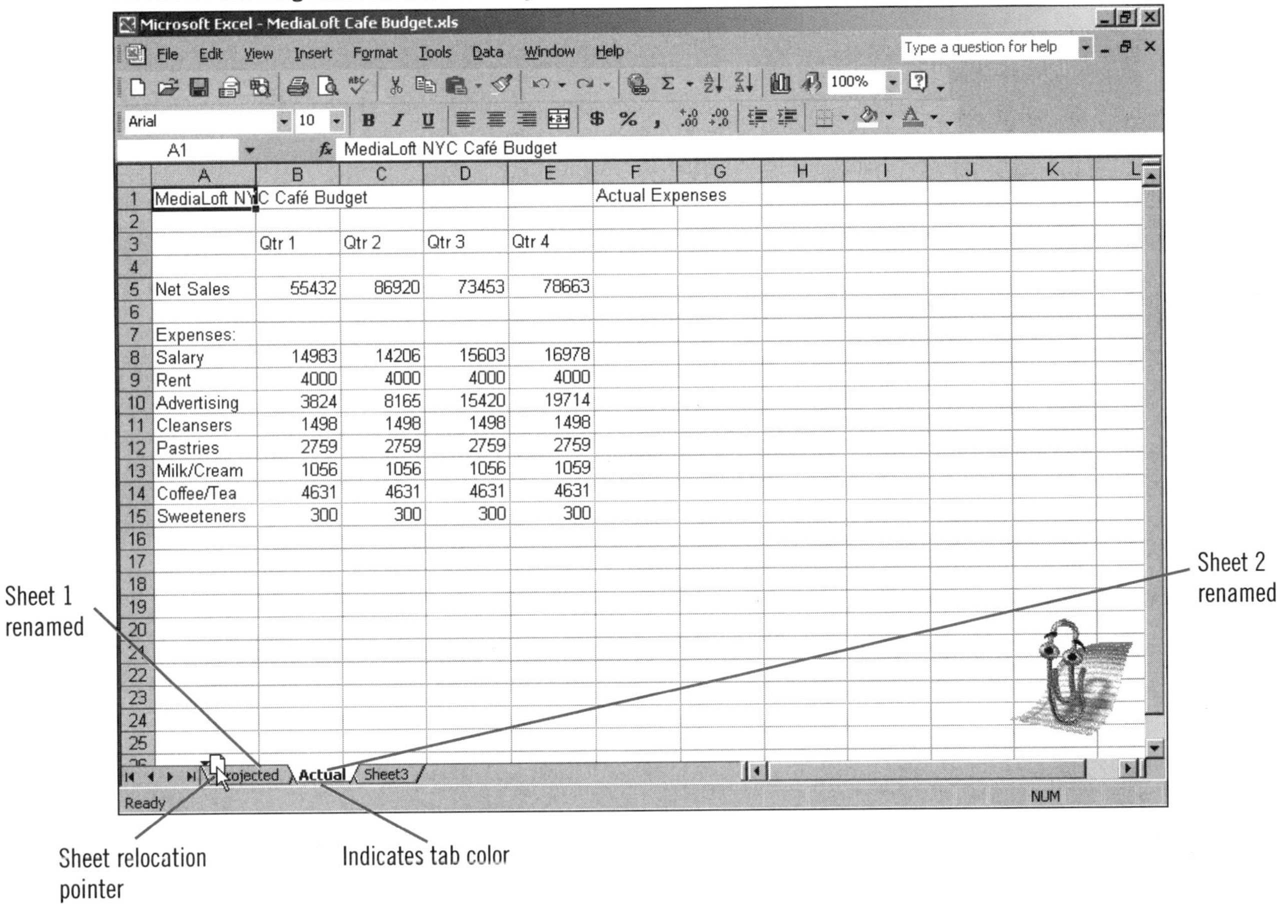

Microsoft Excel - MediaLoft Cafe Budget.xls

File Edit View Insert Format Tools Data Window Help

Type a question for help

A1 MediaLoft NYC Café Budget

	A	B	C	D	E	F
1	MediaLoft NYC Café Budget					Actual Expenses
2						
3		Qtr 1	Qtr 2	Qtr 3	Qtr 4	
4						
5	Net Sales	55432	86920	73453	78663	
6						
7	Expenses:					
8	Salary	14983	14206	15603	16978	
9	Rent	4000	4000	4000	4000	
10	Advertising	3824	8165	15420	19714	
11	Cleansers	1498	1498	1498	1498	
12	Pastries	2759	2759	2759	2759	
13	Milk/Cream	1056	1056	1056	1059	
14	Coffee/Tea	4631	4631	4631	4631	
15	Sweeteners	300	300	300	300	

Projected | Actual | Sheet3

Ready NUM

Sheet 1 renamed

Sheet 2 renamed

Sheet relocation pointer

Indicates tab color

Copying worksheets

There are times when you may want to copy a worksheet. To copy it, press [Ctrl] as you drag the sheet tab and release the mouse button before you release [Ctrl]. You can also move and copy worksheets between workbooks. You must have the workbook that you are copying to, as well as the workbook that you are copying from, open. Select the sheet to copy or move, click Edit on the menu bar, then click Move or Copy sheet. Complete the information in the Move or Copy dialog box. Be sure to click the Create a Copy check box if you are copying rather than moving the worksheet. Carefully check your calculation results whenever you move or copy a worksheet.

Excel 2002

Previewing and Printing a Worksheet

After you complete a worksheet, you may want to print it to have a paper copy for reference or to give to others. You can also print a worksheet that is not complete to review your work when you are not at a computer. Before you print a worksheet, you should save any changes. That way, if anything happens to the file as it is being sent to the printer, you will have your latest work saved. Then you should preview it to make sure it will fit on a page the way you want. When you **preview** a worksheet, you see a copy of the worksheet exactly as it will appear on paper. See Table A-3 for a summary of printing tips. Jim is finished entering the labels and values into the MediaLoft Café budget. He has already saved his changes, so he asks you to preview and print a copy of the worksheet he can review on the way home.

1. **Make sure the printer is on and contains paper**
   If a file is sent to print and the printer is off, an error message appears.

2. **Click the Print Preview button on the Standard toolbar**
   A miniature version of the worksheet appears on the screen, as shown in Figure A-14. If your worksheet requires more than one page, you could click the Next button or the Previous button to move between pages. Because your worksheet is only one page, the Next and Previous buttons are dimmed.

QuickTip

To print the worksheet using existing settings without previewing it, click on the Standard toolbar.

3. **Click Print**
   The Print dialog box opens, as shown in Figure A-15.

4. **Make sure that the Active Sheet(s) option button is selected in the Print what section and that 1 appears in the Number of copies text box in the Copies section**
   Adjusting the value in the Number of copies text box enables you to print multiple copies. You could also print a selected range by clicking the Selection option button.

QuickTip

After previewing or printing a worksheet, dotted lines appear on the screen indicating individual page breaks in the printout. Page break positions vary with each printer.

5. **Click OK**
   A Printing dialog box appears briefly while the file is sent to the printer. Note that the dialog box contains a Cancel button. You can use it to cancel the print job provided you can catch it before the file is sent to the printer.

TABLE A-3: Worksheet printing tips

before you print	recommendation
Save your work	Make sure your work is saved
Check the printer	Make sure that the printer is turned on and is online, that it has paper, and that there are no error messages or warning signals
Preview the worksheet	Check the formatted image for page breaks, page setup (vertical or horizontal), and overall appearance of the worksheet
Check the printer selection	Look in the Print dialog box to verify that the correct printer is selected
Check the Print what options	Verify that you are printing either the active sheet, the entire workbook, or just a selected range

FIGURE A-14: Print Preview screen

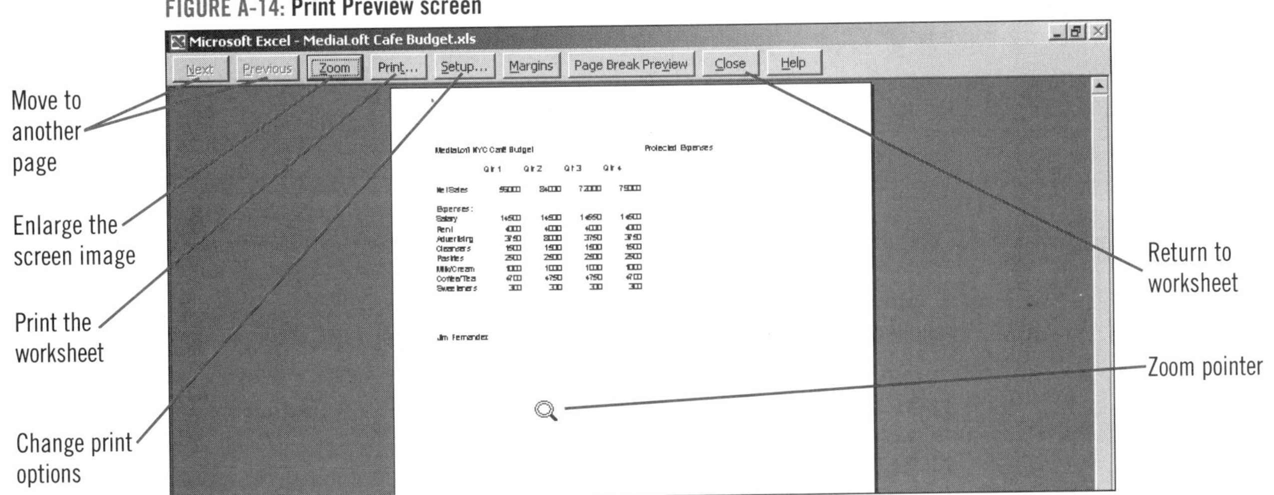

FIGURE A-15: Print dialog box

Your printer may differ

Prints the current worksheet

Indicates the number of copies to be printed

Print
Printer
Name: HP LaserJet 6P
Properties...
Status: Idle
Find Printer...
Type: HP LaserJet 6P
Where: LPT1:
Comment:
Print to file
Print range
All
Page(s) From: To:
Copies
Number of copies: 1
Print what
Selection
Entire workbook
Active sheet(s)
Collate
Preview
OK
Cancel

Using Zoom in Print Preview

When you are in the Print Preview window, you can enlarge the image by clicking the Zoom button. You can also position the Zoom pointer over a specific part of the worksheet page, then click it to view that section of the page. Figure A-16 shows a magnified section of a document. While the image is zoomed in, use the scroll bars to view different sections of the page.

FIGURE A-16: Enlarging the preview using Zoom

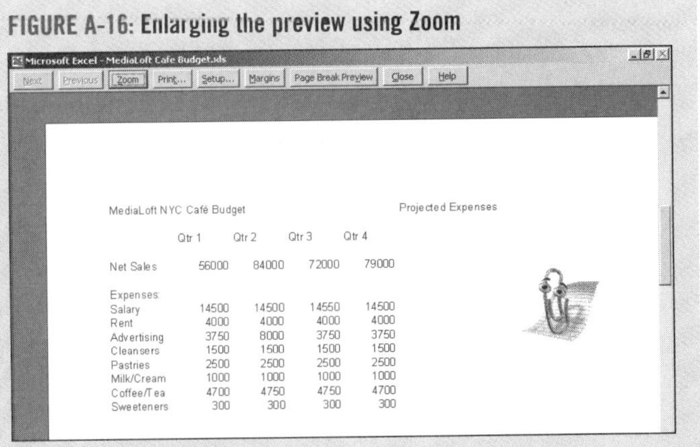

	Qtr 1	Qtr 2	Qtr 3	Qtr 4
Net Sales	56000	84000	72000	79000
Expenses				
Salary	14500	14500	14550	14500
Rent	4000	4000	4000	4000
Advertising	3750	8000	3750	3750
Cleansers	1500	1500	1500	1500
Pastries	2500	2500	2500	2500
Milk/Cream	1000	1000	1000	1000
Coffee/Tea	4700	4750	4750	4700
Sweeteners	300	300	300	300

Excel 2002

Getting Help

Excel features an extensive **Help system** that gives you immediate access to definitions, steps, explanations, and useful tips. The animated Office Assistant provides help in two ways. You can type a **keyword**, a representative word on which Excel can search your area of interest, or you can access a question and answer format to research your Help topic. The Office Assistant provides **Office Assistant Tips** (indicated by a light bulb) on the current action you are performing. You can click the light bulb to display a dialog box containing relevant choices that you can refer to as you work. In addition, you can press [F1] at any time to get immediate help. Alternately, the **Ask a Question list arrow** on the menu bar is always available for asking questions. You can click the text box and type a question at any time to display related help topics. Questions from your current Excel session are stored, and you can access them at any time by clicking the Ask a Question list arrow, then clicking the question of interest. Jim wants to find out more about ranges so he can work more efficiently with them. He asks you to find more information by using the animated Office Assistant.

Steps

QuickTip

If the Office Assistant is displayed, click it to access Help. If it is not displayed, clicking opens the Office Assistant. A previous user may have turned off the Office Assistant. To turn it on, click Help on the menu bar, click Show the Office Assistant, then click the Office Assistant to open the dialog balloon.

QuickTip

Clicking the Print button in the Help window prints the information.

1. Click the **Microsoft Excel Help button** on the Standard toolbar
   An Office Assistant dialog balloon opens, asking what you want to do. You can get information by typing a keyword or question in the white box, known as the **query box**. If the text within the query box is highlighted, your text will automatically replace it. The Office Assistant provides help based on the text in the query box.
2. Type **Define a range**
   See Figure A-18.
3. Click **Search**
   The Office Assistant searches for relevant topics from the Help files in Excel and then displays a list of topics for you to choose from.
4. Click **See More**, then click **Name cells on more than one worksheet**
   A Help window containing information about ranges opens, as shown in Figure A-19.
5. Read the text, then click the **Close button** on the Help window title bar
   The Help window closes.
6. Click the Microsoft Excel button on the taskbar to display it, if necessary.
   The Office Assistant is no longer visible on the worksheet. Hiding the Office Assistant does not turn it off; it only hides it temporarily.

CLUES TO USE

Changing the Office Assistant

The default Office Assistant character is Clippit, but there are others from which you can choose. To change the appearance of the Office Assistant, right-click the Office Assistant, then click Options. Click the Gallery tab shown in Figure A-17, click the Back and Next buttons until you find an Assistant you want to use, then click OK. (You may need to insert your Microsoft Office CD to perform this task.) Each Office Assistant character makes its own unique sounds. Animate any assistant by right-clicking it, then clicking Animate!

FIGURE A-17: Office Assistant dialog box

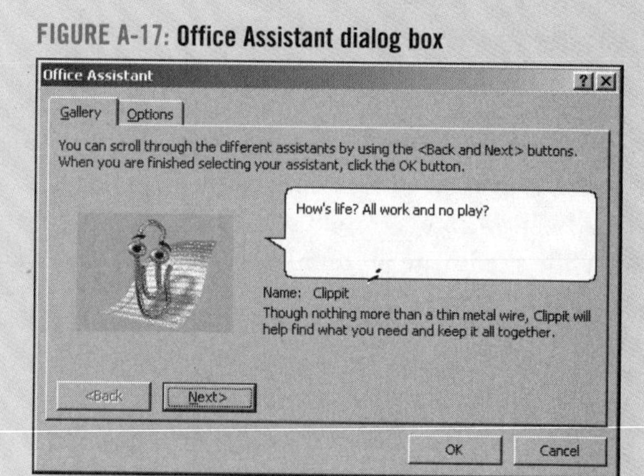

FIGURE A-18: Office Assistant

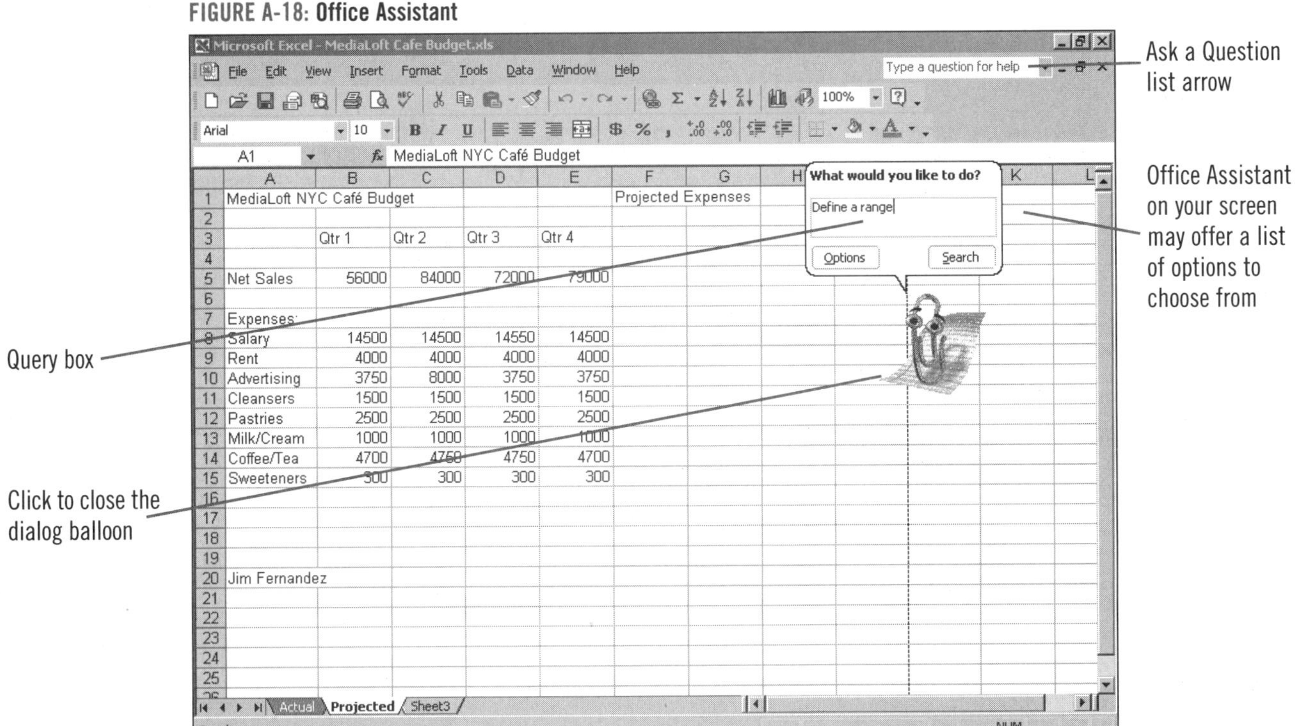

FIGURE A-19: Help window

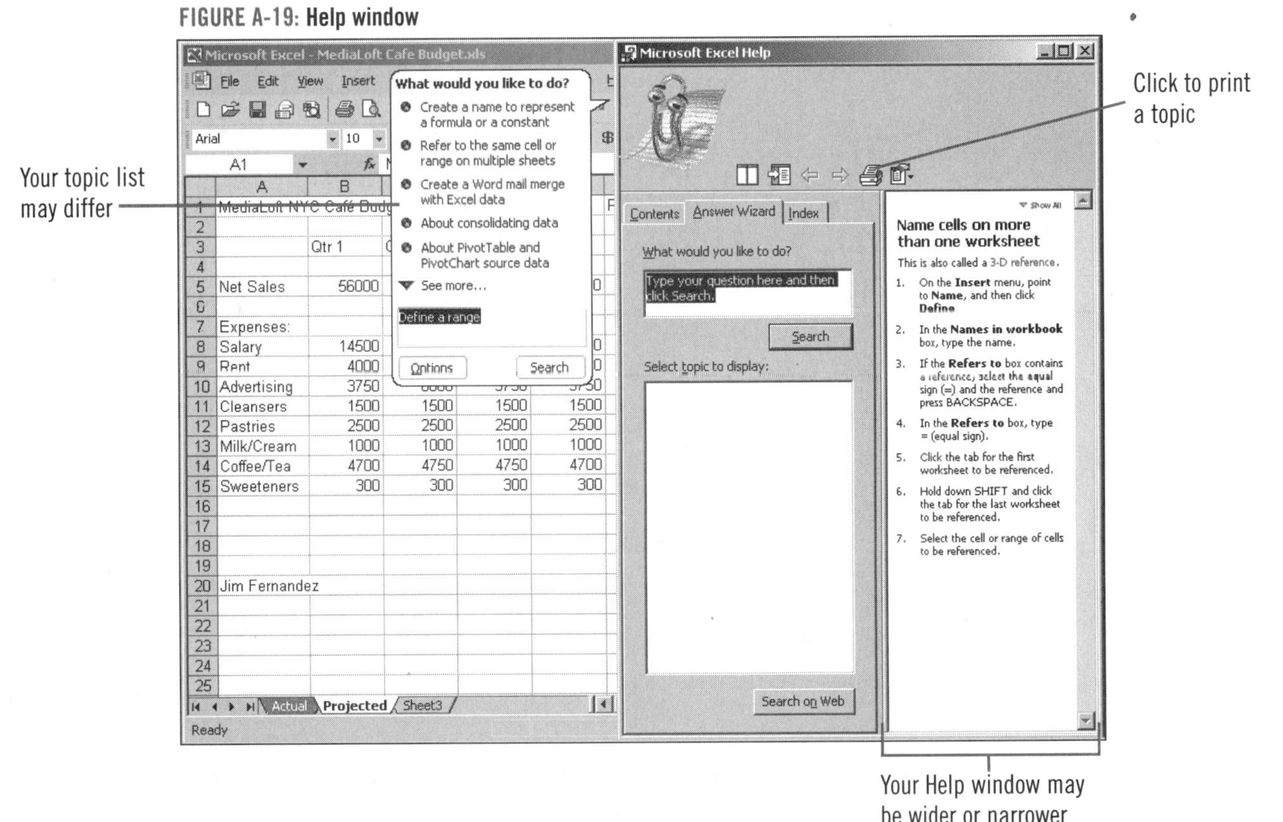

Excel 2002

Closing a Workbook and Exiting Excel

When you have finished working, you need to save the workbook file and close it. When you have completed all your work in Excel you need to exit the program. You can exit Excel by clicking Exit on the File menu. Jim has completed his work on the MediaLoft Café budget. He wants you to close the workbook and then exit Excel.

Steps

1. Click **File** on the menu bar
   The File menu opens. See Figure A-20.

2. Click **Close**
   Excel closes the workbook, asking if you want to save your changes; if you have made any changes be sure to save them. You could also click the workbook Close button instead of using the File menu.

3. Click **File** on the menu bar, then click **Exit**
   You could also click the program Close button to exit the program. Excel closes and you return to the desktop.

QuickTip

To exit Excel and close several files at once, click Exit on the File menu. Excel will prompt you to save changes to each open workbook before exiting.

FIGURE A-20: Closing a workbook using the File menu

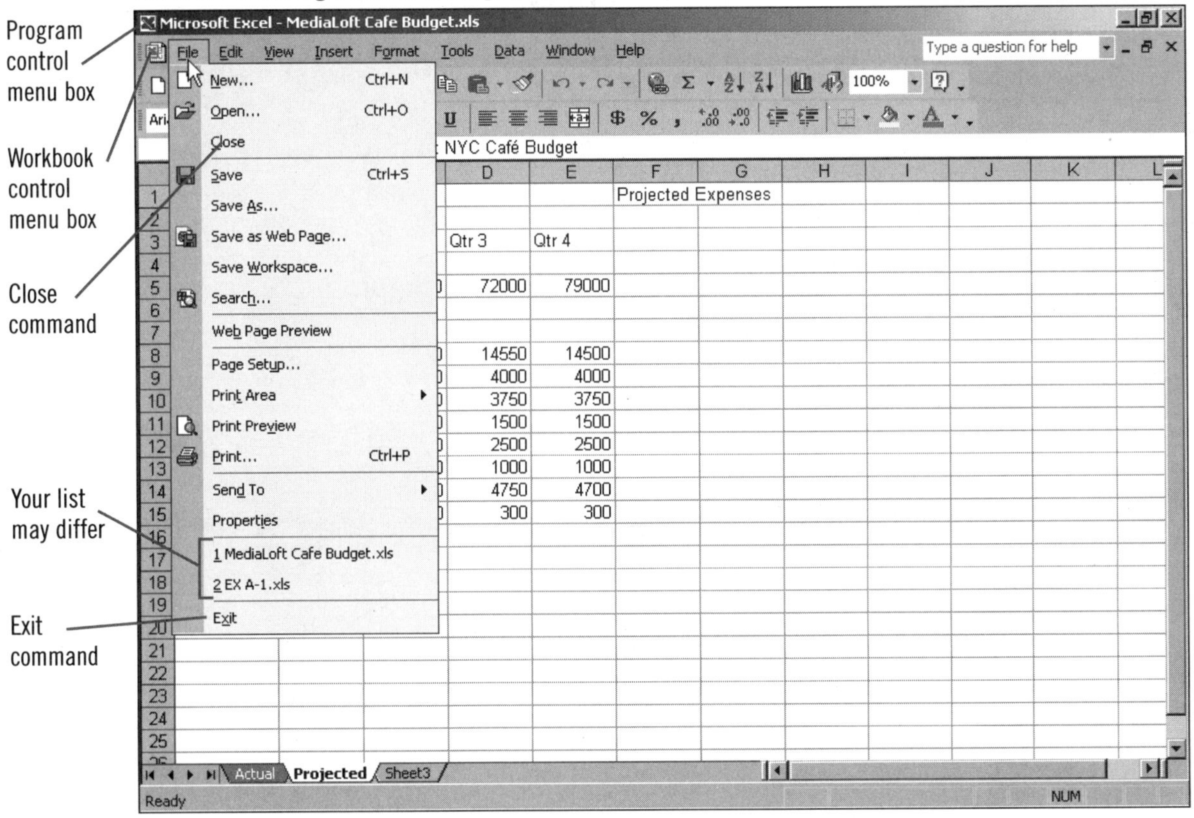

Practice

► Concepts Review

Label the elements of the Excel worksheet window shown in Figure A-21.

FIGURE A-21

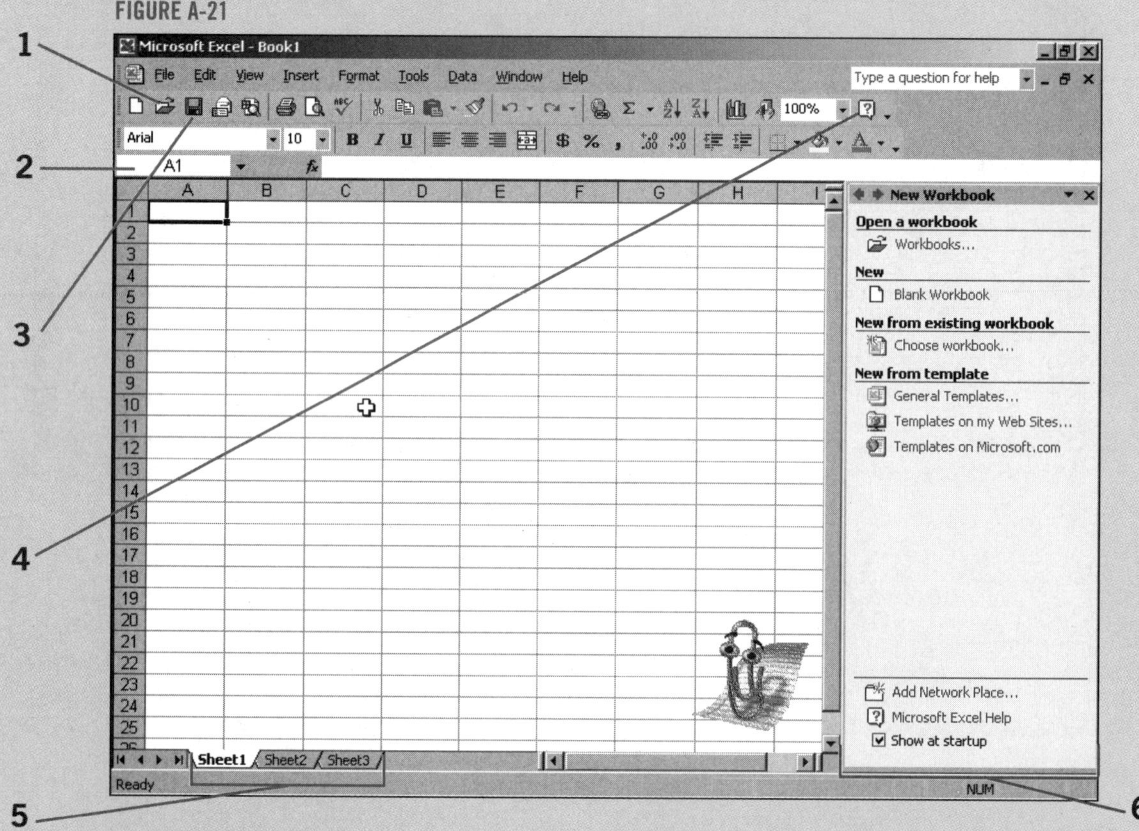

Match each term with the statement that describes it.

7. **Cell pointer**
8. **Formula bar**
9. **Worksheet window**
10. **Name box**
11. **Cell**
12. **Workbook**

- **a.** Area that contains a grid of columns and rows
- **b.** The intersection of a column and row
- **c.** Allows you to enter or edit worksheet data
- **d.** Collection of worksheets
- **e.** Rectangle indicating the active cell
- **f.** Displays the active cell address

Select the best answer from the list of choices.

13. An electronic spreadsheet can perform all of the following tasks, except:

- **a.** Display information visually.
- **b.** Calculate data accurately.
- **c.** Plan worksheet objectives.
- **d.** Recalculate updated information.

14. Each of the following is true about labels, except:

- **a.** They are left-aligned by default.
- **b.** They are not used in calculations.
- **c.** They are right-aligned by default.
- **d.** They can include numerical information.

15. **Each of the following is true about values, except:**
   a. They can include labels.
   b. They are right-aligned by default.
   c. They are used in calculations.
   d. They can include formulas.
16. **What symbol is typed before a number to make the number a label?**
   a. "
   b. !
   c. '
   d. ;
17. **You can get Excel Help in any of the following ways, except:**
   a. Clicking Help on the menu bar, then clicking Microsoft Excel Help.
   b. Pressing [F1].
   c. Clicking [?].
   d. Minimizing the program window.
18. **The following key(s) can be used to confirm cell entries, except:**
   a. [Enter].
   b. [Tab].
   c. [Esc].
   d. [Ctrl][Enter].
19. **Which button is used to preview a worksheet?**
   a. [New]
   b. [Print Preview]
   c. [Save]
   d. [Print]
20. **Which feature is used to enlarge a Print Preview view?**
   a. Magnify
   b. Enlarge
   c. Amplify
   d. Zoom
21. **Each of the following is true about the Office Assistant, except:**
   a. It provides tips based on your work habits.
   b. It provides help using a question-and-answer format.
   c. You can change the appearance of the Office Assistant.
   d. It can complete certain tasks for you.

Skills Review

1. **Start Excel 2002.**
   a. Point to **Programs** in the Start menu.
   b. Click the **Microsoft Excel** program icon.
   c. In what area of the Start menu are all the programs on your computer located?
   d. What appears when Excel opens?
2. **Open and save a workbook.**
   a. Open the workbook EX A-2 from the drive and folder where your Project Files are located.
   b. Save the workbook as **MediaLoft Toronto Cafe** using the Save As command on the File menu; use the New Folder button to save it in a new folder called **Toronto** in the drive and folder where your Project Files are located.
   c. Close the file.
   d. Open it again from the new folder you created.
   e. Open a workbook based on the Balance Sheet template: Display the task pane, select General Templates, display the Spreadsheet Solutions tab, then double-click Balance Sheet.
   f. Save the workbook as **MediaLoft Balance Sheet** in the drive and folder where your Project Files are stored, then close the workbook.

TABLE-4: **MediaLoft Toronto Café**

	On-Hand	Cost Each	Sale Price
Water	32	9.57	
Coffee	52	13.71	
Bread	36	15.22	
Muffins	25	16.99	
Sweets	43	11.72	
Sodas	52	9.61	

3. **Enter labels and values.**
   a. Enter the necessary labels shown in Table A-4.
   b. Enter the values shown in Table A-4.
   c. Clear the contents of cell A9 using the Edit menu, then type **Tea** in cell A9.
   d. Save the workbook using the Save button.
4. **Name and move a sheet.**
   a. Name the Sheet1 tab **Inventory**, then name the Sheet2 tab **Sales**.
   b. Move the Inventory sheet so it comes after the Sales sheet.
   c. Change the tab color of the Inventory sheet to yellow (third column, fifth row).
   d. Change the tab color of the Sales sheet to aqua (fifth column, fourth row).
   e. Save the workbook.
5. **Preview and print a worksheet.**
   a. Make the Inventory sheet active.
   b. View it in Print Preview.
   c. Use the Zoom button to get a better look at your worksheet.
   d. Add your name to cell A11, then print one copy of the worksheet.
6. **Get Help.**
   a. Display the Office Assistant if it is not already displayed.
   b. Ask the Office Assistant for information about creating a formula.
   c. Print the information offered by the Office Assistant, using the Print button in the Help window.
   d. Close the Help window.
7. **Close a workbook and exit Excel.**
   a. Close the file using the Close command.
   b. If asked if you want to save the worksheet, click **No**.
   c. Exit Excel.

► Independent Challenge 1

The Excel Help feature provides definitions, explanations, procedures, and other helpful information. It also provides examples and demonstrations to show you how Excel features work. Topics include elements such as the active cell, status bar, buttons, and dialog boxes, as well as detailed information about Excel commands and options.

a. Start Excel and open a new workbook using the New Workbook task pane.
b. Click the **Office Assistant**; display it if necessary using the Show Office Assistant command on the Help menu.
c. Type a question that will give you information about opening and saving a workbook. (*Hint*: You may have to ask the Office Assistant more than one question.)
d. Print the information, close the Help window, then exit Excel.

► Independent Challenge 2

Spreadsheet software has many uses that can affect the way people work. The beginning of this unit discusses some examples of people using Excel. Use your own personal or business experiences to come up with five examples of how Excel could be used in a business setting.

a. Start Excel.
b. Write down five business tasks that you could complete more efficiently by using an Excel worksheet.
c. Sketch a sample of each worksheet. See Table A-5, a sample payroll worksheet, as a guide.
d. Open a new workbook and save it as **Sample Payroll** in the drive and folder where your Project Files are stored.

e. Give your worksheet a title in cell A1, then type your name in cell B1.
f. Enter the labels shown in Table A-5. Enter Hours Worked in column C and Hourly Wage in Column E.
g. Enter sample data for Hours Worked and Hourly Wage in the worksheet.
h. Save your work, then preview and print the worksheet.
i. Close the worksheet and exit Excel.

TABLE A-5: **Sample payroll**

Employee Name	Hours Worked	Hourly Wage
Dale Havorford		
Chris Wong		
Sharon Armenta		
Belinda Swanson		
Total		

Independent Challenge 3

You are the office manager for Christine's Car Parts, a small auto parts supplier. Although the company is just three years old, it is expanding rapidly, and you are continually looking for ways to make your job easier. Last year you began using Excel to manage and maintain data on inventory and sales, which has greatly helped you to track information accurately and efficiently. The owner of the company has just approved your request to hire an assistant, who will be starting work in a week. You want to create a short training document that acquaints your new assistant with basic Excel skills.

a. Start Excel.
b. Create a new workbook and save it as **Training Workbook** in the drive and folder where your Project Files are located.
c. Enter a title for the worksheet in cell A1.
d. Make up and enter the values and labels for a sample spreadsheet. Make sure you have labels in column A.
e. Enter your name in cell D1.
f. Change the name of Sheet1 to Sample Data, then change the tab color of the Sample Data to another color.
g. Preview the worksheet, then print it.
h. Open a workbook based on a template from the Spreadsheet Solutions tab in the Templates dialog box. (You may need to insert your Office CD in order to do this.)
i. Save the workbook as **Template Sample**, then close the files and exit Excel.

E-QUEST

Independent Challenge 4

You can use the World Wide Web to help make informed purchasing decisions. Your supervisor has just given you approval for buying a new computer. While cost is not a limiting factor, you do need to provide a list of hardware and software requirements. You can use data found on the World Wide Web and use Excel to create a worksheet that details your purchase decision.

a. Connect to the Internet, then go to the CNET site at computers.com.
b. Use any of the links to locate information about the type of computer you want to purchase.
c. Locate data for the type of system you want using at least two vendors from within this site. When you find systems that meet your needs, print out the information. Be sure to identify each system's key features, such as the processor chip, hard drive capacity, RAM, and monitor size.
d. When you are finished gathering data, disconnect from the Internet.
e. Start Excel, open a new workbook and save it in the drive and folder where your Project Files are stored as **New Computer Data**.
f. Enter the manufacturers' names in columns and computer features (RAM, etc.) in rows. List the systems you found through your research, including the features you want (e.g., CD-ROM drive, etc.) and the cost for each system.
g. List the tax and shipping costs the manufacturer charges.
h. Indicate on the worksheet your final purchase decision by including descriptive text in a prominent cell. Enter your name in one of the cells.
i. Save, preview, and then print your worksheet.
j. Close the file and exit Excel.

► Visual Workshop

Create a worksheet similar to Figure A-22 using the skills you learned in this unit. Save the workbook as **Carrie's Camera and Darkroom** to the drive and folder where your Project Files are stored. Type your name in cell A11, then preview and print the worksheet.

FIGURE A-22

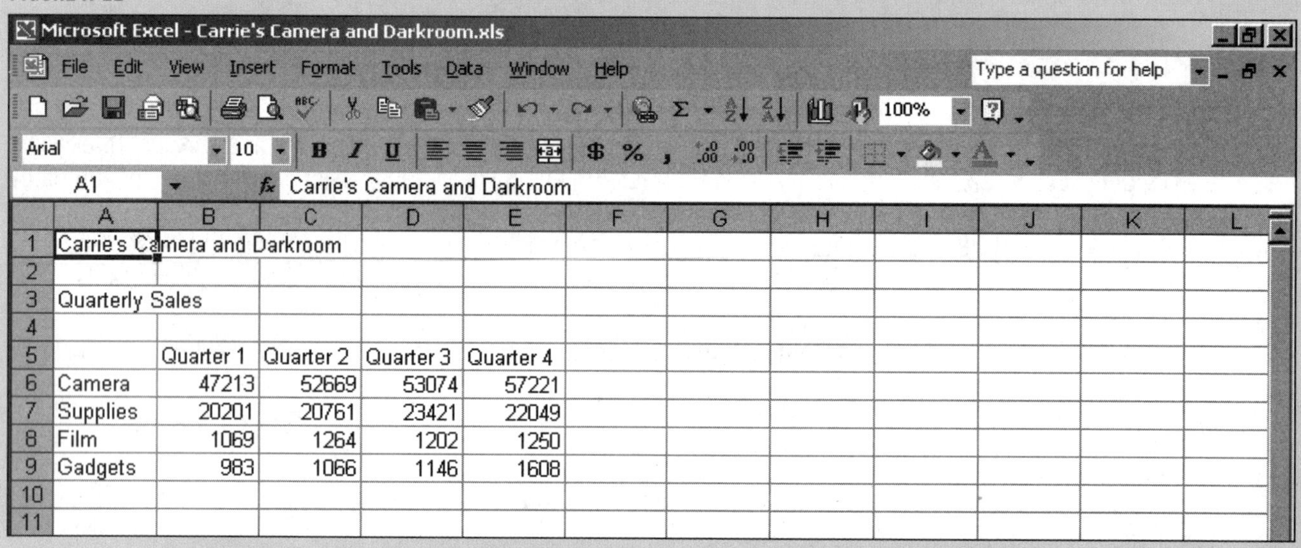

	A	B	C	D	E	F	G	H	I	J	K	L
1	Carrie's Camera and Darkroom											
2												
3	Quarterly Sales											
4												
5		Quarter 1	Quarter 2	Quarter 3	Quarter 4							
6	Camera	47213	52669	53074	57221							
7	Supplies	20201	20761	23421	22049							
8	Film	1069	1264	1202	1250							
9	Gadgets	983	1066	1146	1608							
10												
11												

Excel 2002

Unit B

Building and Editing Worksheets

Objectives

- ▶ Plan and design a worksheet
- MOUS ▶ Edit cell entries
- MOUS ▶ Enter formulas
- MOUS ▶ Create complex formulas
- MOUS ▶ Introduce Excel functions
- MOUS ▶ Copy and move cell entries
- MOUS ▶ Understand relative and absolute cell references
- MOUS ▶ Copy formulas with relative cell references
- MOUS ▶ Copy formulas with absolute cell references

Using your understanding of Excel basics, you can now plan and build your own worksheets. When you build a worksheet, you enter labels, values, and formulas into worksheet cells. Once you create a worksheet, you can save it in a workbook file and then print it. The MediaLoft marketing department has asked Jim Fernandez for an estimate of the average number of author appearances this summer. Marketing hopes that the number of appearances will increase 20% over last year's figures. Jim asks you to create a worksheet that summarizes appearances for last year and forecasts the summer appearances for this year.

Excel 2002

Planning and Designing a Worksheet

Before you start entering data into a worksheet, you need to know the purpose and approximate layout of the worksheet. To increase store traffic and sales, MediaLoft encourages authors to come to stores and sign their books. Jim wants to forecast MediaLoft's 2003 summer author appearances. The goal, already identified by the Marketing department, is to increase the year 2002 signings by 20%. Using the planning guidelines below, work with Jim as he plans this worksheet.

In planning and designing a worksheet it is important to:

- **Determine the purpose of the worksheet and give it a meaningful title**
  Jim needs to forecast summer appearances for 2003. Jim titles the worksheet "Summer 2003 MediaLoft Author Events Forecast."

- **Determine your worksheet's desired results, or "output"**
  Jim needs to begin scheduling author events and will use these forecasts to determine staffing and budget needs if the number of author events increases by 20%. He also wants to calculate the average number of author events because the Marketing department uses this information for corporate promotions.

- **Collect all the information, or "input," that will produce the results you want**
  Jim gathers together the number of author events that occurred at four stores during the 2002 summer season, which runs from June through August.

- **Determine the calculations, or formulas, necessary to achieve the desired results**
  First, Jim needs to total the number of events at each of the selected stores during each month of the summer of 2002. Then he needs to add these totals together to determine the grand total of summer appearances. Because he needs to determine the goal for the 2003 season, the 2002 monthly totals and grand total are multiplied by 1.2 to calculate the projected 20% increase for the 2003 summer season. He'll use the Average function to determine the average number of author appearances for the Marketing department.

- **Sketch on paper how you want the worksheet to look; identify where to place the labels and values**
  Jim decides to put the store locations in rows and the months in columns. He enters the data in his sketch and notes the location of the monthly totals and the grand total. Below the totals, he writes out the formula for determining a 20% increase in 2002 appearances. He also includes a label for the average number of events calculations. Jim's sketch of his worksheet is shown in Figure B-1.

- **Create the worksheet**
  Jim enters the labels first, to establish the structure of the worksheet. He then enters the values—the data summarizing the events—into his worksheet. Finally, he enters the formulas necessary to calculate totals, averages, and forecasts. These values and formulas will be used to calculate the necessary output. The worksheet Jim creates is shown in Figure B-2.

FIGURE B-1: **Worksheet sketch showing labels, values, and calculations**

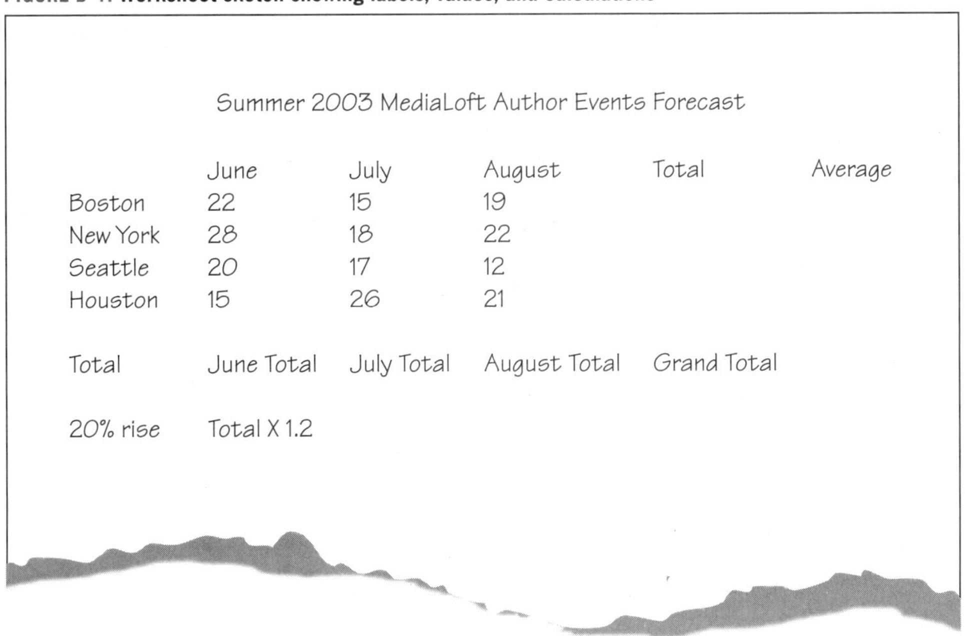

Summer 2003 MediaLoft Author Events Forecast
June July August Total Average
Boston 22 15 19
New York 28 18 22
Seattle 20 17 12
Houston 15 26 21
Total June Total July Total August Total Grand Total
20% rise Total X 1.2

FIGURE B-2: **Jim's forecasting worksheet**

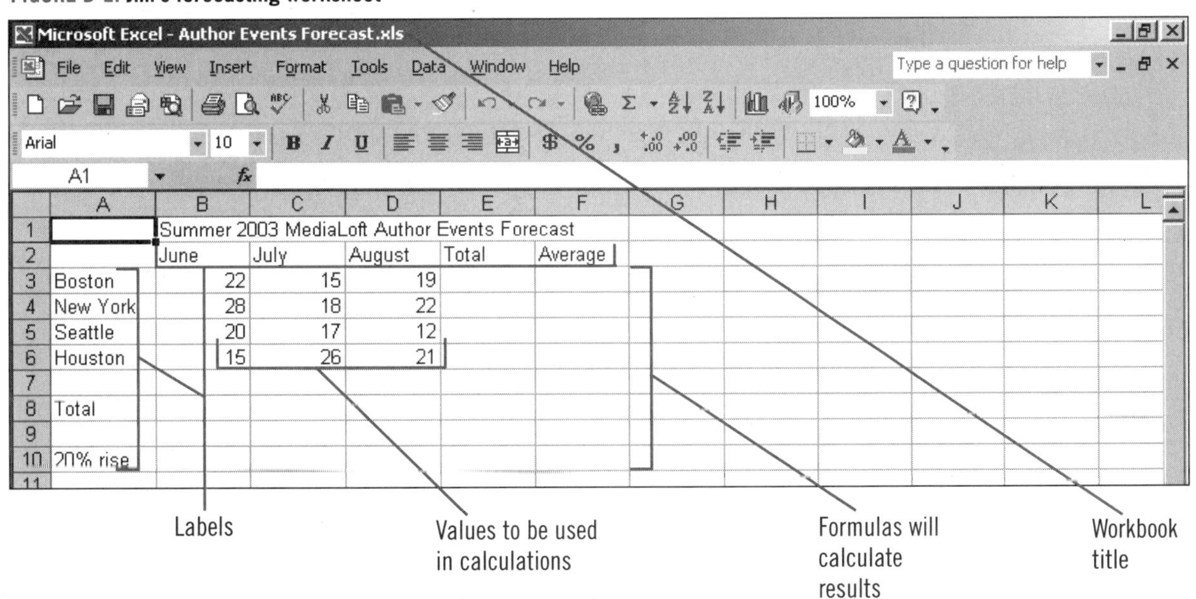

Excel 2002

Excel 2002

Editing Cell Entries

You can change the contents of a cell at any time. To edit the contents of a cell, you first select the cell you want to edit. Then you have two options: you can click the formula bar or press [F2]. This puts Excel into Edit mode. Alternately, you can double-click any cell and start editing. To make sure you are in Edit mode, look at the **mode indicator** on the far-left side of the status bar. After planning and creating his worksheet, Jim notices that he entered the wrong value for the August Seattle events, and that Houston should replace San Diego. He asks you to edit these entries to correct them.

Steps

QuickTip

In the Open dialog box, you can double-click the filename to open the workbook in one step.

1. Start Excel, open the workbook **EX B-1** from the drive and folder where your Project Files are stored, then save it as **Author Events Forecast**
2. Click cell **D5**
   This cell contains August events for the Seattle store, which you want to change to reflect the correct numbers.
3. Click to the right of **12** in the formula bar
   Excel goes into Edit mode, and the mode indicator on the status bar displays "Edit." A blinking vertical line called the **insertion point** appears in the formula bar, and if you move the mouse pointer to the formula bar, the pointer changes to I , which is used for editing. See Figure B-3.
4. Press **[Backspace]**, type **8**, then click the **Enter button** on the formula bar
   The value in cell D5 is changed from 12 to 18, and cell D5 remains selected.
5. Click cell **A6**, then press **[F2]**
   Excel returns to Edit mode, and the insertion point appears in the cell.

QuickTip

The Undo button allows you to reverse up to 16 previous actions, one at a time.

6. Press **[Backspace]** nine times, type **Houston**, then press **[Enter]**
   The label changes to Houston, and cell A7 becomes the active cell. If you make a mistake, you can click the Cancel button on the formula bar *before* confirming the cell entry. If you notice the mistake *after* you have confirmed the cell entry, click the Undo button on the Standard toolbar.
7. Double-click cell **C6**
   Double-clicking a cell also puts Excel into Edit mode with the insertion point in the cell.
8. Press **[Delete]** twice, then type **19**
   The number of book signings for July in Houston has been corrected. See Figure B-4.
9. Click to confirm the entry, then click the **Save button** on the Standard toolbar

FIGURE B-3: **Worksheet in Edit mode**

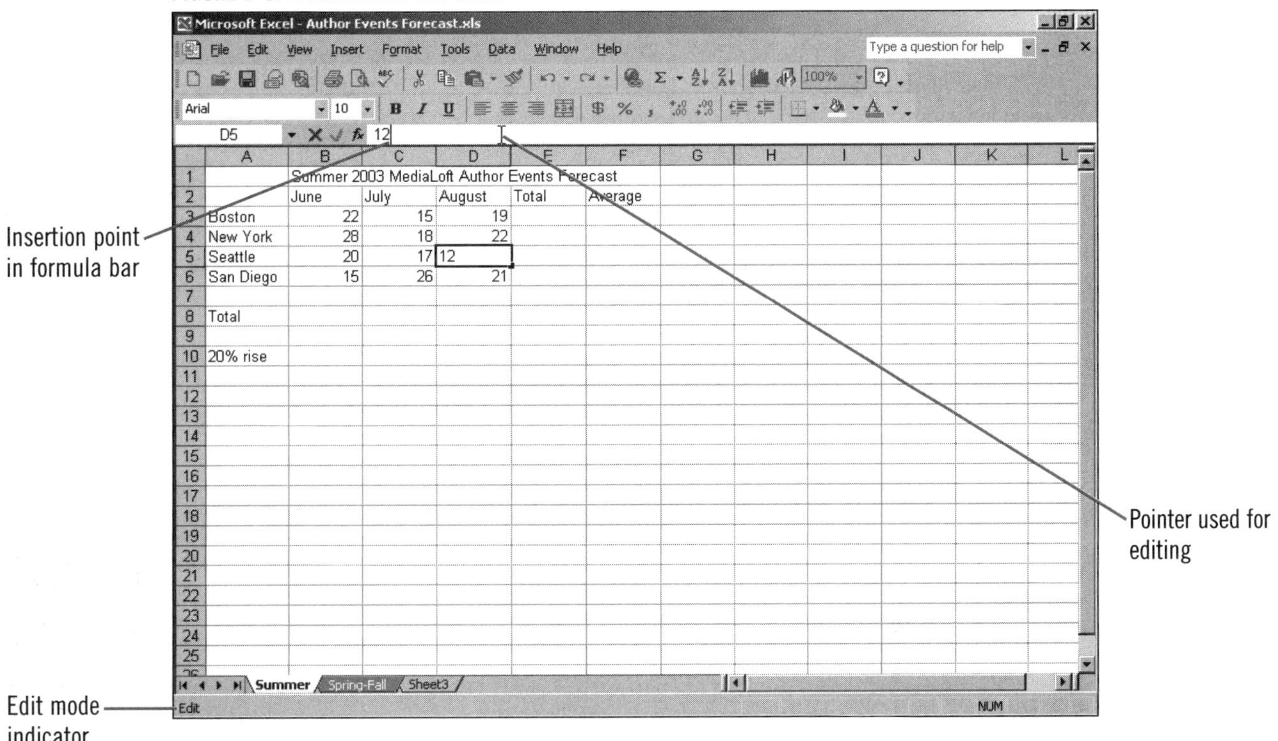

FIGURE B-4: **Edited worksheet**

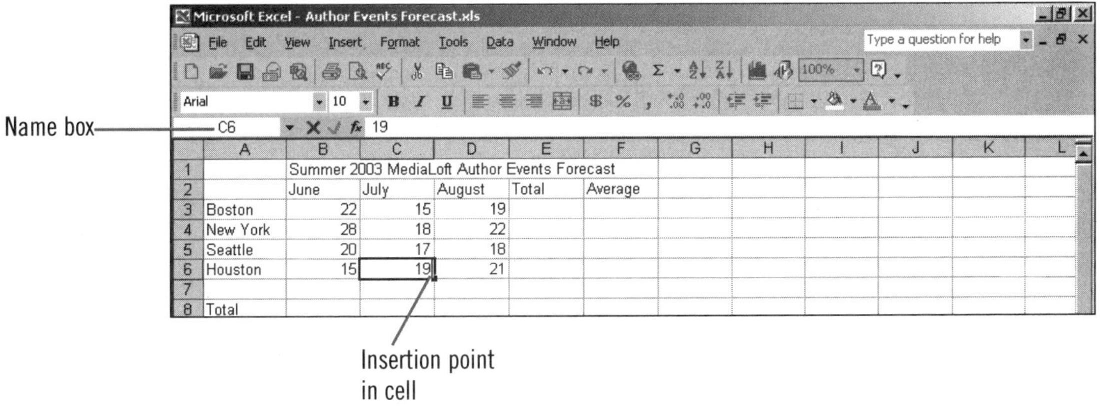

Recovering a lost workbook file

Sometimes while you are using Excel, you may experience a power failure or your computer may "freeze," making it impossible to continue working. If this type of interruption occurs, Excel has a built-in recovery feature that allows you to open and save files that were open at the time of the interruption. When you restart Excel after an interruption, the Document Recovery task pane opens on the left side of your screen displaying both original and recovered versions of the files that were open. If you're not sure which file to open (original or recovered), it's usually better to open the recovered file because it will have retained the latest information. You can, however, open and review all the versions of the file that were recovered and save the best one. Each file listed in the Document Recovery task pane has a list arrow with options that allow you to open the file, save the file, delete the file, or show repairs made to the file.

Excel 2002

Entering Formulas

You use **formulas** to perform numeric calculations such as adding, multiplying, and averaging. Formulas in an Excel worksheet usually start with the equal sign (=), called the **formula prefix**, followed by cell addresses and range names. Arithmetic formulas use one or more **arithmetic operators** to perform calculations; see Table B-1. Using a cell address or range name in a formula is called **cell referencing**. If you change a value in a cell, any formula containing that cell reference will be automatically recalculated using the new value. Jim needs to total the values for the monthly author events for June, July, and August. He asks you to create formulas to perform these calculations.

Steps

1. **Click cell B8**
   This is the cell where you want to enter the calculation that totals the number of June events.

2. **Type = (the equal sign)**
   Placing an equal sign at the beginning of an entry tells Excel that a formula is about to be entered, rather than a label or a value. "Enter" appears on the status bar. The total number of June events is equal to the sum of the values in cells B3, B4, B5, and B6.

3. **Type b3+b4+b5+b6**
   Compare your worksheet to Figure B-5. Each cell address in the equation is shown in a matching color in the worksheet. For example, the cell address B3 is written in blue in the equation and is outlined in blue in the worksheet. This makes it easy to identify each cell in a formula.

4. **Click the Enter button on the formula bar**
   The result, 85, appears in cell B8. Cell B8 remains selected, and the formula appears in the formula bar. Excel is not case-sensitive: it doesn't matter if you type uppercase or lowercase characters when you enter cell addresses. Typing cell addresses is only one way of creating a formula. A more accurate method involves **pointing** at cells using the mouse, then using the keyboard to supply arithmetic operators.

5. **Click cell C8, type =, click cell C3, type +, click cell C4, type +, click cell C5, type +, click cell C6, then click the Enter button on the formula bar**
   When you clicked cell C3, a moving border surrounded the cell. This **moving border** indicates the cell used in the calculation. Moving borders can appear around a single cell or a range of cells. The total number of author appearances for July, 69, appears in cell C8. The pointing method of creating a formula is more accurate than typing, because it is easy to type a cell address incorrectly. Cell D8 also needs a total.

6. **Click cell D8, type =, click cell D3, type +, click cell D4, type +, click cell D5, type +, click cell D6, then click the Enter button on the formula bar**
   The total number of appearances for August, 80, appears in cell D8. Compare your worksheet to Figure B-6.

7. **Click the Save button on the Standard toolbar**

Trouble?

If you type an incorrect character, press [Backspace].

Trouble?

If the formula instead of the result appears in the cell after you click, make sure you began the formula with = (the equal sign).

FIGURE B-5: Worksheet showing cells in a formula

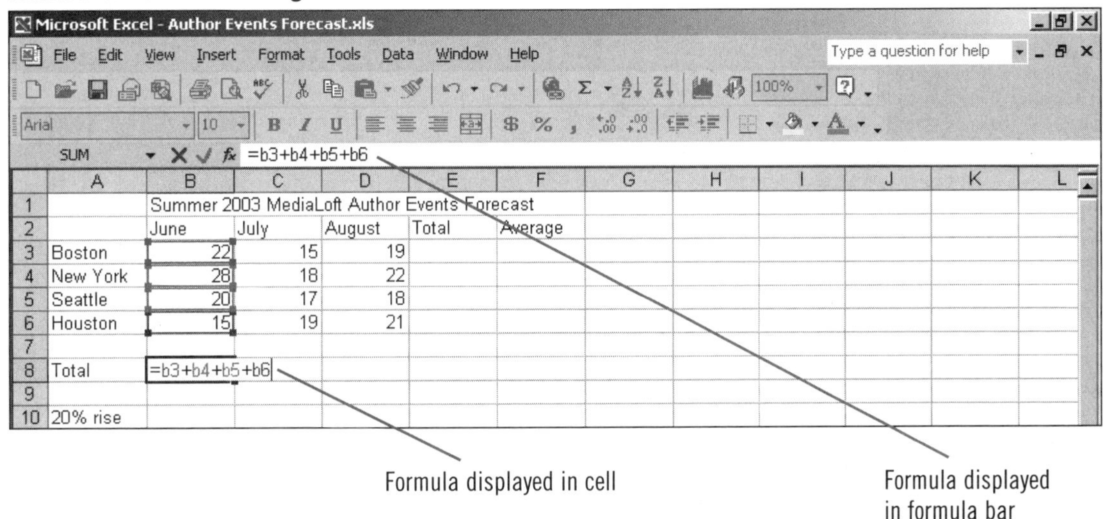

FIGURE B-6: Completed formulas

D8 =D3+D4+D5+D6

	A	B	C	D	E	F
1		Summer 2003 MediaLoft Author Events Forecast				
2		June	July	August	Total	Average
3	Boston	22	15	19		
4	New York	28	18	22		
5	Seattle	20	17	18		
6	Houston	15	19	21		
7						
8	Total	85	69	80		
9						
10	20% rise					

TABLE B-1: Excel arithmetic operators

operator	purpose	example
+	Addition	=A5+A7
–	Subtraction or negation	=A5–10
*	Multiplication	=A5*A7
/	Division	=A5/A7
%	Percent	=35%
^ (caret)	Exponent	=6^2 (same as 6^2)

Excel 2002

Creating Complex Formulas

The formula you entered is a simple formula containing one arithmetic operator, the plus sign. You can create a **complex formula**—an equation that uses more than one type of arithmetic operator. For example, you may need to create a formula that uses addition and multiplication. You can use arithmetic operators to separate tasks within a complex equation. In formulas containing more than one arithmetic operator, Excel uses the order of precedence rules to determine which operation to perform first. Jim wants you to total the values for the monthly author events for June, July, and August, and forecast what the 20% increase in appearances will be. You create a complex formula to perform these calculations.

1. Click cell **B10**, type =, click cell **B8**, then type ***.2**
   This part of the formula calculates 20% of the cell contents by multiplying the June total by .2 (or 20%). Because this part of the formula uses multiplication, it will be calculated first according to the rules of precedence.
2. Type +, then click cell **B8**
   The second part of the formula adds the 20% increase to the original value of the cell. The mode indicator says Point, indicating you can add more cell references. Compare your worksheet to Figure B-7.
3. Click on the formula bar
   The result, 102, appears in cell B10.
4. Click cell **C10**, type =, click cell **C8**, type ***.2**, type +, click cell **C8**, then click
   The result, 82.8, appears in cell C10.
5. Click cell **D10**, type =, click cell **D8**, type ***.2**, type +, click **D8**, then click
   The result, 96, appears in cell D10. Compare your completed worksheet to Figure B-8.
6. Click the **Save button** on the Standard toolbar

QuickTip

Press [Esc] to turn off a moving border.

Clues to Use

Editing formulas

You can edit formulas the same way you edit cell entries: you can click the cell containing the formula then edit it in the formula bar; you can also double-click a cell or press [F2] to enter Edit mode, and then edit the formula in the cell. After you are in Edit mode, use the arrow keys to move the insertion point left or right in the formula. Use [Backspace] or [Delete] to delete characters to the left or right of the insertion point, then type or point to new cell references or operators.

FIGURE B-7: Elements of a complex formula

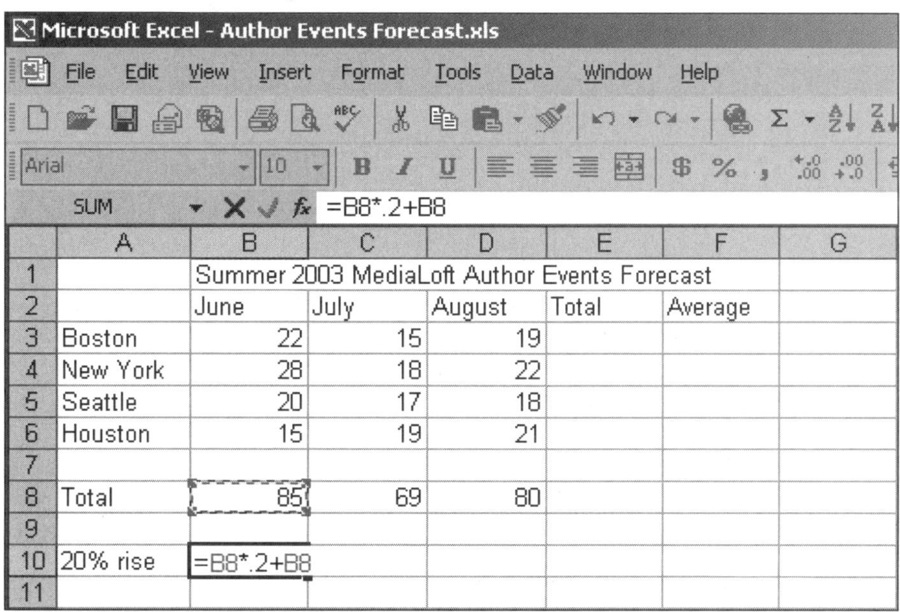

FIGURE B-8: Multiple complex formulas

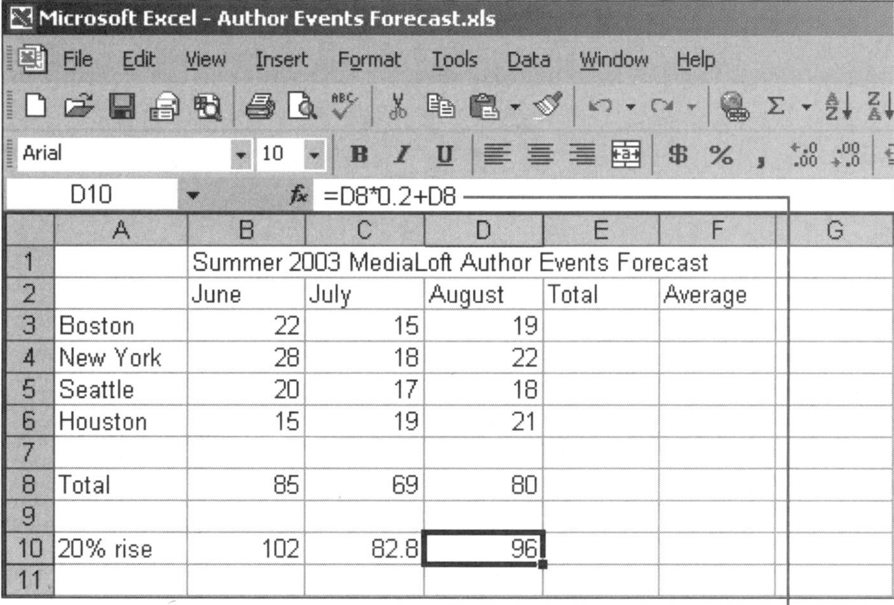

Formula calculates a 20% increase over the value in cell D8 and displays the result in cell D10

Order of precedence in Excel formulas

A formula can include several mathematical operations. When you work with formulas that have more than one operator, the order of precedence is very important. If a formula contains two or more operators, such as 4+.55/4000*25, the computer performs the calculations in a particular sequence based on these rules: Operations inside parentheses are calculated before any other operations. Exponents are calculated next, then any multiplication and division—from left to right. Finally, addition and subtraction are calculated from left to right. In the example 4+.55/4000*25, Excel performs the arithmetic operations by first dividing 4000 into .55, then multiplying the result by 25, then adding 4. You can change the order of calculations by using parentheses. For example, in the formula (4+.55)/4000*25, Excel would first add 4 and .55, then divide that amount by 4000, then finally multiply by 25.

Excel 2002

Introducing Excel Functions

Functions are predefined worksheet formulas that enable you to perform complex calculations easily. Like formulas, functions always begin with the formula prefix = (the equal sign). You can type functions, or you can use the Insert Function button to select the function you need from a list. The **AutoSum** button on the Standard toolbar enters the most frequently used function, SUM. A function can be used by itself within a cell, or as part of a formula. For example, to calculate monthly sales tax, you could create a formula that adds a range of cells (using the SUM function) and then multiplies the total by a decimal. Jim asks you to use the SUM function to calculate the grand totals in his worksheet and the AVERAGE function to calculate the average number of author events per store.

1. Click cell **E3**
   This is where you want the total of all Boston author events for June, July, and August.
2. Click the **AutoSum button** on the Standard toolbar, then click the **Enter button** on the formula bar
   The formula =SUM(B3:D3) appears in the formula bar and the result, 56, appears in cell E3. By default, AutoSum adds the values in the cells above the cell pointer. If there are one or fewer values there, AutoSum adds the values to its left—in this case, the values in cells B3, C3, and D3. The information inside the parentheses is the **argument**, or the information Excel uses to calculate the function result. In this case, the argument is the range B3:D3.
3. Click cell **E4**, click , then click
   The total for the New York events appears in cell E4.
4. Click cell **E5**, then click
   AutoSum sets up a function to add the two values in the cells above the active cell, but this time the default argument is not correct.
5. Click cell **B5** and hold down the mouse button, drag to cell **D5** to select the range **B5:D5**, then click
   As you drag, the argument in the SUM function changes to reflect the selected range, and a yellow Argument ToolTip shows the function syntax. You can click any part of the ToolTip to display Help on the function.
6. Click cell **E6**, type **=SUM(**, click cell **B6** and drag to cell **D6**, click , click cell **E8**, type **=SUM(**, click cell **B8** and drag to cell **D8**, click , click cell **E10**, type **=SUM(**, click cell **B10** and drag to cell **D10**, then click
   Compare your screen to Figure B-9. Excel adds the closing parenthesis.
7. Click cell **F3**, then click the **Insert Function button** on the formula bar
   The Insert Function dialog box and Wizard opens. Here you can select a function from a list. See Table B-2 for frequently used functions. The function you need to calculate averages—named AVERAGE—appears in the Most Recently Used function category.
8. Click **AVERAGE** in the Select a function list box, click **OK**; the Function Arguments dialog box opens; type **B3:D3** in the Number 1 text box, as shown in Figure B-10, then click **OK**
9. Click cell **F4**, click , verify that **AVERAGE** is selected, click **OK**, type **B4:D4**, click **OK**, click cell **F5**, click , click **AVERAGE**, click **OK**, type **B5:D5**, click **OK**, click cell **F6**, click , click **AVERAGE**, click **OK**, type **B6:D6**, then click **OK**
   The result for Boston (cell F3) is 18.66667; the result for New York (cell F4) is 22.66667; the result for Seattle (cell F5) is 18.33333; and the result for Houston (cell F6) is 18.33333, giving you the averages for all four stores.
10. Enter your name in cell **A25**, click the **Save button** on the Standard toolbar, then click the **Print button** on the Standard toolbar

QuickTip

The ScreenTip 1R x 3C tells you the size of the range is 1 row and 3 columns.

Trouble?

If the Office Assistant opens, click No, don't provide help now.

QuickTip

Modify a function's range by clicking the Collapse dialog box button, defining the range with your mouse, then clicking the Expand dialog box button to return to the Function Arguments dialog box.

FIGURE B-9: **Worksheet with SUM functions entered**

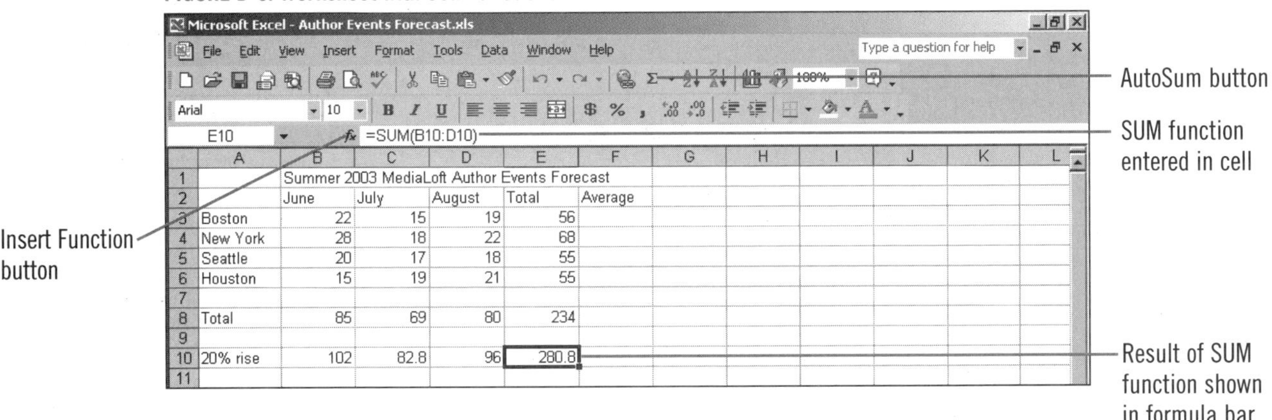

FIGURE B-10: **Using Insert Function to create a formula**

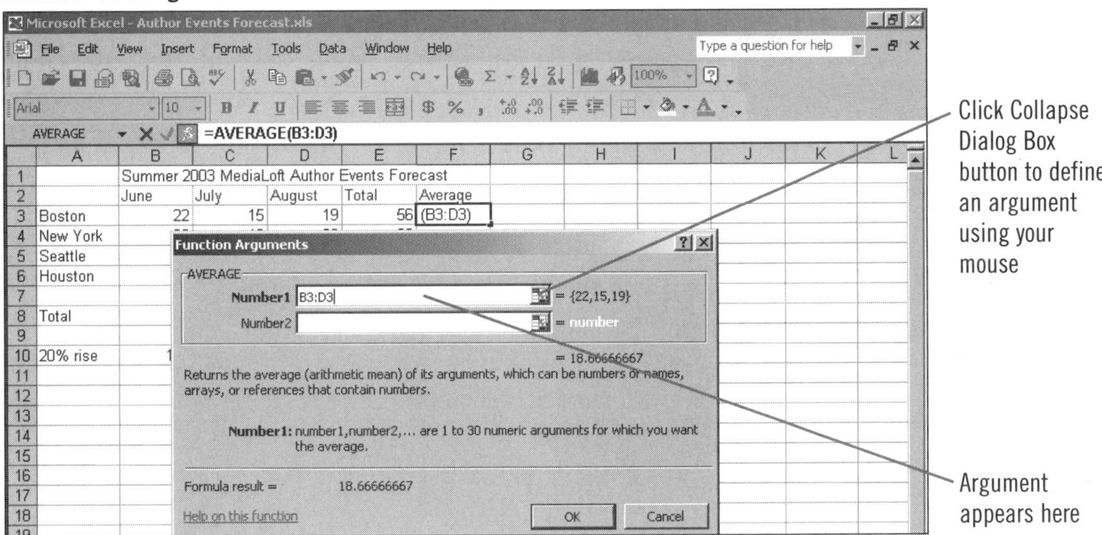

TABLE B-2: **Frequently used functions**

function	description
SUM (*argument*)	Calculates the sum of the arguments
AVERAGE (*argument*)	Calculates the average of the arguments
MAX (*argument*)	Displays the largest value among the arguments
MIN (*argument*)	Displays the smallest value among the arguments
COUNT (*argument*)	Calculates the number of values in the arguments

Using the MIN and MAX functions

Other commonly used functions include MIN and MAX. You use the MIN function to calculate the minimum, or smallest, value in a selected range; the MAX function calculates the maximum, or largest, value in a selected range. The MAX function is included in the Most Recently Used function category in the Insert Function dialog box, while both the MIN and MAX function can be found in the Statistical category. These functions are particularly useful in larger worksheets.

Excel 2002

Copying and Moving Cell Entries

Using the Cut, Copy, and Paste buttons or the Excel drag-and-drop feature, you can copy or move information from one cell or range in your worksheet to another. When you cut or move information, the original data does not remain in the original location. You can also cut, copy, and paste labels and values from one worksheet to another. Jim needs to include the 2003 forecast for spring and fall author events. He's already entered the spring data and will finish entering the labels and data for the fall. He asks you to copy information from the spring report to the fall report.

Steps

1. Click the **Spring-Fall sheet tab** of the Author Events Forecast workbook
   The store names in cells A6:A7 are incorrect.
2. Click the **Summer sheet tab**, select the range **A5:A6**, then click the **Copy button** on the Standard toolbar
   The selected range (A5:A6) is copied to the **Office Clipboard**, a temporary storage area that holds the selected information you copy or cut. A moving border surrounds the selected range until you press [Esc] or copy additional information to the Clipboard. The information you copied remains in the selected range.
3. Click the **Spring-Fall sheet tab**, select the range **A6:A7**, click the **Paste button** on the Standard toolbar, select the range **A4:A9**, then click
   The Clipboard task pane opens when you copy a selection to the already-occupied Clipboard. You can use the Clipboard task pane to copy, cut, store, and paste up to 24 items. Each item in the pane displays its contents.
4. Click cell **A13**, click Boston New York Seattle Houston Total in the Clipboard Task Pane to paste the contents in cell A13, then click the **Close button** in the Task Pane title bar to close it
   The item is copied into the range A13:A18. When pasting an item from the Clipboard into the worksheet, you only need to specify the top-left cell of the range where you want to paste the selection. The Total label in column E is missing from the fall forecast.
5. Click cell **E3**, position the pointer on any edge of the cell until the pointer changes to , then press and hold down **[Ctrl]**
   The pointer changes to the copy pointer .
6. While still pressing **[Ctrl]**, press and hold the **left mouse button**, drag the cell contents to cell **E12**, release the mouse button, then release **[Ctrl]**
   This **drag-and-drop technique** is useful for copying cell contents. As you dragged, an outline of the cell moved with the pointer, as shown in Figure B-11, and a ScreenTip appeared tracking the current position of the item as you moved it. When you released the mouse button, the Total label appeared in cell E12. You can also use drag and drop to move data to a new cell.
7. Click cell **C1**, position the pointer on the edge of the cell until it changes to , then drag the cell contents to **A1**
   You don't use [Ctrl] when moving information with drag and drop. You can easily enter the fall events data into the range B13:D16.
8. Using the information shown in Figure B-12, enter the author events data for the fall into the range B13:D16
9. Click the **Save button** on the Standard toolbar

Trouble?

If the Clipboard task pane does not open, click Edit on the menu bar, then click Office Clipboard.

QuickTip

After you paste an item, the Paste Options button appears. If you move the pointer over it, the Paste Options list arrow appears, letting you choose whether to paste the contents or only the formatting.

Trouble?

When you use drag and drop to move data into occupied cells, Excel asks if you want to replace the existing cells. Click OK to replace the contents with those of the cell you are moving.

FIGURE B-11: **Using drag-and-drop to copy information**

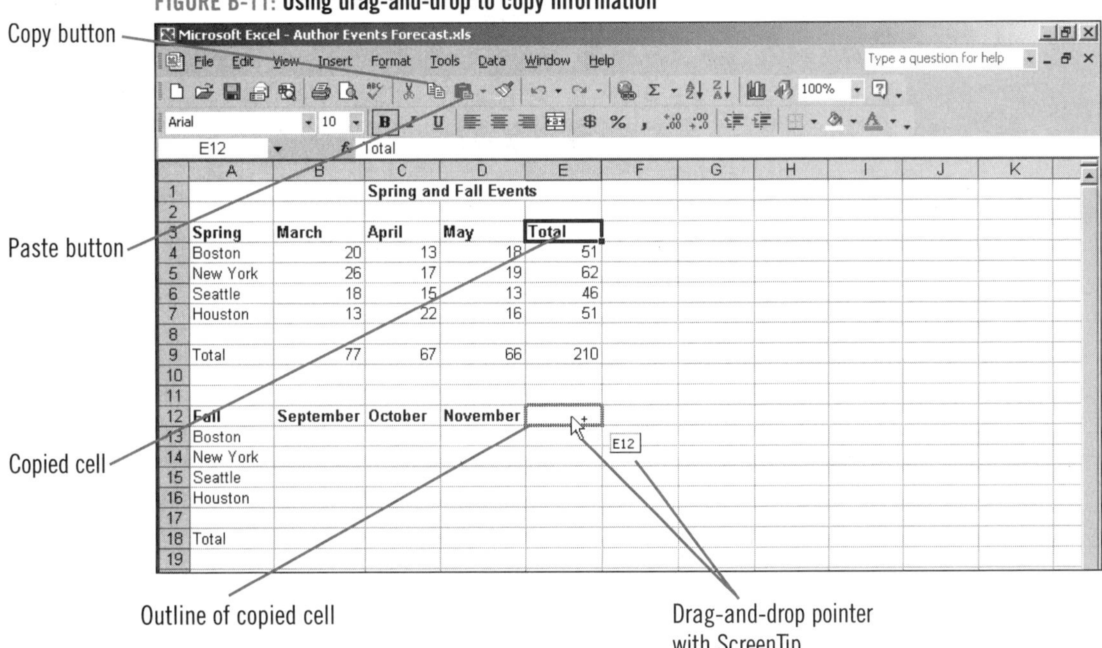

FIGURE B-12: **Worksheet with fall author event data entered**

10					
11					
12	**Fall**	**September**	**October**	**November**	**Total**
13	Boston	22	17	20	
14	New York	27	16	24	
15	Seattle	19	19	18	
16	Houston	15	25	18	
17					
18	Total				
19					
20					
21					
22					
23					
24					
25					

Summer | Spring-Fall | Sheet3

Ready — Sum=240

Sum of selected range appears in status bar

CLUES TO USE

Using the Office Clipboard

The Office Clipboard, shown in the task pane in Figure B-13, lets you copy and paste multiple items such as text, images, tables, or Excel ranges within or between Microsoft Office applications. The Office Clipboard can hold up to 24 items copied or cut from any Office program. The Clipboard task pane displays the items stored on the Office Clipboard. You choose whether to delete the first item from the Clipboard when you copy the 25th item. The collected items remain in the Office Clipboard and are available to you until you close all open Office programs. You can specify when and where to show the Office Clipboard task pane by clicking the options list arrow at the bottom of the Clipboard pane.

FIGURE B-13: **Office Clipboard task pane**

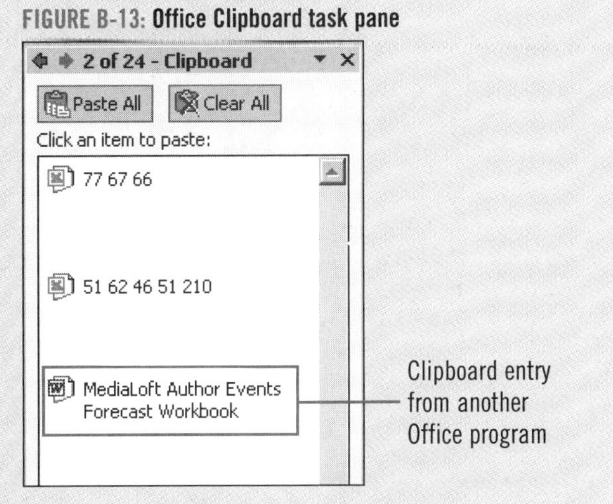

Excel 2002

Understanding Relative and Absolute Cell References

As you work in Excel, you will often want to reuse formulas in different parts of the worksheet. This will save you time because you won't have to retype them. For example, you may want to perform a what-if analysis showing one set of sales figures using a lower forecast in one part of the worksheet and another set using a higher forecast in another area. But when you copy formulas, it is important make sure that they refer to the correct cells. To do this, you need to understand relative and absolute cell references. Jim often reuses formulas in different parts of his worksheets to examine different possible outcomes, so he wants you to understand relative and absolute cell references.

Details

- **Use relative references when cell relationships remain unchanged.**
  When you create a formula that references other cells, Excel normally does not "record" the exact cell references, but instead the relationship to the cell containing the formula. For example, in Figure B-14, cell E5 contains the formula: =SUM(B5:D5). When Excel retrieves values to calculate the formula in cell E5, it actually looks for "the cell three columns to the left of the formula, which in this case is cell B5", "the cell two columns to the left of the formula" and so on. This way, if you copy the cell to a new location such as cell E6, the results will reflect the new formula location, and will automatically retrieve the values in cells B6, C6, and D6. This is called **relative cell referencing**, because Excel is recording the input cells *in relation to* the formula cell.

  In most cases, you will use relative cell references, which is the Excel default. In Figure B-14, the formulas in E5:E9 and in B9:E9 contain relative cell references. They total the "three cells to the left of" or the "four cells above" the formulas.

- **Use absolute cell references when one relationship changes.**
  There are times when you want Excel to retrieve formula information from a specific cell, and you don't want that cell to change when you copy the formula to a new location. For example, you might have a price in a specific cell that you want to use in all formulas, regardless of their location. If you used relative cell referencing, the formula results would be incorrect, because Excel would use a different cell every time you copied the formula. Therefore you need to use an **absolute cell reference**, a reference that does not change when you copy the formula.

  You create an absolute cell reference by placing a $ (dollar sign) before both the column letter and the row number for the cell's address, using the [F4] function key on the keyboard. Figure B-15 displays the formulas used in Figure B-14. The formulas in cells B15 to D18 use absolute cell references to refer to a potential sales increase of 50%, shown in cell B12.

FIGURE B-14: Location of relative references

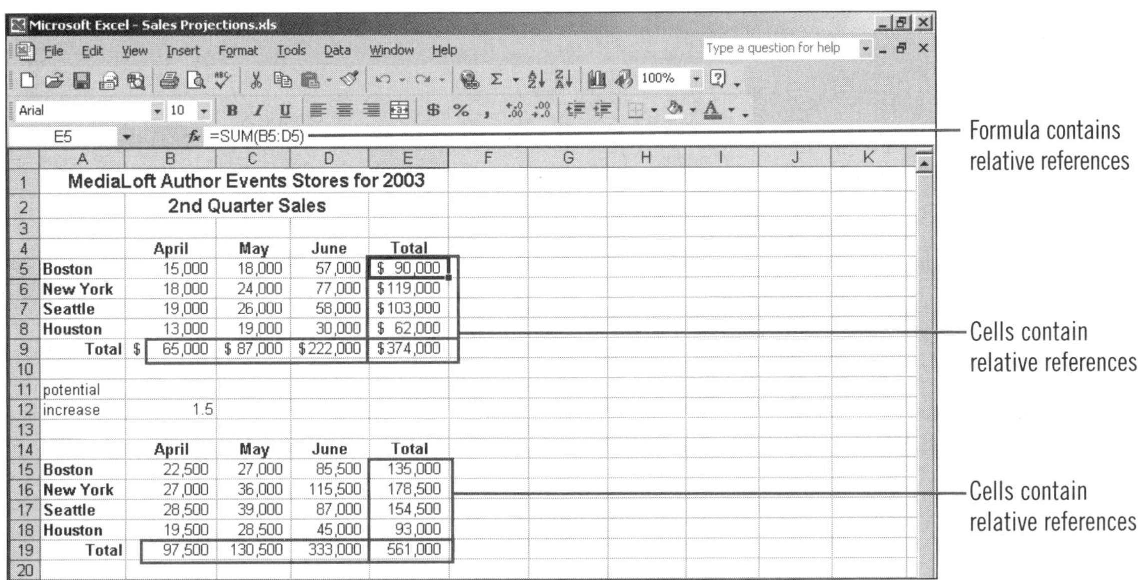

FIGURE B-15: Absolute and relative reference formulas

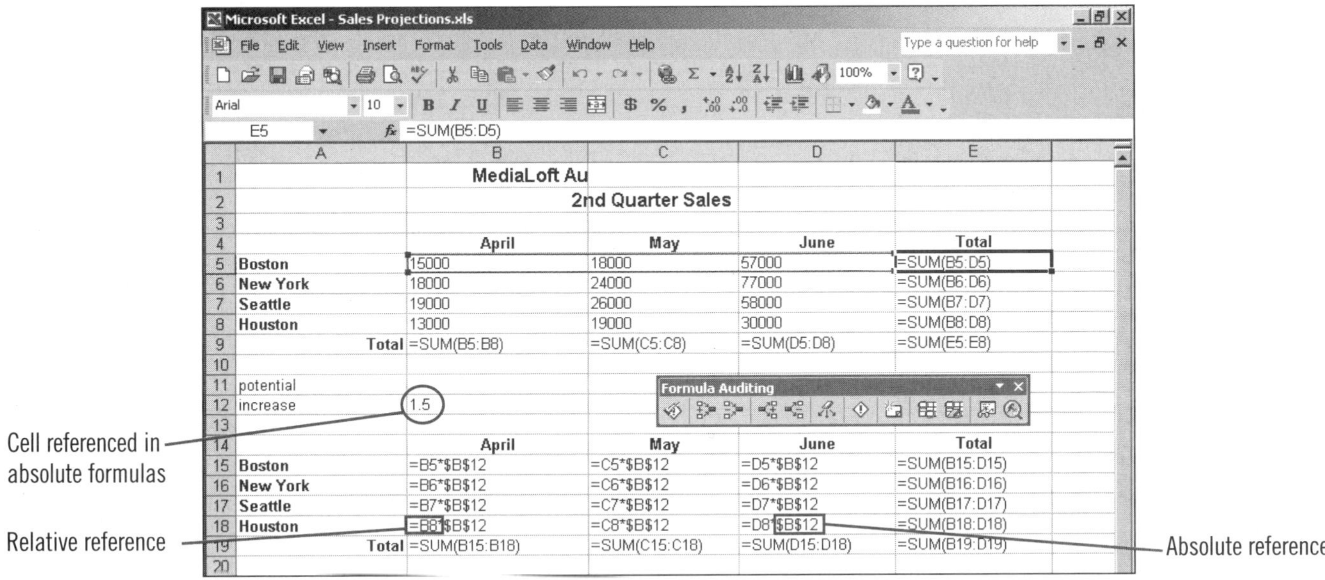

Using a mixed reference

Sometimes when you copy a formula, you'll want to change the row reference but keep the column reference the same. This type of cell referencing combines elements of both absolute and relative referencing and is called a mixed reference. When copied, the mixed reference C$14 changes the column relative to its new location but prevents the row from changing. In the mixed reference $C14, the column would not change but the row would be updated relative to its location. Like the absolute reference, a mixed reference can be created using the [F4] function key. With each press of the [F4] key, you cycle through all the possible combinations of relative, absolute, and mixed references ($C$14, C$14, $C14, C14).

Excel 2002

Copying Formulas with Relative Cell References

Copying and moving formulas allows you to reuse formulas you've already created. Copying formulas, rather than retyping them, is faster and helps to prevent typing errors. You can use the Copy and Paste commands or the Fill Right method to copy formulas. Jim wants you to copy the formulas that total the appearances by region and by month from the spring to the fall.

Steps

1. **Click cell E4, then click the Copy button on the Standard toolbar**
   The formula for calculating the total number of spring Boston author events is copied to the Clipboard. Notice that the formula =SUM(B4:D4) appears in the formula bar.

2. **Click cell E13, then click the Paste button on the Standard toolbar**
   The formula from cell E4 is copied into cell E13, where the new result of 59 appears. Notice in the formula bar that the cell references have changed, so that the range B13:D13 appears in the formula. This formula contains **relative cell references**, which tell Excel to copy the formula to a new cell, but to substitute new cell references so that the relationship of the cells to the formula in its new location remains unchanged. In this case, Excel adjusted the formula so that cells D13, C13, and B13—the three cell references immediately to the left of E13—replaced cells D4, C4, and B4, the three cell references to the left of E4. Notice that the bottom-right corner of the active cell contains a small square, called the **fill handle**. You can use the fill handle to copy labels, formulas, and values. This option is called **AutoFill**.

3. **Position the pointer over the fill handle until it changes to +, press and hold the left mouse button, then drag the fill handle to select the range E13:E16**
   See Figure B-16.

4. **Release the mouse button**
   A formula similar to the one in cell E13 now appears in the range E14:E16. Again, because the formula uses relative cell references, cells E14 through E16 correctly display the totals for the fall author events. After you release the mouse button, the **AutoFill Options button** appears. If you move the pointer over it and click its list arrow, you can specify what you want to fill and whether or not you want to include formatting.

5. **Click cell B9, click Edit on the menu bar, then click Copy**

6. **Click cell B18, click Edit on the menu bar, then click Paste**
   See Figure B-17. The formula for calculating the September events appears in the formula bar. You also need totals to appear in cells C18, D18, and E18. You could use the fill handle again, but another option is to use a menu command.

7. **Select the range B18:E18**

8. **Click Edit on the menu bar, point to Fill, then click Right**
   The rest of the totals are filled in correctly. Compare your worksheet to Figure B-18.

9. **Click the Save button on the Standard toolbar**

QuickTip

To specify components of the copied cell or range prior to pasting, click Edit on the menu bar, then click Paste Special. You can selectively copy formulas, values, comments, validation, and formatting attributes, and specify calculations, as well as transpose cells or paste the contents as a link.

Trouble?

If the Clipboard task pane opens, click the Close button. If the Office Assistant appears, right-click it, then click Hide.

FIGURE B-16: Using the fill handle

12	Fall	September	October	November	Total
13	Boston	22	17	20	59
14	New York	27	16	24	
15	Seattle	19	19	18	
16	Houston	15	25	18	
17					
18	Total				

Formula in cell E13 will be copied to E14:E16

Fill handle

Mouse pointer

FIGURE B-17: Copied formula

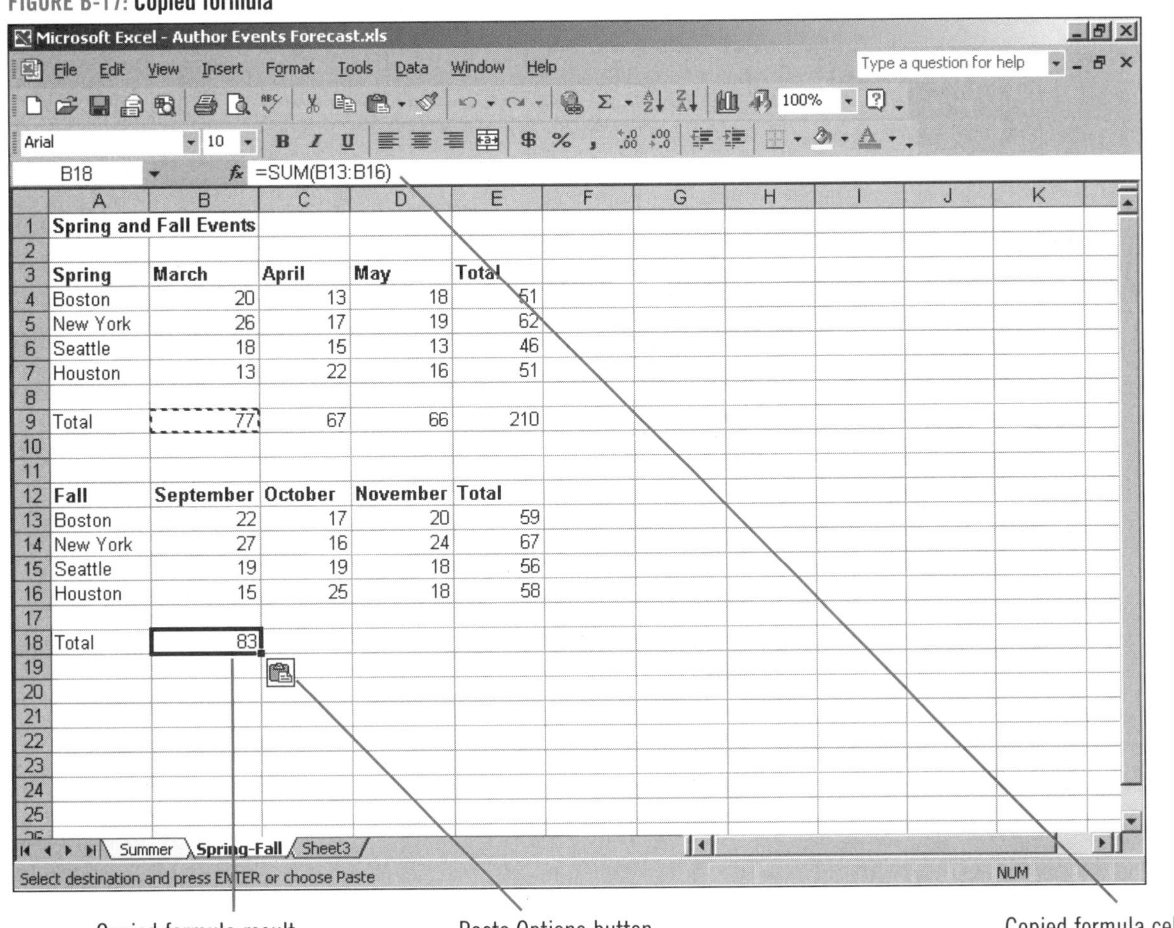

FIGURE B-18: Completed worksheet with all formulas copied

12	Fall	September	October	November	Total
13	Boston	22	17	20	59
14	New York	27	16	24	67
15	Seattle	19	19	18	56
16	Houston	15	25	18	58
17					
18	Total	83	77	80	240

Filling cells with sequential text or values

Often, you'll need to fill cells with sequential text: months of the year, days of the week, years, or text plus a number (Quarter 1, Quarter 2, . . .). You can easily fill cells using sequences by dragging the fill handle. As you drag the fill handle, Excel automatically extends the existing sequence. (The contents of the last filled cell appear in the ScreenTip.) Use the Fill Series command on the Edit menu to examine all of the available fill series options.

Excel 2002

Excel 2002

Copying Formulas with Absolute Cell References

When copying formulas, you might want a cell reference to always refer to a particular cell address. In such an instance, you would use an absolute cell reference. An **absolute cell reference** always refers to a specific cell address when the formula is copied. You create an absolute reference by placing a dollar sign ($) before the row letter and column number of the address (for example $A$1). The staff in the Marketing department hopes the number of author events will increase by 20% over last year's figures. Jim wants you to add a column that calculates a possible increase in the number of spring events in 2003. He asks you to do a what-if analysis and recalculate the spreadsheet several times, changing the percentage by which the number of appearances might increase each time.

Steps

1. Click cell **G1**, type **Change**, then press [→]
   You can store the increase factor that will be used in the what-if analysis in cell H1.
2. Type **1.1**, then press **[Enter]**
   The value in cell H1 represents a 10% increase in author events.
3. Click cell **G3**, type **What if?**, then press **[Enter]**
4. Click cell **G4**, type =, click **E4**, type *, click **H1**, then click the **Enter button** on the formula bar
   The result, 56.1, appears in cell G4. This value represents the total spring events for Boston if there is a 10% increase. Jim wants to perform a what-if analysis for all the stores.
5. Drag the fill handle to extend the selection from **G4** to **G7**
   The resulting values in the range G5:G7 are all zeros. When you copy the formula it adjusts so that the formula in cell G5 is =E5*H2. Because there is no value in cell H2, the result is 0, an error. You need to use an absolute reference in the formula to keep the formula from adjusting itself. That way, it will always reference cell H1. You can change the relative cell reference to an absolute cell reference by using [F4].
6. Click cell **G4**, press **[F2]** to change to Edit mode, then press **[F4]**
   When you press [F2], the **range finder** outlines the equation's arguments in blue and green. When you press [F4], dollar signs appear, changing the H1 cell reference to an absolute reference. See Figure B-19.
7. Click on the formula bar, then drag the fill handle to extend the selection to range **G5:G7**
   The formula correctly contains an absolute cell reference, and the value of G4 remains unchanged at 56.1. The correct values for a 10% increase appear in cells G4:G7. You complete the what-if analysis by changing the value in cell H1 to indicate a 25% increase in events.
8. Click cell **H1**, type **1.25**, then click
   The values in the range G4:G7 change to reflect the 25% increase. Compare your completed worksheets to Figure B-20. Because events only occur in whole numbers, the numbers' appearance can be changed later.
9. Enter your name in cell **A25**, click the **Save button** on the Standard toolbar, click the **Print button** on the Standard toolbar, close the workbook, then exit Excel

QuickTip

Before you copy or move a formula, check to see if you need to use an absolute cell reference.

FIGURE B-19: Absolute cell reference in cell G4

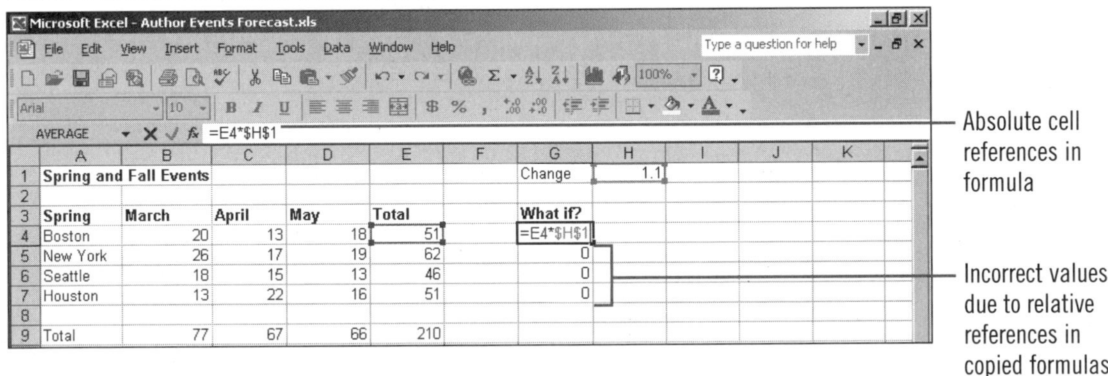

	A	B	C	D	E	F	G	H
1	Spring and Fall Events						Change	1.1
2								
3	Spring	March	April	May	Total		What if?	
4	Boston	20	13	18	51		=E4*$H$1	
5	New York	26	17	19	62		0	
6	Seattle	18	15	13	46		0	
7	Houston	13	22	16	51		0	
8								
9	Total	77	67	66	210			

FIGURE B-20: Completed worksheets

Summer 2003 MediaLoft Author Events Forecast

	June	July	August	Total	Average
Boston	22	15	19	56	18.66667
New York	28	18	22	68	22.66667
Seattle	20	17	18	55	18.33333
Houston	15	19	21	55	18.33333
Total	85	69	80	234	
20% rise	102	82.8	96	280.8	

Spring and Fall Events — Change 1.25

Spring	**March**	**April**	**May**	**Total**	**What if?**
Boston	20	13	18	51	63.75
New York	26	17	19	62	77.5
Seattle	18	15	13	46	57.5
Houston	13	22	16	51	63.75
Total	77	67	66	210	

Fall	**September**	**October**	**November**	**Total**
Boston	22	17	20	59
New York	27	16	24	67
Seattle	19	19	18	56
Houston	15	25	18	58
Total	83	77	80	240

Inserting and deleting selected cells

As you add formulas to your workbook, you may need to insert or delete cells, not entire rows or columns. When you do this, Excel automatically adjusts cell references to reflect their new locations. To insert cells, click Insert on the menu bar, then click Cells. The Insert dialog box opens, asking if you want to insert a cell and move the selected cell down or to the right of the new one. To delete one or more selected cells, click Edit on the menu bar, click Delete, and, in the Delete dialog box, indicate which way you want to move the adjacent cells. When using this option, be careful not to disturb row or column alignment that may be necessary to make sense of the worksheet.

Practice

► Concepts Review

Label each element of the Excel worksheet window shown in Figure B-21.

FIGURE B-21

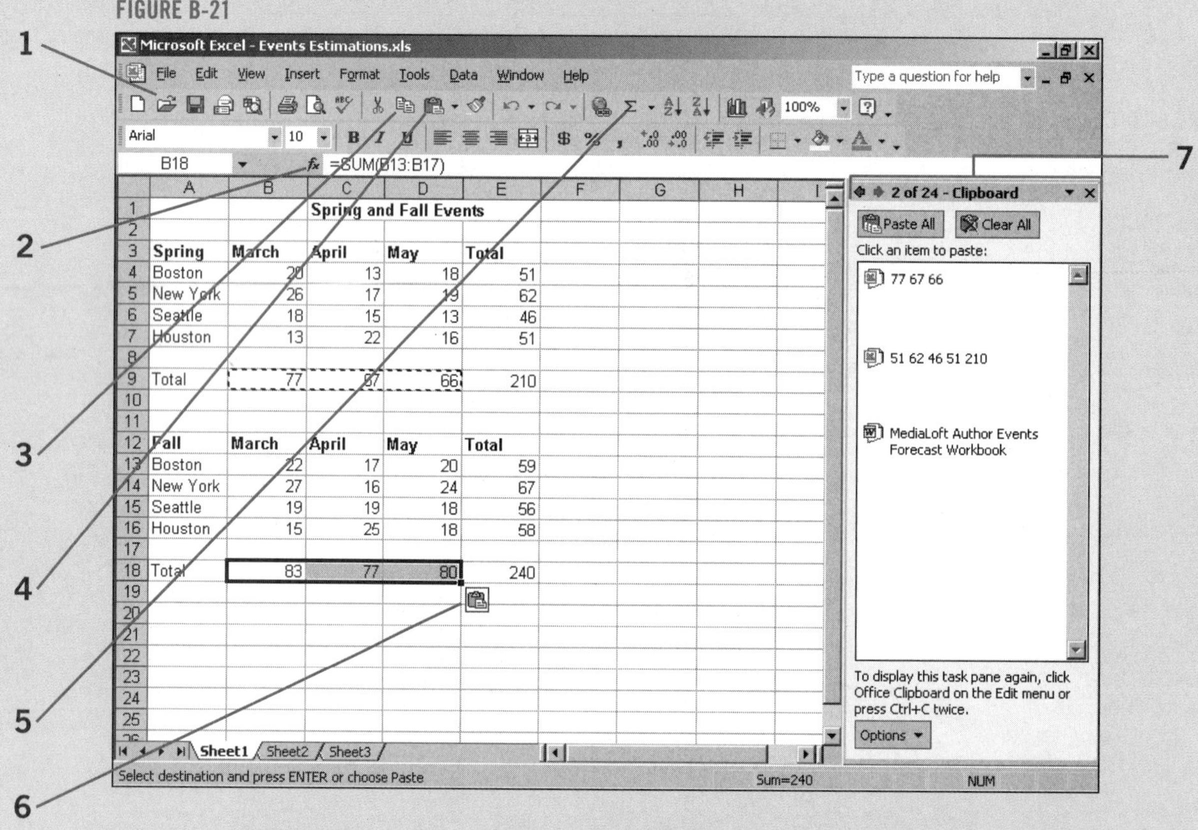

Match the term or button with the statement that describes it.

8. Fill handle
9. Function
10.
11.
12. Formula

a. A predefined formula that provides a shortcut for commonly used calculations
b. A cell entry that performs a calculation in an Excel worksheet
c. Used to copy labels, formulas, and values
d. Adds the selected range to the Office Clipboard.
e. Used to paste cells

Select the best answer from the list of choices.

13. What type of cell reference changes when it is copied?
a. Absolute
b. Circular
c. Looping
d. Relative

14. What character is used to make a reference absolute?
a. &
b. ^
c. $
d. @

15. Which button is used to enter data in a cell?

a. [undo button]
b. [X button]
c. [copy button]
d. [check button]

Skills Review

1. **Edit cell entries and work with ranges.**
   a. Start Excel, open the workbook EX B-2 from the drive and folder where your Project Files are stored then save it as **Office Furnishings**.
   b. Change the quantity of Tables to **27**.
   c. Change the price of Desks to **285**.
   d. Change the quantity of Easels to **18**.
   e. Enter your name in cell A40, then save the workbook.
2. **Enter formulas.**
   a. In cell B6, use the pointing method to enter the formula **B2+B3+B4+B5**.
   b. In cell D2, use the pointing method to enter the formula **B2*C2**.
   c. Save your work.
3. **Create complex formulas.**
   a. In cell B8, enter the formula **(B2+B3+B4+B5)/4**.
   b. In cell C8, enter the formula **(C2+C3+C4+C5)/4**.
   c. Save your work.
4. **Introduce Excel functions.**
   a. Enter the label **Min Price** in cell A9.
   b. In cell C9, enter the function **MIN(C2:C5)**.
   c. Enter the label **Max Price** in cell A10.
   d. Create a formula in cell C10 that determines the maximum price.
   e. Save your work.
5. **Copy and move cell entries.**
   a. Select the range **A1:C6**, then copy the range to cell A12.
   b. Select the range **D1:E1**, then use drag and drop to copy the range to cell D12.
   c. Move the contents of cell G1 to cell E9, then save your work.
6. **Copy formulas with relative cell references.**
   a. Copy the formula in D2 into cells D3:D5.
   b. Copy the formula in D2 into cells D13:D16.
   c. Save the worksheet.
7. **Copy formulas with absolute cell references.**
   a. In cell E10, enter the value **1.375**.
   b. In cell E2, create a formula containing an absolute reference that multiplies D2 and E10.
   c. Use the fill handle to copy the formula in E2 into cells **E3:E5**.
   d. Use the copy and paste buttons to copy the formula in E2 into cells **E13:E16**.
   e. Delete cells A13:E13, shifting the cells up, then edit the formula in cell B16 so the missing reference is removed.
   f. Change the amount in cell E10 to **2.873**.
   g. Select cells A1:E1 and insert cells, shifting cells down.
   h. Enter **Inventory Estimate** in cell A1.
   i. Save, preview, print, and close the workbook, then exit Excel.

Independent Challenge 1

You are the box office manager for the Young Brazilians Jazz Band, a popular new group. Your responsibilities include tracking seasonal ticket sales for the band's concerts and anticipating ticket sales for the next season. The group sells four types of tickets: reserved, general, senior, and student tickets.

The 2003–2004 season includes five scheduled concerts: Spring, Summer, Fall, Winter, and Thaw. You will plan and build a worksheet that tracks the sales of each of the four ticket types for all five concerts.

FIGURE B-22

	A	B	C	D	E	F	G	H
1			2003-2004 Season					
2			Young Brazilians Jazz Band					Increase
3								1.05
4		Reserved	General	Senior	Student			
5	Concerts	Seating	Admission	Citizens	Tickets	Totals		What if?
6	Spring	285	50	30	20	385		404.25
7	Summer	135	25	35	20	215		225.75
8	Fall	130	50	25	20	225		236.25
9	Winter	160	100	30	20	310		325.5
10	Thaw	250	60	35	20	365		383.25
11	Total	960	285	155	100	1500		1575

- **a.** Think about the results you want to see, the information you need to build into these worksheets, and what types of calculations must be performed.
- **b.** Sketch sample worksheets on a piece of paper to indicate how the information should be laid out. What information should go in the columns? In the rows?
- **c.** Start Excel, open a new workbook, then save it as **Young Brazilians** in the drive and folder where your Project Files are stored.
- **d.** Plan and build a worksheet that tracks the sales of each of the four ticket types for all five concerts. Build the worksheets by entering a title, row labels, column headings, and formulas.
- **e.** Enter your own sales data. No concert sold more than 400 tickets, and the Reserved category was the most popular.
- **f.** Calculate the total ticket sales for each concert, the total sales for each of the four ticket types, and the total sales for all tickets.
- **g.** Name the worksheet **Sales Data** and color the tab Red.
- **h.** Copy the Sales Data worksheet to a blank worksheet, name the copied worksheet **5% Increase**, and color the tab aqua.
- **i.** Modify the 5% increase sheet so that a 5% increase in sales of all ticket types is shown in a separate column. See Figure B-22 for a sample worksheet.
- **j.** Enter your name in a worksheet cell.
- **k.** Save your work, preview and print the worksheets, then close the workbook and exit Excel.

Independent Challenge 2

The Beautiful You Salon is a small but growing beauty salon that has hired you to organize its accounting records using Excel. The owners want you to track its expenses using Excel. Before you were hired, one of the bookkeepers entered last year's expenses in a workbook, but the analysis was never completed.

- **a.** Start Excel, open the workbook EX B-3 then save it as **Beautiful You Finances** in the drive and folder where your Project Files are stored. The worksheet includes labels for functions such as the Average, Maximum, and Minimum amounts of each of the expenses in the worksheet.
- **b.** Think about what information would be important for the bookkeeping staff to know.
- **c.** Create your sketch using the existing worksheet as a foundation.
- **d.** Create formulas in the Total column and row using the AutoSum function.
- **e.** Create formulas in the Average, Maximum, and Minimum columns and rows using the appropriate functions, dragging to select the range.
- **f.** Rename Sheet1 **Expenses** and add a color to the tab.
- **g.** Enter your name in a worksheet cell.
- **h.** Save your work, preview and print the worksheet, then close the workbook and exit Excel.

▶ Independent Challenge 3

You have been promoted to computer lab manager at Learn-It-All, a local computer training center. It is your responsibility to make sure there are enough computers for students during scheduled classes. Currently, you have five classrooms: four with IBM PCs and one with Macintoshes. Classes are scheduled Monday, Wednesday, and Friday in two-hour increments from 9 a.m. to 5 p.m. (the lab closes at 7 p.m.), and each room can currently accommodate 30 computers.

You plan and build a worksheet that tracks the number of students who can currently use the available computers per room. You create your enrollment data. Using an additional worksheet, you show the impact of an enrollment increase of 25%.

a. Think about how to construct these worksheets to create the desired output.
b. Sketch sample paper worksheets to indicate how the information should be laid out.
c. Start Excel, open a new workbook, then save it as **Learn-it-All** in the drive and folder where your Project Files are stored.
d. Create a worksheet by entering a title, row labels, column headings, data, and formulas. Name the sheet to easily identify its contents.
e. Create a second sheet by copying the information from the initial sheet.
f. Name the second sheet to easily identify its contents.
g. Add color to each sheet tab.
h. Enter your name in a cell in each sheet.
i. Save your work, preview and print each worksheet, then close the workbook and exit Excel.

Independent Challenge 4

Your company is opening a branch office in Great Britain and your boss is a fanatic about keeping the thermostats at a constant temperature during each season of the year. Because she grew up in the U.S., she is only familiar with Fahrenheit temperatures and doesn't know how to convert them to Celsius. She has asked you to find out the Celsius equivalents for the thermostatic settings she wants to use. She prefers the temperature to be 65 degrees F in the winter, 62 degrees F in the spring, 75 degrees in the summer, and 70 degrees F in the fall. You can use the Web and Excel to determine the new settings.

a. Start Excel, open a new workbook, then save it as **Temperature Conversions** in the drive and folder where your Project Files are stored.
b. Go to the Alta Vista search engine at www.altavista.com and enter search text such as "temperature conversions". You can also use Yahoo!, Excite, Infoseek, or another search engine of your choice. Locate a site that tells you how to convert Fahrenheit temperatures to Celsius. (*Hint*: One possible site you can use to determine these conversions is http://home.clara.net/brianp/, then click on the Temperature link.)
c. Think about how to create an Excel equation that will perform the conversion.
d. Create column and row titles using Table B-3 to get started.
e. In the appropriate cell, create an equation that calculates the conversion of a Fahrenheit temperature to a Celsius temperature.
f. Copy the equation, then paste it in the remaining Celsius cells.
g. Enter your name in a worksheet cell.
h. Save and print your work.

TABLE B-3

Temperature Conversions

Season	Fahrenheit	Celsius
Spring	62	
Winter	68	
Summer	75	
Fall	70	

Visual Workshop

Create a worksheet similar to Figure B-23 using the skills you learned in this unit. Save the workbook as **Annual Budget** in the drive and folder where your Project Files are stored. Enter your name in cell A13, then preview and print the worksheet.

FIGURE B-23

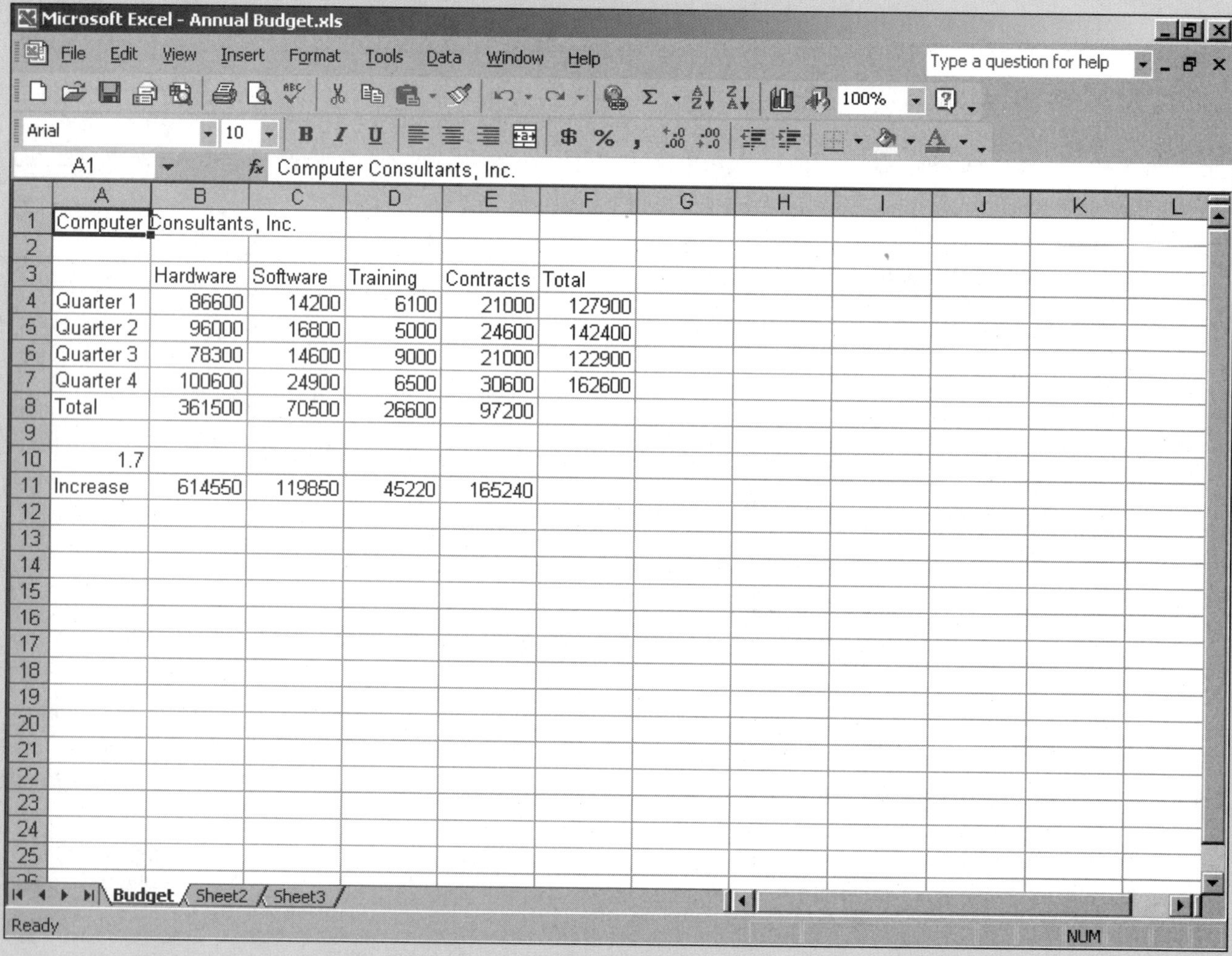

Microsoft Excel - Annual Budget.xls

A1 Computer Consultants, Inc.

	A	B	C	D	E	F
1	Computer Consultants, Inc.					
2						
3		Hardware	Software	Training	Contracts	Total
4	Quarter 1	86600	14200	6100	21000	127900
5	Quarter 2	96000	16800	5000	24600	142400
6	Quarter 3	78300	14600	9000	21000	122900
7	Quarter 4	100600	24900	6500	30600	162600
8	Total	361500	70500	26600	97200	
9						
10	1.7					
11	Increase	614550	119850	45220	165240	

Budget / Sheet2 / Sheet3

Ready NUM

Formatting a Worksheet

Objectives

- MOUS ► Format values
- MOUS ► Use fonts and font sizes
- MOUS ► Change attributes and alignment
- MOUS ► Adjust column widths
- MOUS ► Insert and delete rows and columns
- MOUS ► Apply colors, patterns, and borders
- MOUS ► Use conditional formatting
- MOUS ► Check spelling

You can use Excel formatting features to make a worksheet more attractive, to make it easier to read, or to emphasize key data. You do this by using different colors and fonts for the cell contents, adjusting column and row widths, and inserting and deleting columns and rows. The marketing managers at MediaLoft have asked Jim Fernandez to create a workbook that lists advertising expenses for all MediaLoft stores. Jim has prepared a worksheet for the New York City store containing this information, which he can adapt later for use in other stores. He asks you to use formatting to make the worksheet easier to read and to call attention to important data.

Excel 2002

Formatting Values

If you enter a value in a cell and you don't like the way the data appears, you can adjust the cell's format. **Formatting** determines how labels and values appear in cells, such as boldface, italic, with or without dollar signs or commas, and the like. Formatting changes only the way a value or label appears; it does not alter cell data in any way. To format a cell, first select it, then apply the formatting. You can format cells and ranges before or after you enter data. The Marketing department has requested that Jim begin by listing the New York City store's advertising expenses. Jim developed a worksheet that lists advertising invoices. He entered all the information and now wants you to format some of the labels and values. Because some of the changes might also affect column widths, you make all formatting changes before widening the columns.

Steps 1 2 3 4

QuickTip

Recall that to save a workbook in a different location, you click File on the menu bar, click Save As, click the Save in list arrow and navigate to a new drive or folder, type a new filename if necessary, then click Save.

1. **Start Excel, open the Project File EX C-1 from the drive and folder where your Project Files are stored, then save it as Ad Expenses**
   The store advertising worksheet appears in Figure C-1. You can display numeric data in a variety of ways, such as with decimals or leading dollar signs. Excel provides a special format for currency, which adds two decimal places and a dollar sign.
2. **Select the range E4:E32, then click the Currency Style button on the Formatting toolbar**
   Excel adds dollar signs and two decimal places to the Cost data. Excel automatically resizes the column to display the new formatting. Another way to format dollar values is to use the comma format, which does not include the $ sign.
3. **Select the range G4:I32, then click the Comma Style button on the Formatting toolbar**
   The values in columns G, H, and I display the comma format. You can also format percentages by using the Formatting toolbar.
4. **Select the range J4:J32, click the Percent Style button on the Formatting toolbar, then click the Increase Decimal button on the Formatting toolbar to show one decimal place**
   The % of Total column is now formatted with a percent sign (%) and one decimal place. You decide that you prefer the percentages rounded to the nearest whole number.
5. **Click the Decrease Decimal button**
   You can also apply a variety of formats to dates in a worksheet.
6. **Select the range B4:B31, click Format on the menu bar, click Cells, then if necessary click the Number tab**
   The Format Cells dialog box opens with the Number tab in front and the Date category already selected. See Figure C-2.
7. **Select the format 14-Mar-01 in the Type list box, then click OK**
   The dates in column B appear in the format you selected. You decide you don't need the year to appear in the Inv. Due column.
8. **Select the range C4:C31, click Format on the menu bar, click Cells, click 14-Mar in the Type list box, then click OK**
   Compare your worksheet to Figure C-3.
9. **Click the Save button on the Standard toolbar**

QuickTip

Select any range of contiguous cells by clicking the top-left cell, pressing and holding [Shift], then clicking the bottom-right cell. Add a row to the selected range by continuing to hold down [Shift] and pressing [↓], add a column by pressing [→].

QuickTip

The 3-14-01 format displays a single-digit day (such as 5/9/03) just as 9-May-03 does. The format below it displays the same day as 5/09/03.

FIGURE C-1: Advertising expense worksheet

Microsoft Excel - Ad Expenses.xls

A1 — MediaLoft NYC Advertising Expenses

	A	B	C	D	E	F	G	H	I	J	K	L
1	MediaLoft NYC Advertising Expenses										Sales Tax	0.084
2												
3	Type	Inv. Date	Inv. Due	Placed wit	Cost ea.	Quantity	Ext. Cost	Sales Tax	Total	% of Total		
4	Newspape	1/1/2003	1/31/2003	Village Re	65.11	5	325.55	27.37876	352.9288	0.018241		
5	Radio spot	1/7/2003	2/6/2003	WHAT	11	15	165	13.8765	178.8765	0.009245		
6	Subway	1/20/2003	2/19/2003	Advertising	35	30	1050	88.305	1138.305	0.058833		
7	Yellow Pag	1/1/2003	1/31/2003	NYNEX	152.94	4	611.76	51.44902	663.209	0.034278		
8	Blow-in ca	1/13/2003	2/12/2003	Advertising	0.172	230	39.56	3.326996	42.887	0.002217		
9	Magazine	1/7/2003	2/6/2003	Young Ups	100.92	12	1211.04	101.8485	1312.888	0.067856		
10	Pens	1/5/2003	2/4/2003	Mass App	0.123	250	30.75	2.586075	33.33608	0.001723		
11	Radio spot	1/15/2003	2/14/2003	WHAT	11	15	165	13.8765	178.8765	0.009245		
12	Billboard	1/12/2003	2/11/2003	Advertising	101.87	20	2037.4	171.3453	2208.745	0.114158		

FIGURE C-2: Format Cells dialog box

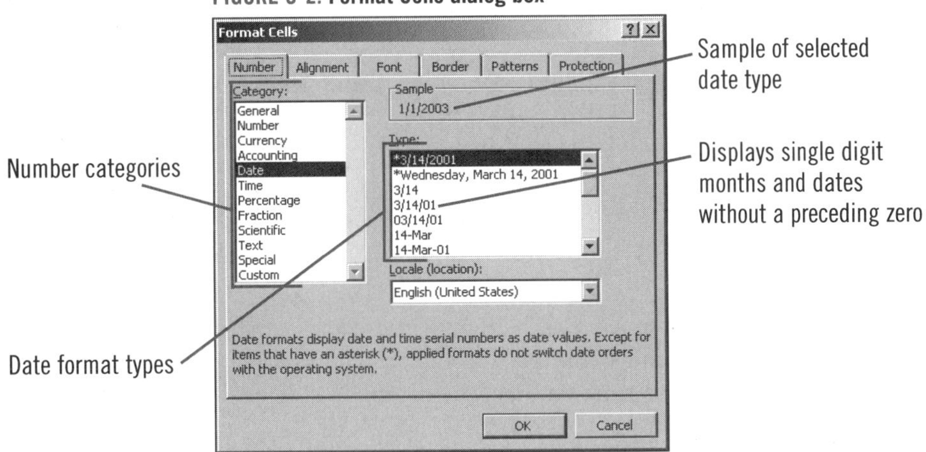

FIGURE C-3: Worksheet with formatted values

Microsoft Excel - Ad Expenses.xls

C4 — =B4+30

	A	B	C	D	E	F	G	H	I	J	K
1	MediaLoft NYC Advertising Expenses										Sales Tax
2											
3	Type	Inv. Date	Inv. Due	Placed wit	Cost ea.	Quantity	Ext. Cost	Sales Tax	Total	% of Total	
4	Newspape	1-Jan-03	31-Jan	Village Re	$ 65.11	5	325.55	27.38	352.93	2%	
5	Radio spot	7-Jan-03	6-Feb	WHAT	$ 11.00	15	165.00	13.88	178.88	1%	
6	Subway	20-Jan-03	19-Feb	Advertising	$ 35.00	30	1,050.00	88.31	1,138.31	6%	
7	Yellow Pag	1-Jan-03	31-Jan	NYNEX	$ 152.94	4	611.76	51.45	663.21	3%	
8	Blow-in ca	13-Jan-03	12-Feb	Advertising	$ 0.17	230	39.56	3.33	42.89	0%	
9	Magazine	7-Jan-03	6-Feb	Young Ups	$ 100.92	12	1,211.04	101.85	1,312.89	7%	
10	Pens	5-Jan-03	4-Feb	Mass App	$ 0.12	250	30.75	2.59	33.34	0%	
11	Radio spot	15-Jan-03	14-Feb	WHAT	$ 11.00	15	165.00	13.88	178.88	1%	
12	Billboard	12-Jan-03	11-Feb	Advertising	$ 101.87	20	2,037.40	171.35	2,200.75	11%	

Date formats appear without year

Using the Format Painter

You can "paint" a cell's format into other cells by using the Format Painter button on the Standard toolbar. This is similar to using copy and paste to copy information, but instead of copying cell contents, you copy only the cell format. Select the cell containing the desired format, then click. The pointer changes to. Use this pointer to select the cell or range you want to contain the new format. You can paint a cell's format onto multiple cells by double-clicking, then clicking each cell that you want to paint with. When you are finished painting formats, you can turn off the Format Painter by pressing [Esc] or by clicking again.

Using Fonts and Font Sizes

A **font** is the name for a collection of characters (letters, numerals, symbols, and punctuation marks) with a similar, specific design. The **font size** is the physical size of the text, measured in units called points. A **point** is equal to 1/72 of an inch. The default font in Excel is 10-point Arial. You can change the font, the size, or both of any worksheet entry or section by using the Format command on the menu bar or by using the Formatting toolbar. Table C-1 shows several fonts in different sizes. Now that the data is formatted, Jim wants you to change the font and size of the labels and the worksheet title so that they stand out more from the data.

Steps

QuickTip

You can also open the Format Cells dialog box by right-clicking selected cells, then clicking Format Cells.

1. Press **[Ctrl][Home]** to select cell A1
2. Click **Format** on the menu bar, click **Cells**, then click the **Font tab** in the Format Cells dialog box

   See Figure C-4.
3. Scroll down the **Font list** to see an alphabetical listing of the fonts available on your computer, click **Times New Roman** in the Font list box, click **24** in the Size list box, then click **OK**

   The title font appears in 24-point Times New Roman, and the Formatting toolbar displays the new font and size information. You can also change a font and increase the font size by using the Formatting toolbar. The column headings should stand out more from the data.
4. Select the range **A3:J3**, then click the **Font list arrow** Arial on the Formatting toolbar

   Notice that the fonts on this font list actually look like the font they represent.
5. Click **Times New Roman** in the Font list, click the **Font Size** list arrow 10, then click **14** in the Font Size list

   Compare your worksheet to Figure C-5. Notice that some of the column headings are now too wide to appear fully in the column. Excel does not automatically adjust column widths to accommodate cell formatting; you have to adjust column widths manually. You'll learn to do this in a later lesson.
6. Click the **Save button** on the Standard toolbar

TABLE C-1: Types of fonts

font	12 point	24 point	font	12 point	24 point
Arial	Excel	Excel	Playbill	Excel	Excel
Comic Sans MS	Excel	Excel	Times New Roman	Excel	Excel

FIGURE C-4: Font tab in the Format Cells dialog box

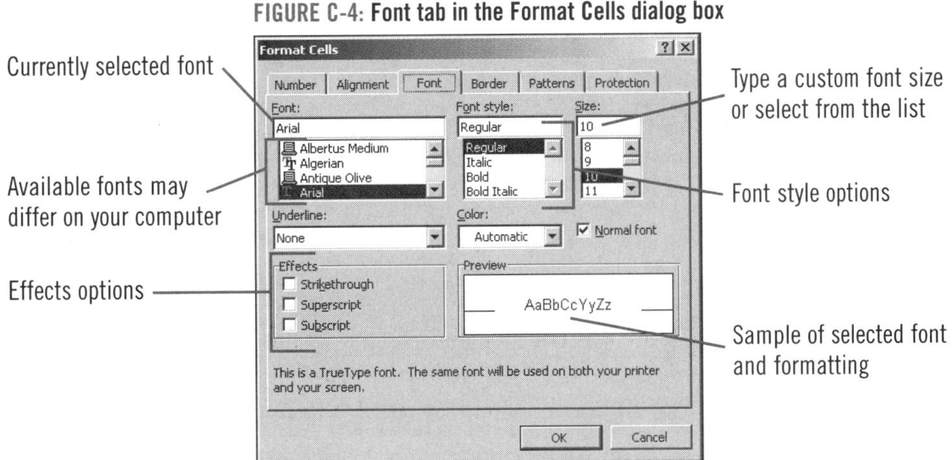

FIGURE C-5: Worksheet with formatted title and labels

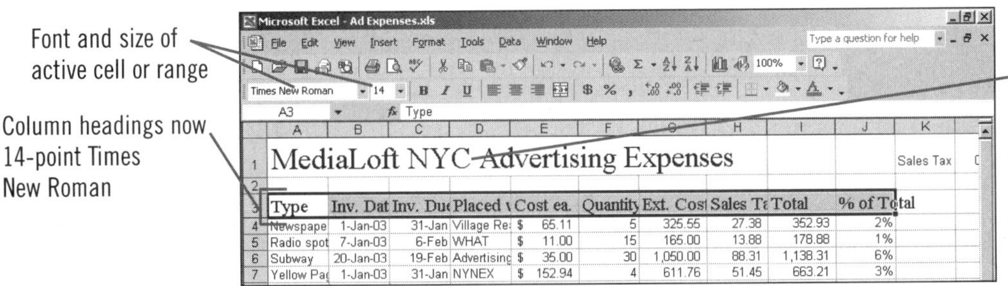

Excel 2002

CLUES TO USE

Inserting Clip Art

You can add clips to your worksheets to make them look more professional. A **clip** is an individual media file, such as art, sound, animation, or a movie. **Clip art** refers to images such as a corporate logo, a picture, or a photo; Excel comes with many clips that you can use. To add clip art to your worksheet, click Insert on the menu bar, point to Picture, then click Clip Art. The Insert Clip Art task pane appears. Here you can search for clips by typing one or more **keywords** (words related to your subject) in the Search text box, then clicking Search. Clips that relate to your keywords appear in the Clip Art task pane, as shown in Figure C-6. Click the image you want. (If you have a standard Office installation and have a dial-up Internet connection, you will have fewer images available.) You can also add your own images to a worksheet by clicking Insert on the menu bar, pointing to Picture, then clicking From File. Navigate to the file you want, then click Insert. To resize an image, drag its lower right corner. To move an image, drag it to a new location.

FIGURE C-6: Results of search on keyword "magic"

Excel 2002

Changing Attributes and Alignment

Attributes are styling formats such as bold, italics, and underlining that you can apply to affect the way text and numbers look in a worksheet. You can also change the **alignment** of labels and values in cells to be left, right, or center. You can apply attributes and alignment options from the Formatting toolbar or from the Alignment tab of the Format Cells dialog box. See Table C-2 for a list and description of the available attribute and alignment toolbar buttons. Now that you have applied new fonts and font sizes to his worksheet labels, Jim wants you to further enhance the worksheet's appearance by adding bold and underline formatting and centering some of the labels.

Steps

1. Press **[Ctrl][Home]** to move to cell A1, then click the **Bold button** on the Formatting toolbar
   The title appears in bold.
2. Select the range **A3:J3**, then click the **Underline button** on the Formatting toolbar
   Excel underlines the text in the column headings in the selected range.
3. Click cell **A3**, click the **Italics button** on the Formatting toolbar, then click
   The word "Type" appears in boldface italic type. Notice that the Bold, Italics, and Underline buttons are selected.
4. Click
   Excel removes italics from cell A3 but the bold and underline formatting attributes remain.
5. Select the range **B3:J3**, then click
   Bold formatting is added to the rest of the labels in the column headings. The title would look better if it were centered over the data columns.
6. Select the range **A1:J1**, then click the **Merge and Center button** on the Formatting toolbar
   The Merge and Center button creates one cell out of the 10 cells across the row, then centers the text in that newly created large cell. The title "MediaLoft NYC Advertising Expenses" is centered across the 10 columns you selected. You can change the alignment within individual cells using toolbar buttons; you can split merged cells into their original components by selecting the merged cells, then clicking .
7. Select the range **A3:J3**, then click the **Center button** on the Formatting toolbar
   Compare your screen to Figure C-7. Although they may be difficult to read, notice that all the headings are centered within their cells.
8. Click the **Save button** on the Standard toolbar

QuickTip

Overuse of any attribute can be distracting and make a workbook less readable. Be consistent, adding emphasis the same way throughout.

QuickTip

Use formatting shortcuts on any selected range: [Ctrl][B] to bold, [Ctrl][I] to italicize, and [Ctrl][U] to underline.

QuickTip

To clear all formatting, click Edit on the menu bar, point to Clear, then click Formats.

Rotating and indenting cell entries

In addition to applying fonts and formatting attributes, you can rotate or indent cell data within a cell to further change its appearance. You can rotate text within a cell by altering its alignment. To change alignment, select the cells you want to modify, click Format on the menu bar, click Cells, then click the Alignment tab. Click a position in the Orientation box, or type a number in the degrees text box to change from the default horizontal alignment, then click OK. You can indent cell contents using the Increase Indent button on the Formatting toolbar, which moves cell contents to the right one space, or the Decrease Indent button , which moves cell contents to the left one space.

FIGURE C-7: Worksheet with formatting attributes applied

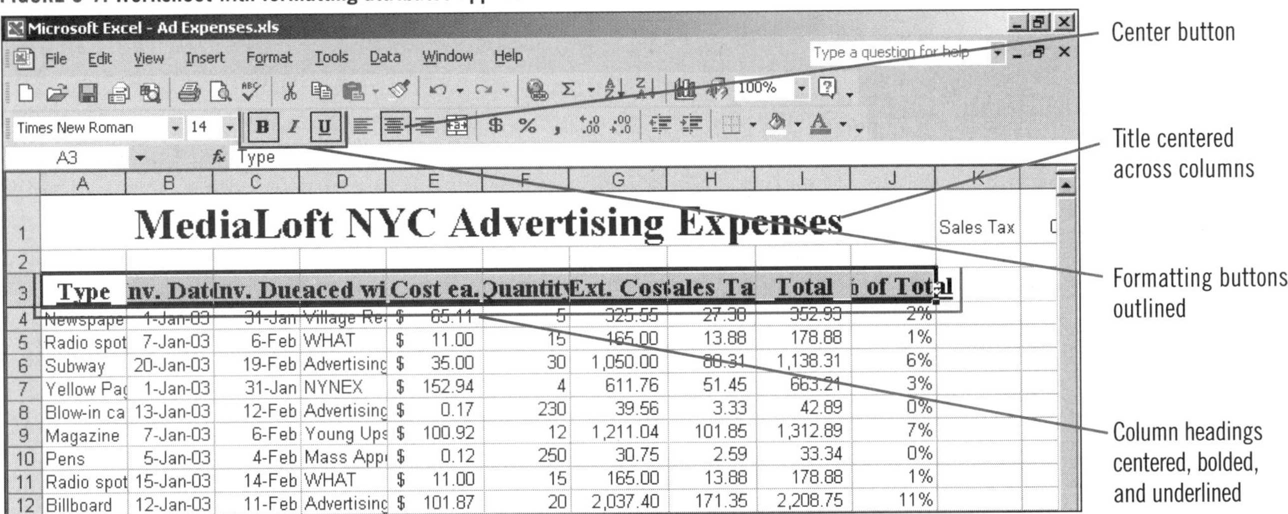

TABLE C-2: Attribute and Alignment buttons on the Formatting toolbar

button	description	button	description
B	**Bolds text**		**Aligns text on the left side of the cell**
I	**Italicizes text**		**Centers text horizontally within the cell**
U	**Underlines text**		**Aligns text on the right side of the cell**
	Adds lines or borders		**Centers text across columns, and combines two or more selected adjacent cells into one cell**

Using AutoFormat

Excel has 17 predefined worksheet formats to make formatting easier and to give you the option of consistently styling your worksheets. AutoFormats are designed for worksheets with labels in the left column and top rows, and totals in the bottom row or right column. To use AutoFormat, select the data to be formatted—or place your mouse pointer anywhere within the range to be selected (Excel can automatically detect a range of cells)—click Format on the menu bar, click AutoFormat, select a format from the sample boxes, as shown in Figure C-8, then click OK.

FIGURE C-8: AutoFormat dialog box

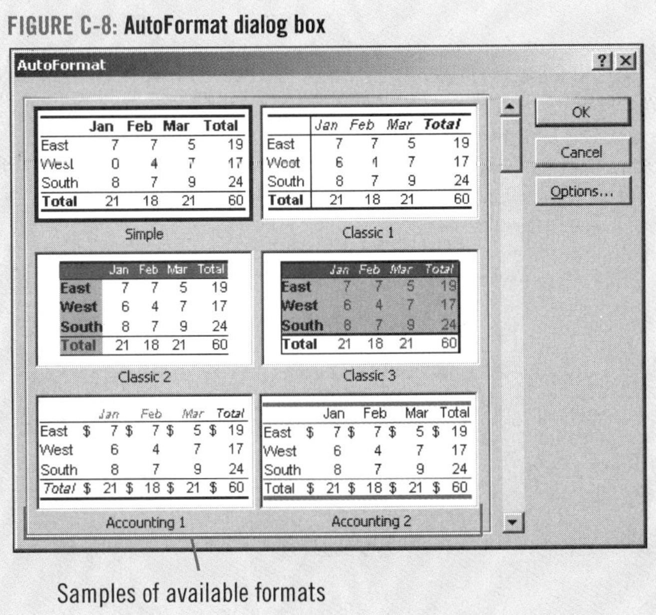

Excel 2002

Adjusting Column Widths

As you continue formatting a worksheet, you might need to adjust column widths to accommodate a larger font size or style. The default column width is 8.43 characters wide, a little less than one inch. With Excel, you can adjust the column width for one or more columns by using the mouse or the Column command on the Format menu. Table C-3 describes the commands available on the Format Column menu. Jim notices that some of the labels in column A have been truncated and don't fit in the cells. He asks you to adjust the widths of the columns so that the labels appear in their entirety.

Steps 1 2 3 4

1. **Position the pointer on the line between the column A and column B headings**
   The **column heading** is the gray box at the top of each column containing a letter. The pointer changes to ✛, as shown in Figure C-9. You position the pointer on the right edge of the column that you are adjusting. The Yellow Pages entries are the widest in the column.
2. **Click and drag the ✛ pointer to the right until the column displays the Yellow Pages entries fully**
   The **AutoFit** feature lets you use the mouse to resize a column so it automatically accommodates the widest entry in a cell.
3. **Position the pointer on the column line between columns B and C headings until it changes to ✛, then double-click**
   Column B automatically widens to fit the widest entry, in this case, the column label.
4. **Use AutoFit to resize columns C, D, and J**
   You can also use the Column Width command on the Format menu to adjust several columns to the same width.
5. **Select the range F5:I5**
   Columns can be adjusted by selecting any cell in the column.
6. **Click Format on the menu bar, point to Column, then click Width**
   The Column Width dialog box appears. Move the dialog box, if necessary, by dragging it by its title bar so you can see the selected columns. The column width measurement is based on the number of characters in the Normal font (in this case, Arial).
7. **Type 11 in the Column Width text box, then click OK**
   The column widths change to reflect the new setting. See Figure C-10.
8. **Click the Save button on the Standard toolbar**

QuickTip

To reset columns to the default width, click the column headings to select the columns, click Format on the menu bar, point to Column, click Standard Width, then click OK.

Trouble?

If "#######" appears after you adjust a column of values, the column is too narrow to display the contents. Increase the column width until the values appear.

TABLE C-3: Format Column commands

command	description	command	description
Width	Sets the width to a specific number of characters	**Unhide**	Unhide(s) column(s)
AutoFit Selection	Fits to the widest entry	**Standard Width**	Resets width to default widths
Hide	Hide(s) column(s)		

FIGURE C-9: **Preparing to change the column width**

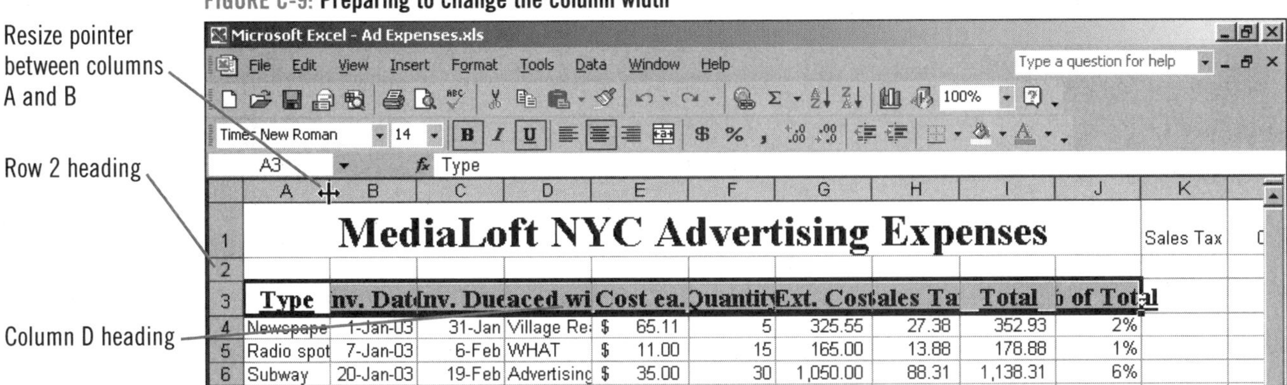

FIGURE C-10: **Worksheet with column widths adjusted**

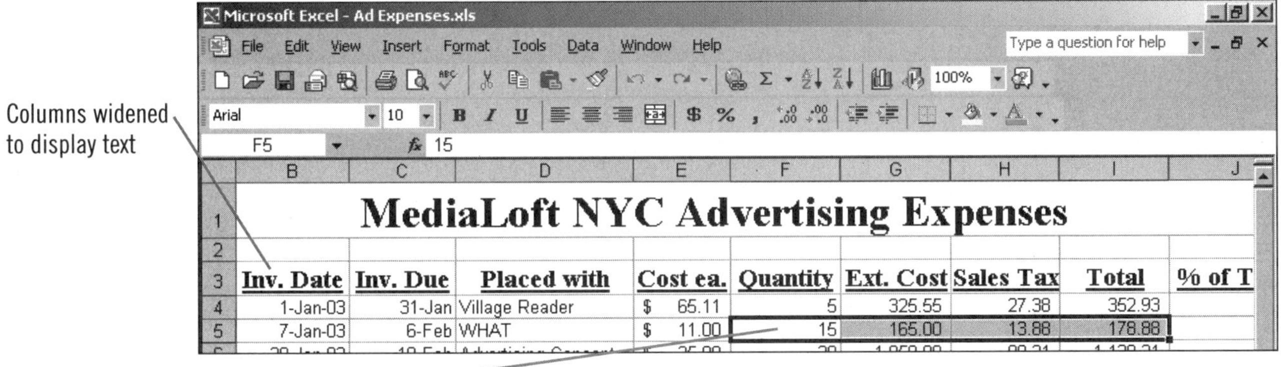

Specifying row height

The Row Height command on the Format menu allows you to customize row height to improve readability. Row height is calculated in points, the same units of measure used for fonts. The row height must exceed the size of the font you are using. Normally, you don't need to adjust row heights manually. If you format something in a row to be a larger point size, Excel will adjust the row to fit the largest point size in the row. You can also adjust row height by placing the ✛ pointer under the row heading and dragging to the desired height.

Excel 2002

Excel 2002

Inserting and Deleting Rows and Columns

As you modify a worksheet, you might find it necessary to insert or delete rows and columns to keep your worksheet current. For example, you might need to insert rows to accommodate new inventory products or remove a column of yearly totals that are no longer necessary. Jim has already improved the appearance of his worksheet by formatting the labels and values in the worksheet. Now he decides to improve the overall appearance of the worksheet by inserting a row between the last row of data and the totals. Jim has located a row of inaccurate data and an unnecessary column that he wants you to delete.

1. **Right-click cell A32, then click Insert**
   The Insert dialog box opens. See Figure C-11. You can choose to insert a column or a row, or you can shift the data in the cells in the active column right or in the active row down. An additional row between the last row of data and the totals will visually separate the totals.

QuickTip

Inserting or deleting rows or columns can cause problems in formulas that contain absolute cell references. After adding rows or columns to a worksheet, be sure to proof your formulas.

2. **Click the Entire row option button, then click OK**
   A blank row appears between the totals and the Billboard data. Excel inserts rows above the cell pointer and inserts columns to the left of the cell pointer. When you insert a new row, the contents of the worksheet shift down from the newly inserted row. The formula result in cell E33 has not changed. When you insert a new column, the contents of the worksheet shift to the right from the point of the new column. To insert a single row, you can also right-click the row heading immediately below where you want the new row, then click Insert. To insert multiple rows, drag across row headings to select the same number of rows as you want to insert. The Insert Options button appears beside cell A33. When you place over , you can click the list arrow and select from the following options: Format Same As Above, Format same As Below, or Clear Formatting.

3. **Click the row 27 heading**
   Hats from Mass Appeal Inc. will no longer be part of the advertising campaign. All of row 27 is selected, as shown in Figure C-12.

QuickTip

Use the Edit menu, or right-click the selected row and click Delete, to remove a selected row. Pressing [Delete] removes the contents of a selected row; the row itself remains.

4. **Click Edit in the menu bar, then click Delete**
   Excel deletes row 27, and all rows below this shift up one row.

5. **Click the column J heading**
   The percentage information is calculated elsewhere and is no longer necessary in this worksheet.

6. **Click Edit in the menu bar, then click Delete**
   Excel deletes column J. The remaining columns to the right shift left one column.

7. **Click the Save button on the Standard toolbar**

FIGURE C-11: Insert dialog box

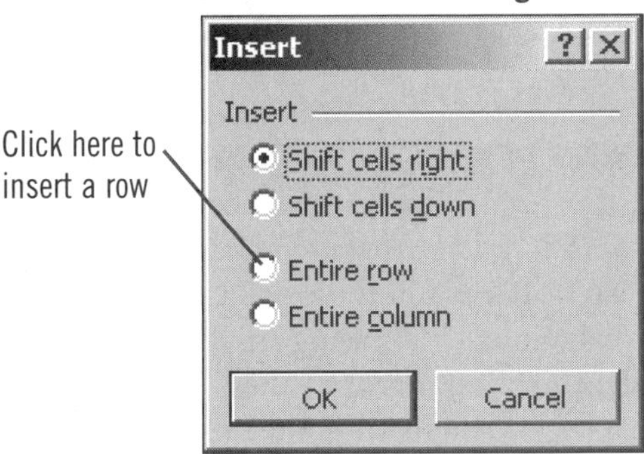

FIGURE C-12: Worksheet with row 27 selected

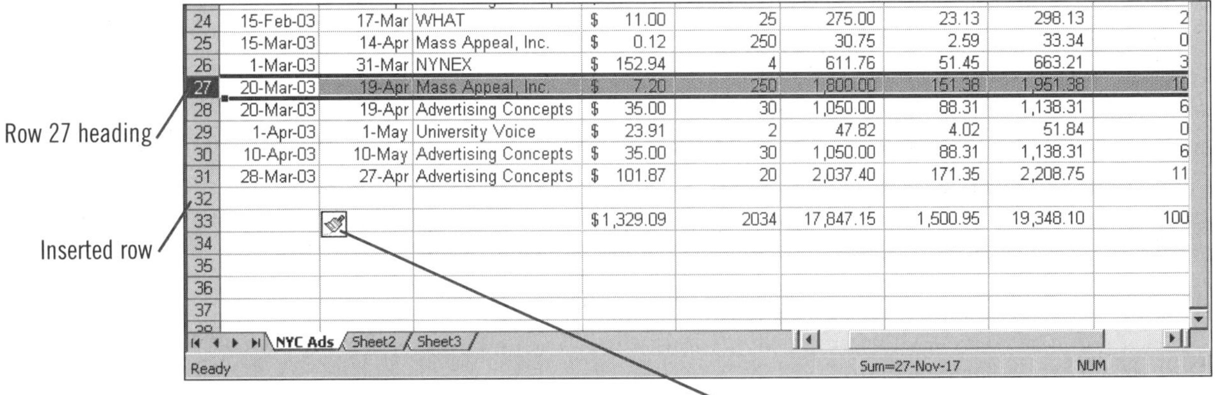

24	15-Feb-03	17-Mar	WHAT	$ 11.00	25	275.00	23.13	298.13	2
25	15-Mar-03	14-Apr	Mass Appeal, Inc.	$ 0.12	250	30.75	2.59	33.34	0
26	1-Mar-03	31-Mar	NYNEX	$ 152.94	4	611.76	51.45	663.21	3
27	20-Mar-03	19-Apr	Mass Appeal, Inc.	$ 7.20	250	1,800.00	151.38	1,951.38	10
28	20-Mar-03	19-Apr	Advertising Concepts	$ 35.00	30	1,050.00	88.31	1,138.31	6
29	1-Apr-03	1-May	University Voice	$ 23.91	2	47.82	4.02	51.84	0
30	10-Apr-03	10-May	Advertising Concepts	$ 35.00	30	1,050.00	88.31	1,138.31	6
31	28-Mar-03	27-Apr	Advertising Concepts	$ 101.87	20	2,037.40	171.35	2,208.75	11
32									
33				$1,329.09	2034	17,847.15	1,500.95	19,348.10	100
34									
35									
36									
37									

Insert Options button may appear in a different location, or may not be visible

Adding and editing comments

Much of your Excel work may be in collaboration with teammates with whom you share worksheets. You can share ideas with other worksheet users by adding comments within selected cells. To include a comment in a worksheet, click the cell where you want to place the comment, click Insert on the menu bar, then click Comment. A resizable text box containing the computer's user name opens where you can type your comments. A small, red triangle appears in the upper-right corner of a cell containing a comment. If the comments are not already displayed, workbook users can point to the triangle to display the comment. To see all worksheet comments, as shown in Figure C-13, click View on the menu bar, then click Comments. To edit a comment click the cell containing the comment, click Insert on the menu bar, then click Edit Comment. To delete a comment, right-click the cell containing the comment, then click Delete Comment.

FIGURE C-13: Comments in worksheet

20	Subway	22-Feb-03	24-Mar	Advertising Concepts	$ 35.00
21	Radio spot	1-Feb-03	3-Mar	WHAT	$ 11.00
22	Newspaper	25-Feb-03	27-Mar	Village Reader	$ 65.11
23	Blow-in cards	10-Mar-03	9-Apr		$ 0.17
24	Radio spot	15-Feb-03	17-Mar		$ 11.00
25	Pens	15-Mar-03	14-Apr		$ 0.12
26	Yellow Pages	1-Mar-03	31-Mar		$ 152.94
27	Subway	20-Mar-03	19-Apr	Advertising Concepts	$ 35.00
28	Newspaper	1-Apr-03	1-May		$ 23.91
29	Subway	10-Apr-03	10-May		$ 35.00
30	Billboard	28-Mar-03	27-Apr		$ 101.87
31					
32					$1,321.89
33					
34					

Jim Fernandez: Should we continue with these ads, or expand to other publications?

Jim Fernandez: We need to evaluate whether we should continue these ads.

NYC Ads / Sheet2 / Sheet3

Ready

Excel 2002

Excel 2002

Applying Colors, Patterns, and Borders

You can use colors, patterns, and borders to enhance the overall appearance of a worksheet and to make it easier to read. You can add these enhancements by using the Patterns or Borders tabs in the Format Cells dialog box or by using the Borders and Color buttons on the Formatting toolbar. You can apply color or patterns to the background of a cell, to a range, or to cell contents. You can also apply borders to all the cells in a worksheet or only to selected cells to call attention to individual or groups of cells. See Table C-4 for a list of border buttons and their functions. Jim asks you to add a pattern, a border, and color to the title of the worksheet to give it a more professional appearance.

1. **Press [Ctrl][Home] to select cell A1, then click the Fill Color list arrow on the Formatting toolbar**
   The color palette appears.

2. **Click the Turquoise color (fourth row, fifth column)**
   Cell A1 has a turquoise background, as shown in Figure C-14. Cell A1 spans columns A through I because of the Merge and Center command used for the title.

> **QuickTip**
> Use color sparingly. Too much color can divert the reader's attention from the worksheet data.

3. **Click Format on the menu bar, then click Cells**
   The Format Cells dialog box opens.

4. **Click the Patterns tab if it is not already displayed**
   See Figure C-15. A high contrast between foreground and background increases the readability of cell contents.

5. **Click the Pattern list arrow, click the Thin Diagonal Crosshatch pattern (third row, last column), then click OK**
   A border also enhances a cell's appearance. Unlike underlining, which is a text formatting tool, borders extend the width of the cell.

6. **Click the Borders list arrow on the Formatting toolbar, then click the Thick Bottom Border (second row, second column) on the Borders palette**
   It can be difficult to view a border in a selected cell.

> **QuickTip**
> You can also draw cell borders using the mouse pointer. Click the Borders list arrow on the Formatting toolbar. Click Draw Borders, then drag to create borders or boxes.

7. **Click cell A3**
   The border is a nice enhancement. Font color can also help distinguish information in a worksheet.

8. **Select the range A3:I3, click the Font Color list arrow on the Formatting toolbar, then click Blue (second row, third column from the right) on the palette**
   The text changes color, as shown in Figure C-16.

> **QuickTip**
> The default color on the Fill Color and Font Color buttons changes to the last color you selected.

9. **Click the Print Preview button on the Standard toolbar, preview the first page, click Next to preview the second page, click Close on the Print Preview toolbar, then click the Save button on the Standard toolbar**

FIGURE C-14: Background color added to cell

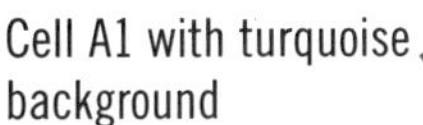

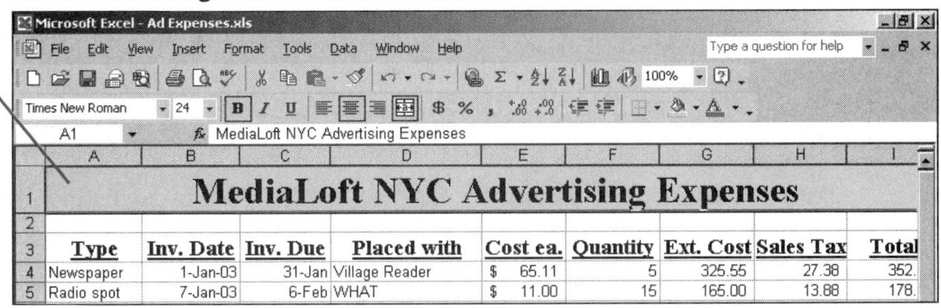

FIGURE C-15: Patterns tab in the Format Cells dialog box

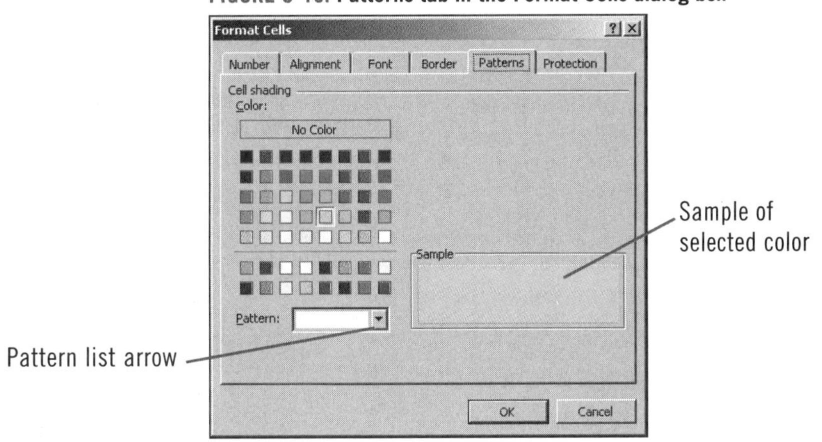

FIGURE C-16: Worksheet with colors, patterns, and border

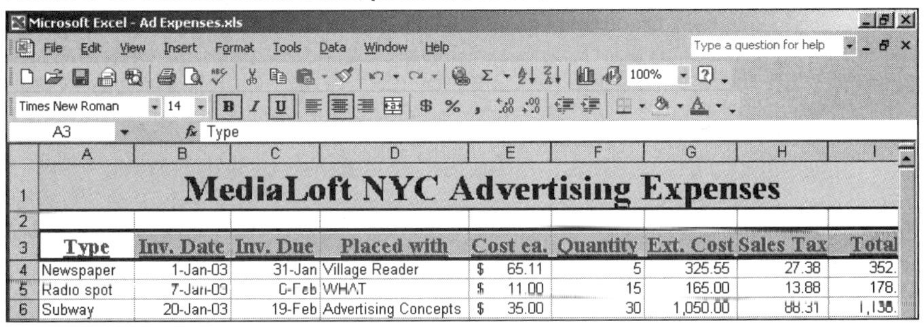

TABLE C-4: Border buttons

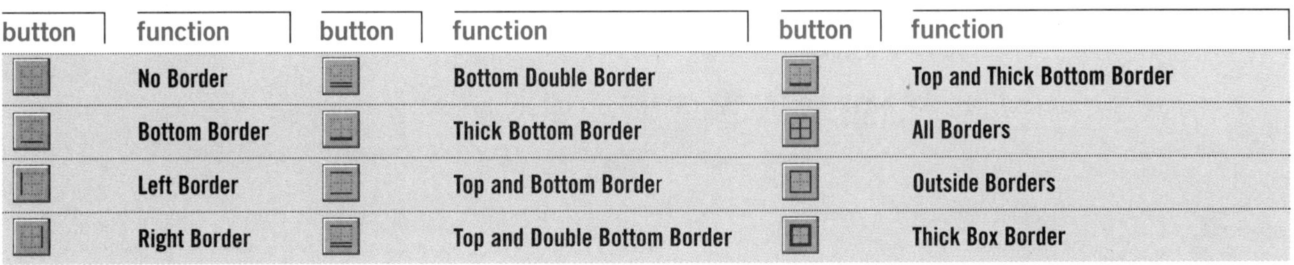

button	function	button	function	button	function
	No Border		**Bottom Double Border**		**Top and Thick Bottom Border**
	Bottom Border		**Thick Bottom Border**		**All Borders**
	Left Border		**Top and Bottom Border**		**Outside Borders**
	Right Border		**Top and Double Bottom Border**		**Thick Box Border**

Excel 2002

Using Conditional Formatting

Formatting makes worksheets look professional and helps distinguish different types of data. You can have Excel automatically apply formatting depending on specific outcomes in cells. You might, for example, want advertising costs above a certain number to appear in red boldface and lower values to appear in blue. Automatically applying formatting attributes based on cell values is called **conditional formatting**. If the data meets your criteria, Excel applies the formats you specify. Jim wants the worksheet to include conditional formatting so that total advertising costs greater than $175 appear in boldface red type. He asks you to create the conditional format in the first cell in the Total cost column.

1. **Click cell G4**
   Use the scroll bars if necessary, to make column G visible.

2. **Click Format on the menu bar, then click Conditional Formatting**
   The Conditional Formatting dialog box opens. Depending on the logical operator you've selected (such as "greater than" or "not equal to"), the Conditional Formatting dialog box displays different input boxes. You can define up to three different conditions that let you determine the outcome, and then assign formatting attributes to each one. You define the condition first. The default setting for the first condition is "Cell Value Is" "between."

3. **To change the current condition, click the Operator list arrow, then click greater than or equal to**
   Because you changed the operator from "between," which required text boxes for two values, only one value text box now appears. The first condition is that the cell value must be greater than or equal to some value. See Table C-5 for a list of options. The value can be a constant, formula, cell reference, or date. That value is set in the third box.

4. **Click the Value text box, then type 175**
   Now that you have assigned the value, you need to specify what formatting you want for cells that meet this condition.

5. **Click Format, click the Color list arrow, click Red (third row, first column), click Bold in the Font style list box, click OK, compare your settings to Figure C-17, then click OK to close the Conditional Formatting dialog box**
   The value in cell G4, 325.55, is formatted in bold red numbers because it is greater than 175, meeting the condition to apply the format. You can copy conditional formats the same way you would copy other formats.

6. **With cell G4 selected, click the Format Painter button on the Standard toolbar, then drag to select the range G5:G30**

7. **Click cell G4**
   Compare your results to Figure C-18. All cells with values greater than or equal to 175 in column G appear in bold red text.

8. **Press [Ctrl][Home] to move to cell A1**

9. **Click the Save button on the Standard toolbar**

Trouble?

If the Office Assistant appears, close it by clicking the No, don't provide help now button.

FIGURE C-17: **Completed Conditional Formatting dialog box**

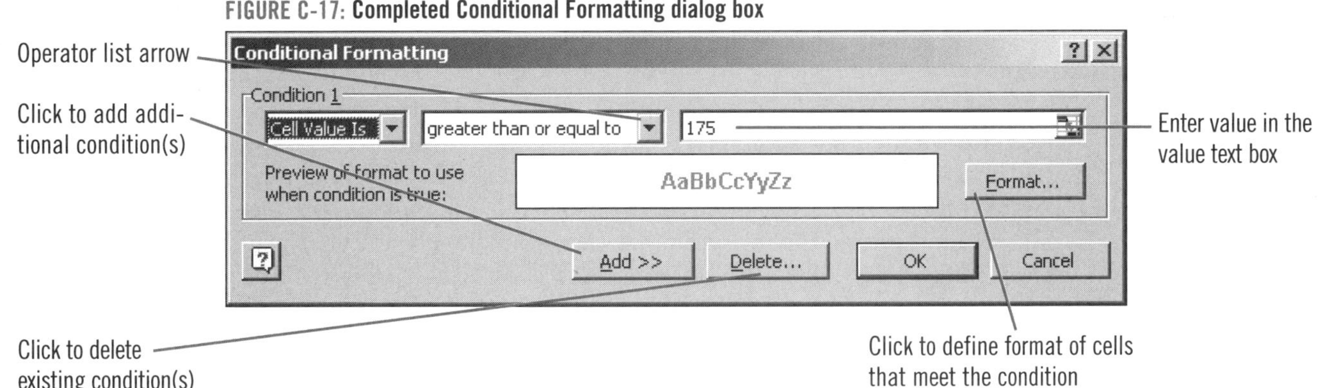

FIGURE C-18: **Worksheet with conditional formatting**

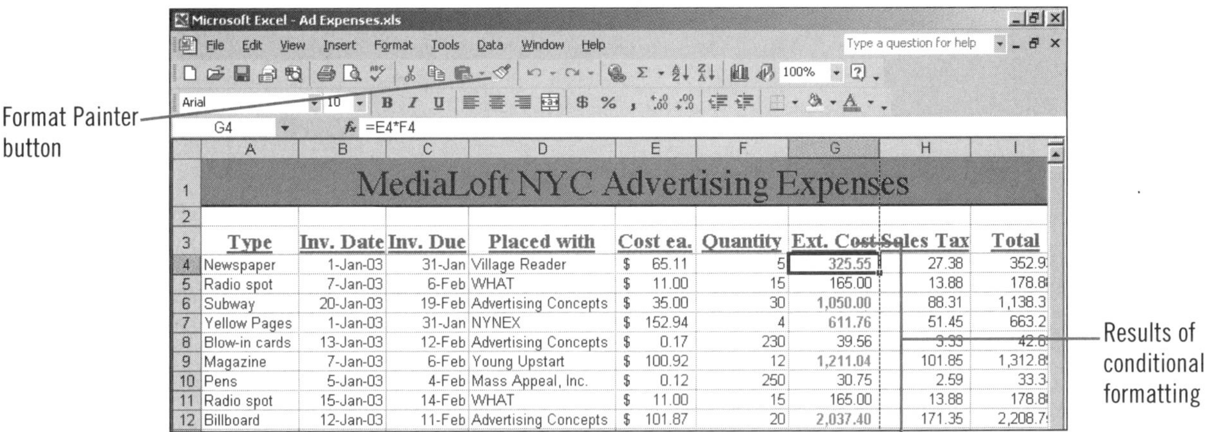

TABLE C-5: **Conditional formatting options**

option	mathematical equivalent	option	mathematical equivalent
Between	X>Y<Z	**Greater than**	Z>Y
Not between	B≯C≮A	**Less than**	Y<Z
Equal to	A=B	**Greater than or equal to**	A≧B
Not equal to	A≠B	**Less than or equal to**	Z≦Y

Deleting conditional formatting

Because it's likely that the conditions you define will change, you can delete any conditional format you define. Select the cell(s) containing conditional formatting, click Format on the menu bar, click Conditional Formatting, then click Delete. The Delete Conditional Format dialog box opens, as shown in Figure C-19. Select the check boxes for any of the conditions you want to delete, click OK, then click OK again. The previously assigned formatting is deleted—leaving the cell's contents intact.

FIGURE C-19: **Delete Conditional Format dialog box**

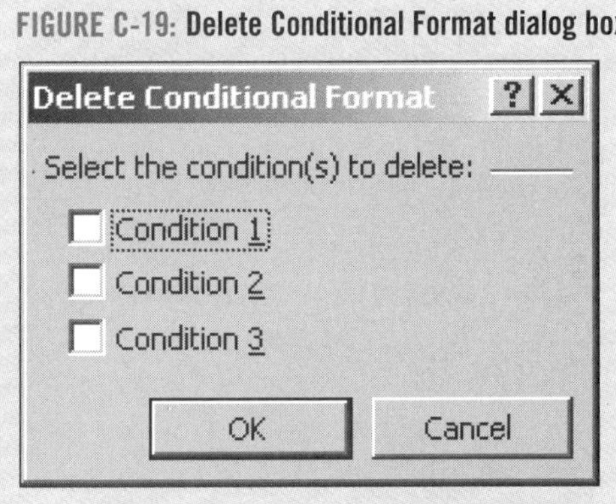

Checking Spelling

A single misspelled word can cast doubt on the validity and professional value of your entire workbook. Excel includes a spelling checker to help you ensure workbook accuracy. The spelling checker scans your worksheet, displays words it doesn't find in its built-in dictionary, and when possible suggests replacements. To check other sheets in a multiple-sheet workbook, you need to display each sheet and run the spelling checker again. Because the built-in dictionary cannot possibly include all the words that each of us needs, you can add words to the dictionary, such as your company name, an acronym, or an unusual technical term. The spelling checker will no longer consider that word misspelled. Any words you've added to the dictionary using Word, Access, or PowerPoint are also available in Excel. Because he will distribute this workbook to the marketing managers, Jim asks you to check its spelling.

Trouble?

If a language other than English is being used, the Spelling English dialog box will list the name of that language.

1. Click the **Spelling button** on the Standard toolbar
   The Spelling English (U.S.) dialog box opens, as shown in Figure C-21, with MediaLoft selected as the first misspelled word in the worksheet. For any word you have the option to Ignore or Ignore All cases the spell checker flags, or Add the word to the dictionary.
2. Click **Ignore All** for MediaLoft
   The spell checker found the word "cards" misspelled and offers "crabs" as an alternative.
3. Scroll through the Suggestions list, click **cards**, then click **Change**
   The word "Concepts" is also misspelled and the spell checker suggests the correct spelling.
4. Click **Change**
   When no more incorrect words are found, Excel displays a message indicating that all the words on that worksheet have been checked.
5. Click **OK**
6. Enter your name in cell **A34**, then press **[Ctrl][Home]**
7. Click the **Save button** on the Standard toolbar, then preview the worksheet
8. In the Preview window, click **Setup**, under Scaling click **Fit to option button** to print the worksheet on one page, click **OK**, click **Print**, then click **OK**
   Compare your printout to Figure C-22.
9. Click **File** on the menu bar, then click **Exit** to close the workbook without saving changes and exit Excel

QuickTip

You can set the Excel AutoCorrect feature to correct spelling as you type. Click Tools on the menu bar, then click AutoCorrect Options.

Using e-mail to send a workbook

You can use e-mail to send an entire workbook from within Excel. To send a workbook as an e-mail message attachment, open the workbook, click File, point to Send to, then click Mail Recipient (as Attachment). You supply the To and (optional) Cc information, as shown in Figure C-20, then click Send. You can also route a workbook to one or more recipients on a routing list. Click File, point to Send to, then click Routing Recipient. Click Create New Contact and enter contact information, then fill in the Routing slip. Depending on your e-mail program and Web browser, you may have to follow a different procedure.

FIGURE C-20: E-mailing an Excel workbook

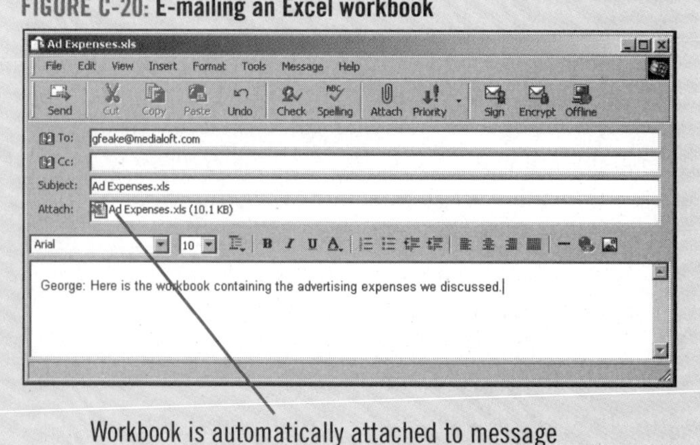

FIGURE C-21: **Spelling English dialog box**

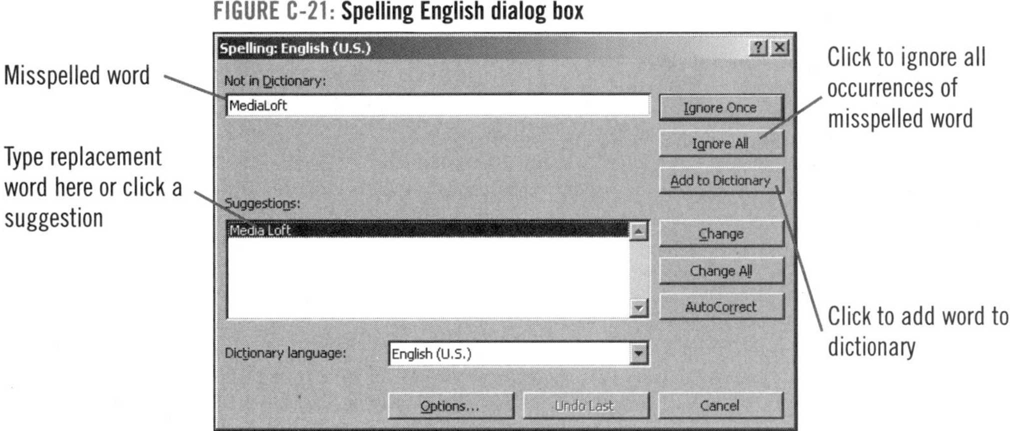

FIGURE C-22: **Completed worksheet**

MediaLoft NYC Advertising Expenses Sales Tax 0.0841

Type	Inv. Date	Inv. Due	Placed with	Cost ea.	Quantity	Ext. Cost	Sales Tax	Total
Newspaper	1-Jan-03	31-Jan	Village Reader	$ 65.11	5	325.55	27.38	352.93
Radio spot	7-Jan-03	6-Feb	WHAT	$ 11.00	15	165.00	13.88	178.88
Subway	20-Jan-03	19-Feb	Advertising Concepts	$ 35.00	30	1,050.00	88.31	1,138.31
Yellow Pages	1-Jan-03	31-Jan	NYNEX	$ 152.94	4	611.76	51.45	663.21
Blow-in cards	13-Jan-03	12-Feb	Advertising Concepts	$ 0.17	230	39.56	3.33	42.89
Magazine	7-Jan-03	6-Feb	Young Upstart	$ 100.92	12	1,211.04	101.85	1,312.89
Pens	5-Jan-03	4-Feb	Mass Appeal, Inc.	$ 0.12	250	30.75	2.59	33.34
Radio spot	15-Jan-03	14-Feb	WHAT	$ 11.00	15	165.00	13.88	178.88
Billboard	12-Jan-03	11-Feb	Advertising Concepts	$ 101.87	20	2,037.40	171.35	2,208.75
Newspaper	25-Jan-03	24-Feb	Village Reader	$ 65.11	6	390.66	32.85	423.51
Newspaper	1-Feb-03	3-Mar	University Voice	$ 23.91	2	47.82	4.02	51.84
T-Shirts	3-Feb-03	5-Mar	Mass Appeal, Inc.	$ 5.67	200	1,134.00	95.37	1,229.37
Yellow Pages	1-Feb-03	3-Mar	NYNEX	$ 152.94	4	611.76	51.45	663.21
Newspaper	1-Mar-03	31-Mar	University Voice	$ 23.91	2	47.82	4.02	51.84
Blow-in cards	28-Feb-03	30-Mar	Advertising Concepts	$ 0.17	275	47.30	3.98	51.28
Magazine	27-Feb-03	29-Mar	Young Upstart	$ 100.92	12	1,211.04	101.85	1,312.89
Subway	22-Feb-03	24-Mar	Advertising Concepts	$ 35.00	30	1,050.00	88.31	1,138.31
Radio spot	1-Feb-03	3-Mar	WHAT	$ 11.00	30	330.00	27.75	357.75
Newspaper	25-Feb-03	27-Mar	Village Reader	$ 65.11	6	390.66	32.85	423.51
Blow-in cards	10-Mar-03	9-Apr	Advertising Concepts	$ 0.17	275	47.30	3.98	51.28
Radio spot	15-Feb-03	17-Mar	WHAT	$ 11.00	25	275.00	23.13	298.13
Pens	15-Mar-03	14-Apr	Mass Appeal, Inc.	$ 0.12	250	30.75	2.59	33.34
Yellow Pages	1-Mar-03	31-Mar	NYNEX	$ 152.94	4	611.76	51.45	663.21
Subway	20-Mar-03	19-Apr	Advertising Concepts	$ 35.00	30	1,050.00	88.31	1,138.31
Newspaper	1-Apr-03	1-May	University Voice	$ 23.91	2	47.82	4.02	51.84
Subway	10-Apr-03	10-May	Advertising Concepts	$ 35.00	30	1,050.00	88.31	1,138.31
Billboard	28-Mar-03	27-Apr	Advertising Concepts	$ 101.87	20	2,037.40	171.35	2,208.75
name				$ 1,321.89	1784	16,047.15	1,349.57	17,396.72

Practice

Concepts Review

Label each element of the Excel worksheet window shown in Figure C-23.

FIGURE C-23

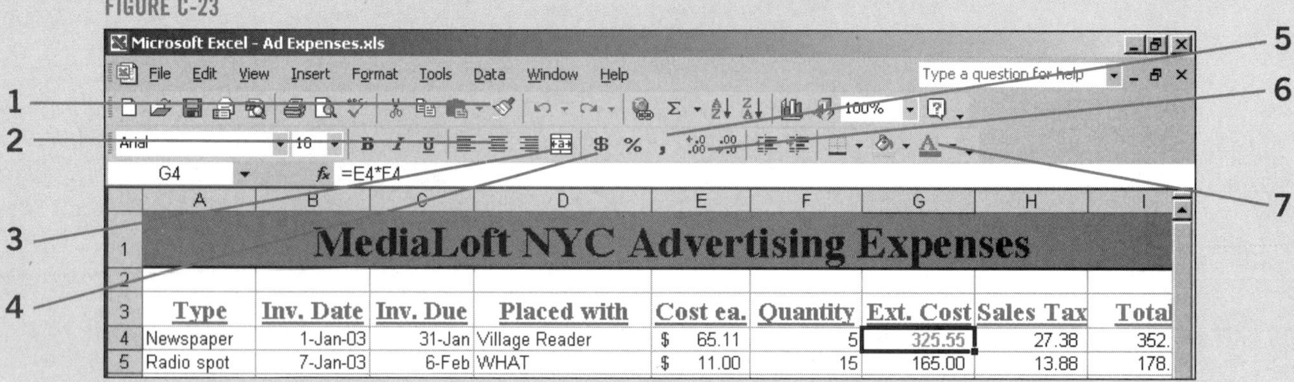

Match each command or button with the statement that describes it.

8. Cells command on the Format menu
9. Delete command on the Edit menu
10. Conditional Formatting
11.
12.
13.

a. Changes appearance of cell depending on result
b. Erases the contents of a cell
c. Used to check the spelling in a worksheet
d. Used to change the appearance of selected cells
e. Pastes the contents of the Clipboard into the current cell
f. Changes the format to Currency

Select the best answer from the list of choices.

14. Which button increases the number of decimal places in selected cells?
- **a.**
- **b.**
- **c.**
- **d.**

15. Each of the following operators can be used in conditional formatting, ***except*****:**
- **a.** Equal to.
- **b.** Greater than.
- **c.** Similar to.
- **d.** Not between.

16. How many conditional formats can be created in any cell?
- **a.** 1
- **b.** 2
- **c.** 3
- **d.** 4

17. Which button center-aligns the contents of a single cell?
- **a.**
- **b.**
- **c.**
- **d.**

18. **Which of the following is an example of the comma format?**
    a. $5,555.55
    b. 5555.55
    c. 55.55%
    d. 5,555.55
19. **What is the name of the feature used to resize a column to its widest entry?**
    a. AutoResize
    b. AutoFormat
    c. AutoFit
    d. AutoAdjust
20. **Which feature applies formatting attributes according to cell contents?**
    a. Conditional Formatting
    b. Comments
    c. AutoFormat
    d. Merge and Center

Skills Review

1. **Format values.**
    a. Start Excel and open a new workbook.
    b. Enter the information from Table C-6 in your worksheet. Begin in cell A1, and do not leave any blank rows or columns.

TABLE C-6

MediaLoft Great Britain
Quarterly Sales Projection

Department	Average Price	Quantity	Totals
Sports	25	2250	
Computers	40	3175	
History	35	1295	
Personal Growth	25	2065	

    c. Save this workbook as **MediaLoft GB Inventory** in the drive and folder where your Project Files are stored.
    d. Add the bold attribute to the data in the Department column.
    e. Use the Format Painter to paste the format from the data in the Department column to the Department and Totals labels.
    f. Add the italics attribute to the Average Price and Quantity labels.
    g. Apply the Comma format to the Price and Quantity data and reduce the number of decimals in the Quantity column to 0.
    h. Insert formulas in the Totals column (multiply the average price by the Quantity).
    i. Apply the Currency format to the Totals data.
    j. Save your work.
2. **Use fonts and font sizes.**
    a. Select the range of cells containing the column titles.
    b. Change the font of the column titles to Times New Roman.
    c. Increase the font size of the column titles and the title in cell A1 to 14-point.
    d. Resize the columns as necessary.
    e. Select the range of values in the Average Price column.
    f. Format the range using the Currency Style button.
    g. Save your changes.
3. **Change attributes and alignment.**
    a. Select the worksheet title **MediaLoft Great Britain**, then use the Bold button to boldface it.
    b. Use the Merge and Center button to center the title and the Quarterly Sales Projection labels over columns A through D.

c. Select the label **Quarterly Sales Projection**, then apply underlining to the label.
d. Select the range of cells containing the column titles, then center them.
e. Return the underlined, merged and centered Quarterly Sales Projection label to its original alignment.
f. Move the Quarterly Sales Projection label to cell D2 and change the alignment to Align Right.
g. Save your changes, then preview and print the workbook.

4. Adjust column widths.

a Use the Format menu to change the size of the Average Price column to **25**.
b. Use the AutoFit feature to resize the Average Price column.
c. Use the Format menu to resize the Department column to **18** and the Sold column to **11**.
d. Change the text in cell C3 to **Sold**, use AutoFit to resize the column, then change the column size to 11.
e. Save your changes.

5. Insert and delete rows and columns.

a. Insert a new row between rows 4 and 5.
b. Add MediaLoft Great Britain's newest department—**Children's Corner**—in the newly inserted row. Enter **35** for the average price and **1225** for the number sold.
c. Add the following comment to cell A5: **New department**.
d. Add a formula in cell D5 that multiplies the Average Price column by the Sold column.
e. Add a new column between the Department and Average Price columns with the title **Location**.
f. Delete the History row.
g. Edit the comment so it reads "New department. Needs promotion."
h. Save your changes.

6. Apply colors, patterns, and borders.

a. Add an outside border around the Average Price and Sold data.
b. Apply a light green background color to the labels in the Department column.
c. Apply a gold background to the column labels in cells **B3:E3**.
d. Change the color of the font in the column labels in cells B3:E3 to blue.
e. Add a 12.5% Gray pattern fill to the title in Row 1. (*Hint*: Use the Patterns tab in the Format Cells dialog box to locate the 12.5% Gray pattern.)
f. Enter your name in cell A20, then save your work.
g. Preview and print the worksheet, then close the workbook.

7. Use conditional formatting.

a. Open the Project File EX C-2 from the drive and folder where your Project Files are stored, then save it as **Monthly Operating Expenses**.
b. Create conditional formatting that changes the monthly data entry to blue if a value is **greater than 2500**, and changes it to red if **less than 700**.
c. Create a third conditional format that changes the monthly data to green if a value is **between 1000 and 2000**.
d. Use the Bold button and Center button to format the column headings and row titles.
e. Make Column A wide enough to accommodate the contents of cells **A4:A9**.
f. AutoFit the remaining columns.
g. Use Merge and Center in Row 1 to center the title over columns A–E.
h. Format the title in cell A1 using 14-point Times New Roman text. Fill the cell with a color and pattern of your choice.
i. Delete the third conditional format.
j. Enter your name in cell A20, then apply a green background to it and make the text color yellow.
k. Use the Edit menu to clear the cell formats from the cell with your name, then save your changes.

8. Check spelling.

a. Check the spelling in the worksheet using the spell checker, correcting any spelling errors.
b. Save your changes, then preview and print the workbook.
c. Close the workbook, then exit Excel.

► Independent Challenge 1

Beautiful You, a small beauty salon, has been using Excel for several months. Now that the salon's accounting records are in Excel, the manager would like you to work on the inventory. Although more items will be added later, the worksheet has enough items for you to begin your modifications.

- **a.** Start Excel, open the Project File EX C-3 from the drive and folder where your Project Files are stored, then save it as **BY Inventory**.
- **b.** Create a formula that calculates the value of the inventory on hand for each item.
- **c.** Use an absolute reference to calculate the sale price of each item, using the markup percentage shown.
- **d.** Add the bold attribute to the column headings.
- **e.** Make sure all columns are wide enough to display the data and headings.
- **f.** Add a row under #2 Curlers for **Nail Files**, price paid **$0.25**, sold **individually (each)**, with **59** on hand.
- **g.** Verify that all the formulas in the worksheet are correct. Adjust any items as needed, check the spelling, then save your work.
- **h.** Use conditional formatting to call attention to items with a quantity of 25 or fewer on hand. Use boldfaced red text.
- **i.** Add an outside border around the data in the Item column.
- **j.** Delete the row with #3 Curlers.
- **k.** Enter your name in an empty cell, then save the file.
- **l.** Preview and print the worksheet, close the workbook, then exit Excel.

► Independent Challenge 2

You volunteer several hours each week with the Community Action Center. You would like to examine the membership list, and decide to use formatting to make the existing data look more professional and easier to read.

- **a.** Start Excel, open the Project File EX C-4 from the drive and folder where your Project Files are stored, then save it as **Community Action**.
- **b.** Remove any blank columns.
- **c.** Format the Annual Revenue figures using the Currency format.
- **d.** Make all columns wide enough to fit their data and headings.
- **e.** Use formatting enhancements, such as fonts, font sizes, and text attributes to make the worksheet more attractive.
- **f.** Center-align the column labels.
- **g.** Use conditional formatting so that Number of Employees data greater than 50 employees appears in a contrasting color.
- **h.** Before printing, preview the file so you know what the worksheet will look like. Adjust any items as necessary, check spelling, enter your name in an empty cell, save your work, then print a copy.
- **i.** Close the workbook then exit Excel.

 Independent Challenge 3

Classic Instruments is a Miami-based company that manufactures high-quality pens and markers. As the finance manager, one of your responsibilities is to analyze the monthly reports from your five district sales offices. Your boss, Joanne Bennington, has just asked you to prepare a quarterly sales report for an upcoming meeting. Because several top executives will be attending this meeting, Joanne reminds you that the report must look professional. In particular, she asks you to emphasize the company's surge in profits during the last month and to highlight the fact that the Northeastern district continues to outpace the other districts.

a. Plan a worksheet that shows the company's sales during the first quarter. Assume that all pens are the same price. Make sure you include:
  - The number of pens sold (units sold) and the associated revenues (total sales) for each of the five district sales offices. The five sales districts include: Northeastern, Midwestern, Southeastern, Southern, and Western
  - Calculations that show month-by-month totals and a three-month cumulative total
  - Calculations that show each district's share of sales (percent of Total Sales)
  - Formatting enhancements to emphasize the recent month's sales surge and the Northeastern district's sales leadership

b. Ask yourself the following questions about the organization and formatting of the worksheet: How will you calculate the totals? What formulas can you copy to save time and keystrokes? Do any of these formulas need to use an absolute reference? How will you show dollar amounts? What information should be shown in bold? Do you need to use more than one font? Should you use more than one point size?

c. Start Excel, then build the worksheet with your own price and sales data. Enter the titles and labels first, then enter the numbers and formulas. You can use the form in Table C-7 to get started.

d. Save the workbook as **Classic Instruments** in the drive and folder where your Project Files are stored.

e. Adjust the column widths as necessary.

f. Change the height of row 1 to 30 points.

g. Format labels and values, and change the attributes and alignment.

h. Use the AutoFormat feature to add color and formatting to the data.

i. Resize columns and adjust the formatting as necessary.

j. Add a column that calculates a 22% increase in sales dollars. Use an absolute cell reference in this calculation.

k. Create a new column named Increased Sales that adds the projected increase to the Total Sales. (*Hint*: Make sure the current formatting is applied to the new information.)

l. Insert a ClipArt image in an appropriate location, adjusting its size and position as necessary.

m. Enter your name in an empty cell.

n. Check the spelling, then save your work.

o. Preview, then print the file in landscape orientation.

p. Close the file then exit Excel.

TABLE C-7

Classic Instruments

1st Quarter Sales Report

		January		February		March		Total	
Office	Price	Units Sold	Sales	Units Sold	Sales	Units Sold	Sales	Units Sold	Sales
Northeastern									
Midwestern									
Southeastern									
Southern									
Western									

Independent Challenge 4

After saving for many years, you now have enough funds to take that international trip you have always dreamed about. Your well-traveled friends have told you that you should always have the local equivalent of $100 U.S. dollars in cash with you when you enter a country. You decide to use the Web to determine how much money you will need in each country.

a. Start Excel, open a new workbook, then save it as **Currency Conversions** in the drive and folder where your Project Files are stored.

b. Enter column and row labels using the following table to get started.

Currency Equivalents			
$100 in US dollars			
Country	$1 Equivalent	$100 US	Name of Units
Australia			
Canada			
France			
Germany			
Sweden			
United Kingdom			

c. Go to the Alta Vista search engine at www.altavista.com and locate information on currency conversions. (*Hint*: One possible site where you can determine currency equivalents is www.oanda.com/. Use the Quick Converter.)

d. Find out how much cash is equivalent to **$1** in U.S. dollars for the following countries: **Australia**, **Canada**, **France**, **Germany**, **Sweden**, and the **United Kingdom**. Also enter the name of the currency used in each country.

e. Create an equation that calculates the equivalent of **$100** in U.S. dollars for each country in the list, using an absolute value in the formula.

f. Format the entries in columns B and C using the correct currency unit for each country, with two decimal places. (*Hint*: Use the Numbers tab in the Format cells dialog box; choose the appropriate currency format from the Symbol list, using 2 decimal places. For example, use the **F (French) Standard** format for the France row, and so forth.)

g. Create a conditional format that changes the font attributes of the calculated amount in the "$100 US" column to bold and red if the amount is equals or exceeds **500 units** of the local currency.

h. Merge and center the title over the column headings.

i. Add a background color to the title.

j. Apply the AutoFormat of your choice to the conversion table.

k. Enter your name in an empty worksheet cell.

l. Spell check, save, preview, then print the worksheet.

m. If you have access to an e-mail account, e-mail your workbook to your instructor as an attachment.

n. Close the workbook and exit Excel.

Visual Workshop

Create the worksheet shown in Figure C-24, using skills you learned in this unit. Open the Project File EX C-5 from the drive and folder where your Project Files are stored, then save it as **Projected March Advertising Invoices**. Create a conditional format in the Cost ea. column so that entries greater than 60 appear in red. (*Hint*: The only additional font used in this exercise is Times New Roman. It is 22 points in row 1, and 16 points in row 3.) Spell check the worksheet, then save and print your work.

FIGURE C-24

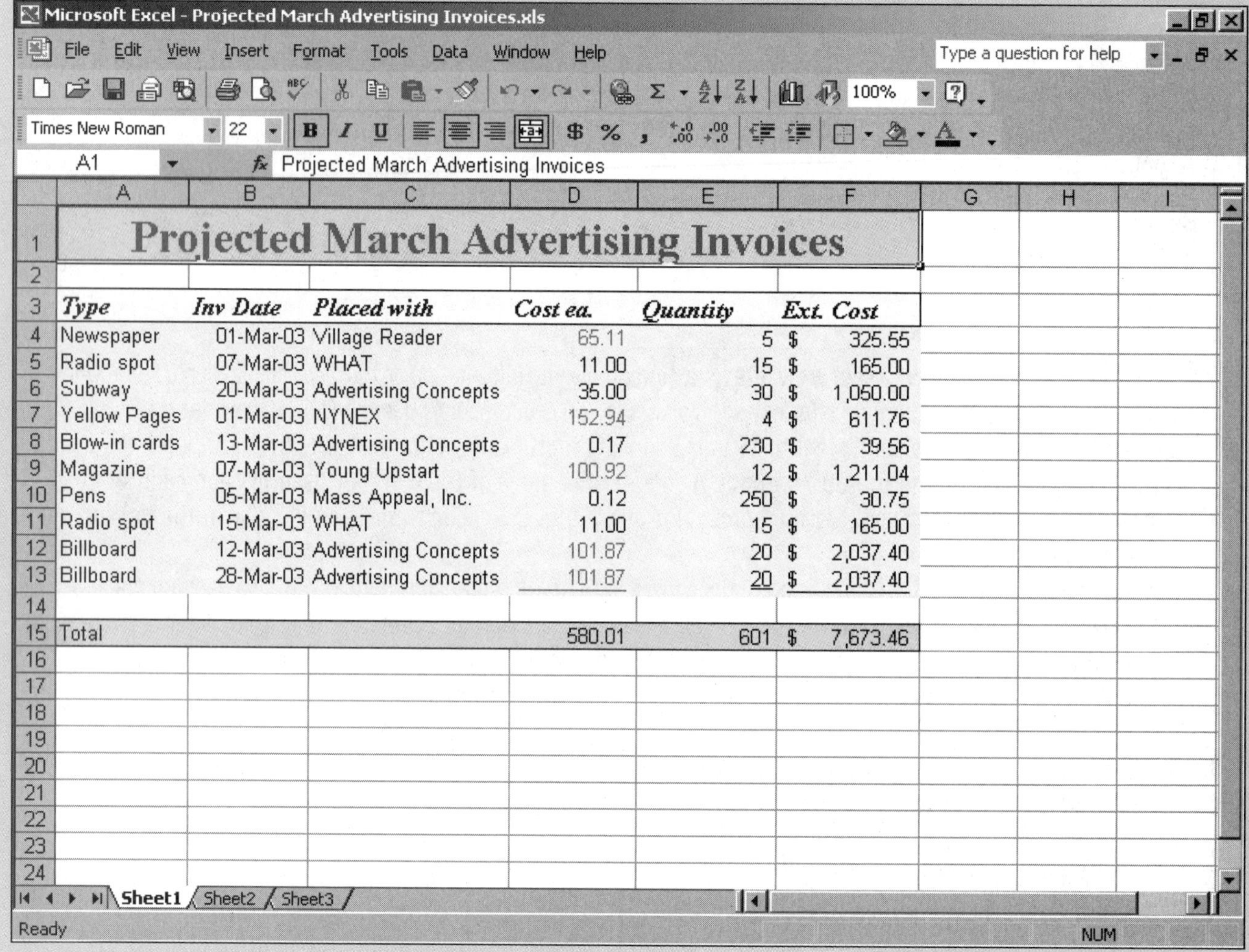

Microsoft Excel - Projected March Advertising Invoices.xls

A1 | Projected March Advertising Invoices

	A	B	C	D	E	F
1	**Projected March Advertising Invoices**					
2						
3	***Type***	***Inv Date***	***Placed with***	***Cost ea.***	***Quantity***	***Ext. Cost***
4	Newspaper	01-Mar-03	Village Reader	65.11	5	$ 325.55
5	Radio spot	07-Mar-03	WHAT	11.00	15	$ 165.00
6	Subway	20-Mar-03	Advertising Concepts	35.00	30	$ 1,050.00
7	Yellow Pages	01-Mar-03	NYNEX	152.94	4	$ 611.76
8	Blow-in cards	13-Mar-03	Advertising Concepts	0.17	230	$ 39.56
9	Magazine	07-Mar-03	Young Upstart	100.92	12	$ 1,211.04
10	Pens	05-Mar-03	Mass Appeal, Inc.	0.12	250	$ 30.75
11	Radio spot	15-Mar-03	WHAT	11.00	15	$ 165.00
12	Billboard	12-Mar-03	Advertising Concepts	101.87	20	$ 2,037.40
13	Billboard	28-Mar-03	Advertising Concepts	101.87	20	$ 2,037.40
14						
15	Total			580.01	601	$ 7,673.46

Sheet1 / Sheet2 / Sheet3

Ready NUM

Excel 2002

Working with Charts

Objectives

- Plan and design a chart
- MOUS Create a chart
- MOUS Move and resize a chart
- MOUS Edit a chart
- MOUS Format a chart
- MOUS Enhance a chart
- MOUS Annotate and draw on a chart
- MOUS Preview and print a chart

Worksheets provide an effective way to organize information, but they are not always the best format for presenting data to others. Information in a selected range or worksheet can easily be displayed as a chart. Charts, often called graphs, allow you to communicate the relationships in your worksheet data in readily understandable pictures. In this unit, you will learn how to create a chart, how to edit a chart and change the chart type, how to add text annotations and arrows to a chart, and how to preview and print a chart. For the annual meeting Jim Fernandez needs you to create a chart showing the six-month sales history for the MediaLoft stores in the eastern division. He wants to illustrate the growth trend in this division.

Excel 2002

Planning and Designing a Chart

Before creating a chart, you need to plan the information you want your chart to show and how you want it to look. In early June, the Marketing Department launched a regional advertising campaign for the eastern division. The results of the campaign were increased sales during the fall months. Jim wants his chart for the annual meeting to illustrate the growth trend for sales in MediaLoft's eastern division stores and to highlight this sales increase.

Jim wants you to use the worksheet shown in Figure D-1 and the following guidelines to plan the chart:

- **Determine the purpose of the chart and identify the data relationships you want to communicate graphically**
  You want to create a chart that shows sales throughout MediaLoft's eastern division from July through December. In particular, you want to highlight the increase in sales that occurred as a result of the advertising campaign.

- **Determine the results you want to see, and decide which chart type is most appropriate to use**
  Different charts display data in distinctive ways. Some chart types are more appropriate for particular types of data and analyses. How you want your data displayed—and how you want that data interpreted—can help you determine the best chart type to use. Table D-1 describes several different types of charts and indicates when each one is best used. Because you want to compare data (sales in multiple locations) over a time period (the months July through December), you decide to use a column chart.

- **Identify the worksheet data you want the chart to illustrate**
  You are using data from the worksheet titled "MediaLoft Eastern Division Stores" shown in Figure D-1. This worksheet contains the sales data for the four stores in the eastern division from July through December.

- **Sketch the chart, then use your sketch to decide where the chart elements should be placed**
  You sketch your chart as shown in Figure D-2. You put the months on the horizontal axis (the **x-axis**) and the monthly sales figures on the vertical axis (the **y-axis**). The x-axis is often called the **category axis** because it often contains the names of data groups, such as months or years. The y-axis is called the **value axis** because it often contains numerical values that help you interpret the size of chart elements. (In a 3-D chart, the y-axis is referred to as the z-axis.) The area inside the horizontal and vertical axes is called the **plot area**. The **tick marks** on the y-axis create a scale of measure for each value. Each value in a cell you select for your chart is a **data point**. In any chart, a **data marker** visually represents each data point, which in this case is a column. A collection of related data points is a **data series**. In this chart, there are four data series (Boston, Chicago, Kansas City, and New York), so you include a **legend** to make it easy to identify them.

FIGURE D-1: Worksheet containing sales data

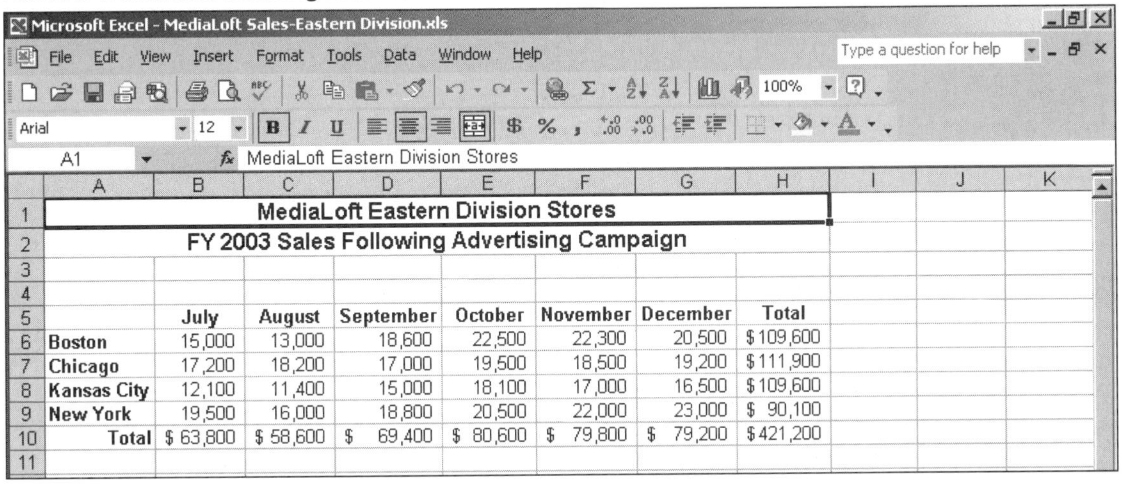

Microsoft Excel - MediaLoft Sales-Eastern Division.xls
File Edit View Insert Format Tools Data Window Help
Type a question for help
Arial
12
100%
A1
MediaLoft Eastern Division Stores
MediaLoft Eastern Division Stores
FY 2003 Sales Following Advertising Campaign
July August September October November December Total
Boston 15,000 13,000 18,600 22,500 22,300 20,500 $109,600
Chicago 17,200 18,200 17,000 19,500 18,500 19,200 $111,900
Kansas City 12,100 11,400 15,000 18,100 17,000 16,500 $109,600
New York 19,500 16,000 18,800 20,500 22,000 23,000 $ 90,100
Total $ 63,800 $ 58,600 $ 69,400 $ 80,600 $ 79,800 $ 79,200 $421,200

FIGURE D-2: Column chart sketch

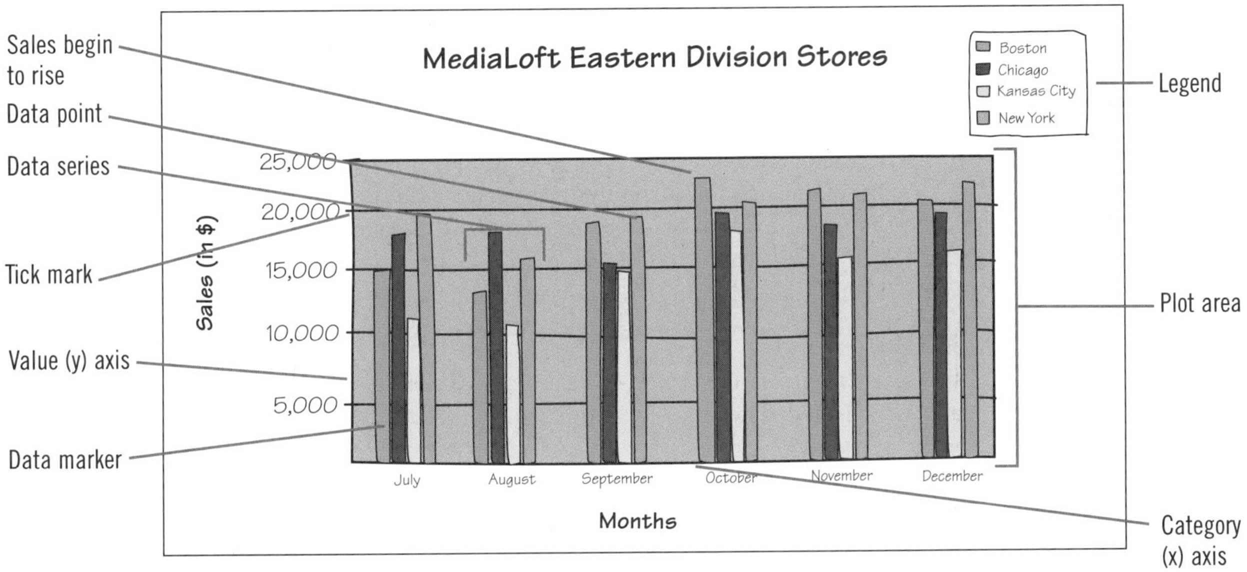

Sales begin to rise
Data point
Data series
Tick mark
Value (y) axis
Data marker
MediaLoft Eastern Division Stores
Boston
Chicago
Kansas City
New York
Legend
Sales (in $)
25,000
20,000
15,000
10,000
5,000
July
August
September
October
November
December
Months
Plot area
Category (x) axis

TABLE D-1: Commonly used chart types

type	button	description
Area		Shows how individual volume changes over time in relation to total volume
Bar		Compares distinct object levels over time using a horizontal format; sometimes referred to as a horizontal bar chart in other spreadsheet programs
Column		Compares distinct object levels over time using a vertical format; the Excel default; sometimes referred to as a bar chart in other spreadsheet programs
Line		Compares trends over even time intervals; appears similar to an area chart, but does not emphasize total
Pie		Compares sizes of pieces as part of a whole; used for a single series of numbers
XY (scatter)		Compares trends over uneven time or measurement intervals; used in scientific and engineering disciplines for trend spotting and extrapolation
Combination	none	Combines a column and line chart to compare data requiring different scales of measure

Excel 2002

Creating a Chart

To create a chart in Excel, you first select the range containing the data you want to chart. Once you've selected a range, you can use the Excel Chart Wizard to lead you through the process of creating the chart. Using the worksheet containing the sales data for the eastern division, Jim asks you to create a chart that shows the growth trend that occurred as a result of the advertising campaign.

Steps

QuickTip

When charting any data for a given time period, make sure all series are for the same time period, so you don't misrepresent your data.

Trouble?

You can create a chart from non-contiguous cells by pressing the Option key and selecting each range.

1. **Start Excel, open the Project File EX D-1 from the drive and location where your Project Files are stored, then save it as MediaLoft Sales - Eastern Division**
   You want the chart to include the monthly sales figures for each of the eastern division stores, as well as month and store labels. You don't include the Total column and row because the monthly figures make up the totals, and these figures would skew the chart.
2. **Select the range A5:G9, then click the Chart Wizard button on the Standard toolbar**
   The selected range contains the data you want to chart. The Chart Wizard opens. The Chart Wizard - Step 1 of 4 - Chart Type dialog box lets you choose the type of chart you want to create. The default chart type is a Clustered Column, as shown in Figure D-3. You can see a preview of the chart using your selected data by clicking, then holding the **Press and Hold to View Sample** button.
3. **Click Next to accept Clustered Column, the default chart type**
   The Chart Wizard - Step 2 of 4 - Chart Source Data dialog box lets you choose the data to chart and whether the series appear in rows or columns. You want to chart the effect of sales for each store over the time period. Currently, the rows are accurately selected as the data series, as specified by the Series in option button located under the Data range. Because you selected the data before clicking the Chart Wizard button, Excel converted the range to absolute values and the correct range, =Sheet1!$A$5:$G$9, appears in the Data range text box.
4. **Click Next**
   The Chart Wizard - Step 3 of 4 - Chart Options dialog box shows a sample chart using the data you selected. The store locations (the rows in the selected range) are plotted against the months (the columns in the selected range), and Excel added the months as labels for each data series. A legend shows each location and its corresponding color on the chart. The Titles tab lets you add titles to the chart and its axes. Other tabs let you modify the axes, legend, and other chart elements.
5. **Click the Chart title text box, then type MediaLoft Sales - Eastern Division**
   After a moment, the title appears in the Sample Chart box. See Figure D-4.
6. **Click Next**
   In the Chart Wizard - Step 4 of 4 - Chart Location dialog box, you determine the placement of the chart in the workbook. You can display a chart as an object on the current sheet, on any other existing sheet, or on a newly created chart sheet. A **chart sheet** in a workbook contains only a chart, which is linked to the worksheet data. The default selection—displaying the chart as an object in the sheet containing the data—will help Jim emphasize his point at the annual meeting.

QuickTip

If you want to delete a chart, select it, then press [Delete].

7. **Click Finish**
   The column chart appears and the Chart toolbar opens, either docked or floating, as shown in Figure D-5. Your chart might be in a different location and look slightly different. You will adjust the chart's location and size in the next lesson. The **selection handles**, the small squares at the corners and sides of the chart's border, indicate that the chart is selected. Anytime a chart is selected, as it is now, a blue border surrounds the worksheet data range, a green border surrounds the row labels, and a purple border surrounds the column labels.
8. **Click the Save button on the Standard toolbar**

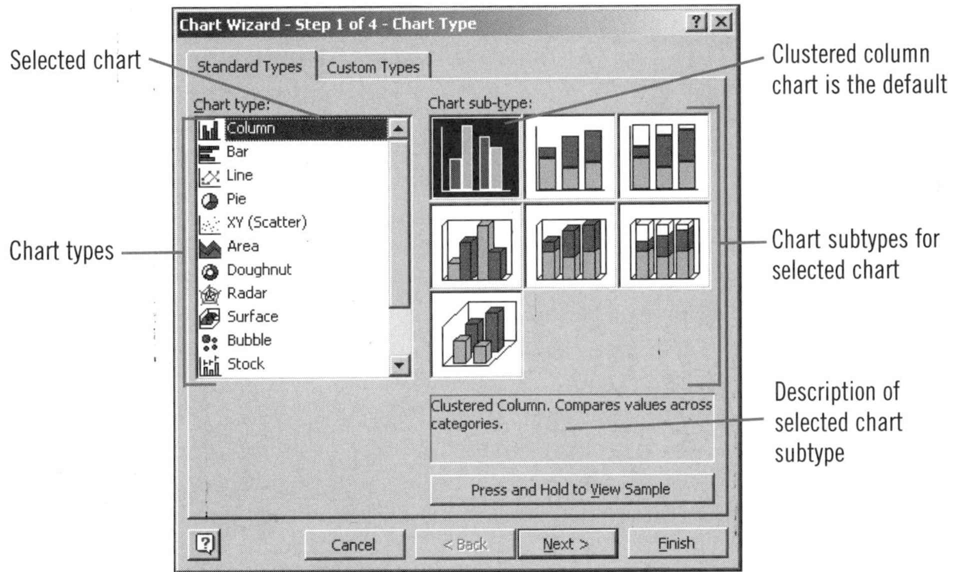

FIGURE D-3: First Chart Wizard dialog box

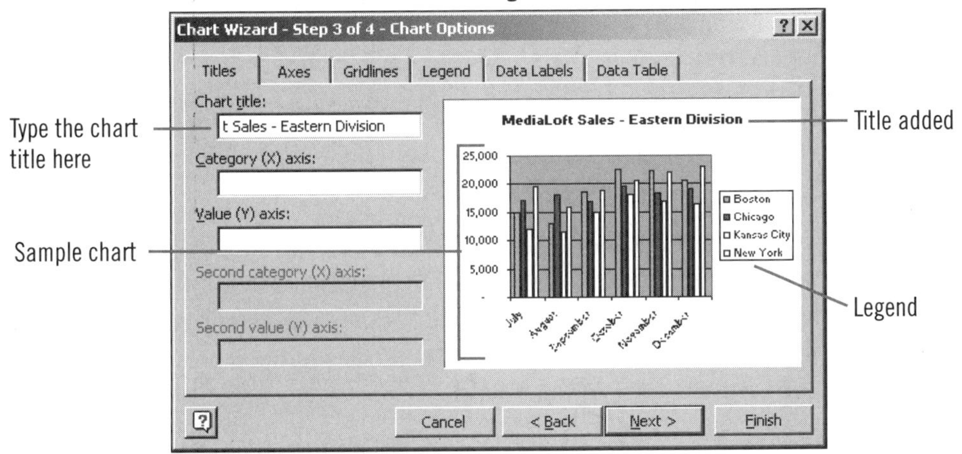

FIGURE D-4: Third Chart Wizard dialog box

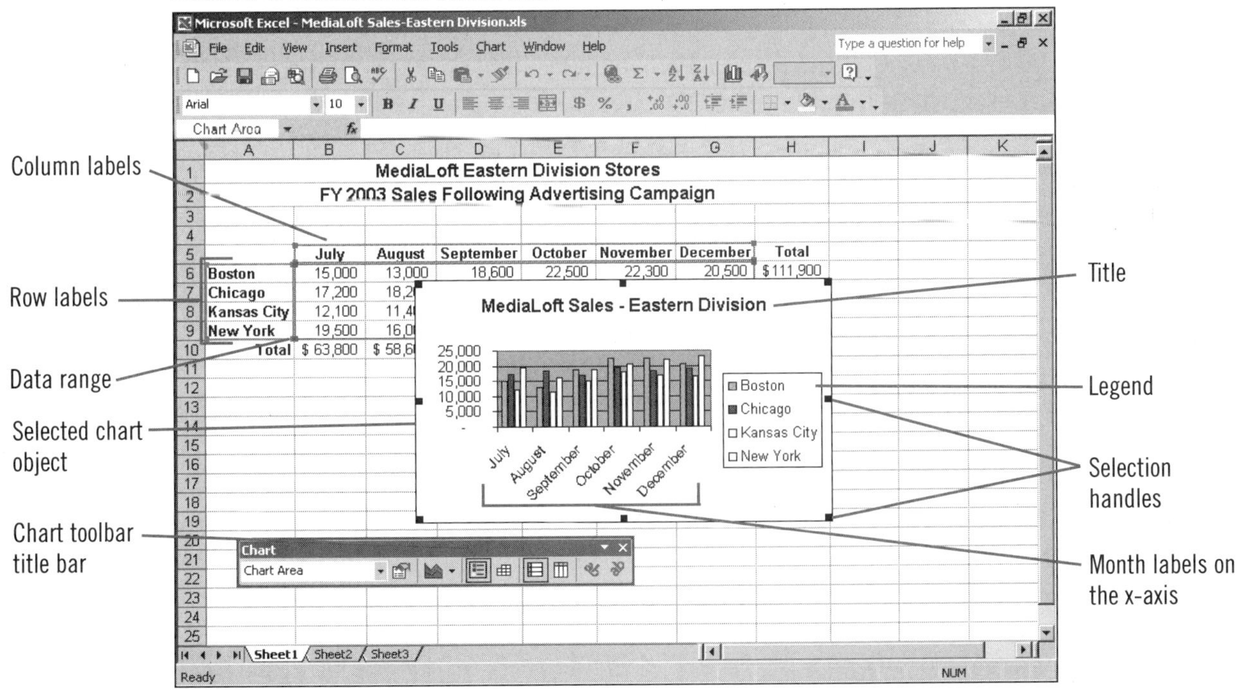

FIGURE D-5: Worksheet with column chart

Excel 2002

Moving and Resizing a Chart

Charts are graphics, or drawn objects, and are not located in a specific cell or at a specific range address. An **object** is an independent element on a worksheet. You can select an object by clicking within its borders to surround it with selection handles. You can move a selected chart object anywhere on a worksheet without affecting formulas or data in the worksheet. However, any data changed in the worksheet will automatically be updated in the chart. You can resize a chart to improve its appearance by dragging its selection handles. You can even put a chart on another sheet, and it will still reflect the original data. Chart objects contain other objects, such as a title and legend, which you can move and resize. To move an object, select it, then drag it or cut and copy it to a new location. When you select a chart object, the name of the selected object appears in the Chart Objects list box on the Chart toolbar and in the name box. Jim wants you to increase the size of the chart, position it below the worksheet data, then change the position of the legend.

Steps

QuickTip

The Chart menu only appears on the menu bar when a chart or one of its objects is selected.

1. **Make sure the chart is still selected, then position the pointer over the chart**
   The pointer shape indicates that you can move the chart or use a selection handle to resize it. For a table of commonly used chart pointers, refer to Table D-2. On occasion, the Chart toolbar obscures your view. You can dock the toolbar to make it easier to see your work.

2. **If the chart toolbar is floating, click the Chart toolbar's title bar, drag it to the right edge of the status bar until it docks, then release the mouse button**
   The toolbar is docked on the bottom of the screen.

QuickTip

Resizing a chart doesn't affect the data in the chart, only the way the chart looks on the sheet.

3. **Place on a blank area near the edge of the chart, press and hold the left mouse button, using , drag it until the upper-left edge of the chart is at the top of row 13 and the left edge of the chart is at the left border of column A, then release the mouse button**
   As you drag the chart, you can see a dotted outline representing the chart's perimeter. The chart appears in the new location.

4. **Position the pointer on the right-middle selection handle until it changes to ↔, then drag the right edge of the chart to the right edge of column H**
   The chart is widened. See Figure D-6.

5. **Position the pointer over the top-middle selection handle until it changes to ↕, then drag it to the top of row 12**

6. **If the labels for the months do not fully appear, position the pointer over the bottom middle selection handle until it changes to ↕, then drag down to display the months**
   You can move the legend to improve the chart's appearance. You want to align the top of the legend with the top of the plot area.

7. **Click the legend to select it, then drag the legend upward using so the top of the legend aligns with the top of the plot area**
   Selection handles appear around the legend when you click it; "Legend" appears in the Chart Objects list box on the Chart toolbar as well as in the name box, and a dotted outline of the legend perimeter appears as you drag. Changing any label will modify the legend text.

QuickTip

Because the chart is no longer selected, the chart toolbar no longer appears.

8. **Click cell A9, type NYC, then click**
   See Figure D-7. The legend changes to the text you entered.

9. **Click the Save button on the Standard toolbar**

FIGURE D-6: Worksheet with resized and repositioned chart

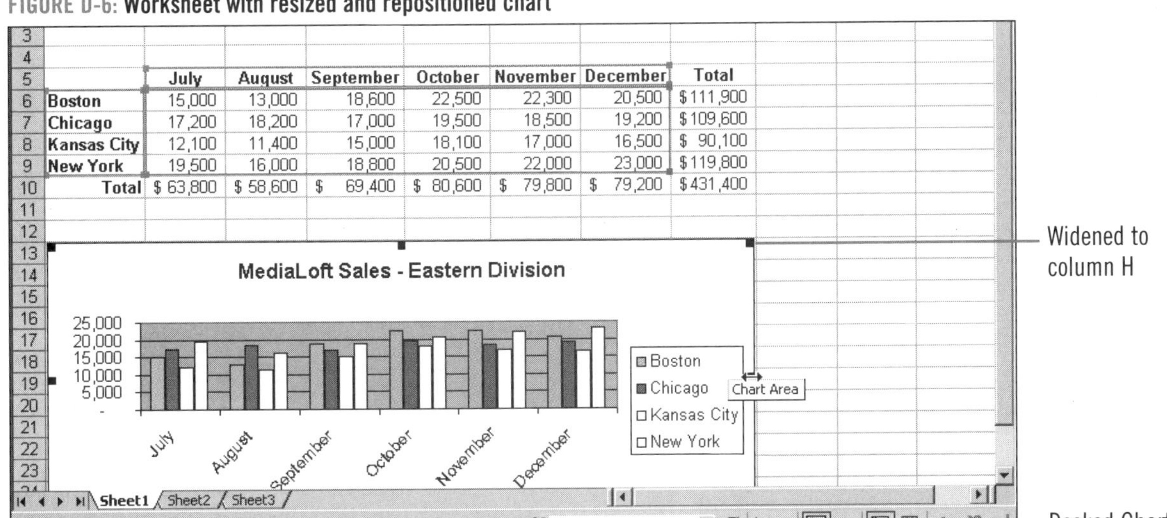

FIGURE D-7: Worksheet with repositioned legend

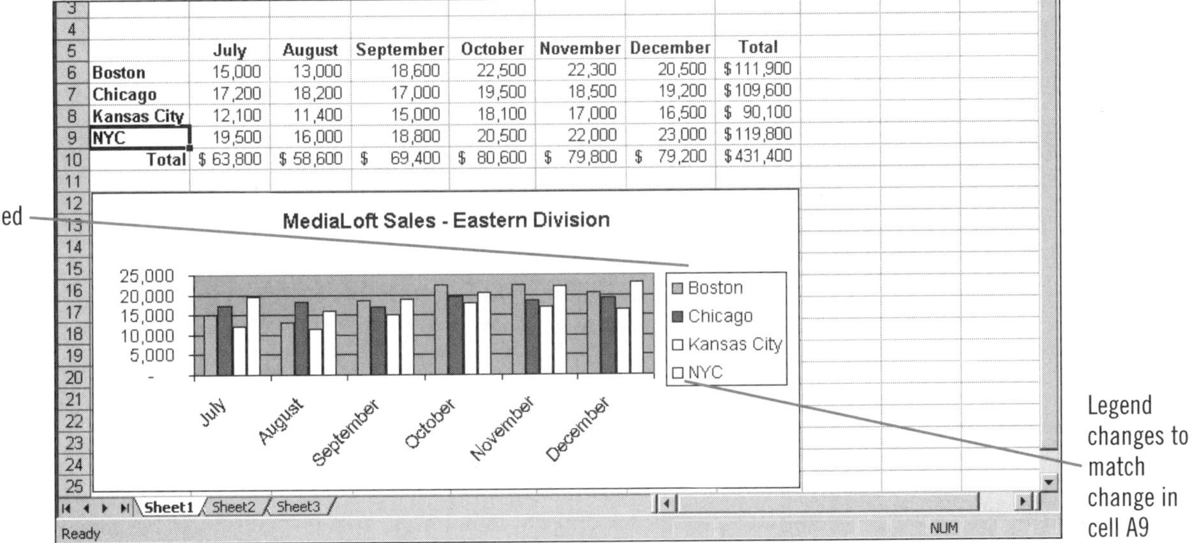

TABLE D-2: Commonly used pointers

name	pointer	use	name	pointer	use
Diagonal resizing	⤢ or ⤡	Change chart shape	**I-beam**	I	Edit chart text from corners
Draw	+	Create shapes	**Move chart**	✥	Change chart location
Horizontal resizing	↔	Change chart shape from left to right	**Vertical resizing**	↕	Changes chart shape from top to bottom

Identifying chart objects

There are many objects within a chart, such as bars and axes; Excel makes it easy to identify each of them. Placing the mouse pointer over a chart object displays a ScreenTip identifying it, whether the chart is selected or not. If a chart—or any object in it—is selected, the ScreenTips still appear. In addition, the name of the selected chart object appears in the Chart Object list box on the Chart toolbar and in the name box .

Excel 2002

Editing a Chart

Once you've created a chart, it's easy to modify it. You can change data values in the worksheet, and the chart will automatically be updated to reflect the new data. You can also easily change the type of chart displayed by using the buttons on the Chart toolbar. Jim looks over his worksheet and realizes that he entered the wrong data for the Kansas City store in November and December. After you correct this data, he wants to see how the same data looks using different chart types.

Steps

Trouble?

If you cannot see the chart and data together on your monitor, click View on the menu bar, click Zoom, then click 75%.

1. If necessary, scroll the worksheet so that you can see both the chart and row 8, containing the Kansas City sales figures, then place your mouse pointer over the December data point to display **Series "Kansas City" Point "December" Value: 16,500**
2. Click cell **F8**, type **19000** to correct the November sales figure, press [→], type **20500** in cell **G8**, then click
   The Kansas City columns for November and December reflect the increased sales figures. See Figure D-8. The totals in column H and row 10 are also updated.
3. Select the chart by clicking on a blank area within the chart border, then click the **Chart Type list arrow** on the Chart toolbar
   The chart type buttons appear on the Chart Type palette. Table D-3 describes the principal chart types available.
4. Click the **Bar Chart button** on the palette
   The column chart changes to a bar chart. See Figure D-9. You look at the bar chart, take some notes, then decide to convert it back to a column chart. You now want to see if the large increase in sales would be better presented with a three-dimensional column chart.
5. Click the **Chart Type list arrow**, then click the **3-D Column Chart button** on the palette
   A three-dimensional column chart appears. You notice that the three-dimensional column format is more crowded than the two-dimensional format but gives you a sense of volume.
6. Click the **Chart Type list arrow**, then click the **Column Chart button** on the palette
7. Click the **Save button** on the Standard toolbar

QuickTip

As you work with charts, experiment with different formats for your charts until you get just the right look.

QuickTip

The chart type button displays the last chart type selected.

TABLE D-3: Commonly used chart type buttons

click to display a	click to display a	click to display a	click to display a
area chart	pie chart	3-D area chart	3-D pie chart
bar chart	(XY) scatter chart	3-D bar chart	3-D surface chart
column chart	doughnut chart	3-D column chart	3-D cylinder chart
line chart	radar chart	3-D line chart	3-D cone chart

FIGURE D-8: Worksheet with new data entered for Kansas City

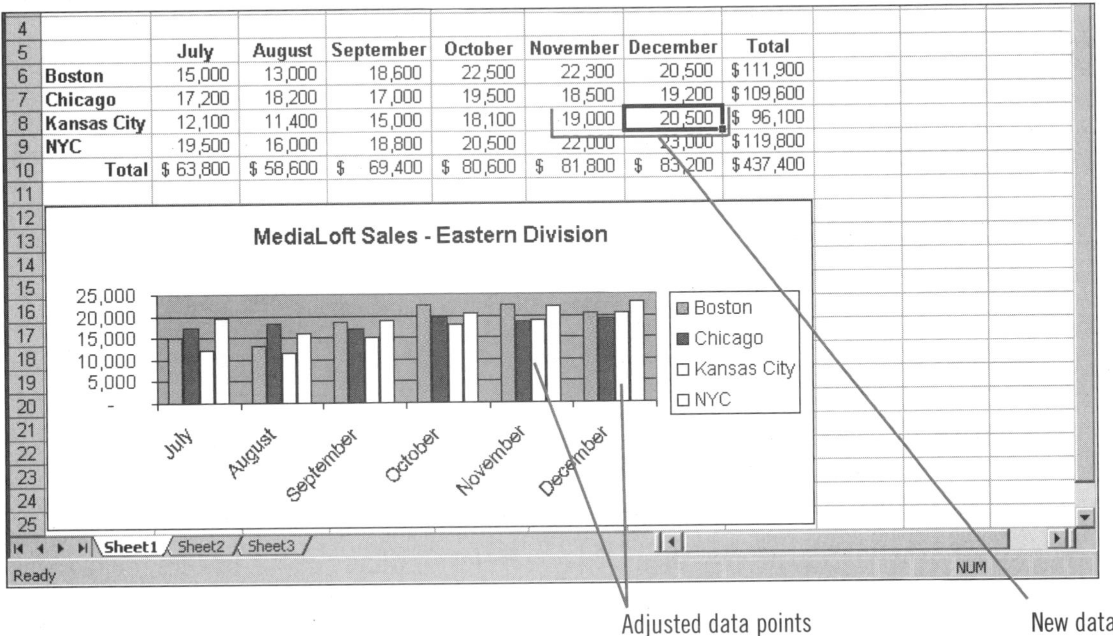

	July	August	September	October	November	December	Total
Boston	15,000	13,000	18,600	22,500	22,300	20,500	$111,900
Chicago	17,200	18,200	17,000	19,500	18,500	19,200	$109,600
Kansas City	12,100	11,400	15,000	18,100	19,000	20,500	$ 96,100
NYC	19,500	16,000	18,800	20,500	22,000	23,000	$119,800
Total	$ 63,800	$ 58,600	$ 69,400	$ 80,600	$ 81,800	$ 83,200	$437,400

FIGURE D-9: Bar chart

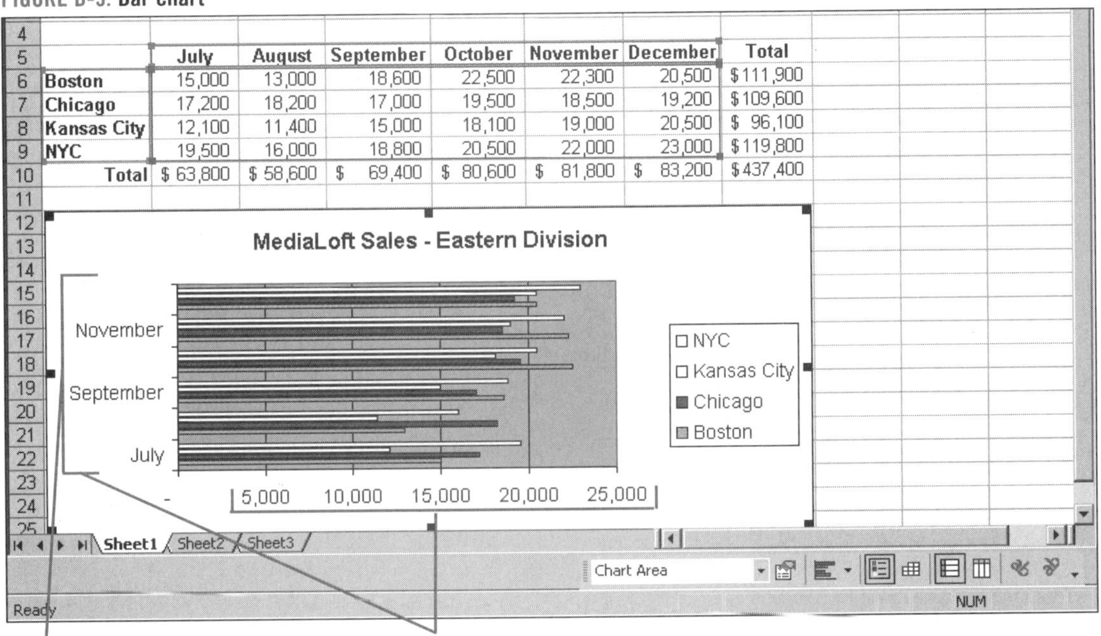

	July	August	September	October	November	December	Total
Boston	15,000	13,000	18,600	22,500	22,300	20,500	$111,900
Chicago	17,200	18,200	17,000	19,500	18,500	19,200	$109,600
Kansas City	12,100	11,400	15,000	18,100	19,000	20,500	$ 96,100
NYC	19,500	16,000	18,800	20,500	22,000	23,000	$119,800
Total	$ 63,800	$ 58,600	$ 69,400	$ 80,600	$ 81,800	$ 83,200	$437,400

Rotating a 3-D chart

In a three-dimensional chart, other data series in the same chart can sometimes obscure columns or bars. You can rotate the chart to obtain a better view. Click the chart, click the tip of one of its axes (select the Corners object), then drag the handles until a more pleasing view of the data series appears. See Figure D-10.

FIGURE D-10: 3-D chart rotated with improved view of data series

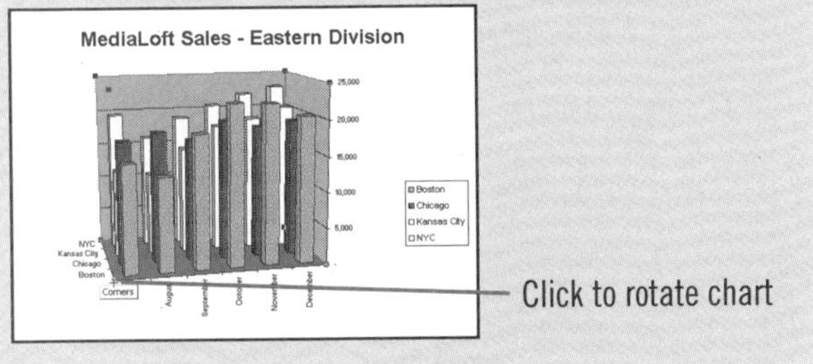

Excel 2002

Formatting a Chart

After you've created a chart using the Chart Wizard, you can easily modify its appearance. You can use the Chart toolbar and Chart menu to change the colors of data series and to add or eliminate a legend and gridlines. **Gridlines** are the horizontal and vertical lines in the chart that enable the eye to follow the value on an axis. The Chart toolbar buttons are listed in Table D-4. Jim wants you to make some changes in the appearance of his chart. He wants to see if the chart looks better without gridlines, and he wants to change the color of a data series.

Steps

1. Make sure the chart is still selected
   Horizontal gridlines currently extend from the y-axis tick marks across the chart's plot area.
2. Click **Chart** on the menu bar, click **Chart Options,** click the **Gridlines tab** in the Chart Options dialog box, then click the **Major Gridlines check box** for the Value (Y) axis to remove the check
   The gridlines disappear from the sample chart in the dialog box, as shown in Figure D-11.
3. Click the **Major Gridlines check box** for the Value (Y) axis to reselect it, then click the **Minor Gridlines check box** for the Value (Y) axis
   Both major and minor gridlines appear in the sample. **Minor gridlines** show the values between the tick marks.
4. Click the **Minor Gridlines check box** for the Value (Y) axis, then click **OK**
   The minor gridlines disappear, leaving only the major gridlines on the Value axis. You can change the color of the columns to better distinguish the data series.
5. With the chart selected, double-click any **light blue column** in the NYC data series
   Handles appear on all the columns in the NYC data series, and the Format Data Series dialog box opens, as shown in Figure D-12.
6. Click the **fuchsia box** (fourth row, first column) in the Patterns tab, then click **OK**
   All the columns for the series become fuchsia, and the legend changes to match the new color. Compare your finished chart to Figure D-13.
7. Click the **Save button** on the Standard toolbar

QuickTip

Add labels, values, and percentages to your chart by using the Data Labels tab in the Chart Options dialog box.

TABLE D-4: Chart enhancement buttons

button	use
	Displays formatting dialog box for the selected object on the chart
	Selects chart type (chart type on button changes to last chart type selected)
	Adds/deletes legend
	Creates a data table within the chart
	Charts data by row
	Charts data by column
	Angles selected text downward (clockwise)
	Angles selected text upward (counter clockwise)

FIGURE D-11: Chart Options dialog box

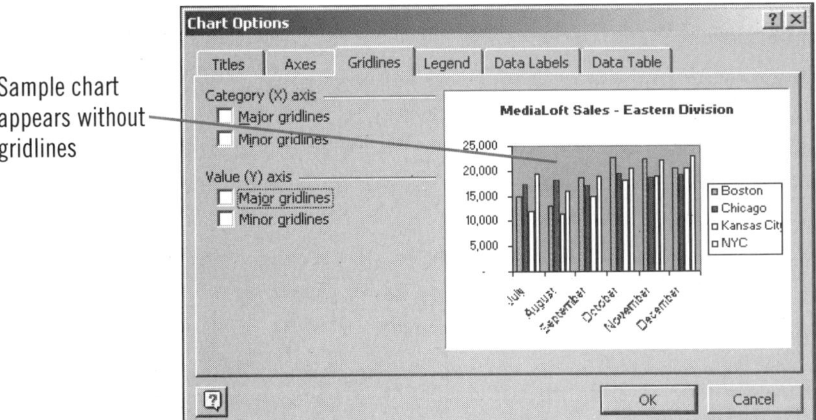

FIGURE D-12: Format Data Series dialog box

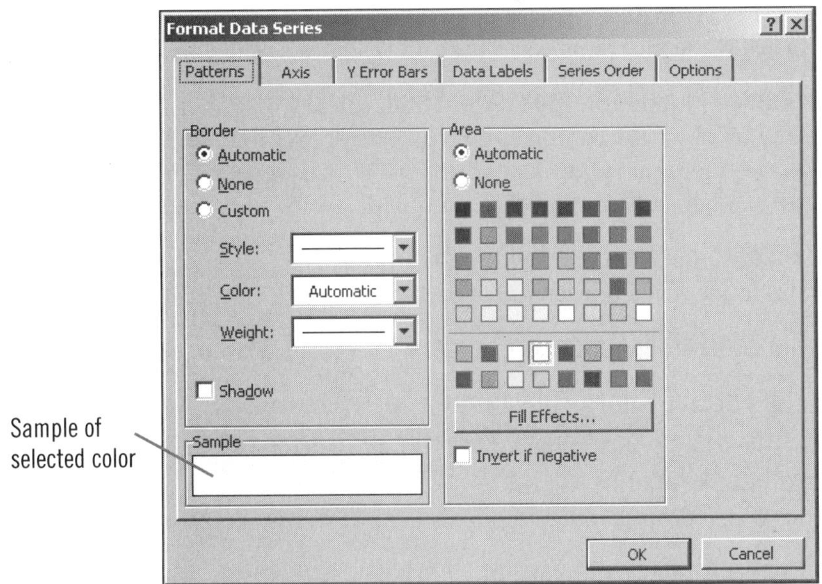

FIGURE D-13: Chart with formatted data series

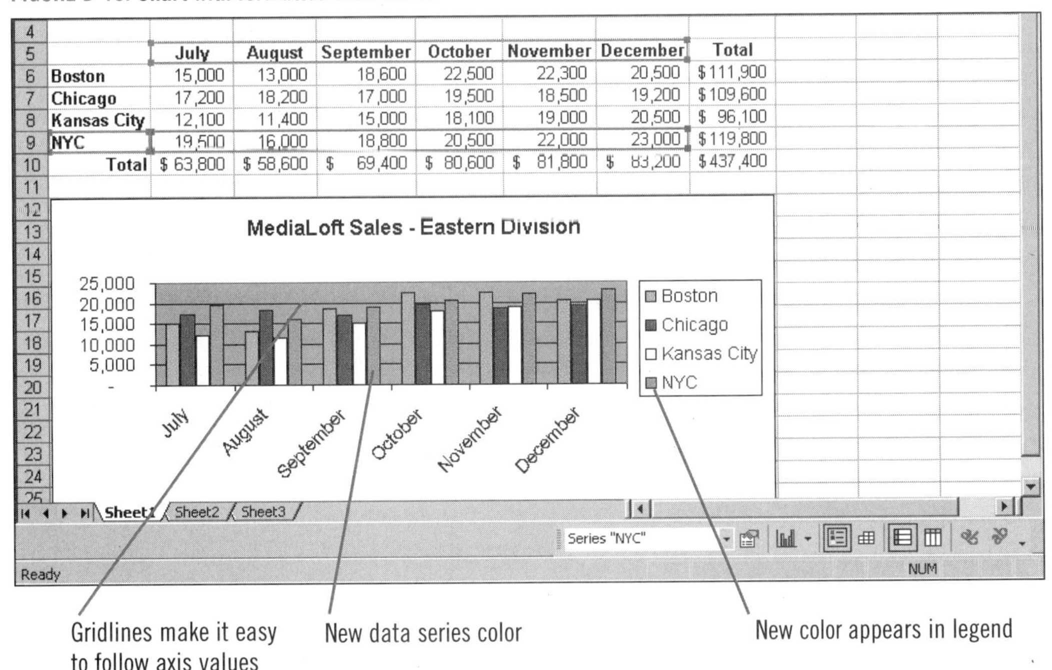

	July	August	September	October	November	December	Total
Boston	15,000	13,000	18,600	22,500	22,300	20,500	$111,900
Chicago	17,200	18,200	17,000	19,500	18,500	19,200	$109,600
Kansas City	12,100	11,400	15,000	18,100	19,000	20,500	$ 96,100
NYC	19,500	16,000	18,800	20,500	22,000	23,000	$119,800
Total	$ 63,800	$ 58,600	$ 69,400	$ 80,600	$ 81,800	$ 83,200	$437,400

Excel 2002

Enhancing a Chart

There are many ways to enhance a chart to make it easier to read and understand. You can create titles for the x-axis and y-axis, add graphics, or add background color. You can even format the text you use in a chart. Jim wants you to improve the appearance of his chart by creating titles for the x-axis and y-axis and adding a drop shadow to the title.

Steps

QuickTip

To edit the text, position the pointer over the selected text box until it changes to I, click, then edit the text.

QuickTip

The Format button opens a dialog box with the appropriate formatting options for the selected chart element. The ScreenTip for the button changes, depending on the selected object.

QuickTip

You can also double-click the Category axis title to open the Format Axis Titles dialog box.

1. Click a blank area of the chart to select it, click **Chart** on the menu bar, click **Chart Options**, click the **Titles tab** in the Chart Options dialog box, then type **Months** in the **Category (X) axis text box**
   Descriptive text on the x-axis helps readers understand the chart. The word "Months" appears below the month labels in the sample chart, as shown in Figure D-14.
2. In the **Value (Y) axis text box**, type **Sales (in $)**, then click **OK**
   A selected text box containing "Sales (in $)" appears rotated 90 degrees to the left of the y-axis. Once the Chart Options dialog box is closed, you can move the Value or Category axis title to a new position by clicking on an edge of the object then dragging it.
3. Press **[Esc]** to deselect the Value-axis title
   Next you decide that a border with a drop shadow will enhance the chart title.
4. Click the chart title, **MediaLoft Sales – Eastern Division**, to select it
5. Click the **Format Chart Title button** on the Chart toolbar to open the Format Chart Title dialog box, make sure the **Patterns tab** is selected, then click the **Shadow check box** to select it
   A border with a drop shadow surrounds the title in the Sample area.
6. Click the **Font tab** in the Format Chart Title dialog box, click **Times New Roman** in the Font list, click **Bold Italic** in the Font style list, click **OK**, then press **[Esc]** to deselect the chart title
   A border with a drop shadow appears around the chart title, and the chart title text is reformatted.
7. Click **Months** (the Category axis title), click , click the **Font tab** if necessary, select **Times New Roman** in the Font list, then click **OK**
   The Category axis title appears in the Times New Roman font.
8. Click **Sales (in $)** (the Value axis title), click , click the **Font tab** if necessary, click **Times New Roman** in the Font list, click **OK**, then press **[Esc]** to deselect the title
   The Value axis title appears in the Times New Roman font. Compare your chart to Figure D-15.
9. Click the **Save button** on the Standard toolbar

FIGURE D-14: **Sample chart with Category (X) axis text**

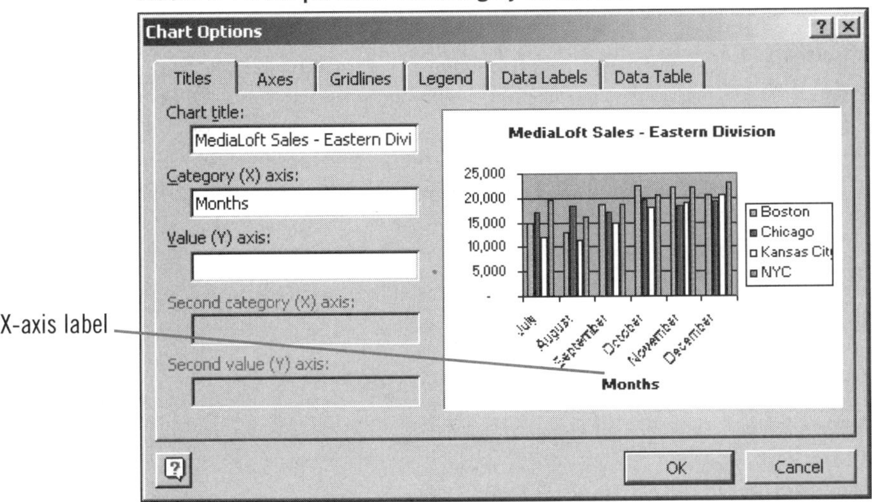

FIGURE D-15: **Enhanced chart**

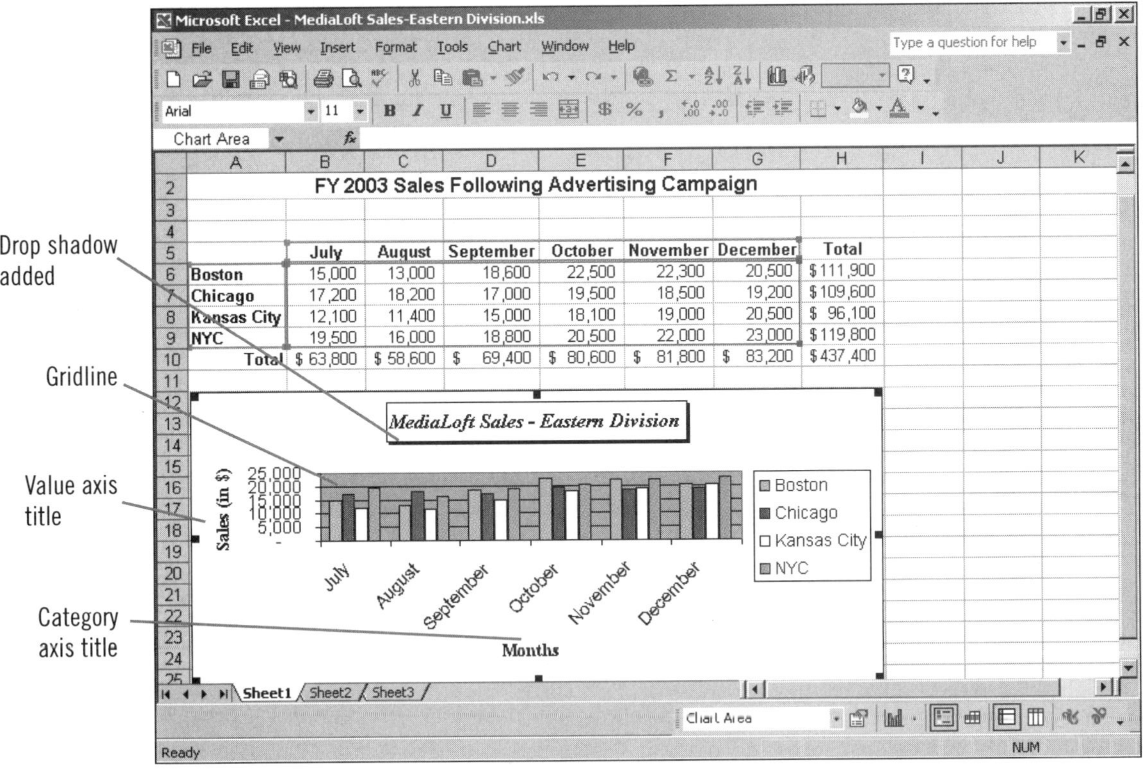

Changing text alignment in charts

You can modify the alignment of axis text to make it fit better within the plot area. With a chart selected, double-click the axis text to be modified. The Format Axis dialog box opens. Click the Alignment tab, then change the alignment by typing the number of degrees in the Degrees text box, or by clicking a marker in the Degrees sample box. When you have made the desired changes, click OK.

Excel 2002

Annotating and Drawing on a Chart

You can add arrows and text annotations to point out critical information in your charts. **Text annotations** are labels that you add to a chart to further describe your data. You can draw lines and arrows that point to the exact locations you want to emphasize. Jim wants you to add a text annotation and an arrow to highlight the October sales increase.

Steps

1. Make sure the chart is selected
   To call attention to the Boston October sales increase, you can draw an arrow that points to the top of the Boston October data series with the annotation, "Due to ad campaign." With the chart selected, simply typing text in the formula bar creates annotation text.

2. Type **Due to ad campaign**, then click the **Enter button**
   As you type, the text appears in the formula bar. After you confirm the entry, the text appears in a selected text box within the chart window.

3. Point to an edge of the text box so that the pointer changes to

4. Drag the **text box** above the chart, as shown in Figure D-16, then release the mouse button
   You can add an arrow to point to a specific area or item in a chart by using the Drawing toolbar.

5. Click the **Drawing button** on the Standard toolbar
   The Drawing toolbar appears below the worksheet.

6. Click the **Arrow button** on the Drawing toolbar, then move the pointer over the chart
   The pointer changes to +, and the status bar displays "Click and drag to insert an AutoShape." When you draw an arrow, the point farthest from where you start will have the arrowhead.

7. Position + under the **t** in the word "to" in the text box, press and hold the left mouse button, drag the line to the Boston column in the October sales series, then release the mouse button
   An arrow appears, pointing to Boston October sales. The arrow is a selected object in the chart; you can resize, format, or delete it just like any other object. Compare your finished chart to Figure D-17.

8. Click to close the Drawing toolbar

9. Click the **Save button** on the Standard toolbar

Trouble?

If the pointer changes to I or ↔, release the mouse button, click outside the text box area to deselect it, select the text box, then repeat Step 3.

QuickTip

To annotate charts, you can also use the Callout shapes on the AutoShapes menu in the Drawing toolbar.

QuickTip

You can also insert text and an arrow in the data section of a worksheet by clicking the Text Box button on the Drawing toolbar, drawing a text box, typing the text, then adding the arrow.

FIGURE D-16: Repositioning text annotation

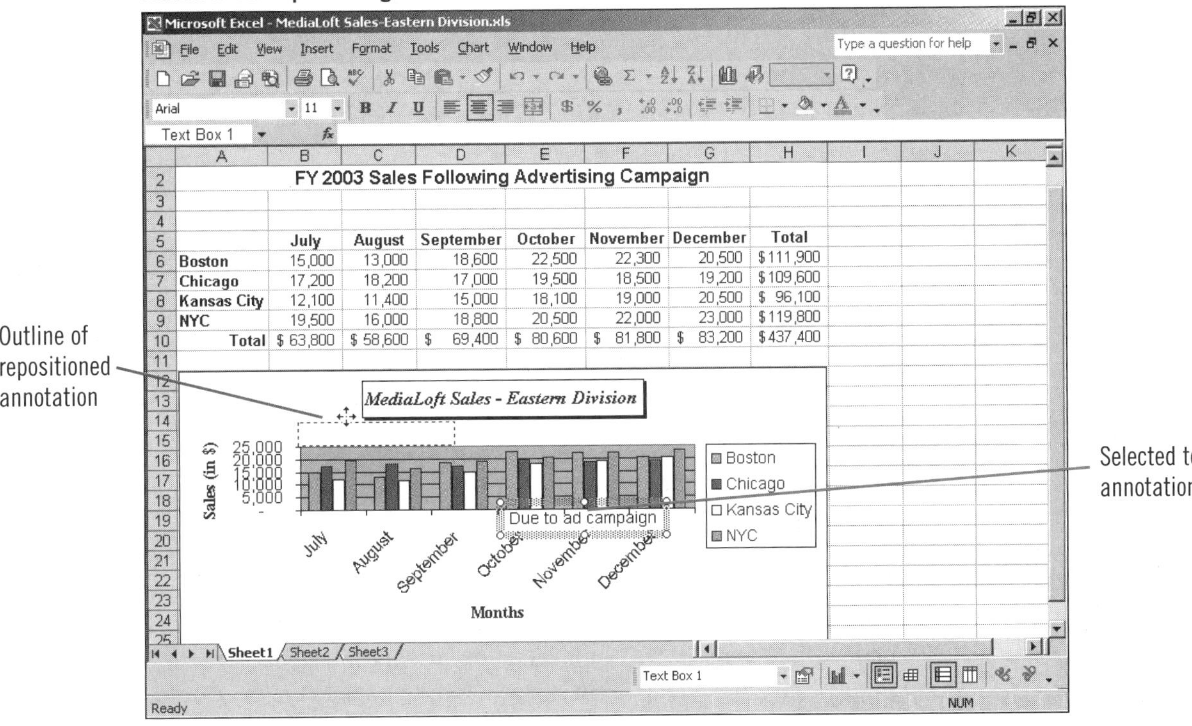

FIGURE D-17: Completed chart with text annotation and arrow

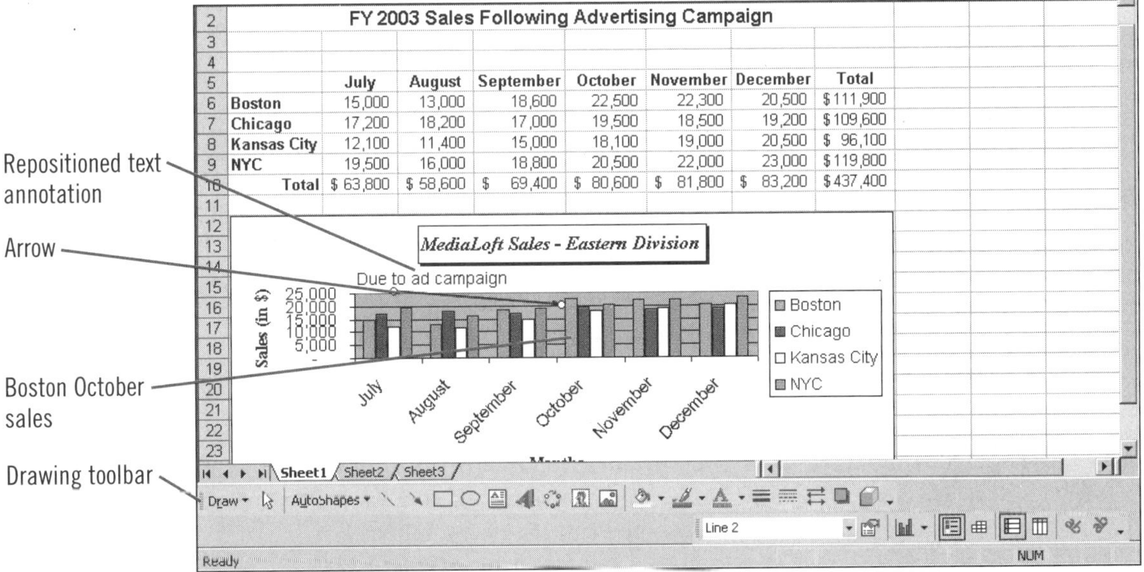

Exploding a pie slice

Just as an arrow can call attention to a data series, you can emphasize a pie slice by exploding, or pulling it away from, the pie chart. Once the pie chart is selected, click the pie to select it, click the desired slice to select only that slice, then drag the slice away from the pie, as shown in Figure D-18. After you change the chart type, you may need to adjust arrows within the chart.

FIGURE D-18: Exploded pie slice

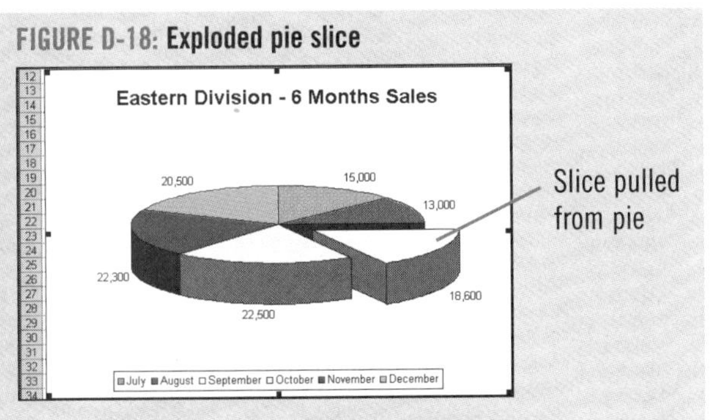

Excel 2002

Excel 2002

Previewing and Printing a Chart

After you complete a chart, you will often need to print it. Like previewing a worksheet, previewing a chart lets you see what your chart looks like before you print it. You can print a chart by itself or as part of the worksheet. Jim wants a printed version of the chart for the annual meeting. He wants you to print the worksheet and the chart together, so that the shareholders can see the actual sales numbers for the eastern division stores.

Steps

1. Press **[Esc]** to deselect the arrow and the chart, enter your name in cell **A35**, then press **[Ctrl][Home]**
2. Click the **Print Preview button** on the Standard toolbar
   The Print Preview window opens. You decide the chart and data would make better use of the page if they were printed in **landscape** orientation—that is, with the text running the long way on the page. You will use Page Setup to change the page orientation.
3. Click **Setup** on the Print Preview toolbar to open the Page Setup dialog box, then click the **Page tab**, if necessary
4. Click the **Landscape option button** in the Orientation section, as shown in Figure D-19, then click **OK**
   Because each page has a default left margin of 0.75", the chart and data will print too far over to the left of the page. You can change this setting using the Margins tab.
5. Click **Setup** on the Print Preview toolbar, click the **Margins tab**, click the **Horizontally check box** (under Center on page), then click **OK**
   The data and chart are positioned horizontally on the page. See Figure D-20.
6. Click **Print** to display the Print dialog box, then click **OK**
   The data and chart print, and you are returned to the worksheet. If you want, you can choose to preview (and print) only the chart.
7. Select the **chart**, then click the **Print Preview button**
   The chart appears in the Print Preview window. If you wanted to, you could print the chart by clicking the Print button on the Print Preview toolbar.
8. Click **Close** on the Print Preview toolbar
9. Click the **Save button** on the Standard toolbar, close the workbook, then exit Excel

QuickTip

The preview will show in color if you have a color printer selected.

QuickTip

The printer you have selected may affect the appearance of the preview screen.

FIGURE D-19: **Page tab of the Page Setup dialog box**

Landscape option button selected

Depending on your printer, your settings may differ

Page Setup

Page | Margins | Header/Footer | Sheet

Orientation

Portrait

Landscape

Options...

Scaling

Adjust to: 100 % normal size

Fit to: 1 page(s) wide by 1 tall

Paper size: Letter

Print quality: 600 dpi

First page number: Auto

OK | Cancel

FIGURE D-20: **Chart and data ready to print**

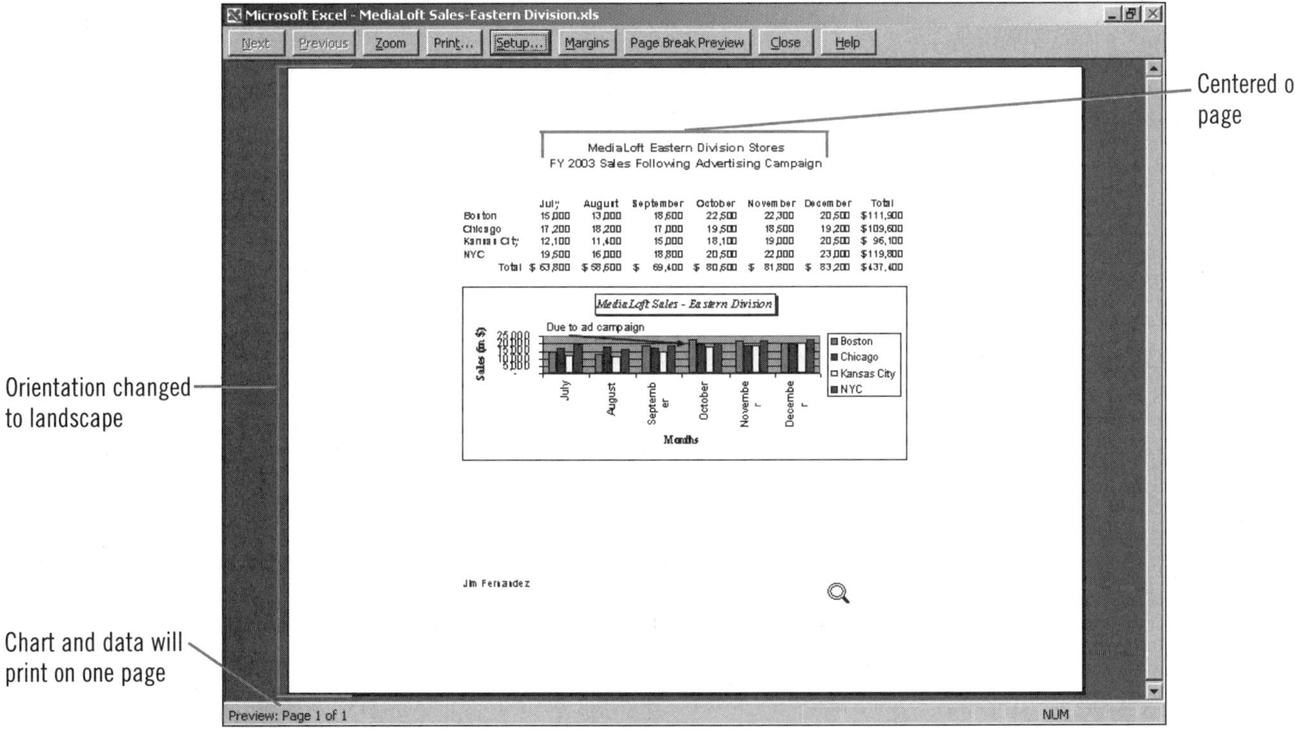

Excel 2002

Using the Page Setup dialog box for a chart

When a chart is selected, a different Page Setup dialog box opens than when neither the chart nor data is selected. The Center on Page options are not always available. To accurately position a chart on the page, you can click the Margins button on the Print Preview toolbar. Margin lines appear on the screen and show you exactly how the margins will appear on the page. The exact placement appears in the status bar when you press and hold the mouse button on the margin line. You can drag the lines to the exact settings you want.

Excel 2002

Practice

► Concepts Review

Label each element of the Excel chart shown in Figure D-21.

FIGURE D-21

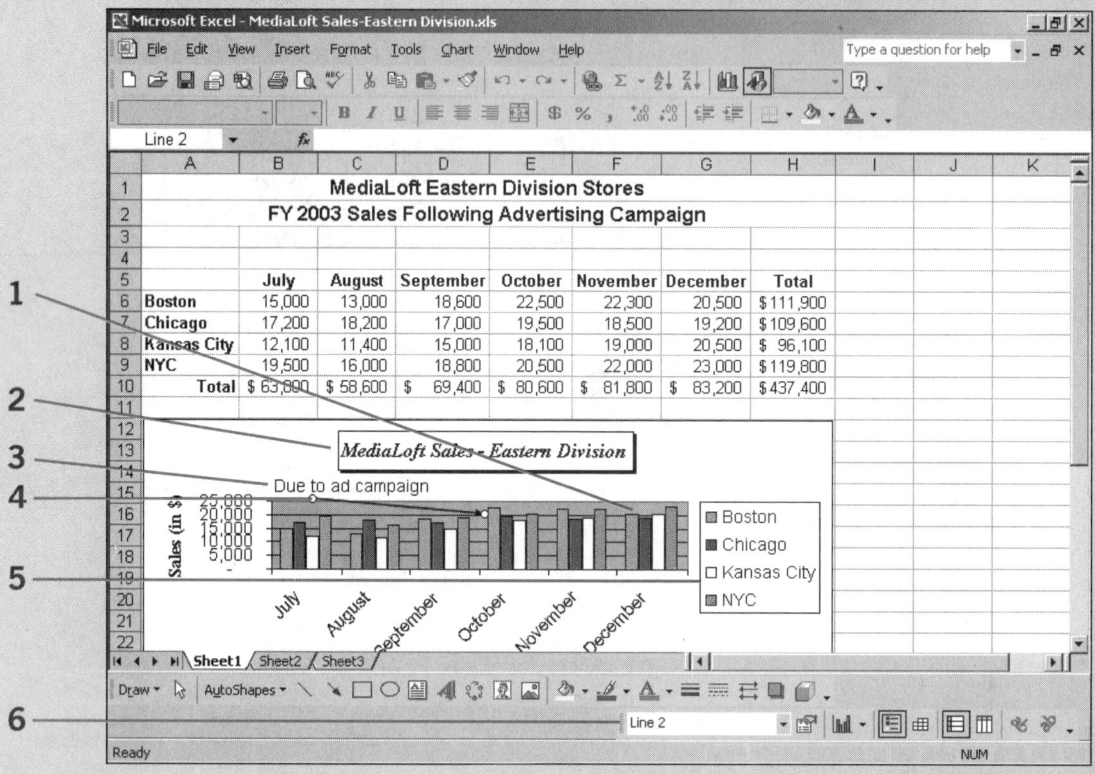

Match each chart type with the statement that describes it.

7. Column	**a.** Shows how volume changes over time
8. Area	**b.** Compares data as parts of a whole
9. Pie	**c.** Displays a column and line chart using different scales of measurement
10. Combination	**d.** Compares trends over even time intervals
11. Line	**e.** Compares data over time—the Excel default

Select the best answer from the list of choices.

12. The object in a chart that identifies patterns used for each data series is a:

- **a.** Data point.
- **b.** Plot.
- **c.** Legend.
- **d.** Range.

13. What is the term for a row or column on a chart?
- **a.** Range address
- **b.** Axis title
- **c.** Chart orientation
- **d.** Data series

14. The orientation of a page whose dimensions are 11" wide by 8½" tall is:
- **a.** Sideways.
- **b.** Longways.
- **c.** Portrait.
- **d.** Landscape.

15. In a 2-D chart, the Value axis is the:
- **a.** X-axis.
- **b.** Z-axis.
- **c.** D-axis.
- **d.** Y-axis.

16. In a 2-D chart, the Category axis is the:
- **a.** X-axis.
- **b.** Z-axis.
- **c.** D-axis.
- **d.** Y-axis.

17. Which pointer is used to resize a chart object?
- **a.** I
- **b.** ⤡
- **c.** ✥
- **d.** +

Skills Review

1. Create a chart.
- **a.** Start Excel, open a new workbook, then save it as **MediaLoft Vancouver Software Usage** in the drive and folder where your Project Files are stored.
- **b.** Enter the information from the following table in your worksheet in range A1:F6. Resize columns as necessary.

	Excel	Word	PowerPoint	Access	Publisher
Accounting	27	15	2	7	1
Marketing	13	35	35	15	35
Engineering	25	5	3	1	5
Personnel	15	25	10	10	27
Production	6	5	22	0	25

Excel 2002

c. Save your work.
d. Select the range containing the data and headings.
e. Start the Chart Wizard.
f. In the Chart Wizard, select a clustered column chart, then verify that the series are in rows; add the chart title **Software Usage by Department**, and make the chart an object on the worksheet.
g. After the chart appears, save your work.

2. Move and resize a chart.

a. Make sure the chart is still selected.
b. Move the chart beneath the data.
c. Resize the chart so it extends to column L.
d. Move the legend below the charted data. (*Hint*: Change the legend's position by using the Legend tab in the Chart Options dialog box.)
e. Save your work.

3. Edit a chart.

a. Change the value in cell B3 to **6**. Notice the change in the chart.
b. Select the chart.
c. Resize the chart so the bottom is at row 24.
d. Use the Chart Type list arrow to change the chart to a 3-D Column Chart.
e. Rotate the chart to move the data.
f. Change the chart back to a column chart.
g. Save your work.

4. Format a chart.

a. Make sure the chart is still selected.
b. Use the Chart Options dialog box to turn off the displayed gridlines.
c. Change the font used in the Category and Value labels to Times New Roman. (*Hint*: Click the axis to select it, then proceed as you would to change an axis title.)
d. Turn on the major gridlines for the Value axis.
e. Change the title's font to Times New Roman.
f. Save your work.

5. Enhance a chart.

a. Make sure the chart is selected, then select the **Titles tab** in the Chart Options dialog box.
b. Enter **Software** as the x-axis title.
c. Enter **Users** as the y-axis title.
d. Change **Production** in the legend to **Art**. (*Hint*: Change the text entry in the worksheet.)
e. Add a drop shadow to the title.
f. Save your work.

6. Annotate and draw on a chart.

- **a.** Make sure the chart is selected, then create the text annotation **Needs More Users**.
- **b.** Position the text annotation beneath the title.
- **c.** Below the text annotation, use the Drawing toolbar to create an arrow similar to the one in Figure D-22 that points to the area containing the Access data.
- **d.** Save your work.

FIGURE D-22

	Excel	Word	PowerPoint	Access	Publisher
Accounting	27	15	2	7	1
Marketing	6	35	35	15	35
Engineering	25	5	3	1	5
Personnel	15	25	10	10	27
Art	6	5	22	0	25

7. Preview and print a chart.

- **a.** In the worksheet, enter your name in cell A30.
- **b.** Preview the chart and data.
- **c.** Change the page orientation to landscape.
- **d.** Center the page contents horizontally and vertically on the page.
- **e.** Print the data and chart from the Print Preview window.
- **f.** Save your work.
- **g.** Preview only the chart, then print it.
- **h.** Close the workbook, then exit Excel.

Excel 2002

Independent Challenge 1

You are the operations manager for the Springfield, Oregon Theater Group. Each year the group applies to various state and federal agencies for matching funds. For this year's funding proposal, you need to create charts to document the number of productions in previous years.

- **a.** Sketch a sample worksheet on a piece of paper describing how you will create the charts. Which type of chart is best suited for the information you need to display? What kind of chart enhancements do you want to use? Will a 3-D effect make your chart easier to understand?
- **b.** Start Excel, open the Project File EX D-2, then save it as **Springfield Theater Group** in the drive and folder where your Project Files are stored.
- **c.** Create a column chart for the data, accepting all Chart Wizard defaults.
- **d.** Change at least one of the colors used in a data series.
- **e.** Create at least two additional charts for the same data to show how different chart types display the same data. (*Hint*: Move each chart to a new location, then deselect each chart before using the Wizard to create the next one.)
- **f.** After creating the charts, make the appropriate enhancements. Include chart titles, legends, and value and category axis titles, using the suggestions in the following table:

suggested chart enhancements	
Title	Types and Number of Plays
Legend	Year 1, Year 2, Year 3, Year 4
Value axis title	Number of Plays
Category axis title	Play Types

g. Add data labels.
h. Enter your name in a worksheet cell.
i. Save your work. Before printing, preview the file so you know what the charts will look like. Adjust any items as necessary.
j. Print the worksheet (charts and data).
k. Close the workbook, then exit Excel.

► Independent Challenge 2

Beautiful You, a small beauty salon, has been using Excel for several months. One of your responsibilities at the Beautiful You Salon is to re-create the company's records using Excel. Another is to convince the current staff that Excel can help them make daily operating decisions more easily and efficiently. To do this, you've decided to create charts using the previous year's operating expenses, including rent, utilities, and payroll. The manager will use these charts at the next monthly meeting.

a. Decide which data in the worksheet should be charted. Sketch two sample charts. What type of charts are best suited for the information you need to show? What kind of chart enhancements will be necessary?
b. Start Excel, open the Project File EX D-3 from the drive and folder where your Project Files are stored, then save it as **BY Expense Charts**.
c. Create a column chart on the worksheet, containing the expense data for all four quarters.
d. Using the same data, create an area chart and one additional chart using any other appropriate chart type. (*Hint*: move each chart to a new location, then deselect it before using the Wizard to create the next one.)
e. Add annotated text and arrows to the column chart that highlight any important data or trends.
f. In one chart, change the color of a data series, then in another chart, use black-and-white patterns only. (*Hint*: use the Fill Effects button in the Format Data Series dialog box. Then display the Patterns tab. Adjust the Foreground color to black and the Background color to white, then select a pattern.
g. Enter your name in a worksheet cell.
h. Save your work. Before printing, preview each chart so you know what the charts will look like. Adjust any items as needed.
i. Print the charts.
j. Close the workbook, then exit Excel.

Independent Challenge 3

You are working as an account representative at the Bright Light Ad Agency. You have been examining the expenses charged to clients of the firm. The Board of Directors wants to examine certain advertising expenses and has asked you to prepare charts that can be used in this evaluation.

a. Start Excel, open the Project File EX D-4 from the drive and folder where your Project Files are stored, then save it as **Bright Light**.
b. Decide what types of charts would be best suited for the data in the range A16:B24. Sketch two sample charts. What kind of chart enhancements will be necessary?
c. Use the Chart Wizard to create at least three different types of charts that show the distribution of advertising expenses. (*Hint*: Move each chart to a new location, then deselect it before using the Wizard to create the next one.)
d. Add annotated text and arrows highlighting important data, such as the largest expense.
e. Change the color of at least one data series.
f. Add chart titles and Category and Value axis titles. Format the titles with a font of your choice. Place a drop shadow around the chart title.

g. Enter your name in a worksheet cell.
h. Save your work. Before printing, preview the file so you know what the charts will look like. Adjust any items as needed. Be sure the chart is placed appropriately on the page.
i. Print the charts, close the workbook then exit Excel.

Independent Challenge 4

Your company, Film Distribution, is headquartered in Montreal, and is considering opening a new office in the U.S. They would like you to begin investigating possible locations. You can use the Web to find and compare median pay scales in specific cities to see how relocating will affect the standard of living for those employees who move to the new office.

a. Start Excel, open a new workbook, then save it as **New Location Analysis** in the drive and folder where your Project Files are located.
b. Connect to the Internet, use your browser to go to homeadvisor.msn.com/pickaplace/comparecities.asp. (If this address is no longer current, go to homeadvisor.msn.com or www.homefair.com, and follow links for **Moving and Relocation**, **Compare Cost of Living**, or similar links to find the information needed for your spreadsheet. You can also use your favorite search engine to locate other sites on cost of living comparisons.)
c. Determine the median incomes for Seattle, San Francisco, Dallas, Salt Lake City, Memphis, and Boston. Record this data on a sheet named Median Income in your workbook. (*Hint*: See the table below for suggested data layout.)

Location	Income
Seattle	
San Francisco	
Dallas	
Salt Lake City	
Memphis	
Boston	

d. Format the data so it looks attractive and professional.
e. Create any type of column chart, with the data series in columns, on the same worksheet as the data. Include a descriptive title.
f. Determine how much an employee would need to earn in Seattle, San Francisco, Dallas, Memphis, and Boston to maintain the same standard of living as if the company chose to relocate to Salt Lake City and pay $75,000. Record this data on a sheet named **Standard of Living** in your workbook.
g. Format the data so it looks attractive and professional.
h. Create any type of chart you feel is appropriate on the same worksheet as the data. Include a descriptive title.
i. Do not display the legends in either chart.
j. Change the color of the data series in the Standard of Living chart to bright green.
k. Remove the major gridlines in the Median Income chart.
l. Format the Value axis in both charts so that the salary income displays a 1000 separator (comma) but no decimal places.
m. Enter your name in a cell in both worksheets.
n. Save the workbook. Preview the chart and change margins as necessary.
o. Print each worksheet, including the data and chart, making setup modifications as necessary.
p. Close the workbook, then exit Excel.

Visual Workshop

Modify a worksheet, using the skills you learned in this unit and using Figure D-23 for reference. Open the Project File EX D-5 from the drive and folder where your Project Files are stored, then save it as **Quarterly Advertising Budget**. Create the chart, then change the chart to reflect Figure D-23. Enter your name in cell A13, save, preview, then print your results.

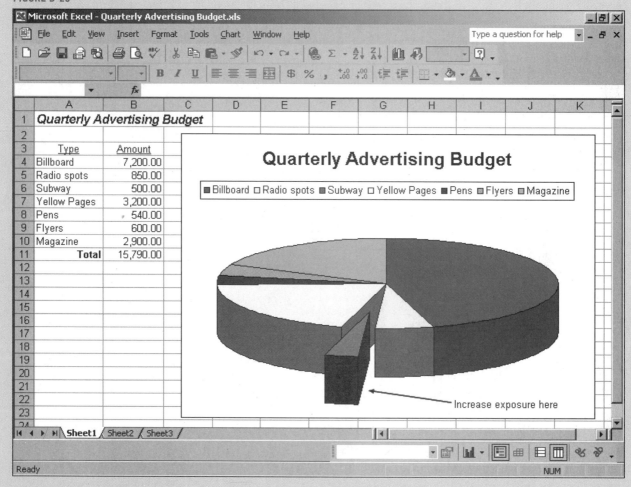

FIGURE D-23

Microsoft Excel - Quarterly Advertising Budget.xls

Quarterly Advertising Budget

Type	Amount
Billboard	7,200.00
Radio spots	850.00
Subway	500.00
Yellow Pages	3,200.00
Pens	540.00
Flyers	600.00
Magazine	2,900.00
Total	15,790.00

Quarterly Advertising Budget

Billboard Radio spots Subway Yellow Pages Pens Flyers Magazine

Increase exposure here

Excel 2002

Unit E

Working with Formulas and Functions

Objectives

- MOUS ► Create a formula with several operators
- MOUS ► Use names in a formula
- ► Generate multiple totals with AutoSum
- MOUS ► Use dates in calculations
- MOUS ► Build a conditional formula with the IF function
- MOUS ► Use statistical functions
- MOUS ► Calculate payments with the PMT function
- MOUS ► Display and print formula contents

Without formulas, Excel would simply be an electronic grid with text and numbers. Used with formulas, Excel becomes a powerful data analysis software tool. As you learn how to analyze data using different types of formulas, including those that call for functions, you will discover more ways to use Excel. In this unit, you will gain a further understanding of Excel formulas and learn how to build several Excel functions. Top management at MediaLoft has asked Jim Fernandez to analyze various company data. To do this, Jim creates several worksheets that require the use of formulas and functions. Because management is considering raising salaries for store managers, Jim has asked you to create a report that compares the payroll deductions and net pay for store managers before and after a proposed raise.

Excel 2002

Creating a Formula with Several Operators

You can create formulas that contain a combination of cell references (for example, Z100 and B2), operators (for example, * [multiplication] and - [subtraction]), and values (for example, 99 or 1.56). Formulas can also contain functions. You have used AutoSum to insert the Sum function into a cell. You can also create a single formula that performs several calculations. If you enter a formula with more than one operator, Excel performs the calculations in a particular sequence based on algebraic rules, called the order of precedence (also called the order of operations); that is, Excel performs the operation(s) within the parentheses first, then performs the other calculations in a specific order. See Table E-1. Jim has been given the gross pay and payroll deductions for the monthly payroll and needs to complete his analysis. He has also preformatted, with the Comma style, any cells that are to contain values. He asks you to enter a formula for net pay that subtracts the payroll deductions from gross pay.

Steps

1. **Start Excel if necessary, open the Project File EX E-1 from the drive and folder where your Project Files are stored, then save it as Company Data**
   The first part of the net pay formula will go in cell B11.
2. **Click Edit on the menu bar, click Go To, type B11 in the Reference box, then click OK**
   Cell B11 is now the active cell. The Go To command is especially useful when you want to select a cell in a large worksheet.
3. **Type =, click cell B6, type -, then click the Insert Function button on the formula bar to open the Insert Function dialog box**
   You type the equal sign (=) to tell Excel that a formula follows. B6 references the cell containing the gross pay, and the minus sign (-) indicates that the next entry, a sum, will be subtracted from cell B6. The Function Wizard begins by displaying the Insert Function dialog box, which allows you to choose from a list of available functions or search for a specific function. See Figure E-1.
4. **Type Sum in the Search for a function text box, click Go, make sure Sum is selected in the Select a function list, then click OK**
   B6:B10 appears in the Number1 text box. You want to sum the range B7:B10.
5. **With the Number1 argument selected in the Function Arguments dialog box, click the Number1 Collapse Dialog box button, select the range B7:B10 in the worksheet, click the Redisplay Dialog Box button, then click OK**
   Collapsing the dialog box allows you to select the worksheet range. The net pay for Payroll Period 1 appears in cell B11.
6. **Copy the formula in cell B11 into cells C11:F11, then return to cell A1**
   The formula in cell B11 is copied to the range C11:F11 to complete row 11. See Figure E-2.
7. **Save the workbook**

Trouble?

If you make a mistake while building a formula, press [Esc] and begin again.

FIGURE E-1: Insert Function dialog box

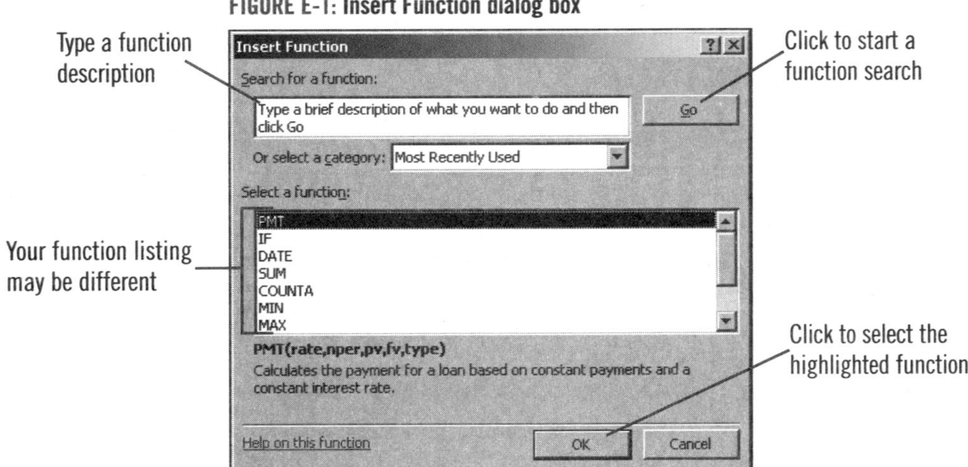

FIGURE E-2: Worksheet with copied formulas

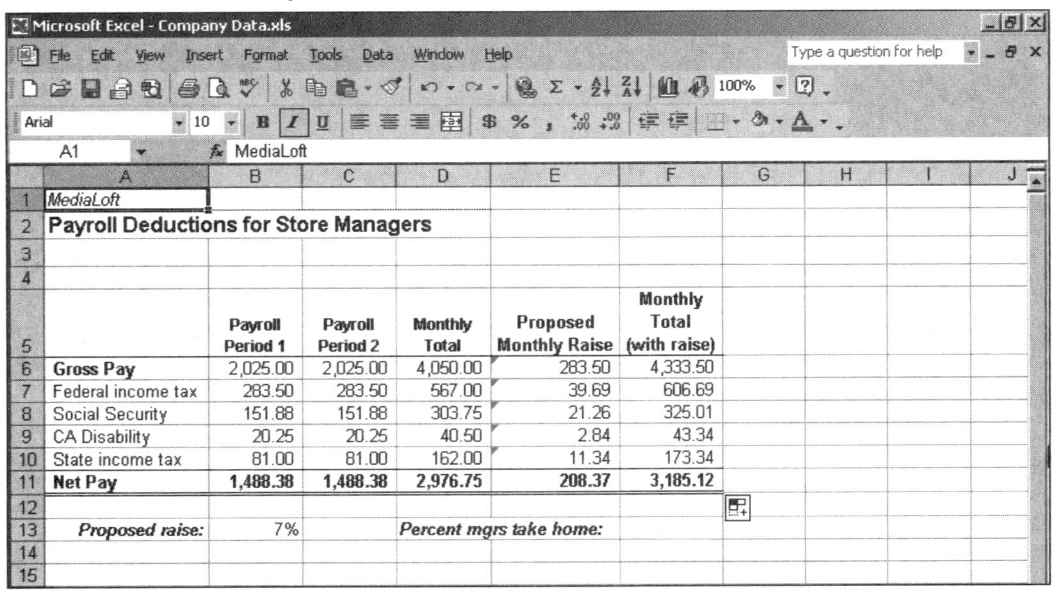

	A	B	C	D	E	F
1	MediaLoft					
2	Payroll Deductions for Store Managers					
3						
4						
5		Payroll Period 1	Payroll Period 2	Monthly Total	Proposed Monthly Raise	Monthly Total (with raise)
6	Gross Pay	2,025.00	2,025.00	4,050.00	283.50	4,333.50
7	Federal income tax	283.50	283.50	567.00	39.69	606.69
8	Social Security	151.88	151.88	303.75	21.26	325.01
9	CA Disability	20.25	20.25	40.50	2.84	43.34
10	State income tax	81.00	81.00	162.00	11.34	173.34
11	Net Pay	1,488.38	1,488.38	2,976.75	208.37	3,185.12
12						
13	Proposed raise:	7%		Percent mgrs take home:		

TABLE E-1: Sample formulas using parentheses and several operators

formula	order of precedence	calculated result
=10-20/10-5	Divide 20 by 10; subtract the result from 10, then subtarct 5	3
=(10-20)/10-5	Subtract 20 from 10; divide that by 10; then subtract 5	-6
=(10*2)*(10+2)	Multiply 10 by 2; add 10 to 2; then multiply the results	240

Using Paste Special to paste formulas and values and to perform calculations

You can use the Paste Special command to quickly enter formulas and values or even to perform quick calculations. Click the cell(s) containing the formula or value you want to copy, click the Copy button on the Standard toolbar, then right-click the cell where you want the result to appear. In the pop-up menu, choose Paste Special, choose the feature you want to paste, then click OK.

Excel 2002

Using Names in a Formula

To reduce errors and make your worksheet easier to follow, you can assign names to cells and ranges. You can also use names in formulas to make formulas easier to build. For example, the formula Revenue-Cost is much easier to understand than the formula A2-D3. When used in formulas, names become absolute cell references by default. Names can use uppercase or lowercase letters as well as digits. After you name a cell or range, you can use the name on any sheet in the workbook. If you move a named cell or range, its name moves with it. Jim wants to include a formula that calculates the percentage of monthly gross pay the managers would actually take home (their net pay) if they received a 7% raise. He asks you to name the cells you'll use in the calculation.

Steps

QuickTip

You can also assign names to ranges of cells. Select the range, click the name box, then type in the range name. You can also name a range by pointing to Name on the Insert menu then choosing Define to provide the name.

QuickTip

You can use the Label Ranges dialog box (Insert menu, Name submenu, Label command) to designate existing column or row headings as labels. Then instead of using cell references for the column or row in formulas, you can use the labels. (If this feature is not turned on, go to Tools/Options/Calculation tab/Accept labels in formulas.)

QuickTip

To delete a cell or range name, click Insert on the menu bar, point to Name, then click Define. Select the name, click Delete, then click OK.

1. Click cell **F6**, click the **name box** on the formula bar to select the active cell reference, type **Gross_with_Raise**, then press **[Enter]**
   The name assigned to cell F6, Gross_with_Raise, appears in the name box. Note that you must type underscores instead of spaces between words. Cell F6 is now named Gross_with_Raise to refer to the monthly gross pay amount that includes the 7% raise. The name box displays as much of the name as fits (Gross_with_...). The net pay cell needs a name.

2. Click cell **F11**, click the **name box**, type **Net_with_Raise**, then press **[Enter]**
   The new formula will use names instead of cell references.

3. Click cell **F13**, type **=Net_with_Raise/Gross_with_Raise**, then click the **Enter button** on the formula bar (make sure you begin the formula with an equal sign)
   Notice that as you finish typing each name, the name changes color to match the outline around the cell reference. The formula bar now shows the new formula, and the result, 0.735, appears in the cell. You can also insert names in a formula by clicking Insert on the menu bar, pointing to Name, then clicking Paste. If you want to replace existing formula references with the corresponding names you have added, click Insert on the menu bar, point to Name, click Apply, click the name or names, then click OK. Cell F13 needs to be formatted in Percent style.

4. Select cell **F13** if necessary, click **Format** on the menu bar, click **Style**, click the **Style name list arrow**, click **Percent**, then click **OK**
   The result shown in cell F13, 74%, is rounded to the nearest whole percent, as shown in Figure E-3. A **style** is a combination of formatting characteristics, such as bold, italic, and underlined. You can use the Style dialog box instead of the Formatting toolbar to apply styles. You can also use it to remove styles: select the cell that has a style and select Normal in the Style name list. To define your own style (such as bold, italic, and 14 point), select a cell, format it using the Formatting toolbar, open the Style dialog box and type a name for your style, then click Add. Later, you can apply all those formatting characteristics by applying your new style from the dialog box.

5. Add your name to cell A20, save the workbook, then preview and print the worksheet

FIGURE E-3: **Worksheet formula that includes cell names**

Microsoft Excel - Company Data.xls

F13 | =Net_with_Raise/Gross_with_Raise

	A	B	C	D	E	F
1	*MediaLoft*					
2	**Payroll Deductions for Store Managers**					
3						
4						
5		**Payroll Period 1**	**Payroll Period 2**	**Monthly Total**	**Proposed Monthly Raise**	**Monthly Total (with raise)**
6	**Gross Pay**	2,025.00	2,025.00	4,050.00	283.50	4,333.50
7	Federal income tax	283.50	283.50	567.00	39.69	606.69
8	Social Security	151.88	151.88	303.75	21.26	325.01
9	CA Disability	20.25	20.25	40.50	2.84	43.34
10	State income tax	81.00	81.00	162.00	11.34	173.34
11	**Net Pay**	**1,488.38**	**1,488.38**	**2,976.75**	**208.37**	**3,185.12**
12						
13	***Proposed raise:***	7%		***Percent mgrs take home:***		74%
14						

Name box

Formula with cell names

Cell named Gross_with_Raise

Result of calculation

Cell named Net_with_Raise

Producing a list of names

You might want to verify the names you have in a workbook and the cells they reference. To paste a list of names in a workbook, select a blank cell that has several blank cells beside and beneath it. Click Insert on the menu bar, point to Name, then click Paste. In the Paste Name dialog box, click Paste List. Excel produces a list of names that includes the sheet name and the cell or range the name identifies. See Figure E-4.

FIGURE E-4: **Worksheet with pasted list of names**

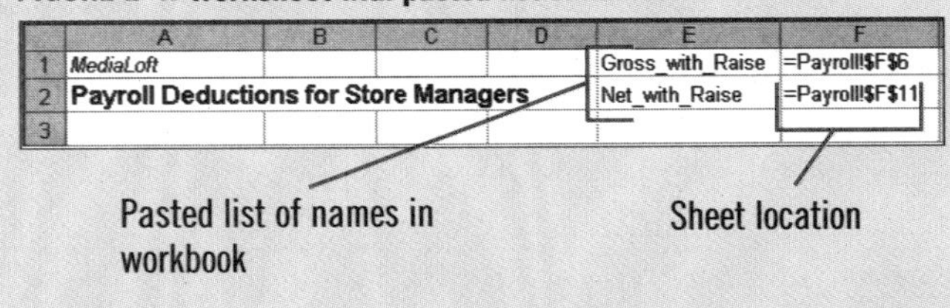

	A	B	C	D	E	F
1	*MediaLoft*				Gross_with_Raise	=Payroll!$F$6
2	**Payroll Deductions for Store Managers**				Net_with_Raise	=Payroll!$F$11
3						

Generating Multiple Totals with AutoSum

In most cases, the result of a function is a value derived from a single calculation. You have used AutoSum to produce a total of a single range of numbers; you can also use it to total multiple ranges. If you include blank cells to the right or at the bottom of a selected range, AutoSum will generate several totals and enter the results in the blank cells. You can have Excel generate grand totals of worksheet subtotals by selecting a range of cells and using the AutoSum function. Maria Abbott, MediaLoft's general sales manager, has given Jim a worksheet summarizing store sales. He asks you to complete the worksheet totals.

Trouble?

If you select the wrong combination of cells, click on a single cell and begin again.

1. **Make the Sales sheet active, select range B5:E9, press and hold [Ctrl], then select range B11:E15**
   To select nonadjacent cells, you must press and hold [Ctrl] while selecting the additional cells. Compare your selections with Figure E-6. The totals will appear in the last line of each selection.

2. **Click the AutoSum button Σ on the Standard toolbar**
   When the selected range you want to sum (B5:E9 and B11:E15, in this example) includes a blank cell with data values above it, AutoSum enters the total in the blank cell.

3. **Select the range B5:F17, then click Σ**
   Whenever the selected range you want to sum includes a blank cell in the bottom row or right column, AutoSum enters the total in the blank cell. In this case, Excel ignores the data values and totals only the sums. Although Excel generates totals when you click the AutoSum button, it is a good idea to check the results.

4. **Click cell B17**
   The formula bar reads =SUM(B15,B9). See Figure E-7. When generating grand totals, Excel references the cells contained in SUM functions with a comma separator between cell references. Excel uses commas to separate multiple arguments in all functions, not just in SUM.

5. **Enter your name into cell A20, save the workbook, then preview and print the worksheet**

Quick calculations with AutoCalculate

To view a total quickly without entering a formula, just select the range you want to sum, and the answer appears in the status bar next to SUM=. You also can perform other quick calculations, such as averaging or finding the minimum value in a selection. To do this, right-click the AutoCalculate area in the status bar and select from the list of options. The option you select remains in effect and in the status bar until you make another selection. See Figure E-5.

FIGURE E-5: Using AutoCalculate

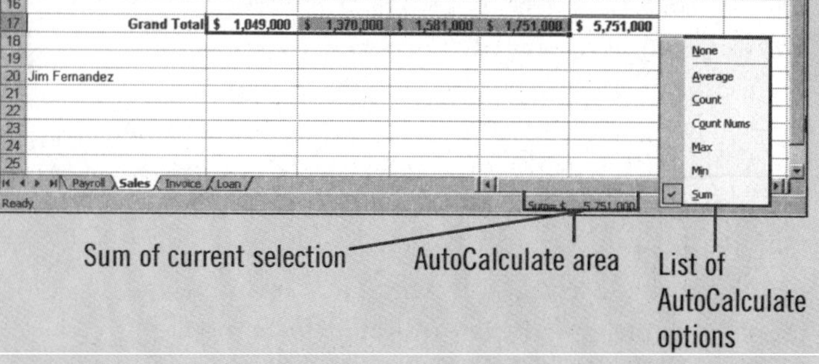

FIGURE E-6: Selecting nonadjacent ranges using [Ctrl]

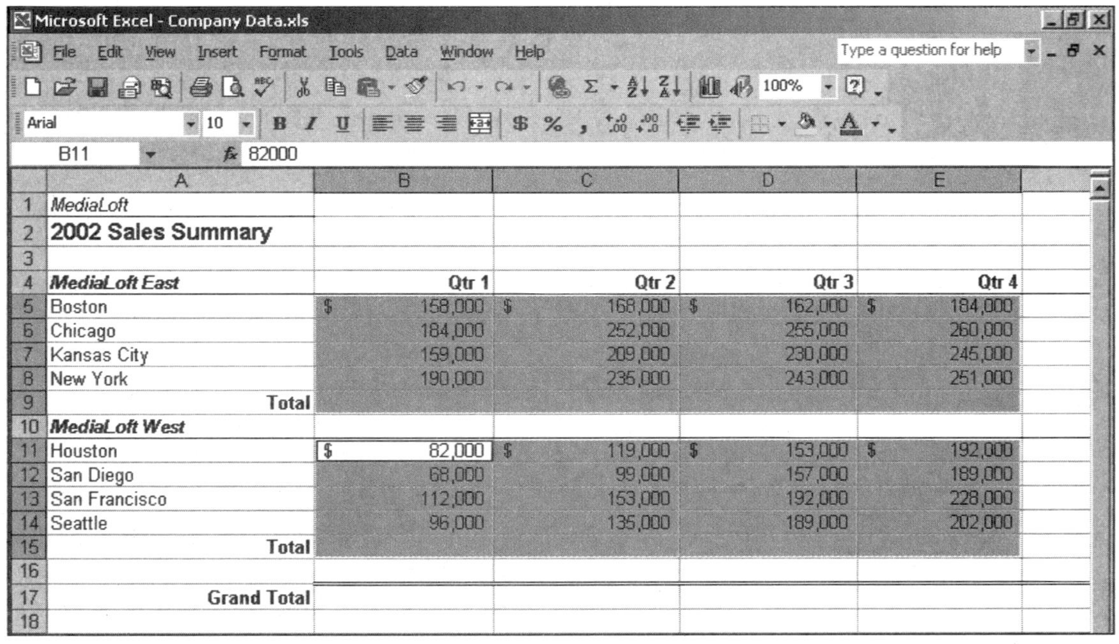

	A	B	C	D	E
1	MediaLoft				
2	2002 Sales Summary				
3					
4	MediaLoft East	Qtr 1	Qtr 2	Qtr 3	Qtr 4
5	Boston	$ 158,000	$ 168,000	$ 162,000	$ 184,000
6	Chicago	184,000	252,000	255,000	260,000
7	Kansas City	159,000	209,000	230,000	245,000
8	New York	190,000	235,000	243,000	251,000
9	Total				
10	MediaLoft West				
11	Houston	$ 82,000	$ 119,000	$ 153,000	$ 192,000
12	San Diego	68,000	99,000	157,000	189,000
13	San Francisco	112,000	153,000	192,000	228,000
14	Seattle	96,000	135,000	189,000	202,000
15	Total				
16					
17	Grand Total				
18					

FIGURE E-7: Completed worksheet

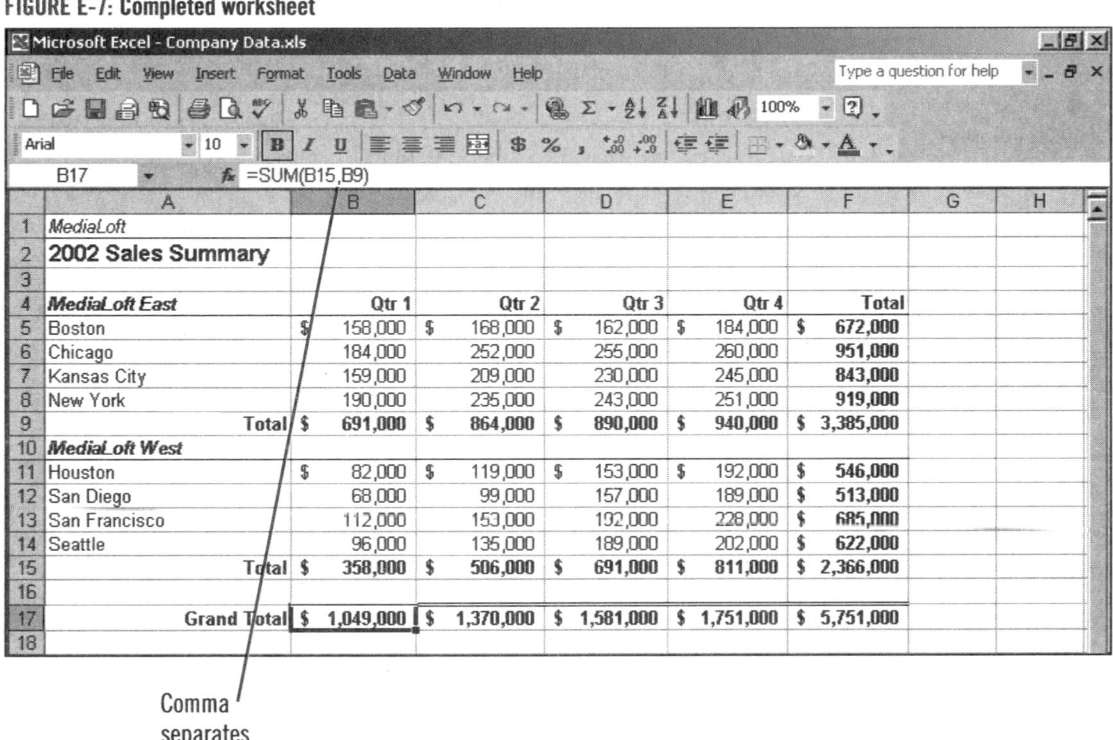

	A	B	C	D	E	F
1	MediaLoft					
2	2002 Sales Summary					
3						
4	MediaLoft East	Qtr 1	Qtr 2	Qtr 3	Qtr 4	Total
5	Boston	$ 158,000	$ 168,000	$ 162,000	$ 184,000	$ 672,000
6	Chicago	184,000	252,000	255,000	260,000	951,000
7	Kansas City	159,000	209,000	230,000	245,000	843,000
8	New York	190,000	235,000	243,000	251,000	919,000
9	Total	$ 691,000	$ 864,000	$ 890,000	$ 940,000	$ 3,385,000
10	MediaLoft West					
11	Houston	$ 82,000	$ 119,000	$ 153,000	$ 192,000	$ 546,000
12	San Diego	68,000	99,000	157,000	189,000	$ 513,000
13	San Francisco	112,000	153,000	192,000	228,000	$ 685,000
14	Seattle	96,000	135,000	189,000	202,000	$ 622,000
15	Total	$ 358,000	$ 506,000	$ 691,000	$ 811,000	$ 2,366,000
16						
17	Grand Total	$ 1,049,000	$ 1,370,000	$ 1,581,000	$ 1,751,000	$ 5,751,000
18						

Excel 2002

Using Dates in Calculations

If you enter dates in a worksheet in a format that Excel recognizes as a date, you can sort them and perform date calculations. When you enter an Excel date format, Excel converts it to a serial number so it can be used in calculations. A date's serial number is the number of days it is from January 1, 1900. Excel assigns the serial number of "1" to January 1, 1900 and counts up from there; the serial number of January 1, 2003, for example, is 37,622. Jim's next task is to calculate the due date and age of each invoice on the worksheet. He reminds you to enter the worksheet dates in a format that Excel recognizes, so he can use date calculations.

Steps

1. **Make the Invoice sheet active, click cell C4, click the Insert Function button on the formula bar, type Date in the Search for a function text box, click Go, click Date in the Select a function list, then click OK**
   The calculations will be based on a current date of 4/1/03, the date that Jim is revising his worksheet.

Trouble?

If the year appears with four digits instead of two, your system administrator may have set a four-digit year display. You can continue with the lesson.

2. **Enter 2003 in the Year text box, enter 4 in the month text box, enter 1 in the Day text box, then click OK**
   The date appears in cell C4 as 4/1/03. The Date function uses the format DATE(year, month, day). You want to enter a formula that calculates the invoice due date, which is 30 days from the invoice date. The formula adds 30 days to the invoice date.

3. **Click cell E7, type =, click cell B7, type +30, then click the Enter button on the formula bar**
   Excel calculates the result by converting the 3/1/03 invoice date to a serial date number, adding 30 to it, then automatically formatting the result as the date 3/31/03, as shown in Figure E-8. You can use the same formula to calculate the due dates of the other invoices.

QuickTip

You can also perform time calculations in Excel. For example, you can enter an employee's starting and ending time, then calculate how long he or she worked. You must enter time in an Excel time format.

4. **Drag the fill handle to copy the formula in cell E7 into cells E8:E13**
   Relative cell referencing adjusts the copied formula to contain the appropriate cell references. Now you are ready to enter the formula that calculates the age of each invoice. You do this by subtracting the invoice date from the current date. Because each invoice age formula must refer to the current date, you must make cell C4, the current date cell, an absolute reference in the formula.

5. **Click cell F7, type =, click cell C4, press [F4] to add the absolute reference symbols ($), type -, click B7, then click**
   The formula bar displays the formula $C$4-B7. The numerical result, 31, appears in cell F7 because there are 31 days between 3/1/03 and 4/1/03. You can use the same formula to calculate the age of the remaining invoices.

QuickTip

You can also insert the current date into a worksheet by using the TODAY() function. The NOW() function inserts the current date and time into a cell.

6. **Drag the fill handle to copy the formula in F7 to the range F8:F13, then return to cell A1**
   The age of each invoice appears in column F, as shown in Figure E-9.

7. **Save the workbook**

FIGURE E-8: Worksheet with formula for invoice due date

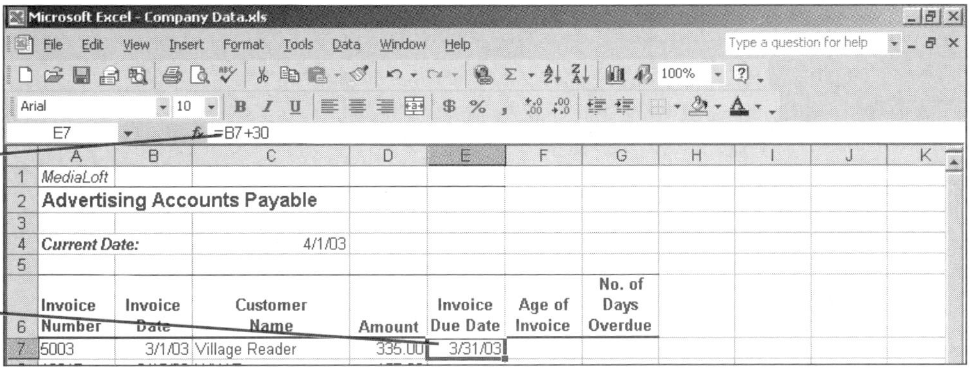

Formula is invoice date +30

Formula result automatically calculated as date

FIGURE E-9: Worksheet with copied formulas

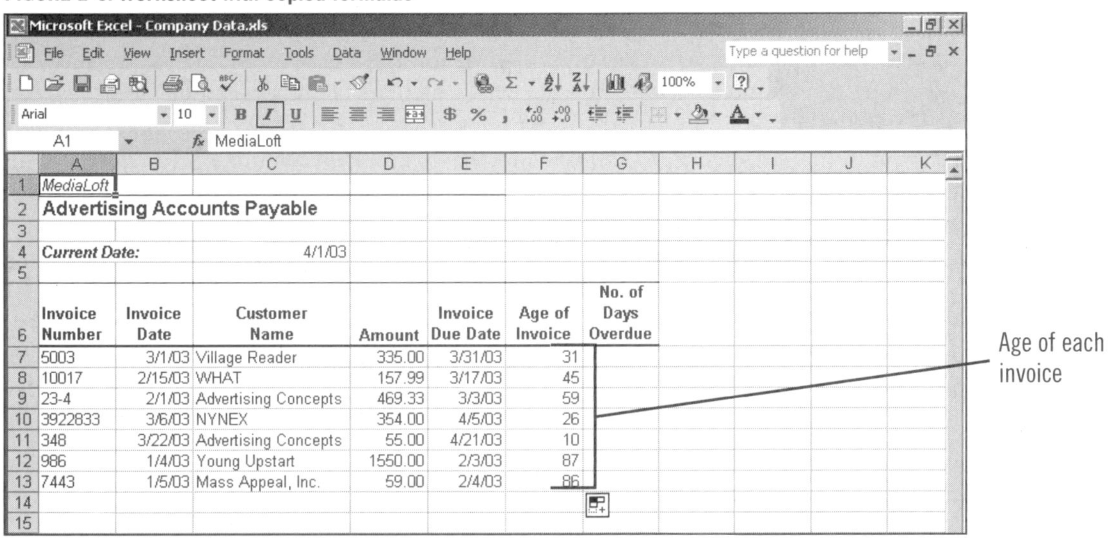

Custom number and date formats

When you use numbers and dates in worksheets or calculations, you can use built-in Excel formats or create your own. For example, 9/1/03 uses the Excel format m/d/yy, but you could change it to the format d-mmm, or 1-Sep. The value $3,789 uses the number format $#,### where # represents positive numbers. To apply number formats, click Format on the menu bar, click Cells, then click the Number tab. In the category list, click a category, then specify the exact format in the list or scroll box to the right. To create a custom format, click Custom in the category list, then click a format that resembles the one you want. In the Type box, edit the symbols until they represent the format you want, then click OK. See Figure E-10.

FIGURE E-10: Custom formats on the Number tab in the Format Cells dialog box

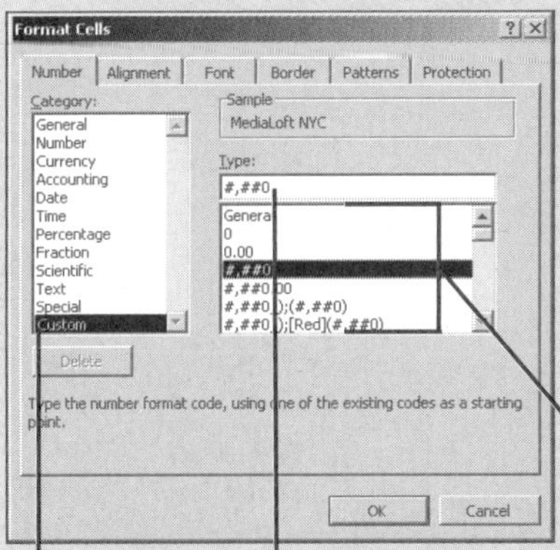

Custom formats category

Edit these symbols to customize this format

Custom formats

Excel 2002

Building a Conditional Formula with the IF Function

You can build a conditional formula using an IF function. A **conditional formula** is one that makes calculations based on stated conditions. For example, you can build a formula to calculate bonuses based on a person's performance rating. If a person is rated a 5 (the stated condition) on a scale of 1 to 5, with 5 being the highest rating, he or she receives 10% of his or her salary as a bonus; otherwise, there is no bonus. A condition that can be answered with a true or false response is called a **logical test**. The IF function has three parts, separated by commas: a condition or logical test, an action to take if the logical test or condition is true, then an action to take if the logical test or condition is false. Another way of expressing this is: IF(test_cond,do_this,else_this). Translated into an Excel IF function, the formula to calculate bonuses would look something like this: IF(Rating=5,Salary*0.10,0). The translation would be: If the rating equals 5, multiply the salary by 0.10 (the decimal equivalent of 10%), then place the result in the selected cell; if the rating does not equal 5, place a 0 in the cell. When entering the logical test portion of an IF statement, you typically use some combination of the comparison operators listed in Table E-2. You are almost finished with the invoice worksheet. To complete it, you need to use an IF function that calculates the number of days each invoice is overdue.

Steps

1. Click cell **G7**, click the **Insert Function button** on the formula bar, enter **Conditional** in the Search for a function text box, click **Go**, click **IF** in the Select a function list, then click **OK**

   You want the function to calculate the number of days overdue as follows: If the age of the invoice is greater than 30, calculate the days overdue (Age of Invoice - 30), and place the result in cell G7; otherwise, place a 0 (zero) in the cell.

2. Enter **F7>30** in the Logical_test text box

   The symbol (>) represents "greater than". So far, the formula reads: If Age of Invoice is greater than 30 (in other words, if the invoice is overdue). The next part of the function tells Excel the action to take if the invoice is over 30 days old.

3. Enter **F7-30** in the Value_if_true text box

   This part of the formula is what you want Excel to do if the logical test is true (that is, if the age of the invoice is over 30). Continuing the translation of the formula, this part means: Take the Age of Invoice value and subtract 30. The last part of the formula tells Excel the action to take if the logical test is false (that is, if the age of the invoice is 30 days or less).

4. Enter **0** in the Value_if_false text box, then click **OK**

   The function is complete, and the result, 1 (the number of days overdue), appears in cell G7. See Figure E-11.

5. Copy the formula in cell G7 into cells **G8:G13** and return to cell A1

   Compare your results with Figure E-12.

6. Save the workbook

FIGURE E-11: Worksheet with IF function

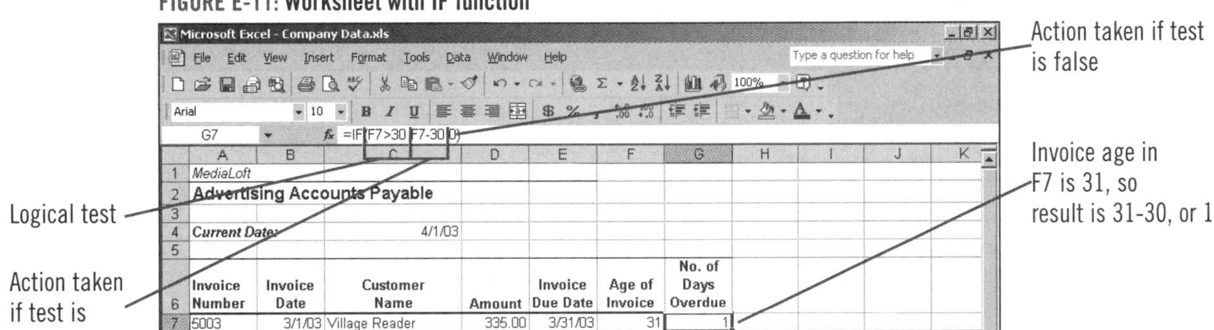

FIGURE E-12: Completed worksheet

	A	B	C	D	E	F	G
1	MediaLoft						
2	Advertising Accounts Payable						
3							
4	Current Date:		4/1/03				
5							
6	Invoice Number	Invoice Date	Customer Name	Amount	Invoice Due Date	Age of Invoice	No. of Days Overdue
7	5003	3/1/03	Village Reader	335.00	3/31/03	31	1
8	10017	2/15/03	WHAT	157.99	3/17/03	45	15
9	23-4	2/1/03	Advertising Concepts	469.33	3/3/03	59	29
10	3922833	3/6/03	NYNEX	354.00	4/5/03	26	0
11	348	3/22/03	Advertising Concepts	55.00	4/21/03	10	0
12	986	1/4/03	Young Upstart	1550.00	2/3/03	87	57
13	7443	1/5/03	Mass Appeal, Inc.	59.00	2/4/03	86	56
14							
15							

TABLE E-2: Comparison operators

operator	function	operator	function
<	Less than	<=	Less than or equal to
>	Greater than	>=	Greater than or equal to
=	Equal to	<>	Not equal to

Correcting circular references

A cell with a circular reference contains a formula that refers to its own cell location. If you accidentally enter a formula with a circular reference, a warning box will open alerting you to the problem. Click OK to display the Circular Reference toolbar or HELP to open a Help window explaining how to find the circular reference. In simple formulas, a circular reference is easy to spot. To correct it, edit the formula to remove any reference to the cell where the formula is located.

Excel 2002

Excel 2002

Using Statistical Functions

Excel offers several hundred worksheet functions. A small group of these functions calculates statistics such as averages, minimum values, and maximum values. See Table E-3 for a brief description of these commonly used functions. Now that you have experience using the Function Wizard, you'll type in a few of the more common functions. Jim wants to present summary information about open accounts payable. To do this, he asks you to add some statistical functions to the worksheet. You begin by using the MAX function to calculate the maximum value in a range.

Steps

1. **Click cell D19, type =MAX(, select range G7:G13, then press [Enter]**
   Excel automatically adds the closing parenthesis. The age of the oldest invoice (or maximum value in range G7:G13) is 57 days, as shown in cell D19. Jim needs to know the largest dollar amount among the outstanding invoices.
2. **In cell D20, type =MAX(, select range D7:D13, then press [Enter]**
   The largest outstanding invoice, of 1550.00, is shown in cell D20. The MIN function finds the smallest dollar amount and the age of the newest invoice.
3. **In cell D21, type =MIN(, select range D7:D13, then press [Enter]; in cell D22, type =MIN(, select range F7:F13, then press [Enter]**
   The smallest dollar amount owed is 55.00, as shown in cell D21, and the newest invoice is 10 days old. The COUNT function calculates the number of invoices by counting the number of entries in column A.
4. **In cell D23, click the Insert Function button on the formula bar to open the Insert Function dialog box**
5. **Click the Select a category list arrow, choose Statistical, then in the Select a function box, click COUNT**
   After selecting the function name, notice that the description of the COUNT function reads, "Counts the number of cells that contain numbers…" Because the invoice numbers are formatted in General rather than in the Number format, they are considered text entries, not numerical entries, so the COUNT function will not work. There is another function, COUNTA, that counts the number of cells that are not empty and therefore can be used to count the number of invoice number entries.
6. **Under Select a function, click COUNTA, then click OK**
   The Function Arguments dialog box opens and automatically references the range above the active cell as the first argument (in this case, range D19:D22, which is not the range you want to count). See Figure E-13. You need to select the correct range of invoice numbers.
7. **With the Value1 argument selected in the Function Arguments dialog box, click the Value1 Collapse Dialog Box button, select range A7:A13 in the worksheet, click the Redisplay Dialog Box button, click OK, then return to cell A1**
   Cell D23 confirms that there are seven invoices. Compare your worksheet with Figure E-14.
8. **Enter your name in cell A26, save the workbook, then print the worksheet**

Trouble?

If your results do not match those shown here, check your formulas and make sure you did not type a comma following each open parenthesis. The formula in cell D20, for example, should be =MAX(D7:D13).

QuickTip

If you don't see the desired function in the Function name list, scroll to display more function names.

QuickTip

Instead of using the Collaspe dialog box button, you can click the desired worksheet cell to insert a cell address.

FIGURE E-13: Formula Palette showing COUNTA function

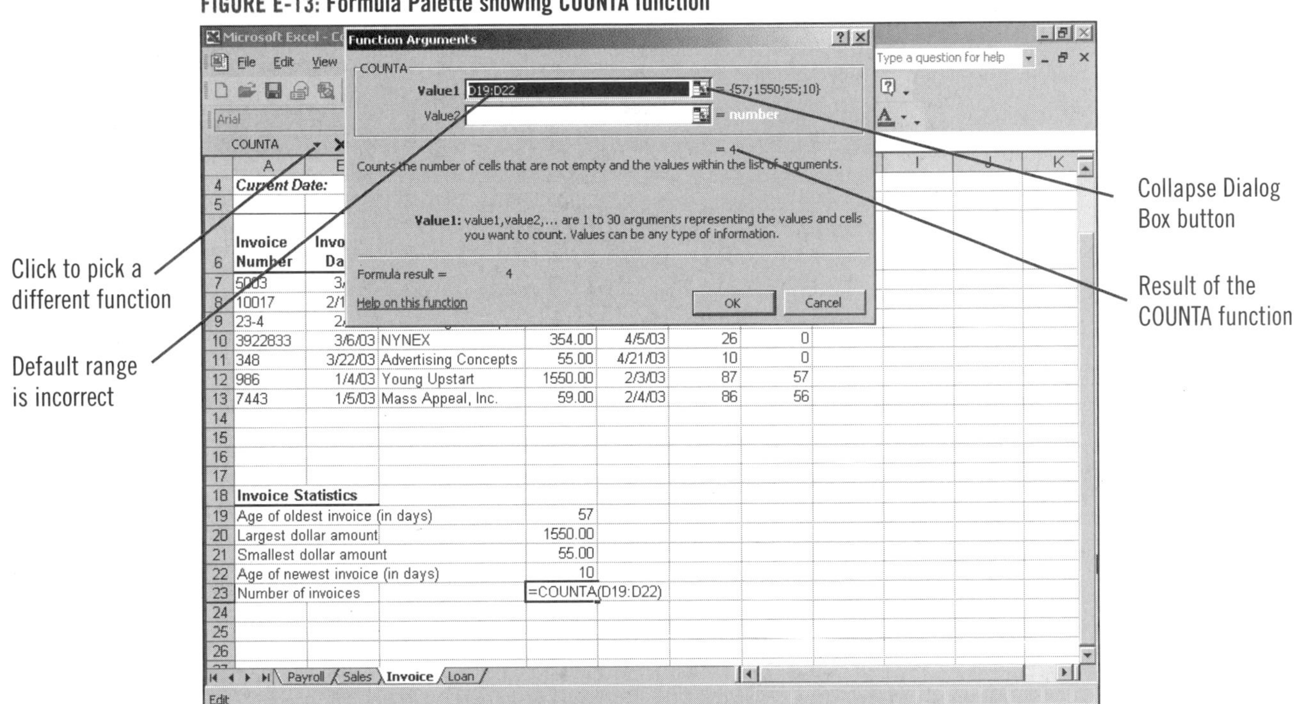

FIGURE E-14: Worksheet with invoice statistics

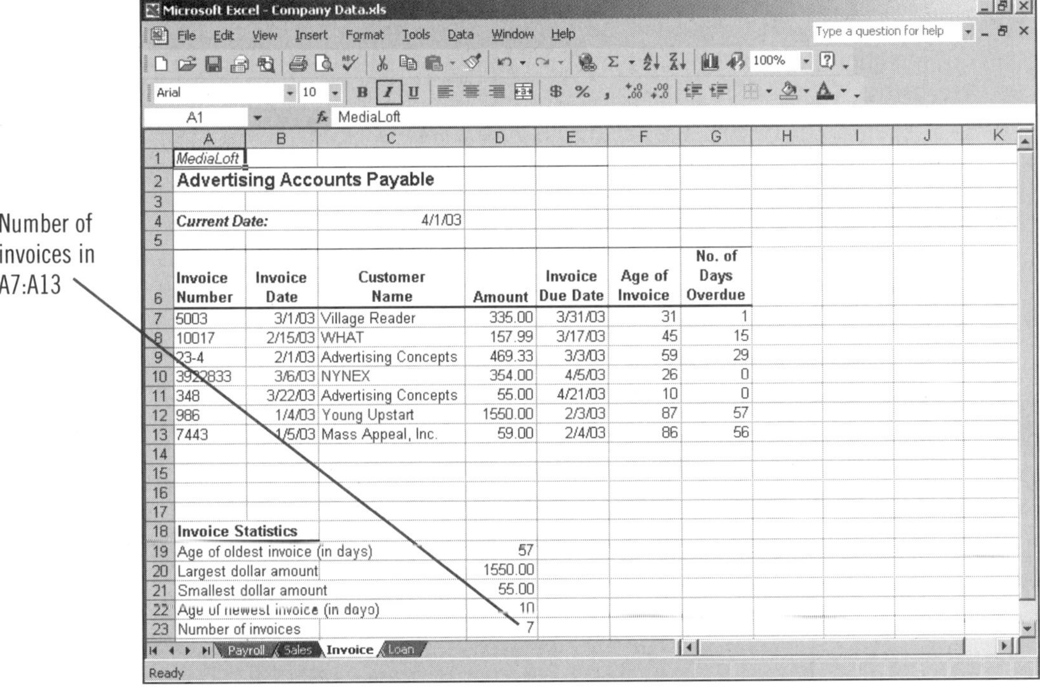

TABLE E-3: Commonly used statistical functions

function	worksheet action	function	worksheet action
AVERAGE	Calculates an average value	**MAX**	Finds the largest value
COUNT	Counts the number of values	**MIN**	Finds the smallest value
COUNTA	Counts the number of nonblank entries	**MEDIAN**	Finds the middle value

Excel 2002

Calculating Payments with the PMT Function

PMT is a financial function that calculates the periodic payment amount for money borrowed. For example, if you want to borrow money to buy a car, the PMT function can calculate your monthly payment on the loan. Let's say you want to borrow $15,000 at 8.5% interest and pay the loan off in five years. The Excel PMT function can tell you that your monthly payment will be $311.38. The parts of the PMT function are: PMT(rate, nper, pv, fv, type). See Figure E-15 for an illustration of a PMT function that calculates the monthly payment in the car loan example. For several months, MediaLoft management has been discussing the expansion of the San Diego store. Jim has obtained quotes from three different lenders on borrowing $27,000 to begin the expansion. He obtained loan quotes from a commercial bank, a venture capitalist, and an investment banker. He wants you to summarize the information, using the Excel PMT function.

1. Make the Loan sheet active, click cell **E5**, click the **Insert Function button** on the formula bar, enter **PMT** in the Search for a function text box, click **Go**, click **PMT** in the Select a function list if necessary, then click **OK**
2. Move the Function Arguments dialog box to display row 5 of the worksheet; with the cursor in the Rate text box, click cell **C5** on the worksheet, type **/12**, then press **[Tab]**
3. With the cursor in the Nper text box, click cell **D5**; click the PV text box, click cell **B5**, then click **OK**
   You must divide the annual interest by 12 because you are calculating monthly, not annual, payments. The FV and Type are optional arguments. Note that the payment of ($587.05) in cell E5 appears in red, indicating that it is a negative amount. Excel displays the result of a PMT function as a negative value to reflect the negative cash flow the loan represents to the borrower. To show the monthly payment as a positive number, you place a minus sign in front of the PV cell reference in the function.

QuickTip

You must be consistent about the units you use for rate and nper. If you express nper as the number of monthly payments, then you must express the interest rate as a monthly rate.

4. Edit cell E5 so it reads **=PMT(C5/12,D5,-B5)**, then click
   A positive value of $587.05 now appears in cell E5. See Figure E-16. You can use the same formula to generate the monthly payments for the other loans.
5. With cell **E5** selected, drag the fill handle to fill the range **E6:E7**
   A monthly payment of $883.95 for the venture capitalist loan appears in cell E6. A monthly payment of $1,270.98 for the investment banker loan appears in cell E7. The loans with shorter terms have much higher payments. You will not know the entire financial picture until you calculate the total payments and total interest for each lender.

QuickTip

You can cut, copy, and paste functions from one worksheet area to another or from one workbook to another.

6. Click cell **F5**, type **=E5*D5**, then press **[Tab]**; in cell G5, type **=F5-B5**, then click
7. Copy the formulas in cells F5:G5 into the range **F6:G7**, then return to cell **A1**
   You can experiment with different interest rates, loan amounts, or terms for any one of the lenders; the PMT function generates a new set of values automatically. Compare your results with those in Figure E-17.
8. Enter your name in cell A13, save the workbook, then preview and print the worksheet

FIGURE E-15: Example of PMT function for car loan

PMT(.085/12,60,15000) = $311.38

FIGURE E-16: PMT function calculating monthly loan payment

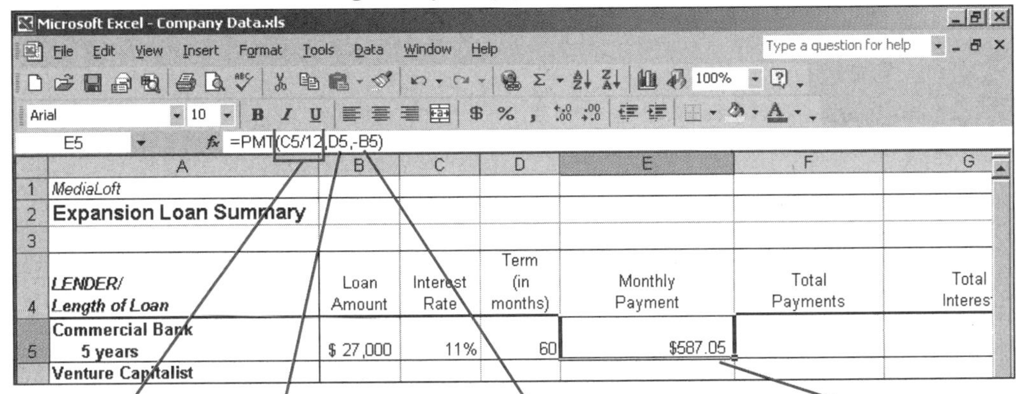

FIGURE E-17: Completed worksheet

	A	B	C	D	E	F	G
1	*MediaLoft*						
2	**Expansion Loan Summary**						
3							
4	*LENDER/ Length of Loan*	Loan Amount	Interest Rate	Term (in months)	Monthly Payment	Total Payments	Total Interest
5	**Commercial Bank 5 years**	$ 27,000	11%	60	$587.05	$ 35,222.73	$ 8,222.73
6	**Venture Capitalist 3 years**	$ 27,000	11%	36	$883.95	$ 31,822.03	$ 4,822.03
7	**Investment Banker 2 years**	$ 27,000	12%	24	$1,270.98	$ 30,503.61	$ 3,503.61

Calculating future value with the FV function

You can use the FV (Future Value) function to determine the amount of money a given monthly investment will amount to, at a given interest rate after a given number of payment periods. The syntax is similar to that of the PMT function: FV(rate,nper,pmt,pv,type). For example, suppose you want to invest $1,000 every month for the next 12 months into an account that pays 12% a year, and you want to know how much you will have at the end of 12 months (that is, its future value). You would enter the function FV(.01,12,-1000), and Excel would return the value $12,682.50 as the future value of your investment. As with the PMT function, the units for the rate and nper must be consistent. If you made monthly payments on a three-year loan at 6% annual interest, you would use the rate .06/12 and 36 periods (12*3). The arguments pv and type are optional; pv is the present value, or the total amount the series of payments is worth now. If you omit it, Excel assumes the pv is 0. The "type" argument indicates when the payments are made; 0 is the end of the period, and 1 is the beginning of the period.

Excel 2002

Displaying and Printing Formula Contents

Excel usually displays the result of formula calculations in the worksheet area and displays formula contents for the active cell in the formula bar. However, you can instruct Excel to display the formulas directly in the worksheet cells in which they were entered. You can document worksheet formulas by first displaying the formulas, then printing them. These formula printouts are valuable paper-based worksheet documentation. Because formulas are often longer than their corresponding values, landscape orientation is the best choice for printing formulas. Jim wants you to produce a formula printout to submit with the worksheet.

Steps 1 2 3 4

1. **Click Tools on the menu bar, click Options, then click the View tab**
   The View tab of the Options dialog box appears, as shown in Figure E-18.
2. **Under Window options, click the Formulas check box to select it, then click OK**
   The columns widen and retain their original formats.
3. **Scroll horizontally to bring columns E through G into view**
   Instead of displaying formula results in the cells, Excel shows the actual formulas and automatically adjusts the column widths to accommodate them.
4. **Click the Print Preview button on the Standard toolbar**
   The status bar reads Preview: Page 1 of 2, indicating that the worksheet will print on two pages. You want to print it on one page and include the row number and column letter headings.
5. **Click Setup in the Print Preview window, then click the Page tab**
6. **Under Orientation, click the Landscape option button; then under Scaling, click the Fit to option button and note that the wide and tall check boxes contain the number "1".**
   Selecting Landscape instructs Excel to print the worksheet sideways on the page. The Fit to option ensures that the document is printed on a single page.
7. **Click the Sheet tab, under Print click the Row and column headings check box to select it, click OK, then position the Zoom pointer over column A and click**
   The worksheet formulas now appear on a single page, in landscape orientation, with row (number) and column (letter) headings. See Figure E-19.
8. **Click Print in the Print Preview window, then click OK**
   After you retrieve the printout, you want to return the worksheet to displaying formula results. You can do this easily by using a key combination.
9. **Press [Ctrl][`] to redisplay formula results**
   [Ctrl][`] (grave accent mark) toggles between displaying formula results and displaying formula contents.
10. **Save the workbook, then close it and exit Excel**
   The completed figure for the payroll worksheet is displayed in Figure E-3; the completed sales worksheet is displayed in Figure E-7; and the completed invoice worksheet is shown in Figure E-14.

QuickTip

Move the Formula Auditing toolbar if necessary.

QuickTip

All Page Setup options—such as Landscape orientation, Fit to scaling—apply to the active worksheet and are saved with the workbook.

QuickTip

To print row and column labels on every page of a multiple-page worksheet, click the Sheet tab, and fill in the Rows to repeat at top and the Columns to repeat at left in the Print titles section.

FIGURE E-18: View tab of the Options dialog box

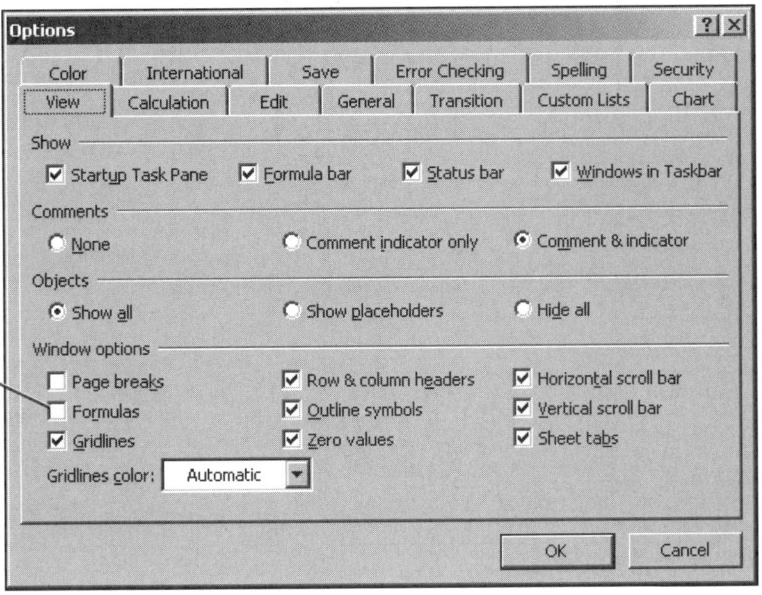

Options

Color | International | Save | Error Checking | Spelling | Security
View | Calculation | Edit | General | Transition | Custom Lists | Chart

Show

Startup Task Pane | Formula bar | Status bar | Windows in Taskbar

Comments

None | Comment indicator only | Comment & indicator

Objects

Show all | Show placeholders | Hide all

Window options

Page breaks | Row & column headers | Horizontal scroll bar

Formulas | Outline symbols | Vertical scroll bar

Gridlines | Zero values | Sheet tabs

Gridlines color: Automatic

OK | Cancel

Select this option to view formulas

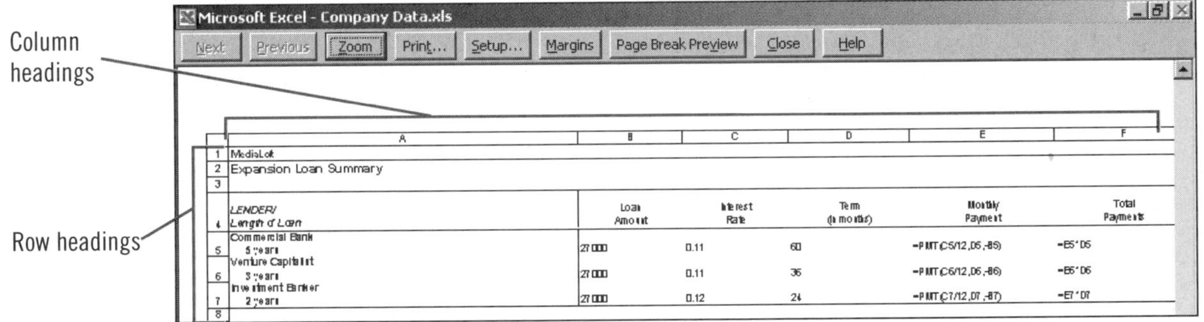

FIGURE E-19: Print Preview window

Setting margins and alignment when printing part of a worksheet

CLUES TO USE

You can set custom margins to print smaller sections of a worksheet. Select the range you want to print, click File on the menu bar, click Print, under Print what click Selection, then click Preview. In the Print Preview window, click Setup, then click the Margins tab. See Figure E-20. Double-click the margin numbers and type new ones. Use the Center on page check boxes to center the range horizontally or vertically. If you plan to print the range again, save the view after you print: Click View on the menu bar, click Custom Views, click Add, then type a view name and click OK.

FIGURE E-20: Margins tab in the Page Setup dialog box

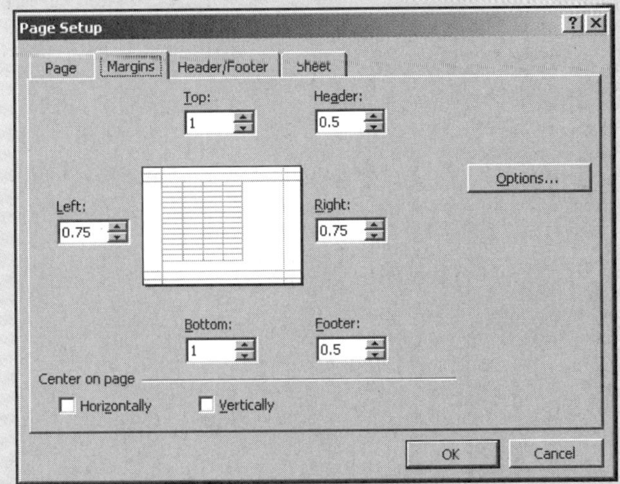

Practice

► Concepts Review

Label each element of the Excel screen shown in Figure E-21.

FIGURE E-21

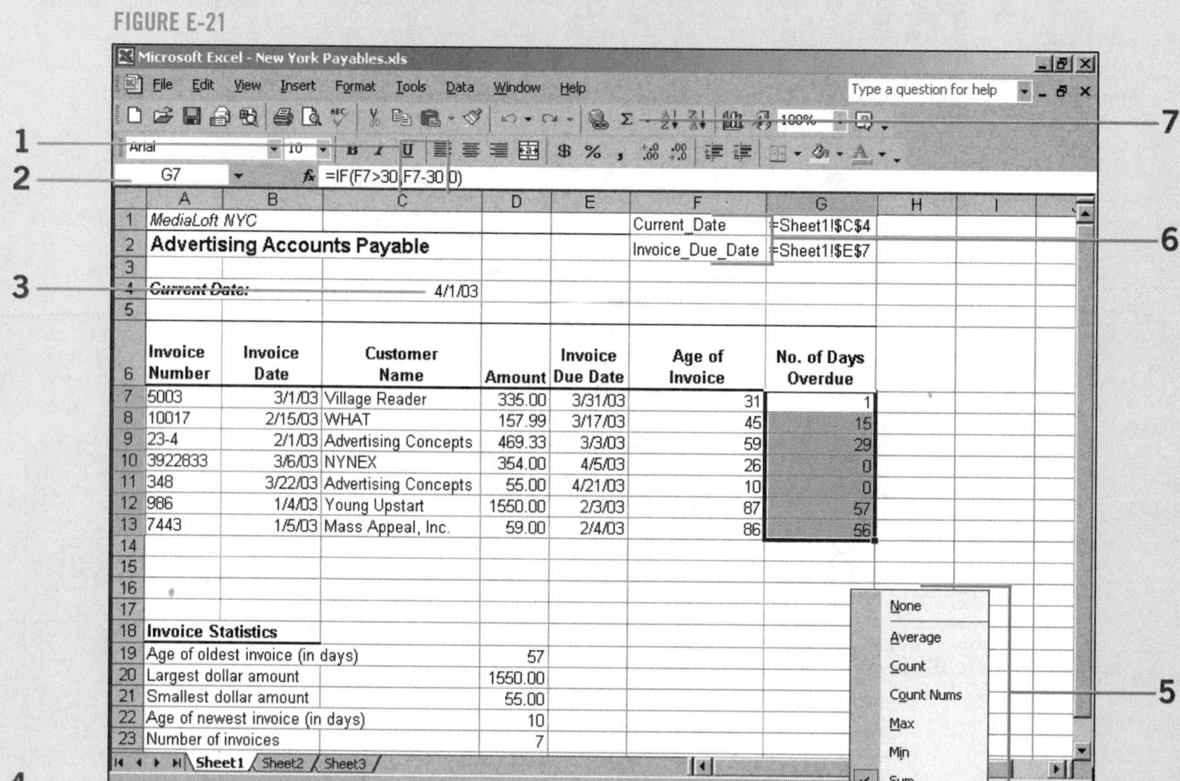

Match each term with the statement that best describes its function.

8. Style
9. COUNTA
10. test_cond
11. COUNT
12. pv

a. Part of the IF function in which the conditions are stated
b. Function used to count the number of numerical entries
c. Part of the PMT function that represents the loan amount
d. Function used to count the number of nonblank entries
e. A combination of formatting characteristics

Select the best answer from the list of choices.

13. To generate a positive payment value when using the PMT function, you must:
- **a.** Enter the function arguments as positive values.
- **b.** Enter the function arguments as negative values.
- **c.** Enter the amount being borrowed as a negative value.
- **d.** Enter the interest rate divisor as a negative value.

14. When you enter the rate and nper arguments in a PMT function, you must:
- **a.** Multiply both units by 12.
- **b.** Be consistent in the units used.
- **c.** Divide both values by 12.
- **d.** Use monthly units instead of annual units.

15. To express conditions such as less than or equal to, you can use a(n):
- **a.** IF function.
- **b.** Comparison operator.
- **c.** AutoCalculate formula.
- **d.** PMT function.

16. Which of the following statements is false?
- **a.** $#,### is an Excel number format.
- **b.** You can create custom number and date formats in Excel.
- **c.** You can use only existing number and date formats in Excel.
- **d.** m/d/yy is an Excel date format.

Skills Review

1. Create a formula with several operators.
- **a.** Start Excel, open the Project File EX E-2 from the drive and folder where your Project Files are stored, then save the workbook as **Manager Bonuses**.
- **b.** On the Bonuses worksheet, select cell **C15** using the Go To command.
- **c.** Enter the formula **C13+(C14*7)**.
- **d.** Use the Paste Special command to paste the values and formats in B4:B10 to G4:G10, then save your work.

2. Use names in a formula.
- **a.** Name cell C13 **Dept_Bonus**.
- **b.** Name cell C14 **Project_Bonus**.
- **c.** Select the range **C4:C10** and name it **Base_Pay**.
- **d.** In cell E4, enter the formula **Dept_Bonus*D4+Project_Bonus**.
- **e.** Copy the formula in cell E4 into the range E5:E10.
- **f.** Format range E4:E10 with the Comma style, using the Style dialog box.
- **g.** Select the range **E4:E10** and name it **Bonus_Total**.
- **h.** In cell F4, enter a formula that sums Base_Pay and Bonus_Total.
- **i.** Copy the formula in cell F4 into the range F5:F10.
- **j.** Format range F4:F10 with the Comma style, using the Style dialog box.
- **k.** Save your work.

3. **Generate multiple totals with AutoSum.**
   a. Select range **E4:F11**.
   b. Enter the totals using AutoSum.
   c. Format range E11:F11 with the Currency style, using the Style dialog box.
   d. Enter your name in cell A18, save your work, then preview and print this worksheet.

4. **Use dates in calculations.**
   a. Make the Merit Pay sheet active.
   b. In cell D6, enter the formula **B6+183**.
   c. Copy the formula in cell D6 into the range D7:D14.
   d. Use the NOW function to insert the date and time in cell A3, widening the column as necessary.
   e. In cell E18, enter the text **Next Pay Date**, and, in cell G18, use the Date function to enter the date **10/1/03**. (*Hint*: You must enter the year as 2003. You can format it as a two-digit year using the Modify button on the Style dialog box and choosing Date in the Category list on the Number tab.)
   f. Save your work.

5. **Build a conditional formula with the IF function.**
   a. In cell F6, use the Function Wizard to enter the formula **IF(C6=5,E6*0.05,0)**.
   b. Copy the formula in cell F6 into the range F7:F14.
   c. Apply the comma format with no decimal places to F6:F14.
   d. Select the range **A4:G4** and delete the cells, using the Delete command on the Edit menu. Shift the remaining cells up.
   e. Repeat the procedure to delete the cells A15:G15.
   f. Use the Cells command on the Insert menu to insert a cell between Department Statistics and Average Salary, moving the remaining cells down.
   g. Check your formulas to make sure the cell references have been updated.
   h. Save your work.

6. **Use statistical functions.**
   a. In cell C18, enter a function to calculate the average salary in the range E5:E13 with no decimal places. Use dragging to select the cells.
   b. In cell C19, enter a function to calculate the largest bonus in the range F5:F13.
   c. In cell C20, enter a function to calculate the lowest performance rating in the range C5:C13.
   d. In cell C21, enter a function to calculate the number of entries in range A5:A13.
   e. Enter your name into cell A28, then save, preview, and print the worksheet.

7. **Calculate payments with the PMT function.**
   a. Make the Loan sheet active.
   b. In cell B9, use the Function Wizard to enter the formula **PMT(B5/12,B6,-B4)**.
   c. In cell B10, enter the formula **B9*B6**.
   d. AutoFit column B, if necessary.
   e. In cell B11, enter the formula **B10-B4**.
   f. Enter your name in cell A15, then save, preview, and print the worksheet.

8. **Display and print formula contents.**
   a. Use the View tab in the Options dialog box to display formulas.
   b. Adjust the column widths as necessary.
   c. Save, preview, and print this worksheet in landscape orientation with the row and column headings.
   d. Redisplay the formula results in the worksheet.
   e. Close the workbook, then exit Excel.

► Independent Challenge 1

As manager of Mike's Ice Cream Parlor, you have been asked to create a worksheet that totals the monthly sales of all store products. Your monthly report should include the following:

- Sales totals for the current month for each product
- Sales totals for the last month for each product
- The percent change in sales from last month to this month

To document the report further, you decide to include a printout of the worksheet formulas.

a. Start Excel, open the Project File EX E-3 from the drive and folder where your Project Files are stored, then save it as **Mike's Sales**.
b. Use the TODAY function to enter today's date in cell A3. Create and apply a custom format for the date entry.
c. Complete the headings for weeks 2 through 4. Enter totals for each week, and current month totals for each product. Calculate the percent change in sales from last month to this month. (*Hint*: The formula in words would be (Current Month-Last Month)/Last Month.)
d. After you enter the percent change formula for regular ice cream, copy the formula down the column and format the column with the Percent style.
e. Apply a comma format with no decimal places to all numbers and totals.
f. Enter your name into cell A15, then save, preview, and print the worksheet on a single page. If necessary, print in landscape orientation. If you make any page setup changes, save the worksheet again.
g. Display and print the worksheet formulas, then print the formulas on one page with row and column headings.
h. Close the workbook without saving the changes for displaying formulas, then exit Excel.

► Independent Challenge 2

You are an auditor with a certified public accounting firm. Fly Away, a manufacturer of skating products, has contacted you to audit its financial records. The management at Fly Away is considering opening a branch in Great Britain and needs its records audited to prepare the business plan. The managers at Fly Away have asked you to assist them in preparing their year-end sales summary as part of this audit. Specifically, they want to add expenses and show the percent of annual expenses that each expense category represents. They also want to show what percent of annual sales each expense category represents. You should include a formula calculating the difference between sales and expenses and another formula calculating expenses divided by sales. The expense categories and their respective dollar amounts are as follows: Building Lease $46,000; Equipment $208,000; Office $25,000; Salary $355,000; Taxes $310,000. Use these expense amounts to prepare the year-end sales and expenses summary for Fly Away.

a. Start Excel, open the Project File EX E-4 from the drive and folder where your Project Files are stored, then save the workbook as **Fly Away Sales**.
b. Name the cell containing the formula for total annual expenses **Annual_Expenses**. Use the name Annual_Expenses in cell C12 to create a formula calculating percent of annual expenses. Copy this formula as appropriate and apply the Percent style. Make sure to include a formula that sums all the values for percent of annual expenses, which should equal 100%.

c. Enter a formula calculating the percent of annual sales each expense category represents. Use the name **Annual_Sales** in the formula and format it appropriately. Copy this formula as appropriate and apply the Percent style. Make sure to include a formula that sums all the values for percent of annual sales.
d. Enter the formula calculating Net Profit, using the names Annual_Sales and Annual_Expenses.
e. Enter the formula for Expenses as a percent of sales, using the names Annual_Sales and Annual_Expenses.
f. Format the cells using the Currency, Percent, or Comma style as appropriate. Widen the columns as necessary to display cell contents.
g. Set the top and bottom margins at 4 inches and center the worksheet horizontally so the worksheet will print on two pages. *(Hint:* Use the Margins tab on the Page Setup dialog box.)
h. Print the first row containing the company name on each page. (*Hint*: Use the Sheet tab on the Page Setup dialog box and specify row 1 to repeat at the top.)
i. Enter your name into cell A22, then save, preview, and print the worksheet. Save any page setup changes you make.
j. Close the workbook then exit Excel.

▶ Independent Challenge 3

As the owner of Custom Fit, a general contracting firm specializing in home-storage projects, you are facing yet another business challenge at your firm. Because jobs are taking longer than expected, you decide to take out a loan to purchase some new power tools. According to your estimates, you need a $7,000 loan to purchase the tools. You check three loan sources: the Small Business Administration (SBA), your local bank, and a consortium of investors. The SBA will lend you the money at 8% interest, but you have to pay it off in three years. The local bank offers you the loan at 8.75% interest over four years. The consortium offers you a 7.75% loan, but they require you to pay it back in two years. To analyze all three loan options, you decide to build a tool loan summary worksheet. Using the loan terms provided, build a worksheet summarizing your options.

a. Start Excel, open a new workbook, then save it as **Custom Fit Loan Options** in the drive and folder where your Project Files are stored.
b. Enter today's date in cell A3, using the TODAY function.
c. Enter labels and worksheet data. You need headings for the loan source, loan amount, interest rate, term or number of payments, monthly payment, total payments, and total interest. Fill in the data provided for the three loan sources.
d. Enter formulas as appropriate: a PMT formula for the monthly payment, a formula calculating the total payments based on the monthly payment and term values, and a formula for total interest based on the total payments and the loan amount.
e. Format the worksheet as desired.
f. Enter your name in cell A14, then save, preview, and print the worksheet on a single page using landscape orientation. Print the worksheet formulas showing row and column headings. Do not save the worksheet with the formula settings.
g. Close the workbook then exit Excel.

Independent Challenge 4

The MediaLoft management wants to start IRAs for its employees. The company plans to deposit $2,000 in the employees' accounts at the beginning of each year. You have been asked to research current rates at financial institutions. You will use the Web to find this information.

a. Go to the Alta Vista search engine at www.altavista.com and enter "IRA rates" in the Search box. You can also use Yahoo, Excite, Infoseek or another search engine of your choice. Find IRA rates offered by three institutions for a $2,000 deposit, then write down the institution name, the rate, and the minimum deposit in the table below.

b. Start Excel, open a new workbook, then save it as **IRA Rates** in the drive and folder where your Project Files are stored.

c. Enter the column headings, row headings, and, research results from the table below into your IRA Rates workbook.

IRA WORKSHEET

Institution	Rate	Minimum Deposit	Number of Years	Amount Deposited (Yearly)	Future Value
			35	2000	
			35	2000	
			35	2000	
Highest Rate					
Average Rate					
Highest Future Value					

d. Use the FV function to calculate the future value of a $2,000 yearly deposit over 35 years for each institution, making sure it displays as a positive number. Assume that the payments are made at the beginning of the period, so the Type argument equals 1.

e. Use Excel functions to enter the highest rate, the average rate, and the highest future value into the workbook.

f. Enter your name in cell A15, then save, preview, and print the worksheet on a single page.

g. Display and print the formulas for the worksheet on a single page using landscape orientation. Do not save the worksheet with the formulas displayed.

h. Close the workbook then exit Excel.

Visual Workshop

Create the worksheet shown in Figure E-22. (Hint: Enter the items in range C9:C11 as labels by typing an apostrophe before each formula.) Enter your name in row 15, and save the workbook as **Car Payment Calculator**. Preview, then print, the worksheet.

FIGURE E-22

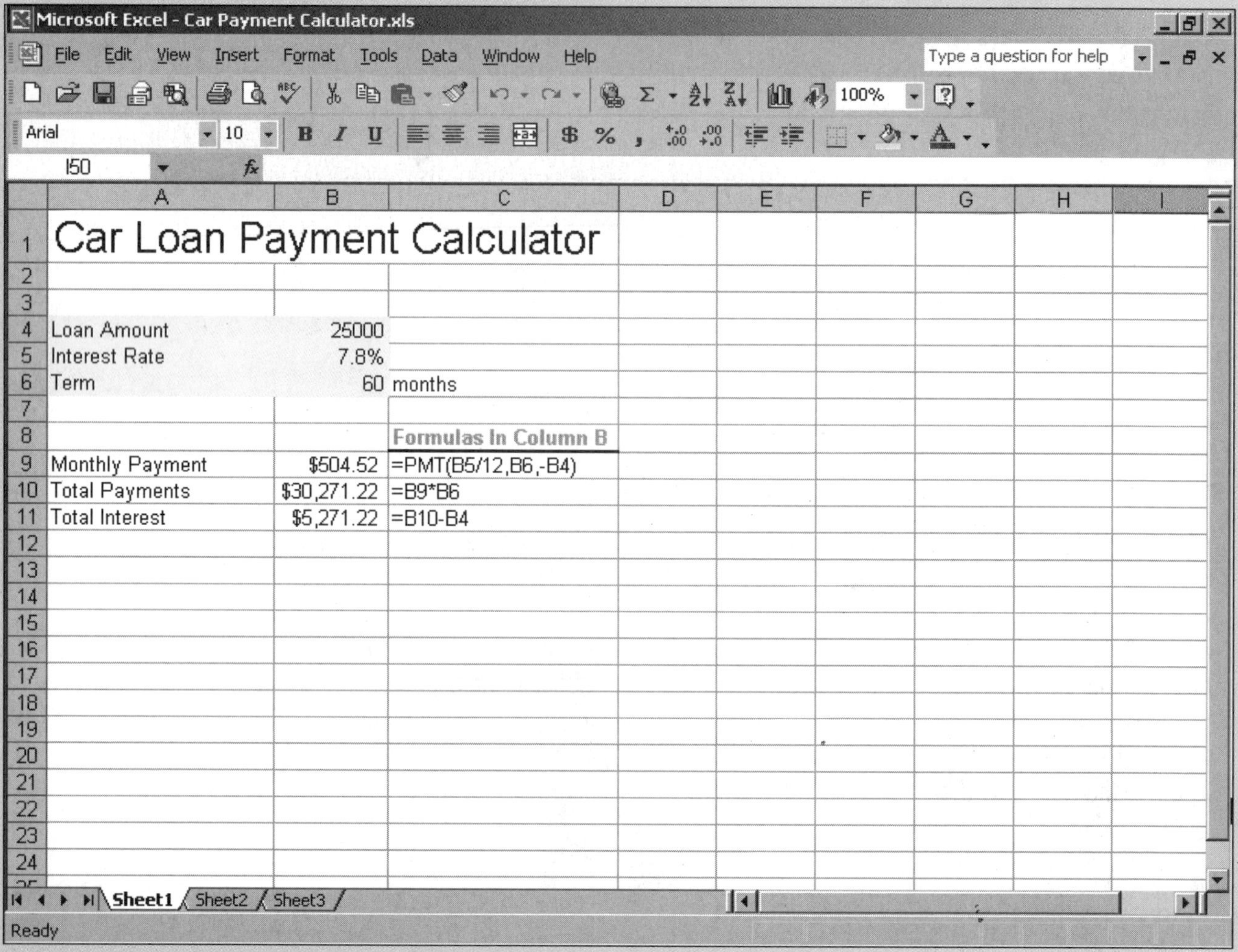

Microsoft Excel - Car Payment Calculator.xls

File Edit View Insert Format Tools Data Window Help | Type a question for help

Arial | 10 | 100%

I50

	A	B	C	D	E	F	G	H	I
1	Car Loan Payment Calculator								
2									
3									
4	Loan Amount	25000							
5	Interest Rate	7.8%							
6	Term	60	months						
7									
8			**Formulas In Column B**						
9	Monthly Payment	$504.52	=PMT(B5/12,B6,-B4)						
10	Total Payments	$30,271.22	=B9*B6						
11	Total Interest	$5,271.22	=B10-B4						
12									
13									
14									
15									
16									
17									
18									
19									
20									
21									
22									
23									
24									

Sheet1 / Sheet2 / Sheet3

Ready

Managing

Workbooks and Preparing Them for the Web

Objectives

- MOUS ► Freeze columns and rows
- MOUS ► Insert and delete worksheets
- MOUS ► Consolidate data with 3-D references
- MOUS ► Hide and protect worksheet areas
- MOUS ► Save custom views of a worksheet
- ► Control page breaks and page numbering
- MOUS ► Create a hyperlink between Excel files
- MOUS ► Save an Excel file as a Web page

In this unit you will learn several Excel features to help you manage and print workbook data. You will also learn how to prepare workbooks for publication on the World Wide Web. MediaLoft's accounting department asks Jim Fernandez to design a timecard summary worksheet to track salary costs for hourly workers. He asks you to design a worksheet using some employees from the MediaLoft Houston store. When the worksheet is complete, the accounting department will add the rest of the employees and place it on the MediaLoft intranet site for review by store managers. Jim wants you to save the worksheet in HTML format for viewing on the site.

Excel 2002

Freezing Columns and Rows

As rows and columns fill up with data, you might need to scroll through the worksheet to add, delete, modify, and view information. Looking at information without row or column labels can be confusing. In Excel, you can temporarily freeze columns and rows, which enables you to view separate areas of your worksheets at the same time. **Panes** are the columns and rows that **freeze**, or remain in place, while you scroll through your worksheet. Freezing rows and columns is especially useful when you're dealing with large worksheets. Jim needs to verify the total hours worked, hourly pay rate, and total pay for salespeople Paul Cristifano and Virginia Young. Because the worksheet is becoming more difficult to read as its size increases, Jim wants you to freeze the column and row labels.

1. **Start Excel if necessary, open the Project File EX F-1 from the drive and folder where your Project Files are stored, then save it as Timecard Summary**
2. **Scroll through the Monday worksheet to view the data, then click cell D6**
   You move to cell D6 because Excel freezes the columns to the left and the rows above the cell pointer. You want to freeze columns A, B, and C as well as rows 1 through 5. By doing so, you will be able to see each employee's last name, first name, and timecard number on the screen when you scroll to the right, and you will also be able to read the labels in rows 1 through 5.
3. **Click Window on the menu bar, then click Freeze Panes**
   A thin line appears along the column border to the left of the active cell, and another line appears along the row above the active cell, indicating that columns A through C and rows 1 through 5 are frozen.
4. **Scroll to the right until columns A through C and L through O are visible**
   Because columns A, B, and C are frozen, they remain on the screen; columns D through K are temporarily hidden from view. Notice that the information you are looking for in row 13 (last name, total hours, hourly pay rate, and total pay for Paul Cristifano) is readily available. Paul's data appears to be correct, but you still need to verify Virginia Young's information.
5. **Scroll down until row 26 is visible**
   In addition to columns A through C, rows 1 through 5 remain on the screen. See Figure F-1. Jim jots down the information for Virginia Young. Even though a pane is frozen, you can click in the frozen area of the worksheet and edit the contents of the cells there, if necessary.
6. **Press [Ctrl][Home]**
   Because the panes are frozen, the cell pointer moves to cell D6, not A1.
7. **Click Window on the menu bar, then click Unfreeze Panes**
   The panes are unfrozen.
8. **Return to cell A1, then save the workbook**

FIGURE F-1: Scrolled worksheet with frozen rows and columns

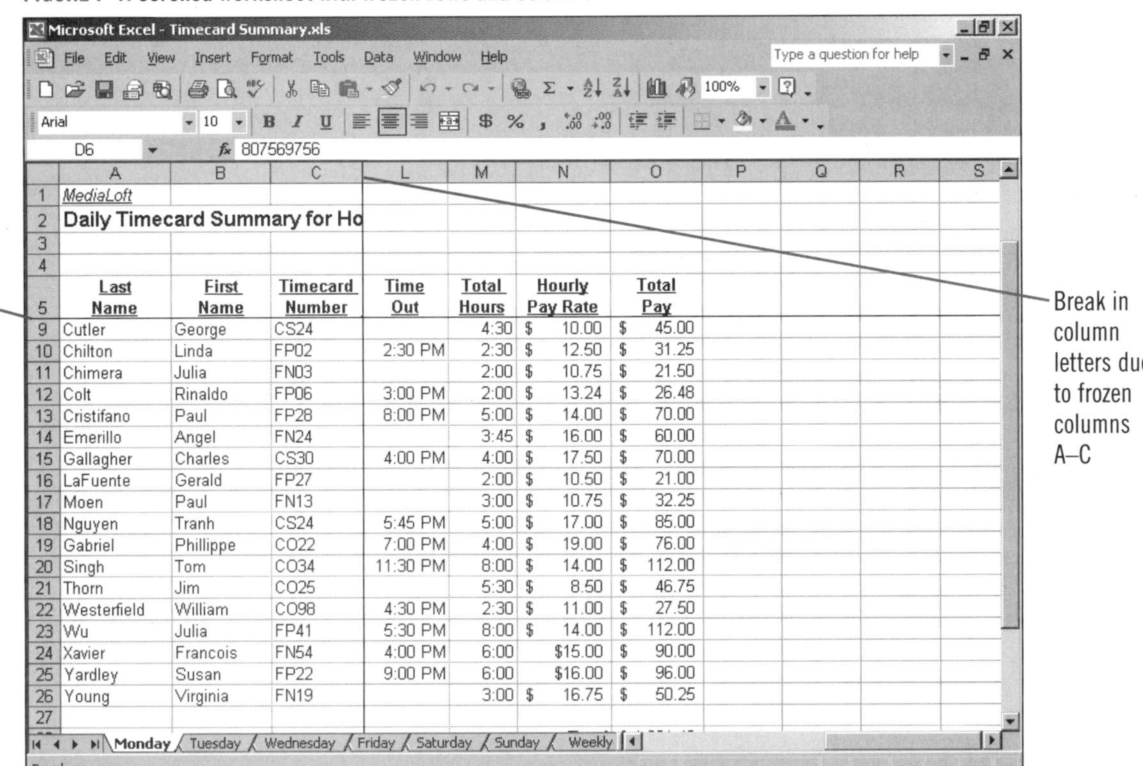

Splitting the worksheet into multiple panes

Excel provides a way to split the worksheet area into vertical and/or horizontal panes, so that you can click inside any one pane and scroll to locate information in that pane while the other panes remain in place. See Figure F-2. To split a worksheet area into multiple panes, drag the split box (the small box at the top of the vertical scroll bar or at the right end of the horizontal scroll bar) in the direction you want the split to appear. To remove the split, move the mouse over the split until the pointer changes to a double pointed arrow ╪, then double-click.

FIGURE F-2: Worksheet split into two horizontal panes

Upper pane

Lower pane

Horizontal split box

Vertical split box

Inserting and Deleting Worksheets

You can insert and delete worksheets in a workbook at any time. For example, because new workbooks open with only three sheets available (Sheet1, Sheet2, and Sheet3), you need to insert at least one more sheet if you want to have four quarterly worksheets in an annual financial budget workbook. You can do this by using commands on the menu bar or shortcut menu. Jim was in a hurry when he added the sheet tabs to the Timecard Summary workbook. He wants you to insert a sheet for Thursday and delete the sheet for Sunday because Houston workers do not work on Sundays.

Steps 1 2 3 4

QuickTip

You can copy a selected worksheet by clicking Edit on the menu bar, then clicking Move or Copy Sheet. Choose the sheet the copy will precede, then select the Create a copy check box.

1. Click the **Friday sheet tab**, click **Insert** on the menu bar, then click **Worksheet**
   Excel inserts a new sheet tab labeled Sheet1 to the left of the Friday sheet.
2. Double-click the Sheet1 tab and rename it **Thursday**
   Now the tabs read Monday, Tuesday, Wednesday, Thursday, Friday, and Saturday. The tab for the Weekly Summary is not visible. You still need to delete the Sunday worksheet.
3. Right-click the **Sunday sheet tab**, then click **Delete** on the shortcut menu shown in Figure F-3
   The shortcut menu allows you to insert, delete, rename, move, or copy sheets; select all the sheets; change tab color; and view any Visual Basic programming code in a worksheet.
4. Move the mouse pointer over any tab scrolling button, then right-click
   Excel opens a menu of the worksheets in the active workbook. Compare your list with Figure F-4.
5. Return to the Monday sheet, then save the workbook

QuickTip

You can scroll several tabs at once by pressing [Shift] while clicking one of the middle tab scrolling buttons.

Previewing and printing multiple worksheets

To preview and print multiple worksheets, press and hold down [Ctrl] and click the tabs for the sheets you want to print, then click the Preview or Print button. In Print Preview, the multiple worksheets will appear as separate pages in the Preview window, which you can display by clicking Next and Previous. To preview and print an entire workbook, click File on the menu bar, click Print, click to select the Entire Workbook option button, then click Preview. In the Preview window, you can page through the entire workbook. (Blank worksheets will not appear as pages in Print Preview.) When you click Print, the entire workbook will print.

FIGURE F-3: **Worksheet shortcut menu**

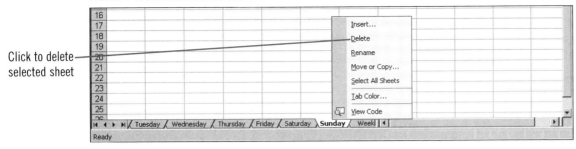

Click to delete selected sheet

Insert...
Delete
Rename
Move or Copy...
Select All Sheets
Tab Color...
View Code

Tuesday / Wednesday / Thursday / Friday / Saturday / Sunday / Week
Ready

FIGURE F-4: **Workbook with worksheets menu**

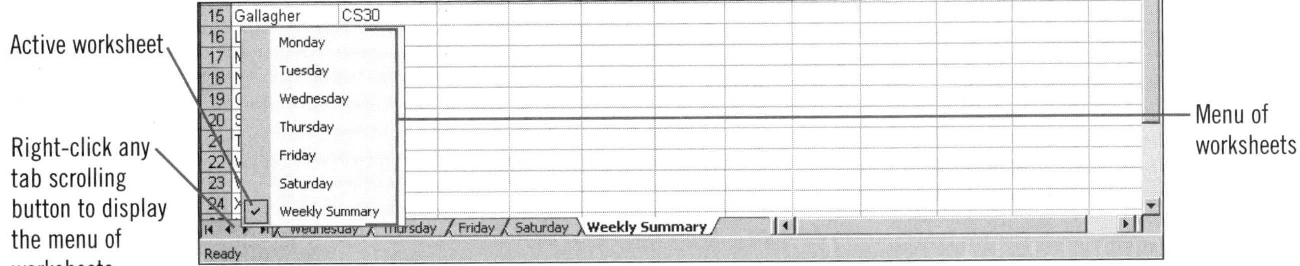

CLUES TO USE

Specifying headers and footers

As you prepare a workbook for others to view, it is helpful to provide as much data as possible about the worksheets such as the number of pages, who created it, and when. You can do this easily in a **header** or **footer**, information that prints at the top or bottom of each printed page. Headers and footers are visible on the screen only in Print Preview. To add a header, for example, click View on the menu bar, click Header and Footer, then click Custom Header. You will see a dialog box similar to that in Figure F-5. Both the header and the footer are divided into three sections, and you can enter information in any or all of them. You can type information, such as your name, and click the icons to enter the page number, total pages, date, time, file path, filename or sheet name. You can insert a picture by clicking the Insert Picture icon, and you can format the picture by clicking the Format picture icon and selecting formatting options. When you click an icon, Excel inserts a symbol in the footer section containing an ampersand (&) and the element name in brackets. When you are finished, click OK, click the Print Preview button on the Header/Footer tab to see your header and footer, then click Close.

FIGURE F-5: **Header dialog box**

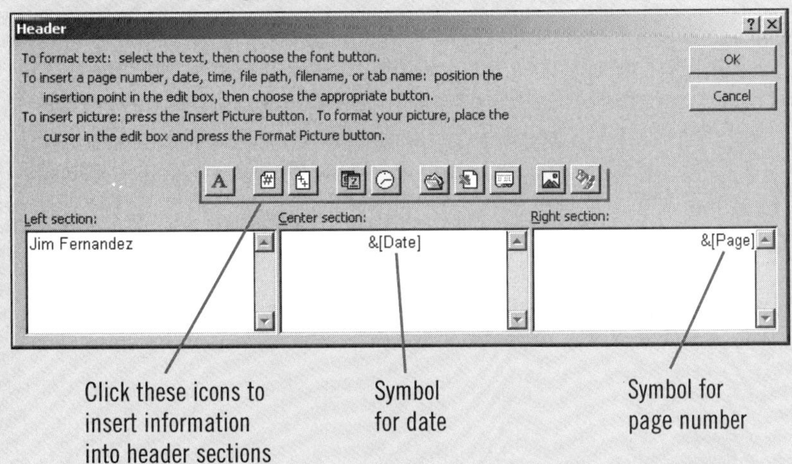

Excel 2002

Excel 2002

Consolidating Data with 3-D References

When you want to summarize similar data that exists in different sheets or workbooks, you can combine and display it in one sheet. For example, you might have departmental sales figures on four different store sheets that you want to consolidate on one summary sheet showing total departmental sales for all stores. The best way to consolidate data is to use cell references to the various sheets on a consolidation, or summary, sheet. Because they reference other sheets that are usually behind the summary sheet, such references effectively create another dimension in the workbook and are called **3-D references.** You can reference data in other sheets and in other workbooks. Referencing cells is a better method than retyping calculated results because the data values on which calculated totals depend might change. If you reference the values instead, any changes to the original values are automatically reflected in the consolidation sheet. Although Jim does not have timecard data for the remaining days of the week, he wants you to test the Weekly Summary sheet that will consolidate the timesheet data. He asks you to do this by creating a reference from the total pay data in the Monday sheet to the Weekly Summary sheet. You will freeze panes to improve the view of the worksheet before initiating the reference between them.

Steps 1 2 3 4

1. On the Monday sheet, click cell **D6**, click **Window** on the menu bar, click **Freeze Panes**, then scroll horizontally to bring columns L through O into view
2. Right-click a **tab scrolling button**, then click **Weekly Summary**
   Because the Weekly Summary sheet (which is the consolidation sheet) will contain the reference, the cell pointer must reside there when you initiate the reference. A **simple reference** displays the contents of another cell.
3. While in the Weekly Summary sheet, click cell **C6**, type =, activate the Monday sheet, click cell **O6**, then click the **Enter button** on the formula bar
   The Weekly Summary sheet becomes active, and formula bar reads =Monday!O6. See Figure F-6. *Monday* references the Monday sheet. The ! (exclamation point) is an **external reference indicator,** meaning that the cell referenced is outside the active sheet; O6 is the actual cell reference in the external sheet. The result, $34.20, appears in cell C6 of the Weekly Summary sheet, showing the reference to the value in cell O6 of the Monday sheet.
4. In the Weekly Summary sheet, copy cell **C6** into cells **C7:C26**
   Excel copies the contents of cell C6 with its relative reference to the Monday sheet data. You can test a reference by changing one cell value on which the reference is based and seeing if the reference changes.
5. Activate the Monday sheet, edit cell L6 to read **6:30 PM**, then activate the Weekly Summary sheet
   Cell C6 now shows $42.75. Changing Beryl Arenson's "time out" from 5:30 to 6:30 increased her pay from $34.20 to $42.75. This makes sense because Beryl's hours went from four to five, and her hourly salary is $8.55. The reference to Monday's total pay was automatically updated in the Weekly Summary sheet. See Figure F-7.
6. Enter your name in the left section of the footer, preview the worksheet, then print it
7. Activate the Monday sheet, unfreeze the panes, then save the workbook

QuickTip

If you have difficulty referencing cells between sheets, press [Esc] and begin again.

FIGURE F-6: Worksheet showing referenced cell

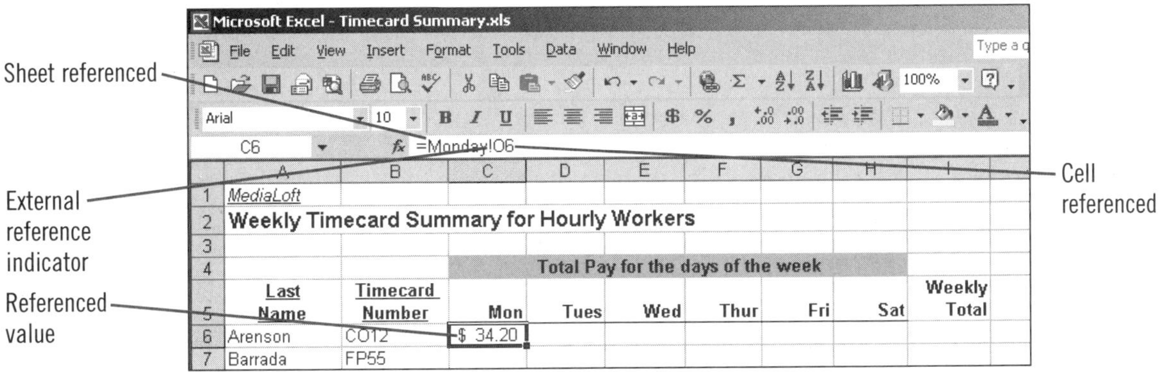

FIGURE F-7: Weekly Summary worksheet with updated reference

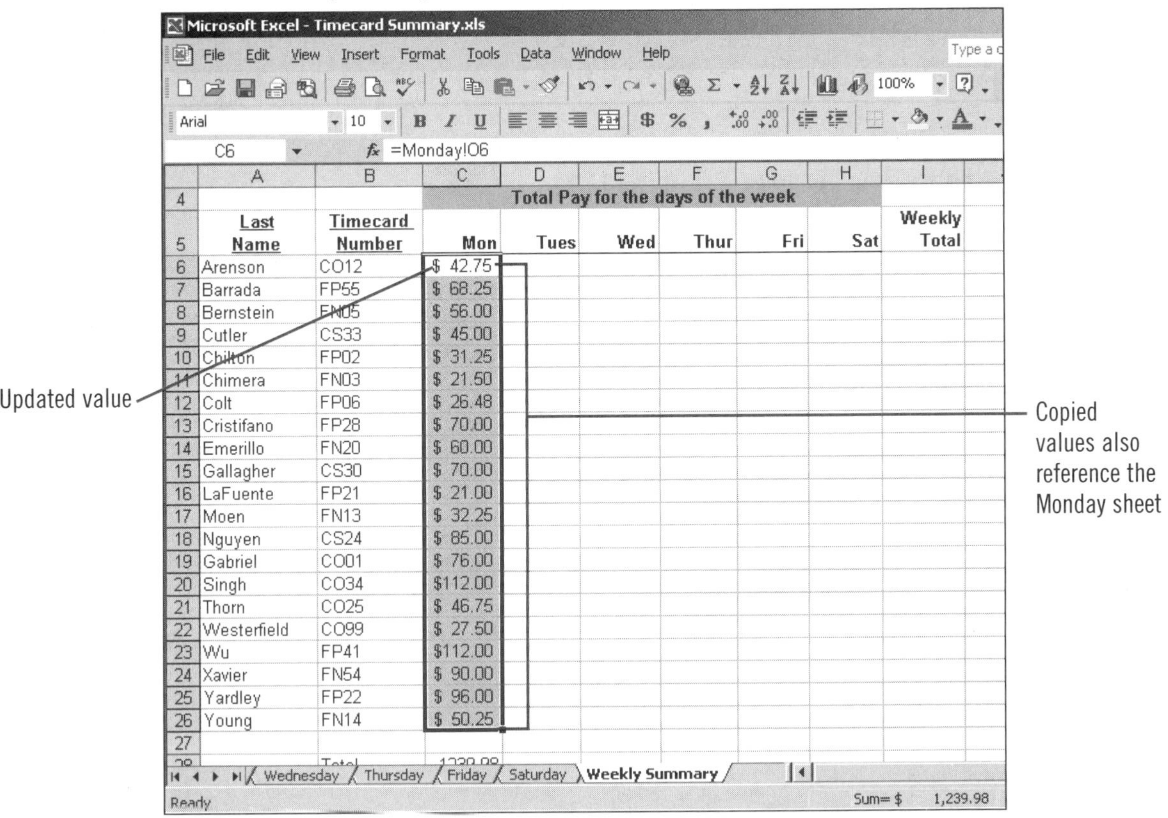

CLUES TO USE

Linking data between workbooks

Just as you can reference data between cells in a worksheet and between sheets, you can reference data between workbooks dynamically so that changes made in referenced cells in one workbook are reflected in the consolidation sheet in the other workbook. This dynamic referencing is called **linking.** To link a single cell between workbooks, open both workbooks, select the cell to receive the linked data, type = (the equal sign), select the cell in the other workbook containing the data to be linked, then press [Enter]. Excel automatically inserts the name of the referenced workbook in the cell reference. For example if the linked data is contained in cell C7 of worksheet New in the Products workbook, the cell entry will read ='[Product.xls]New'!$C$7. To perform calculations, enter formulas on the consolidation sheet using cells in the supporting sheets. If you are linking more than one cell, you can copy the linked data to the Clipboard, select the upper-left cell in the workbook to receive the link, click Edit on the menu bar, click Paste Special, then click Paste Link.

Hiding and Protecting Worksheet Areas

Worksheets can contain sensitive information that you don't want others to view or alter. To protect such information, Excel gives you two options. You can **hide** the formulas in selected cells (or rows, columns, or entire sheets), and you can **lock** selected cells, in which case other people will be able to view the data (values, numbers, labels, formulas, etc.) in those cells but not to change it. See Table F-1 for a list of options you can use to protect a worksheet. You set the lock and hide options in the Format Cells dialog box. Excel locks all cells by default but this protection is not in effect until you activate the Excel protection feature via the Tools menu. A common worksheet protection strategy is to unlock cells in which data will be changed, sometimes referred to as the **data entry area**, and to lock cells in which the data should not be changed. Then, when you protect the worksheet, the unlocked areas can still be changed. Because Jim will assign someone to enter the sensitive timecard information into the worksheet, he wants you to hide and lock selected areas of the worksheet.

1. On the Monday sheet, select the range **I6:L27**, click **Format** on the menu bar, click **Cells**, then click the **Protection tab**
   You include row 27, even though it does not contain data, in the event that new data is added to the row later. Notice that the Locked box in the Protection tab is already checked, as shown in Figure F-8. The Locked check box is selected by default, meaning that all the cells in a new workbook start out locked. (Note, however, that cell locking is not applied unless the protection feature is also activated. The protection feature is inactive by default.)
2. Click the **Locked check box** to deselect it, then click **OK**
   Excel stores time as a fraction of a 24-hour day. In the formula for total pay, hours must be multiplied by 24. This concept might be confusing to the data entry person, so you hide the formulas.
3. Select range **O6:O26**, click **Format** on the menu bar, click **Cells**, click the **Protection tab**, click the **Hidden check box** to select it, then click **OK**
   The data remains the same (unhidden and unlocked) until you set the protection in the next step.
4. Click **Tools** on the menu bar, point to **Protection**, then click **Protect Sheet**
   The Protect Sheet dialog box opens. The default options allow you to protect the worksheet while allowing users to select locked or unlocked cells only. You choose not to use a password.
5. Click **OK**
   You are ready to test the new worksheet protection.
6. Click cell **O6**
   The formula bar is empty because of the hidden formula setting.
7. In cell O6, type **T** to confirm that locked cells cannot be changed, then click **OK**
   When you attempt to change a locked cell, a message box reminds you of the protected cell's read-only status. See Figure F-9.
8. Click cell **I6**, type **9**, and notice that Excel allows you to begin the entry, press **[Esc]** to cancel the entry, then save the workbook
   Because you unlocked the cells in columns I through L before you protected the worksheet, you can make changes to these cells. Jim is satisfied that the Time In and Time Out data can be changed as necessary.

QuickTip

To turn off worksheet protection, click Tools on the menu bar, point to Protection, then click Unprotect Sheet. If prompted for a password, type the password, then click OK.

FIGURE F-8: Protection tab in Format Cells dialog box

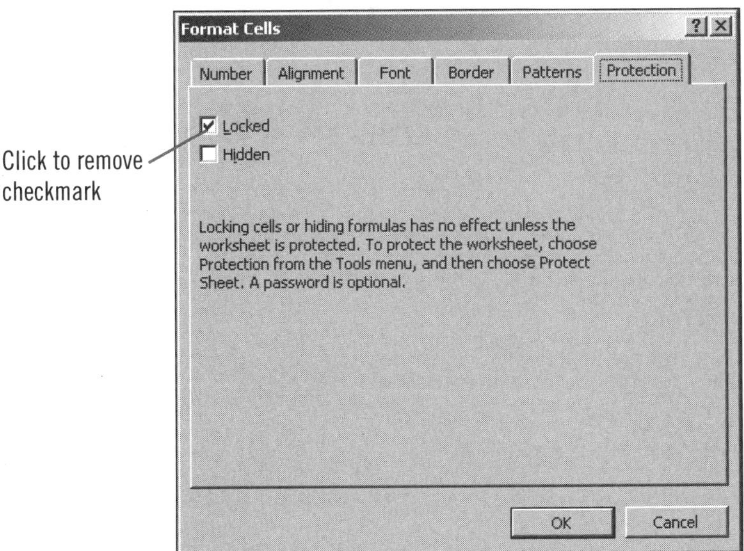

FIGURE F-9: Reminder of protected cell's read-only status

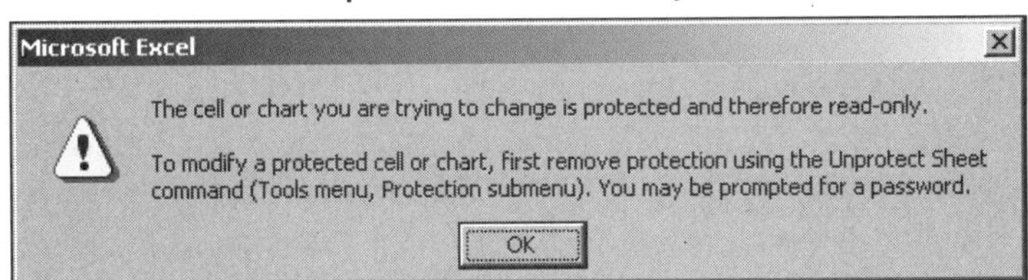

Excel 2002

TABLE F-1: Options for hiding and protecting worksheet elements

task	menu commands
Hide/Unhide a column	Format, Column, Hide or Unhide
Hide/Unhide a formula	Format, Cells, Protection tab, select/deselect Hidden check box
Hide/Unhide a row	Format, Row, Hide or Unhide
Hide/Unhide a sheet	Format, Sheet, Hide or Unhide
Protect workbook	Tools, Protection, Protect Workbook, assign optional password
Protect worksheet	Tools, Protection, Protect Sheet, assign optional password
Unlock/Relock cells	Format, Cells, Protection tab, deselect/select Locked check box

Note: Some of the hide and protect options do not take effect until protection is enabled.

Changing workbook properties

You can also password-protect an entire workbook from being opened or modified by changing its file properties. Click File on the menu bar, click Save As, click Tools, then click General Options. Specify the password(s) for opening or modifying the workbook. To remove a workbook password, you can double-click the asterisks in the Password to open or Password to modify text boxes and press [Delete]. You can also use this dialog text box to offer users an option to open the workbook in read-only format so that users can open but not change it. Another way to make an entire workbook read-only is to right-click Start on the Taskbar, then click Explore (or Explore All Users). Locate and right-click the filename, click Properties, click the General tab, then, in the Attributes section, select the Read-only check box.

Excel 2002

Saving Custom Views of a Worksheet

A **view** is a set of display and/or print settings that you can name and save, then access at a later time. By using the Excel Custom Views feature, you can create several different views of a worksheet without having to create separate sheets. For example, if you often switch between portrait and landscape orientations when printing different parts of a worksheet, you can create two views with the appropriate print settings for each view. You set the display and/or print settings first, then name the view. Because Jim will generate several reports from his data, he asks you to save the current print and display settings as a custom view. To better view the data, he wants you to use the Zoom box to display the entire worksheet on one screen.

Steps

1. With the Monday sheet active, select range **A1:028**, click the **Zoom list arrow** on the Standard toolbar, click **Selection**, then press **[Ctrl][Home]** to return to cell A1
   Excel adjusts the display magnification so that the data selected fits on one screen. See Figure F-10. After selecting the **Zoom box**, you can also pick a magnification percentage from the list or type the desired percentage.
2. Click **View** on the menu bar, then click **Custom Views**
   The Custom Views dialog box opens. Any previously defined views for the active worksheet appear in the Views box. In this case, Jim had created a custom view named Generic containing default print and display settings. See Figure F-11.
3. Click **Add**
   The Add View dialog box opens, as shown in Figure F-12. Here, you enter a name for the view and decide whether to include print settings and hidden rows, columns, and filter settings. You want to include the selected options.
4. In the Name box, type **Complete Daily Worksheet**, then click **OK**
   After creating a custom view of the worksheet, you return to the worksheet area. You are ready to test the two custom views. In case the views require a change to the worksheet, it's a good idea to turn off worksheet protection.
5. Click **Tools** on the menu bar, point to **Protection**, then click **Unprotect Sheet**
6. Click **View** on the menu bar, then click **Custom Views**
   The Custom Views dialog box opens, listing both the Complete Daily Worksheet and Generic views.
7. Click **Generic** in the Views list box, click **Show**, preview the worksheet, then close the Preview window
   The Generic custom view returns the worksheet to the Excel default print and display settings. Now you are ready to test the new custom view.
8. Click **View** on the menu bar, click **Custom Views**, click **Complete Daily Worksheet** in the Views list box, then click **Show**
   The entire worksheet fits on the screen.
9. Return to the Generic view, then save your work

QuickTip

To delete views from the active worksheet, select the view in the Views list box, then click Delete.

Trouble?

If you receive the message "Some view settings could not be applied," repeat Step 5 to ensure that worksheet protection is turned off.

FIGURE F-10: Selected data fitted to one screen

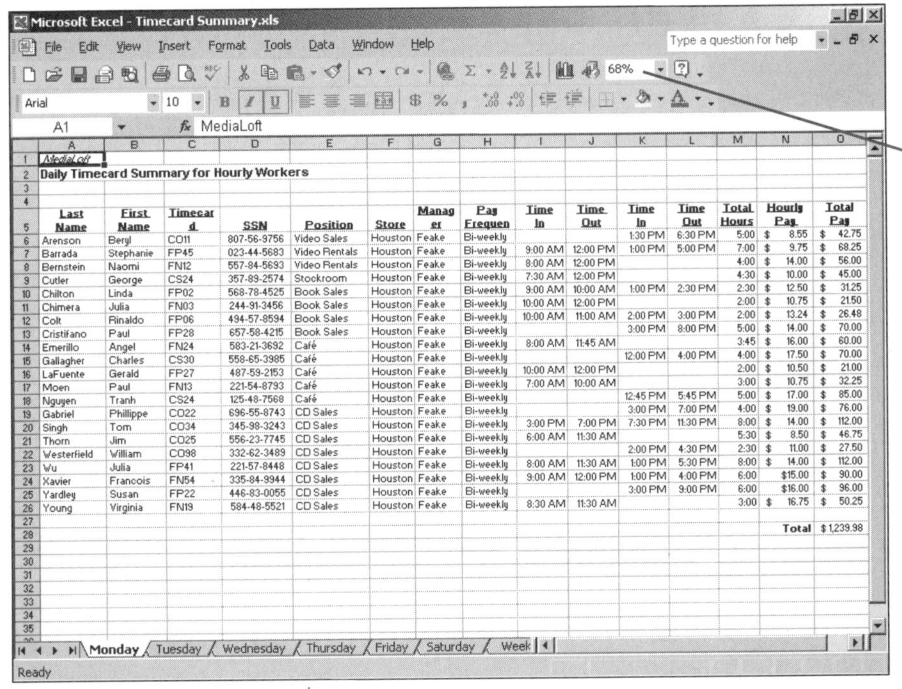

FIGURE F-11: Custom Views dialog box

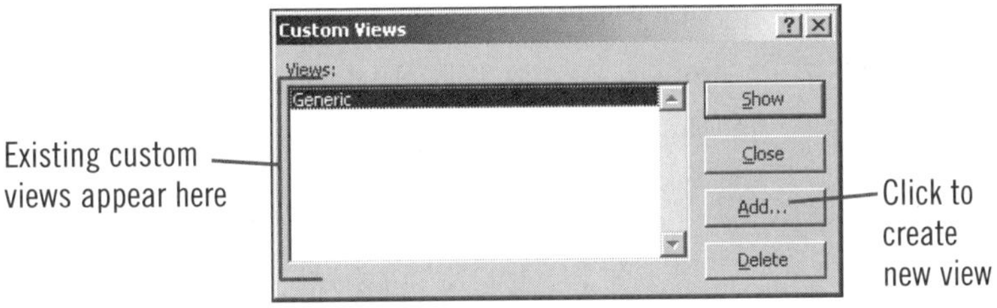

FIGURE F-12: Add View dialog box

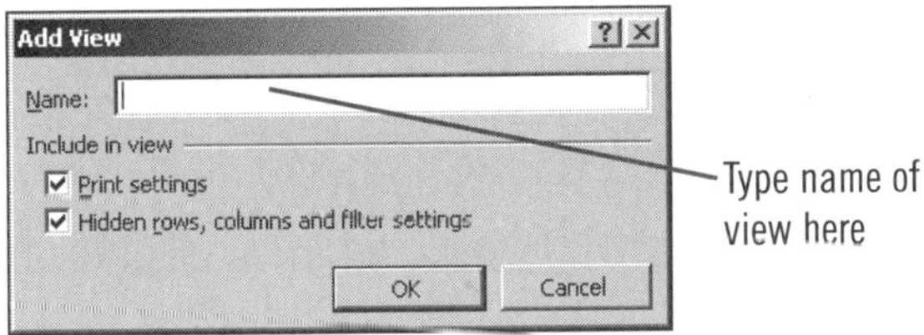

Creating a workspace

If you work with several workbooks at a time, you can group them so you can open them in one step by creating a **workspace**, a file with an .xlw extension. Then, instead of opening each workbook individually, you can open the workspace. To create a workspace, open the workbooks you wish to group and locate and size them as you would like them to appear. Click File on the menu bar, click Save Workspace, type a name for the workspace file, then click Save. Remember, however, that the workspace file does not contain the workbooks themselves, so you still have to save any changes you make to the original workbook files. To open the workbooks in the workspace automatically when you start Excel, place the workspace file in your XLStart folder (C:\Program Files\Microsoft Office\Office\XLStart).

Excel 2002

Controlling Page Breaks and Page Numbering

The vertical and horizontal dashed lines in worksheets indicate page breaks. Excel automatically inserts a page break when your worksheet data doesn't fit on one page. These page breaks are **dynamic**, which means they adjust automatically when you insert or delete rows and columns and when you change column widths or row heights. Everything to the left of the first vertical dashed line and above the first horizontal dashed line is printed on the first page. You can override the automatic breaks by choosing the Page Break command on the Insert menu. Table F-2 describes the different types of page breaks you can use. Jim wants another report displaying no more than half the hourly workers on each page. To accomplish this, he asks you to insert a manual page break.

1. **Click cell A16, click Insert on the menu bar, then click Page Break**
   A dashed line appears between rows 15 and 16, indicating a horizontal page break. See Figure F-13. After you set page breaks, it's a good idea to preview each page.
2. **Preview the worksheet, then click Zoom**
   Notice that the status bar reads "Page 1 of 4" and that the data for the employees up through Charles Gallagher appears on the first page. Jim decides to place the date in the footer.
3. **While in the Print Preview window, click Setup, click the Header/Footer tab, click Custom Footer, click the Right section box, click the Date button**
4. **Click the Left section box, type your name, then click OK**
   Your name, the page number, and the date appear in the Footer preview area.
5. **In the Page Setup dialog box, click OK, and while still in Print Preview, check to make sure that all the pages show your name, the page numbers, and the date, click Close, save the workbook, then print the worksheet**
6. **Click View on the menu bar, click Custom Views, click Add, type Half and Half, then click OK**
   Your new custom view has the page breaks and all current print settings.
7. **Make sure cell A16 is selected, then click Insert on the menu bar and click Remove Page Break**
   Excel removes the manual page break above or to the left of the active cell.
8. **Save the workbook**

TABLE F-2: Page break options

type of page break	where to position cell pointer
Both horizontal and vertical page breaks	Select the cell below and to the right of the gridline where you want the breaks to occur
Only a horizontal page break	Select the cell in column A that is directly below the gridline where you want the page to break
Only a vertical page break	Select a cell in row 1 that is to the right of the gridline where you want the page to break

FIGURE F-13: Worksheet with horizontal page break

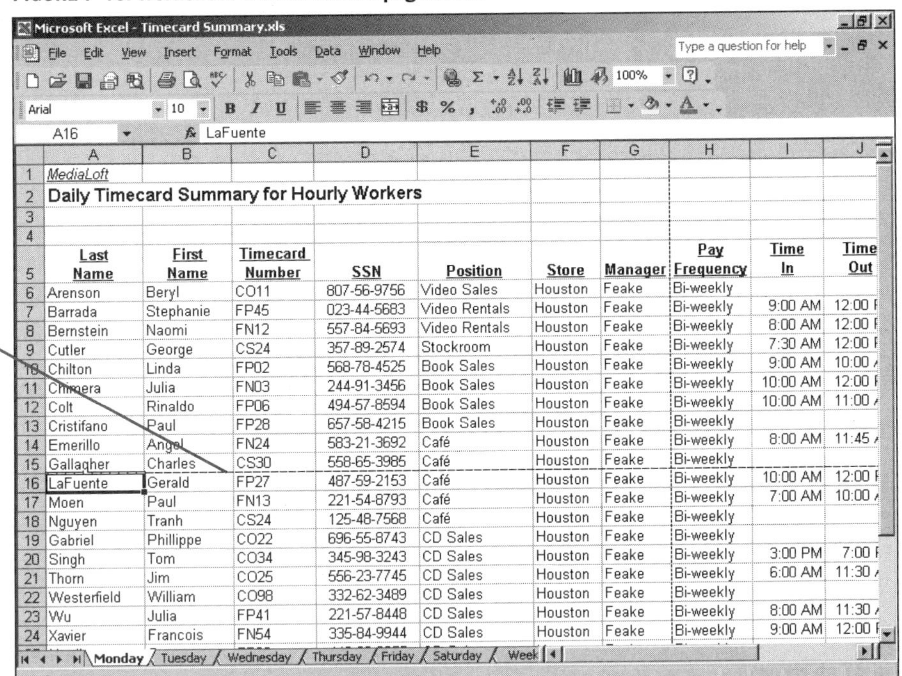

Microsoft Excel - Timecard Summary.xls

A16 LaFuente

	A	B	C	D	E	F	G	H	I	J
1	MediaLoft									
2	Daily Timecard Summary for Hourly Workers									
3										
4										
5	Last Name	First Name	Timecard Number	SSN	Position	Store	Manager	Pay Frequency	Time In	Time Out
6	Arenson	Beryl	CO11	807-56-9756	Video Sales	Houston	Feake	Bi-weekly		
7	Barrada	Stephanie	FP45	023-44-5683	Video Rentals	Houston	Feake	Bi-weekly	9:00 AM	12:00
8	Bernstein	Naomi	FN12	557-84-5693	Video Rentals	Houston	Feake	Bi-weekly	8:00 AM	12:00
9	Cutler	George	CS24	357-89-2574	Stockroom	Houston	Feake	Bi-weekly	7:30 AM	12:00
10	Chilton	Linda	FP02	568-78-4525	Book Sales	Houston	Feake	Bi-weekly	9:00 AM	10:00
11	Chimera	Julia	FN03	244-91-3456	Book Sales	Houston	Feake	Bi-weekly	10:00 AM	12:00
12	Colt	Rinaldo	FP06	494-57-8594	Book Sales	Houston	Feake	Bi-weekly	10:00 AM	11:00
13	Cristifano	Paul	FP28	657-58-4215	Book Sales	Houston	Feake	Bi-weekly		
14	Emerillo	Angel	FN24	583-21-3692	Café	Houston	Feake	Bi-weekly	8:00 AM	11:45
15	Gallagher	Charles	CS30	558-65-3985	Café	Houston	Feake	Bi-weekly		
16	LaFuente	Gerald	FP27	487-59-2153	Café	Houston	Feake	Bi-weekly	10:00 AM	12:00
17	Moen	Paul	FN13	221-54-8793	Café	Houston	Feake	Bi-weekly	7:00 AM	10:00
18	Nguyen	Tranh	CS24	125-48-7568	Café	Houston	Feake	Bi-weekly		
19	Gabriel	Phillippe	CO22	696-55-8743	CD Sales	Houston	Feake	Bi-weekly		
20	Singh	Tom	CO34	345-98-3243	CD Sales	Houston	Feake	Bi-weekly	3:00 PM	7:00
21	Thorn	Jim	CO25	556-23-7745	CD Sales	Houston	Feake	Bi-weekly	6:00 AM	11:30
22	Westerfield	William	CO98	332-62-3489	CD Sales	Houston	Feake	Bi-weekly		
23	Wu	Julia	FP41	221-57-8448	CD Sales	Houston	Feake	Bi-weekly	8:00 AM	11:30
24	Xavier	Francois	FN54	335-84-9944	CD Sales	Houston	Feake	Bi-weekly	9:00 AM	12:00

Monday / Tuesday / Wednesday / Thursday / Friday / Saturday / Week

Ready

Dashed line indicates horizontal break after row 15

FIGURE F-14: Page Break Preview window

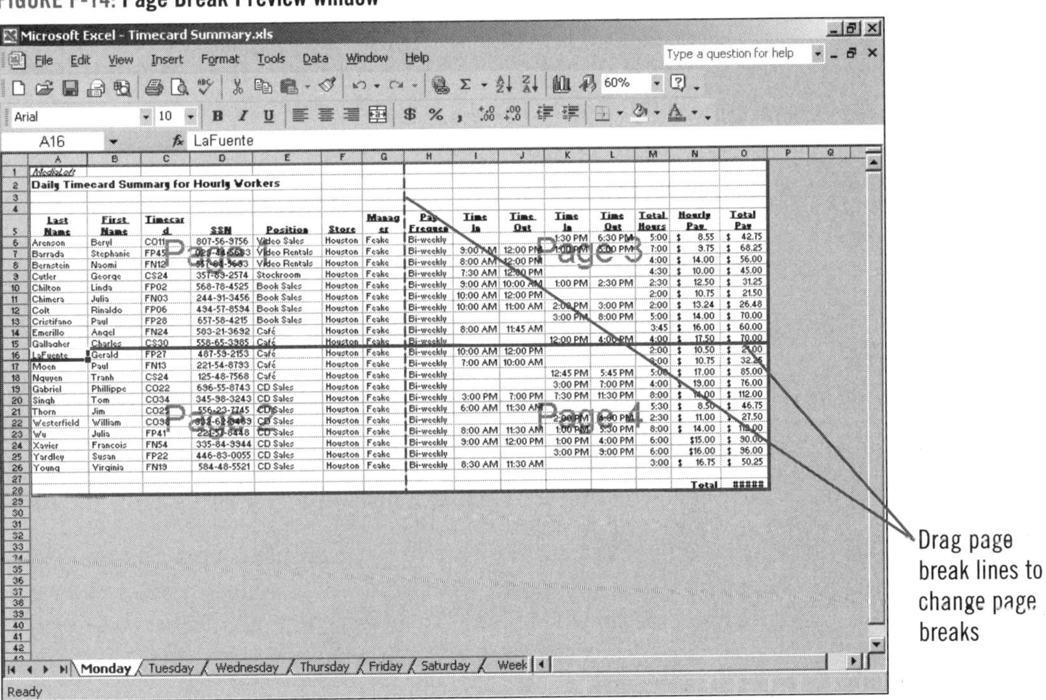

Drag page break lines to change page breaks

Using Page Break Preview

You can view and change page breaks manually by clicking View on the menu bar, then clicking Page Break Preview, or clicking Page Break Preview in the Print Preview window. (If you see a Welcome to Page Break Preview dialog box, click OK to close it.) Drag the page break lines to the desired location. See Figure F-14. To exit Page Break Preview, click View on the menu bar, then click Normal.

Excel 2002

Creating a Hyperlink Between Excel Files

As you manage the content and appearance of your workbooks, you may want the workbook user to view information in another workbook. It might be nonessential information or data that is too detailed to place in the workbook itself. In these cases, you can create a **hyperlink**, an object (a filename, a word, a phrase, or a graphic) in a worksheet that, when you click it, will display, or "jump to," another worksheet, called the **target**. The target can also be a document or a site on the World Wide Web. Hyperlinks are navigational tools between worksheets and are not used to exchange information. For example, in a worksheet that lists customer invoices, at each customer's name, you might create a hyperlink to an Excel file containing payment terms for each customer. Jim wants managers who view the Timecard Summary workbook to be able to view the pay categories for MediaLoft store employees. He asks you to create a hyperlink at the Hourly Pay Rate column heading. Users will click the hyperlink to view the Pay Rate worksheet.

1. Display the Monday worksheet
2. Click **Edit**, click **Go To**, type **N5** (the cell containing the text Hourly Pay Rate), then click **OK**
3. Click the **Insert Hyperlink button** on the Standard toolbar, then click **Existing File or Web Page**, if it is not already selected
   The Insert Hyperlink dialog box opens. See Figure F-15. The icons under "Link to" on the left side of the dialog box let you specify the type of location you want the link to jump to: an existing file or Web page, a place in the same document, a new document, or an e-mail address. Because Jim wants users to display a document he has created, the first icon, Existing File or Web Page, is correct.
4. Click the **Look in list arrow** to navigate to the location where your Project Files are stored, then click **Pay Rate Classifications** in the file list
   The filename you selected appears in the Address text box. This is the document users will see when they click this hyperlink. You can also specify the ScreenTip that users will see when they hold the pointer over the hyperlink.
5. Click **ScreenTip**, type **Click here to see MediaLoft pay rate classifications**, click **OK**, then click **OK** again
   Cell N5 now contains underlined blue text, indicating that it is a hyperlink. After you create a hyperlink, you should check it to make sure that it jumps to the correct destination.
6. Move the pointer over the **Hourly Pay Rate text**, view the ScreenTip, then click once
   Notice that when you move the pointer over the text, the pointer changes to , indicating that it is a hyperlink, and the ScreenTip appears. After you click, the Pay Rate Classifications worksheet appears. See Figure F-16. The Web toolbar appears beneath the Standard and Formatting toolbars.
7. Click the **Back button** on the Web toolbar, save the workbook, then print the worksheet

QuickTip

To remove a hyperlink or change its target, right-click it, point to Hyperlink, then click Remove Hyperlink or Edit Hyperlink.

QuickTip

If you link to a Web page you must open a connection to the Internet to test the link.

CLUES TO USE

Using hyperlinks to navigate large worksheets

Hyperlinks are useful in navigating large worksheets or workbooks. You can create a hyperlink from a cell to another cell in the same worksheet, a cell in another worksheet, or a defined name anywhere in the workbook. Under "Link to" in the Insert Hyperlink dialog box, click Place in This Document. Then type the cell reference and indicate the sheet, or select a named location.

FIGURE F-15: Insert Hyperlink dialog box

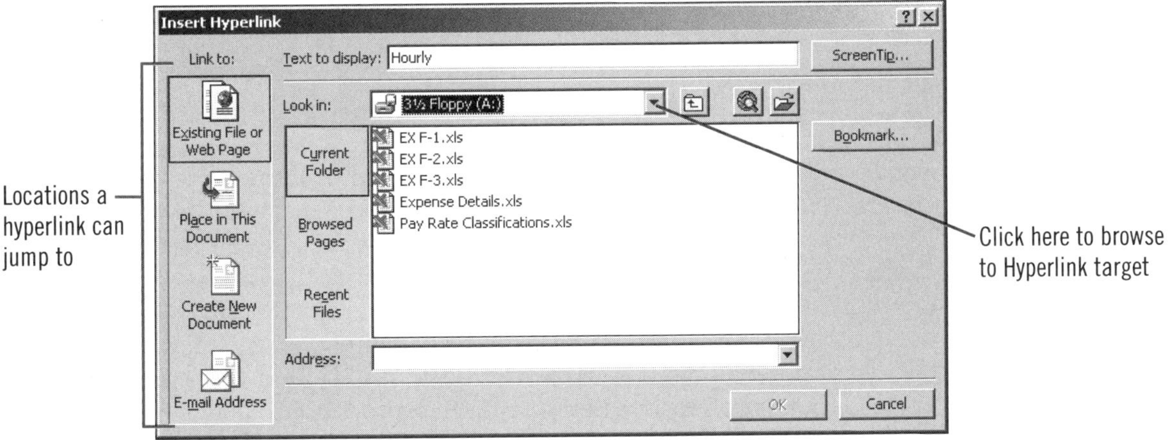

FIGURE F-16: Target document

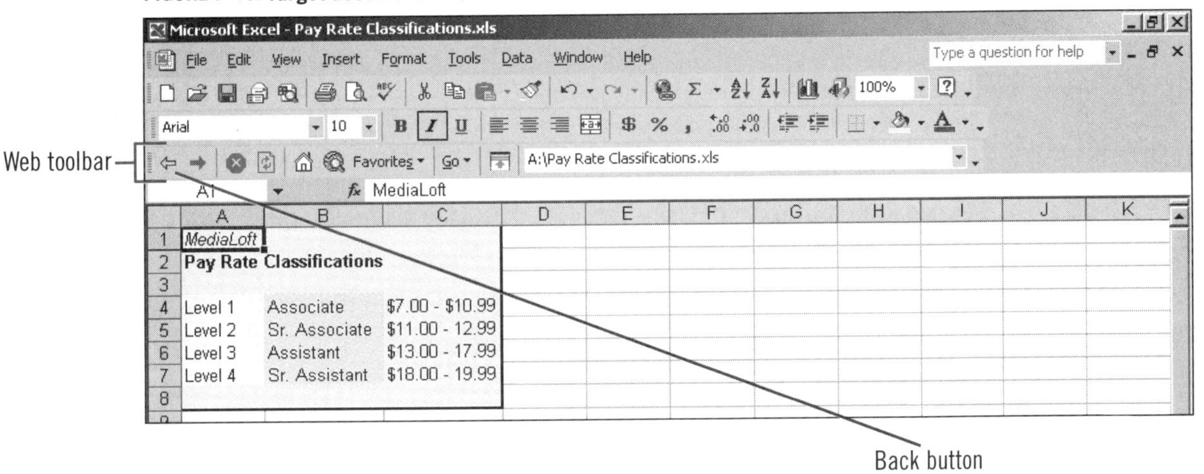

Finding and replacing data and formats

You can easily change worksheet data by using the find-and-replace feature in Excel. Click Edit on the menu bar, click Replace, enter the text you want to find, press [Tab], then enter the text you want to replace it with. Use the Find Next, Find All, Replace, and Replace All buttons to find and replace any or all occurrences of the specified text. You can specify a data format for your search criteria by clicking the Options button, clicking the Format list arrow, and selecting a format.

Excel 2002

Saving an Excel File as a Web Page

One way to share Excel data is to place, or **publish**, it over a network or on the Web so that others can access it using their Web browsers. The network can be an **intranet**, which is an internal network site used by a particular group of people who work together. If you post an entire workbook, users can click worksheet tabs to view each sheet. You can make the workbook interactive, meaning that users can enter, format, and calculate data. To publish an Excel document to an intranet or the Web, you must first save it as an **HTML (Hypertext Markup Language)** document, so it can be interpreted by a Web browser. Jim asks you to save the entire Timecard Summary workbook in HTML format so he can publish it on the MediaLoft intranet for managers to use.

Steps

QuickTip

You can use the Save As option on the File menu to save a workbook in formats that can be opened in earlier versions of Excel as well as in databases and other spreadsheet programs.

1. Click **File** on the menu bar, then click **Save as Web Page**
   The Save As dialog box opens. By default, the Entire Workbook option button is selected, which is what Jim wants. However, he wants the title bar of the Web page to be more descriptive than the filename.
2. Click **Change Title**
   The Set Page Title dialog box opens.
3. Type **MediaLoft Houston Timecard Summary**, then click **OK**
   The new title appears in the Page title area. The Save as type list box indicates that the workbook will be saved as a Web page, which is in HTML format. See Figure F-17.

QuickTip

To avoid problems when publishing your pages to a Web server, it is best to use lowercase characters, omit special characters and spaces, and limit your filename to eight characters.

4. Change the filename to **timesum**, then click the **Save in list arrow** to navigate to the drive and folder where your Project Files are stored
5. Click **Save**
   A dialog box appears, indicating that the custom views you saved earlier will not be part of the HTML file.
6. Click **Yes**
   Excel saves the workbook as an HTML file in the folder location you specified in the Save As dialog box, and in the same place creates a folder in which it places associated files, such as a file for each worksheet. To make the workbook available to others, you would publish all these files on an intranet or Web server. When the save process is complete, the original XLS file closes and the HTML file opens on your screen.
7. Click **File** on the menu bar, click **Web Page Preview**, then maximize the browser window
   The workbook opens in your default Web browser, which could be Internet Explorer or Netscape, showing you what it would look like if you opened it on an intranet or on the Web. See Figure F-18. The Monday worksheet appears as it would if it were on a Web site or intranet, with tabs at the bottom of the screen for each sheet.
8. Click the **Weekly Summary Sheet tab** then print the worksheet using your browser
9. Close the Web browser window, then close the timesum workbook and the Pay Rate Classifications workbook

FIGURE F-17: Save As dialog box

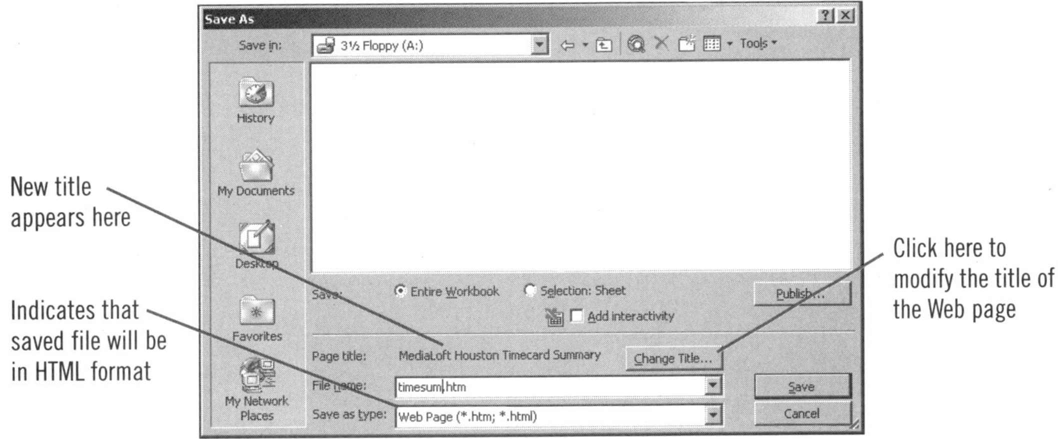

FIGURE F-18: Workbook in Web page preview

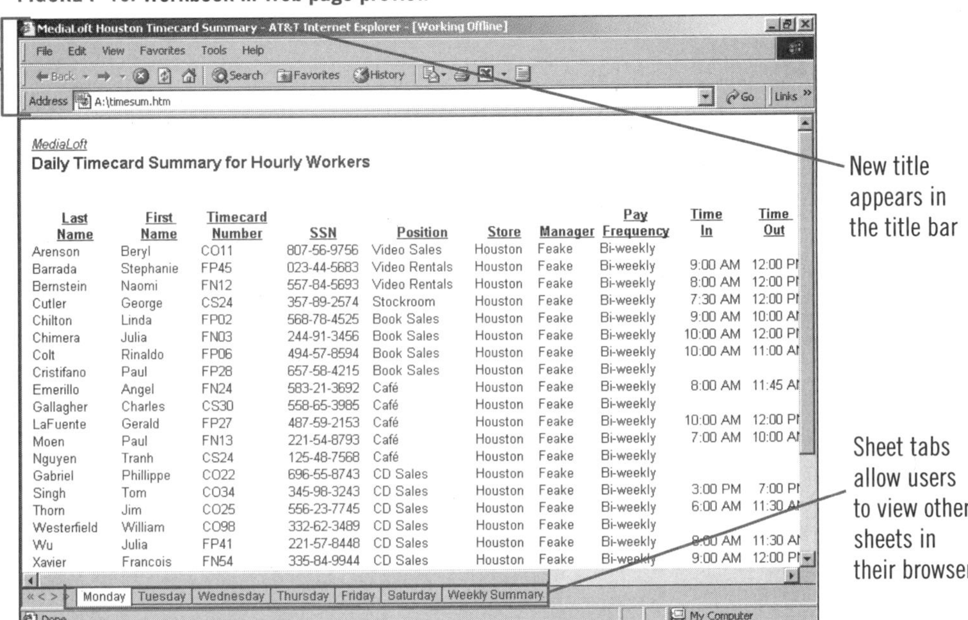

Last Name	First Name	Timecard Number	SSN	Position	Store	Manager	Pay Frequency	Time In	Time Out
Arenson	Beryl	CO11	807-56-9756	Video Sales	Houston	Feake	Bi-weekly		
Barrada	Stephanie	FP45	023-44-5683	Video Rentals	Houston	Feake	Bi-weekly	9:00 AM	12:00 P
Bernstein	Naomi	FN12	557-84-5693	Video Rentals	Houston	Feake	Bi-weekly	8:00 AM	12:00 P
Cutler	George	CS24	357-89-2574	Stockroom	Houston	Feake	Bi-weekly	7:30 AM	12:00 P
Chilton	Linda	FP02	568-78-4525	Book Sales	Houston	Feake	Bi-weekly	9:00 AM	10:00 A
Chimera	Julia	FN03	244-91-3456	Book Sales	Houston	Feake	Bi-weekly	10:00 AM	12:00 P
Colt	Rinaldo	FP06	494-57-8594	Book Sales	Houston	Feake	Bi-weekly	10:00 AM	11:00 A
Cristifano	Paul	FP28	657-58-4215	Book Sales	Houston	Feake	Bi-weekly		
Emerillo	Angel	FN24	583-21-3692	Café	Houston	Feake	Bi-weekly	8:00 AM	11:45 A
Gallagher	Charles	CS30	558-65-3985	Café	Houston	Feake	Bi-weekly		
LaFuente	Gerald	FP27	487-59-2153	Café	Houston	Feake	Bi-weekly	10:00 AM	12:00 P
Moen	Paul	FN13	221-54-8793	Café	Houston	Feake	Bi-weekly	7:00 AM	10:00 A
Nguyen	Tranh	CS24	125-48-7568	Café	Houston	Feake	Bi-weekly		
Gabriel	Phillippe	CO22	696-55-8743	CD Sales	Houston	Feake	Bi-weekly		
Singh	Tom	CO34	345-98-3243	CD Sales	Houston	Feake	Bi-weekly	3:00 PM	7:00 P
Thorn	Jim	CO25	556-23-7745	CD Sales	Houston	Feake	Bi-weekly	6:00 AM	11:30 A
Westerfield	William	CO98	332-62-3489	CD Sales	Houston	Feake	Bi-weekly		
Wu	Julia	FP41	221-57-8448	CD Sales	Houston	Feake	Bi-weekly	8:00 AM	11:30 A
Xavier	Francois	FN54	335-84-9944	CD Sales	Houston	Feake	Bi-weekly	9:00 AM	12:00 P

Excel 2002

Holding Web discussions

You can attach a discussion comment to an Excel worksheet that you will save as an HTML document. This allows people viewing your worksheet on the Web to review and reply to your comments. To insert a discussion comment in Excel, click Tools on the menu bar, point to Online Collaboration, then click Web Discussions. This will display the Web Discussions Toolbar. See Figure F-19. You can add comments that others can view on the Web by clicking the Insert Discussion about the Workbook button on the Web Discussions Toolbar. Your comments, which are stored on a discussion server, will appear with the worksheet when it is saved and published as a Web document. People viewing your worksheet on the Web can reply by clicking the Discuss button on the Standard Buttons toolbar in Internet Explorer to display the Discussions Toolbar. Then they can click the Insert Discussion in the Document button. *Note*: You must specify a discussion server to use this feature.

FIGURE F-19: Web Discussion toolbar

Web Discussion Toolbar

Monday Tuesday Wednesday Thursday Friday Saturday Week
Discussions Subscribe... Close
Ready

Practice

▶ Concepts Review

Label each element of the Excel screen shown in Figure F-20.

FIGURE F-20

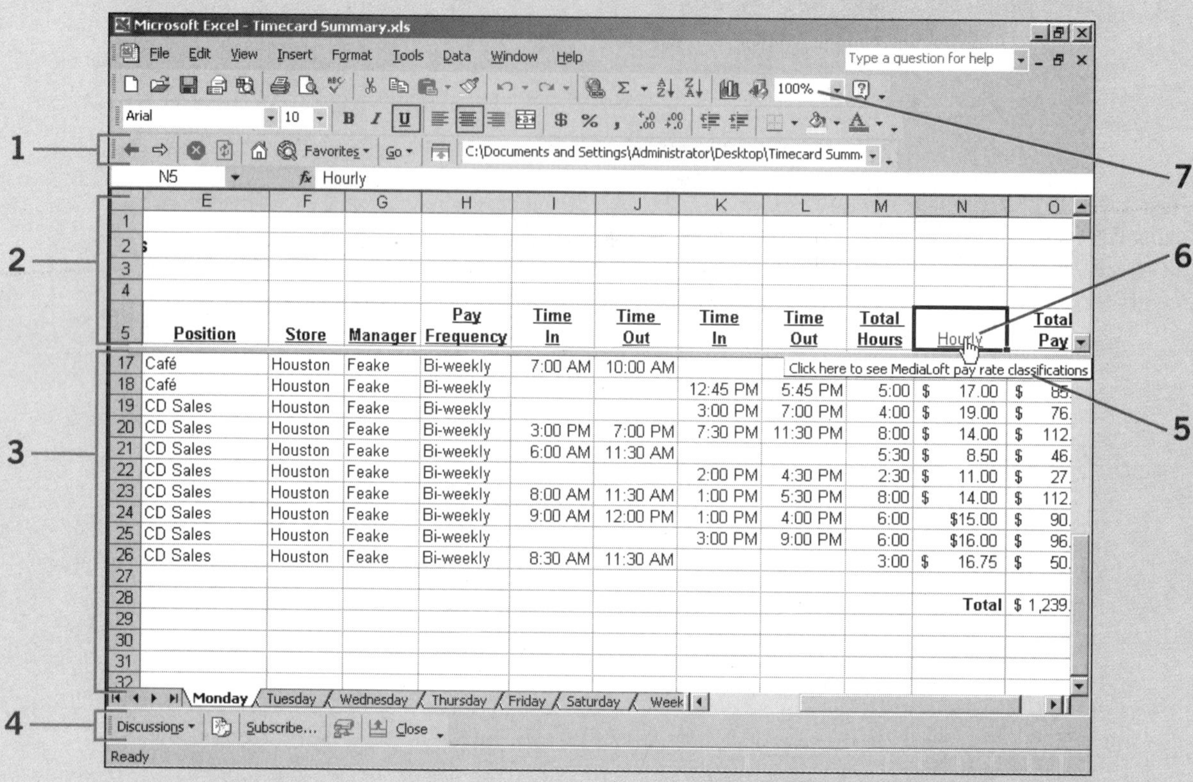

Match each of the terms with the statement that describes its function.

8. Dashed line
9. Hyperlink
10. 3-D reference
11.
12.

a. Inserts a picture into header or footer.
b. Uses values from different worksheets or workbooks
c. Indicates a page break
d. Inserts a code to print the sheet name in a header or footer
e. A navigational tool for use between worksheets or workbooks

Select the best answer from the list of choices.

13. You can save frequently used display and print settings by using the ____________ feature.

a. HTML
b. View menu
c. Custom Views
d. Save command

14. You can group several workbooks in a ____________ so they can be opened together rather than individually.

a. Workgroup
b. Workspace
c. Consolidated workbook
d. Work unit

15. You can specify data formats in the Find and Replace dialog box by clicking the ____________ button.

a. Format
b. Options >>
c. Data
d. Tools

Skills Review

1. Freeze columns and rows.

a. Start Excel, open the Project File EX F-2 from the drive and folder where your Project Files are stored, then save it as **San Francisco Budget**.
b. Activate the 2003 sheet, then freeze columns A and B and rows 1 through 3 for improved viewing. (*Hint*: Click cell C4 prior to issuing the Freeze Panes command.)
c. Scroll until columns A and B and F through H are visible.
d. Press **[Ctrl][Home]** to return to cell C4.
e. Unfreeze the panes.

2. Insert and delete worksheets.

a. With the 2003 sheet active, use the sheet shortcut menu to insert a new sheet to its left.
b. Delete the 2002 sheet, rename the new sheet 2005 and move it after the 2004 sheet.
c. Add a custom footer to the 2003 sheet with your name on the left side and the page number on the right side.
d. Add a custom header with the worksheet name on the left side.
e. Save and preview the worksheet, compare your results to Figure F-21, then print it.

3. Consolidate data with 3-D references.

a. In cell C22, enter a reference to cell G7.
b. In cell C23, enter a reference to cell G18.
c. Activate the 2004 worksheet.
d. In cell C4, enter a reference to cell C4 on the 2003 worksheet.

FIGURE F-21

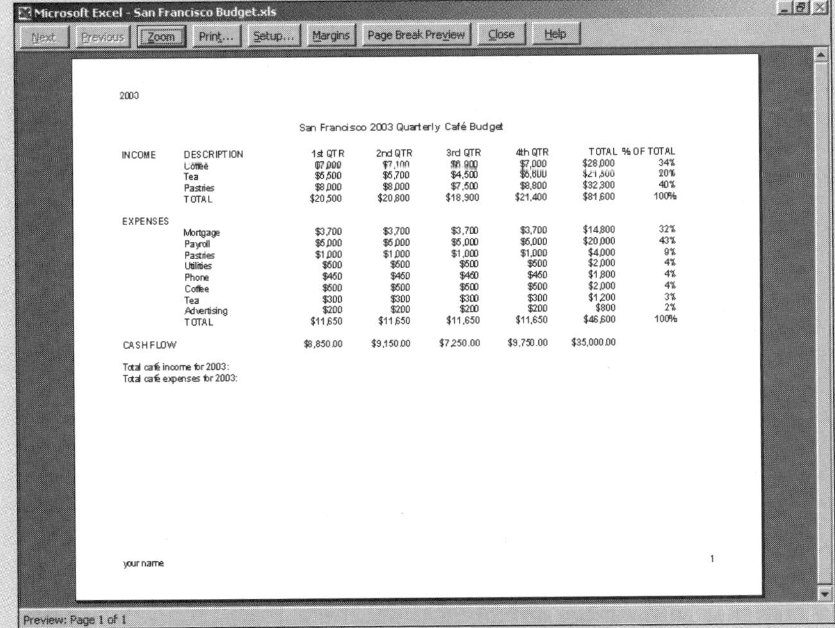

2003

San Francisco 2003 Quarterly Café Budget

INCOME	DESCRIPTION	1st QTR	2nd QTR	3rd QTR	4th QTR	TOTAL	% OF TOTAL
	Coffee	$7,000	$7,100	$6,900	$7,000	$28,000	34%
	Tea	$5,500	$5,700	$4,500	$5,600	$21,300	20%
	Pastries	$8,000	$8,000	$7,500	$8,800	$32,300	40%
	TOTAL	$20,500	$20,800	$18,900	$21,400	$81,600	100%
EXPENSES							
	Mortgage	$3,700	$3,700	$3,700	$3,700	$14,800	32%
	Payroll	$5,000	$5,000	$5,000	$5,000	$20,000	43%
	Pastries	$1,000	$1,000	$1,000	$1,000	$4,000	9%
	Utilities	$500	$500	$500	$500	$2,000	4%
	Phone	$450	$450	$460	$450	$1,800	4%
	Coffee	$500	$500	$500	$500	$2,000	4%
	Tea	$300	$300	$300	$300	$1,200	3%
	Advertising	$200	$200	$200	$200	$800	2%
	TOTAL	$11,650	$11,650	$11,650	$11,650	$46,600	100%
CASHFLOW		$8,850.00	$9,150.00	$7,250.00	$9,750.00	$35,000.00	

Total café income for 2003:
Total café expenses for 2003:

your name 1

e. In the 2004 worksheet, copy the contents of cell C4 into cells C5:C6.
f. Preview the 2004 worksheet, then use the Setup button to add your name to the footer.
g. Print the 2004 worksheet, then save your work.

4. **Hide and protect worksheet areas.**
   a. On the 2003 sheet, unlock the expense data in the range C10:F17.
   b. On the 2003 sheet, hide the percent of total formulas in column H and the cash flow formulas in row 20.
   c. Protect the sheet without using a password.
   d. To make sure the other cells are locked, attempt to make an entry in cell D4. You should see the error message displayed in Figure F-22.
   e. Change the first quarter mortgage expense to $3,900.
   f. Verify the formulas in column H and row 20 are hidden.
   g. Unprotect the worksheet.
   h. Save the workbook.

FIGURE F-22

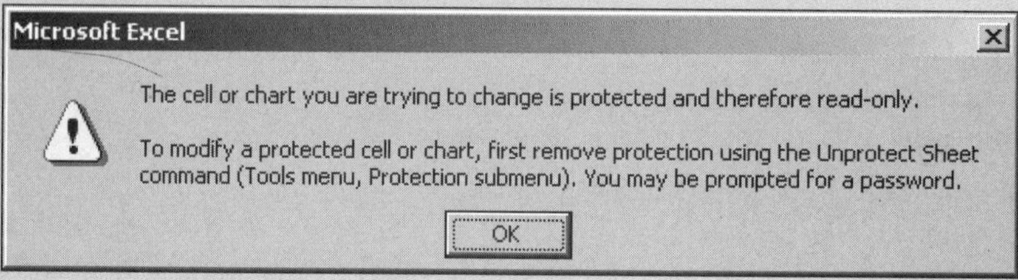

5. **Save custom views of a worksheet.**
   a. Set the zoom on the 2003 worksheet so that all the data fits on your screen.
   b. Make this a new view called **Entire 2003 Budget**.
   c. Use the Custom Views dialog box to return to Generic view. (*Note*: Using custom views may affect your headers, footers, and page orientation.)
   d. Save the workbook.
6. **Control page breaks and page numbering.**
   a. Insert a page break above cell A10.
   b. Save the view as **Halves**.
   c. Save the workbook.
7. **Create a hyperlink between Excel files.**
   a. On the 2003 worksheet, make cell A9 a hyperlink to the file **Expense Details**.
   b. Test the link, then print the Expense Details worksheet.
   c. Edit the hyperlink in cell A9, adding a ScreenTip that reads **Click here to see expense assumptions**.
   d. Return to the San Francisco Budget worksheet by using the Web toolbar.
   e. On the 2004 worksheet, enter the text **Based on 2003 budget** in cell A2.
   f. Make the text in cell A2 a hyperlink to cell A1 in the 2003 worksheet. (*Hint*: Use the Place in This Document button and note the cell reference in the Type the cell reference text box.)
   g. Test the hyperlink.
   h. Save the workbook and protect it with the password **pass**.
   i. Close and reopen the workbook to test the password.
   j. Remove the password and save the workbook again.
8. **Save an Excel file as a Web page.**
   a. If you have access to a Web discussion server, attach a discussion comment to the 2003 worksheet with your name and the date you reviewed the budget. (If you don't have access to discussion server, proceed to step b.)

b. Save the entire budget workbook as a Web page with a title bar that reads **Our Budget** and the file named **sfbudget**.
c. Preview the Web page in your browser. If your browser doesn't open automatically, check your taskbar.
d. Test the worksheet tabs in the browser to make sure they work.
e. Print the 2003 worksheet from your browser.
f. Close your browser.
g. Return to Excel, close the HTML document and the Expense Details workbook, then exit Excel.

► Independent Challenge 1

As a new employee at SoftSales, a computer software retailer, you are responsible for tracking the sales of different product lines and determining which computer operating system generates the most software sales each month. Although sales figures vary from month to month, the format in which data is entered does not. You decide to create a worksheet tracking sales across platforms by month. Use a separate worksheet for each month and create data for three months. Use your own data for the number of software packages sold in the Windows and Macintosh columns for each product.

a. Start Excel, create a new workbook, then save it as **Software Sales Summary** in the drive and folder where your Project Files are stored.
b. Create three worksheets to hold software sales information for the months of January, February, and March. Use Table F-3 as a guide to enter row and column labels, your own data, and formulas for the totals.
c. Create a summary sheet that totals the information in all three sheets.
d. Add headers to all four worksheets that includes your name, the sheet name, and the date.
e. Format the worksheet appropriately.
f. Save the workbook, preview and print the four worksheets, then exit Excel.

Excel 2002

TABLE F-3

	Windows	Macintosh	Total
Games Software			
Combat Flight Simulator			
Safari			
NASCAR Racing			
Total			
Business Software			
Word Processing			
Spreadsheet			
Presentation			
Graphics			
Page Layout			
Total			
Utilities			
Antivirus			
File Recovery			
Total			

 Independent Challenge 2

You own PC Assist, a software training company located in Montreal, Canada. You have added several new entries to the August check register and are ready to enter September's check activity. Because the sheet for August will include much of the same information you need for September, you decide to copy it. Then you will edit the new sheet to fit your needs for the September check activity. You will use sheet referencing to enter the beginning balance and beginning check number. Using your own data, you will complete five checks for the September register.

a. Start Excel, open the Project File EX F-3 from the drive and folder where your Project Files are stored, then save it as **Update to Check Register**. The expense amounts in the worksheet include the Goods and Services tax (GST)/(TPS), the Harmonized Sales Tax (HST)/(TVH), and the Quebec sales tax (TVQ).
b. Delete Sheet 2 and Sheet 3, then create a worksheet for September by copying the August sheet and renaming it.
c. With the September sheet active, delete the data in range A6:E24.
d. To update the balance at the beginning of the month, use sheet referencing from the last balance entry in the August sheet.
e. Generate the first check number. (*Hint*: Use a formula that references the last check number in August and adds one.)
f. Enter data for five checks using September 2003 dates. For the check number, use the number above it and add 1.
g. Add a footer to both sheets that includes your name on the left side of the printout and the system date on the right side. Add a header for the worksheets that displays the sheet name centered on the printout. (*Hint*: Select both sheets using the Shift key, then apply the header and footer)
h. Save the workbook.
i. Use the Find and Replace dialog box to change the beginning balance for August from **20000** to **25000**, formatted as a number with two decimal places. (*Hint*: The Options >> button will allow you to change the data format)
j. Select both worksheets, preview the entire workbook, then close the Preview window.
k. Print the September worksheet in landscape orientation on a single page.
l. Save and close the workbook, then exit Excel.

 Independent Challenge 3

You are a college student with two roommates. Each month you receive your long-distance telephone bill. Because no one wants to figure out who owes what, you split the bill three ways. You are sure that one of your roommates makes most of the long-distance calls. To make the situation more equitable, you decide to create a spreadsheet to track the long-distance phone calls each month. You will create a workbook with a separate sheet for each roommate and track the following information for each month's long-distance calls: date of call, time of call (AM or PM), call minutes, location called, state called, area code, phone number, and call charge. Then you will total the charges for each roommate and create a summary sheet of all three roommates' charges for the month. Since your roommate is working with an older version of Excel, you'll also save the workbook in a format he can open.

a. Start Excel, create a new workbook, then save it as **Monthly Long Distance** in the drive and folder where your Project Files are stored.
b. Enter column headings and row labels to track each call.
c. Use your own data, entering at least three long-distance calls for each roommate.
d. Create totals for minutes and charges on each roommate's sheet.
e. Create a summary sheet that shows each name and uses cell references to display the total minutes and total charges for each person.
f. On the summary sheet, create a hyperlink from each person's name to cell A1 of their respective worksheet. Enter your name on all worksheet footers, then save the workbook.
g. Create a workbook with the same type of information for the two people in the apartment next door. Save it as **Next Door**.

h. Use linking to create a 3-D reference that displays the neighbors' totals on your summary sheet so your roommates can compare their expenses with the neighbors'.
i. Create a workspace that groups the workbooks Monthly Long Distance and Next Door. Name the workspace **Phonebill**. (*Hint*: Save Workspace is an option on the File menu.)
j. Change the workbook properties of the Next Door workbook to Read-only.
k. Save the Monthly Long Distance Excel file again in Microsoft Excel 5.0 worksheet format. Name the workbook **Monthly Long Distance-5**. (*Hint*: Use the Save As command on the file menu.) Notice that the links don't work in Excel 5.0.
l. Close your browser then close any open files and exit Excel.

Independent Challenge 4

Lynne Watson, the creative director at WebProductions, a web design company, is considering purchasing digital cameras for the New York and Montreal offices. You have been asked to research this purchase by comparing features and current prices in US and Canadian currencies. Lynne would like you to prepare a worksheet containing the following information about each camera: Product Description, Manufacturer, Platform (MacOS, Windows), Max Resolution, Image Capacity, and Price in both US and Canadian currencies. You decide to investigate online vendors for this information. You will also use an online currency converter to display the price information in Canadian currency.

a. Find features and pricing for five digital cameras that you think would be appropriate for commercial images. Go to the Alta Vista search engine at www.altavista.com or Yahoo at www.yahoo.com and use their shopping directories. You can also use Excite, Hotbot, Infoseek, or another search engine of your choice. Use your search engine to find a currency converter site, then convert the prices you found from the online vendors into Canadian currency.
b. Start Excel, create a new workbook, then save it as **Camera Research** in the drive and folder where your Project Files are stored.
c. Enter the information you found on the Web in the table below. The image capacity and price information may include ranges of values.

Description	Manufacturer	Platform	Max Resolution	Image Capacity	Price $USD	Price $CAD

d. Enter the information from the table into your Camera Research workbook. Name the worksheet **Online Vendors.**
e. Add a custom header that displays the sheet name centered on the printout.
f. Add a custom footer that includes your name on the left side of the printout.
g. Make the cells in the Manufacturer column hyperlinks to the manufacturer's Web site. Save the workbook.
h. Save the workbook with the name **camera** in HTML format for management's use and preview it in your Web browser.
i. Print the worksheet from your browser.
j. Exit your browser then close any open files and exit Excel.

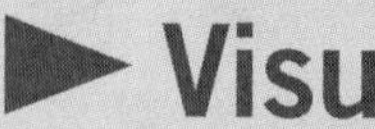

▶ Visual Workshop

Create the worksheet shown in Figure F-23, then save it as **Martinez.xls**. Enter your name in the footer, save the workbook and print the worksheet. Then save the workbook as a Web page using the name **martinez.htm**. Preview the worksheet in your Web browser, then print the sheet from the browser. Notice that the text in cell A1 is a hyperlink to the Our History worksheet; the graphic is from the Clip Gallery. If you don't have this graphic, substitute the graphic of your choice.

FIGURE F-23

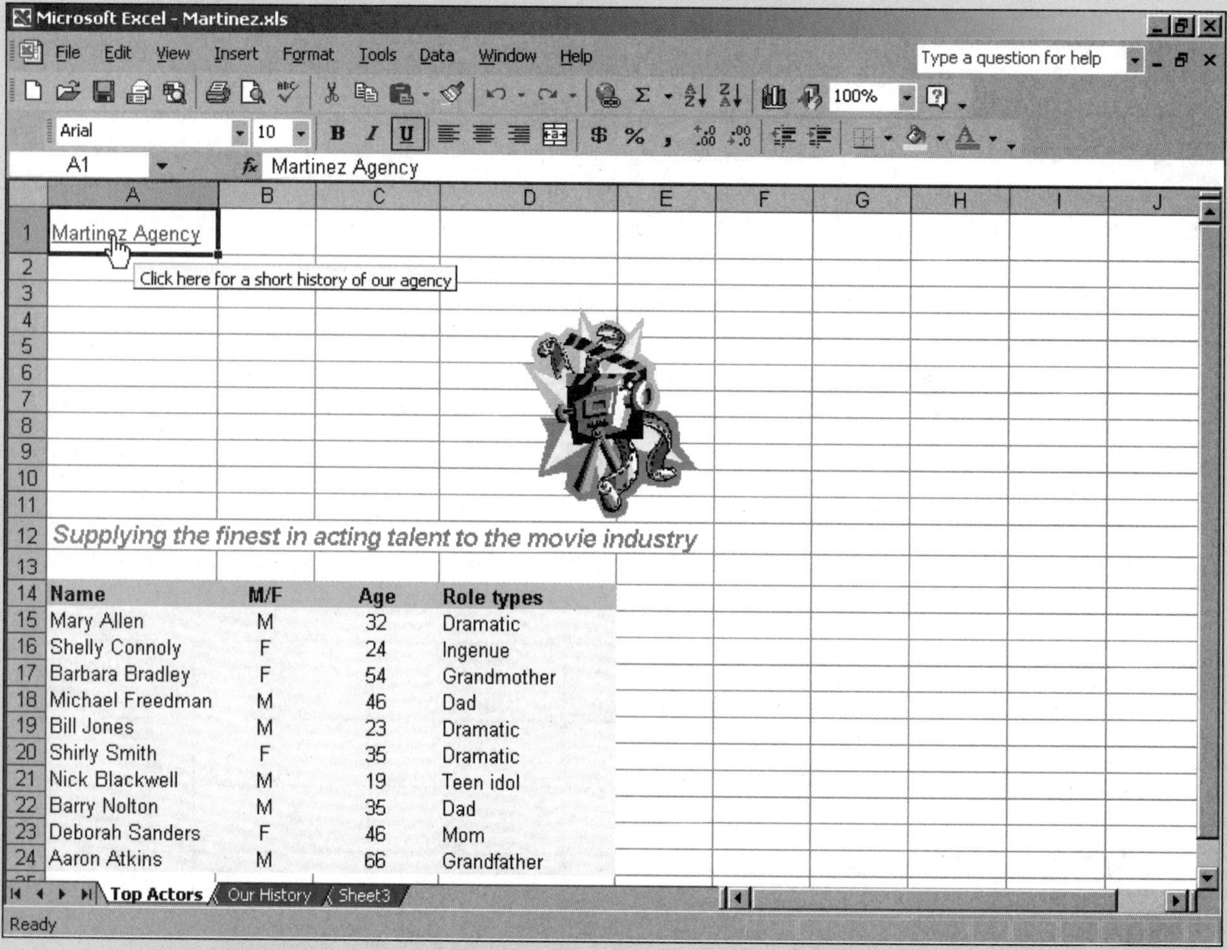

Microsoft Excel - Martinez.xls
File Edit View Insert Format Tools Data Window Help
Type a question for help
100%
Arial
10
A1
Martinez Agency
Martinez Agency
Click here for a short history of our agency
Supplying the finest in acting talent to the movie industry
Name M/F Age Role types
Mary Allen M 32 Dramatic
Shelly Connoly F 24 Ingenue
Barbara Bradley F 54 Grandmother
Michael Freedman M 46 Dad
Bill Jones M 23 Dramatic
Shirly Smith F 35 Dramatic
Nick Blackwell M 19 Teen idol
Barry Nolton M 35 Dad
Deborah Sanders F 46 Mom
Aaron Atkins M 66 Grandfather
Top Actors
Our History
Sheet3
Ready

Automating Worksheet Tasks

Objectives

- MOUS ► Plan a macro
- MOUS ► Record a macro
- MOUS ► Run a macro
- MOUS ► Edit a macro
- ► Use shortcut keys with macros
- ► Use the Personal Macro Workbook
- MOUS ► Add a macro as a menu item
- MOUS ► Create a toolbar for macros

A **macro** is a set of instructions that performs tasks in the order you specify. You create macros to automate frequently performed Excel tasks that require a series of steps. For example, if you usually enter your name and date in a worksheet footer, you can record the keystrokes in an Excel macro that enters the text and inserts the current date automatically. In this unit, you will plan and design a simple macro, then record and run it. Then you will edit the macro. You will also assign shortcut keys to a macro, store a macro in the Personal Macro Workbook, add a macro option to the Tools menu, and create a new toolbar for macros. Jim wants you to create a macro for the Accounting Department. The macro will automatically insert text that will identify the worksheet as an Accounting Department document.

Planning a Macro

You create macros for tasks that you perform on a regular basis. For example, you can create a macro to enter and format text or to save and print a worksheet. To create a macro, you record the series of actions or write the instructions in a special programming language. Because the sequence of actions is important, you need to plan the macro carefully before you record it. You use the Macro command on the Tools menu to record, run, and modify macros. Jim wants you to create a macro for the Accounting Department that inserts the text "Accounting Department" in the upper-left corner of any worksheet. You work with him to plan the macro using the following guidelines:

Details

- **Assign the macro a descriptive name**
  The first character of a macro name must be a letter; the remaining characters can be letters, numbers, or underscores. Spaces are not allowed in macro names; use underscores in place of spaces. (Press [Shift][-] to enter an underscore character.) Jim wants you to name the macro "DeptStamp". See Table G-1 for a list of macros Jim might create to automate other tasks.

- **Write out the steps the macro will perform**
  This planning helps eliminate careless errors. Jim writes a description of the macro he wants, as shown in Figure G-1.

- **Decide how you will perform the actions you want to record**
  You can use the mouse, the keyboard, or a combination of the two. Jim wants you to use both the mouse and the keyboard.

- **Practice the steps you want Excel to record, and write them down**
  Jim wrote down the sequence of actions he wants you to include in the macro.

- **Decide where to locate the description of the macro and the macro itself**
  Macros can be stored in an unused area of the active workbook, in a new workbook, or in the Personal Macro Workbook, a special workbook used only for macro storage. Jim wants you to store the macro in a new workbook.

TABLE G-1: Possible macros and their descriptive names

description of macro	descriptive name
Enter a frequently used proper name, such as Jim Fernandez	JimFernandez
Enter a frequently used company name, such as MediaLoft	CompanyName
Print the active worksheet on a single page, in landscape orientation	FitToLand
Turn off the header and footer in the active worksheet	HeadFootOff
Show a frequently used custom view, such as a generic view of the worksheet, setting the print and display settings back to the Excel defaults	GenericView

FIGURE G-1: Paper description of planned macro

Macro to create stamp with the department name

Name:	DeptStamp
Description:	Adds a stamp to the top left of the worksheet, identifying it as an Accounting Department worksheet
Steps:	1. Position the cell pointer in cell A1. 2. Type Accounting Department, then click the Enter button. 3. Click Format on the menu bar, then click Cells. 4. Click Font tab, under Font style click Bold, under Underline click Single, and under Color click Red, then click OK.

Macros and viruses

When you open an Excel workbook that has macros, you will see a message asking you if you want to enable or disable macros. This is because macros can contain viruses, destructive software programs that can damage your computer files. If you know your workbook came from a trusted source, click Enable macros. If you are not sure of the workbook's source, click Disable macros. If you disable the macros in a workbook, you will not be able to use them. For more information about macro security and security levels type "About macro security" in the Type a question for help text box.

Excel 2002

Recording a Macro

The easiest way to create a macro is to record it using the Excel Macro Recorder. You turn the Macro Recorder on, name the macro, enter the keystrokes and select the commands you want the macro to perform, then stop the recorder. As you record the macro, each action is translated into program code you can later view and modify. You can take as long as you want to record the macro; a recorded macro contains only your actions, not the amount of time you took to record it. Jim wants you to create a macro that enters a department stamp in cell A1 of the active worksheet. You create this macro by recording your actions.

Trouble?

If the task pane is not visible, click View on the menu bar, then click Task Pane. You can also open a blank workbook by clicking the New button on the Standard toolbar.

Trouble?

If the Stop Recording toolbar is not displayed, click View, point to Toolbars, then click Stop Recording.

Trouble?

If your results differ from Figure G-4, clear the contents of cell A1, then slowly and carefully repeat Steps 2 through 10. When prompted to replace the existing macro at the end of Step 5, click Yes.

1. Start Excel, click the **Blank Workbook button** on the New Workbook task pane, save the blank workbook as **My Excel Macros** in the drive and folder where your Project Files are stored, then close the task pane.
   You are ready to start recording the macro.
2. Click **Tools** on the menu bar, point to **Macro**, then click **Record New Macro**
   The Record Macro dialog box opens. See Figure G-2. The default name Macro1 is selected. You can either assign this name or enter a new name. This dialog box also allows you to assign a shortcut key for running the macro and assign a storage location for the macro.
3. Type **DeptStamp** in the Macro name text box
4. If the "Store macro" in list box does not display "This Workbook", click the **list arrow** and select **This Workbook**
5. If the Description text box does not contain your name, select the existing name, type your own name, then click **OK**
   The dialog box closes. A small Stop Recording toolbar appears containing the Stop Recording button, and the word "Recording" appears on the status bar. Take your time performing the steps below. Excel records every keystroke, menu selection, and mouse action that you make.
6. Press **[Ctrl][Home]**
   When you begin an Excel session, macros record absolute cell references. By beginning the recording in cell A1, you ensure that the macro includes the instruction to select cell A1 as the first step, even if cell A1 is already selected.
7. Type **Accounting Department** in cell A1, then click the **Enter button** on the formula bar
8. Click **Format** on the menu bar, then click **Cells**
9. Click the **Font tab**, in the Font style list box click **Bold**, click the **Underline list arrow** and click **Single**, then click the **Color list arrow** and click **red** (third row, first color on left)
   See Figure G-3.
10. Click **OK**, click the **Stop Recording button** on the Stop Recording toolbar, click **cell D1** to deselect cell A1, then save the workbook
    Compare your results with Figure G-4.

FIGURE G-2: Record Macro dialog box

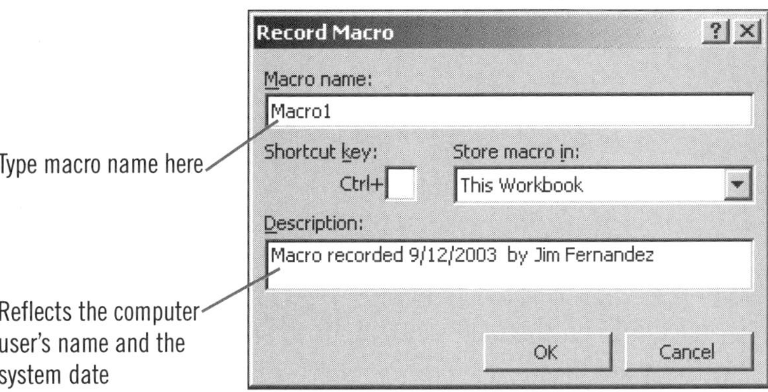

FIGURE G-3: Font tab of the Format Cells dialog box

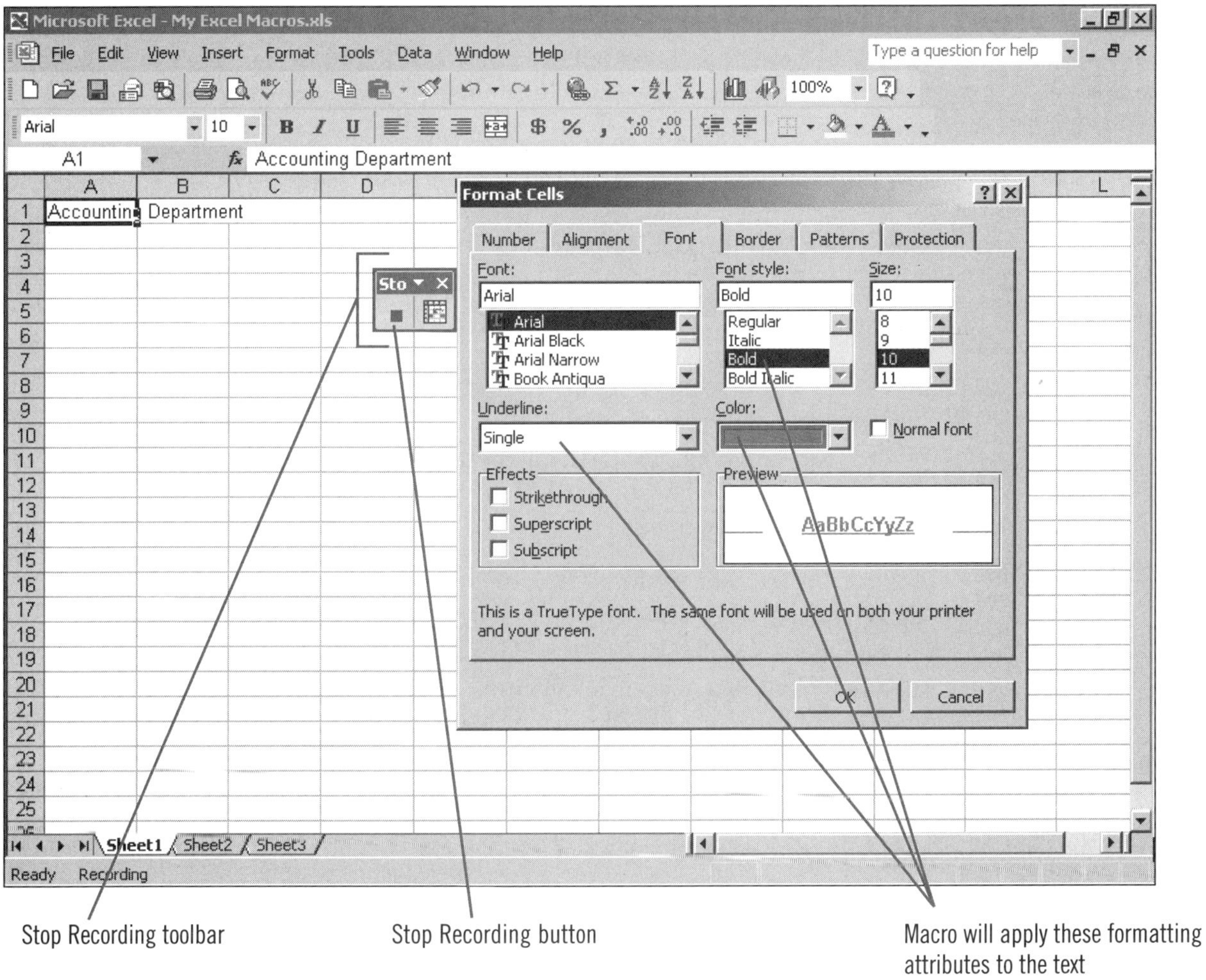

Stop Recording toolbar

Stop Recording button

Macro will apply these formatting attributes to the text

FIGURE G-4: Accounting Department stamp

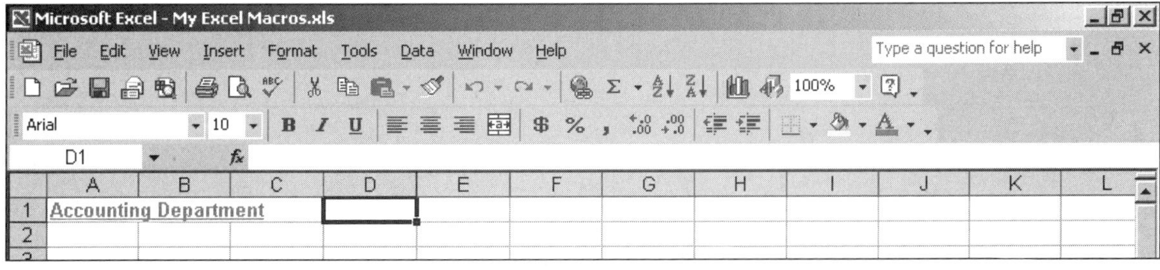

Excel 2002

Excel 2002

Running a Macro

Once you record a macro, you should test it to make sure that the actions it performs are correct. To test a macro, you **run**, or execute, it. One way to run a macro is to select the macro in the Macros dialog box, then click Run. Jim asks you to clear the contents of cell A1 then test the DeptStamp macro. After you run the macro in the My Excel Macros workbook, he asks you to test the macro once more from a newly opened workbook.

1. Click **cell A1**, click **Edit** on the menu bar, point to **Clear**, click **All**, then click any other cell to deselect cell A1

   When you delete only the contents of a cell, any formatting still remains in the cell. By using the Clear All option on the Edit menu, you can be sure that the cell is free of contents and formatting.

2. Click **Tools** on the menu bar, point to **Macro**, then click **Macros**

   The Macro dialog box, shown in Figure G-5, lists all the macros contained in the open workbooks. If other people have used your computer, other macros may be listed.

3. Make sure **DeptStamp** is selected, click **Run**, then deselect cell A1

   Watch your screen as the macro quickly plays back the steps you recorded in the previous lesson. When the macro is finished, your screen should look like Figure G-6. As long as the workbook containing the macro remains open, you can run the macro in any open workbook.

4. Click the **New button** on the Standard toolbar

   Because the new workbook automatically fills the screen, it is difficult to be sure that the My Excel Macros workbook is still open.

5. Click **Window** on the menu bar

   A list of open workbooks appears underneath the menu options. The active workbook name (in this case, Book2) appears with a check mark to its left. The My Excel Macros workbook appears on the menu, so you know it's open. See Figure G-7.

6. Deselect cell A1, click **Tools** on the menu bar, point to **Macro**, click **Macros**, make sure **'My Excel Macros.xls'!DeptStamp** is selected, click **Run**, then deselect cell A1

   When multiple workbooks are open, the macro name in the Macro dialog box includes the workbook name between single quotation marks, followed by an exclamation point, indicating that the macro is outside the active workbook. Because you only used this workbook to test the macro, you don't need to save it.

7. Close Book2 without saving changes

   The My Excel Macros workbook reappears.

QuickTip

To delete a macro, select the macro name in the Macro dialog box, click Delete, then click Yes to confirm the action.

QuickTip

To stop a macro while it is running, press [Esc] then click End.

Trouble?

If you get a security error message when attempting to run your macro, the security level may be set too high in the workbook. You can enable macros for the workbook by clicking the Macro option on the Tools menu and selecting Security. Set the security level to Medium or Low, then close and reopen the workbook.

FIGURE G-5: **Macro dialog box**

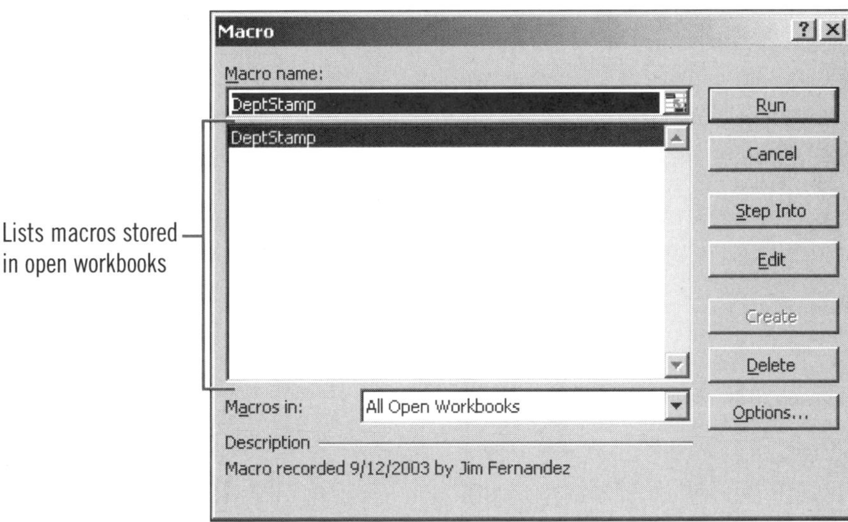

FIGURE G-6: **Result of running DeptStamp macro**

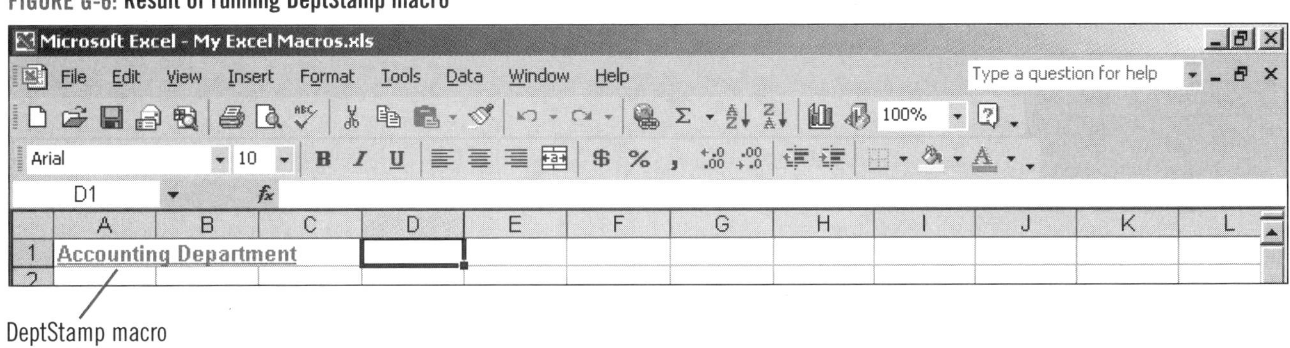

FIGURE G-7: **Window menu showing the list of open workbooks**

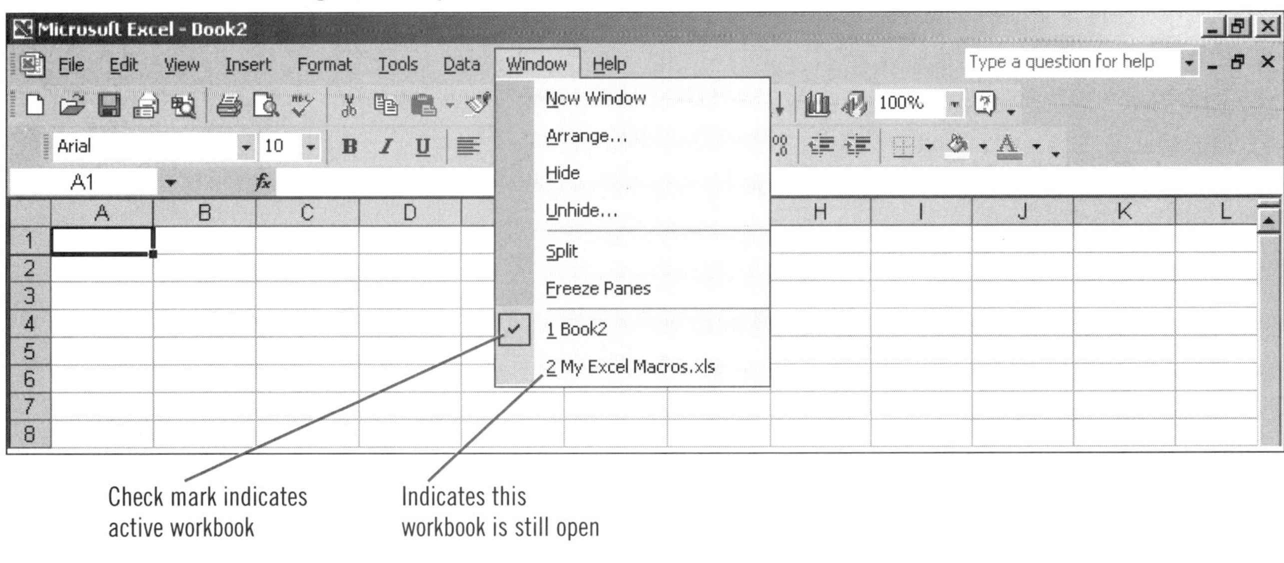

Excel 2002

Editing a Macro

When you use the Macro Recorder to create a macro, the program instructions, called **program code**, are recorded automatically in the Visual Basic for Applications (VBA) programming language. Each macro is stored as a **module**, or program code container, attached to the workbook. After you record a macro, you might need to change it. If you have a lot of changes to make, it might be best to rerecord the macro. If you need to make only minor adjustments, you can edit the macro code directly using the Visual Basic Editor. Jim wants you to modify his macro to change the point size of the department stamp to 12.

Steps 1 2 3 4

QuickTip

Another way to start the Visual Basic Editor is to click Tools on the menu bar, point to Macro, then click Visual Basic Editor, or press [Alt][F11].

1. Make sure the My Excel Macros workbook is open, click **Tools** on the menu bar, point to **Macro**, click **Macros**, make sure **DeptStamp** is selected, then click **Edit**
   The Visual Basic Editor starts, showing the DeptStamp macro steps in a numbered module window (in this case, Module1).
2. If necessary, maximize the window titled **My Excel Macros.xls – [Module1(Code)]**, then examine the steps in the macro
   The name of the macro and the date it was recorded appear at the top of the module window. Below that, Excel has translated your keystrokes and commands into macro code. When you open and make selections in a dialog box during macro recording, Excel automatically stores all the dialog box settings in the macro code. For example, the line .FontStyle = "Bold" was generated when you clicked Bold in the Format Cells dialog box. You also see lines of code that you didn't generate directly while recording the DeptStamp macro; for example, .Name = "Arial".
3. In the line .Size = 10, double-click **10** to select it, then type **12**
   See Figure G-8. Because Module1 is attached to the workbook and not stored as a separate file, any changes to the module are saved automatically when you save the workbook.
4. In the Visual Basic Editor, click **File** on the menu bar, click **Print**, click **OK** to print the module, then review the printout

QuickTip

You can return to Excel without closing the module by clicking the View Microsoft Excel button on the standard toolbar.

5. Click **File** on the menu bar, then click **Close and Return to Microsoft Excel**
   You want to rerun the DeptStamp macro to make sure the macro reflects the change you made using the Visual Basic Editor.
6. Click cell **A1**, click **Edit** on the menu bar, point to **Clear**, click **All**, deselect cell **A1**, click **Tools** on the menu bar, point to **Macro**, click **Macros**, make sure **DeptStamp** is selected, click **Run**, then deselect cell **A1**
   Compare your results to Figure G-9. The department stamp is now in 12-point type.
7. Save the workbook

FIGURE G-8: **Visual Basic Editor showing Module1**

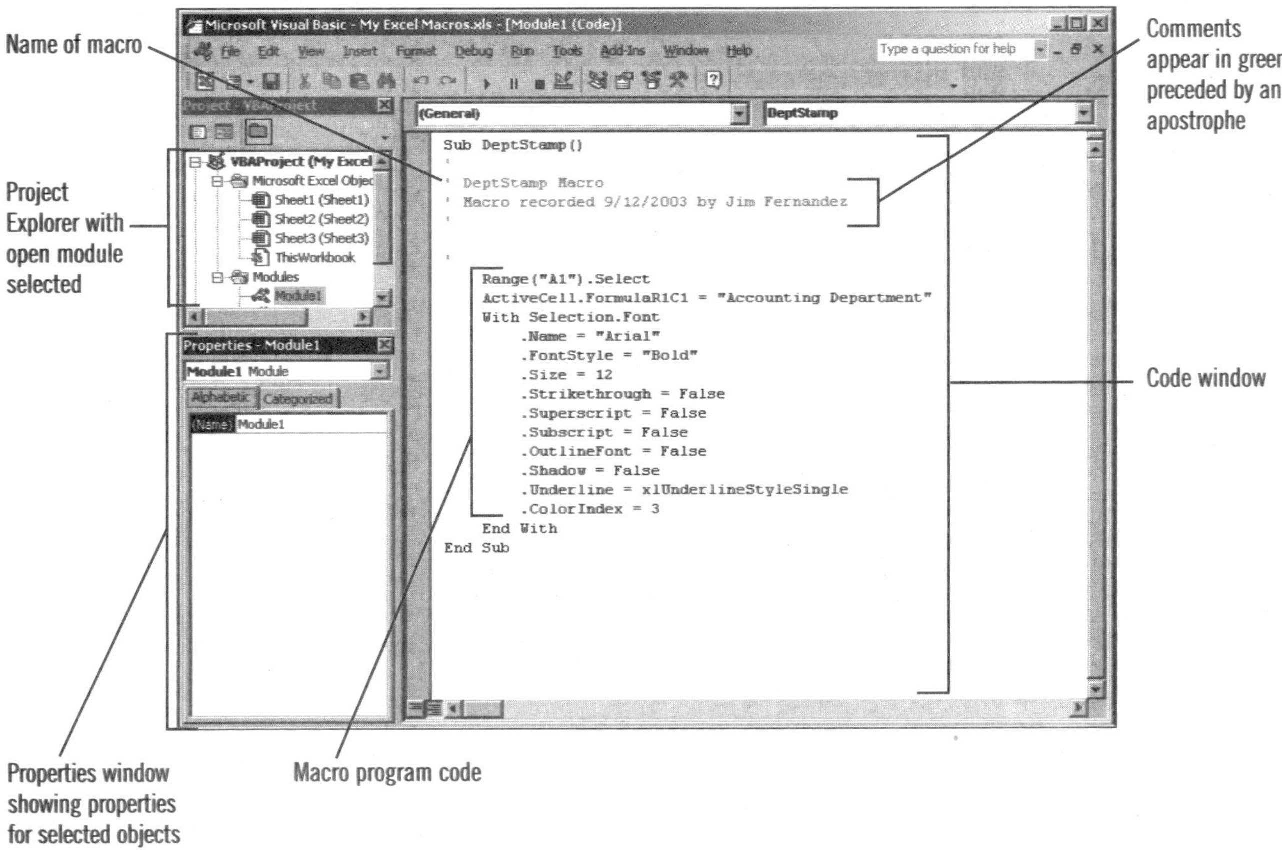

Name of macro
Project Explorer with open module selected
Properties window showing properties for selected objects
Macro program code
Comments appear in green preceded by an apostrophe
Code window
Microsoft Visual Basic - My Excel Macros.xls - [Module1 (Code)]
Sub DeptStamp()
'
' DeptStamp Macro
' Macro recorded 9/12/2003 by Jim Fernandez
'
'
Range("A1").Select
ActiveCell.FormulaR1C1 = "Accounting Department"
With Selection.Font
.Name = "Arial"
.FontStyle = "Bold"
.Size = 12
.Strikethrough = False
.Superscript = False
.Subscript = False
.OutlineFont = False
.Shadow = False
.Underline = xlUnderlineStyleSingle
.ColorIndex = 3
End With
End Sub

FIGURE G-9: **Result of running edited DeptStamp macro**

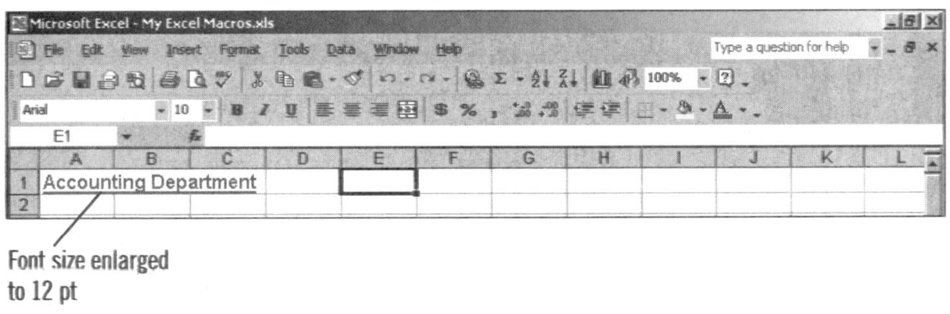

Microsoft Excel - My Excel Macros.xls
Accounting Department
Font size enlarged to 12 pt

CLUES TO USE

Adding comments to Visual Basic code

With practice, you will be able to interpret the lines of code within your macro. Others who use your macro, however, might want to know the function of a particular line. You can explain the code by adding comments to the macro. Comments are explanatory text added to the lines of code. When you enter a comment, you must type an apostrophe (') before the comment text. Otherwise, the program will try to interpret it as a command. On the screen, comments appear in green after you press [Enter]. See Figure G-8. You also can insert blank lines as comments in the macro code to make the code more readable. To do this, type an apostrophe, then press [Enter].

Excel 2002

Using Shortcut Keys with Macros

In addition to running a macro from the Macro dialog box, you can run a macro by assigning a shortcut key combination to it. Using shortcut keys to run macros reduces the number of actions required to begin macro playback. You assign shortcut key combinations in the Record Macro dialog box. Jim also wants you to create a macro called CompanyName to enter the company name into a worksheet. You will assign a shortcut key combination to run the macro.

Steps

1. **Click cell B2**

   You will record the macro in cell B2. You want the macro to enter the company name anywhere in a worksheet. Therefore, you will not begin the macro with an instruction to position the cell pointer, as you did in the DeptStamp macro.

2. **Click Tools on the menu bar, point to Macro, then click Record New Macro**

   The Record Macro dialog box opens. Notice the option Shortcut key: Ctrl+ followed by a blank box. You can type a letter (A–Z) in the Shortcut key text box to assign the key combination of [Ctrl] plus that letter to run the macro. You use the key combination [Ctrl][Shift] plus a letter to avoid overriding any of the Excel [Ctrl] [letter] shortcut keys, such as [Ctrl][C] for Copy.

3. **With the default macro name selected, type CompanyName, click the Shortcut key text box, press and hold [Shift], type C, then, if necessary, replace the name in the Description box with your name**

   Compare your screen with Figure G-10. You are ready to record the CompanyName macro.

4. **Click OK to close the dialog box**

   By default, Excel records absolute cell references in macros. Beginning the macro in cell B2 causes the macro code to begin with a statement to select cell B2. Because you want to be able to run this macro in any active cell, you need to instruct Excel to record relative cell references while recording the macro.

5. **Click the Relative Reference button on the Stop Recording toolbar**

   The Relative Reference button is now selected. See Figure G-11. This button is a toggle and retains the relative reference setting until you click it again to turn it off or you exit Excel.

6. **Type MediaLoft in cell B2, click the Enter button on the formula bar, press [Ctrl][I] to italicize the text, click the Stop Recording button on the Stop Recording toolbar, then deselect cell B2**

   MediaLoft appears in italics in cell B2. You are ready to run the macro in cell A5 using the shortcut key combination.

7. **Click cell A5, press and hold [Ctrl][Shift], type C, then deselect the cell**

   The company name appears in cell A5. See Figure G-12. Because the macro played back in the selected cell (A5) instead of the cell where it was recorded (B2), you know that the macro recorded relative cell references.

8. **Save the workbook**

FIGURE G-10: Record Macro dialog box with shortcut key assigned

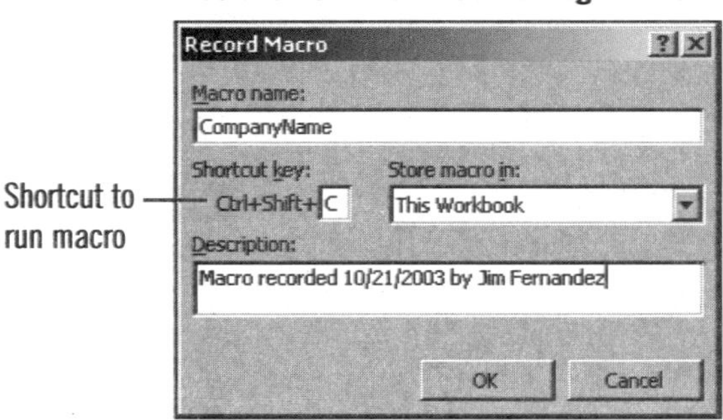

FIGURE G-11: Stop Recording toolbar with Relative Reference button selected

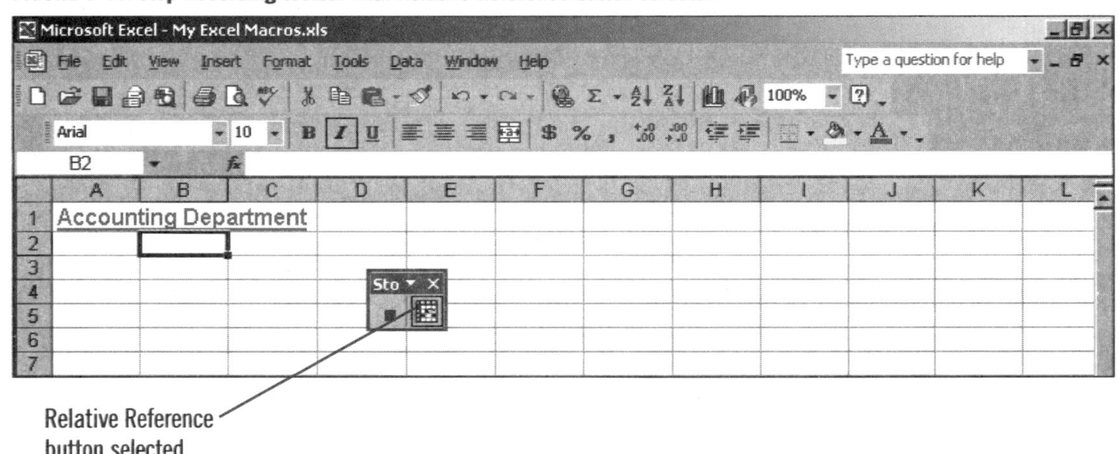

FIGURE G-12: Result of running the CompanyName macro

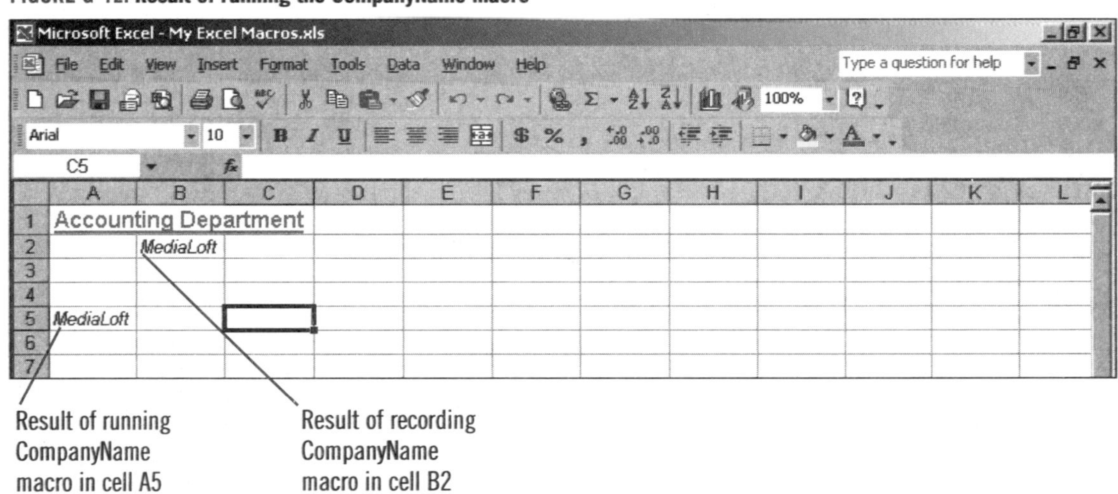

Excel 2002

Excel 2002

Using the Personal Macro Workbook

You can store commonly used macros in a **Personal Macro Workbook**. The Personal Macro Workbook is always available, unless you specify otherwise, and gives you access to all the macros it contains, regardless of which workbooks are open. The Personal Macro Workbook file is created automatically the first time you choose to store a macro in it. You can add additional macros to the Personal Macro Workbook by saving them there. Jim often likes to add a footer to his worksheets identifying his department, the workbook name, the worksheet name, his name, and the current date. He wants you to create a macro that automatically inserts this footer. Because he wants to use this macro in future worksheets, he asks you to store this macro in the Personal Macro Workbook.

Steps

1. **From any cell in the active worksheet, click Tools on the menu bar, point to Macro, then click Record New Macro**
   The Record Macro dialog box opens.

2. **Type FooterStamp in the Macro name text box, click the Shortcut key text box, press and hold [Shift], type F, then click the Store macro in list arrow**
   You have named the macro FooterStamp and assigned it the shortcut combination [Ctrl][Shift][F]. Notice that This Workbook is selected by default, indicating that Excel automatically stores macros in the active workbook. See Figure G-13. You also can choose to store the macro in a new workbook or in the Personal Macro Workbook.

3. **Click Personal Macro Workbook, replace the existing name in the Description text box with your own name, if necessary, then click OK**
   The recorder is on, and you are ready to record the macro keystrokes. If you are prompted to replace an existing macro named FooterStamp, click Yes.

4. **Click File on the menu bar, click Page Setup, click the Header/Footer tab (make sure to do this even if it is already active), click Custom Footer, in the Left section box, type Accounting; click the Center section box, click the File Name button, press [Spacebar], type /, press [Spacebar], click the Tab Name button to insert the sheet name; click the Right section box, type your name followed by a comma, press [Spacebar], click the Date button, click OK to return to the Header/Footer tab**
   The footer stamp is set up, as shown in Figure G-14.

5. **Click OK to return to the worksheet, then click the Stop Recording button on the Stop Recording toolbar**
   You want to ensure that the macro will set the footer stamp in any active worksheet.

6. **Activate Sheet2, in cell A1 type Testing the FooterStamp macro, press [Enter], press and hold [Ctrl][Shift], then type F**
   The FooterStamp macro plays back the sequence of commands.

7. **Preview the worksheet to verify that the new footer was inserted, then close the Preview window**

8. **Save the workbook, then print the worksheet**
   Jim is satisfied that the FooterStamp macro works in any active worksheet.

QuickTip

If you see a message saying that the Personal Macro Workbook needs to be opened, open it, then begin again from Step 1. The Personal Macro Workbook file is usually stored in the Documents and Settings/Administrator/Application Data/Microsoft/Excel/XLSTART folder under the name "Personal.xls" and opens when you open Excel.

QuickTip

You can copy or move macros stored in other workbooks to the Personal Macro Workbook by using the Visual Basic Editor.

FIGURE G-13: Record Macro dialog box showing macro storage options

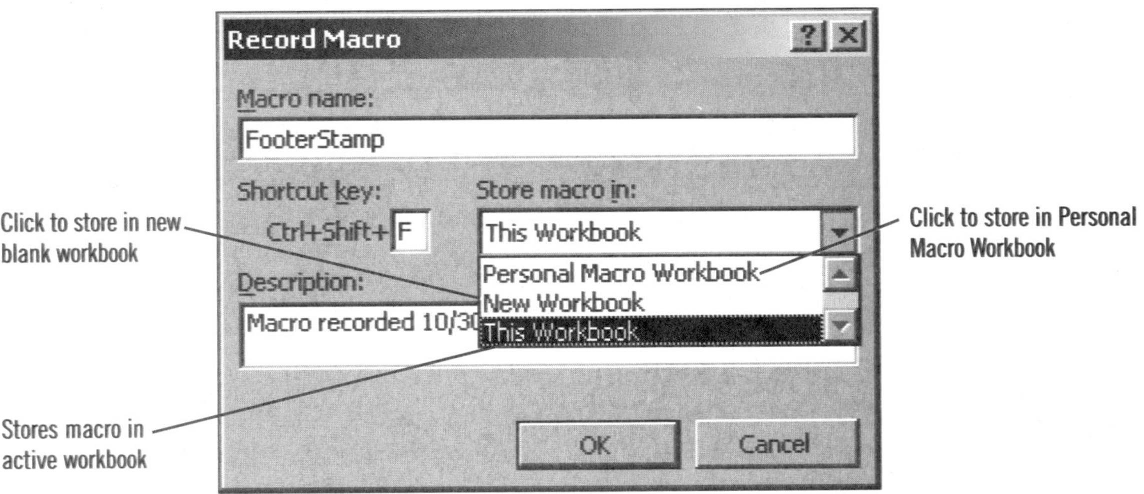

FIGURE G-14: Header/Footer tab showing custom footer settings

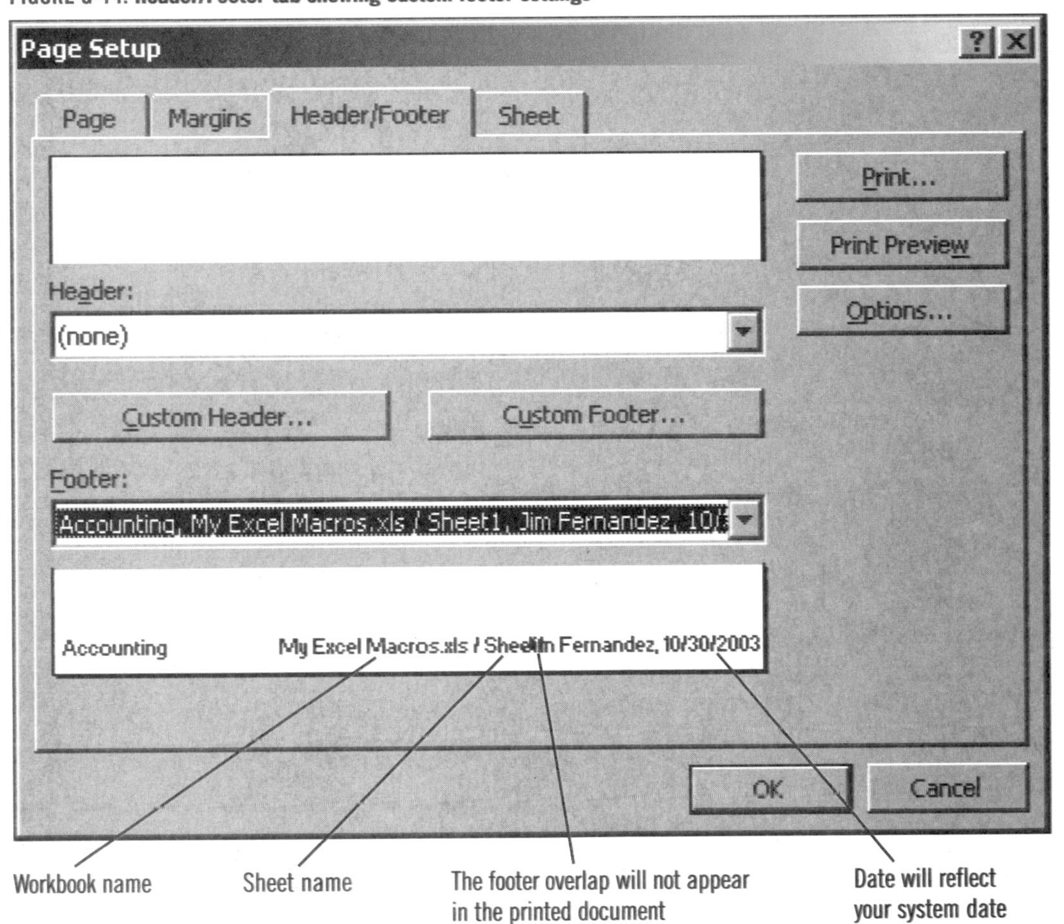

Working with the Personal Macro Workbook

Once you use the Personal Macro Workbook, it opens automatically each time you start Excel so you can add macros to it. By default, the Personal Macro Workbook is hidden as a precautionary measure so you don't accidentally delete anything from it. If you need to delete a macro from the Personal Macro Workbook, click Unhide on the Window menu, click Personal.xls, then click OK.

Adding a Macro as a Menu Item

In addition to storing macros in the Personal Macro Workbook so that they are always available, you can add macros as items on the Excel Worksheet menu bar. The **Worksheet menu bar** is the toolbar at the top of the Excel screen. To increase the availability of the FooterStamp macro, Jim decides to add it as an item on the Tools menu. He wants you to add a custom menu item to the Tools menu, then assign the macro to that menu item.

Steps

1. **With Sheet2 active, click Tools on the menu bar, click Customize, click the Commands tab, then under Categories, click Macros**
   See Figure G-15.

QuickTip

You may need to reposition the Customize dialog box to make the Tools option on the Worksheet menu bar visible.

2. **Click Custom Menu Item under Commands, drag the selection to Tools on the menu bar (the menu opens), then point just under the last menu option, but do not release the mouse button**
   Compare your screen to Figure G-16.
3. **Release the mouse button**
   Now, Custom Menu Item is the last item on the Tools menu.
4. **With the Tools menu still open, right-click Custom Menu Item, select the text in the Name box (&Custom Menu Item), type Footer Stamp, then click Assign Macro**
   Unlike a macro name, the name of a custom menu item can have spaces between words like all standard menu items. The Assign Macro dialog box opens.
5. **Click PERSONAL.XLS!FooterStamp under Macro name, click OK, then click Close**
   You have assigned the FooterStamp macro to the new menu command.
6. **Click the Sheet3 tab, in cell A1 type Testing macro menu item, press [Enter], then click Tools on the menu bar**
   The Tools menu appears with the new menu option at the bottom. See Figure G-17.
7. **Click Footer Stamp, preview the worksheet to verify that the footer was inserted, then close the Print Preview window**
   The Print Preview window appears with the footer stamp. Because others using your computer might be confused by the macro on the menu, it's a good idea to remove it.
8. **Click Tools on the menu bar, click Customize, click the Toolbars tab, click Worksheet Menu Bar to highlight it, click Reset, click OK to confirm, click Close, click Tools on the menu bar to make sure that the custom item has been deleted, then save the workbook**

Adding a custom menu

You can create a custom menu on an existing toolbar and assign macros to it. To do this, click Tools on the menu bar, click Customize, click the Commands tab, click New Menu in the Categories list, then drag the New Menu from the Commands box to the toolbar. To name the new menu, right-click, then enter a name in the Name box.

FIGURE G-15: Commands tab of the Customize dialog box

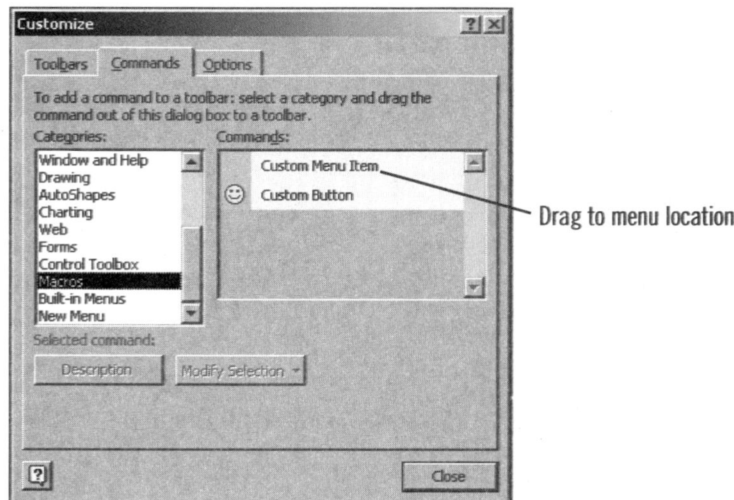

FIGURE G-16: Tools menu showing placement of the Custom Menu Item

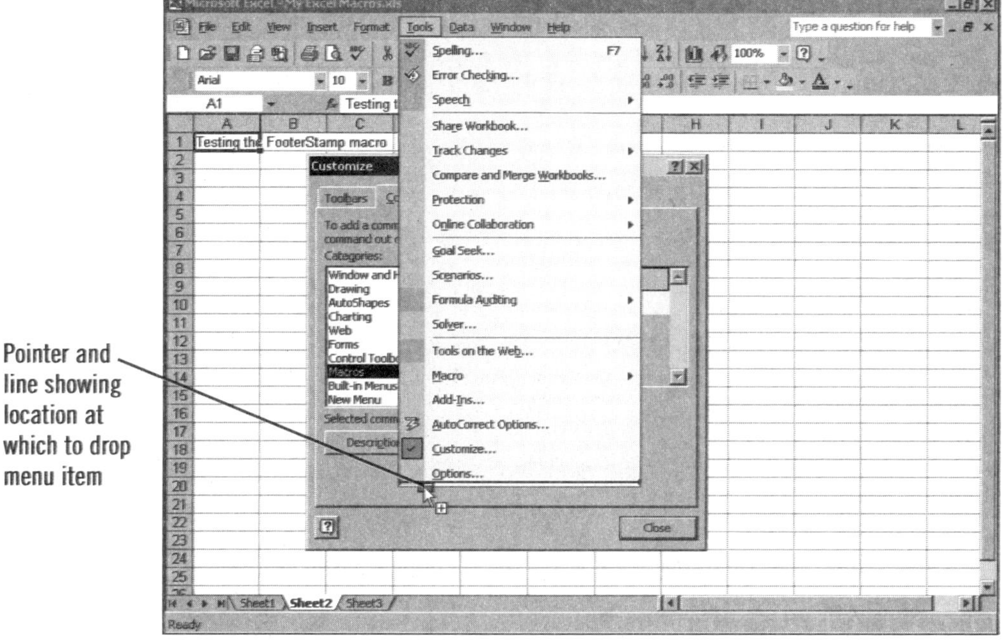

FIGURE G-17: Tools menu with new Footer Stamp item

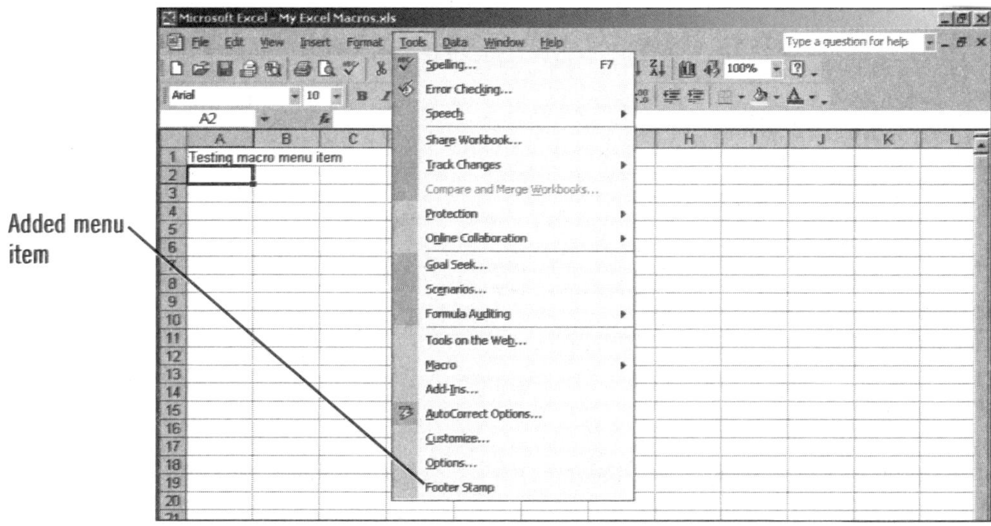

Excel 2002

Excel 2002

Creating a Toolbar for Macros

Toolbars contain buttons that allow you to access commonly used commands. You can create your own custom toolbars to organize commands so that you can find and use them quickly. Once you create a toolbar, you can add buttons to access Excel commands such as macros. Jim asks you to create a custom toolbar called Macros that will contain buttons to run two of his macros.

Steps

QuickTip

Toolbars you create or customize are available to all workbooks on your computer. You can ensure that a custom toolbar is visible in a specific workbook by attaching the toolbar to the workbook using the Toolbars tab in the Customize dialog box.

1. With Sheet3 active, click **Tools** on the menu bar, click **Customize**, click the **Toolbars tab**, then click **New**
   The New Toolbar dialog box opens, as shown in Figure G-18. Under Toolbar name, a default name of Custom1 is selected.
2. Type **Macros**, then click **OK**
   Excel adds the new toolbar named Macros to the bottom of the Toolbars list, and a small, empty toolbar named Macros opens. See Figure G-19. You cannot see the entire toolbar name. A toolbar starts out small and expands to fit the buttons you assign to it.
3. Click the **Commands tab** in the Customize dialog box, click **Macros** under Categories, then drag the **Custom button** over the new Macros toolbar and release the mouse button
   The Macros toolbar contains one button. You want the toolbar to contain two macros, so you need to add one more button.
4. Drag the **Custom button** over the Macros toolbar again
   With the two buttons in place, you are ready to customize the buttons and assign macros to them.
5. Right-click the left button on the Macros toolbar, select **&Custom Button** in the Name box, type **Department Stamp**, click **Assign Macro**, click **DeptStamp**, then click **OK**
   With the first toolbar button customized, you are ready to customize the second button.
6. With the Customize dialog box open, right-click the right button on the Macros toolbar, edit the name to read **Company Name**, click **Change Button Image**, click (seventh row, first column), right-click , click **Assign Macro**, click **CompanyName** to select it, click **OK**, then close the Customize dialog box
   The Macros toolbar appears with the two customized macro buttons.
7. Move the mouse pointer over on the Macros toolbar to display the macro name (Department Stamp), then click to run the macro; click **cell B2**, move the mouse pointer over on the Macros toolbar to display the macro name (Company Name), then click to run that macro; deselect the cell
   Compare your screen with Figure G-20. The DeptStamp macro automatically replaces the contents of cell A1. Because others using your computer might be confused by the new toolbar, it's a good idea to remove it.
8. Click **Tools** on the menu bar, click **Customize**, click the **Toolbars tab** if necessary, in the Toolbars window click **Macros** to highlight it, click **Delete**, click **OK** to confirm the deletion, then click **Close**
9. Save the workbook, print Sheet 3, then close the document and exit Excel
   The completed figure for Sheet1 is shown in Figure G-12.

FIGURE G-18: New Toolbar dialog box

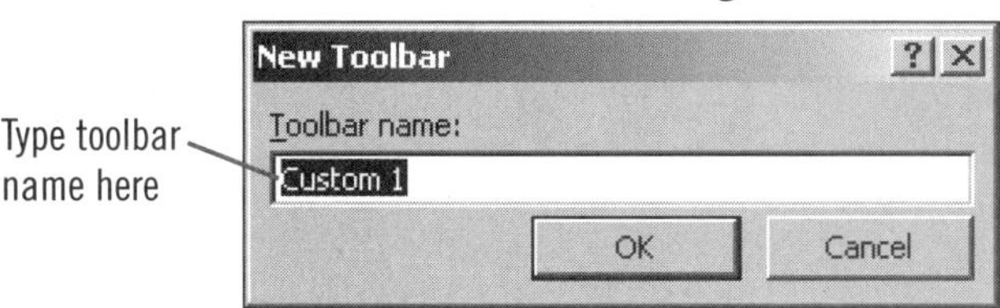

FIGURE G-19: Customize dialog box with new Macros toolbar

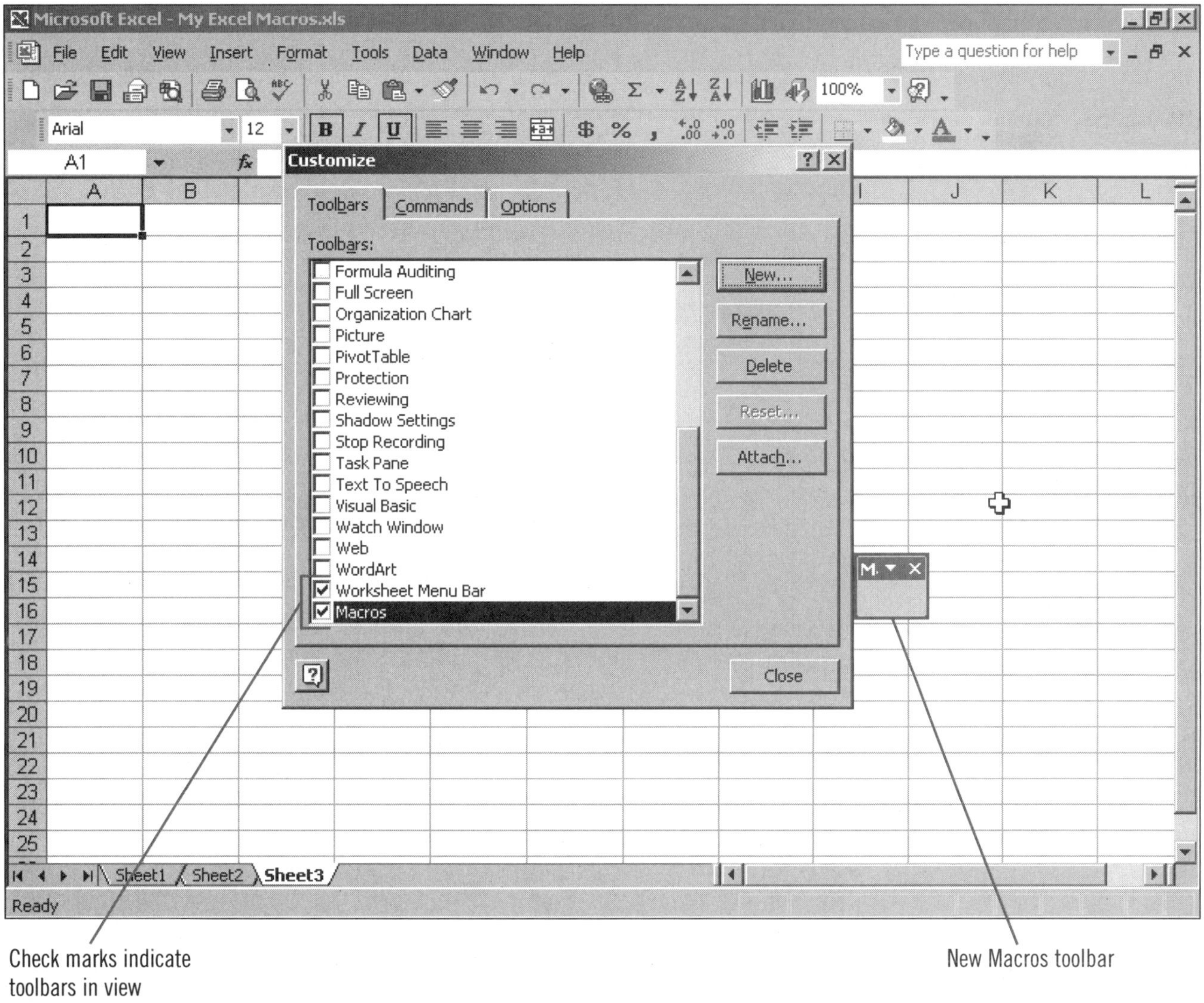

Check marks indicate toolbars in view

New Macros toolbar

FIGURE G-20: Worksheet showing Macros toolbar with two customized buttons

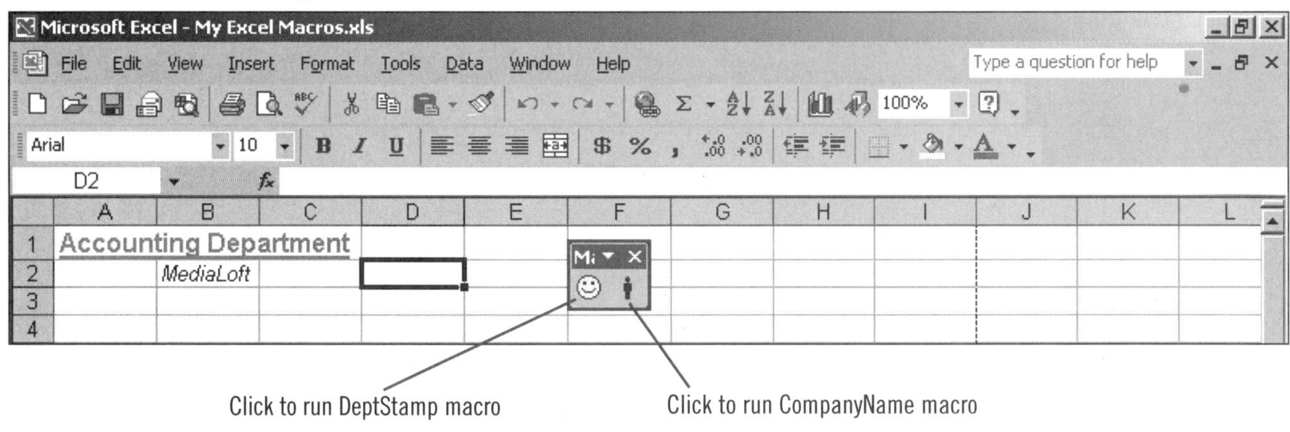

Excel 2002

Excel 2002

Practice

► Concepts Review

Label each element of the Excel screen shown in Figure G-21.

FIGURE G-21

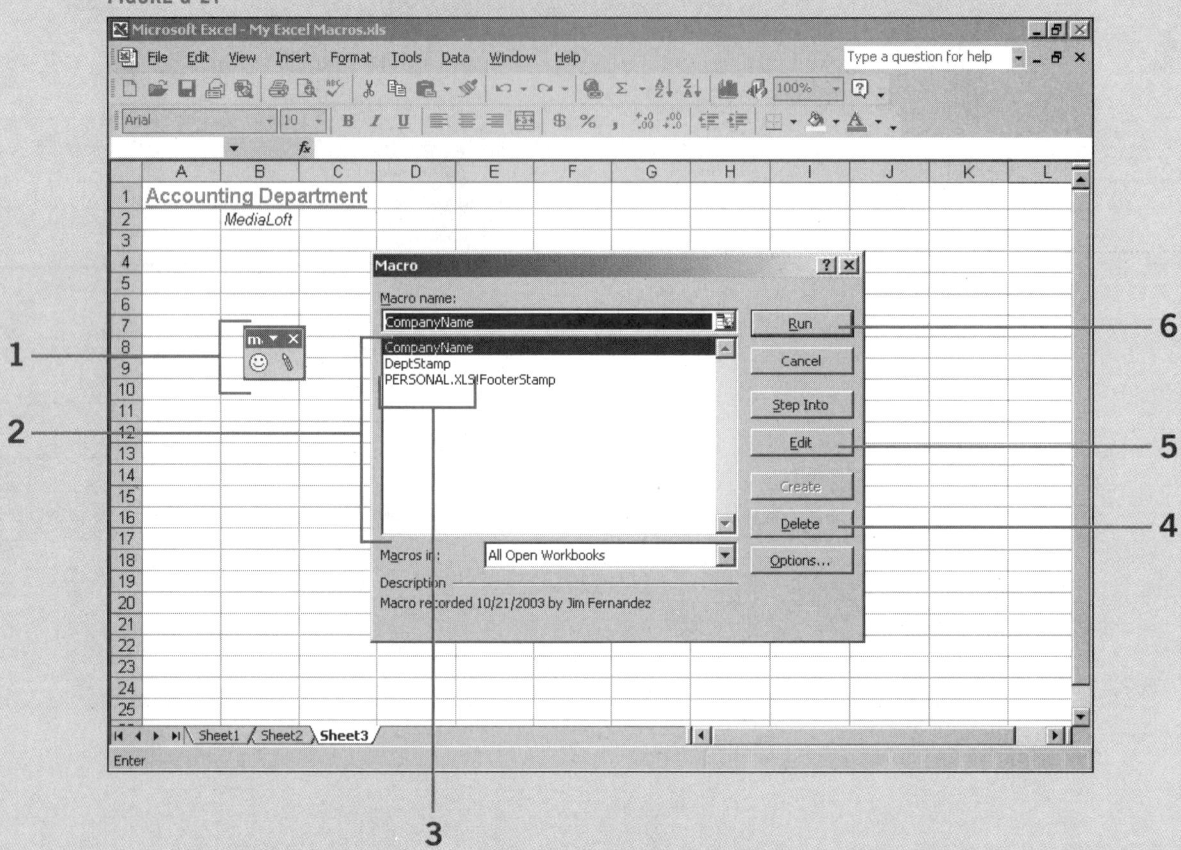

Match each term or button with the statement that describes it.

7. Visual Basic Editor	a. Statements that appear in green explaining macro code
8. Macro comments	b. Used to store commonly used macros
9. Personal Macro Workbook	c. Used to make changes to macro code
10. [button icon]	d. Used to record relative cell references
11. [smiley button icon]	e. Used to add a custom button on a macros toolbar

Select the best answer from the list of choices.

12. Which of the following is the best candidate for a macro?

a. One-button or one-keystroke commands.
b. Often-used sequences of commands or actions.
c. Seldom-used commands or tasks.
d. Nonsequential tasks.

13. When you are recording a macro, you can execute commands by using:

a. Only the keyboard.
b. Only the mouse.
c. Any combination of the keyboard and the mouse.
d. Only menu commands.

14. Commonly used macros should be stored in:

a. The Common Macro Workbook.
b. The Master Macro Workbook.
c. The Personal Macro Workbook.
d. The Custom Macro Workbook.

15. Which of the following is *not* true about editing a macro?

a. You edit macros using the Visual Basic Editor.
b. A macro cannot be edited and must be recorded again.
c. You can type changes directly in the existing program code.
d. You can make more than one editing change in a macro.

16. Why is it important to plan a macro?

a. Macros won't be stored if they contain errors.
b. Planning helps prevent careless errors from being introduced into the macro.
c. It is impossible to edit a macro.
d. Macros can't be deleted.

17. Macros are recorded with relative references:

a. Only if the Relative Reference button is selected.
b. In all cases.
c. Only if relative references are chosen while recording the macro.
d. Only if the Absolute Reference button is not selected.

18. You can run macros:

a. From the Macro dialog box.
b. From shortcut key combinations.
c. As items on menus.
d. Using all of the above.

Skills Review

1. **Record a macro.**
   a. Start Excel, open a new workbook, then save it as **Macros** in the drive and folder where your Project Files are stored. You will record a macro titled **MyAddress** that enters and formats your name, address, and telephone number in a worksheet.
   b. Store the macro in the current workbook.
   c. Record the macro, entering your name in cell A1, your street address in cell A2, your city, state, and ZIP code in cell A3, and your telephone number in cell A4.
   d. Format the information in 12-point Arial bold.
   e. Add a border and make the text red.
   f. Stop the recorder and save the workbook.

2. **Run a macro.**
   a. Clear cell entries and formats in the range affected by the macro.
   b. Run the MyAddress macro in cell A1.
   c. On the worksheet, clear all the cell entries and formats generated by running the MyAddress macro.
   d. Save the workbook.

3. **Edit a macro.**
   a. Open the MyAddress macro in the Visual Basic Editor.
   b. Locate the line of code that defines the font size, then change the size to 16 point.
   c. Edit the Range in the fifth line of macro to A1:D4 to accommodate the increased label size.
   d. Add a comment line that describes this macro.
   e. Save and print the module, then return to Excel.
   f. Test the macro in Sheet1.
   g. Save the workbook.

4. **Use shortcut keys with macros.**
   a. Record a macro called **MyName** in the current workbook that enters your full name in boldface in the selected cell of a worksheet. (*Hint*: You will need to record a relative cell reference).
   b. Assign your macro the shortcut key combination [Ctrl][Shift][Q] and store it in the current workbook.
   c. After you record the macro, clear the cell containing your name that you used to record the macro.
   d. Use the shortcut key combination to run the MyName macro.
   e. Save the workbook.

5. **Use the Personal Macro Workbook.**
   a. Record a new macro called **FitToLand** that sets print orientation to landscape, with content scaled to fit on one page.
   b. Store the macro in the Personal Macro Workbook. If you are prompted to replace the existing FitToLand macro, click Yes.
   c. After you record the macro, activate Sheet2, and enter some test data in row 1 that exceeds one page width.
   d. In the Page Setup dialog box, make sure the orientation is set to portrait and the scaling is 100 percent of normal size.
   e. Run the macro.

f. Preview Sheet2 and verify that it's in landscape view and fits on one page.
g. Save the workbook.

6. Add a macro as a menu item.

a. On the Commands tab in the Customize dialog box, specify that you want to create a Custom Menu Item for macros.
b. Place the Custom Menu Item at the bottom of the Tools menu.
c. Rename the Custom Menu Item **Fit to Landscape**.
d. Assign the macro PERSONAL.XLS!FitToLand to the command.
e. Go to Sheet3 and make sure the orientation is set to portrait, then enter some test data in column A.
f. Run the Fit to Landscape macro from the Tools menu.
g. Preview the worksheet and verify that it is in landscape view.
h. Reset the Worksheet Menu bar.
i. Verify that the Fit to Landscape command has been removed from the Tools menu.
j. Save the workbook.

7. Create a toolbar for macros.

a. With the Macros workbook still open, you will create a new custom toolbar, titled My Info.
b. Display the Macros command category in the customize dialog box, then drag the Custom Button to the My Info toolbar.
c. Drag the Custom Button to the My Info toolbar a second time to create another button.
d. Rename the first button **My Address**, and assign the MyAddress macro to it.
e. Rename the second button **My Name**, and assign the MyName macro to it.
f. Change the second button image to one of your choice.
g. On Sheet3, clear the existing cell data, then test both macro buttons on the My Info toolbar.
h. Use the Toolbars tab of the Customize dialog box to delete the toolbar named My Info.
i. Save the workbook, print the worksheet, close the workbook, then exit Excel.

▶ Independent Challenge 1

As a computer-support employee of Boston Accounting Solutions, you need to develop ways to help your fellow employees work more efficiently. Employees have asked for Excel macros that will do the following:

- Delete the current row and insert a blank row
- Delete the current column and insert a blank column
- Place the department name of Accounting in a 14-point red font in cell A1 (The width of A1 should be increased if necessary)

a. Plan and write the steps necessary for each macro.
b. Start Excel, create a new workbook, then save it as **Excel Utility Macros** in the drive and folder where your Project Files are stored.
c. Create a new toolbar called **Helpers**.
d. Create a macro for each employee request described above, name them DeleteRow, DeleteColumn, and DepartmentName, then save them in the Excel Utility Macros workbook.
e. Add comment lines to each module, describing the function of the macro and your name, then return to Excel.
f. Add each macro to the Tools menu.

g. On the Helpers toolbar, install buttons to run the macros.
h. Test each macro by using the Run command, the menu command, and the new buttons.
i. Delete the new toolbar, then reset the Worksheet menu bar.
j. Save the workbook, print the module containing the program code for all three macros, then close the workbook and exit Excel.

► Independent Challenge 2

You are an analyst in the Loan Department of Atlantic Bank. Every quarter, you produce a number of single-page quarterly budget worksheets. Your manager has informed you that certain worksheets need to contain a footer stamp indicating that the worksheet was produced in the Loan Department. The footer should also show the current page number out of the total number of pages, (for example, 1 of 5) and the workbook filename. It's tedious to add the footer stamp to the numerous worksheets you produce. You will record a macro to do this.

a. Plan and write the steps to create the macro.
b. Start Excel, create a new workbook, then save it as **Header and Footer Stamp** in the drive and folder where your Project Files are stored.
c. Create the macro described above, name it footerstamp, assign it the shortcut key combination [Ctrl][Shift][F], and store it in the current workbook. Make sure it adds the footer with the department name and the other required information.
d. Add a descriptive comment line to the macro code with your name.
e. Add the macro to the Tools menu.
f. Create a toolbar titled **Stamp**, then add a button to the toolbar to run the macro.
g. Enter the text **Footer Test** in cell A1. Test the macro using the shortcut key combination, the menu command, and the new button.
h. Delete the new toolbar, then reset the Worksheet menu bar.
i. Save the workbook, print the module for the macro, close the module and the workbook, then exit Excel.

► Independent Challenge 3

You are an administrative assistant at the Sydney, Australia, branch of Computers Inc. A major part of your job is to create spreadsheets that project sales results in different markets. It seems that you are constantly changing the print settings so that workbooks print in landscape orientation and are scaled to fit on one page. You have decided that it's time to create a macro to streamline this process.

a. Plan and write the steps necessary to create the macro.
b. Start Excel, create a new workbook, then save it as **Computers Inc Macro** in the drive and folder where your Project Files are stored.
c. Create a macro that changes the page orientation to landscape and scales the worksheet to fit on one page.
d. Name the macro **Landscape**, assign it the shortcut key combination [Ctrl][Shift][L], and store it in the current workbook.
e. Add the macro to the Tools menu.
f. Enter the text **Macro test** in cell A1 and add your name. Test the macro using the new menu command.
g. Reset the Worksheet menu bar and change the page orientation back to portrait.
h. Edit the macro to include the company name, Computers Inc, in the center footer and add your name as a comment. Test the macro using the shortcut key combination, making sure the footer was added.

i. Add a custom menu to the standard toolbar and name it **Macros**. Add a custom menu item to the new Macros menu, name the menu option **Page Orientation**, and assign the landscape macro to it.
j. Delete the footer and change the page orientation to portrait, then test the macro using the new menu.
k. Reset the standard toolbar.
l. Save the workbook, print the module for the macro; close the workbook, then exit Excel.

Independent Challenge 4

PC Assist, a software training company, has decided to begin purchasing its branch office supplies through online vendors. One of the products the company needs to purchase is toner for the Hewlett-Packard LaserJet 2100 printers in the offices. You have been asked to research vendors and prices on the Web. You will create a workbook to hold office supply vendor information that you can use for various products. You will add a macro to this workbook to find the lowest price of the product, format the information, and add a descriptive footer to the worksheet.

Go to the AltaVista search engine at www.altavista.com and enter **Office Supplies** in the Search box. You can also use Yahoo!, Excite, Infoseek, or another search engine of your choice. You may want to use the shopping directories on the search engines as another source of information. Find three online suppliers of toner for the company's printers and note their prices.

a. Start Excel, open the Project File EX G-1 from the drive and folder where your Project Files are stored, enter your name into cell A15, then save the workbook as **Office Supplies**.
b. Complete the table below with three online suppliers of office products you found in your search.

Office Product	
Vendor	Price
Lowest Price	

c. Enter three vendors and their prices from your table into the Excel worksheet. Enter the Product name **Toner** in the cell next to Office Product.
d. Create a macro named **Toner** in the Office Supplies workbook that can be activated by the [Ctrl][Shift][T] key combination. The macro should do the following:
   - Find the lowest price for the office product and insert it to the right of the Lowest Price label.
   - Boldface the Lowest Price text and the cell to its right that will contain the lowest value.
   - Place a thick box border around all the information.
   - Fill the information area with a light turquoise color.
   - Add a footer with the company name **PC Assist** on the left and the workbook name on the right.
   - Include your name in a comment line.
e. Clear all the formatting, the footer, and the lowest price from the worksheet.
f. Test the macro using the key combination [Ctrl][Shift][T].
g. Save your workbook, print the results of the macro, then open the macro in the Visual Basic Editor and print the macro code.
h. Return to Excel, close the workbook, then exit Excel.

Excel 2002

 Visual Workshop

Create the macro shown in Figure G-22. (*Hint*: Save a blank workbook as **File Utility Macros**, then create a macro in the current workbook called **SaveClose** that saves a previously named workbook. Finally, include the line **ActiveWorkbook.Close** in the module, as shown in the figure.) Print the module. Test the macro. If the "Macro recorded" comment doesn't contain your name, edit it accordingly.

FIGURE G-22

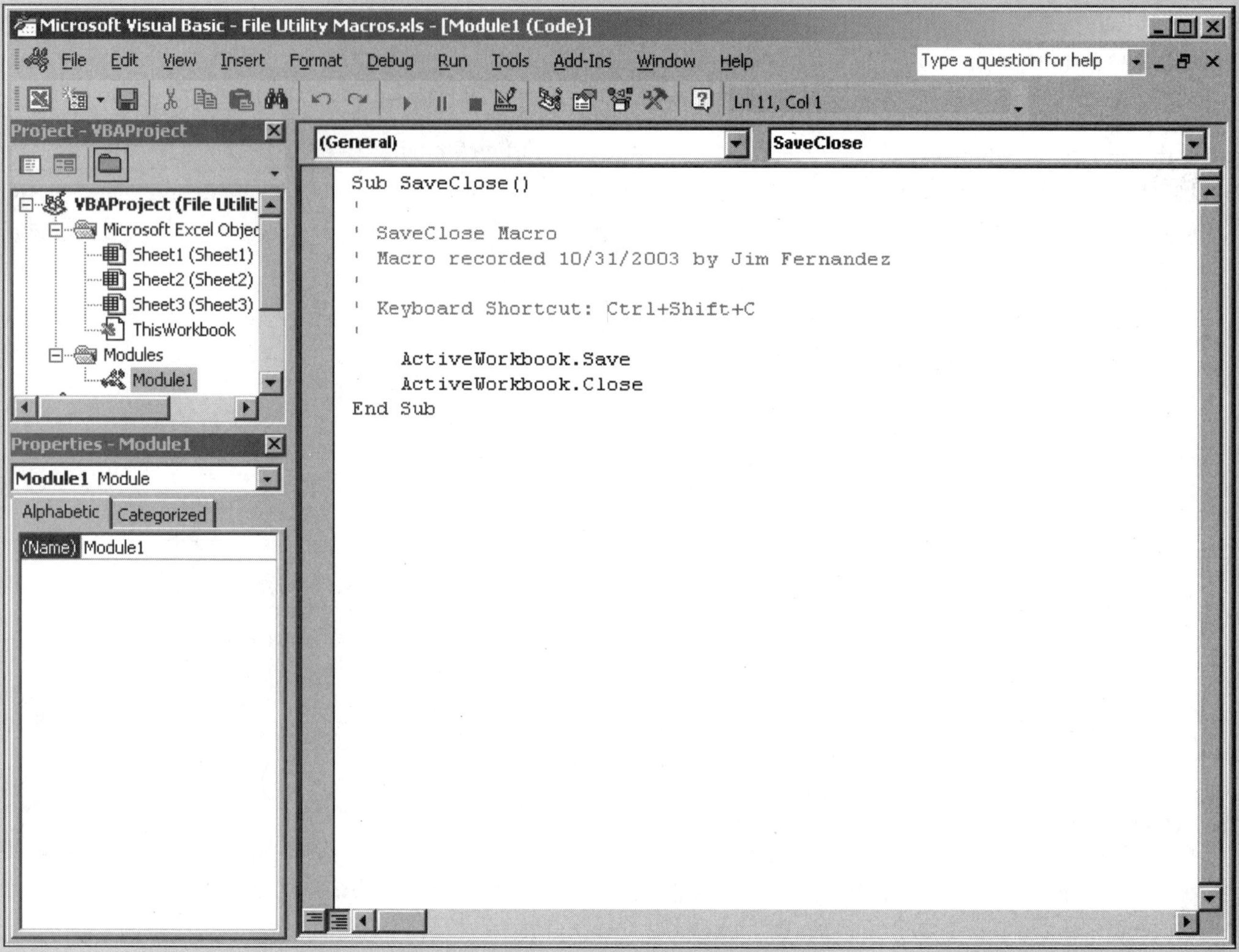

```
Sub SaveClose()
'
' SaveClose Macro
' Macro recorded 10/31/2003 by Jim Fernandez
'
' Keyboard Shortcut: Ctrl+Shift+C
'
    ActiveWorkbook.Save
    ActiveWorkbook.Close
End Sub
```

Using Lists

Objectives

- Plan a list
- MOUS Create a list
- Add records with the data form
- Find records
- Delete records
- Sort a list on one field
- Sort a list on multiple fields
- MOUS Print a list

A **database** is an organized collection of related information. Examples of databases include a telephone book, a card catalog, and a roster of company employees. Excel refers to a database as a **list**. Using an Excel list, you can organize and manage worksheet information so that you can quickly find data for projects, reports, and charts. In this unit, you'll learn how to plan and create a list; add, change, find, and delete information in a list; and then sort and print a list.

MediaLoft uses lists to analyze new customer information. Jim Fernandez has asked you to help him build and manage a list of new customers as part of the ongoing strategy to focus on the expenditure of the company's advertising dollars.

Excel 2002

Planning a List

When planning a list, consider what information the list will contain and how you will work with the data now and in the future. Lists are organized into records. A **record** contains data about an object or person. Records are rows in the list and are comprised of fields. **Fields** are columns in the list; each field describes a characteristic about the record, such as a customer's last name or street address. Each field has a **field name**, a column label that describes the field. See Table H-1 for additional planning guidelines. Jim has asked you to compile a list of new customers. Before entering the data into an Excel worksheet, you will plan the list using the following guidelines:

Details

- **Identify the purpose of the list**
  Determine the kind of information the list should contain. Jim will use the list to identify areas of the country in which new customers live.
- **Plan the structure of the list**
  Determine the fields that make up a record. Jim has customer cards that contain information about each new customer. Figure H-1 shows a typical card. Each customer in the list will have a record. The fields in the record correspond to the information on the cards.
- **Write down the names of the fields**
  Field names can be up to 255 characters long (the maximum column width), although shorter names are easier to see in the cells. Field names appear in the first row of a list. Jim writes down field names that describe each piece of information shown in Figure H-1.
- **Determine any special number formatting required in the list**
  Most lists contain both text and numbers. When planning a list, consider whether any fields require specific number formatting or prefixes. Jim notes that some ZIP codes begin with zero. Because Excel automatically drops a leading zero, Jim must type an apostrophe (') when he enters a ZIP code that begins with 0 (zero). The apostrophe tells Excel that the cell contains a label rather than a value. If a column contains a combination of numbers and text, you should format the field as text. Otherwise, the numbers are sorted first, and the numbers that contain text characters are sorted after that; for example, 11542, 60614, 87105, '01810, '02115. To instruct Excel to sort the ZIP codes properly, Jim enters all ZIP codes with a leading apostrophe and formats the field as text.

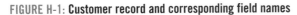

FIGURE H-1: Customer record and corresponding field names

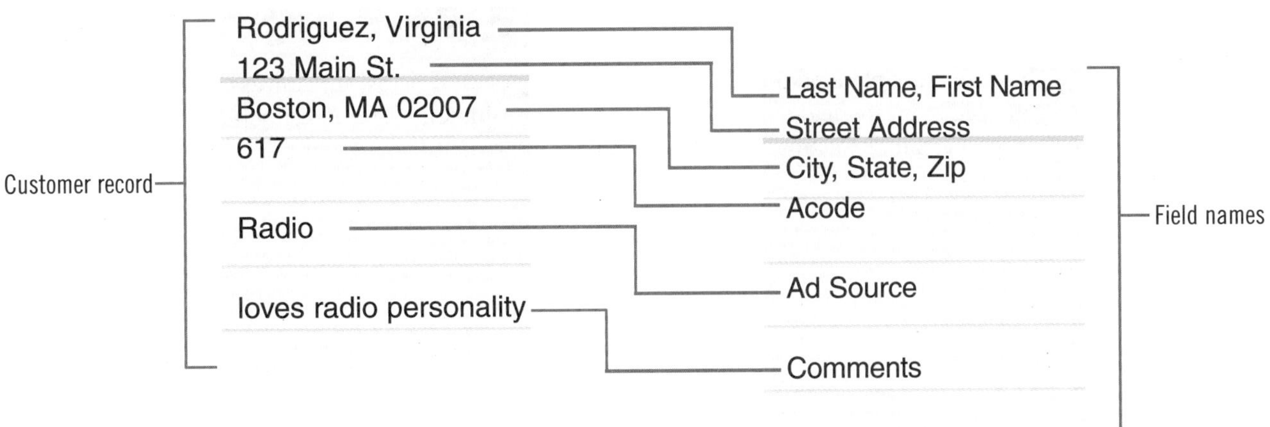

TABLE H-1: Guidelines for planning a list

size and location guidelines	row and column content guidelines
Devote an entire worksheet to your list and list summary information because some list management features can be used on only one list at a time.	Plan and design your list so that all rows have similar items in the same column.
Leave at least one blank column and one blank row between your list and list summary data. Doing this helps Excel select your list when it performs list management tasks such as sorting.	Do not insert extra spaces at the beginning of a cell because that can affect sorting and searching.
Avoid placing critical data to the left or right of the list.	Use the same format for all cells in a column.
	Instead of blank rows or columns between your labels and your data, use formatting to make column labels stand out from the data.

Using lists versus databases

If your list contains more records than can fit on one worksheet (that is, more than 65,536), you should consider using database software rather than spreadsheet software.

Excel 2002

Creating a List

Once you have planned the list structure, the sequence of fields, and any appropriate formatting, you need to create field names. Table H-2 provides guidelines for naming fields. You are ready to create the list using the field names you wrote down earlier.

Steps

1. Start Excel if necessary, open the Project File **EX H-1** from the drive and folder where your Project Files are stored, then save it as **New Customer List**

2. Rename Sheet1 **Practice**, then if necessary maximize the Excel window
   It is a good idea to devote an entire worksheet to your list.

3. Beginning in cell A1 and moving horizontally, enter each field name in a separate cell, as shown in Figure H-2
   Always put field names in the first row of the list. Don't worry if your field names are wider than the cells; you will fix this later.

4. Select the field headings in range **A1:I1**, then click the **Bold button** on the Formatting toolbar; with range A1:I1 still selected, click the **Borders list arrow**, then click the **Thick Bottom Border** (second column, second row)

5. Enter the information from Figure H-3 in the rows immediately below the field names, using a leading apostrophe (') for all ZIP codes; do not leave any blank rows
   If you don't type an apostrophe, Excel deletes the leading zero (0) in the ZIP code. The data appears in columns organized by field name.

6. Select the range **A1:I4**, click **Format** on the menu bar, point to **Column**, click **AutoFit Selection**, click anywhere in the worksheet to deselect the range, then save the workbook
   Resizing the column widths this way is faster than double-clicking the column divider lines between each pair of columns. Compare your screen with Figure H-4.

QuickTip

If the field name you plan to use is wider than the data in the column, you can turn on Wrap Text on the Alignment tab in the Format Cells dialog box to stack the heading in the cell. You can also press [Alt][Enter] to force a line break while entering field names.

Trouble?

Cells F2:F4 may have a green error indicator in the upper-left corner of the cell, and an error button may appear. This warning is a result of storing the ZIP code numbers as text. To remove the warnings and prevent similar ones in the future, select Options from the Tools menu, click the Error Checking tab, and remove the check next to Number stored as text.

TABLE H-2: Guidelines for naming fields

guideline	explanation
Use labels to name fields	Numbers can be interpreted as parts of formulas
Do not use duplicate field names	Duplicate field names can cause information to be incorrectly entered and sorted
Format the field names to stand out from the list data	Use a font, alignment, format, pattern, border, or capitalization style for the column labels that are different from the format of your list data
Use descriptive names	Avoid names that might be confused with cell addresses, such as Q4

FIGURE H-2: Field names entered and formatted in row 1

Microsoft Excel - New Customer List.xls

	A	B	C	D	E	F	G	H	I	J	K	L
1	Last Name	First Name	Street Address	City	State	Zip	Acode	Ad Source	Comments			

FIGURE H-3: Cards with customer information

Rodriguez, Virginia	Wong, Sam	Frei, Carol
123 Main St.	2120 Central NE.	123 Elm St.
Boston, MA 02007	San Francisco, CA 93772	Salem, MA 01970
617	415	978
Radio	Newspaper	Newspaper
loves radio personality	graphics caught eye	no comments

FIGURE H-4: List with three records

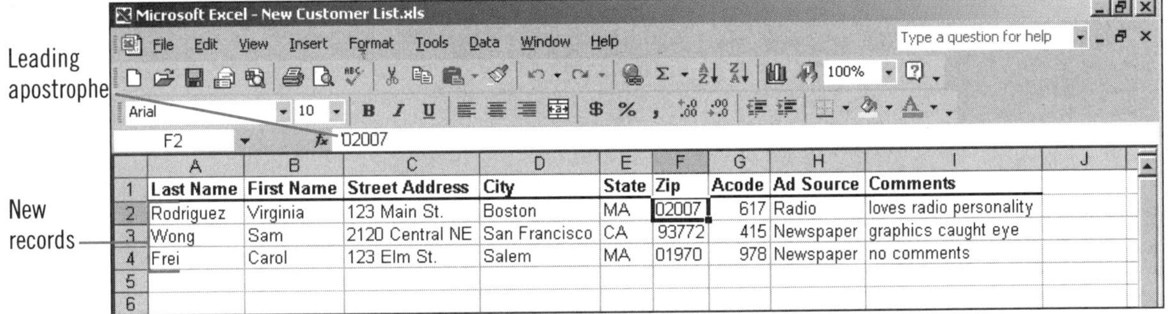

	A	B	C	D	E	F	G	H	I	J
1	Last Name	First Name	Street Address	City	State	Zip	Acode	Ad Source	Comments	
2	Rodriguez	Virginia	123 Main St.	Boston	MA	02007	617	Radio	loves radio personality	
3	Wong	Sam	2120 Central NE	San Francisco	CA	93772	415	Newspaper	graphics caught eye	
4	Frei	Carol	123 Elm St.	Salem	MA	01970	978	Newspaper	no comments	
5										
6										

CLUES TO USE

Filtering lists using AutoFilter

You can filter a list to show only the rows that meet specific criteria. For example, you might want to display only the records of customers in a certain ZIP code, or only residents of California. (A filter is different from a sort, which rearranges list records.) The AutoFilter feature is the easiest way to apply a filter.

To use AutoFilter, click Data on the menu bar, point to Filter, then click AutoFilter. List arrows will appear next to the field names, allowing you to select criteria for a field. For example, if you specify MA as the criteria in a State field, Excel displays only the records where MA is entered as the state.

Excel 2002

Adding Records with the Data Form

You can add records to a list by typing data directly into the cells within the list range. Once the field names are created, you can also use the data form as a quick, easy method of data entry. A **data form** is a dialog box that displays one record at a time. You have entered all the customer records Jim had on his cards, but he receives the names of two additional customers. You decide to use the Excel data form to add the new customer information.

Steps

1. Make sure the New Customer List file is open, then activate **Sheet2** and rename it **Working List**
   Working List contains the nearly completed customer list.
2. Select any cell in the customer list, click **Data** on the menu bar, then click **Form**
   A data form containing the first record appears, as shown in Figure H-5.
3. Click **New**
   A blank data form appears with the insertion point in the first field.
4. Type **Chavez** in the Last Name box, then press **[Tab]** to move the insertion point to the next field
5. Enter the rest of the information for Jeffrey Chavez, as shown in Figure H-6
   Press [Tab] to move the insertion point to the next field, or click in the next field box to move the insertion point there.
6. Click **New** to add Jeffrey Chavez's record and open another blank data form, enter the record for Cathy Relman as shown in Figure H-6, then click **Close**
   The records that you added with the data form are placed at the end of the list and are formatted in the same way as the previous records.
7. If necessary, scroll down the worksheet to bring rows 46 and 47 into view, check both new records, return to cell A1, then save the workbook

Trouble?

If you accidentally press [↑] or [↓] while in a data form and find that you displayed the wrong record, press [↑] or [↓] until you return to the desired record.

QuickTip

Excel automatically extends formatting and formulas in lists.

FIGURE H-5: **Data form showing first record in the list**

Working List

Last Name:	Rodriguez
First Name:	Virginia
Street Address:	123 Main St.
City:	Boston
State:	MA
Zip:	02007
ACode:	617
Ad Source:	Radio
Comments on ads:	loves radio personality

1 of 44

New | Delete | Restore | Find Prev | Find Next | Criteria | Close

Current record number

Total number of records

Leading apostrophe not visible in data form after records are added

Click to open a blank data form for adding a record

FIGURE H-6: **Two data forms with information for two new records**

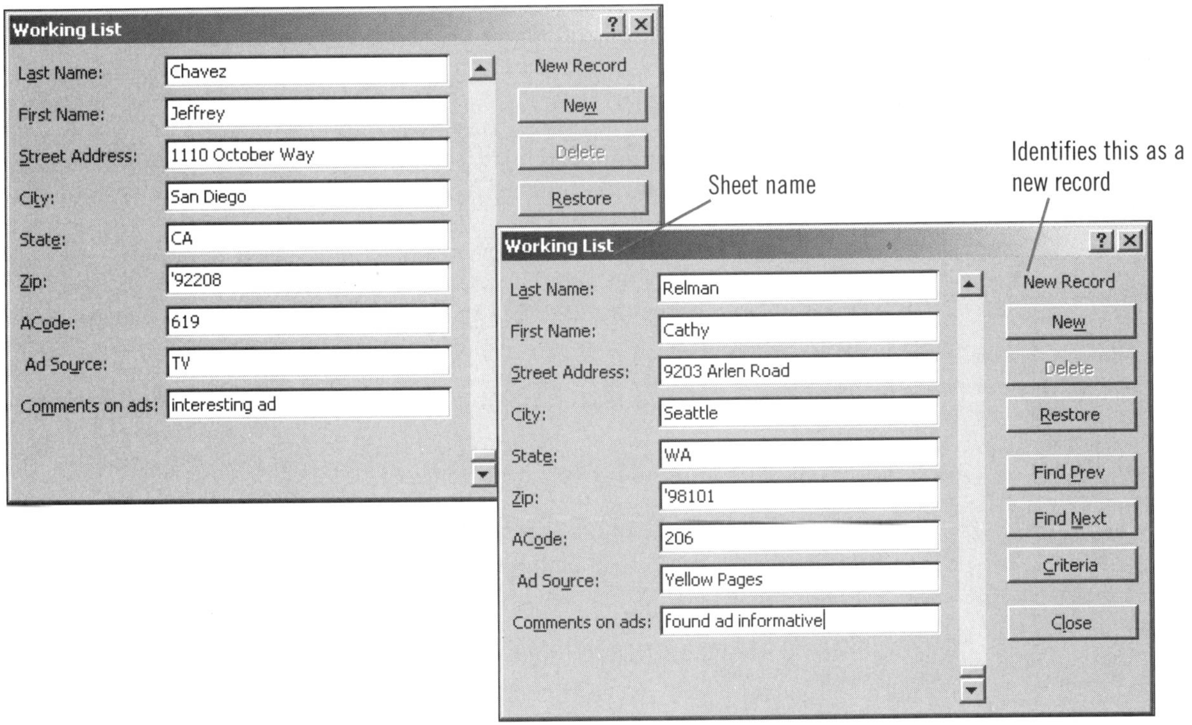

Excel 2002

Finding Records

From time to time, you need to locate specific records in your list. You can use the Excel Find command on the Edit menu or the data form to search your list. You can also use the Replace command on the Edit menu to locate and replace existing entries or portions of entries with specified information. Jim wants to be more specific about the radio ad source, so he asks you to replace "Radio" with "KWIN Radio." He also wants to know how many of the new customers originated from the company's TV ads. You begin by searching for those records with the ad source "TV".

Steps

Trouble?

If you receive the message "No list found," select any cell within the list, then repeat Step 1.

1. **Click any cell within the list, click Data on the menu bar, click Form, then click Criteria**
   The data form changes so that all fields are blank and "Criteria" appears in the upper-right corner. See Figure H-7. You want to search for records whose Ad Source field contains the label "TV".

2. **Click in the Ad Source text box, type TV, then click Find Next**
   Excel displays the first record for a customer who learned about the company through its TV ads. See Figure H-8.

QuickTip

You can also use comparison operators when performing a search using the data form. For example, you could specify >50,000 in a Salary field box to return those records in the Salary field with a value greater than $50,000.

3. **Click Find Next until there are no more matching records, then click Close**
   There are six customers whose ad source is TV.

4. **Return to cell A1, click Edit on the menu bar, then click Replace**
   The Find and Replace dialog box opens with the Replace tab selected and the insertion point in the Find what box. See Figure H-9.

5. **Type Radio in the Find what text box, then click the Replace with text box**
   Jim wants you to search for entries containing "Radio" and replace them with "KWIN Radio".

6. **Type KWIN Radio in the Replace with text box**
   Because you notice that there are other list entries containing the word "radio" with a lowercase "r" (in the Comments column), you need to make sure that only capitalized instances of the word are replaced.

QuickTip

Be sure to clear this option for future searches, where you may not want to use it.

7. **Click Options >>, click the Match case check box to select it, click Options <<, then click Find Next**
   Excel moves the cell pointer to the first occurrence of "Radio".

8. **Click Replace All, click OK, then click Close**
   The dialog box closes. Note that in the Comments column, each instance of the word "radio" remains unchanged.

9. **Make sure there are no entries in the Ad Source column that read "Radio", then save the workbook**

Using wildcards to fine-tune your search

You can use special symbols called **wildcards** when defining search criteria in the data form or Replace dialog box. The question mark (?) wildcard stands for any single character. For example, if you do not know whether a customer's last name is Paulsen or Paulson, you can specify Pauls?n as the search criteria to locate both options. The asterisk (*) wildcard stands for any group of characters. For example, if you specify Jan* as the search criteria in the First Name field, Excel locates all records with first names beginning with Jan (for instance, Jan, Janet, Janice).

FIGURE H-7: Criteria data form

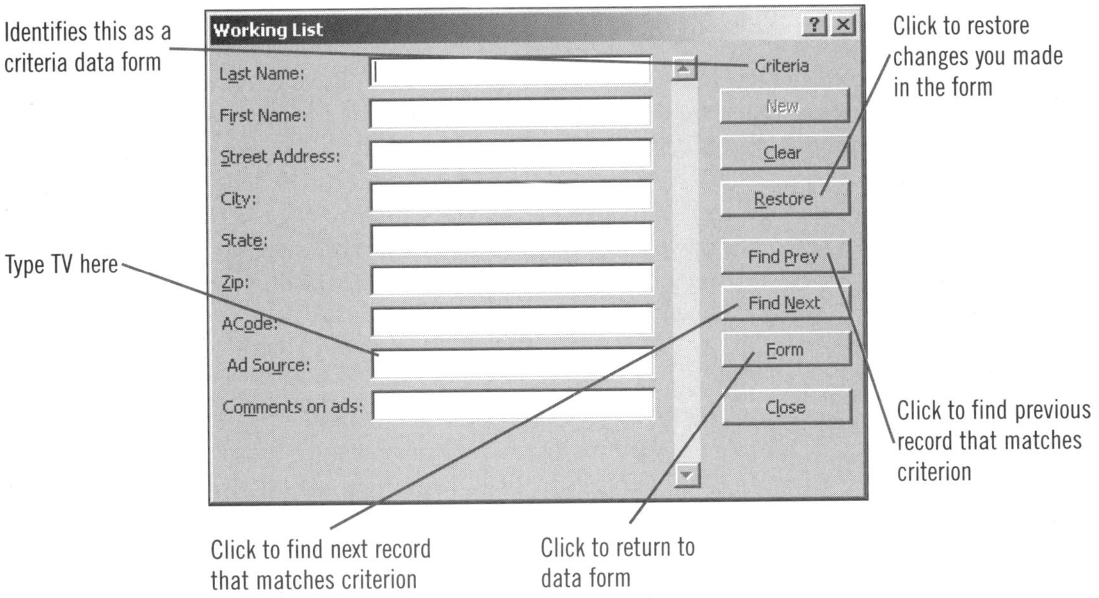

Identifies this as a criteria data form

Type TV here

Click to restore changes you made in the form

Click to find previous record that matches criterion

Click to find next record that matches criterion

Click to return to data form

FIGURE H-8: Finding a record using the data form

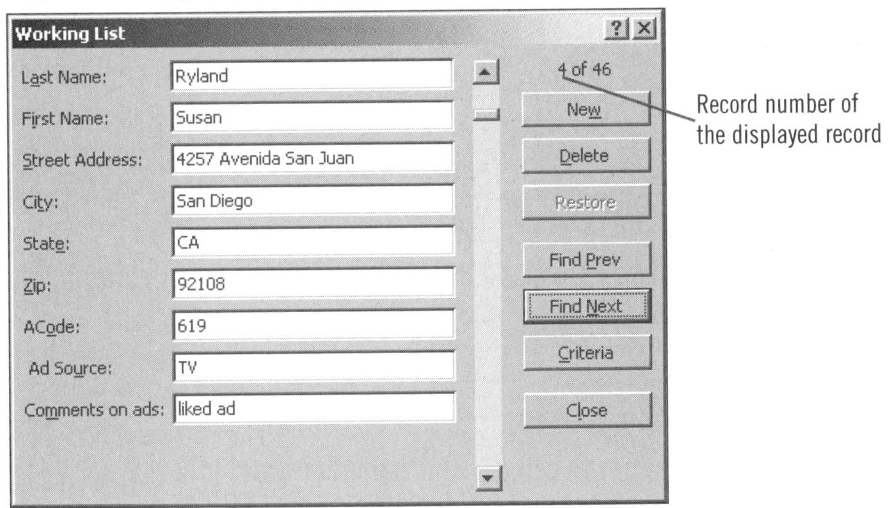

FIGURE H-9: Find and Replace dialog box

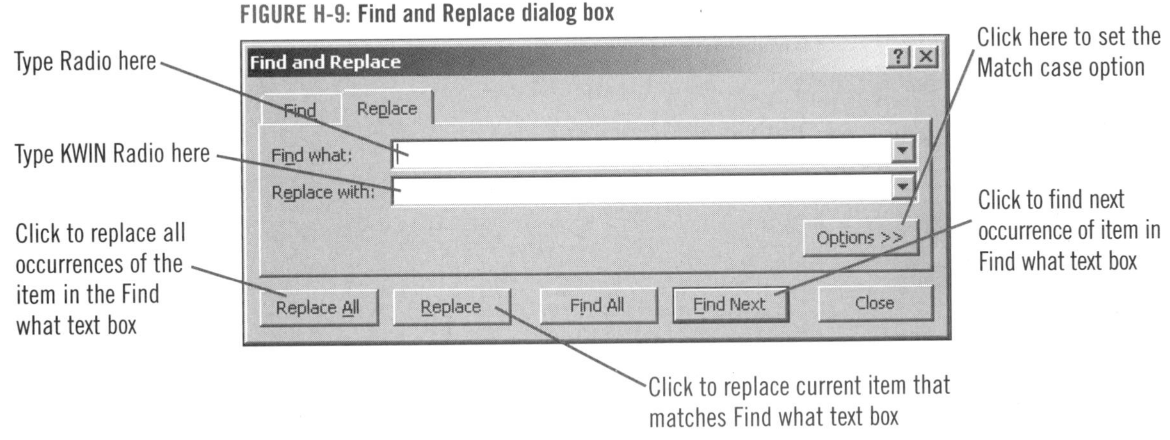

Excel 2002

Deleting Records

You need to keep your list up to date by removing obsolete records. One way to remove records is to use the Delete button on the data form. You can also delete all records that share something in common—that is, records that meet certain criteria. For example, you can specify a criterion for Excel to find the next record containing ZIP code 01879, then remove the record by using the Delete button. If specifying one criterion does not meet your needs, you can set multiple criteria. Jim notices two entries for Carolyn Smith, and wants you to check the list for additional duplicate entries. You will use the data form to delete the duplicate record.

Steps

QuickTip

You can use the data form to edit records as well as to add, search for, and delete them. Just find the desired record and edit the data directly in the appropriate box.

QuickTip

Clicking Restore on the data form will undo your changes when you are adding a new record, as long as you click it before you press Enter or click Close. Restore will not restore deleted record(s).

1. Click **Data** on the menu bar, click **Form**, then click **Criteria**
   The Criteria data form opens.
2. Type **Smith** in the **Last Name text box**, press Tab to move the insertion point to the **First Name text box**, type **Carolyn**, then click **Find Next**
   Excel displays the first record for a customer whose name is Carolyn Smith. You decide to leave the initial entry for Carolyn Smith (record 5 of 46) and delete the second one, once you confirm that it is a duplicate.
3. Click **Find Next**
   The duplicate record for Carolyn Smith, number 40, appears as shown in Figure H-10. You are ready to delete the duplicate entry.
4. Click **Delete**, then click **OK** to confirm the deletion
   The duplicate record for Carolyn Smith is deleted, and all the other records move up one row. The data form now shows the record for Julio Manuel.
5. Click **Close** to return to the worksheet, scroll down until rows 41–46 are visible, then read the entry in row 41
   Notice that the duplicate entry for Carolyn Smith is gone and that Manuel Julio moved up a row and is now in row 41. You also notice a record for K. C. Splint in row 43, which is a duplicate entry.
6. Return to cell A1, and read the record information for K. C. Splint in row 8
   After confirming the duplicate entry, you decide to delete the row.
7. Click cell **A8**, click **Edit** on the menu bar, then click **Delete**
   The Delete dialog box opens, as shown in Figure H-11.
8. Click the **Entire row option button**, then click **OK**
   You have deleted the entire row. The duplicate record for K. C. Splint is deleted and the other records move up to fill in the gap.
9. Save the workbook

FIGURE H-10: **Data form showing duplicate record for Carolyn Smith**

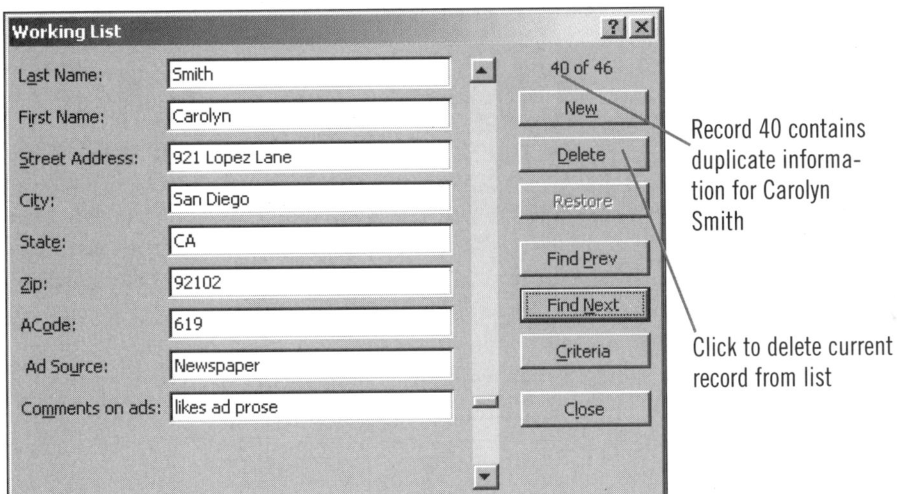

FIGURE H-11: **Delete dialog box**

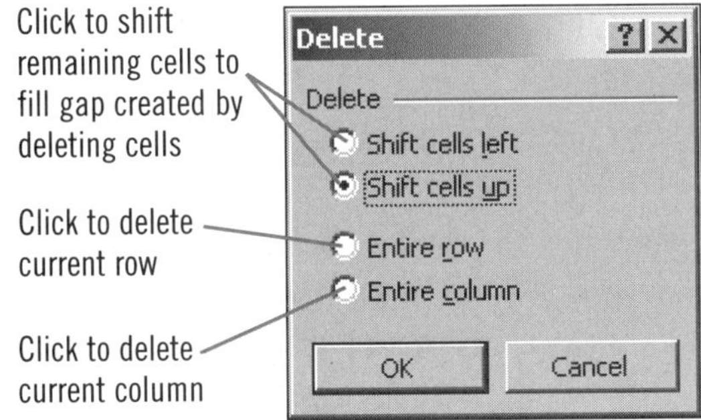

Excel 2002

Deleting records using the worksheet

When you delete a record using the data form, you cannot undo your deletion. When you delete a record by deleting its row in the worksheet, however, you can immediately retrieve it; use the Undo command on the Edit menu, click the Undo button, or press [Ctrl][Z].

Excel 2002

Sorting a List on One Field

Usually, you enter records in the order in which they are received, rather than in alphabetical or numerical order. When you add records to a list using the data form, the records are added to the end of the list. Using the Excel sorting feature, you can rearrange the order of the records. You can use the sort buttons on the Standard toolbar to sort records by one field, or you can use the Sort command on the Data menu to perform more advanced sorts. Alternately, you can sort an entire list or any portion of a list, and you can arrange sorted information in ascending or descending order. In ascending order, the lowest value (the beginning of the alphabet, for instance, or the earliest date) appears at the top of the list. In a field containing labels and numbers, numbers come first. In descending order, the highest value (the end of the alphabet or the latest date) appears at the top of the list. In a field containing labels and numbers, labels come first. Table H-3 provides examples of ascending and descending sorts. Because Jim wants to be able to return the records to their original order following any sorts, he wants you to create a new field called Entry Order. You will then perform several single field sorts on the list.

Steps

QuickTip

Before you sort records, it is a good idea to make a backup copy of your list or create a field that numbers the records so you can return them to their original order, if necessary.

1. In cell J1, enter the column heading and format as shown in Figure H-12, then AutoFit column J
2. Type **1** in cell J2, press **[Enter]**, type **2** in cell J3, press **[Enter]**, select cells **J2:J3**, drag the fill handle to cell **J45**

   You are now ready to sort the list in ascending order by last name. You must position the cell pointer within the column you want to sort prior to issuing the sort command.
3. Return to cell A1, then click the **Sort Ascending button** on the Standard toolbar

   Excel rearranges the records in ascending order by last name, as shown in Figure H-13. You can also sort the list in descending order by any field.
4. Click cell **G1**, then click the **Sort Descending button** on the Standard toolbar

   Excel sorts the list, placing those records with higher-digit area codes at the top. You are now ready to return the list to original entry order.
5. Click cell **J1**, click the **Sort Ascending button** on the Standard toolbar, then save the workbook

   The list is back to its original order, and the workbook is saved.

Trouble?

If your sort does not perform as intended, press [Ctrl][Z] immediately to undo the sort.

FIGURE H-12: List with Entry Order field added

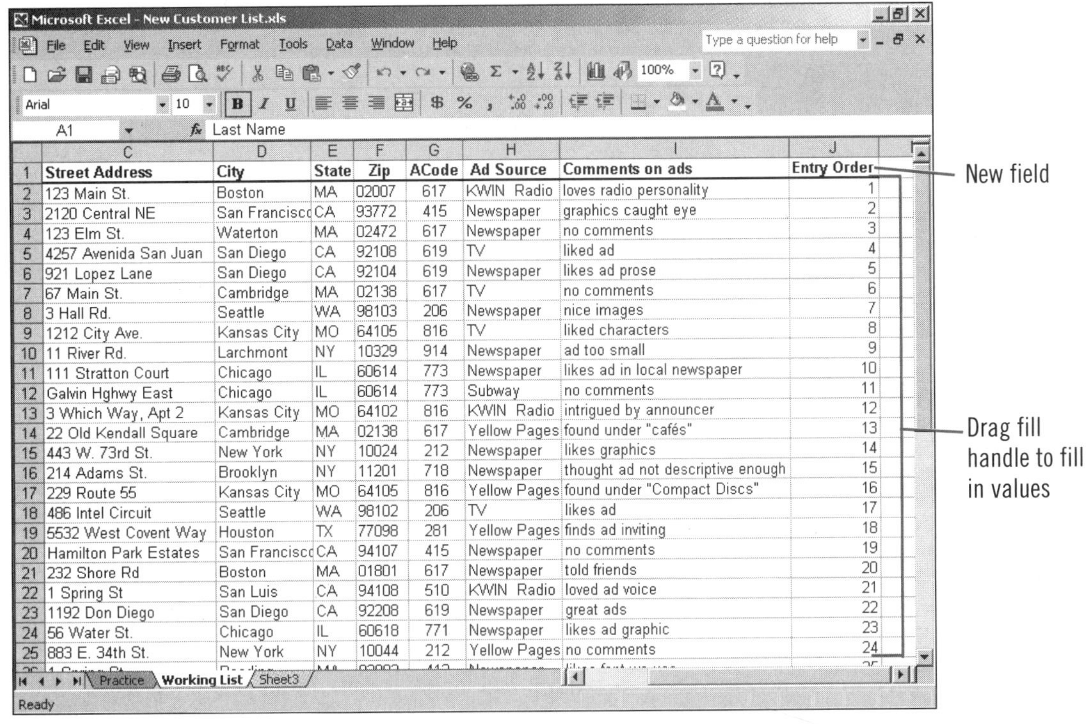

FIGURE H-13: List sorted alphabetically by Last Name

List sorted in ascending order by Last Name

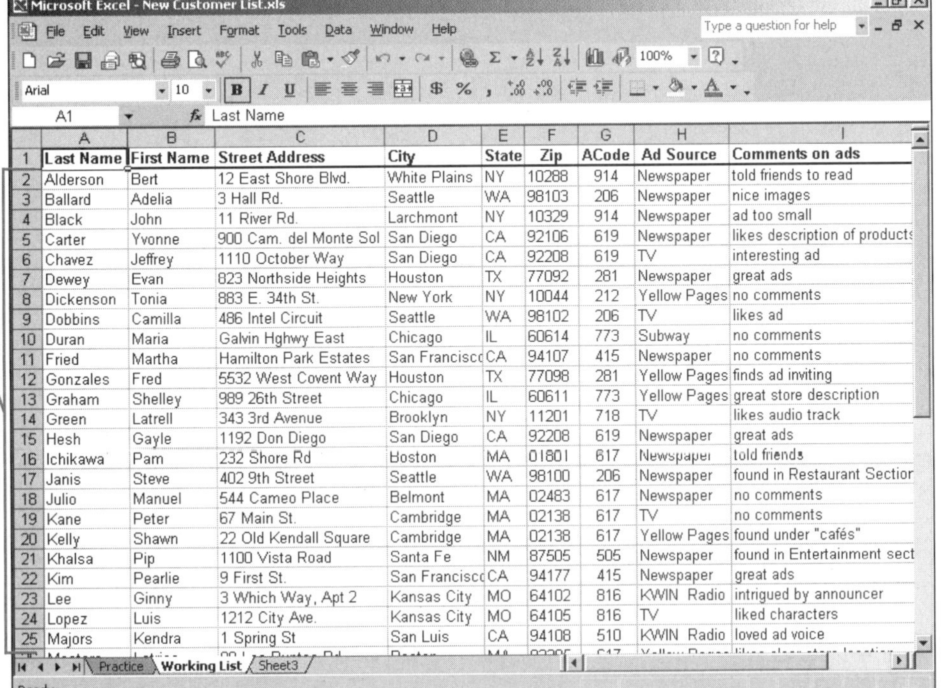

Excel 2002

TABLE H-3: Sort order options and examples

option	alphabetic	numeric	date	alphanumeric
Ascending	A, B, C	7, 8, 9	1/1, 2/1, 3/1	12A, 99B, DX8, QT7
Descending	C, B, A	9, 8, 7	3/1, 2/1, 1/1	QT7, DX8, 99B, 12A

Excel 2002

Sorting a List on Multiple Fields

You can sort lists by as many as three fields by specifying **sort keys**, the criteria on which the sort is based. Up to three column headings can be entered in the Sort dialog box to specify the sort criteria. Jim wants you to sort the records alphabetically by state first, then within the state by ZIP code.

Steps

QuickTip

You can specify a capitalization sort by clicking Options in the Sort dialog box, then selecting the Case sensitive box. When you choose this option, lowercase entries precede uppercase entries.

QuickTip

The Sort warning dialog box will appear if you are sorting a list on a field containing numbers that are formatted as text.

1. Click **Data** on the menu bar, then click **Sort**

   The Sort dialog box opens, as shown in Figure H-14. You want to sort the list by state and then by ZIP code.

2. Click the **Sort by** list arrow, click **State**, then click the **Ascending option button** to select it, if necessary

   The list will be sorted alphabetically in ascending order (A–Z) by the State field. A second sort criterion will sort the entries within each state grouping.

3. Click the top **Then by list arrow**, click **Zip**, then click the **Descending option button**

   You could also sort by a third key by selecting a field in the bottom Then by list box.

4. Click **OK** to perform the sort, click **OK** on the Sort Warning dialog box, press **[Ctrl][Home]**, then scroll through the list to see the result of the sort

   The list is sorted alphabetically by state in ascending order, then within each state by ZIP code in descending order. Compare your results with Figure H-15.

5. Save the workbook

FIGURE H-14: **Sort dialog box**

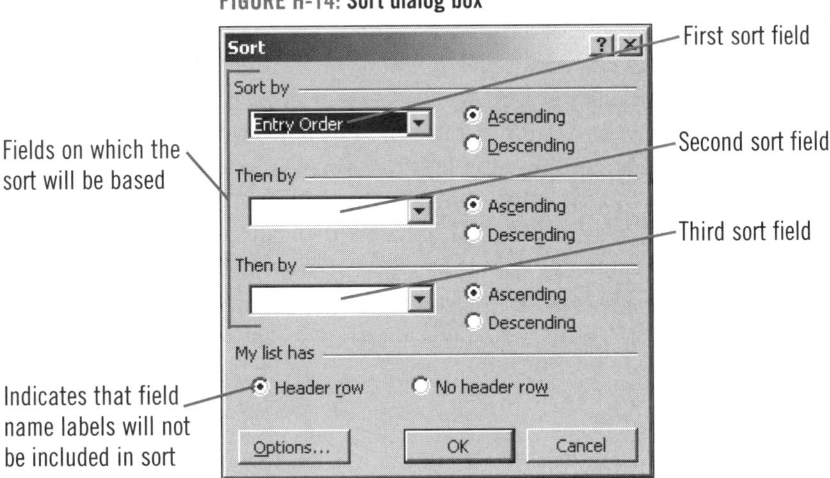

FIGURE H-15: **List sorted by multiple fields**

First sort by state

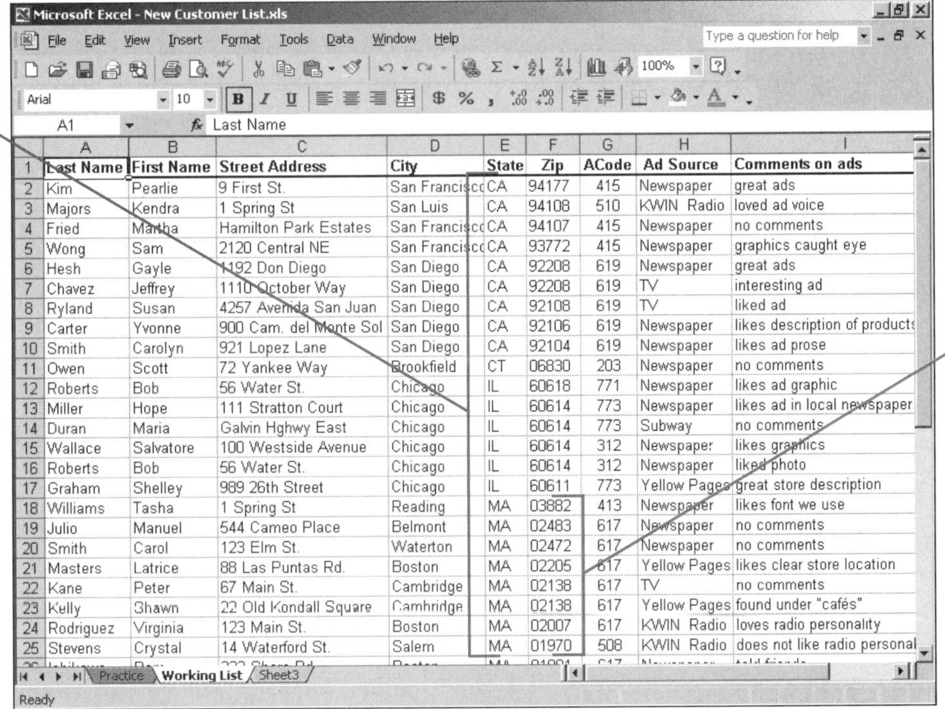

	A	B	C	D	E	F	G	H	I
1	Last Name	First Name	Street Address	City	State	Zip	ACode	Ad Source	Comments on ads
2	Kim	Pearlie	9 First St.	San Francisco	CA	94177	415	Newspaper	great ads
3	Majors	Kendra	1 Spring St	San Luis	CA	94108	510	KWIN Radio	loved ad voice
4	Fried	Martha	Hamilton Park Estates	San Francisco	CA	94107	415	Newspaper	no comments
5	Wong	Sam	2120 Central NE	San Francisco	CA	93772	415	Newspaper	graphics caught eye
6	Hesh	Gayle	1192 Don Diego	San Diego	CA	92208	619	Newspaper	great ads
7	Chavez	Jeffrey	1110 October Way	San Diego	CA	92208	619	TV	interesting ad
8	Ryland	Susan	4257 Avenida San Juan	San Diego	CA	92108	619	TV	liked ad
9	Carter	Yvonne	900 Cam. del Monte Sol	San Diego	CA	92106	619	Newspaper	likes description of products
10	Smith	Carolyn	921 Lopez Lane	San Diego	CA	92104	619	Newspaper	likes ad prose
11	Owen	Scott	72 Yankee Way	Brookfield	CT	06830	203	Newspaper	no comments
12	Roberts	Bob	56 Water St.	Chicago	IL	60618	771	Newspaper	likes ad graphic
13	Miller	Hope	111 Stratton Court	Chicago	IL	60614	773	Newspaper	likes ad in local newspaper
14	Duran	Maria	Galvin Hghwy East	Chicago	IL	60614	773	Subway	no comments
15	Wallace	Salvatore	100 Westside Avenue	Chicago	IL	60614	312	Newspaper	likes graphics
16	Roberts	Bob	56 Water St.	Chicago	IL	60614	312	Newspaper	liked photo
17	Graham	Shelley	989 26th Street	Chicago	IL	60611	773	Yellow Pages	great store description
18	Williams	Tasha	1 Spring St	Reading	MA	03882	413	Newspaper	likes font we use
19	Julio	Manuel	544 Cameo Place	Belmont	MA	02483	617	Newspaper	no comments
20	Smith	Carol	123 Elm St.	Waterton	MA	02472	617	Newspaper	no comments
21	Masters	Latrice	88 Las Puntas Rd.	Boston	MA	02205	617	Yellow Pages	likes clear store location
22	Kane	Peter	67 Main St.	Cambridge	MA	02138	617	TV	no comments
23	Kelly	Shawn	22 Old Kendall Square	Cambridge	MA	02138	617	Yellow Pages	found under "cafés"
24	Rodriguez	Virginia	123 Main St.	Boston	MA	02007	617	KWIN Radio	loves radio personality
25	Stevens	Crystal	14 Waterford St.	Salem	MA	01970	508	KWIN Radio	does not like radio personal

Second sort by ZIP code within state

Specifying a custom sort order

You can identify a custom sort order for the field selected in the Sort by box. To do this, click Options in the Sort dialog box, click the First key sort order list arrow, then click the desired custom order. Commonly used custom sort orders are days of the week (Sun, Mon, Tues, Wed, etc.) and months (Jan, Feb, Mar, etc.); alphabetic sorts do not sort these items properly.

Excel 2002

Excel 2002

Printing a List

If a list is small enough to fit on one page, you can print it as you would any other Excel worksheet. If you have more columns than can fit on a portrait-oriented page, try setting the page orientation to landscape. Because lists often have more rows than can fit on a page, you can define the first row of the list (containing the field names) as the **print title**, which prints at the top of every page. Most lists do not have any descriptive information above the field names on the worksheet. To augment the information contained in the field names, you can use headers and footers to add identifying text, such as the list title or report date. If you want to exclude any fields from your list report, you can hide the selected columns from view so that they do not print. Jim has finished updating his list and would like you to print it. You begin by previewing the list.

Steps

1. Click the **Print Preview button** on the Standard toolbar
   The status bar reads Preview: Page 1 of 2. You want all the fields in the list to fit on a single page, but you'll need two pages to fit all the data.

> **QuickTip**
> To print multiple ranges at the same time, click Page Break Preview on the View menu, drag to select the ranges (use [Ctrl] to select nonadjacent areas), click File, point to Print Area, then click Set Print Area. You can view the ranges included in the print area by using Print Preview.

2. From the Print Preview window, click **Setup**, click the **Page tab**, click the **Landscape option button** under Orientation, click the **Fit to option button** under Scaling, double-click the **tall box** and type **2**, click **OK**
   The list still does not fit on a single page. Because the records on page 2 appear without column headings, you want to set up the first row of the list, which contains the field names, as a repeating print title.
3. Click **Close** to exit the Print Preview window, click **File** on the menu bar, click **Page Setup**, click the **Sheet tab**, click the **Rows to repeat at top text box** under Print titles, click any cell in row 1, compare your screen to Figure H-16, then click **OK**
   When you select row 1 as a print title, Excel automatically inserts an absolute reference to a beginning row to repeat at the top of each page—in this case, the print title to repeat beginning and ending with row 1.
4. Click the **Print Preview** button, click **Next** to view the second page, then click **Zoom**
   Setting up a print title to repeat row 1 causes the field names to appear at the top of each printed page. You can save these print settings by creating a custom view.
5. Click **Close**, click **View** on the menu bar, click **Custom Views**, click **Add**, enter **Print-Title** in the Name text box, then click **OK**
   This creates a custom view named Print-Title that you can use at any time. You can use the worksheet header to provide information about the list.
6. Click , click **Setup**, click the **Header/Footer tab**, click **Custom Header**, click the **Left section box** and enter your name, then click the **Center section box** and enter **MediaLoft -**, press **[Spacebar]**, then click the **Filename button**
7. Select the header information in the Center section box, click the **Font button**, change the font size to **14** and the style to **Bold**, click **OK**, click **OK** again to return to the Header/Footer tab, click **OK** to preview the list, then click **Close**

> **QuickTip**
> To print more than one worksheet, select each sheet tab while holding down [Shift] or [Ctrl], then click .

8. Save the workbook, print the worksheet, then close the workbook
   Compare your printed worksheet with Figure H-17.

FIGURE H-16: **Sheet tab of the Page Setup dialog box**

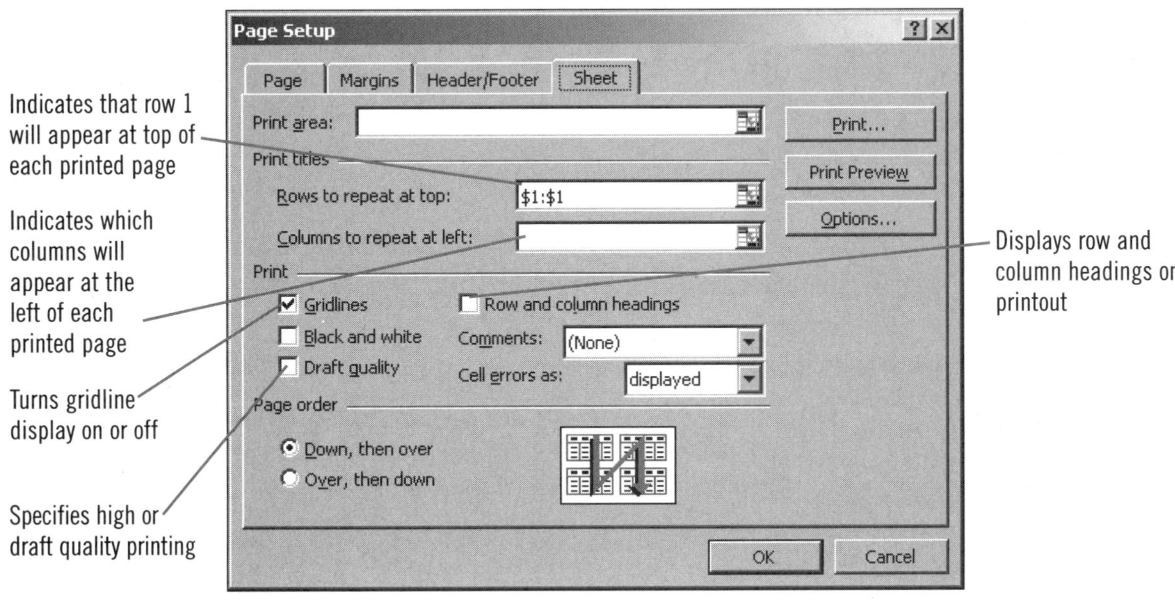

FIGURE H-17: **Completed list**

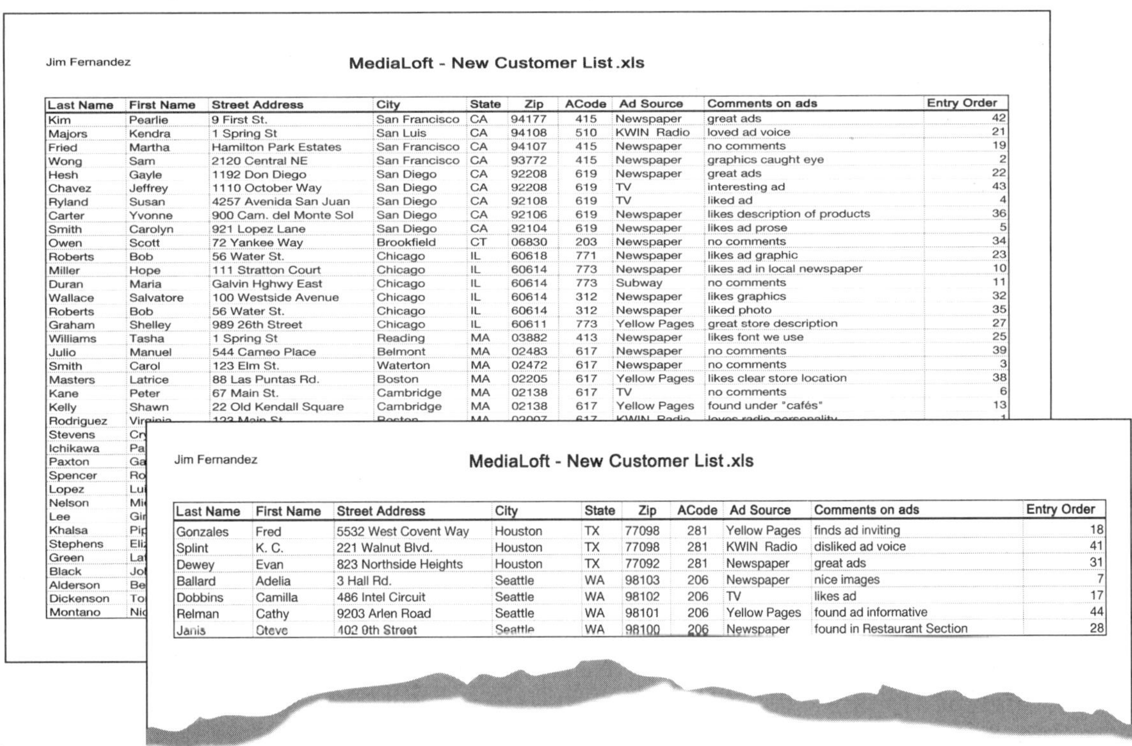

Jim Fernandez

MediaLoft - New Customer List.xls

Last Name	First Name	Street Address	City	State	Zip	ACode	Ad Source	Comments on ads	Entry Order
Kim	Pearlie	9 First St.	San Francisco	CA	94177	415	Newspaper	great ads	42
Majors	Kendra	1 Spring St	San Luis	CA	94108	510	KWIN Radio	loved ad voice	21
Fried	Martha	Hamilton Park Estates	San Francisco	CA	94107	415	Newspaper	no comments	19
Wong	Sam	2120 Central NE	San Francisco	CA	93772	415	Newspaper	graphics caught eye	2
Hesh	Gayle	1192 Don Diego	San Diego	CA	92208	619	Newspaper	great ads	22
Chavez	Jeffrey	1110 October Way	San Diego	CA	92208	619	TV	interesting ad	43
Ryland	Susan	4257 Avenida San Juan	San Diego	CA	92108	619	TV	liked ad	4
Carter	Yvonne	900 Cam. del Monte Sol	San Diego	CA	92106	619	Newspaper	likes description of products	36
Smith	Carolyn	921 Lopez Lane	San Diego	CA	92104	619	Newspaper	likes ad prose	5
Owen	Scott	72 Yankee Way	Brookfield	CT	06830	203	Newspaper	no comments	34
Roberts	Bob	56 Water St.	Chicago	IL	60618	771	Newspaper	likes ad graphic	23
Miller	Hope	111 Stratton Court	Chicago	IL	60614	773	Newspaper	likes ad in local newspaper	10
Duran	Maria	Galvin Hghwy East	Chicago	IL	60614	773	Subway	no comments	11
Wallace	Salvatore	100 Westside Avenue	Chicago	IL	60614	312	Newspaper	likes graphics	32
Roberts	Bob	56 Water St.	Chicago	IL	60614	312	Newspaper	liked photo	35
Graham	Shelley	989 26th Street	Chicago	IL	60611	773	Yellow Pages	great store description	27
Williams	Tasha	1 Spring St	Reading	MA	03882	413	Newspaper	likes font we use	25
Julio	Manuel	544 Cameo Place	Belmont	MA	02483	617	Newspaper	no comments	39
Smith	Carol	123 Elm St.	Waterton	MA	02472	617	Newspaper	no comments	3
Masters	Latrice	88 Las Puntas Rd.	Boston	MA	02205	617	Yellow Pages	likes clear store location	38
Kane	Peter	67 Main St.	Cambridge	MA	02138	617	TV	no comments	6
Kelly	Shawn	22 Old Kendall Square	Cambridge	MA	02138	617	Yellow Pages	found under "cafés"	13
Rodriguez									
Stevens									
Ichikawa									
Paxton									
Spencer									
Lopez									
Nelson									
Lee									
Khalsa									
Stephens									
Green									
Black									
Alderson									
Dickenson									
Montano									

Jim Fernandez

MediaLoft - New Customer List.xls

Last Name	First Name	Street Address	City	State	Zip	ACode	Ad Source	Comments on ads	Entry Order
Gonzales	Fred	5532 West Covent Way	Houston	TX	77098	281	Yellow Pages	finds ad inviting	18
Splint	K. C.	221 Walnut Blvd.	Houston	TX	77098	281	KWIN Radio	disliked ad voice	41
Dewey	Evan	823 Northside Heights	Houston	TX	77092	281	Newspaper	great ads	31
Ballard	Adelia	3 Hall Rd.	Seattle	WA	98103	206	Newspaper	nice images	7
Dobbins	Camilla	486 Intel Circuit	Seattle	WA	98102	206	TV	likes ad	17
Relman	Cathy	9203 Arlen Road	Seattle	WA	98101	206	Yellow Pages	found ad informative	44
Janis	Steve	402 9th Street	Seattle	WA	98100	206	Newspaper	found in Restaurant Section	28

Setting a print area

There are times when you want to print only part of a worksheet. You can do this in the Print dialog box by choosing Selection under Print what. If you want to print a selected area repeatedly, it's best to define a print area, which will print when you click the Print button on the Standard toolbar. To set a print area, click View on the menu bar, then click Page Break Preview. In the preview window, select the area you want to print. Right-click the area, then select Set Print Area. The print area becomes outlined in a blue border. You can drag the border to extend the print area or add nonadjacent cells to it by selecting them, right-clicking them, then selecting Add to Print Area. To clear a print area, click File on the menu bar, point to Print Area, then click Clear Print Area.

Practice

► Concepts Review

Label each of the elements of the Excel screen shown in Figure H-18.

FIGURE H-18

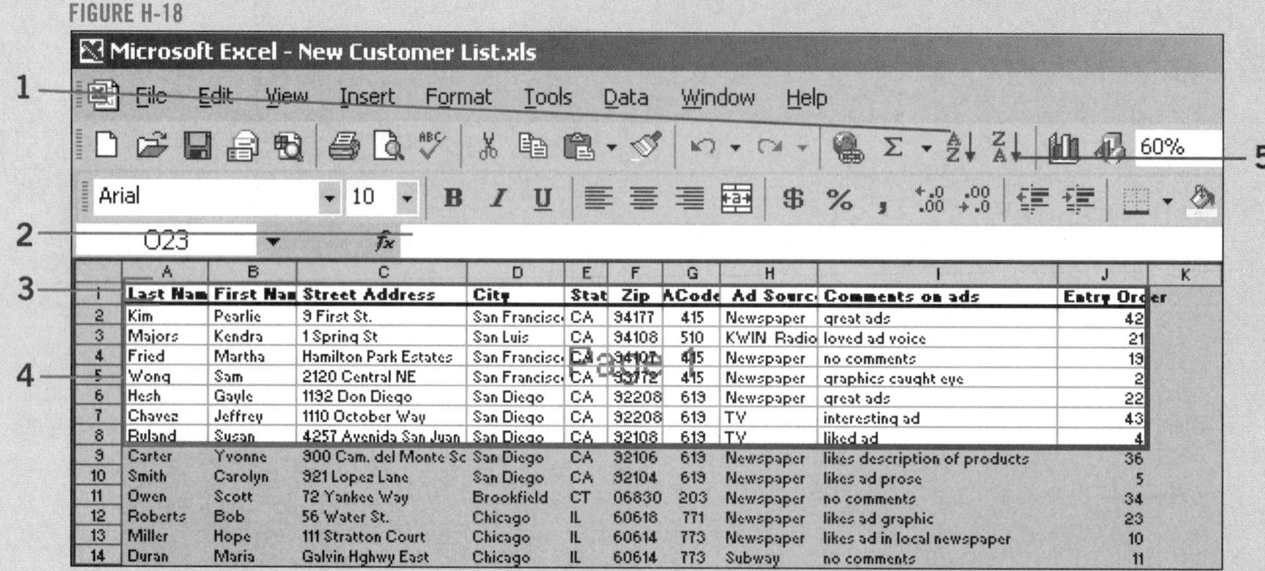

Match each term with the statement that best describes it.

6. List
7. Record
8. Database
9. Sort
10. Field name

a. Arrange records in a particular sequence
b. Organized collection of related information in Excel
c. Row in an Excel list
d. Type of software used for lists containing more than 65,536 records
e. Label positioned at the top of the column identifying data

Select the best answer from the list of choices.

11. Which of the following Excel sorting options do you use to sort a list of employee names in A-to-Z order?
- **a.** Ascending
- **b.** Absolute
- **c.** Alphabetic
- **d.** Descending

12. Which of the following series is in descending order?
- **a.** 4, 5, 6, A, B, C
- **b.** C, B, A, 6, 5, 4
- **c.** 8, 7, 6, 5, 6, 7
- **d.** 8, 6, 4, C, B, A

13. To prevent field name labels from being included in a sort, you need to make sure __________ is selected in the Sort dialog box.
- **a.** Field row
- **b.** No field row
- **c.** No header row
- **d.** Header row

14. When printing a list on multiple pages, you can define a print title containing repeating row(s) to:
- **a.** Include appropriate fields in the printout.
- **b.** Include field names at the top of each printed page.
- **c.** Include the header in list reports.
- **d.** Exclude from the printout all rows under the first row.

Skills Review

1. Create a list.
- **a.** Create a new workbook, then save it as **MediaLoft New York Employee List** in the drive and folder where your Project files are stored.
- **b.** In cell A1, enter the title **MediaLoft New York Employees.**
- **c.** Enter the field names and records, using the information in the following table.

Last Name	First Name	Years	Position	Full/Part Time	Training?
Long	Sarah	3	CD Sales	F	Y
Marino	Donato	2	CD Sales	P	N
Khederian	Jay	4	Video Sales	F	Y
Johnson	Carol	1	Video Sales	F	N
Rabinowicz	Miriam	2	Café Sales	P	Y

- **d.** Apply bold formatting to the field names.
- **e.** Center the entries in the Years, Full/Part Time, and Training? fields.
- **f.** Adjust the column widths to make the data readable.
- **g.** Enter your name in the footer, save, then print the list.

2. **Add records with the data form.**
   a. Click any record in the list.
   b. Open the data form and add a new record for **David Gitano**, a one-year employee in Book Sales. David is full time and has not completed training.
   c. Add a new record for **George Worley**, the café manager. George is full time, has worked there two years, and has completed training.
   d. Save the file.
3. **Find and delete records.**
   a. Use the Find command to find the record for **Carol Johnson**.
   b. Delete the record.
   c. Save the file.
4. **Sort a list by one field.**
   a. Sort the list alphabetically in ascending order by last name.
   b. Save the file.
5. **Sort a list by multiple fields.**
   a. Sort the list alphabetically in ascending order, first by whether or not the employees have completed training and then by last name.
   b. Save the file.
6. **Print a list.**
   a. Add a header that reads **Employee Information** in the center; format the header in bold.
   b. Set the print area to include the range A1:F8.
   c. Save the workbook, print the print area, then close the workbook.
   d. Exit Excel.

► Independent Challenge 1

You own Personalize IT, an advertising firm located in Australia. The firm sells specialty items imprinted with the customer's name and/or logo such as hats, pens, mugs, and T-shirts. Plan and build a list of order information with a minimum of 10 records using the items sold. Your list should contain at least five different customers. (Some customers may place more than one order.) Each record should contain the following fields:

Customer last: Customer last name
Customer first: Customer first name
Item: Item description
Quantity: The number of items purchased
Cost: The item's price

a. Prepare a list plan that states your goal, outlines the data you'll need, and identifies the list elements.
b. Sketch a sample list on a piece of paper, indicating how the list should be built. Which of the data fields will be formatted as labels? As values?
c. Start Excel, create a new workbook, then save it as **Personalize IT** in the drive and folder where your Project Files are stored. Build the list by first entering **Personalize IT** as the worksheet title in cell A1, then enter the following field names in the designated cells:

Cell	Field name
A2	Customer last
B2	Customer first
C2	Item
D2	Quantity
E2	Cost

d. Enter 8 data records using your own data.
e. Add a new record to your list using the data form.
f. Enter **Subtotal** in cell F2, **Total** in cell G2, **Tax** in cell H2, and **.1** in cell I2 (the 10% sales tax).
g. Enter formulas to calculate the subtotal (Quantity*Cost) in cell F3 and the total (including tax) in cell G3. Copy the formulas down the columns.
h. Format the Cost, Subtotal, and Total columns as currency. Adjust the column widths as necessary.
i. Sort the list in ascending order by Item, then by Customer last.
j. Enter your name in the worksheet footer, then save the workbook.
k. Preview the worksheet, print the worksheet on one page, close the workbook, then exit Excel.

▶ Independent Challenge 2

You are taking a class titled Television Shows: Past and Present at a local community college. The instructor has provided you with an Excel list of television programs from the '60s and '70s. She has included fields tracking the following information: the number of years the show was a favorite, favorite character, the show's length in minutes, least favorite character, and comments about the show. The instructor has included data for each show in the list. She has asked you to add a field (column label) and one record (show of your choosing) to the list. Because the list should cover only 30-minute shows, you need to delete any records for shows longer than 30 minutes. Also, your instructor wants you to sort the list by television show and format the list as needed prior to printing. Feel free to change any of the list data to suit your tastes and opinions.

FIGURE H-19

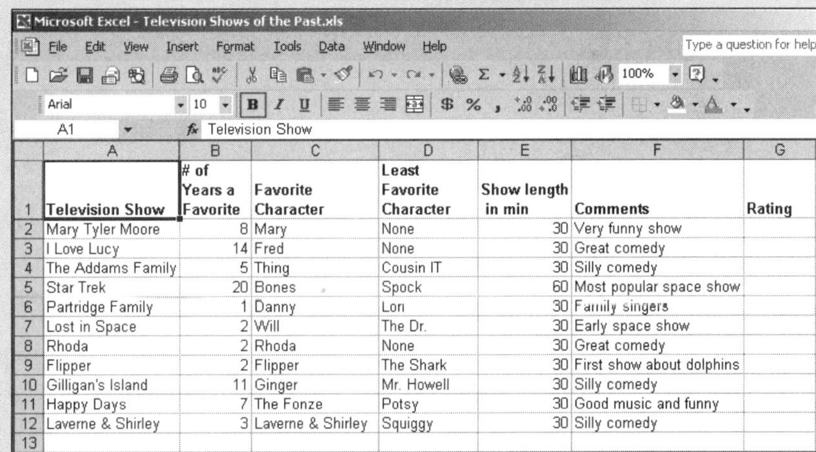

	A	B	C	D	E	F	G
1	Television Show	# of Years a Favorite	Favorite Character	Least Favorite Character	Show length in min	Comments	Rating
2	Mary Tyler Moore	8	Mary	None	30	Very funny show	
3	I Love Lucy	14	Fred	None	30	Great comedy	
4	The Addams Family	5	Thing	Cousin IT	30	Silly comedy	
5	Star Trek	20	Bones	Spock	60	Most popular space show	
6	Partridge Family	1	Danny	Lori	30	Family singers	
7	Lost in Space	2	Will	The Dr.	30	Early space show	
8	Rhoda	2	Rhoda	None	30	Great comedy	
9	Flipper	2	Flipper	The Shark	30	First show about dolphins	
10	Gilligan's Island	11	Ginger	Mr. Howell	30	Silly comedy	
11	Happy Days	7	The Fonze	Potsy	30	Good music and funny	
12	Laverne & Shirley	3	Laverne & Shirley	Squiggy	30	Silly comedy	
13							

a. Start Excel, open the Project File EX H-2 from the drive and folder where your Project Files are stored, then save it as **Television Shows of the Past**.
b. Add a field called **Rating** in column G. Your worksheet should look like Figure H-19. Complete the Rating field for each record with a value of 1–5 that reflects the rating you would give the television show.
c. Use the data form to add one record to the list. Make sure to enter information in every field.
d. Delete any records having show lengths other than 30. (*Hint*: Use the comparison operator <> in the Show length field to find records not equal to 30.)
e. Make any formatting changes to the list as needed and save the list.
f. Sort the list in ascending order by show name.
g. Enter your name in the worksheet footer, save the workbook, then print the nonadjacent columns Television Show and Rating.

h. Sort the list again, this time in descending order by number of years the show was a favorite.
i. Add a centered header that reads **Television Shows of the Past: '60s and '70s**.
j. Save the workbook, then preview the list and print it on a single page modifying its orientation if necessary.
k. Close the workbook and exit Excel.

▶ Independent Challenge 3

You are the assistant manager at Nite Owl Video in Brisbane, Australia. You have assembled an Excel list of the most popular Australian films your store rents, along with information about the Australian Film Institute (AFI) award they won, the release dates, and the film genres. Your customers have suggested that you prepare an in-store handout listing the films with the information sorted in different ways.

FIGURE H-20

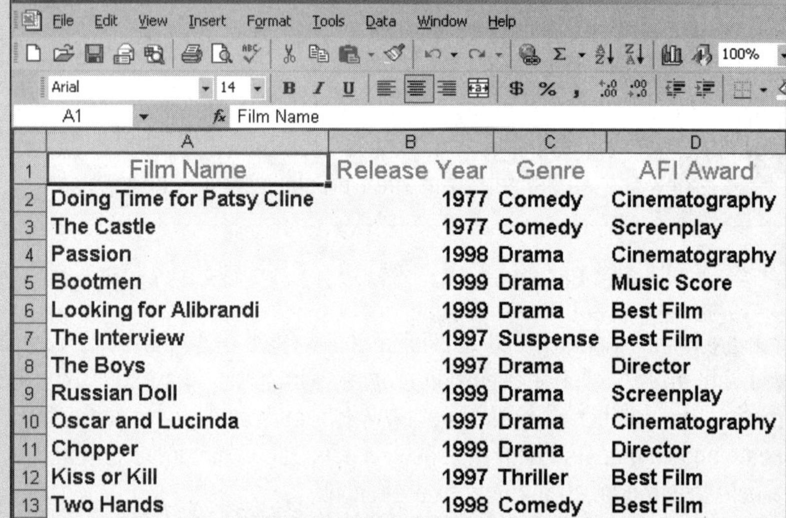

	A	B	C	D
1	Film Name	Release Year	Genre	AFI Award
2	Doing Time for Patsy Cline	1977	Comedy	Cinematography
3	The Castle	1977	Comedy	Screenplay
4	Passion	1998	Drama	Cinematography
5	Bootmen	1999	Drama	Music Score
6	Looking for Alibrandi	1999	Drama	Best Film
7	The Interview	1997	Suspense	Best Film
8	The Boys	1997	Drama	Director
9	Russian Doll	1999	Drama	Screenplay
10	Oscar and Lucinda	1997	Drama	Cinematography
11	Chopper	1999	Drama	Director
12	Kiss or Kill	1997	Thriller	Best Film
13	Two Hands	1998	Comedy	Best Film

a. Start Excel, open the Project File EX H-3 from the drive and folder where your Project Files are stored, then save it as **Best Films**.
b. Format the list using Figure H-20 as a guide.
c. Sort the list in ascending order by Genre. Sort the list again in ascending order by Film Name.
d. Sort the list again using two fields, this time in descending order by the Genre, then in ascending order by Release Year.
e. Enter your name in the worksheet footer, save your work, then print the worksheet.
f. Use the data form to add a record to the list with the following information: Film name: In a Savage Land; Release year: 1998; Genre: Drama; AFI Award: Sound.
g. Use the data form to find and delete the record for the film "Passion."
h. Activate AutoFilter, use it to display only dramas, then print the list.
i. Redisplay all films, then set a print area that includes the range A1:C13.
j. Clear the print area and print the worksheet.
k. Close the workbook and exit Excel.

Independent Challenge 4

The Local newspaper you work for has decided to start publishing the top selling MP3 titles. They would like to list the best-selling titles in the genres of Pop and Rock, Jazz, and Latin music. You have been asked to research the best-selling MP3 music along with price information. You will create a workbook to hold the information about the top three titles for each genre. You will add an AutoFilter to the Genre field to make it easier to view titles by the type of music.

a. Go to the AltaVista search engine at www.altavista.com and enter " MP3" in the Search box, then click the direct link to the MP3 site. You can also use Yahoo!, Excite, Infoseek, or another search engine of your choice. (If you prefer, you can enter the URL www.mp3.com directly in your browser.)

b. Complete the table below with the MP3 title information you found in your search.

Title	Artist	Genre	Price

c. Start Excel, open a new workbook enter your name in the worksheet footer, then save the workbook as **MP3 Titles**.

d. Use your table to enter the top three titles for the three music categories along with the Artist and price information into your Excel worksheet. Save the workbook.

e. Add an AutoFilter to the Genre column then use the filter to display only the Jazz records. (*Hint*: To apply a filter to only one column, select the column before applying the AutoFilter.)

f. Print only the records for the Jazz genre, then use the AutoFilter to display all the records.

g. Save the workbook again, set a print area to print only the Title and Artist columns, then print the print area.

h. Clear the print area, save the worksheet, close the workbook, then exit Excel.

Excel 2002

► Visual Workshop

Create the worksheet shown in Figure H-21. Save the workbook as **Famous Jazz Performers** in the drive and folder where your Project Files are stored. Once you've entered the field names and records, sort the list using two fields. The first sort should be in ascending order by Contribution to Jazz, and the second sort should be in ascending order by Last Name. Change the page setup so that the list is centered on the page horizontally and the header reads "Famous Jazz Performers". Enter your name in the worksheet footer. Preview and print the list, then save the workbook.

FIGURE H-21

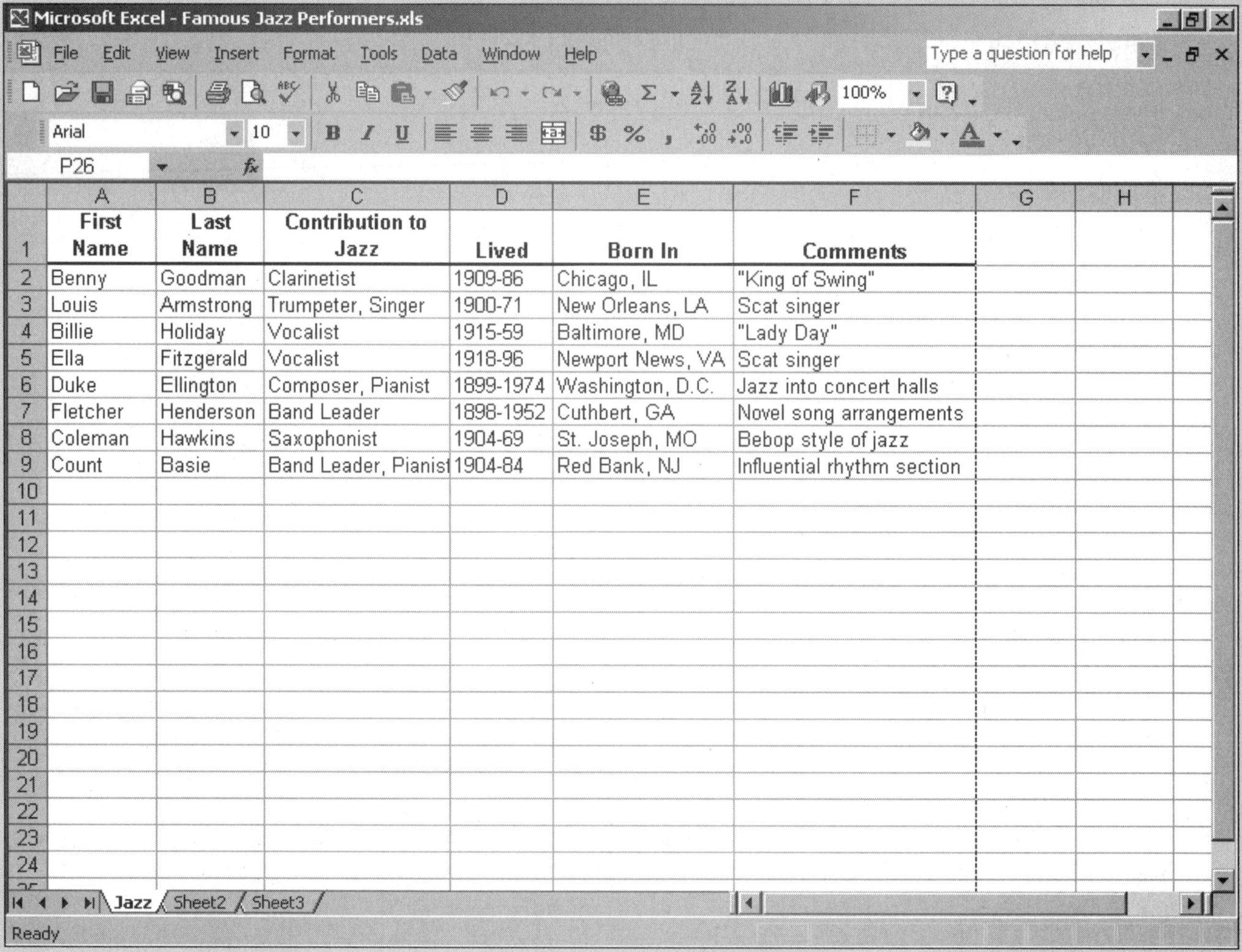

Microsoft Excel - Famous Jazz Performers.xls

First Name	Last Name	Contribution to Jazz	Lived	Born In	Comments
Benny	Goodman	Clarinetist	1909-86	Chicago, IL	"King of Swing"
Louis	Armstrong	Trumpeter, Singer	1900-71	New Orleans, LA	Scat singer
Billie	Holiday	Vocalist	1915-59	Baltimore, MD	"Lady Day"
Ella	Fitzgerald	Vocalist	1918-96	Newport News, VA	Scat singer
Duke	Ellington	Composer, Pianist	1899-1974	Washington, D.C.	Jazz into concert halls
Fletcher	Henderson	Band Leader	1898-1952	Cuthbert, GA	Novel song arrangements
Coleman	Hawkins	Saxophonist	1904-69	St. Joseph, MO	Bebop style of jazz
Count	Basie	Band Leader, Pianist	1904-84	Red Bank, NJ	Influential rhythm section

Excel 2002

Unit I

Analyzing List Data

Objectives

- MOUS ► Retrieve records with AutoFilter
- MOUS ► Create a custom filter
- MOUS ► Filter a list with Advanced Filter
- ► Extract list data
- MOUS ► Create subtotals using grouping and outlines
- MOUS ► Look up values in a list
- ► Summarize list data
- MOUS ► Use data validation for list entries

There are many ways to analyze or manipulate list data with Excel. One way is to filter a list so that only the rows that meet certain criteria are retrieved. In this unit you will retrieve records using AutoFilter, create a custom filter, then filter a list using the Excel Advanced Filter feature. In addition, you will learn to insert automatic subtotals, use lookup functions to locate list entries, then apply database functions to summarize list data that meets specific criteria. You'll also learn how to restrict entries in a column by using data validation. Jim Fernandez recently conducted a survey for the MediaLoft Marketing Department. He mailed questionnaires to a random selection of customers at all stores. After the questionnaires were returned, he entered the data into Excel. He wants you to analyze the data and create reports.

Excel 2002

Retrieving Records with AutoFilter

The Excel AutoFilter feature **retrieves** (searches for and lists) records that meet user-specified criteria. Autofilter provides many filtering options. One option is to **filter** out, or hide, data that fails to meet certain criteria. You can also filter specific values in a column, use the predefined Top 10 option to filter records based on upper or lower values in a column, or create a custom filter. For example, you can filter a customer list to retrieve names of only those customers residing in Canada. You can filter records based on a specific field then request that Excel retrieve only those records having an entry (or no entry) in that field. Once you create a filtered list, you can print it or copy it to another part of the worksheet to manipulate it further. Jim is now ready to work with the survey information. He asks you to retrieve data for customers who live in Chicago, Illinois.

1. Start Excel, open the Project File **EX I-1** from the drive and folder where your Project Files are stored, then save it as **Survey Data**
   The AutoFilter feature will enable you to retrieve the records for the report.
2. Click **Data** on the menu bar, point to **Filter**, then click **AutoFilter**
   List arrows appear to the right of each field name.
3. Click the **City** list arrow
   An AutoFilter list containing the different city options appears below the field name, as shown in Figure I-1. Because you want to retrieve data for only those customers who live in Chicago, "Chicago" will be your **search criterion**.
4. In the AutoFilter list, click **Chicago**
   Only those records containing Chicago in the City field appear, as shown in Figure I-2. The status bar indicates the number of matching records (in this case, 5 of 35), the color of the row numbers changes for the matching records, and the color of the list arrow for the filtered field changes. Next, you want to retrieve information about those customers who purchased the most merchandise.
5. Click **Data** on the menu bar, point to **Filter**, then click **Show All**
   Now that you have cleared the previous filter, all the records reappear.
6. Scroll right until columns G through M are visible, click the **Purchases to Date** list arrow, then click **(Top 10...)**
   The Top 10 AutoFilter dialog box opens. The default is to select the 10 records with the highest value. You need to display only the top two.
7. With **10** selected in the middle box, type **2**, then click **OK**
   The records are retrieved for the two customers who purchased the most merchandise, \$3,200 and \$2,530. See Figure I-3.
8. Click the **Purchases to Date** list arrow, click **(All)**, press **[Ctrl][Home]**
   You have cleared the filter, and all the records reappear.
9. Add your name to the right side of the footer, save the workbook, then print the list

Trouble?

If the column label in cell A1 covers the column headers, making it difficult to find the appropriate columns, select A2 before scrolling.

QuickTip

If a worksheet is arranged with the field names in rows rather in columns, you can transpose the rows to columns so a filter can be used. To do this you need to copy the range containing the list, select the upper-left cell of the paste area, click the Paste button list arrow on the Standard toolbar, then click Transpose.

FIGURE I-1: Worksheet showing AutoFilter options

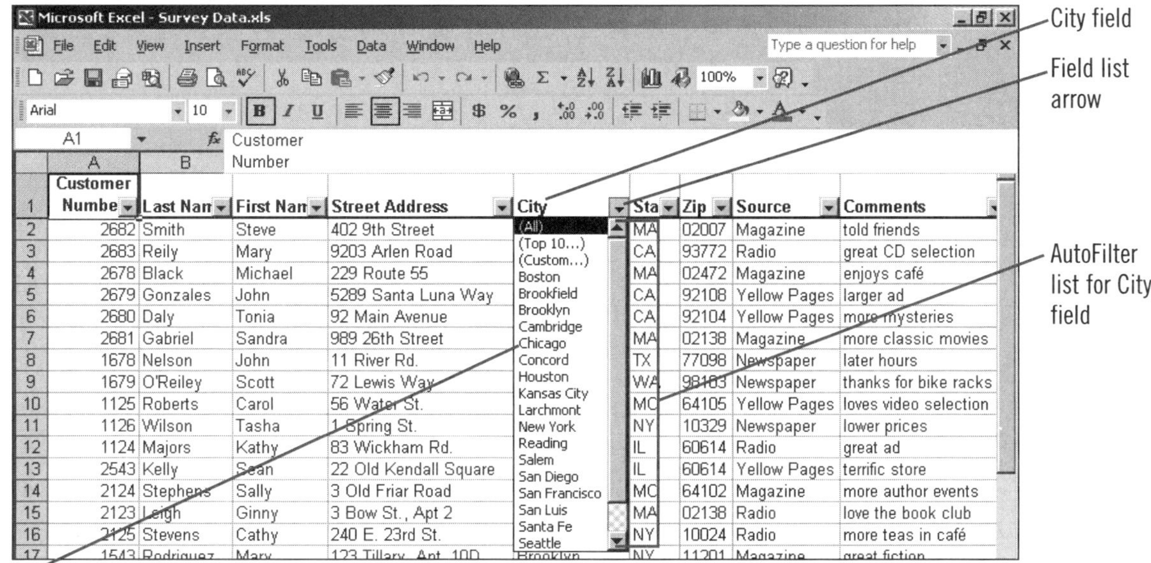

FIGURE I-2: List filtered with AutoFilter

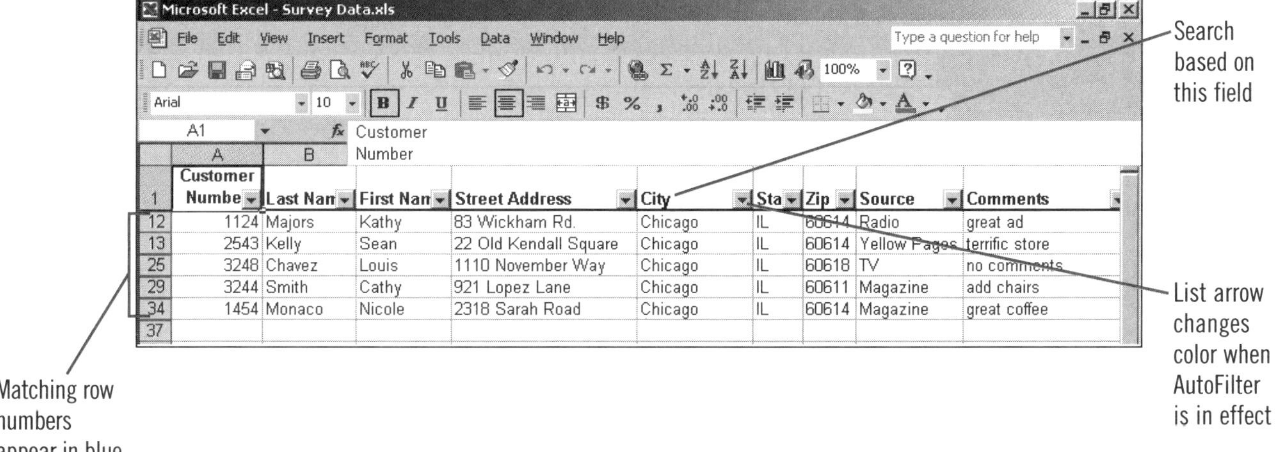

FIGURE I-3: List filtered with Top 2 AutoFilter criteria

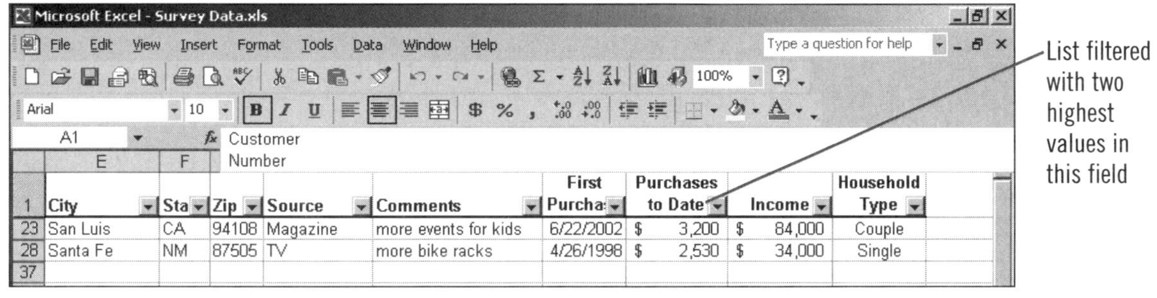

Excel 2002

Creating a Custom Filter

So far, you have used the AutoFilter command to filter rows based on an entry in a single column. You can perform more complex filters by using options in the Custom AutoFilter dialog box. For example, you can filter rows based on two entries in a single column or use comparison operators such as "greater than" or "less than." Jim's next task is to locate those customers who reside west of the Rocky Mountains, in a "family" household, and who heard about MediaLoft through a magazine advertisement. He asks you to create a custom filter to list the customers satisfying these criteria.

QuickTip

When specifying criteria in the Custom AutoFilter dialog box, use the ? wildcard to represent any single character and the * wildcard to represent any series of characters.

Trouble?

If no records are displayed in the worksheet, you may have forgotten to type the apostrophe before the number 81000. Repeat Steps 2 and 3, making sure you include the leading apostrophe.

1. Click the **Zip** list arrow, then click **(Custom . . .)**
   The Custom AutoFilter dialog box opens. Because all residents west of the Rockies have a ZIP code greater than 81000, that will be your criterion. All the ZIP codes in the list were originally entered as labels with leading apostrophes, so you need to include an apostrophe when entering the ZIP code value.
2. Click the **Zip** list arrow, click **is greater than**, press **[Tab]**, then type **'81000**
   Your completed Custom AutoFilter dialog box should match Figure I-4.
3. Click **OK**
   The dialog box closes, and only those records having a ZIP code greater than 81000 appear in the worksheet. Now, you'll narrow the list even further by displaying only those customers who live in a family household.
4. Scroll right until columns G through M are visible, click the **Household Type** list arrow, then click **Family**
   The list of records retrieved has narrowed. Finally, you need to filter out all customers except those who heard about MediaLoft through a magazine advertisement.
5. Click the **Source** list arrow, then click **Magazine**
   Your final filtered list now shows only customers in family households, west of the Rocky Mountains, who heard about MediaLoft through magazine ads. See Figure I-5.
6. Preview, then print the worksheet
   The worksheet prints using the existing print settings—landscape orientation, scaled to fit on a single page.
7. Click **Data** on the menu bar, point to **Filter**, click **AutoFilter** to deselect it, then press **[Ctrl][Home]**
   You have cleared the filter, and all the customer records appear.

FIGURE I-4: Custom AutoFilter dialog box

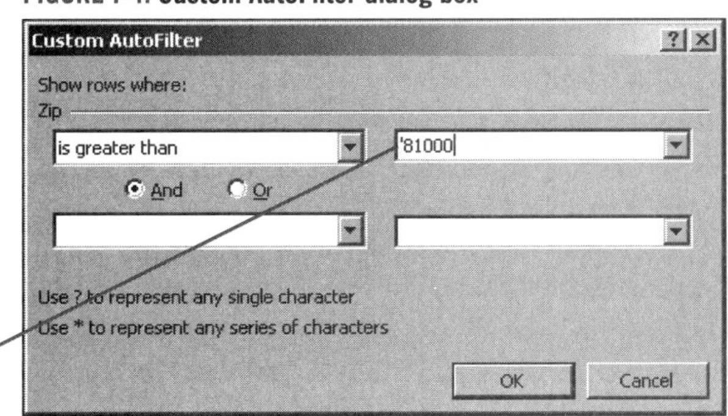

Value includes leading apostrophe

FIGURE I-5: Results of custom filter

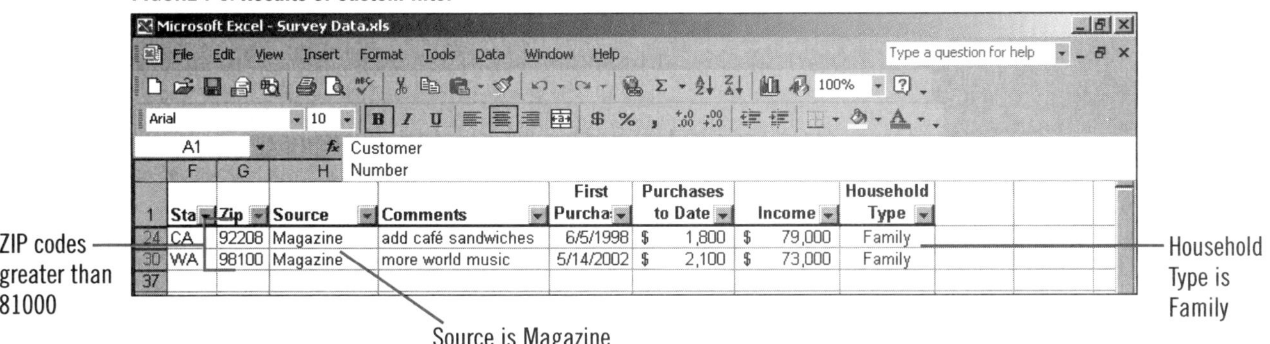

"And" and "Or" logical conditions

You can narrow a search even further by using the And or Or buttons in the Custom AutoFilter dialog box. For example, you can select records for those customers with homes in California *and* Texas as well as select records for customers with homes in California *or* Texas. See Figure I-6. When used in this way, "And" and "Or" are often referred to as **logical conditions**. When you search for customers with homes in California *and* Texas, you are specifying an And condition. When you search for customers with homes in either California *or* Texas, you are specifying an Or condition.

FIGURE I-6: Using the Custom AutoFilter dialog box

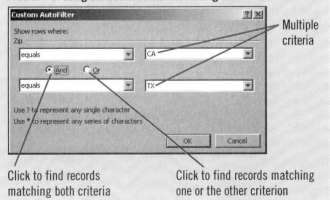

Custom AutoFilter
Show rows where:
Zip
equals — CA
And — Or
equals — TX
Use ? to represent any single character
Use * to represent any series of characters
OK — Cancel

Multiple criteria

Click to find records matching both criteria

Click to find records matching one or the other criterion

Excel 2002

Filtering a List with Advanced Filter

The Advanced Filter command allows you to search for data that matches complicated criteria in more than one column, using And and Or conditions. To use advanced filtering, you must define a criteria range. A **criteria range** is a cell range containing one row of labels (usually a copy of the column labels) and at least one additional row underneath the row of labels that contains the criteria you want to match. Jim's next task is to identify customers who have been MediaLoft customers since before May 1, 2001, and whose total purchases are less than or equal to $1,000. He asks you to use the Advanced Filter command to retrieve this data. You begin by defining the criteria range.

Steps

1. Select **rows 1 through 6**, click **Insert** on the menu bar, then click **Rows**; click cell **A1**, type **Criteria Range**, click cell **A6**, type **List Range**, then click the **Enter button**
   See Figure I-7. Six blank rows are added above the list. Excel does not require the labels "Criteria Range" and "List Range," but they are useful because they help organize the worksheet. It will be helpful to see the column labels.

Trouble?

If the column labels make it difficult for you to drag the pointer to cell M7, try clicking M7 first; then drag the pointer all the way left to cell A7.

2. Select range **A7:M7**, click the **Copy button** on the Standard toolbar, click cell **A2**, then press **[Enter]**
   Next, you want to list records for only those people who have been customers since before May 1, 2001 and who have purchased no more than $1,000.

3. Scroll right until columns H through M are visible, click cell **J3**, type **<5/1/200** (making sure there is no space between the symbol and the 5), click cell **K3**, type **<=1,000**, then click
   This enters the criteria in the cells directly beneath the Criteria Range labels. See Figure I-8. Placing the criteria in the same row indicates that the records you are searching for must match both criteria; that is, it specifies an And condition.

4. Press **[Ctrl][Home]**, click **Data** on the menu bar, point to **Filter**, then click **Advanced Filter**
   The Advanced Filter dialog box opens, with the list range already entered. The default setting under Action is to filter the list in its current location rather than copy it to another location.

Trouble?

If you did not get the filtered list of records, make sure the date in cell J3 has the same date format as the dates in the list range.

5. Click the **Criteria Range text box**, select range **A2:M3** in the worksheet (move the dialog box if necessary), then click **OK**
   You have specified the criteria range. The filtered list contains 12 records that match both the criteria—the first purchase was before 5/1/2001 and the purchases to date total less than $1,000. You'll filter this list even further in the next lesson.

FIGURE I-7: Using the Advanced Filter command

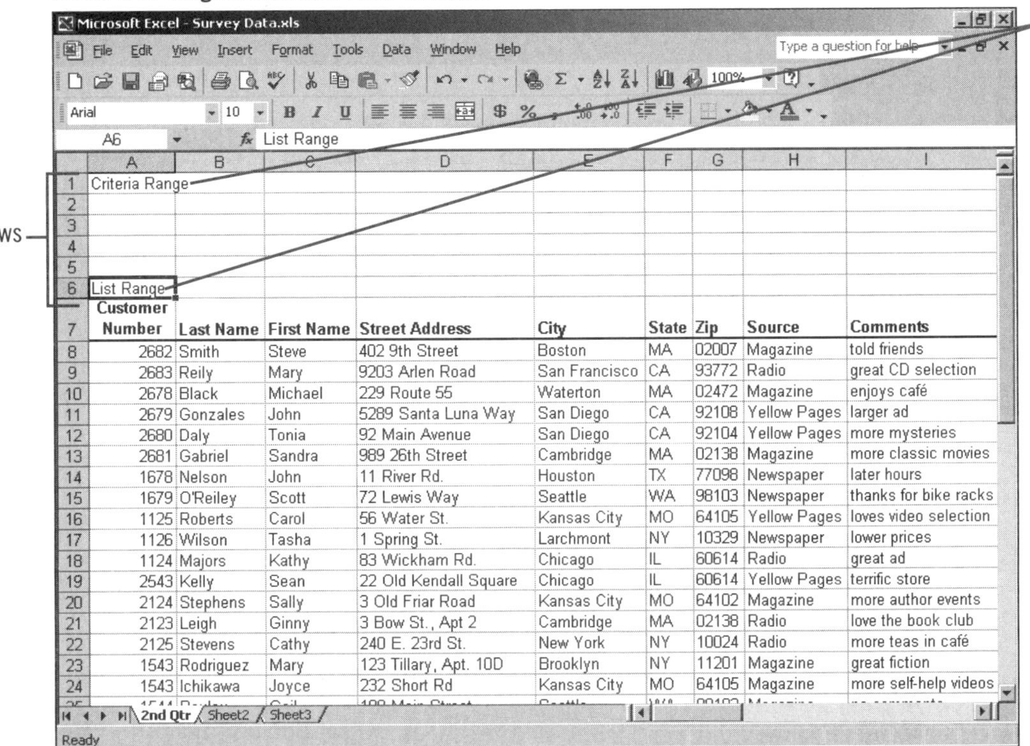

FIGURE I-8: Criteria in the same row

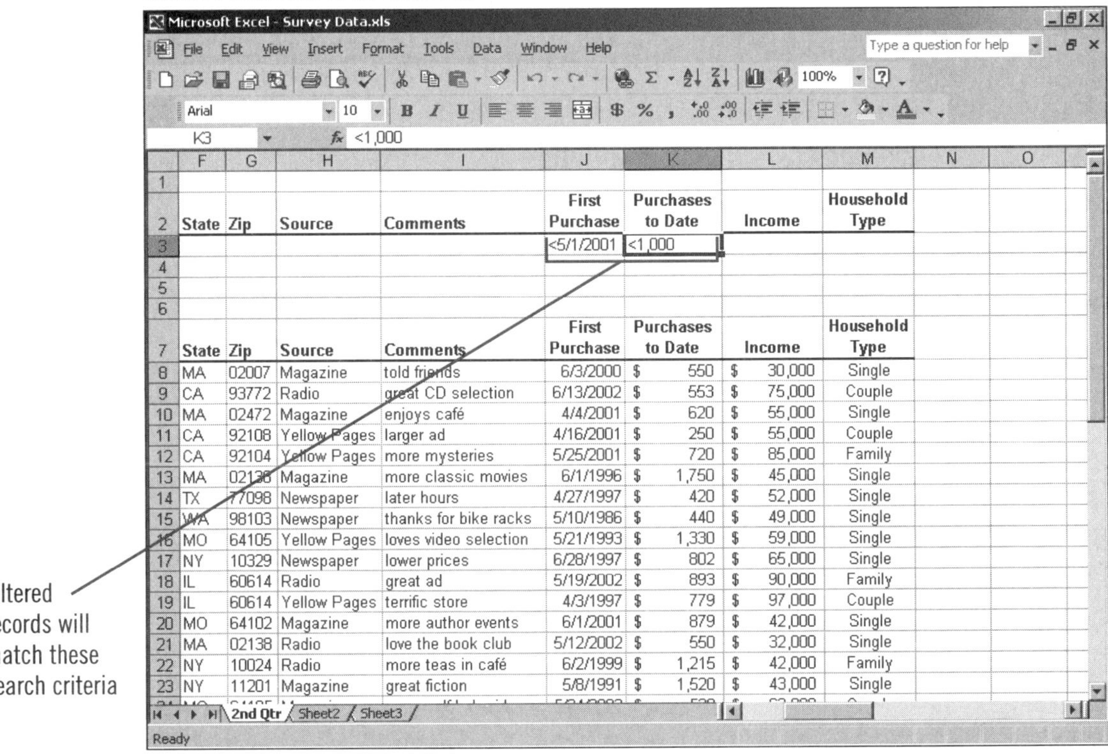

Excel 2002

Extracting List Data

Whenever you take the time to specify a complicated set of search criteria, it's a good idea to extract the matching records. When you **extract** data, you place a copy of a filtered list in a range you specify in the Advanced Filter dialog box. That way, you won't accidentally clear the filter or lose track of the records you spent time compiling. Jim needs to filter the previous list one step further to reflect only those customers in the current filtered list who heard of MediaLoft through TV or a magazine ad. He asks you to complete this filter by specifying an Or condition. You will do this by entering two sets of criteria in two separate rows. You decide to save the matching records by extracting them to a different location in the worksheet.

Steps

1. In cell **H3**, enter **TV**, in cell **H4**, enter **Magazine**
2. Copy the criteria in **J3:K3** to **J4:K4**
   See Figure I-9. This time, you'll indicate that you want to copy the filtered list to a range beginning in cell A50.
3. Click **Data** on the menu bar, point to **Filter**, then click **Advanced Filter**
4. Under Action, click the **Copy to another location option button** to select it, click the **Copy to** text box, then type **A50**
   The last time you filtered the list, the criteria range included only rows 2 and 3, and now you have criteria in row 4.
5. Select the contents of the **Criteria Range text box**, click the Criteria Range **Collapse Dialog Box button**, select the range **A2:M4**
6. Click the **Redisplay Dialog Box button**, click **OK**; then scroll down until row 50 is visible
   Collapsing the dialog box allows you to select the desired range rather than typing it in the Criteria Range text box. You have changed the criteria range to include row 4. The matching records now appear in the range beginning in cell A50. See Figure I-10. The original list, starting in cell A7, contains the records filtered in the previous lesson.
7. Save the workbook, select the range **A50:M56**, click **File** on the menu bar, click **Print**, under Print what, click the **Selection option button**, click **Preview**, then click **Print**
   The selected area prints.
8. Press **[Ctrl][Home]**, click **Data** on the menu bar, point to **Filter**, then click **Show All**
   All the records in the range reappear. You return to the original list, which starts at its new location in cell A7.
9. Close the workbook

Trouble?

Make sure the criteria range in the Advanced Filter dialog box includes the field names and the number of rows underneath the names that contain criteria. If you leave a blank row in the criteria range, Excel filters nothing and shows all records.

FIGURE I-9: Criteria in separate rows

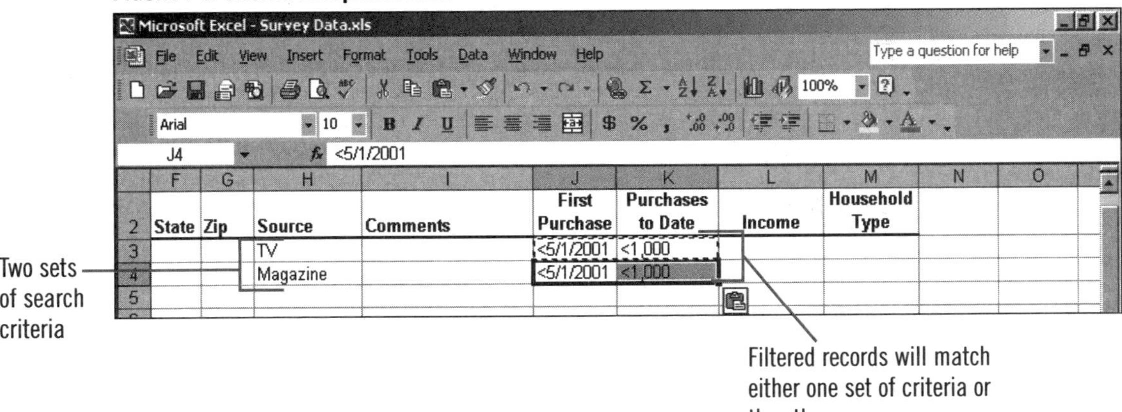

FIGURE I-10: Extracted data records

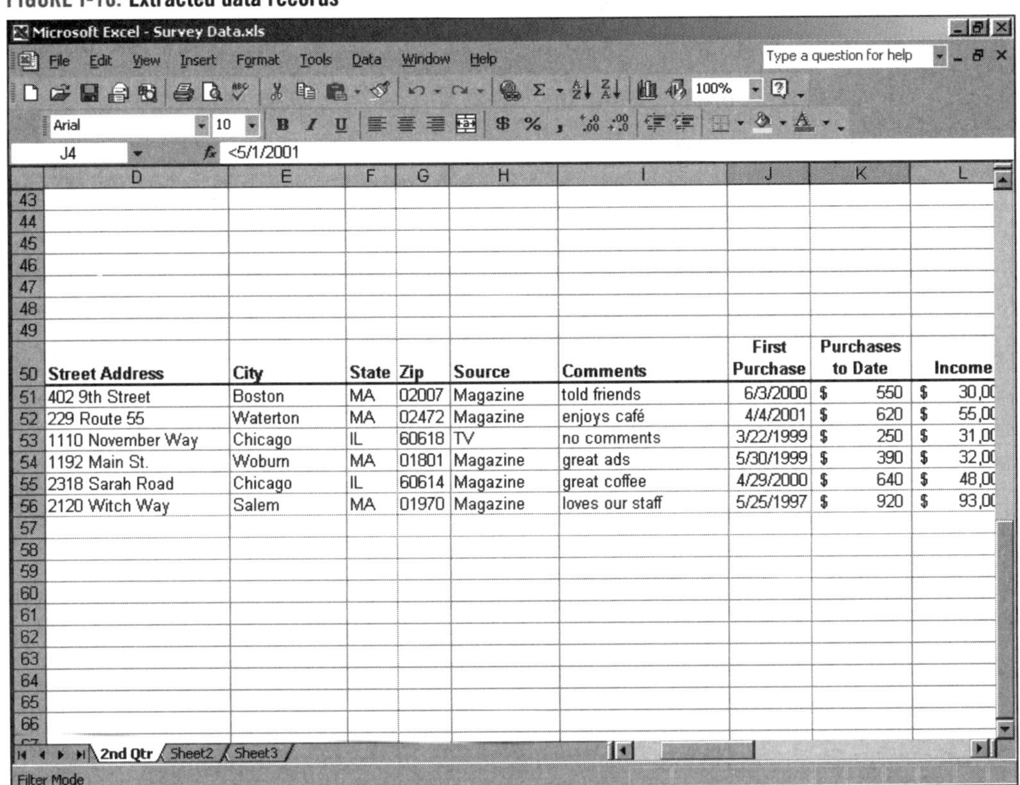

Understanding the criteria range and the copy-to location

When you define the criteria range and the copy-to location in the Advanced Filter dialog box, Excel automatically creates the names Criteria and Extract for these ranges in the worksheet. The criteria range includes the field names and any criteria rows underneath them. The extract range includes just the field names above the extracted list. To extract a different list, select Extract as the copy-to location. Excel deletes the old list in the extract area and generates a new list under the field names. Make sure the worksheet has enough blank rows under the field names for your data.

Excel 2002

Creating Subtotals Using Grouping and Outlines

The Excel subtotals feature provides a quick, easy way to group and summarize data in a list. Usually, you create subtotals with the SUM function but you can also subtotal groups with functions such as COUNT, AVERAGE, MAX, and MIN. Before you can issue the Subtotal command, your list must have field names and be sorted, and the cell pointer must be within the list range. Jim wants you to create a list grouped by advertising source, with subtotals for purchases to date and household income. You begin by sorting the list in ascending order, first by advertising source, then by state, and, finally, by city.

Steps

1. Open the Project File **EX I-1** from the drive and folder where your Project Files are stored, then save it as **Survey Data 2**
2. With the cell pointer positioned in the list range, click **Data** on the menu bar, click **Sort**; click the **Sort by** list arrow, click **Source**
3. Click the first **Then by** list arrow, click **State**, click the **Ascending option button**, click the second **Then by** list arrow, click **City**, then click **OK**
   You have sorted the list in ascending order, first by advertising source, then by state, and, finally, by city.
4. Press **[Ctrl][Home]**, click **Data** on the menu bar, then click **Subtotals**
   The list range is selected, in this case, range A1:M36, and the Subtotal dialog box opens. Here, you specify the items you want subtotaled, the function you want to apply to the values, and the fields you want to summarize.
5. Click the **At each change in** list arrow, click **Source**, click the **Use function** list arrow, click **Sum**; in the "Add subtotal to" list, click the **Purchases to Date** and **Income** check boxes to select them; if necessary, click the **Household Type** check box to deselect it
6. If necessary, click the **Replace current subtotals** and **Summary below data** check boxes to select them
   Your completed Subtotal dialog box should match Figure I-11.
7. Click **OK**, then scroll to and click cell **K41**
   The subtotaled list appears, showing the calculated subtotals and grand total in columns K and L. See Figure I-12. Notice that Excel displays an outline to the left of the worksheet, showing the structure of the subtotaled lists.
8. Save and preview the worksheet, click **Setup**, place your name on the right side of the footer, then print the worksheet
9. Press **[Ctrl][Home]**, click **Data** on the menu bar, click **Subtotals**, then click **Remove All**
   You have turned off the Subtotaling feature. The subtotals are removed, and the Outline feature is turned off automatically.

QuickTip

You can create subtotals for a range of cells in a list. Select the range, click Data, click Subtotals, then complete the Subtotal dialog box for the cell range.

FIGURE I-11: Completed Subtotal dialog box

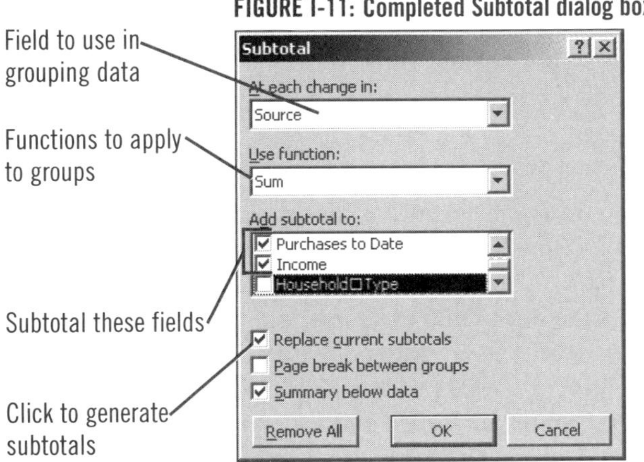

FIGURE I-12: Portion of subtotaled list

Number 9 indicates the SUM function

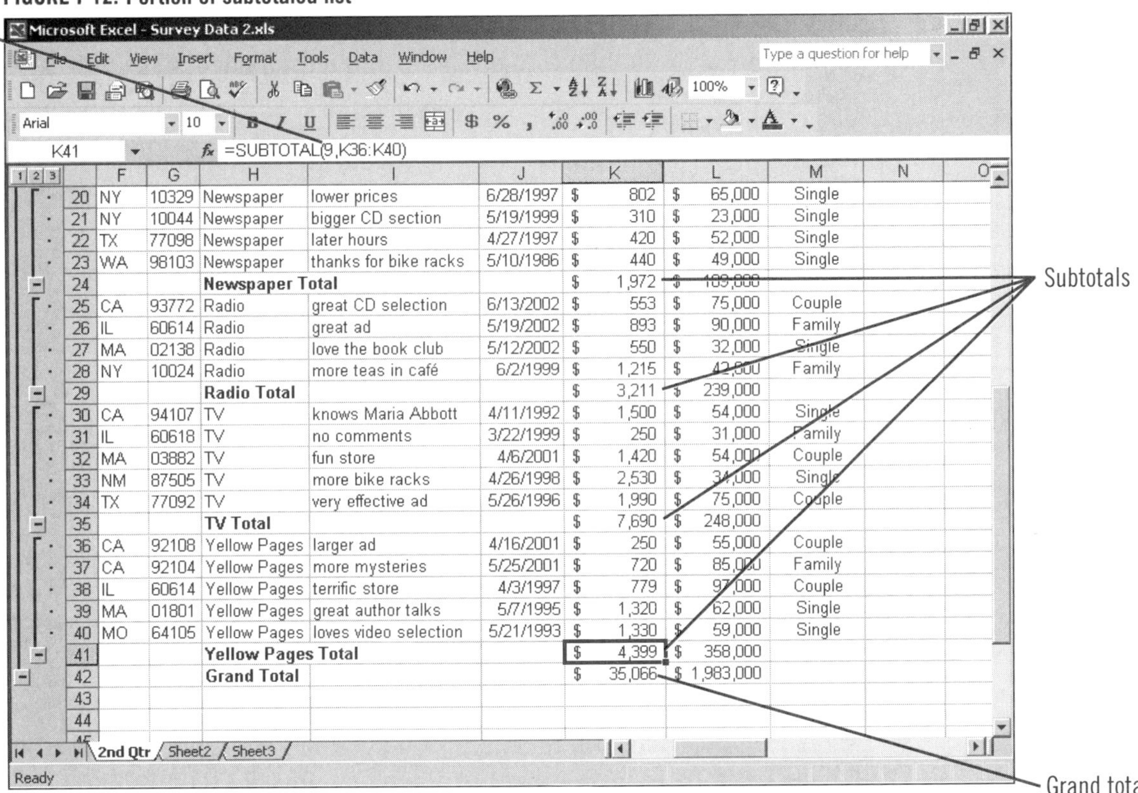

	F	G	H	I	J	K	L	M
20	NY	10329	Newspaper	lower prices	6/28/1997	$ 802	$ 65,000	Single
21	NY	10044	Newspaper	bigger CD section	5/19/1999	$ 310	$ 23,000	Single
22	TX	77098	Newspaper	later hours	4/27/1997	$ 420	$ 52,000	Single
23	WA	98103	Newspaper	thanks for bike racks	5/10/1986	$ 440	$ 49,000	Single
24			Newspaper Total			$ 1,972	$ 189,000	
25	CA	93772	Radio	great CD selection	6/13/2002	$ 553	$ 75,000	Couple
26	IL	60614	Radio	great ad	5/19/2002	$ 893	$ 90,000	Family
27	MA	02138	Radio	love the book club	5/12/2002	$ 550	$ 32,000	Single
28	NY	10024	Radio	more teas in café	6/2/1999	$ 1,215	$ 42,000	Family
29			Radio Total			$ 3,211	$ 239,000	
30	CA	94107	TV	knows Maria Abbott	4/11/1992	$ 1,500	$ 54,000	Single
31	IL	60618	TV	no comments	3/22/1999	$ 250	$ 31,000	Family
32	MA	03882	TV	fun store	4/6/2001	$ 1,420	$ 54,000	Couple
33	NM	87505	TV	more bike racks	4/26/1998	$ 2,530	$ 34,000	Single
34	TX	77092	TV	very effective ad	5/26/1996	$ 1,990	$ 75,000	Couple
35			TV Total			$ 7,690	$ 248,000	
36	CA	92108	Yellow Pages	larger ad	4/16/2001	$ 250	$ 55,000	Couple
37	CA	92104	Yellow Pages	more mysteries	5/25/2001	$ 720	$ 85,000	Family
38	IL	60614	Yellow Pages	terrific store	4/3/1997	$ 779	$ 97,000	Couple
39	MA	01801	Yellow Pages	great author talks	5/7/1995	$ 1,320	$ 62,000	Single
40	MO	64105	Yellow Pages	loves video selection	5/21/1993	$ 1,330	$ 59,000	Single
41			Yellow Pages Total			$ 4,399	$ 358,000	
42			Grand Total			$ 35,066	$ 1,983,000	

Clues to Use

Using Show Details and Hide Details buttons in an outline

Once you have generated subtotals, all detail records appear in an outline. See Figure I-13. You can then click the Hide Details button [−] of your choice to hide that group of records, creating a summary report. You can also create a chart that shows the summary data. Any chart you create will be automatically updated as you show or hide data. You can also click the Show Details button [+] for the group of data you want to display. To show a specific level of detail, click the row or column level button for the lowest level you want to display. For example, to display levels 1 through 3, click [3].

FIGURE I-13: Subtotaled list with level 2 details

Hide Details button
Show Details button
Row level symbols

	State	Zip	Source	Comments	First Purchase	Purchases to Date	Income	Household Type
19			Magazine Total			$ 17,794	$ 949,000	
24			Newspaper Total			$ 1,972	$ 189,000	
29			Radio Total			$ 3,211	$ 239,000	
35			TV Total			$ 7,690	$ 248,000	
41			Yellow Pages Total			$ 4,399	$ 358,000	
42			Grand Total			$ 35,066	$ 1,983,000	

Excel 2002

Look up Values in a List

The Excel VLOOKUP function helps you locate specific values in a list. VLOOKUP searches vertically (V) down the leftmost column of a list then reads across the row to find the value in the column you specify, much as you might look up a number in a phone book: You locate a person's name then read across the row to find the phone number you are looking for. Jim wants to be able to find out what type of household a particular customer lives in simply by entering his or her customer number. He asks you to use the VLOOKUP function to accomplish this task. You begin by creating a special list, called a **table**, containing the customer numbers you will use in the search, then you will copy the names to a separate location.

Steps

QuickTip

Excel also has a Lookup Wizard to help you perform lookups. It is an Excel add-in (or extra) program. Open the Tools menu and click Lookup to use the Lookup Wizard. If you don't see Lookup on the Tools menu, install the Lookup Wizard using the Add-Ins option of the Tools menu.

1. Click cell **C2**, click **Window** on the menu bar, then click **Freeze Panes**; scroll right until columns M through U and rows 1 through 15 are visible
2. Click cell **O1**, type **VLOOKUP**, press **[Alt] [Enter]**, type **Function**, click the **Enter button**, then click the **Bold button**; copy the contents of cell **A1** to cell **Q1**, copy the contents of cell **M1** to cell **R1**, widen the columns as necessary to display the text, then press **Esc**
   See Figure I-14. Jim wants to know the household type for customer number 3247.
3. Click cell **Q2**, type **3247**, then press [→]
   The VLOOKUP function in the Paste Function dialog box will let Jim find the household type for customer number 3247.
4. Make sure cell R2 is selected, click the **Insert Function button**
5. Under "Search for a function" type **Lookup**, click **Go**, click **VLOOKUP** under "Select a function," then click **OK**
   The Function Arguments dialog box opens, with boxes for each of the VLOOKUP arguments. Because the value you want to find is in cell Q2, that will be the Lookup_value. The list you want to search is the customer list, so its name, Database, will be the Table_array.

QuickTip

If you want to find only the closest match for a value, enter TRUE in the Range_lookup text box.

6. Drag the **Function Arguments dialog box** down so that at least rows 1 and 2 of the worksheet are visible; with the insertion point in the Lookup_value text box, click cell **Q2**, click the **Table_array text box**, then type **DATABASE**
   The column you want to search (Household Type) is the 13th column from the left, so the Col_index_num will be 13. Because you want to find an exact match for the value in cell Q2, the Range_lookup argument will be FALSE.
7. Click the **Col_index_num text box**, type **13**, click the **Range_lookup text box**, then type **FALSE**
   Your completed Function Arguments dialog box should match Figure I-15.
8. Click **OK**
   Excel searches down the leftmost column of the customer list until it finds a value matching the one in cell Q2. It finds the household type for that record, Single, then displays it in cell R2. You'll use this function to determine the household type for one other customer.
9. Click cell **Q2**, type **2125**, then click
   The VLOOKUP function returns the value Family in cell R2.
10. Press **[Ctrl][Home]**, then save the workbook.

Trouble?

If an exact match is not found, make sure the Range_lookup is set to FALSE.

FIGURE I-14: Worksheet with headings for VLOOKUP

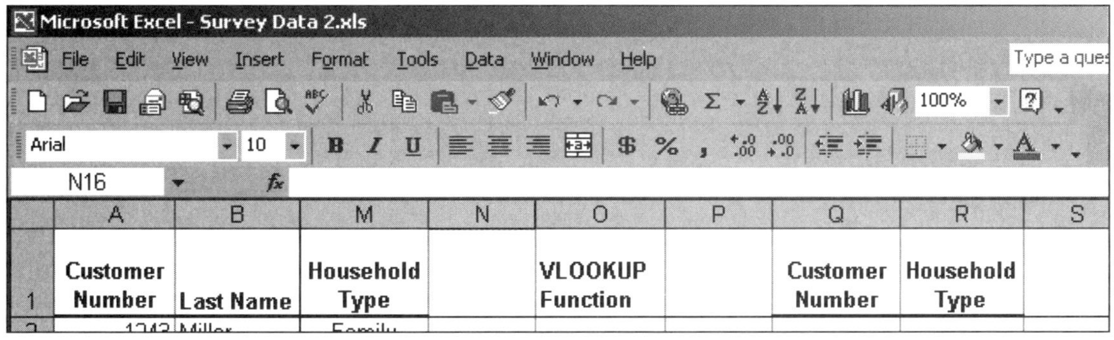

FIGURE I-15: Completed Function Arguments dialog box

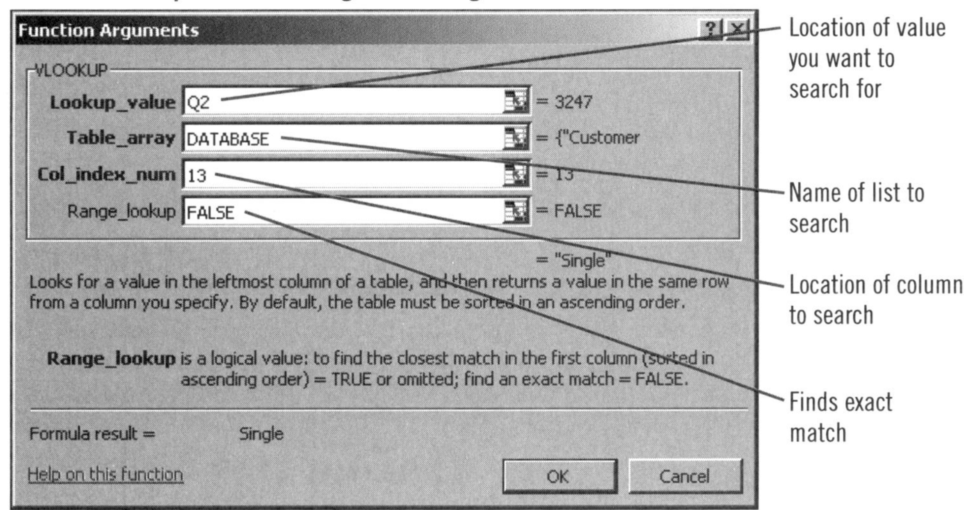

Excel 2002

Using the HLOOKUP and MATCH functions

The VLOOKUP (Vertical Lookup) function is useful when your data is arranged vertically, in columns. The HLOOKUP (Horizontal Lookup) function is useful when your data is arranged horizontally, in rows. HLOOKUP searches horizontally across the topmost row of a list until it finds the matching value, then looks down the number of rows you specify. The arguments for this function are identical to those for the VLOOKUP function, with one exception. Instead of a Col_index_number, HLOOKUP uses a Row_index_number, which indicates the location of the row you want to search. For example, if you want to search the fourth row from the top, the Row_index_number should be 4. You can use the MATCH function when you want the position of an item in a range. The MATCH function uses the syntax: MATCH (**lookup_value,lookup_array**,match_type) where lookup_value is the value you want to match in the lookup_array range. The match type can be 0 for an exact match, 1 for matching the largest value that is less than or equal to lookup_value or a -1, for matching the smallest value that is greater than or equal to lookup_value.

Excel 2002

Summarizing List Data

Database functions allow you to summarize list data in a variety of ways. For example, you can use them to count, average, or total values in a field for only those records that meet specified criteria. When working with a sales activity list, for example, you can use Excel to count the number of client contacts by sales representative or to total the amount sold to specific accounts by month. The format for database functions is explained in Figure I-16. Jim wants you to summarize the information in his list in two ways. First, he wants you to find the total purchases to date for each advertising source. He also wants you to count the number of records for each advertising source. You begin by creating a criteria range that includes a copy of the column label for the column you want to summarize, as well as the criterion itself.

Steps

1. With the panes still frozen, scroll down until row 31 is the top row underneath the frozen headings, then enter and format the five labels shown in Figure I-17 in the range: **H39:J41**

   The criteria range in H40:H41 tells Excel to summarize records with the entry "Yellow Pages" in the Source column. The functions will be in cells K39 and K41.

2. Click cell **K39**, click the **Insert Function button**, under "Search for a function" enter **Database**, click **Go**, click **DSUM** under "Select a function," then click **OK**

3. In the Function Arguments dialog box, enter **Database** in the Database text box, click the **Field text box**, and click cell **K1** "Purchases to Date"

4. Click the **Criteria text box** and select the range **H40:H41**, then click **OK**

   The result in cell K39 is 4399. For the range named Database, Excel totaled the information in the column "Purchases to Date" for those records that meet the criterion Source = Yellow Pages. The DCOUNTA function will help you determine the number of nonblank records meeting the criterion Source = Yellow Pages.

5. Click cell **K41**, click, under "Search for a function" enter **Database**, click **Go,** click **DCOUNTA** under "Select a function," then click **OK**

6. In the Function Arguments dialog box enter **Database** in the Database text box, click the **Field text box** and click cell **A1** "Customer Number," click the **Criteria text box** and select the range **H40:H41**, then click **OK**

   The result in cell K41 is 5, meaning that there are five customers who heard about MediaLoft through the Yellow Pages. This function uses the "Customer Number" field in the list to check for nonblank cells within the criteria range Source = Yellow Pages. You also want to see total purchases and a count for the magazine ads.

7. Click cell **H41**, type **Magazine**, then click the **Enter button**

   With total purchases of $17,794, it's clear that magazine advertising is a more effective way of attracting MediaLoft customers. Compare your results with Figure I-18.

8. Press **[Ctrl][Home]**, then save and close the workbook

Trouble?

If you can't see the cell or range you need to select, you can move the dialog box or collapse it.

FIGURE I-16: Format of database function

DSUM(DATABASE, 11, H40:H41)

- DSUM: Name of database function
- DATABASE: Name of range the function will use
- 11: Column number of the field the function will use
- H40:H41: Range that contains the list criteria

FIGURE I-17: Portion of worksheet showing summary area

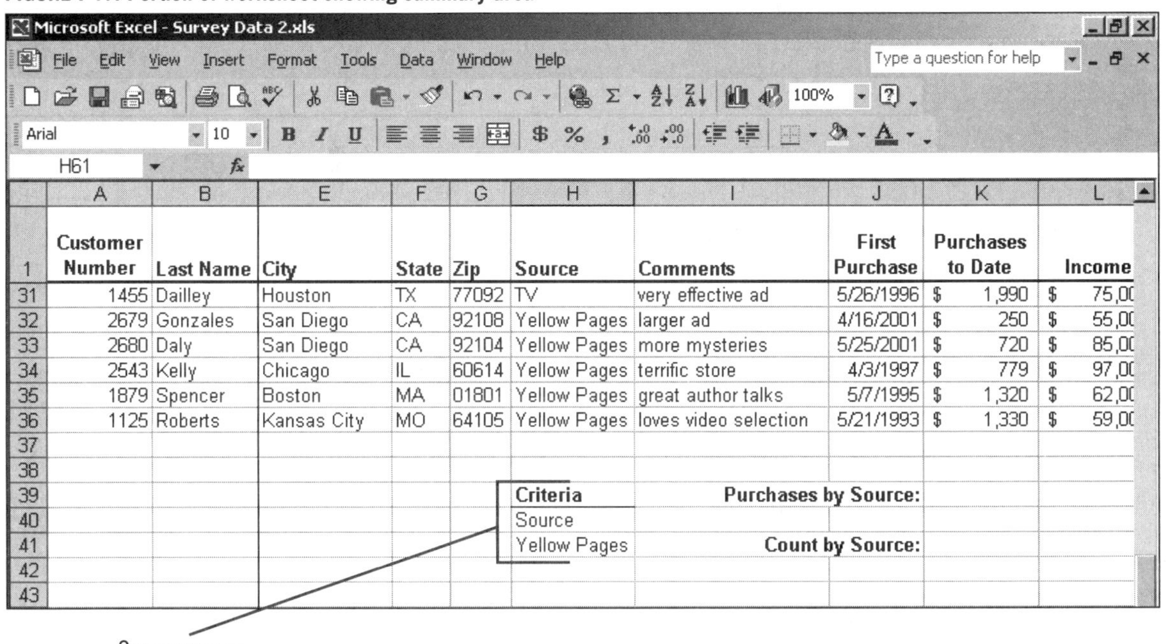

Microsoft Excel - Survey Data 2.xls

H61

	A	B	E	F	G	H	I	J	K	L
1	Customer Number	Last Name	City	State	Zip	Source	Comments	First Purchase	Purchases to Date	Income
31	1455	Dailley	Houston	TX	77092	TV	very effective ad	5/26/1996	$ 1,990	$ 75,0
32	2679	Gonzales	San Diego	CA	92108	Yellow Pages	larger ad	4/16/2001	$ 250	$ 55,0
33	2680	Daly	San Diego	CA	92104	Yellow Pages	more mysteries	5/25/2001	$ 720	$ 85,0
34	2543	Kelly	Chicago	IL	60614	Yellow Pages	terrific store	4/3/1997	$ 779	$ 97,0
35	1879	Spencer	Boston	MA	01801	Yellow Pages	great author talks	5/7/1995	$ 1,320	$ 62,0
36	1125	Roberts	Kansas City	MO	64105	Yellow Pages	loves video selection	5/21/1993	$ 1,330	$ 59,0
37										
38										
39						Criteria	Purchases by Source:			
40						Source				
41						Yellow Pages	Count by Source:			
42										
43										

FIGURE I-18: Result generated by database function

Microsoft Excel - Survey Data 2.xls

H41 Magazine

	A	B	E	F	G	H	I	J	K	L
1	Customer Number	Last Name	City	State	Zip	Source	Comments	First Purchase	Purchases to Date	Income
31	1455	Dailley	Houston	TX	77092	TV	very effective ad	5/26/1996	$ 1,990	$ 75,0
32	2679	Gonzales	San Diego	CA	92108	Yellow Pages	larger ad	4/16/2001	$ 250	$ 55,0
33	2680	Daly	San Diego	CA	92104	Yellow Pages	more mysteries	5/25/2001	$ 720	$ 85,0
34	2543	Kelly	Chicago	IL	60614	Yellow Pages	terrific store	4/3/1997	$ 779	$ 97,0
35	1879	Spencer	Boston	MA	01801	Yellow Pages	great author talks	5/7/1995	$ 1,320	$ 62,0
36	1125	Roberts	Kansas City	MO	64105	Yellow Pages	loves video selection	5/21/1993	$ 1,330	$ 59,0
37										
38										
39						Criteria	Purchases by Source:		17794	
40						Source				
41						Magazine	Count by Source:		17	
42										
43										
44										
45										
46										
47										
48										
49										
50										
51										
52										

2nd Qtr / Sheet2 / Sheet3

Ready

Excel 2002

Excel 2002

Using Data Validation for List Entries

The Excel Data Validation feature allows you to specify what data is valid for a range of cells. You can restrict data to whole numbers, decimal numbers, or text, or you can set limits on entries. You can also specify a list of acceptable entries. Once you've specified what data the program should consider valid for that cell, Excel prevents users from entering any other data, which it considers to be invalid. Jim wants to make sure that information in the Household Type column is entered consistently in the future. He asks you to restrict the entries in that column to three options: Couple, Single, and Family. First, you select the column you want to restrict.

Steps

1. Open the Project File **EX I-1** from the drive and folder where your Project Files are stored, then save it as **Survey Data 3**
2. Scroll right until column M appears, then click the **Column M** column header
   The entire column is selected.
3. Click **Data** on the menu bar, click **Validation**, click the **Settings tab** if necessary, click the **Allow** list arrow, then click **List**
   Selecting the List option enables you to type a list of specific options.
4. Click the **Source** text box, then type **Couple, Single, Family**
   You have entered the list of acceptable entries, separated by commas. See Figure I-19. You want the data entry person to be able to select a valid entry from a drop-down list.
5. Click the **In-cell dropdown check box** to select it if necessary, then click **OK**
   The dialog box closes, and you return to the worksheet. The new data restrictions will apply only to new or replacement entries in the Household Type column, not to existing entries.
6. Click cell **M37**, then click the **list arrow** to display the list of valid entries
   See Figure I-20. You could click an item in the list to have it entered in the cell, but you want to test the data restriction by entering an invalid entry.
7. Click the **list arrow** to close the list, type **Individual**, then press **[Enter]**
   A warning dialog box appears to prevent you from entering the invalid data.
8. Click **Cancel**, click the **list arrow**, then click **Single**
   The cell accepts the valid entry. The data restriction ensures that new records will contain only one of the three correct entries in the Household Type column. The customer list is finished and ready for future data entry.
9. Enter your name in the right section of the worksheet footer, save the workbook, preview and print it, then close the workbook and exit Excel
10. Compare your final document to Figure I-21

QuickTip

To restrict entries to decimal or whole numbers, dates, or times, select the appropriate option in the Allow list. To specify a long list of valid entries, type the list in a column elsewhere in the worksheet, then type the address of the list in the Source text box.

FIGURE I-19: Creating data restrictions

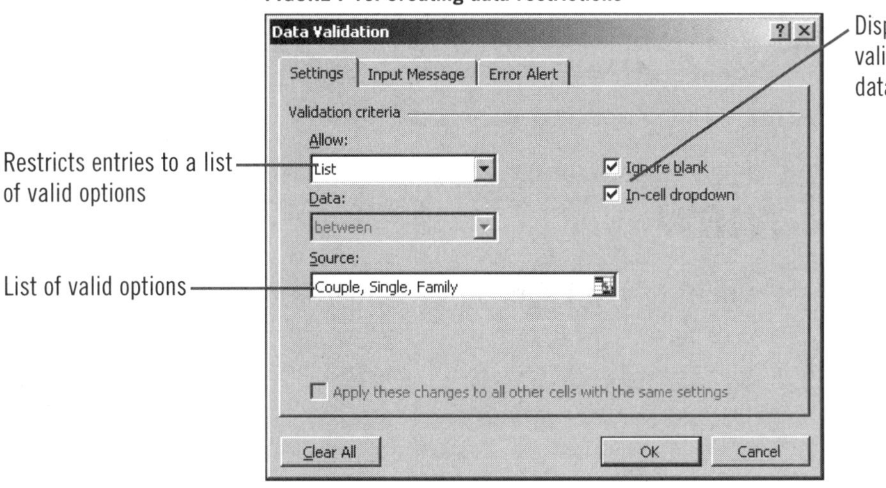

FIGURE I-20: Entering data in restricted cells

36	$ 750	$ 82,000	Couple
37			
38			Couple
39			Single
40			Family

FIGURE I-21: Print Preview of the final document

Survey Data 3.xls

Customer Number	Last Name	First Name	Street Address	City	State	Zip	Source	Comments	First Purchase	Purchases to Date	Income	Household Type
2682	Smith	Steve	402 9th Street	Boston	MA	02007	Magazine	told friends	6/3/00	$ 550	$ 30,000	Single
2683	Reily	Mary	9203 Arlen Road	San Francisco	CA	93772	Radio	great CD selection	6/13/02	$ 553	$ 75,000	Couple
2678	Black	Michael	229 Route 55	Waterton	MA	02472	Magazine	enjoys café	4/4/01	$ 620	$ 55,000	Single
2679	Gonzales	John	5289 Santa Luna Way	San Diego	CA	92108	Yellow Pages	larger ad	4/16/01	$ 250	$ 55,000	Couple
2680	Daly	Tonia	92 Main Avenue	San Diego	CA	92104	Yellow Pages	more mysteries	5/25/01	$ 720	$ 85,000	Family
2681	Gabriel	Sandra	989 26th Street	Cambridge	MA	02138	Magazine	more classic movies	6/1/96	$ 1,750	$ 45,000	Single
1678	Nelson	John	11 River Rd.	Houston	TX	77098	Newspaper	later hours	4/27/97	$ 420	$ 52,000	Single
1679	O'Reiley	Scott	72 Lewis Way	Seattle	WA	98103	Newspaper	thanks for bike racks	5/10/86	$ 440	$ 49,000	Single
1125	Roberts	Carol	56 Water St.	Kansas City	MO	64105	Yellow Pages	loves video selection	5/21/93	$ 1,330	$ 59,000	Single
1126	Wilson	Tasha	1 Spring St.	Larchmont	NY	10329	Newspaper	lower prices	6/28/97	$ 802	$ 65,000	Single
1124	Majors	Kathy	83 Wickham Rd.	Chicago	IL	60614	Radio	great ad	5/19/02	$ 893	$ 90,000	Family
2543	Kelly	Sean	22 Old Kendall Square	Chicago	IL	60614	Yellow Pages	terrific store	4/3/97	$ 779	$ 97,000	Couple
2124	Stephens	Sally	3 Old Friar Road	Kansas City	MO	64102	Magazine	more author events	6/1/01	$ 879	$ 42,000	Single
2123	Leigh	Ginny	3 Bow St., Apt 2	Cambridge	MA	02138	Radio	love the book club	5/12/02	$ 560	$ 72,000	Single
2125	Stevens	Cathy	240 E. 23rd St.	New York	NY	10024	Radio	more teas in café	6/2/99	$ 1,215	$ 42,000	Family
1543	Rodriguez	Mary	123 Tillary, Apt. 10D	Brooklyn	NY	11201	Magazine	great fiction	5/8/91	$ 1,520	$ 43,000	Single
1543	Ichikawa	Joyce	232 Short Rd	Kansas City	MO	64105	Magazine	more self-help videos	5/24/02	$ 530	$ 62,000	Couple
1544	Pauley	Gail	100 Main Street	Seattle	WA	98102	Magazine	no comments	6/16/01	$ 895	$ 45,000	Single
2235	Wong	John	123 Elm St.	Houston	TX	77098	Magazine	salespeople helpful	6/28/01	$ 320	$ 38,000	Single
1878	Kelly	Peter	67 Polk St.	San Francisco	CA	94107	TV	knows Maria Abbott	4/11/92	$ 1,500	$ 54,000	Single
1879	Spencer	Peter	293 Pilgrim Drive	Boston	MA	01801	Yellow Pages	great author talks	5/7/95	$ 1,320	$ 62,000	Single
1324	Belcus	Adelia	3 Hall Rd.	San Luis	CA	94108	Magazine	more events for kids	6/22/02	$ 3,200	$ 84,000	Couple
1243	Miller	Hailey	111 Stratton Court	San Diego	CA	92208	Magazine	add café sandwiches	6/5/98	$ 1,800	$ 79,000	Family
3248	Chavez	Louis	1110 November Way	Chicago	IL	60618	TV	no comments	3/22/99	$ 250	$ 31,000	Family
3247	Khalsa	Paul	130 W. 98th St.	New York	NY	10044	Newspaper	bigger CD section	5/19/99	$ 310	$ 23,000	Single
3243	Rolland	Susan	42 Silver Street	Reading	MA	03882	TV	fun store	4/6/01	$ 1,420	$ 54,000	Couple
3245	Lopez	Maria	1212 Agua Fria	Santa Fe	NM	87505	TV	more bike racks	4/26/98	$ 2,530	$ 34,000	Single
3244	Smith	Cathy	921 Lopez Lane	Chicago	IL	60611	Magazine	add chairs	4/9/02	$ 480	$ 45,000	Single
3246	Friedson	Martha	Hyde Park Estates	Seattle	WA	98100	Magazine	more world music	5/14/02	$ 2,100	$ 73,000	Family
3249	Hesh	Gail	1192 Main St.	Woburn	MA	01801	Magazine	great ads	5/30/99	$ 390	$ 32,000	Single
3250	Carter	Lynne	900 Monument St.	Concord	MA	01742	Magazine	love the book club	6/15/02	$ 450	$ 53,000	Family
1455	Dailley	Camilla	486 Intel Circuit	Houston	TX	77092	TV	very effective ad	5/26/96	$ 1,990	$ 75,000	Couple
1454	Monaco	Nicole	2318 Sarah Road	Chicago	IL	60614	Magazine	great coffee	4/29/00	$ 640	$ 48,000	Single
2423	Pacheco	Scott	2120 Witch Way	Salem	MA	01970	Magazine	loves our staff	5/25/97	$ 920	$ 93,000	Family
2424	Santos	Evan	823 Northside Heights	Brookfield	CT	06830	Magazine	great books	6/12/01	$ 750	$ 82,000	Couple
												Single

Report Date: 8/13/01 [Student Name]

Excel 2002

Practice

▶ Concepts Review

Explain the function of each element of the Excel screen labeled in Figure I-22.

FIGURE I-22

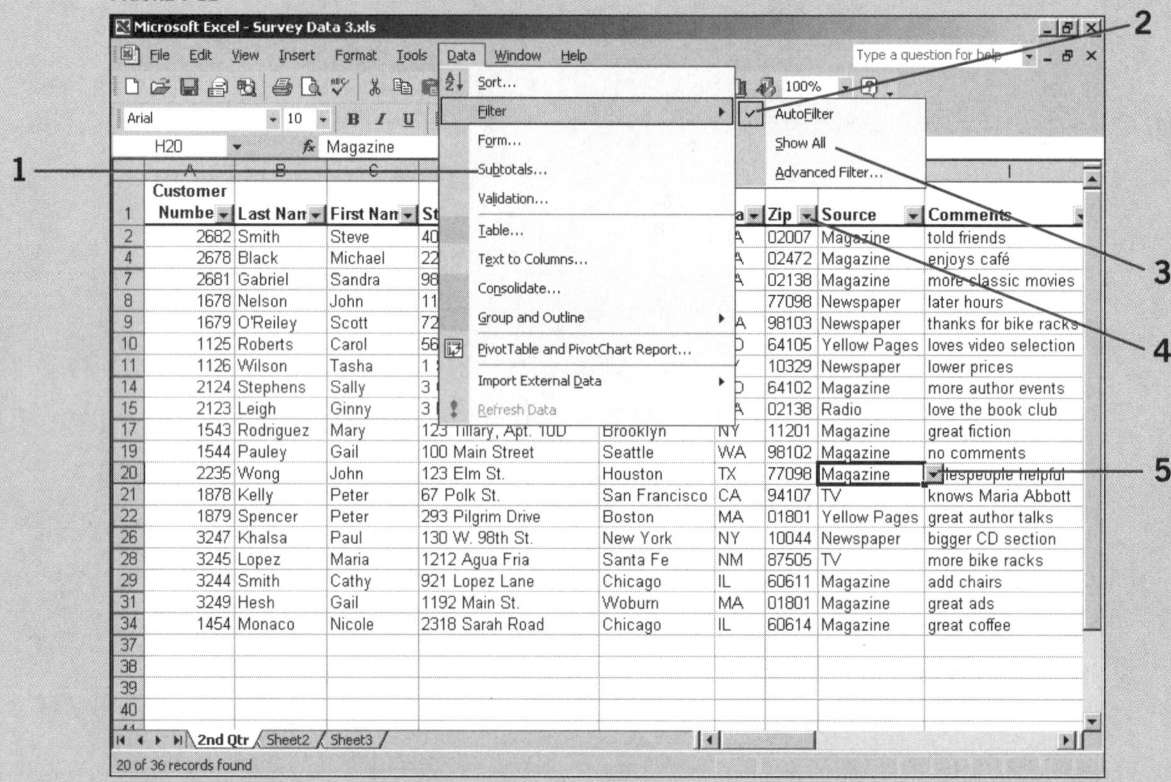

Match each term with the statement that describes it.

6. DSUM	**a.** Cell range when advanced filter results are copied to another location
7. Extracted list	**b.** Range in which search conditions are set
8. Data validation	**c.** Restricts list entries to specified options
9. Criteria range	**d.** Name of the list searched in a VLOOKUP function
10. Table_array	**e.** Function used to total list values that meet specified criteria

Select the best answer from the list of choices.

11. The ____________ logical condition finds records matching both listed criteria.
- **a.** Or
- **b.** And
- **c.** True
- **d.** False

12. What does it mean when you select the Or option when creating a custom filter?
- **a.** Neither criterion has to be 100% true.
- **b.** Either criterion can be true to find a match.
- **c.** Both criteria must be true to find a match.
- **d.** Custom filter requires a criteria range.

13. What must a list have before automatic subtotals can be inserted?
- **a.** Enough records to show multiple subtotals
- **b.** Grand totals
- **c.** Column or field headings
- **d.** Formatted cells

Skills Review

1. Retrieve records with AutoFilter.
- **a.** Start Excel, open the Project File EX I-2 from the drive and folder where your Project Files are stored, then save it as **Compensation Summary**.
- **b.** Use AutoFilter to list records for employees in the Accounting Department.
- **c.** Redisplay all employees, then use AutoFilter to show the three employees with the highest annual salary.
- **d.** Redisplay all the records, then save the workbook.

2. Create a custom filter.
- **a.** Create a custom filter showing employees hired prior to 1/1/1999 or after 1/1/2000.
- **b.** Change the page setup to landscape orientation, fit to a single page, enter your name in the worksheet footer, save the workbook, preview, then print the filtered worksheet.
- **c.** Redisplay all records.
- **d.** Turn off the AutoFilter.

3. Filter and extract a list with Advanced Filter.
- **a.** You will retrieve a list of employees who were hired prior to 1/1/2000 and earn more than $60,000 a year. Define a criteria range by copying the field names in range **A1:J1** to cell **A14**.
- **b.** In cell D15, enter the criterion **<1/1/2000**, then in cell G15 enter **>60,000**.
- **c.** Return to cell A1.
- **d.** Open the Advanced Filter dialog box.
- **e.** Indicate that you want to copy to another location, enter the criteria range **A14:J15**, then indicate that you want to copy it to cell **A18**.
- **f.** Confirm that the retrieved list meets the criteria.
- **g.** Select and print only the extracted list.
- **h.** Use the Edit menu to clear data and formats from the criteria and extracted ranges then save the workbook.

4. Creating subtotals using grouping and outlines.
- **a.** Move to cell A1. Sort the list in ascending order by department, and in descending order by monthly salary.
- **b.** Group and create subtotals by department, using the Sum function; select **Monthly Salary** in the "Add Subtotal to" list box, deselect Annual Comp.

c. Use the outline to display only the subtotals, save the workbook, preview, then print only the subtotaled list in landscape orientation on one page.
d. Remove the subtotals, then save the workbook.
e. Group and create subtotals by department for the Accounting and Information Systems Departments only, using the Sum function; select **Annual Bonus** in the "Add Subtotal to" list box, deselect **Monthly Salary**. (*Hint*: You will need to select the range A1:J8 before adding the subtotals)
f. Use the outline to display only the Accounting and Information Systems subtotals; save the workbook; preview, then print only the subtotals in landscape orientation.
g. Remove the subtotals, if necessary redefine the database range as A1:J11 using the Name/Define Commands on the Insert menu, then save the workbook.

5. **Look up values in a list.**
   a. You will locate annual compensation information by entering a Social Security number. Scroll so that columns F through P are visible.
   b. In cell N2, enter **556-21-4325**.
   c. In cell O2, enter the following function: **=VLOOKUP(N2,A2:J11,10,FALSE)**, then view the results.
   d. Enter another social security number, **334-21-9807**, in cell N2, then view the annual compensation for that employee.
   e. Save the workbook.
6. **Summarize list data.**
   a. You'll enter a database function to average the annual salaries by department, using the Marketing Department as the initial criterion.
   b. Define the criteria area: In cell C14, enter **Criteria**; in cell C15, enter **Dept.** (make sure you type the period); then in cell C16, enter **Marketing**.
   c. In cell E14, enter **Average Annual Salary by Department:**.
   d. In cell H14, enter the following database function: **=DAVERAGE(Database,7,C15:C16)**.
   e. Test the function further by entering the text **Accounting** in cell C16. When the criterion is entered, cell H14 should display 65,250.
   f. Save the workbook, enter your name in the worksheet footer, print the worksheet, then close it.
7. **Use data validation for list entries.**
   a. Open the Project File EX I-2 again, then save it as **Compensation Summary 2** in the drive and folder where your Project Files are stored.
   b. Select **column E**.
   c. For the validation criteria, specify that you want to allow a list of valid options.
   d. Enter a list of valid options that restricts the entries to **Accounting**, **Information Systems**, and **Marketing**. Remember to use a comma between each item in the list.
   e. Indicate that you want the options to appear in an in-cell dropdown list, then close the dialog box.
   f. Go to cell E12, then select **Accounting** in the dropdown list.
   g. Select column F.
   h. Indicate that you want to restrict the data entered to only whole numbers.
   i. In the minimum text box, enter **1000**. In the Maximum text box, enter **20000**. Close the dialog box.
   j. Click cell F12, enter **25000**, then press [Enter].
   k. Click Cancel, then enter **19000.50**.
   l. Click Cancel, then enter **19000**.
   m. Enter your name in the worksheet footer; save, preview, then print the worksheet in landscape orientation, fitting the data to one page.
   n. Close the workbook, then exit Excel.

► Independent Challenge 1

You own Olives, a gourmet food store located in Philadelphia. To help with inventory management, you have created an Excel list of your olive oil inventory. You want to filter the list to show only extra virgin olive oil information. You also want to show information for extra virgin olive oil with a vintage of 2001. You will subtotal the complete list to show total dollar value by type of olive oil. Lastly, you will restrict future data entries for the type of olive oil to three possibilities.

- **a.** Start Excel, open the Project File EX I-3 from the drive and folder where your Project Files are stored, then save it as **Olive Oil**.
- **b.** Use AutoFilter to generate a list of Extra Virgin Olive Oil. Preview, then print the list. Clear the filter.
- **c.** Use Advanced Filter to extract a list to the range of cells beginning in A20 of Extra Virgin olive oil with a vintage of 2001. Preview and print the extracted list, then clear the filter.
- **d.** Sort the list in ascending order by type of olive oil. Insert subtotals by type of olive oil using the Sum function; select **Total $** in the Add Subtotal to list box. Use the outline to display only the subtotals, save the workbook, preview, then print only the subtotaled list in landscape orientation, fitting the data to one page. Turn off subtotaling.
- **e.** Select column B. Open the Data Validation dialog box, then select List in the Allow box. Enter **Extra Virgin, Super Tuscan, Ultra Premium** for the list of olive oil types in the Source text box. Make sure the In-cell dropdown check box is selected.
- **f.** Test the data validation by entering valid and invalid data in cell B20.
- **g.** Sort the list range by vintage and then by unit price, both in ascending order. Enter **Position of $5.75 Olive Oil** in cell C15.
- **h.** Enter a function in cell F15 that obtains the position of the $5.75 bottle of olive oil in the list range. (*Hint:* Use **=MATCH(5.75,D2:D13,0)** Then format the cell in the General format.
- **i.** Enter your name in the worksheet footer, then save the workbook and print the worksheet.
- **j.** Close the workbook then exit Excel.

► Independent Challenge 2

A few months ago, you started your own business, called Custom Books. Your business creates and sells personalized books for special occasions. After purchasing a distributorship from an established book company and the rights to use several of the company's titles, you started creating personalized books. Customers provide you with the name of the book's protagonist and the desired book title, and you generate the book text. You decided to put together an invoice list to track sales, starting in October. Now that you have this list, you would like to manipulate it in several ways. First, you want to filter the list to retrieve only books retailing for more than $12.95 and ordered during the first half of the month (prior to 10/15). Next, you want to subtotal the unit price and total cost columns by book title. Finally, you want to restrict entries in the Order Date column.

- **a.** Start Excel, open the Project File EX I-4 from the drive and folder where your Project Files are stored, then save it as **Custom Books - Invoice DB**.
- **b.** Use the Advanced Filter to show books with a unit price of more than $12.95 ordered prior to 10/15/2002. Save your workbook, print the filtered list in landscape orientation with gridlines and row and column headings. Clear the filter, then save your work again.
- **c.** Sort the list by Book Title, then create subtotals in the Unit Price and Total Cost columns by book title. Save your subtotaled list, print the subtotaled list on a single page without gridlines, row, or column headings. Clear the subtotals.
- **d.** Use the Data Validation dialog box to restrict entries to those with order dates between 10/1/2002 and 10/31/2002. Select **Date** In the Allow list, then enter the appropriate dates in the Start Date and End Date boxes. Test the data restrictions by attempting to enter an invalid date.
- **e.** Enter your name in the worksheet footer, then save and close the workbook.

f. Open the Project File EXI-4, then save it as **Custom Books - Lookup** in the drive and folder where your Project Files are stored.

g. Enter the worksheet labels in the range **F27:G30**, as shown in Figure I-23. Enter a VLOOKUP function in cell G28 to retrieve a customer's book title based on its invoice number entered in cell F28. Enter a second VLOOKUP function in cell G31 to look up an order date based on its invoice number entered in cell F31. If necessary, format the cell displaying the date in a date format, then save your work. Test the functions by entering invoice numbers in cells F28 and F31.

FIGURE I-23

27	Invoice#	Title					Order Date
28							
29							
30	Invoice#	Order Date					

h. Use the database function, DCOUNT, in cell N28 to count the number of books ordered on any given date. Test the functions by entering an order date in cell L28.

i. Enter your name in the worksheet footer, save your work, then print the list in landscape orientation, fitting the data, to one page. Close the workbook then exit Excel.

► Independent Challenge 3

You are the manager of Readers, an independent bookstore located in San Francisco. You have created an Excel list that contains your book inventory, along with the sales figures for each book and the date it went on the bestseller list. You would like to manipulate this list to display product categories, and inventory items meeting specific criteria. You would also like to add subtotals to the list and add database functions to total sales. Finally, you want to restrict entries in the Category column.

a. Start Excel, open the Project File EX I-5 from the drive and folder where your Project Files are stored, then save it as **Bestsellers**. Your worksheet should look like Figure I-24.

FIGURE I-24

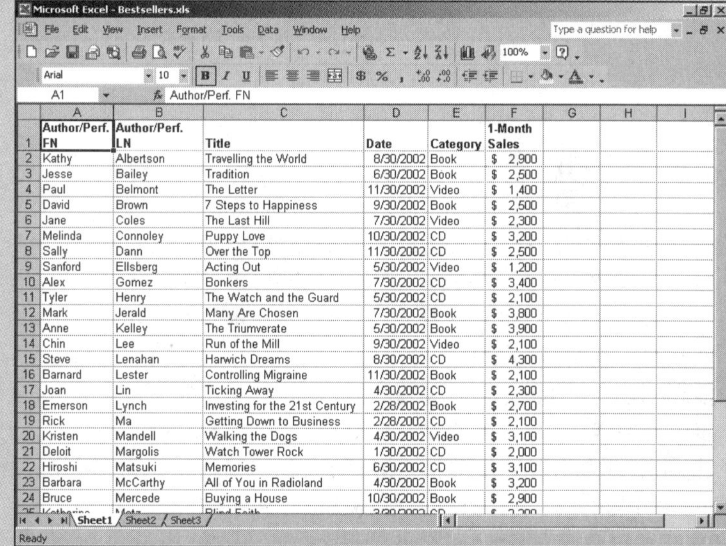

	A	B	C	D	E	F
1	Author/Perf. FN	Author/Perf. LN	Title	Date	Category	1-Month Sales
2	Kathy	Albertson	Travelling the World	8/30/2002	Book	$ 2,900
3	Jesse	Bailey	Tradition	6/30/2002	Book	$ 2,500
4	Paul	Belmont	The Letter	11/30/2002	Video	$ 1,400
5	David	Brown	7 Steps to Happiness	9/30/2002	Book	$ 2,500
6	Jane	Coles	The Last Hill	7/30/2002	Video	$ 2,300
7	Melinda	Connoley	Puppy Love	10/30/2002	CD	$ 3,200
8	Sally	Dann	Over the Top	11/30/2002	CD	$ 2,500
9	Sanford	Ellsberg	Acting Out	5/30/2002	Video	$ 1,200
10	Alex	Gomez	Bonkers	7/30/2002	CD	$ 3,400
11	Tyler	Henry	The Watch and the Guard	5/30/2002	CD	$ 2,100
12	Mark	Jerald	Many Are Chosen	7/30/2002	Book	$ 3,800
13	Anne	Kelley	The Triumverate	5/30/2002	Book	$ 3,900
14	Chin	Lee	Run of the Mill	9/30/2002	Video	$ 2,100
15	Steve	Lenahan	Harwich Dreams	8/30/2002	CD	$ 4,300
16	Barnard	Lester	Controlling Migraine	11/30/2002	Book	$ 2,100
17	Joan	Lin	Ticking Away	4/30/2002	CD	$ 2,300
18	Emerson	Lynch	Investing for the 21st Century	2/28/2002	Book	$ 2,700
19	Rick	Ma	Getting Down to Business	2/28/2002	CD	$ 2,100
20	Kristen	Mandell	Walking the Dogs	4/30/2002	Video	$ 3,100
21	Deloit	Margolis	Watch Tower Rock	1/30/2002	CD	$ 2,000
22	Hiroshi	Matsuki	Memories	6/30/2002	CD	$ 3,100
23	Barbara	McCarthy	All of You in Radioland	4/30/2002	Book	$ 3,200
24	Bruce	Mercede	Buying a House	10/30/2002	Book	$ 2,900

b. Use AutoFilter to display only books.

c. Further filter the list to display only books that were on the bestseller list before 7/30/2002. Clear the filter.

d. Create an advanced filter that retrieves, to its current location, records with dates before 9/1/2002 and whose sales were greater than $2,000. Enter your name in the footer, save the workbook, then print the filtered list. Clear the filter.

e. Create another advanced filter that extracts products whose sales were $3,000 or more and places them in another area of the worksheet.

f. Save the workbook, then print the extracted range with row and column headings.

g. Close the Bestsellers workbook, saving your changes.

h. Open the Project File EX I-5 from the drive and folder where your Project Files are stored, then save it as **Bestsellers 2**.

i. Subtotal the sales by category. Adjust column widths as necessary.

j. Use the outline to display only category names and totals.

k. Redisplay the records and remove the subtotals.

l. Freeze the column headings and scroll to display several blank lines below the last line.

m. Use the DSUM function to let worksheet users find the total sales by category. Format the cell containing the function appropriately.

n. Use data validation to restrict category entries to CD, Book, or Video, then test an entry with valid and invalid entries.

o. Enter your name in the footer, save the workbook, then print the worksheet.
p. Close the workbook then exit Excel.

Independent Challenge 4

You are planning a holiday to Australia during the month of February. Your itinerary includes the cities of Sydney and Cairns. You will research hotel accommodations on the Web, finding three hotels in each city. February is considered high season in Australia, and you will find rates for a double room. You will then enter information about hotel locations, prices and amenities in an Excel worksheet and manipulate it to locate hotels satisfying specific rate criteria. You will also use a reference function to locate a phone number when you provide a hotel name in your list. Finally, you will restrict the entries in certain fields to values in drop-down lists to simplify data entry and reduce errors.

a. Go to the AltaVista search engine at www.altavista.com then enter "hotels AND Australia" in the Search text box. You can also use Yahoo!, Excite, Infoseek, or another search engine of your choice. Some search engines use & or + in place of AND in the search text.
b. Start Excel, open the Project File EX I-6 from the drive and folder where your Project Files are stored, then save the workbook as **Hotels**.
c. Complete a table with the information for six hotels you found in your search. Use the table at right as a guide. The fields Pool, Room Service, Concierge, Gift Shop, Air Conditioning, In-room Movies, and Beach will all have Yes/No entries. You should format the Check-in and Check-out rows with a custom format of h:mm AM/PM. If you are using a listing from a hotel broker, you may need to search for the hotel's Web page to find some of the information.

Hotel Name
Street Addres
City
State
Phone
Fax
Rate AU$
Number of Restaurants
Pool
Room Service
Concierge
Gift Shop
Check-in
Check-out
Air conditioning
In-room Movies
Beach
Health Club

d. Enter the information from the table into your Hotels workbook.
e. Create a custom filter showing only hotels in Sydney charging less than Au$ 300 per night. Place the results of the filter on Sheet2 of the workbook. (*Hint*: You will need to transpose the rows to columns. You should paste the results in Sheet2) and then apply the custom filter. Show all the records.
f. In cells C2 to C15 of Sheet2, restrict the city entries to Cairns or Sydney. Provide an in-cell dropdown list, allowing the selection of these two options. Test the dropdown list.
g. Restrict the Room Service column to Yes or No. Provide an in-cell dropdown list, allowing the selection of these two options. Test the dropdown list.
h. Restrict the Check-in entries to times between 1:00 PM and 4:00 PM. Test the data validation by entering valid and invalid times.
i. Restrict the Check-out entries to times between 10:00 AM and 12:00 PM. Test the data validation by entering valid and invalid times.
j. Enter **Lookup:** in cell B19, enter **Hotel** in cell C19, and enter **Phone number** in cell D19.
k. Enter one of the hotel names you found in cell C20
l. Enter a lookup function in cell D20 to locate the phone number for the hotel in cell C20. (*Hint*: The function is: =VLOOKUP(C20,A1:R7,5)
m. Enter your name in the footer of both worksheets, save the workbook, then print both worksheets.
n. Close the workbook then exit Excel.

▶ Visual Workshop

Create the worksheet shown in Figure I-25. Apply all necessary percentage and currency formatting to the worksheet cells. Save the workbook as **Commission Lookup** in the drive and folder where your Project Files are stored. (*Hints*: The formula in cell D5 accesses the commission from the table. Calculate the commission by multiplying the Amount of Sale by the Commission Rate. If an exact amount for the Amount of Sale does not exist, the next highest or lowest dollar value is used.) Add your name to the worksheet footer, then preview and print the worksheet.

FIGURE I-25

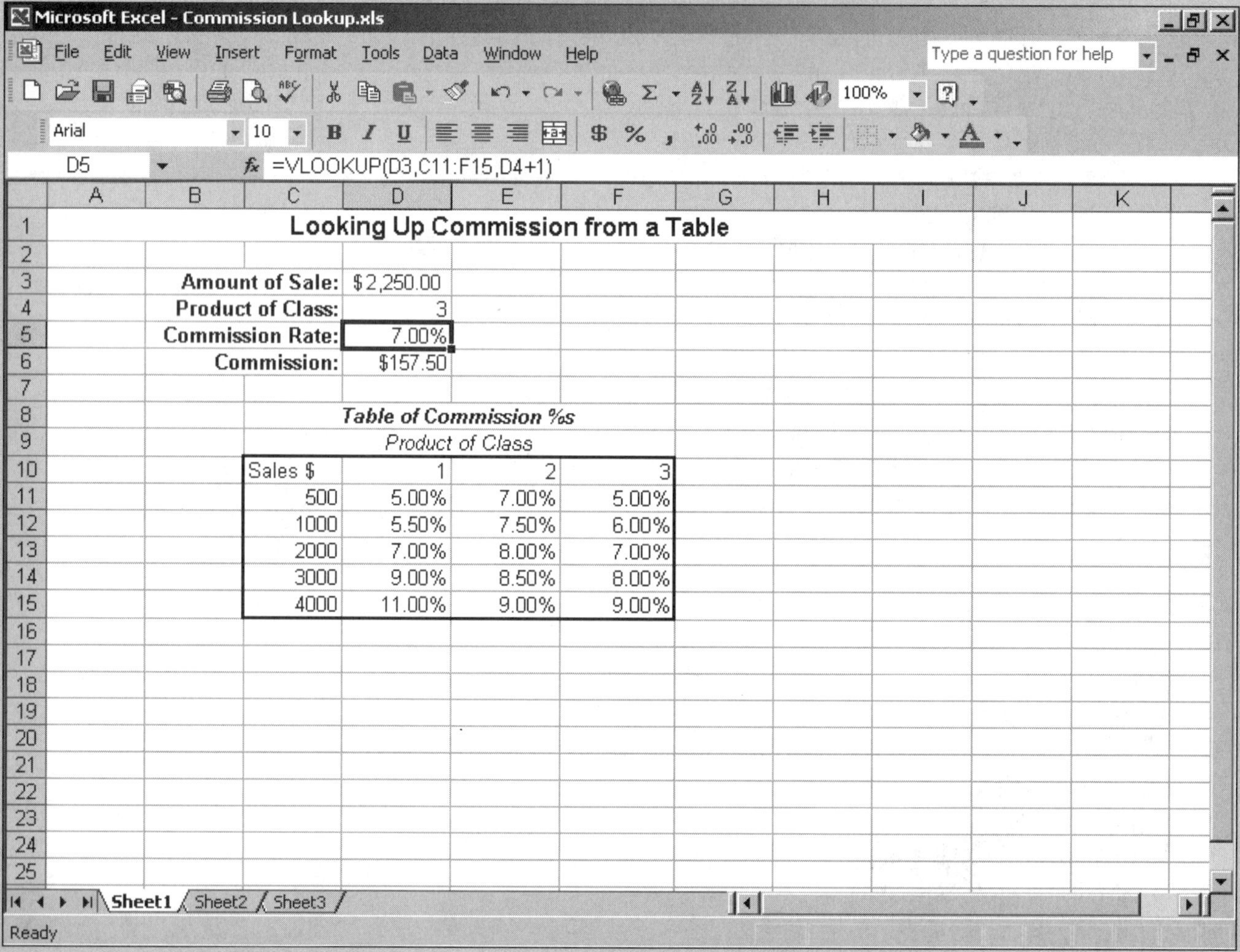
Microsoft Excel - Commission Lookup.xls
File Edit View Insert Format Tools Data Window Help
Type a question for help
100%
Arial
10
D5
=VLOOKUP(D3,C11:F15,D4+1)
Looking Up Commission from a Table
Amount of Sale: $2,250.00
Product of Class: 3
Commission Rate: 7.00%
Commission: $157.50
Table of Commission %s
Product of Class
Sales $ 1 2 3
500 5.00% 7.00% 5.00%
1000 5.50% 7.50% 6.00%
2000 7.00% 8.00% 7.00%
3000 9.00% 8.50% 8.00%
4000 11.00% 9.00% 9.00%
Sheet1 Sheet2 Sheet3
Ready

Excel 2002

Enhancing

Charts and Worksheets

Objectives

- Select a custom chart type
- Customize a data series
- Format a chart axis
- MOUS Add a data table to a chart
- Rotate a chart
- Enhance a chart with WordArt
- Rotate text
- Add a picture to a chart

There are many ways to revise a chart or a worksheet to present its data with greater impact. In this unit, you enhance both charts and worksheets by selecting a custom chart type, customizing a data series, formatting axes, adding a data table, and rotating a chart. You also add special text effects and rotate text. Finally, you enhance the appearance of a chart by adding a picture to its background. However, too much customization can be distracting; your goal in enhancing charts or worksheets is to communicate your data more clearly. MediaLoft's director of café operations, Jeff Shimada, has requested two charts showing the sales of café pastry products in the first two quarters. You will produce these charts and enhance them to improve their appearance and make the worksheet data more accessible.

Excel 2002

Selecting a Custom Chart Type

The Excel Chart Wizard offers a choice between standard and custom chart types. A **standard chart type** is a commonly used column, bar, pie, or area chart with several variations. For each standard chart type, you can choose from several subtypes, such as clustered column or stacked column. You can use the Wizard to add display options, and modify the formatting of any chart element. Excel supplies 20 built-in **custom chart types**, with special formatting already applied. You can also define your own custom chart type by modifying any of the existing Excel chart types. For example, you could define a chart type containing your company's logo and distribute it to other Excel users in your office. Jeff wants you to create a chart showing the amount of each type of pastry sold for the first quarter. To save time, you will use an Excel built-in custom chart.

1. Start Excel, open the Project File **EX J-1** from the drive and folder where your Project Files are stored, then save it as **Pastry Sales**
   The first step is to select the data you want to appear in the chart. In this case, you want the row labels in cells A6:A10 and the data for January and February in cells B5:C10 (You will add the data for March in the next lesson.)
2. Select the range **A5:C10**
3. Click the **Chart Wizard button** on the Standard toolbar, click the **Custom Types tab** in the Step 1 Chart Wizard dialog box, then under Select from, click the **Built-in option button** to select it if necessary
   See Figure J-1. When the built-in option button in the Custom Types tab is selected, all of the Excel custom chart types are displayed in the Chart type box, and a sample of the default chart appears in the Sample box.
4. Click **Columns with Depth** in the Chart type box
   A preview of the chart type appears in the Sample box. This custom chart type displays 3-D bars without gridlines.
5. Click **Next**
6. Make sure ='TotalSales'!$A$5:$C$10 appears as the data range in the Data range box in the Step 2 Chart Wizard dialog box, then click **Next**
7. In the Step 3 Chart Wizard dialog box, click **Next**; if necessary, click the **As object in option button** in the Step 4 Chart Wizard dialog box to select it, then click **Finish**
   The completed chart appears, covering part of the worksheet data, along with the Chart toolbar. The Chart toolbar appears when a chart is selected and anywhere within the worksheet window. As you complete the following steps, you may need to drag the toolbar to a new location.
8. Scroll down the worksheet until rows 13 through 28 are visible, click the chart border and drag the chart left and down until its upper-left corner is at the top of cell **A13**, drag the **middle-right sizing handle** right to the border between column H and column I, then drag its bottom border to the bottom of row 25
   The new chart fills the range A13:H25, as shown in Figure J-2.
9. Save the workbook

Trouble?

If the Chart toolbar does not open, right-click any toolbar and click Chart.

Trouble?

Remember you can drag the Chart toolbar out of the way if it blocks your view of the chart.

FIGURE J-1: Custom Types tab settings

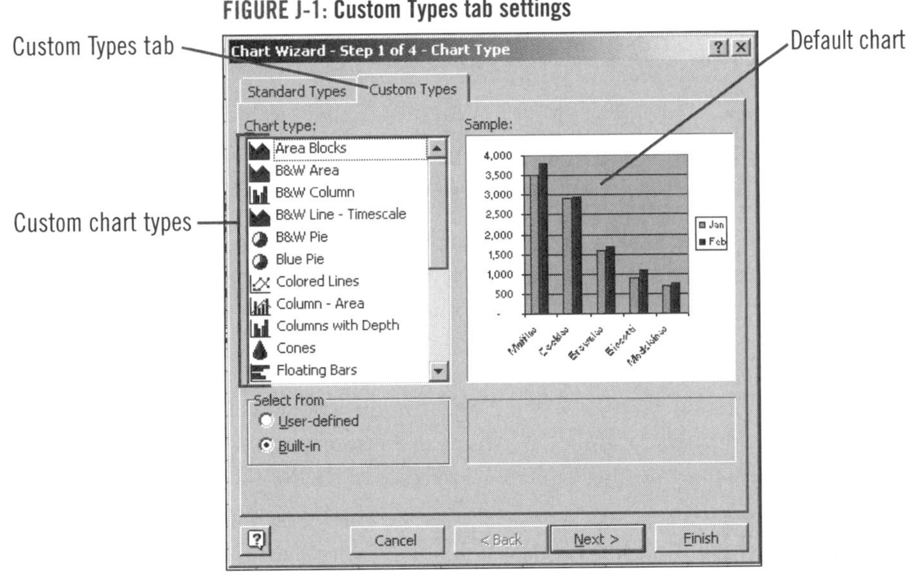

FIGURE J-2: New chart

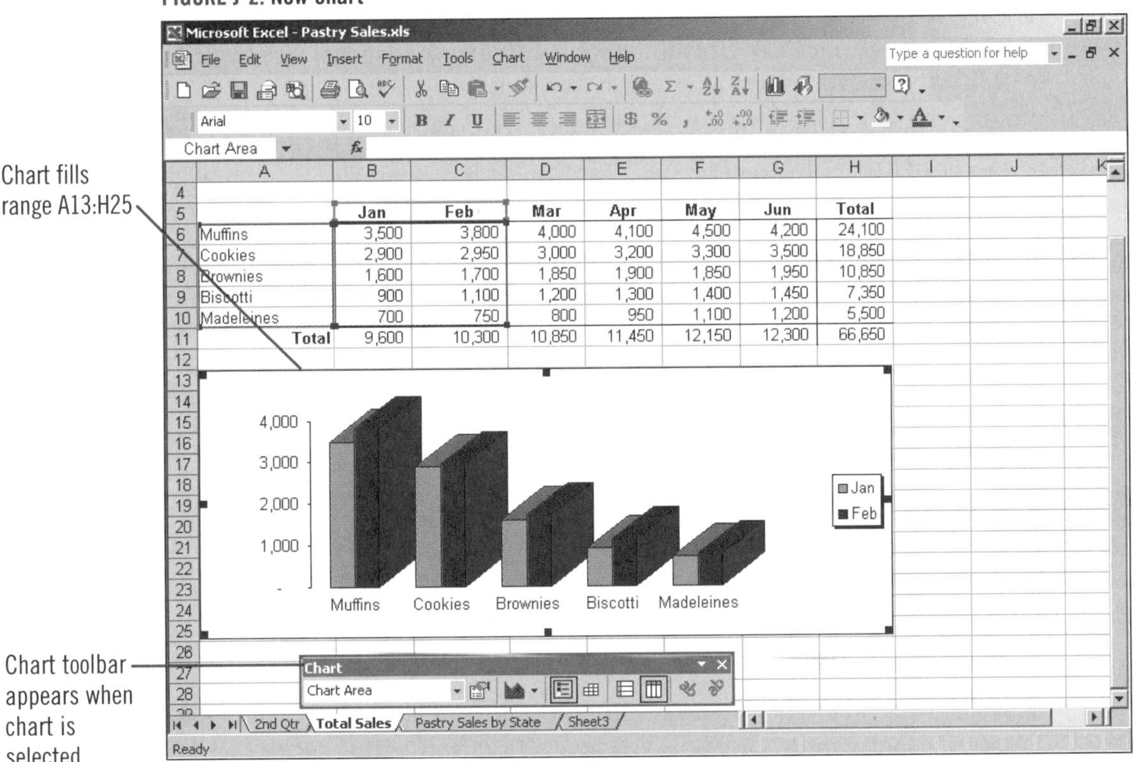

Creating your own custom chart type

You can create your own custom chart type by starting with a standard chart then adding elements, such as a legend, color, or gridlines that suit your needs. After you have finished creating the chart, make sure it is selected, click Chart on the menu bar, click Chart type, click the Custom Types tab, then click User-defined. To make sure that the chart is available for later use, click Add, then type a name for your chart type in the Name box. You can use your custom chart type to create additional charts by opening the Chart Wizard dialog box, then clicking the User-defined button in the Custom Types tab.

Excel 2002

Customizing a Data Series

A **data series** is the information, usually numbers or values, that Excel plots on a chart. You can customize the data series in a chart by altering the spreadsheet range that contains the chart data or by entering descriptive text, called a **data label**, that appears above a data marker in a chart. As with other Excel elements, you can change the borders, patterns, or colors of a data series. Jeff notices that you omitted the data for March when you created his first quarter sales chart. You need to add this information to make the chart accurately reflect the entire first quarter sales. Jeff also wants you to customize the updated chart by adding data labels to one of the data series to make it more specific. You'll also change the color of another data series so its columns will stand out more. You start by adding the March data.

1. If necessary, click the chart to select it, scroll up until row 5 is the top row on your screen, select the range **D5:D10**, position the pointer over the lower border of cell D10 until it changes to
2. Drag the selected range anywhere within the chart area, until the pointer changes to
   The chart now includes data for the entire first quarter: January, February, and March. Next, you will add data labels to the March data series.
3. Click the **Chart Objects list arrow** in the Chart toolbar, then click **Series "Mar"**
   See Figure J-3. Selection handles appear on each of the columns representing the data for March. Now that the data series is selected, you can format it by adding labels.
4. Click the **Format Data Series button** on the Chart toolbar, then click the **Data Labels tab** in the Format Data Series dialog box
   You want the value to appear on top of each selected data marker.
5. Under Label Contains, click the **Value option** to select it, then click **OK**
   The data labels appear on the data markers, as shown in Figure J-4. You want the February data series to stand out more.
6. Click the **Chart Objects list arrow** on the Chart toolbar, click **Series "Feb"**, click , then click the **Patterns tab** in the Format Data Series dialog box
   The Patterns tab opens. See Figure J-5. The maroon color in the Sample box matches the current color displayed in the chart for the February data series. You decide that the series would show up better in a brighter shade of red.
7. Under Area, click the **red box** (third row, first column), click **OK**, press **[Esc]** to deselect the data series, press **[Esc]** again to deselect the entire chart, then save the workbook
   The February data series now appears in a brighter shade of red.

QuickTip

The ScreenTip for the Format Selected Object button changes, depending on what chart object is selected.

QuickTip

You can use the navigation arrows on the keyboard to select chart objects in succession.

Removing, inserting, and formatting legends

To insert or remove a legend, click the Legend button on the Chart toolbar to toggle the legend on or off. To format legend text, click Legend in the Chart Objects list of the Chart toolbar, click the Format Legend button , and choose the options you want in the Font tab.

FIGURE J-3: Selected data series

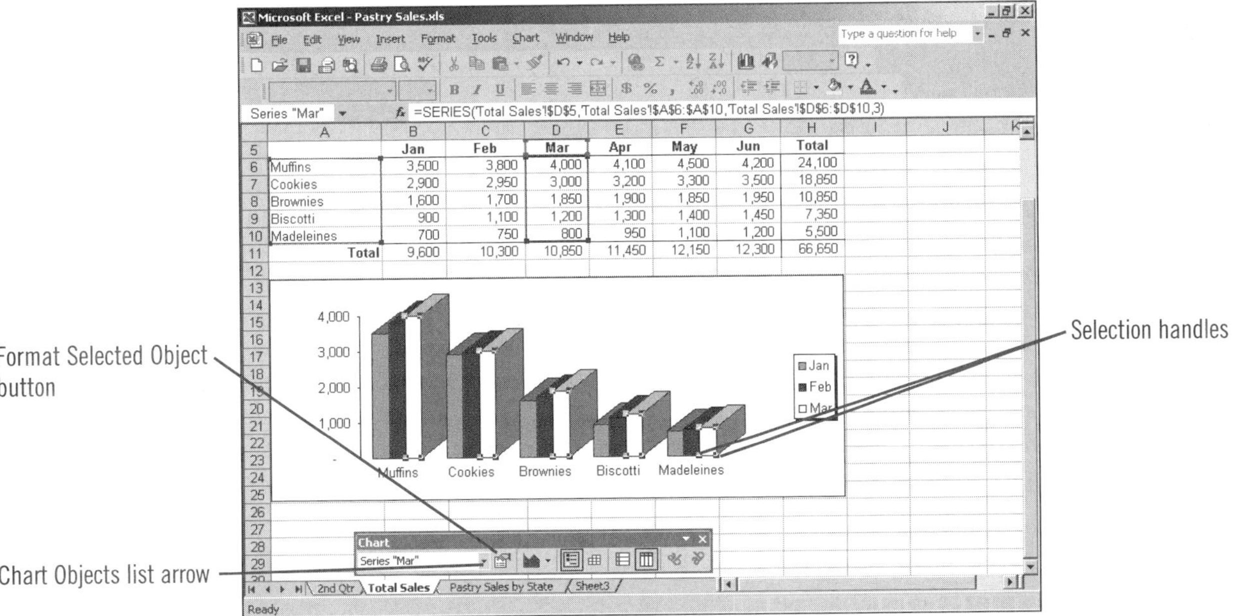

FIGURE J-4: Chart with data labels

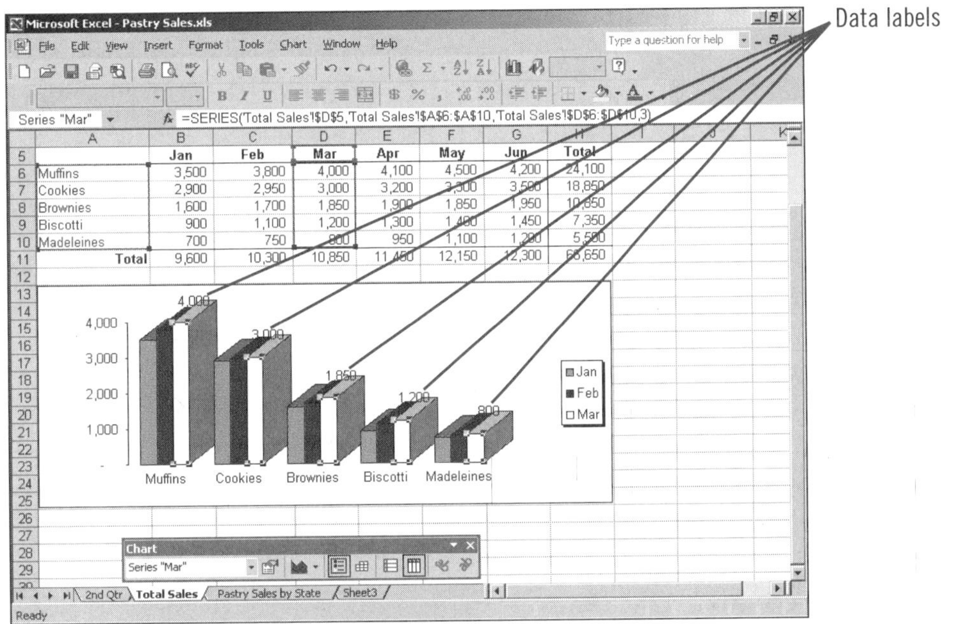

FIGURE J-5: Patterns tab settings

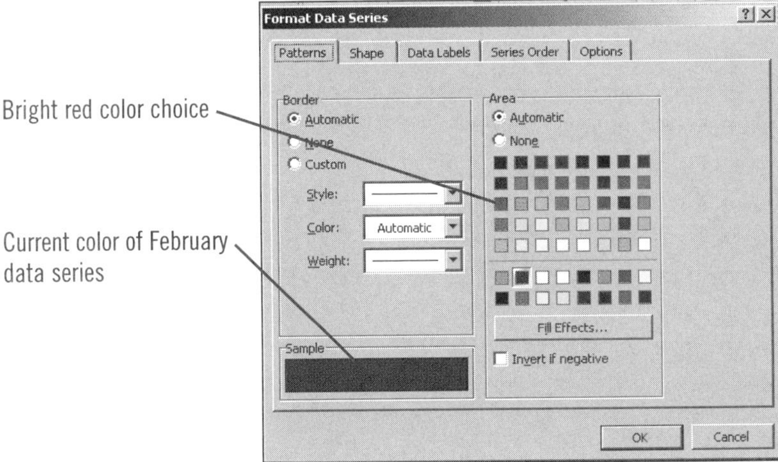

Excel 2002

Formatting a Chart Axis

Excel plots and formats chart data and places the chart axes within the chart's **plot area**. Data values in two-dimensional charts are plotted on the y-axis and categories are plotted on the x-axis. A scale is created for the value (y) axis that is based on the highest and lowest values in the data series, and intervals are placed along the scale. In three-dimensional charts, like the one in Figure J-6, three axes are generated, where *x* remains the category axis, but *z* becomes the value axis and *y* becomes the measure for the chart's depth. In 3-D charts, the value (*z*) axis usually contains the scale. For a list of the axes Excel uses to plot data, see Table J-1. You can override the Excel default formats for chart axes at any time by using the Format Axis dialog box. Jeff notices that the highest column is very close to the top of the chart. He asks you to increase the maximum number on the value axis and change its number format. You begin by selecting the chart object you want to format.

Steps

1. Click the **chart**, click the **Chart Objects list arrow** on the Chart toolbar, then click **Value Axis**

   The vertical axis is selected. Because this is a 3-D chart, this is the z axis.

2. Click the **Format Access button** on the Chart toolbar, then click the **Scale tab**

   The Scale tab of the Format Axis dialog box opens. The check marks under Auto indicate the default scale settings. You can override any of these settings by entering a new value.

3. In the Maximum box select **4000**, type **5000**, then click **OK**

   The chart adjusts so that 5000 appears as the maximum value on the value axis. Next, you want the minimum value to appear as a zero (0) and not as a hyphen (-).

4. With the Value Axis still selected, click on the Chart toolbar, then click the **Number tab**

   The Number tab of the Format Axis dialog box opens. Currently, a custom format is selected under Category, which instructs Excel to use a hyphen instead of 0 as the lowest value.

5. Under Category click **General**, click **OK**, press **[Esc]** twice, then save the workbook

   The chart now shows 0 as the minimum value, as shown in Figure J-7.

FIGURE J-6: Chart elements in a 3-D chart

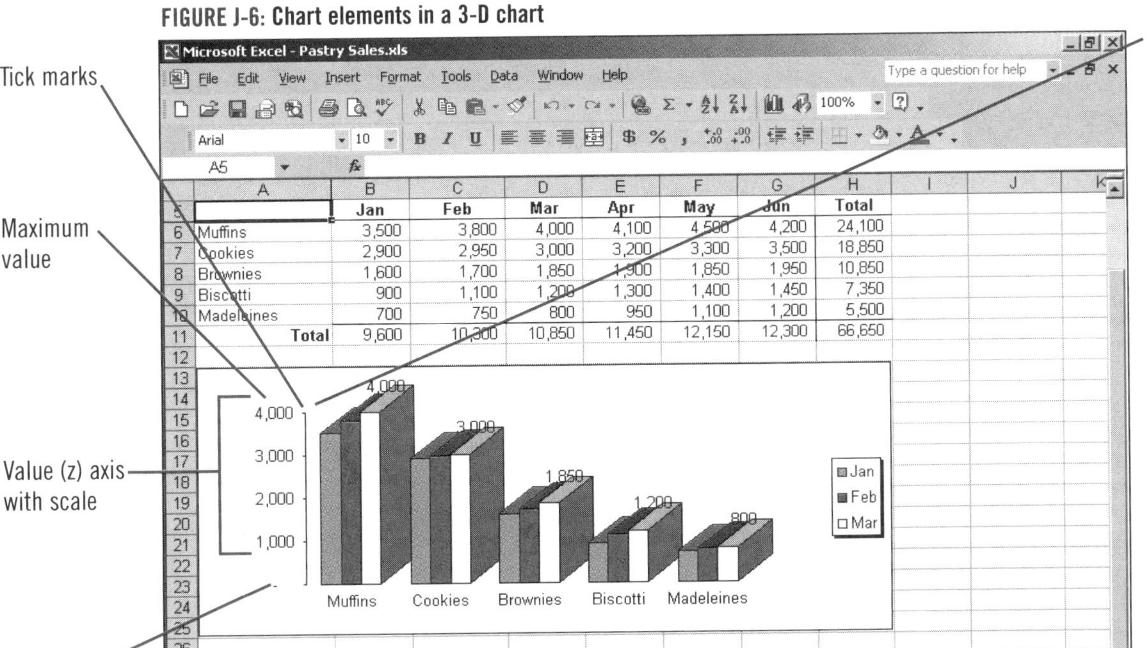

FIGURE J-7: Chart with formatted axis

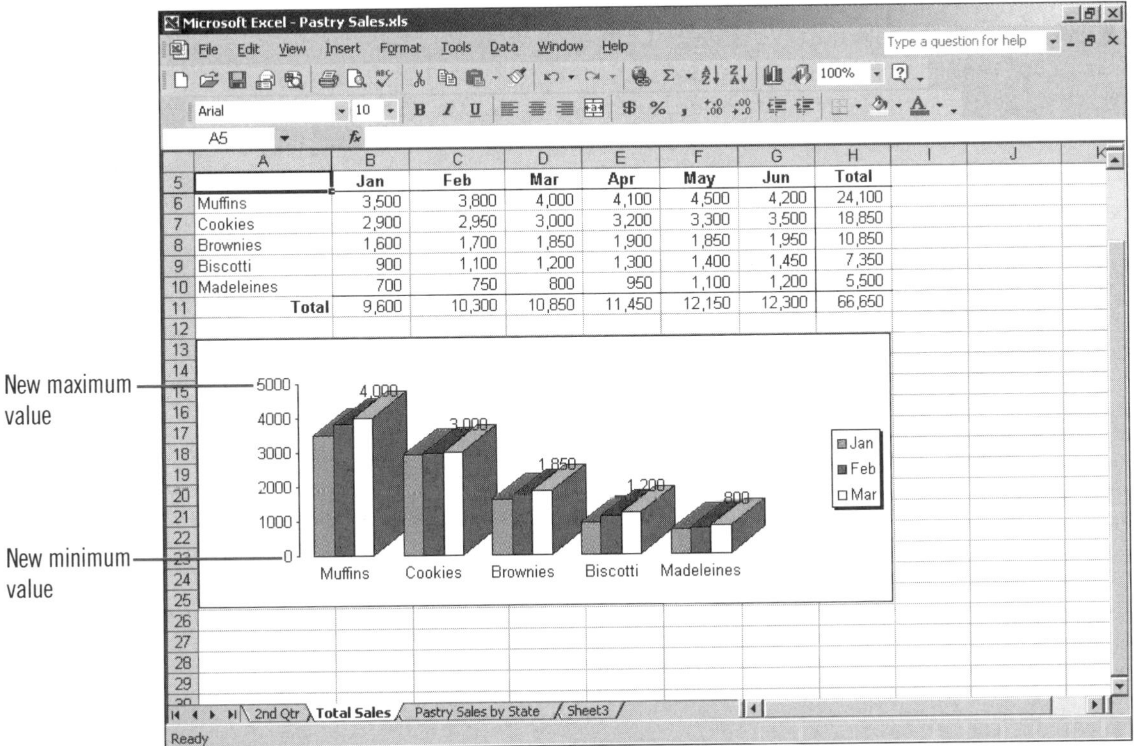

TABLE J-1: Axes used by Excel for chart formatting

axes in a two-dimensional chart	axes in a three-dimensional chart
Category (*x*) axis (horizontal)	Category (*x*) axis (horizontal)
Value (*y*) axis (vertical)	Series (*y*) axis (depth)
	Value (z) axis (vertical)

Excel 2002

Adding a Data Table to a Chart

A **data table** is a grid containing the chart data, attached to the bottom of a chart. Data tables are useful because they highlight the data you used to generate a chart, which might otherwise be difficult to find. Data tables can be displayed in line, area, column, and bar charts, and print automatically along with a chart. It's good practice to add data tables to charts that are stored separately from worksheet data. Jeff wants you to emphasize the first quarter data used to generate the chart. You decide to add a data table.

Steps

1. Click the **chart** to select it, click **Chart** on the menu bar, click **Chart Options**, then click the **Data Table tab**
   The Data Table tab in the Chart Options dialog box opens, as shown in Figure J-8. The preview window displays the selected chart.

2. Click the **Show data table check box** to select it
   The chart in the preview window changes to show what the chart will look like with a data table added to the bottom. See Figure J-9. The data table crowds the chart labels, making them hard to read. (Your chart may look slightly different.) You'll fix this problem after you close the Chart Options dialog box.

QuickTip

You can add a data table when creating a chart in Step 3 of the Chart Wizard.

3. Click **OK**, then, if necessary, scroll down to display the chart
   The chart and the newly added data table look too crowded inside the current chart area. If you were to drag the chart borders to enlarge the chart, you wouldn't be able to see the entire chart displayed on the screen. It's more convenient to move the chart to its own sheet.

QuickTip

To hide a data table, click the Data Table tab in the Chart Options dialog box, then clear the Show data table check box.

4. If necessary, click the **chart** to select it, click **Chart** on the menu bar, click **Location**, click the **As new sheet option button under Place chart, click OK**
   The chart now appears on a new sheet, where it is fully displayed in the worksheet window. See Figure J-10.

5. Enter your name in the sheet footer, save the workbook, then preview and print the chart sheet

Creating a trendline

Trendlines graphically represent data trends. You can add trendlines to data series in unstacked 2-D area, bar, column, line, stock, xy, and bubble charts. To add a trendline to a data series, select the series and select the Add Trendline option on the Chart menu. You can specify the type of trendline you want in the Type tab of the Add Trendline dialog box.

FIGURE J-8: Data Table tab settings

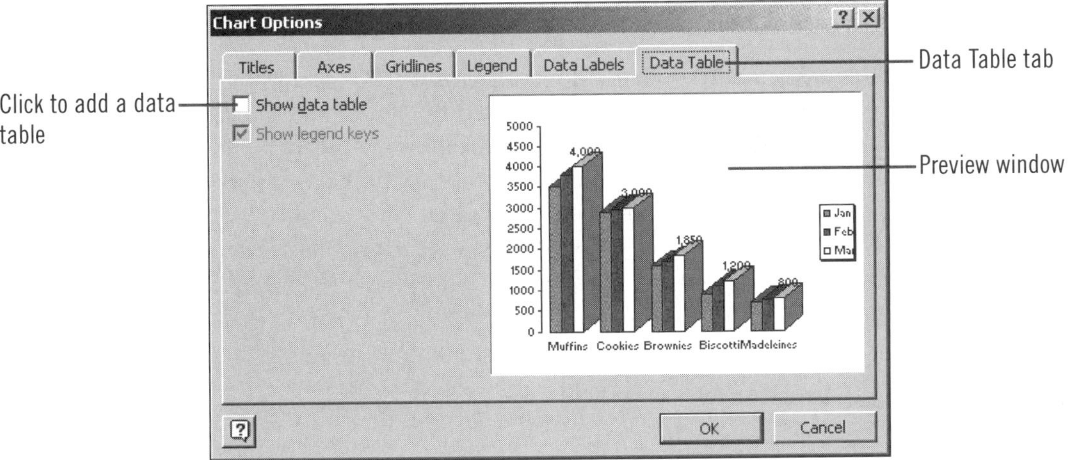

FIGURE J-9: Show Data Table box selected

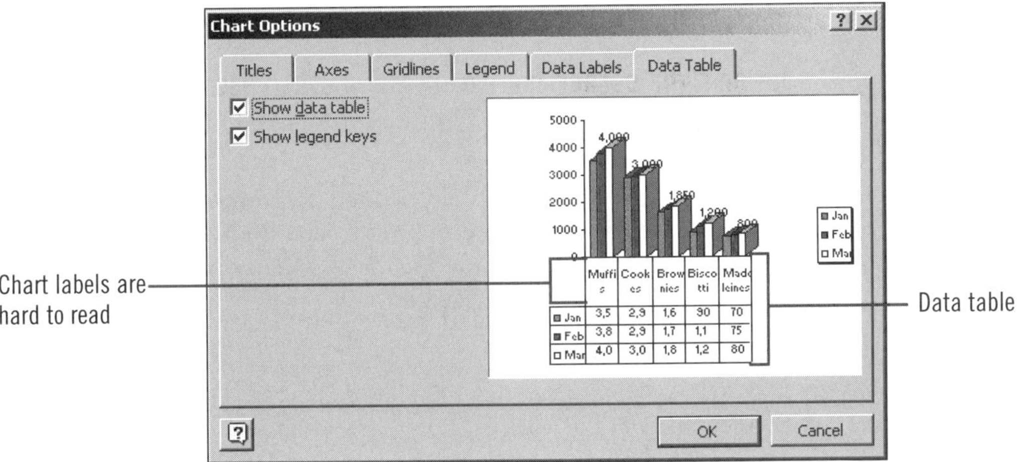

FIGURE J-10: Chart moved to separate chart sheet

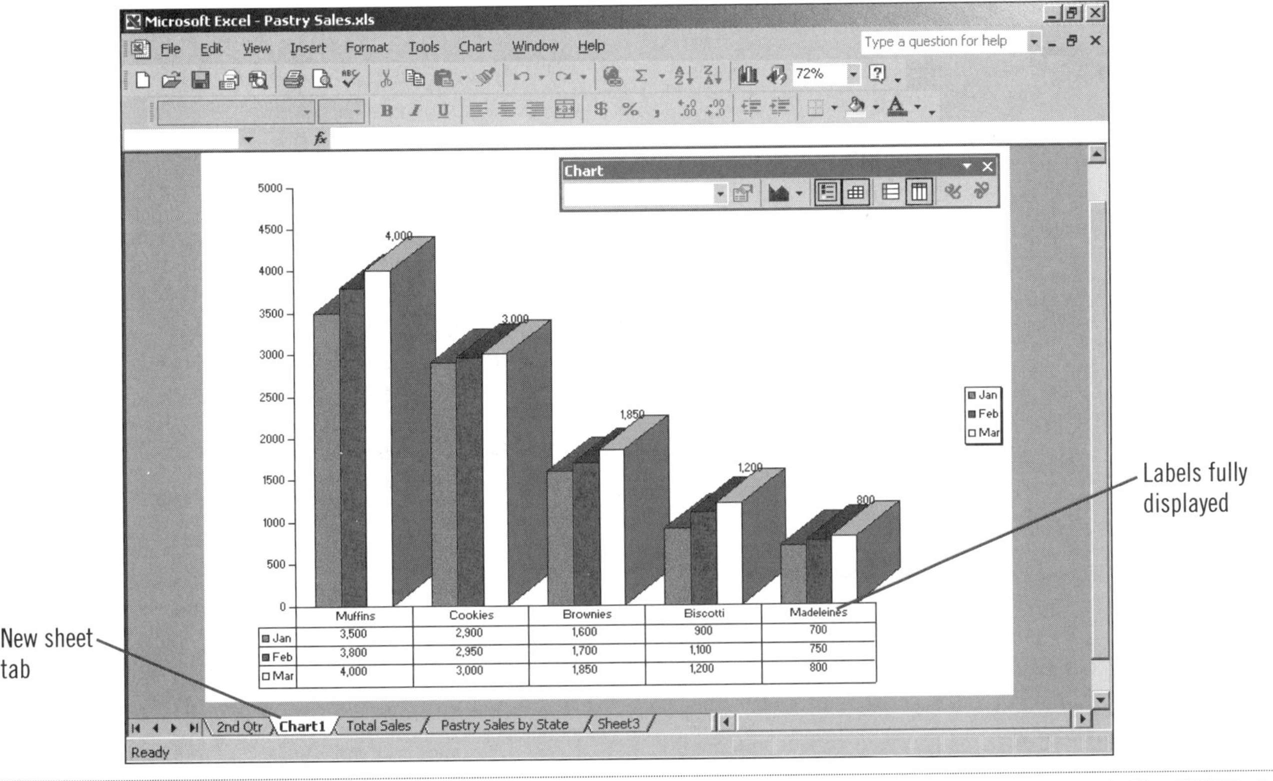

Excel 2002

Rotating a Chart

Three-dimensional (3-D) charts do not always display data in the most effective way. In many cases, data in these charts can be obscured by one or more of the chart's data markers. By rotating and/or elevating the axes, you can improve the visibility of the chart data. You can adjust the rotation and elevation of a 3-D chart by dragging it with the mouse or using the 3-D View command on the Chart menu. Jeff's workbook already contains a 3-D chart illustrating the sales data for the second quarter. He wants you to rotate the chart so the June columns are easier to see.

Steps

1. Click the **2nd Qtr sheet tab**, click the **Chart Objects list arrow** on the Chart toolbar, then click **Corners**
   Selection handles appear on the corners of the chart, as shown in Figure J-11.
2. Click the **lower-right corner handle** of the chart, press and hold the left mouse button and drag left approximately 2" until it looks like the object shown in Figure J-12, then release the mouse button
   The June columns may not be entirely visible. When using the dragging method to rotate a three-dimensional chart, you might need to make several attempts before you're satisfied with the view. It's usually more efficient to use the 3-D View option on the Chart menu.
3. Click **Chart** on the menu bar, click **3-D View**, then drag the **3-D View dialog box** to the upper-right area of the screen
   See Figure J-13. The preview box in the 3-D View dialog box allows you to preview changes to the chart's orientation in the worksheet.
4. Click **Default**
   The chart returns to its original position. Next, you decrease the chart's elevation, the height from which the chart is viewed.
5. To the left of the preview box, click the **Decrease Elevation button**
   Notice how the preview image of the chart changes when you change the elevation.
6. Click **Apply**
   As the number in the Elevation box decreases, the viewpoint shifts downward. Next, you'll change the rotation and **perspective**, or depth, of the chart.
7. In the Rotation box, select the current value, then type **55**; in the Perspective box, select the current value, type **0**, then click **Apply**
   The chart is reformatted. You notice, however, that the columns appear crowded. To correct this problem, you change the height as a percentage of the chart base.
8. In the Height box, select the current value, type **70**, click **Apply**, then click **OK**
   The 3-D View dialog box closes. The chart columns now appear less crowded, making the chart easier to read.
9. Save the workbook

Trouble?

Your 3-D View dialog box settings may be different from the ones shown in Figure J-13.

Trouble?

If you have difficulty locating the Decrease Elevation button, refer to Figure J-13.

FIGURE J-11: Chart corners selected

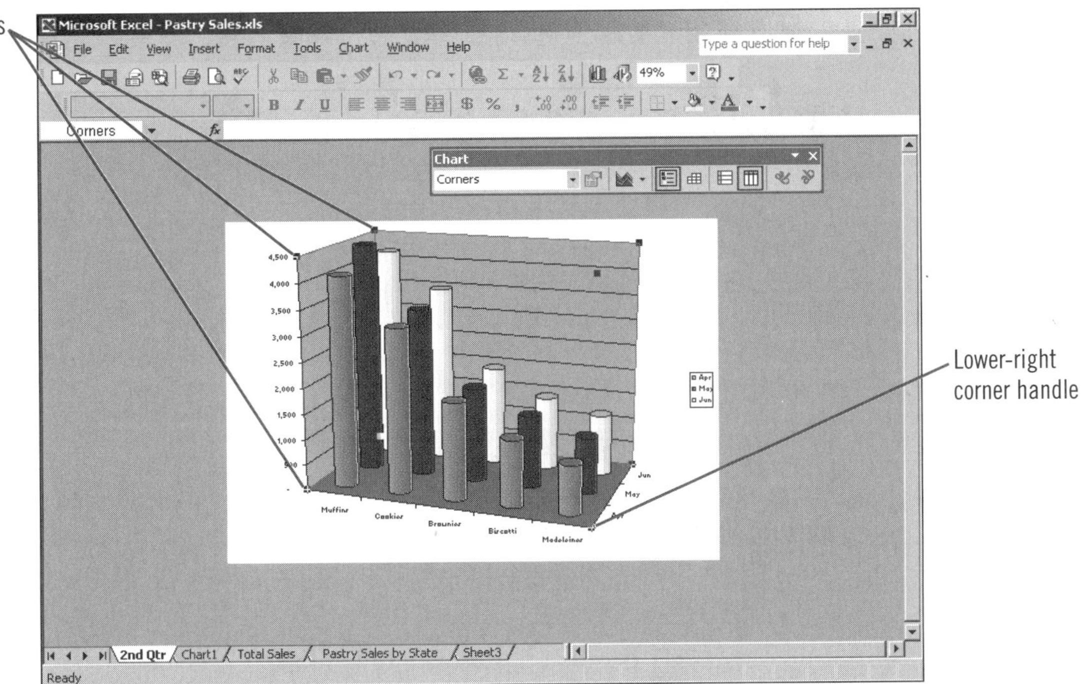

FIGURE J-12: Chart rotation in progress

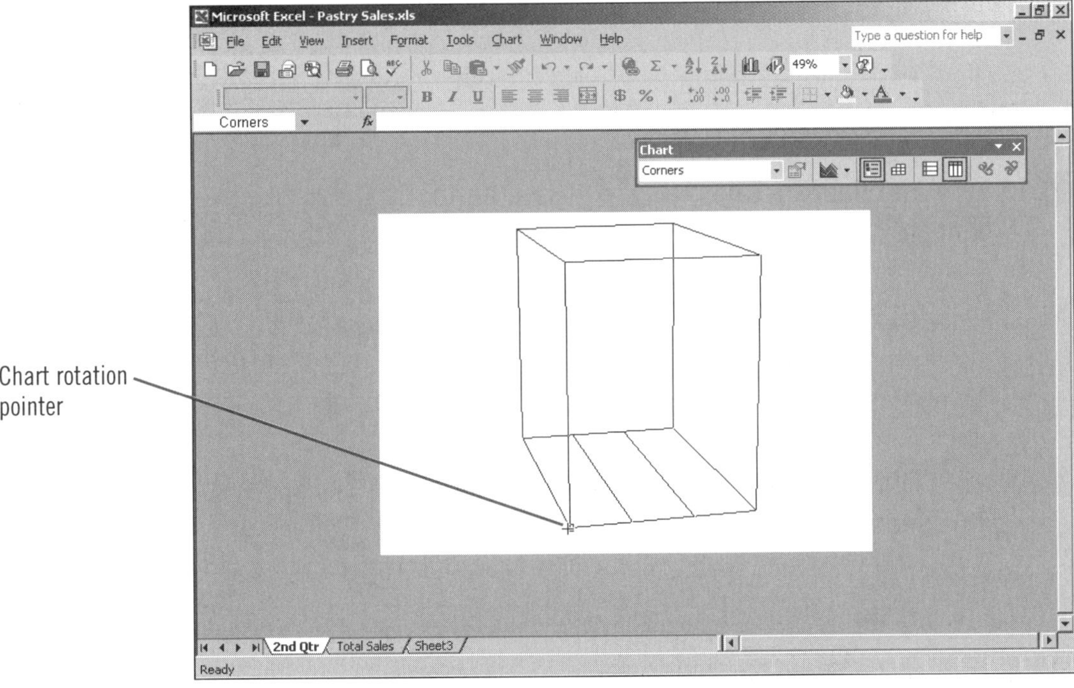

FIGURE J-13: Screen with chart and 3-D View dialog box

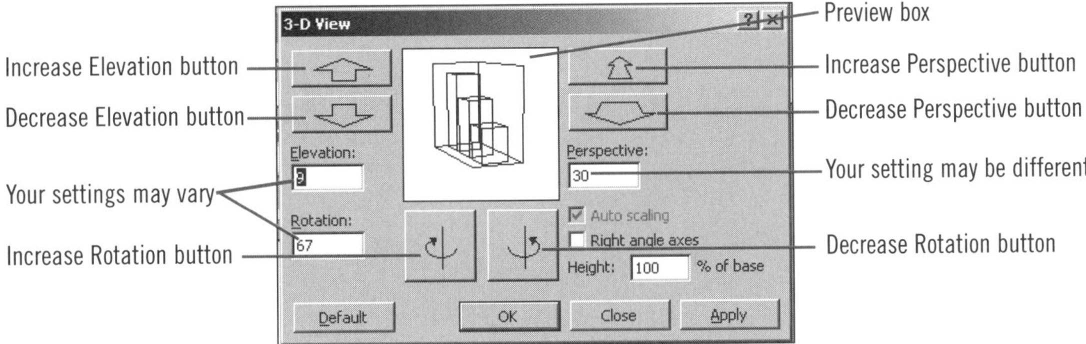

Excel 2002

Excel 2002

Enhancing a Chart with WordArt

You can enhance your chart or worksheet by adding specially formatted text using the WordArt tool on the Drawing toolbar. Once you've added a piece of WordArt to your workbook, you can edit or format it using the tools on the WordArt toolbar. Text formatted as WordArt is considered a drawing object rather than text. This means that WordArt objects cannot be treated as if they were labels entered in a cell; that is, you cannot sort, spell check, or use their cell references in formulas. Jeff wants you to add a WordArt title to the second quarter chart. You begin by displaying the Drawing toolbar.

Steps

1. If the drawing toolbar does not already appear on your screen, click the **Drawing button** on the Standard toolbar
   The Drawing toolbar appears at the bottom of the Excel window. The WordArt text will be your chart title.
2. Click the **Insert WordArt button** on the Drawing toolbar
   The WordArt Gallery dialog box opens. This is where you select the style for your text.
3. In the second row, click the second style from the left, as shown in Figure J-14, then click **OK**
   The Edit WordArt Text dialog box opens, as shown in Figure J-15. This is where you enter the text you want to format as WordArt. You also can adjust the point size or font of the text or select bold or italic styles.
4. Type **2nd Quarter Sales**, click the **Bold button**, if necessary select **Times New Roman** in the Font list box and **36** in the Size list box, then click **OK**
   The dialog box closes, and the chart reappears with the new title in the middle of the chart.
5. Place the pointer over 2nd Quarter Sales (the WordArt title) until the pointer changes to , then drag **2nd Quarter Sales** up until it appears in the upper-right corner of the chart
   The title is repositioned, as shown in Figure J-16. Next, you decide to edit the WordArt to change "2nd" to the word "Second."
6. Click **Edit Text on the WordArt toolbar, double-click 2nd** in the Edit WordArt Text box, type **Second**, then click **OK**
   The dialog box closes, and the edited title appears over the chart.
7. Press **[Esc]** to deselect the WordArt object, then click to hide the Drawing toolbar
8. Enter your name in the chart sheet footer, save the workbook, then preview and print the chart sheet

QuickTip

To delete a WordArt object, click it to make sure it is selected, then press [Delete].

QuickTip

To resize a WordArt object, drag any selection handle. To rotate WordArt, drag the green rotation handle.

QuickTip

To change the style of a WordArt object, click the WordArt Gallery button on the WordArt toolbar, select a new style, then click OK.

FIGURE J-14: Selecting a WordArt style

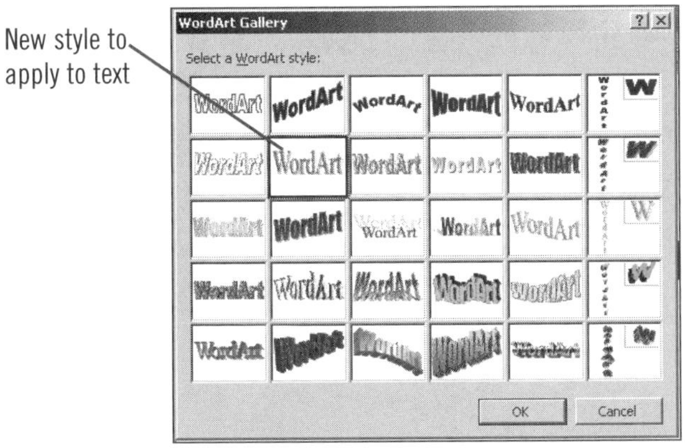

New style to apply to text

WordArt Gallery

Select a WordArt style:

OK Cancel

FIGURE J-15: Entering the WordArt text

FIGURE J-16: Positioning the WordArt object

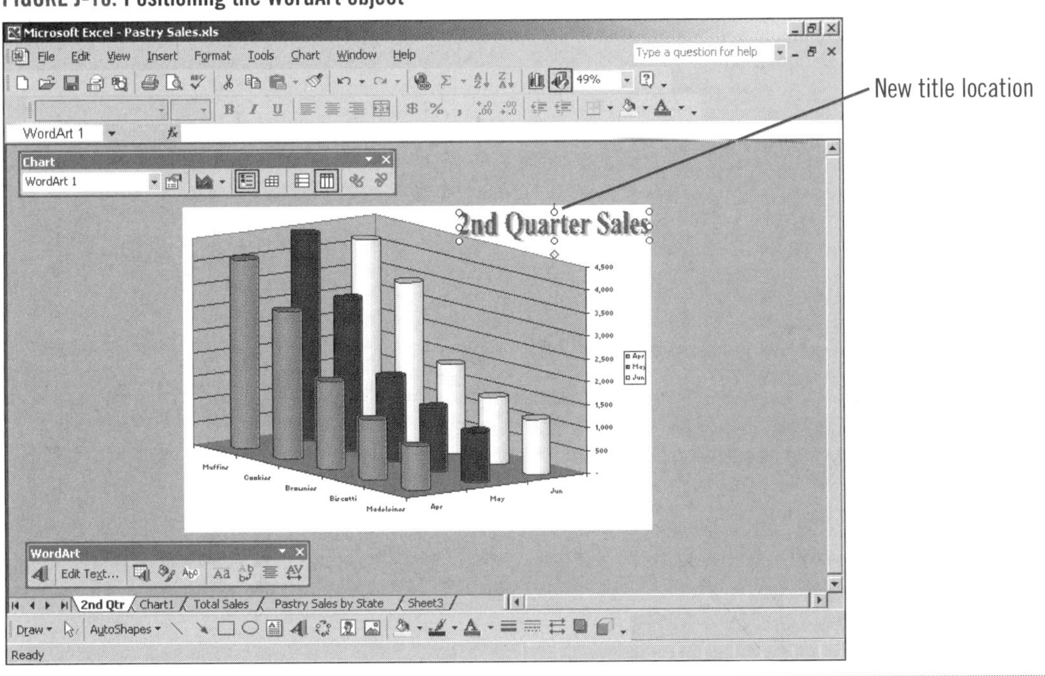

Excel 2002

Rotating Text

By rotating text within a worksheet cell, you can draw attention to column labels or titles without turning the text into a drawing object. Unlike WordArt, rotated text retains its usefulness as a worksheet entry, which means you can still sort it, spell check it, and use its cell reference in formulas. Now that you have finished enhancing the two charts in the workbook, Jeff wants you to improve the worksheet's appearance. You decide to rotate the column labels in cells B5 through G5.

Steps

1. Click the **Total Sales sheet tab**, make sure that row 5 is the top row in the worksheet area, then select cells **B5:G5**
2. Click **Format** on the menu bar, click **Cells**, then click the **Alignment tab**
   The Alignment tab of the Format Cells dialog box opens. See Figure J-17. The settings under Orientation allow you to change the rotation of cell entries. Clicking the narrow left box allows you to display text vertically in the cell. To rotate the text to another angle, drag the rotation indicator in the right box to the angle you want, or type the degree of angle you want in the Degrees box.
3. Double-click the **Degrees text box**, type **45**, then click **OK**
   The Format Cells dialog box closes.
4. Scroll up until row 1 is the top row in the worksheet area, then click cell **A1**
   The column labels for January through June now appear at a 45-degree angle in their cells, as shown in Figure J-18. The worksheet is now finished.
5. Enter your name in the sheet footer, save the workbook, then preview and print the worksheet

Using Speech Recognition

Speech recognition technology lets you enter text and issue commands by talking into a standard microphone connected to your computer. To install the Speech Recognition feature, you need to answer some simple questions in several dialog boxes. The first time you start Speech, you step through the Training Wizard. The Training Wizard is a series of paragraphs that you read into your computer's microphone to teach the Speech program to recognize your voice and to help you learn the correct speed and clarity necessary to use the program. You can complete the training session more than once to improve the program's ability to understand your speech. Once you install the Speech recognition component in Microsoft Word, it is available in all Office applications (except Office Designer). To activate it, click Tools on the menu bar, then click Speech. When Speech recognition is on, the language bar appears in the application title bar.

FIGURE J-17: Alignment tab settings

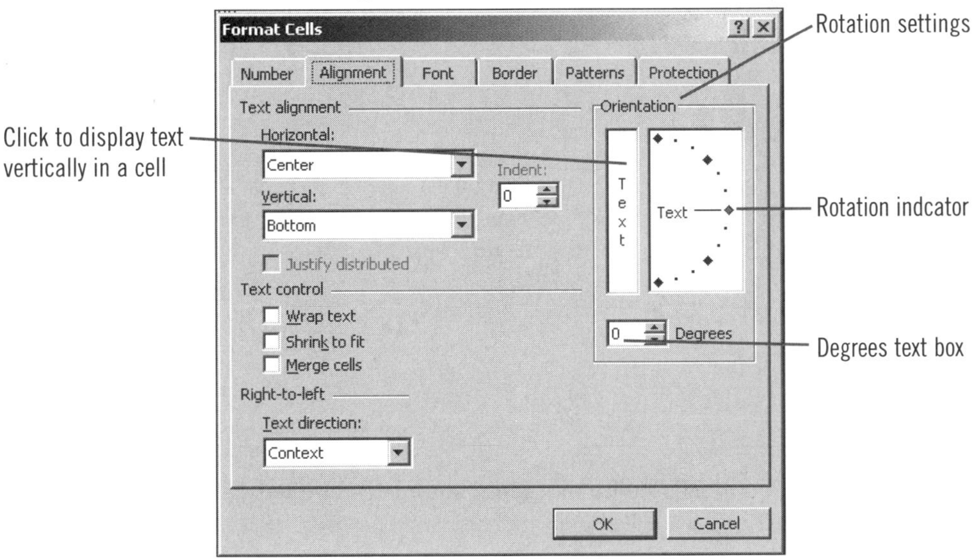

FIGURE J-18: Rotated column labels

Column labels rotated at 45-degree angle

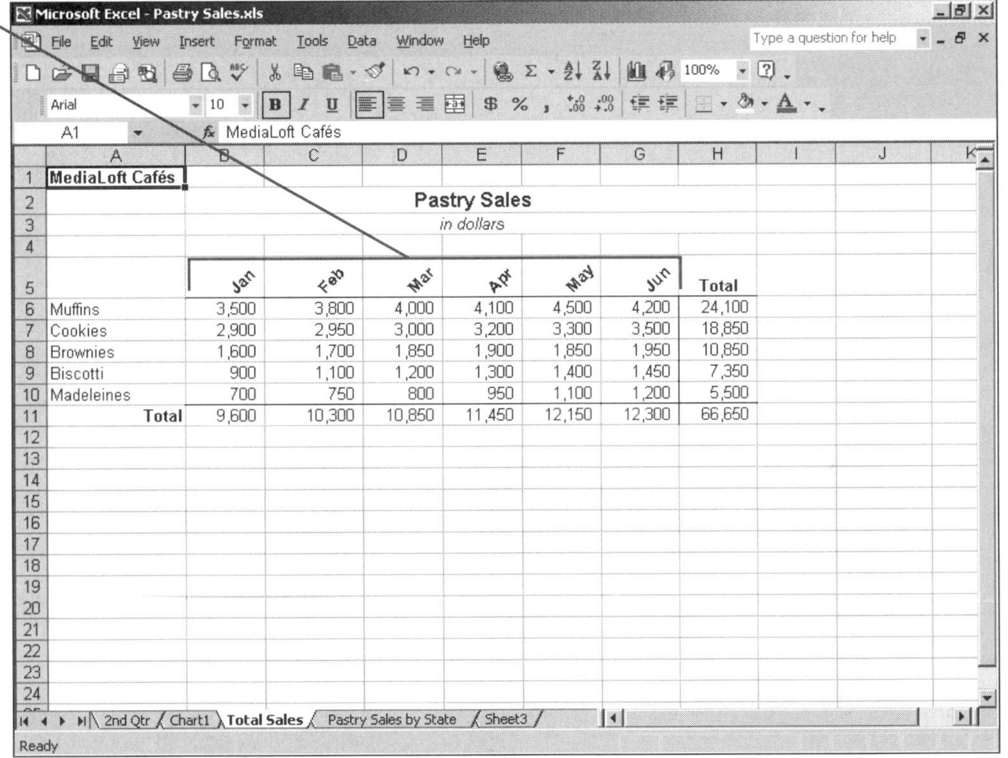

Rotating chart labels

You can rotate the category labels on a chart by using the buttons on the Chart toolbar. First, select the Category Axis in the Chart Objects list box, then click either the Angle Clockwise button or the Angle Counterclockwise button on the Chart toolbar.

Adding a Picture to a Chart

You can enhance your chart by adding a picture to the data markers, chart area, plot area, legend, or chart walls and floors. Jeff wants you to improve the appearance of the second quarter chart by adding a picture to the chart area. He also wants the MediaLoft logo to appear in the chart sheet header. You begin by clearing the formatting from the chart walls.

Steps

1. Click the **2nd Qtr sheet tab**, click one of the gray chart walls, then press **[Delete]**
   The chart wall formatting disappears, and the chart area remains selected.
2. Click the **Fill Color arrow** on the Formatting toolbar
   The fill options for the chart area appear, as shown in Figure J-19.
3. Click **Fill Effects**, then select the **Picture tab** in the Fill Effects dialog box
   You can insert a picture into these chart types by copying the picture and pasting it into the data series.
4. Click **Select Picture**, click the **Look in list arrow**, then navigate to the drive and folder where your Project Files are stored
   The available image files appear in the preview area of the Select Picture dialog box, as shown in Figure J-20.
5. Select the **Coffee** picture, click **Insert**, then click **OK** to close the Fill Effects dialog box
   The coffee picture is inserted in the chart area, as shown in Figure J-21. You also need the MediaLoft logo in the chart sheet header.
6. Click **View** on the menu bar, click **Header and Footer**, then click **Custom Header**
7. With the pointer in the Left section, click the **Insert Picture** button, select the **Logo** picture, click **Insert**, then click **OK** twice to return to your chart
8. Preview the chart, verify that the logo appears, then close the preview and save the workbook
9. Print the chart sheet, close the workbook, then exit Excel
   The final Total Sales worksheet is shown in Figure J-18. The final Chart1 sheet is shown in Figure J-10.

QuickTip

The Fill Effects command is not available for 2-D line, scatter, or unfilled radar chart data markers.

FIGURE J-19: Fill options

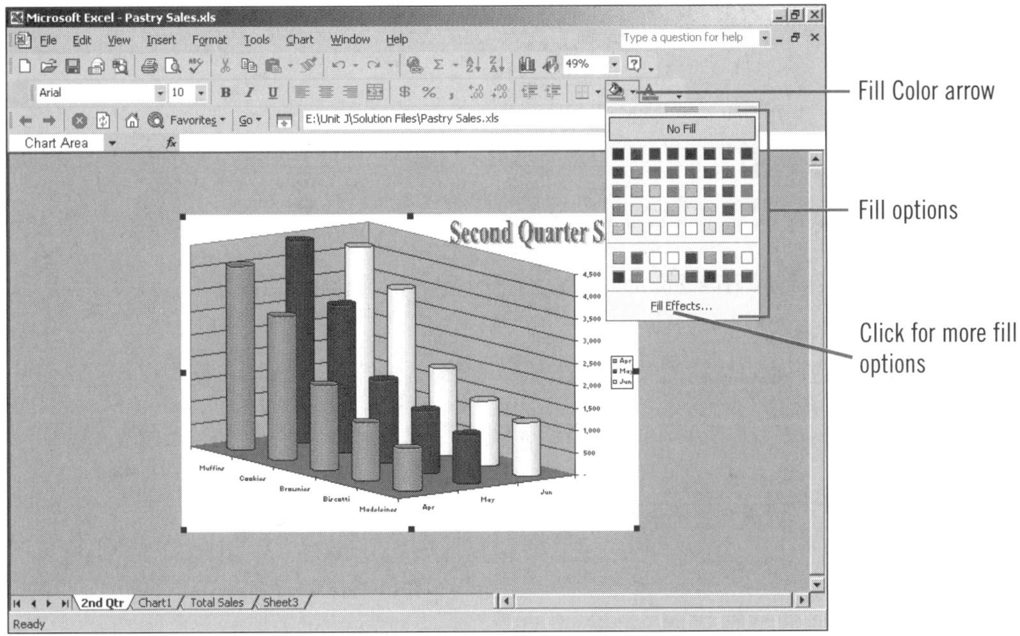

FIGURE J-20: Select Picture dialog box

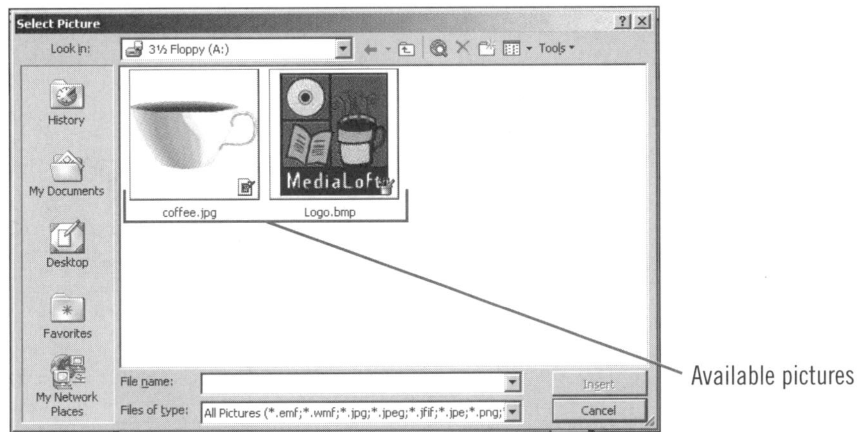

FIGURE J-21: Chart with picture inserted

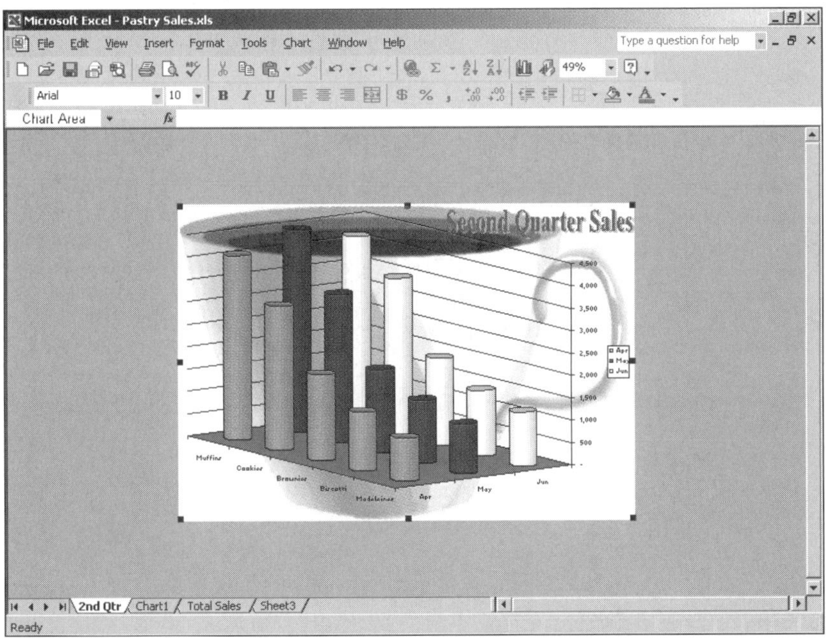

Excel 2002

Practice

► Concepts Review

Label each element of the Excel screen shown in Figure J-22.

FIGURE J-22

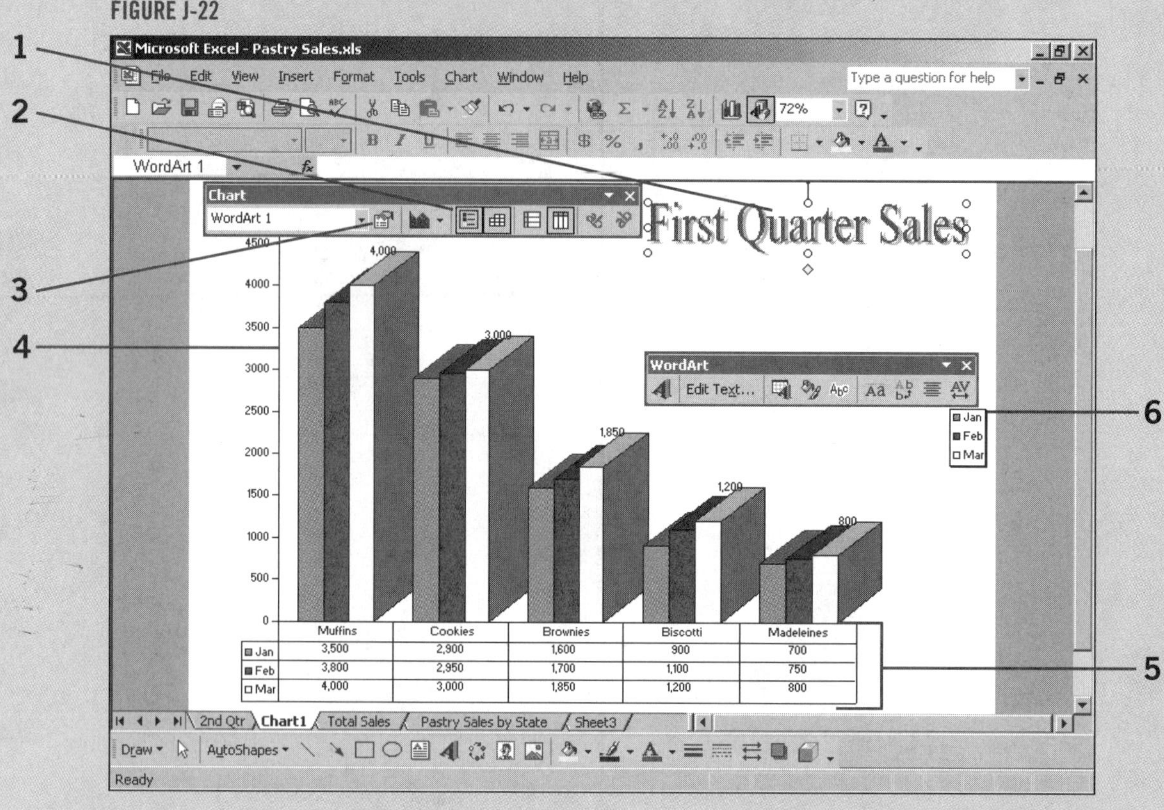

Match each button with the statement that describes it.

7. [button]
8. [button]
9. [button]
10. [button]
11. [button]

a. Opens the WordArt dialog box
b. Use to format the selected chart object
c. Use to rotate category labels on a chart clockwise
d. Use to change the style of a piece of WordArt
e. Use to display the Drawing toolbar

Select the best answer from the list of choices.

12. A chart's scale:
- **a.** Always appears on the (x) axis.
- **b.** Always appears on the (y) axis.
- **c.** Always appears on the (z) axis.
- **d.** Can be adjusted.

13. In 3-dimensional charts, the z-axis is the:
- **a.** Category axis.
- **b.** Value axis.
- **c.** Depth axis.
- **d.** 3-D axis.

14. You can add WordArt to a chart by:
- **a.** Clicking the Insert WordArt button on the Drawing toolbar.
- **b.** Clicking the Insert WordArt button on the Standard toolbar.
- **c.** Clicking the Insert WordArt button on the Chart toolbar.
- **d.** Using the Format Cells dialog box.

15. In 2-dimensional charts, the x-axis plots:
- **a.** Data values.
- **b.** The legend.
- **c.** Depth.
- **d.** Categories.

16. What is a data table?
- **a.** A three-dimensional arrangement of data on the y-axis.
- **b.** Worksheet data arranged geographically.
- **c.** A customized data series.
- **d.** The data used to create a chart displayed in a grid.

17. Excel provides 20 built-in ____________ chart types.
- **a.** Standard
- **b.** Custom
- **c.** Default
- **d.** 3-D

18. To rotate text in a worksheet cell:
- **a.** Adjust settings on the Alignment tab of the Format cells dialog box.
- **b.** Click the Rotate button on the Standard toolbar.
- **c.** Select the text, then drag it to rotate it the desired number of degrees.
- **d.** Format the text as WordArt, then drag the WordArt.

Skills Review

1. Select a custom chart type.
- **a.** Start Excel, open the Project File EX J-2 from the drive and folder where your Project Files are stored, then save it as **MediaLoft Coffee Sales**.
- **b.** With the 1st Quarter sheet active, select the range **A4:B7**.
- **c.** Open the Chart Wizard, and on the Custom Types tab in the Chart Wizard dialog box, make sure the Built-in option button is selected.
- **d.** Select **Blue Pie** in the Chart type box.

- **e.** Advance to the Step 2 Chart Wizard dialog box and make sure that the data range is correct, then proceed to Step 4 and make sure that the As Object In button is selected. Finish the Wizard.
- **f.** Drag the chart to a better location in the worksheet, then resize it as necessary.
- **g.** Save the workbook.

2. Customize a data series.

- **a.** With the 2nd Quarter sheet active, move the June data in D4:D7 into the chart area.
- **b.** Select the April data series and display its data labels (values).
- **c.** Use the Format Data Series dialog box to change the color of the May data series to the shade of green of your choice.
- **d.** Save the workbook.

3. Format a chart axis.

- **a.** With the 2nd Quarter sheet active, select the value axis.
- **b.** Set the value axis maximum to 10000 and minimum to 0.
- **c.** On the Number tab in the Format Axis dialog box under Category, use the Currency format to add a dollar sign and two decimal places to the values, then close the dialog box.
- **d.** Save the workbook.

4. Add a data table to a chart.

- **a.** Show the data table for the 2nd Quarter chart.
- **b.** Use the Location command on the Chart menu to move the chart to its own sheet.
- **c.** Display the 3rd Quarter sheet.
- **d.** Use the Data Table tab in the Chart Options dialog box to hide the data table.
- **e.** Remove the chart legend.
- **f.** Save the workbook.

5. Rotate a chart.

- **a.** Activate the Chart1 sheet, use the Chart Objects list arrow to select the chart corners.
- **b.** Drag a chart corner to rotate the chart.
- **c.** Return the chart to its default rotation using the 3-D View command on the Chart menu.
- **d.** Change the rotation to 315.
- **e.** Change the elevation to 13.
- **f.** Deselect the chart corners.
- **g.** Save the workbook.

6. Enhance a chart with WordArt.

- **a.** With the Chart1 sheet active, display the Drawing toolbar.
- **b.** Open WordArt and select the second style from the right in the second row.
- **c.** In the Edit WordArt Text dialog box, enter the text **Second Quarter Sales** and format it in italic.
- **d.** Position the new title above the chart.
- **e.** Make sure the WordArt object is still selected, then use the WordArt Gallery button on the WordArt toolbar to select the second style from the left in the second row.
- **f.** Save the workbook.
- **g.** Close the Drawing toolbar.

7. Rotate text.

- **a.** Activate the 1st Quarter sheet, select cells **B4:D4**.
- **b.** Change the alignment to 45 degrees.
- **c.** Activate the 2nd Quarter sheet, select the range **B4:D4**.
- **d.** Change the alignment to 45 degrees.
- **e.** Activate the 3rd Quarter sheet tab, rotate the Category Axis labels clockwise.
- **f.** Save the workbook.

8. **Add a picture to a chart.**
   a. Activate the Chart1 sheet, then select the chart walls.
   b. Delete the formatting from the chart walls using the Delete key.
   c. With the chart area selected, open the Fill Effects dialog box.
   d. Insert the **Coffee** picture, from the drive and folder where your Project files are stored, into the chart area.
   e. Enter the MediaLoft logo in the Chart1 sheet header.
   f. Enter **your name** in the footer of each worksheet.
   g. Preview each worksheet, then save the workbook.
   h. Print the four worksheets, then close the workbook.
   i. Exit Excel.

Independent Challenge 1

You are the co-owner of Sandwich Express, a metropolitan delicatessen. Each week, you order several pounds of cheese: Cheddar, Monterey Jack, Swiss, Provolone, and American. Last month was especially busy, and you ordered an increasing amount of cheese each week in every category except American, which seems to be declining in popularity. Recently, your business partner suggested that using Excel could help you more efficiently forecast of the amount of cheese to order each week. You developed a worksheet with a three-dimensional stacked bar chart to analyze last month's cheese orders. Now, you want to enhance the chart by adding data labels, reformatting the value axis, increasing the elevation, adding several titles, and adding pictures.

FIGURE J-23

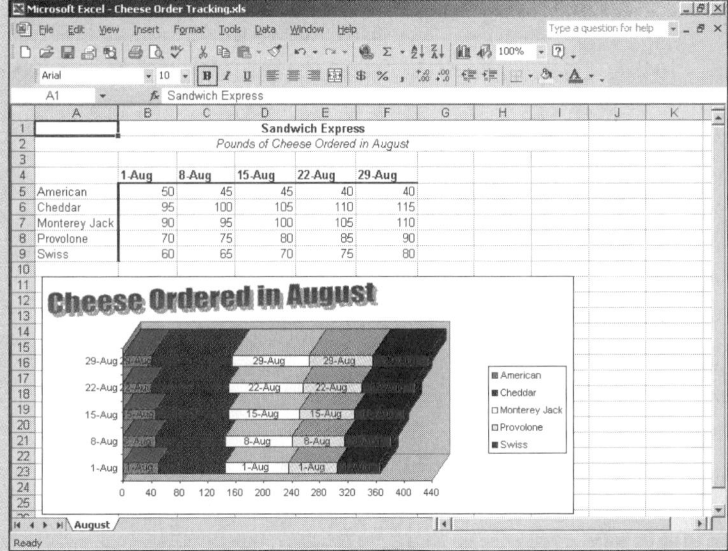

a. Start Excel, open the Project File titled EX J-3 from the drive and folder where your Project Files are stored, then save it as **Cheese Order Tracking**.
b. Add the data for 8/22 and 8/29 to the chart. Add data labels (values) to all data markers.
c. Reformat the value axis to display the scale in increments of 40, instead of 50 pounds. (*Hint*: in a horizontal bar chart, the value axis is the x, or horizontal, axis.)
d. Increase the chart's elevation to 30.
e. Add a WordArt title of **Cheese Ordered in August** to the upper-left corner of the chart. Use the WordArt Gallery to apply the second style from the left in the third row. If necessary, resize the WordArt object so it does not overlap the data. See Figure J-23.
f. Move the chart to its own sheet and add a data table. Name the chart sheet **Cheese**.
g. Enter your name in the footer of each sheet.
h. Save the workbook, preview, then print the worksheet and chart.

▶ Independent Challenge 2

You are the assistant to the VP of Marketing at ProSoft, a software development company, located in Minneapolis, Minnesota. The Vice President has asked you to chart some information from a recent survey of ProSoft customers. Customers provided information about their professions and the number of children in their households. Your administrative assistant has entered the survey data in an Excel worksheet, which you will use to create two charts.

a. Start Excel, open the Project File titled EX J-4 from the drive and folder where your Project Files are stored, then save it as **Customer Survey.**
b. Using the occupational data in columns A and B of the Survey data worksheet, create a pie chart on the worksheet. Select the 3-D visual effect from the standard pie chart types.
c. Enlarge the chart so it is as large as possible while still fitting on the screen.
d. Move the chart to a separate sheet; name the sheet **Occupation**.
e. Select the Professional slice by clicking the chart, then clicking the slice; change the slice color to bright red.
f. On the Survey data worksheet, use the Number of Children data in columns D and E to create a horizontal bar chart. Delete the legend. Place the chart on a new sheet named **Children.**
g. Add a centered WordArt title to the Children and Occupation charts, using appropriate fonts, colors, and font sizes; resize and rotate the WordArt object if you wish.
h. On the Children sheet, rotate the category axis labels clockwise using the Chart toolbar.
i. Insert the MediaLoft logo in the left section of the sheet headers and enter your name in the sheet footers.
j. Save the workbook, then preview and print all three sheets.
k. Close the workbook and exit Excel.

▶ Independent Challenge 3

You are a real estate agent for Galaxy Properties, which specializes in residential real estate. In September, you were voted salesperson of the month. Your sales manager has asked you to assemble a brief presentation on your sales activity during September to show to the new agents in the office. You decide to include a chart showing your sales for September in each of three areas: single-family homes, condominiums, and townhouses. Using your own data, create a worksheet and accompanying chart to present the information. Enhance the chart as outlined in the following:

a. Start Excel, create a new workbook, then save it as **September Sales** in the drive and folder where your Project Files are stored.
b. Enter your own worksheet labels and data. Use the table below as an example of the worksheet layout.

Galaxy Properties	
September Sales	
	Sales in $
Single-family	
Condos	
Townhouses	

c. Create a bar chart showing your September sales figures for single-family homes, condos, and townhouses. Use the clustered bar with a 3-D visual effect from the standard bar types.
d. Include data labels (values) on the data series.

e. Add a WordArt title.
f. Add new data to the worksheet for rental properties, then add the data series to the chart.
g. Move the chart to a chart sheet and add a data table.
h. Display the chart toolbar on the worksheet, then rotate the column label in the worksheet.
i. Create a custom chart type based on the modifications you made to the standard 3-D bar chart you started with. Name the custom chart Custom 3-D Bar and verify that it appears in the user-defined Chart type list.
j. Enter your name in each sheet footer, save the workbook, then preview and print the worksheet and chart.
k. Close the workbook and exit Excel.

Independent Challenges 4

You are the beverage manager at Rosemont Market, a gourmet food store located in London, England. You meet twice annually with the store manager to discuss trends in departmental sales at the store. You decide to use charts to represent the sales trends for the department's beverage products. You will begin by charting the tea sales for the first half of the year. Then you will analyze the sales trend using a trendline. Last, you will enhance the chart by adding a data table, reformatting the value axis, adding several titles, and adding a picture. You will begin by searching the Web to find an appropriate picture for your chart.

Go to the AltaVista search engine at www.altavista.com and enter **free + clip art** in the Search box. Follow the links to find free clip art. You can also use Yahoo!, Excite, Infoseek, or another search engine of your choice. Find a royalty-free picture that would be suitable for a chart of tea information. Follow the instructions on the Web site to download the picture.

a. Start Excel, open the Project File titled EX J-5, then save the workbook as **Tea Sales**.
b. Create a line chart on the worksheet showing the January through May sales information. Use any of the standard line types for your chart.
c. Add the June data from the table below to the worksheet, then add the data series to the chart.

	June
English Breakfast	40
Irish Breakfast	117
Earl Grey	75
Chamomile	90

d. Move the chart to its own sheet and add a data table.
e. Add a WordArt title.
f. Move the legend to the left edge of the chart area and move the plot area to the right edge of the chart area.
g. Remove the chart gridlines.
h. Add the title, **Pounds of Tea Sold**, to the y axis and align it horizontally beside the axis.
i. Reformat the value axis to display a scale in increments of 40.
j. Add linear trendlines to the Irish Breakfast and English Breakfast data series. (*Hint*: Choose Add Trendline from the Chart menu, then select Linear as the type.)
k. Add the picture you downloaded from the Web as the background to the chart legend. Reformat the legend text if necessary for readability.
l. Insert the picture in your chart sheet header.
m. Enter your name in the footer of the chart sheet and the worksheet, save the workbook, preview and print the worksheet and chart.
n. Close the workbook and exit Excel.

Visual Workshop

Create the worksheet and accompanying custom chart shown in Figure J-24. Save the workbook as **The Dutch Garden**. Study the chart and worksheet carefully to make sure you select the displayed chart type with all the enhancements shown. (*Hint*: The source data series is charted in rows.) Enter your name in the sheet footer, preview, then print the worksheet and chart together in landscape orientation.

FIGURE J-24

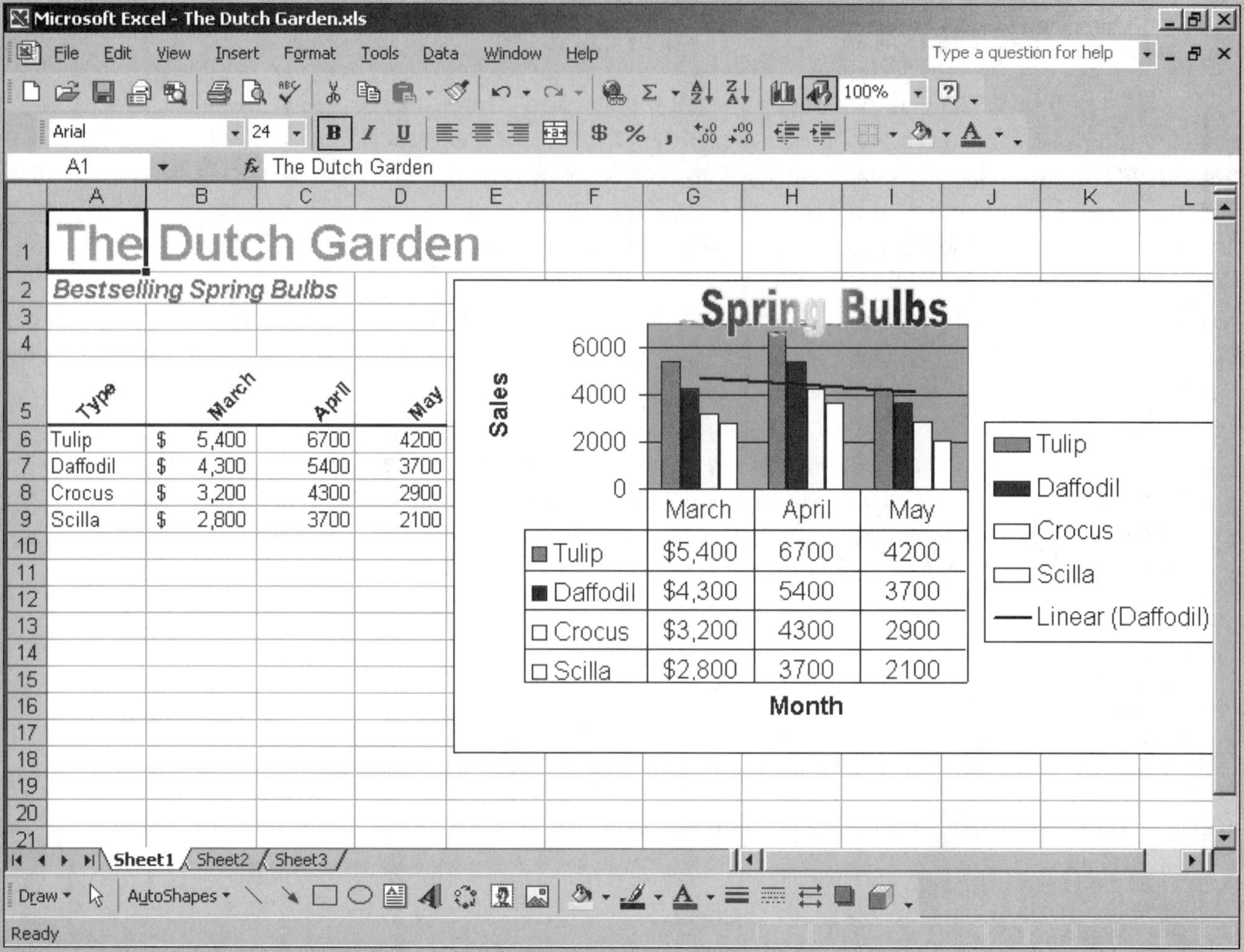

Microsoft Excel - The Dutch Garden.xls

The Dutch Garden

Bestselling Spring Bulbs

Type	March	April	May
Tulip	$ 5,400	6700	4200
Daffodil	$ 4,300	5400	3700
Crocus	$ 3,200	4300	2900
Scilla	$ 2,800	3700	2100

Spring Bulbs

Sales

	March	April	May
Tulip	$5,400	6700	4200
Daffodil	$4,300	5400	3700
Crocus	$3,200	4300	2900
Scilla	$2,800	3700	2100

Month

Tulip
Daffodil
Crocus
Scilla
Linear (Daffodil)

Using What-If Analysis

Objectives

- Define what-if analysis
- MOUS Track a what-if analysis with Scenario Manager
- MOUS Generate a scenario summary
- Project figures using a data table
- Create a two-input data table
- Use Goal Seek
- Set up a complex what-if analysis with Solver
- Run Solver and generate an Answer Report

Each time you use a worksheet to answer the question "what if?" you are performing a **what-if analysis**. For example, what would happen to a firm's overall expense budget if company travel expenses decreased by 30%? Using Excel, you can perform a what-if analysis in many ways. In this unit, you will learn to track what-if scenarios and generate summary reports using the Excel Scenario Manager. You will design and manipulate one-input and two-input data tables to project multiple outcomes. Also, you will use the Goal Seek feature to solve a what-if analysis. Finally, you will use Solver to perform a complex what-if analysis involving multiple variables. The MediaLoft corporate office is considering the purchase of several pieces of capital equipment, as well as several vehicles. They have asked you to help analyze their options using Excel.

Excel 2002

Defining a What-If Analysis

By performing a what-if analysis in a worksheet, you can get immediate answers to questions such as "What happens to profits if we sell 30% more of a certain product?" or "What happens to monthly payments if interest rates rise 2 points?" A worksheet used to produce a what-if analysis is often called a **model** because it acts as the basis for multiple outcomes. To perform a what-if analysis in a worksheet, you change the value in one or more **input cells** (cells that contain data rather than formulas), then observe the effects on dependent cells. A **dependent cell** usually contains a formula whose value changes depending on the values in the input cells. A dependent cell can be located either in the same worksheet as the changing input value or in another worksheet. Jim has created a worksheet model to perform an initial what-if analysis of equipment loan payments. See Figure K-1. You will follow the guidelines below to perform a what-if analysis for him.

Details

- **Understand and state the purpose of the worksheet model**
  The worksheet model is designed to calculate a fixed-rate, monthly equipment loan payment.

- **Determine the data input value(s) that, if changed, affect the dependent cell results**
  The model contains three data input values (labeled Loan Amount, Annual Interest Rate, and Term in Months), in cells B4, B5, and B6, respectively.

- **Identify the dependent cell(s), usually containing formulas, that will contain adjusted results as different data values are entered**
  There are three dependent cell formulas (labeled Monthly Payment, Total Payments, and Total Interest). The results appear in cells B9, B10, and B11, respectively.

- **Formulate questions you want the what-if analysis to answer**
  You want to answer the following questions with this model: (1) What happens to the monthly payments if the interest rate is 10%? (2) What happens to the monthly payments if the loan term is 60 months (5 years) instead of 48 months (4 years)? (3) What happens to the monthly payments if a less-expensive car is purchased with a lower loan amount?

- **Perform the what-if analysis and explore the relationships between the input values and the dependent cell formulas**
  You want to see what effect a 10% interest rate has on the dependent cell formulas. Because the interest rate is located in cell B5, any formula that references cell B5 will be directly affected by a change in interest rate—in this case, the Monthly Payment formula in cell B9. Because the formula in cell B10 references cell B9 and the formula in cell B11 references cell B10, however, a change in the interest rate in cell B5 affects these other two formulas as well. Figure K-2 shows the result of the what-if analysis described in this example.

FIGURE K-1: Worksheet model for a what-if analysis

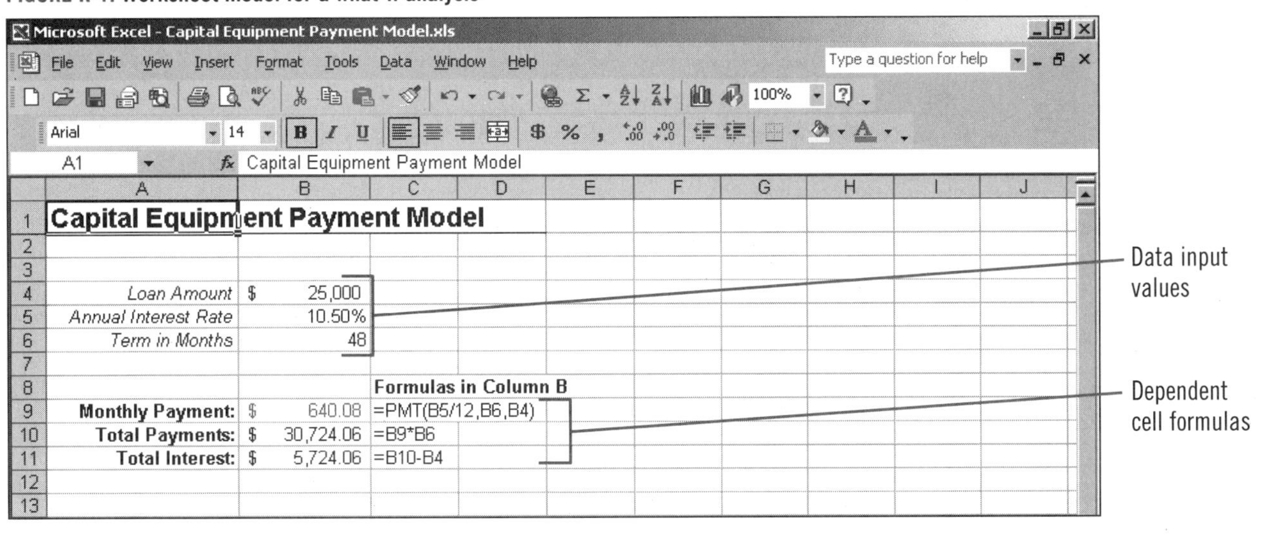

FIGURE K-2: What-if analysis with changed input value and dependent formula results

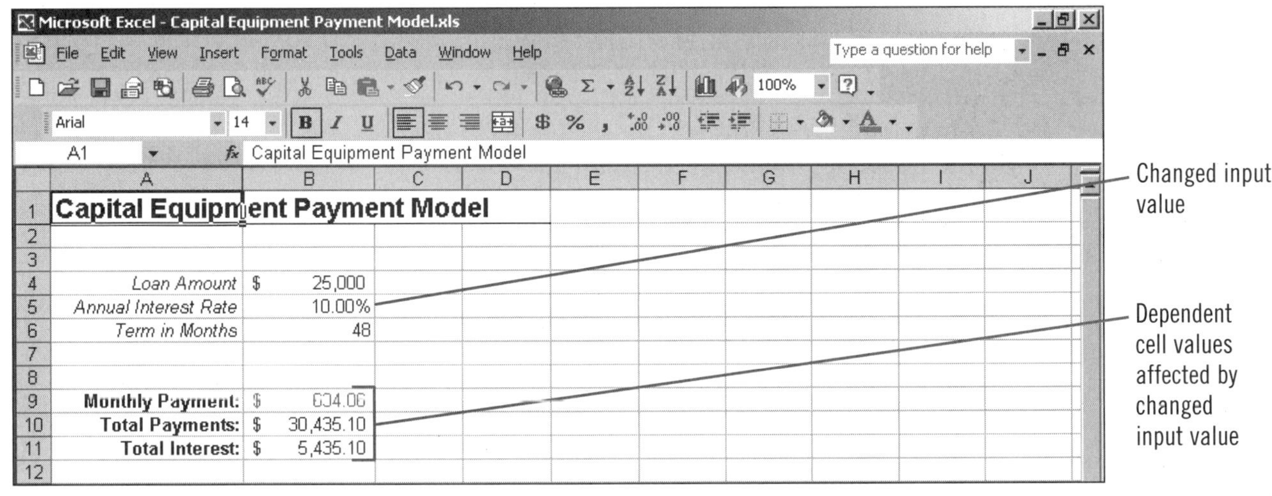

Excel 2002

Excel 2002

Tracking a What-If Analysis with Scenario Manager

A **scenario** is a set of values you use to forecast worksheet results. The Excel Scenario Manager simplifies the process of what-if analysis by allowing you to name and save different scenarios with the worksheet. Scenarios are particularly useful when you work with uncertain or changing variables. If you plan to create a budget, for example, but are uncertain of your revenue, you can assign several different values to the revenue, then switch between the scenarios to perform a what-if analysis. Jim asks you to use Scenario Manager to consider three equipment loan scenarios: (1) the original loan quote, (2) a longer-term loan, and (3) a reduced loan amount.

Steps 1 2 3 4

1. Start Excel, open the Project File **EX K-1** from the drive and folder where your Project Files are stored, then save it as **Capital Equipment Payment Model**

   The first step in defining a scenario is choosing the cells that will vary in the different scenarios; these are known as **changing cells**.

2. With the Single Loan sheet displayed, select range **B4:B6**, click **Tools** on the menu bar, then click **Scenarios**

   The Scenario Manager dialog box opens with the following message: "No Scenarios defined. Choose Add to add scenarios."

3. Click **Add**, drag the Add Scenario dialog box to the right until columns **A** and **B** are visible, then type **Original loan quote** in the Scenario name text box

   The range in the Changing cells box reflects your initial selection, as shown in Figure K-3.

4. Click **OK** to confirm the Add Scenario settings

   The Scenario Values dialog box opens, as shown in Figure K-4. The existing values appear in the changing cell boxes. Because this first scenario reflects the original loan quote input values ($25,000 at 10.5% for 48 months), these values are correct.

5. Click **OK**

   The Scenario Manager dialog box reappears with the new scenario listed in the Scenarios box. You want to examine a second scenario, this one with a loan term of 60 months.

6. Click **Add**; in the Scenario name text box type **Longer term loan**, click **OK**; in the Scenario Values dialog box, select **48**; in the third changing cell box, type **60**, then click **Add**

   You also want to examine a scenario that uses $21,000 as the loan amount.

7. In the Scenario name text box type **Reduced loan amount**, click **OK**; in the Scenario Values dialog box, change the **25000** in the first changing cell box to **21000**, then click **OK**

   The Scenario Manager dialog box reappears. See Figure K-5. All three scenarios are listed, with the most recent—Reduced loan amount—selected. Now that you have defined the three scenarios, you can apply them and see what effect they will have on the monthly payment.

8. Make sure the Reduced loan amount scenario is still selected, click **Show**, notice that the monthly payment in the worksheet changes from $640.08 to $537.67; click **Longer term loan**, click **Show**, notice that the monthly payment is now $537.35; click **Original loan quote**, click **Show** to return to the original values, then click **Close**

9. Save the workbook

FIGURE K-3: Add Scenario dialog box

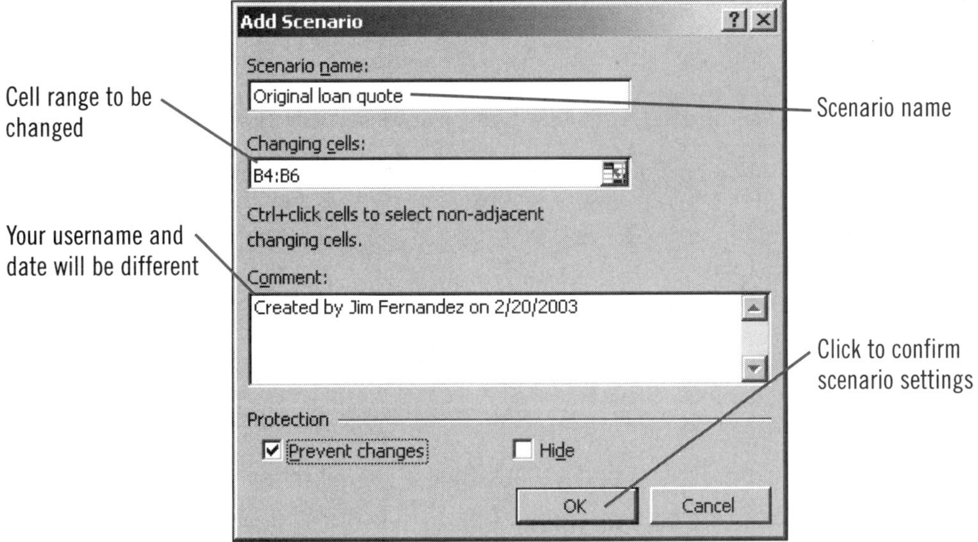

FIGURE K-4: Scenario Values dialog box

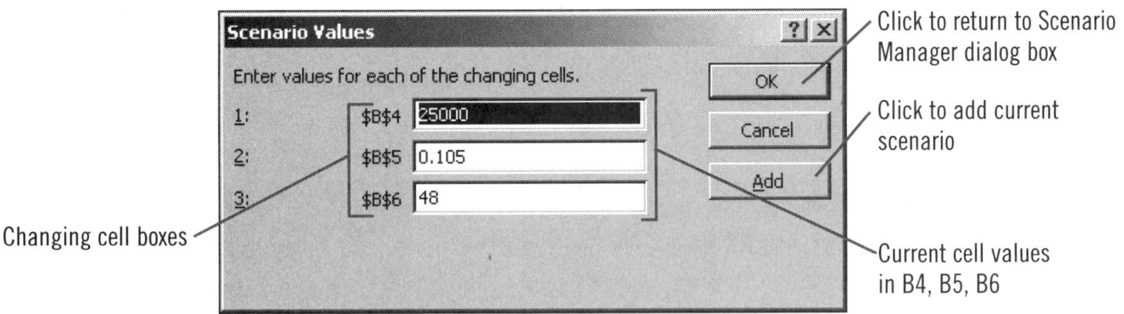

FIGURE K-5: Scenario Manager dialog box with three scenarios listed

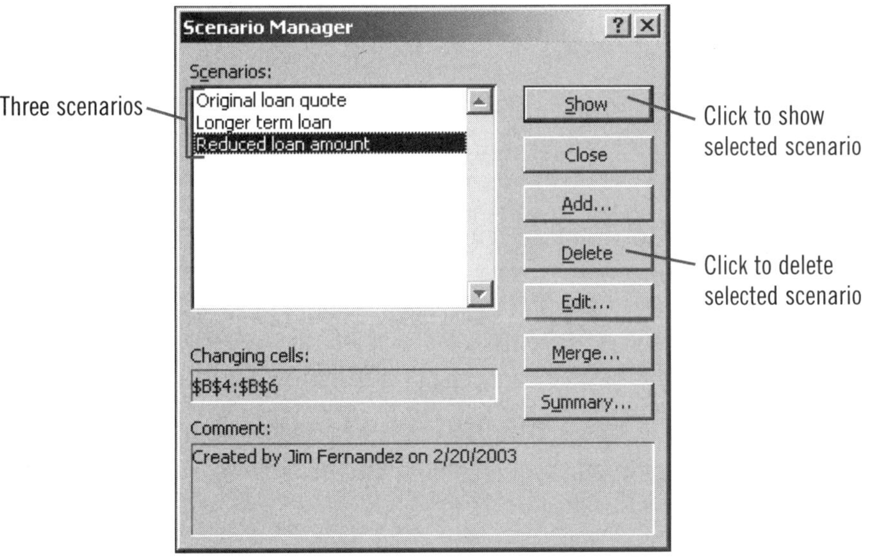

Excel 2002

Merging scenarios

To bring scenarios from another workbook into the current workbook, click the Merge button in the Scenario Manager dialog box. The Merge Scenarios dialog box opens, letting you select scenarios from other workbooks.

Excel 2002

Generating a Scenario Summary

Although it may be useful to switch between different scenarios when analyzing data, in most cases you will want to refer to a single report summarizing the results of the scenarios in a worksheet. A **scenario summary** is an Excel table that compiles data from the changing cells and corresponding result cells for each scenario. You can use a scenario summary to illustrate the best, worst, and most likely scenarios for a particular set of circumstances. Naming the cells makes the summary easier to read because the names, not the cell references, are listed in the report. Now that you have defined Jim's scenarios, he needs you to generate and print a scenario summary report. You begin by creating cell names in column B based on the labels in column A.

Steps

QuickTip

To delete a range name, click Insert on the menu bar, point to Name, click Define, click the range name, then click Delete.

1. Select the range **A4:B11**, click **Insert** on the menu bar, point to **Name**, click **Create**, click the **Left column check box** to select it if necessary, then click **OK**

   Excel creates the names based on the labels in column A.

2. Click cell **B4** to make sure Loan_Amount appears in the Name box, then click the **Name Box list arrow**

   All six labels appear in the Name Box list, confirming that they were created. See Figure K-6. Now you are ready to generate the scenario summary report.

3. Press **[Esc]** to close the Name Box list, click **Tools** on the menu bar, click **Scenarios**, then click **Summary** in the Scenario Manager dialog box

   The Scenario Summary dialog box opens. Scenario summary is selected, indicating that it is the default report type.

4. Select the **Result cells box,** if necessary, then select range **B9:B11** in the worksheet

   With the report type and result cells specified, as shown in Figure K-7, you are now ready to generate the report.

QuickTip

The scenario summary is not linked to the worksheet. If you change the cells in the worksheet, you must generate a new scenario summary.

5. Click **OK**

   The summary of the worksheet's scenarios appears on a new sheet. The report appears in outline format so that you can hide or show report details. Because the Current Values column shows the same values as the Original loan quote column, you decide to delete column D.

6. Press **[Ctrl][Home]**, right-click the **column D header**, then click **Delete** in the shortcut menu

   The column containing the current values is deleted, and the Original loan quote column data shifts to the left. Next, you want to delete the notes at the bottom of the report because they refer to the column that no longer exists. You also want to make the report title more descriptive.

7. Select the range **B13:B15**, press **[Delete]**, select cell **B2**, edit its contents to read **Scenario Summary for Equipment Loan**, then click cell **A1**

   The completed scenario summary is shown in Figure K-8.

8. Add your name to the report footer, save the workbook, then preview and print the report in landscape orientation

FIGURE K-6: List box containing newly created names

Name box list arrow

Names match labels in column A in alphabetical order

Microsoft Excel - Capital Equipment Payment Model.xls

	A	B
1	Equipment Payment Model	
4	Loan Amount	$ 25,000
5	Annual Interest Rate	10.50%
6	Term in Months	48
9	Monthly Payment:	$ 640.08
10	Total Payments:	$ 30,724.06
11	Total Interest:	$ 5,724.06

Annual_Interest_Rate
Loan_Amount
Monthly_Payment
Term_in_Months
Total_Interest
Total_Payments

FIGURE K-7: Scenario Summary dialog box

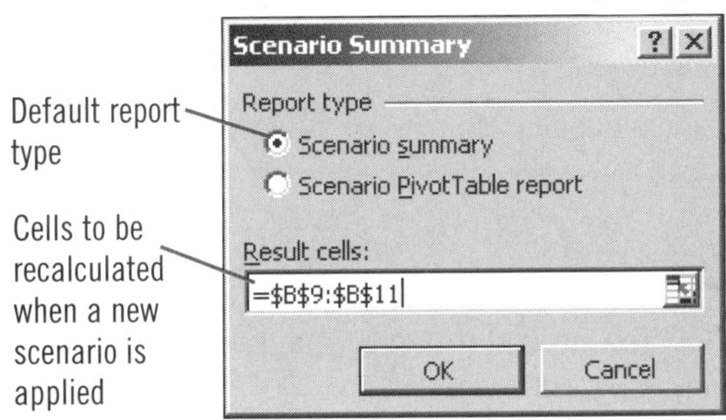

FIGURE K-8: Completed Scenario Summary report

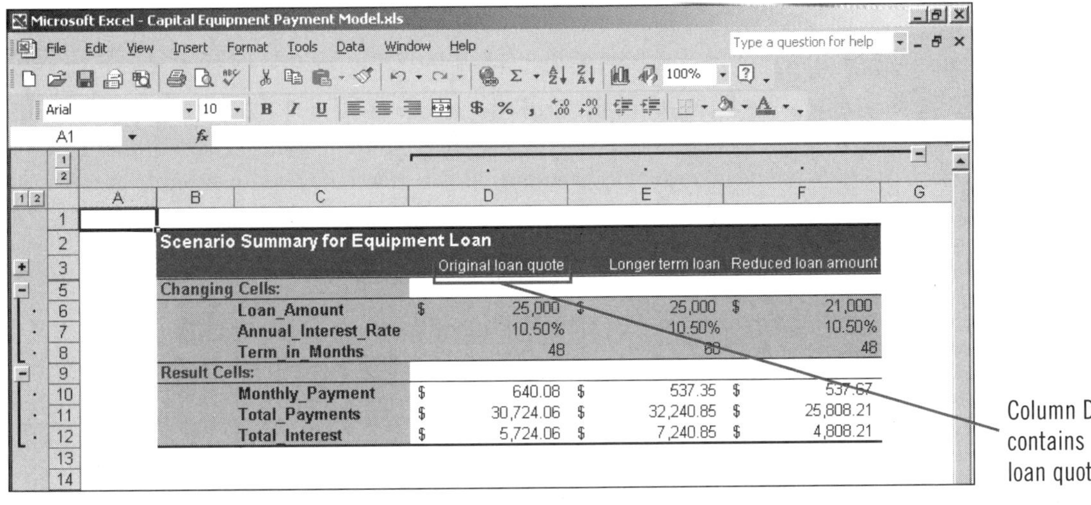

Excel 2002

Excel 2002

Projecting Figures Using a Data Table

Another way to answer what-if questions in a worksheet is by using a data table. A **data table**, sometimes referred to as a **one-input data table**, is a range of cells that shows the resulting values when one input value is varied in a formula. For example, you could use a data table to calculate your monthly mortgage payment based on several different interest rates. Now that you have completed Jim's analysis, he wants you to find out how the monthly equipment payments would change as interest rates increased by increments of 0.25%. He estimates that the lowest interest rate would be about 9.75% and the highest 11.25%. You begin by creating a table structure, with the varying interest rates listed in the left column.

Steps 1 2 3 4

1. Click the **Single Loan sheet tab**, select cell **D4**, type **Interest**, select cell **D5**, type **9.75%**, select cell **D6**, type **10.00%**; select the range **D5:D6**, drag the fill handle to select the range **D7:D11**, then release the mouse button
   With the varying interest rates (input values) listed in column D, you need to enter a formula reference to cell B9. This tells Excel to use the formula in cell B9 to calculate multiple results in column E, based on the changing interest rates in column D.
2. Click cell **E4**, type **=B9**, then click the **Enter button** on the Formula bar
   The value in cell B9, $640.08, now appears in cell E4, and the formula reference (=B9) appears in the formula bar. See Figure K-9. Because the value in cell E4 isn't a part of the data table (Excel only uses it to calculate the values in the table), you want to hide the contents of cell E4 from view.
3. With cell E4 selected, click **Format** on the menu bar, click **Cells**, click the **Number tab** in the Format Cells dialog box if necessary, click **Custom** under Category, select **;;** in the Type box, then click **OK**
   The two semicolons actually specify no format, so the cell is blank. With the table structure in place, you can now generate monthly payment values for the varying interest rates.
4. Select range **D4:E11**, click **Data** on the menu bar, then click **Table**
   You have highlighted the range that makes up the table structure. The Table dialog box opens, as shown in Figure K-10. This is where you indicate in which worksheet cell you want the varying input values (the interest rates in column D) to be substituted. Because the monthly payments formula in cell B9 (which you just referenced in cell E4) uses the annual interest rate in cell B5 as input, you'll enter a reference to cell B5. You'll place this reference in the Column input cell box, rather than in the Row input cell box, because the varying input values are arranged in a column in your data table structure.
5. Click the **Column input cell box**, click cell **B5**, then click **OK**
   Excel generates monthly payments for each interest rate. The monthly payment values appear next to the interest rates in column E. The new data and the heading in cell D4 need formatting.
6. Click cell **D4**, click the **Bold button** on the Formatting toolbar, then click the **Align Right button** on the Formatting toolbar
7. Select the range **E5:E11**, click the **Currency Style button** on the Formatting toolbar, select cell **A1**, add your name to the worksheet footer, save the workbook, then preview and print the worksheet
   The completed data table appears as shown in Figure K-11. Notice that the monthly payment amount for a 10.50% interest rate is the same as the original loan quote in cell B9. You can use this information to cross-check the values that Excel generates in data tables.

Trouble?

If you receive the message "Selection not valid," repeat Step 4, taking care to select the entire range D4:E11.

QuickTip

You cannot delete individual values in a data table; you must clear all values.

FIGURE K-9: One-input data table structure

Reference to formula in cell B9

Varying interest rates are table input values

Value displayed in cell B9

Microsoft Excel - Capital Equipment Payment Model.xls

E4 =B9

	A	B	C	D	E
1	Capital Equipment Payment Model				
2					
3					
4	Loan Amount	$ 25,000		Interest	$640.08
5	Annual Interest Rate	10.50%		9.75%	
6	Term in Months	48		10.00%	
7				10.25%	
8				10.50%	
9	Monthly Payment:	$ 640.08		10.75%	
10	Total Payments:	$ 30,724.06		11.00%	
11	Total Interest:	$ 5,724.06		11.25%	
12					

FIGURE K-10: Table dialog box

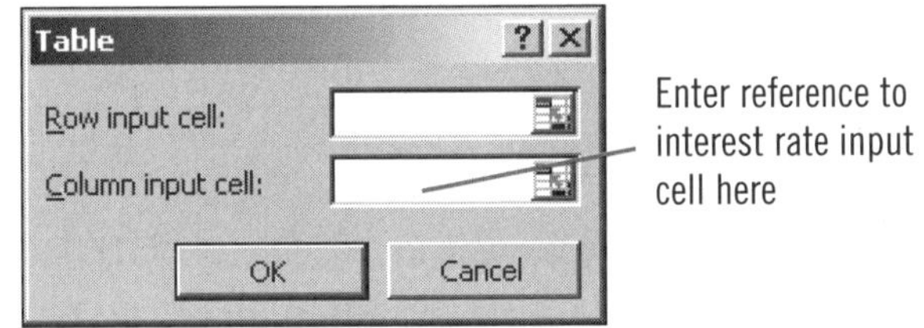

FIGURE K-11: Completed data table with resulting values

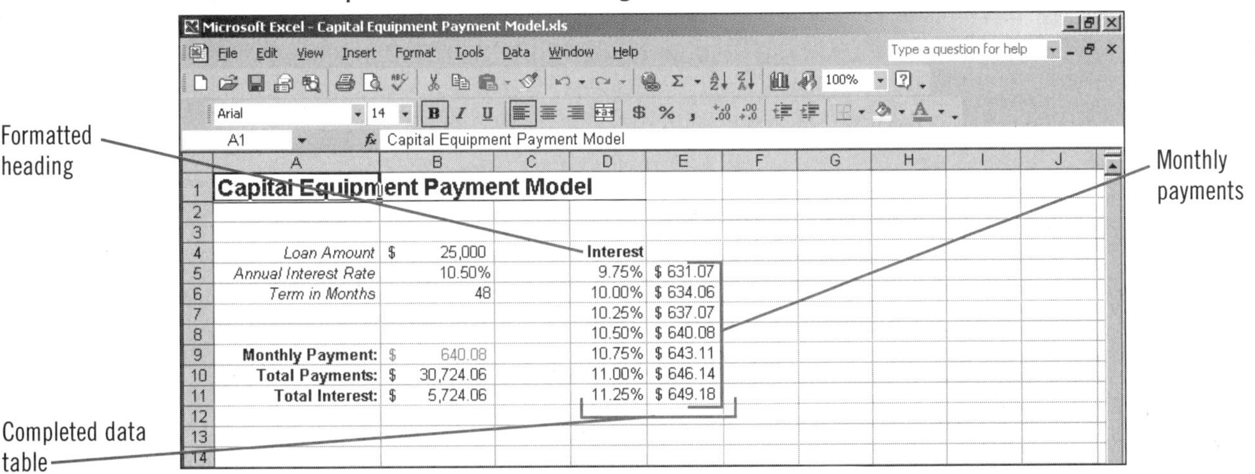

Excel 2002

Excel 2002

Creating a Two-Input Data Table

A **two-input data table** shows the resulting values when two different input values are varied in a formula. You could, for example, use a two-input data table to calculate your monthly mortgage payment based on varying interest rates and varying loan terms. In a two-input data table, different values of one input cell appear across the top row of the table, while different values of the second input cell are listed down the left column of the table. Jim wants you to use a two-input data table to see what happens if the various interest rates are applied across several different loan terms, such as 3, 4, and 5 years. You begin by changing the structure of the one-input data table to accommodate a two-input data table.

Steps

1. With the Single Loan sheet activated, move the contents of cell **D4** to cell **C7**; click cell **C8**, type **Rates**, click the **Enter button** on the Formula bar, click the **Align Right button** on the Formatting toolbar, then click the **Bold button** on the Formatting toolbar
   The left table heading is in place. You don't need the old data table values, and it is best to clear the cell formatting when you delete the old values.
2. Select the range **E4:E11**, click **Edit** on the menu bar, point to **Clear**, then click **All**
3. Click cell **F3**, type **Months**, click , click , click cell **E4**, type **36**, click , click cell **F4**, type **48**, click cell **G4**, then type **60**
   With both top row and left column values and headings in place, you are ready to reference the monthly payment formula. This is the formula Excel will use to calculate the values in the table. Because it is not part of the table (Excel uses it only to calculate the values in the table), it is best to hide the cell contents from view.
4. Click cell **D4**, type **=B9**, click , click **Format** on the menu bar, click **Cells**, in the Format Cells dialog box click the **Number tab** if necessary, click **Custom**, select **;;** in the Type box, then click **OK**
   The two-input data table structure is complete, as shown in Figure K-12. You are ready to have Excel calculate the table values.
5. Select the range **D4:G11**, click **Data** on the menu bar, then click **Table**
   The Table dialog box opens. The loan terms are arranged in a row, so you'll enter a reference to the loan term input cell (B6) in the Row input cell box. The interest rates are arranged in a column, so you'll enter a reference to the interest rate input cell (B5) in the Column input cell box.
6. With the insertion point positioned in the Row input cell text box, click cell **B6** in the worksheet, click the **Column input cell text box**, then click cell **B5**
   See Figure K-13. The row input cell (B6) references the loan term, and the column input cell (B5) references the interest rate. Now, you can generate the data table values and format the results.
7. Click **OK**, select the range **E5:G11**, click the **Currency Style button** on the Formatting toolbar, then click cell **F8**
   The resulting values appear, as shown in Figure K-14. The value in cell F8 matches the original quote: a monthly payment of $640.08 for a 48-month loan of $25,000 at a 10.50% interest rate.
8. Save the workbook, then preview and print the worksheet

Trouble?

If the Table dialog box obstructs your view of the worksheet, drag it out of the way.

FIGURE K-12: Two-input data table structure

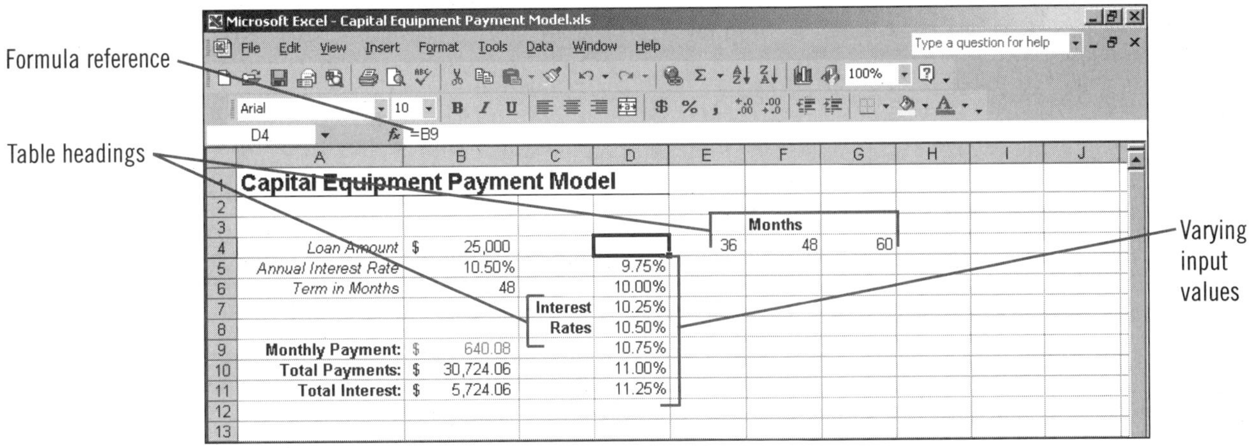

Microsoft Excel - Capital Equipment Payment Model.xls
Formula reference
Table headings
Varying input values
D4
=B9
Capital Equipment Payment Model
Months
36
48
60
Loan Amount $ 25,000
Annual Interest Rate 10.50%
Term in Months 48
Interest Rates
9.75%
10.00%
10.25%
10.50%
10.75%
11.00%
11.25%
Monthly Payment: $ 640.08
Total Payments: $ 30,724.06
Total Interest: $ 5,724.06

FIGURE K-13: Table dialog box

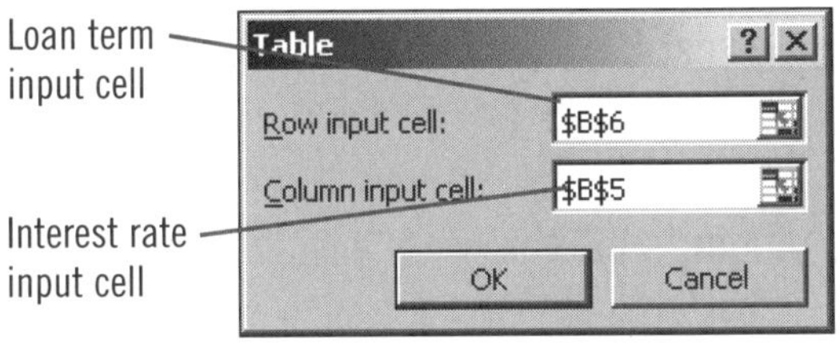

Loan term input cell
Interest rate input cell
Table
Row input cell: $B$6
Column input cell: $B$5
OK
Cancel

FIGURE K-14: Completed two-input data table

Microsoft Excel - Capital Equipment Payment Model.xls
Hidden reference to cell B9
Monthly payments for varying rates and terms
Original loan quote information
F8
{=TABLE(B6,B5)}
Capital Equipment Payment Model
Months
36
48
60
Loan Amount $ 25,000
Annual Interest Rate 10.50%
Term in Months 48
Interest Rates
9.75% $ 803.75 $ 631.07 $ 528.11
10.00% $ 806.68 $ 634.06 $ 531.18
10.25% $ 809.62 $ 637.07 $ 534.26
10.50% $ 812.56 $ 640.08 $ 537.35
10.75% $ 815.51 $ 643.11 $ 540.45
11.00% $ 818.47 $ 646.14 $ 543.56
11.25% $ 821.43 $ 649.18 $ 546.68
Monthly Payment: $ 640.08
Total Payments: $ 30,724.06
Total Interest: $ 5,724.06

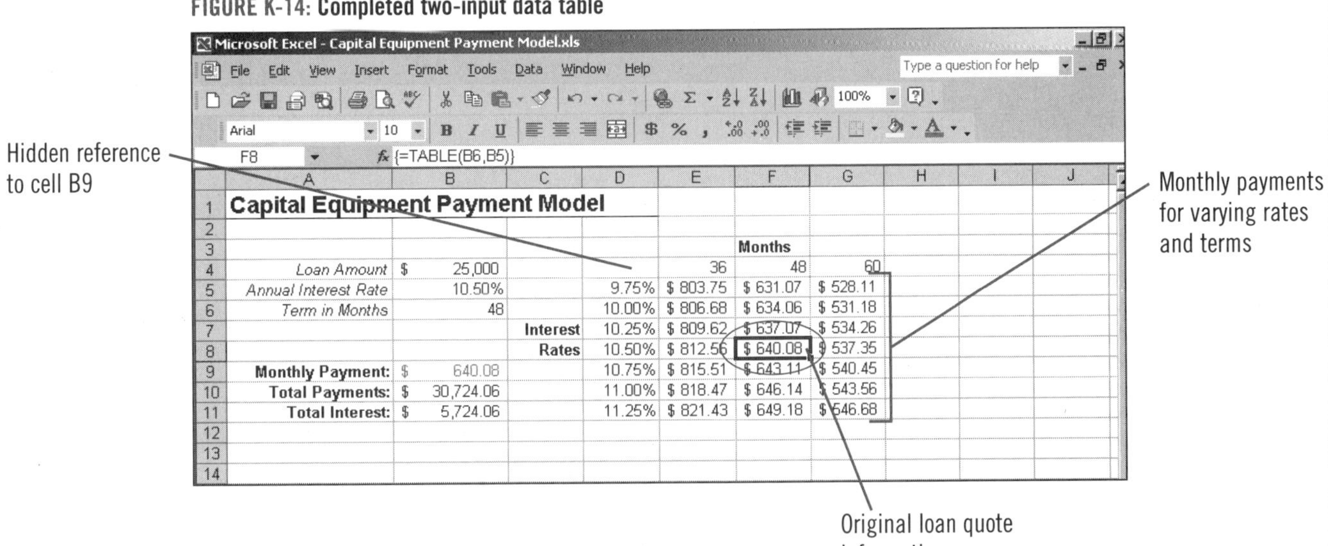

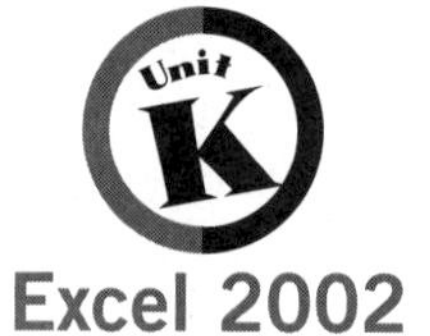

Excel 2002

Using Goal Seek

You can think of goal seeking as a what-if analysis in reverse. In a what-if analysis, you might try many sets of values to achieve a certain solution. To **goal seek**, you specify a solution, then find the input value that produces the answer you want. "Backing into" a solution in this way, sometimes referred to as **backsolving**, can save a significant amount of time. For example, you can use Goal Seek to determine how many units must be sold to reach a particular sales goal or to determine the expenses that must be cut to meet a budget. After reviewing his data table, Jim has a follow-up question: How much money could MediaLoft borrow if the company wanted to keep the total payment amount of all the equipment to $28,000? You use Goal Seek to answer his question.

Steps

1. **On the Single Loan worksheet, click cell B10**
   The first step in using Goal Seek is to select a goal cell. A **goal cell** contains a formula in which you can substitute values to find a specific value, or goal. You use cell B10 as the goal cell because it contains the formula for total payments.
2. **Click Tools on the menu bar, then click Goal Seek**
   The Goal Seek dialog box opens. The Set cell box contains a reference to cell B10, the Total Payments cell you selected in Step 1. You need to indicate that the figure in cell B10 should not exceed 28000.
3. **Click the To value text box, then type 28000**
   The 28000 figure represents the desired solution you want to reach by substituting different values in the goal cell.
4. **Click the By changing cell box, then click cell B4**
   You have specified that you want cell B4 to change to reach the 28000 solution. See Figure K-15.
5. **Click OK, then move the dialog box as needed so that column B is visible**
   The Goal Seek Status dialog box opens with the following message: "Goal Seeking with Cell B10 found a solution." By changing the Loan Amount figure in cell B4 from $25,000 to $22,783, Goal Seek achieves a Total Payments goal of $28,000.
6. **Click OK**
   Changing the loan amount value in cell B4 changes all the values in the worksheet, including the data table. See Figure K-16.
7. **Save the workbook, then preview and print the worksheet**

QuickTip

Before you select another command, you can return the worksheet to its status prior to the Goal Seek by pressing [Ctrl][Z].

FIGURE K-15: Completed Goal Seek dialog box

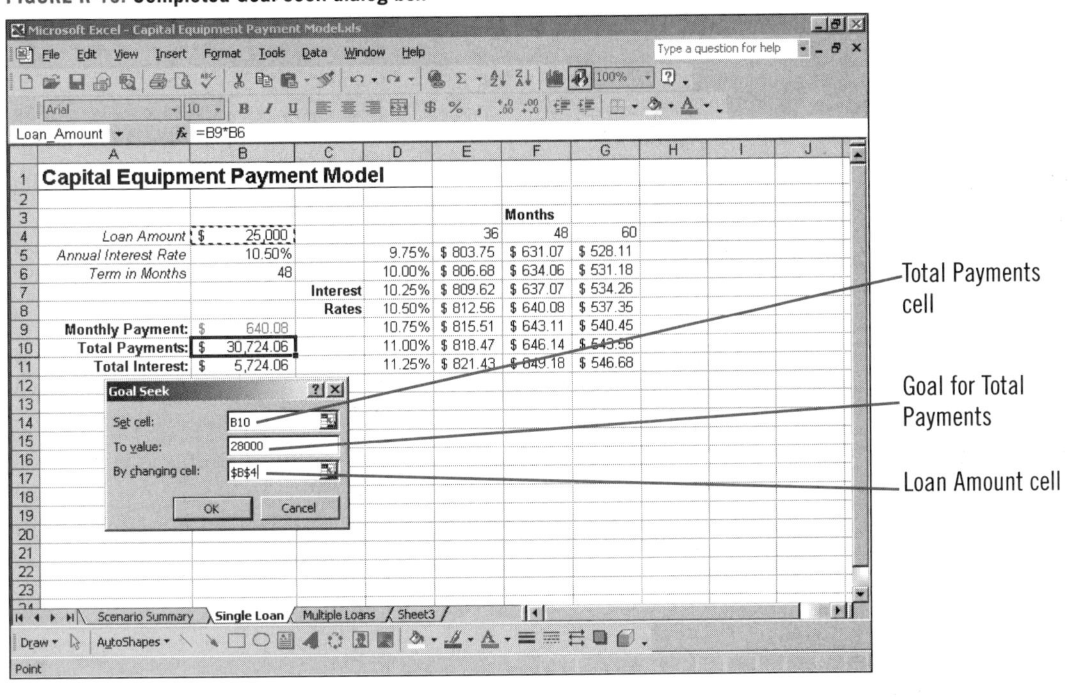

FIGURE K-16: Worksheet with new values

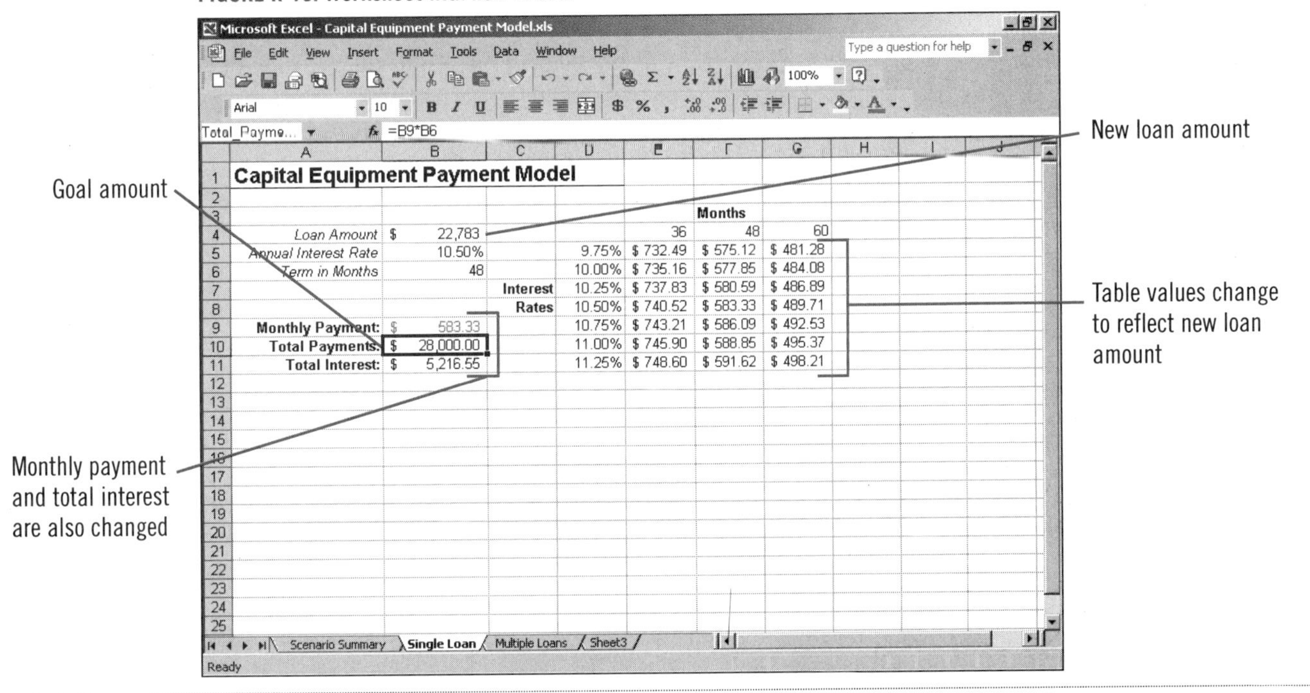

Excel 2002

Setting up a Complex What-If Analysis with Solver

The Excel Solver finds the most appropriate value for a formula by changing the input values in the worksheet. The cell containing the formula is called the **target cell**. As you learned earlier, cells containing the values that change are called changing cells. Solver is helpful when you need to perform a complex what-if analysis involving multiple input values or when the input values must conform to specific constraints. After seeing the analysis of interest rates and payments, Jim decides to address the vehicle purchase order for the MediaLoft shuttle service. He decides that the best plan is to purchase a combination of vans, sedans, and compact cars that will accommodate a total of 44 passengers. The total monthly payments for the vehicles should not exceed $3,700. You use Solver to help Jim find the best possible combination of vehicles.

Steps

Trouble?

If Solver is not on your Tools menu, install the Solver add-in. Click Tools, click Add-Ins, then select the Solver Add-in check box. See your technical support person for assistance.

Trouble?

If your Solver Parameters dialog box has entries in the By Changing Cells box or in the Subject to the Constraints box, click Reset All, click OK, then continue with Step 3.

1. Click the **Multiple Loans sheet tab**
   See Figure K-17. This worksheet is designed to calculate the total loan amount, total monthly payments, and total number of passengers for a combination of vans, sedans, and compact cars. It assumes an annual interest rate of 10% and a loan term of 48 months. You will use Solver to change the purchase quantities in cells B7:D7 (the changing cells) to achieve your target of 44 passengers in cell B15 (the target cell). Your solution will include a constraint on cell B14, specifying that the total monthly payments must be less than or equal to $3,700.
2. Click **Tools**, then click **Solver**
   The Solver Parameters dialog box opens. This is where you indicate the target cell, the changing cells, and the constraints under which you want Solver to work. You begin by changing the value in the target cell.
3. With the **Set Target Cell text box** selected in the Solver Parameters dialog box, click cell **B15** in the worksheet, click the **Value of option button**, double-click the **Value of text box,** then type **44**
4. Select the text in the By Changing Cells text box, then select cells **B7:D7** in the worksheet
   You need to specify the constraints on the worksheet values in the Add Constraint dialog box.
5. Click **Add,** with the insertion point in the Cell Reference text box in the Add Constraint dialog box, click cell **B14** in the worksheet, click the list arrow, select <=, click the **Constraint text box**, type **3700**
   See Figure K-18. The Add Constraint dialog box specifies that cell B14 should contain a value that is less than or equal to 3700. Next, you need to specify that the purchase quantities should be as close as possible to integers.
6. Click **Add**, with the insertion point in the Cell Reference text box, select range **B7:D7** in the worksheet, click the list arrow, then select **int**
   Integer appears in the Constraint text box. Next, you need to specify that the purchase quantities should be greater than or equal to zero.
7. Click **Add**, with the insertion point in the Cell Reference box, select cells **B7:D7**, select >=, click the **Constraint text box**, type **0**, then click **OK**
   The Solver Parameters dialog box reappears, with the constraints listed as shown in Figure K-19. In the next lesson, you will run Solver and generate an answer report.

FIGURE K-17: Worksheet set up for a complex what-if analysis

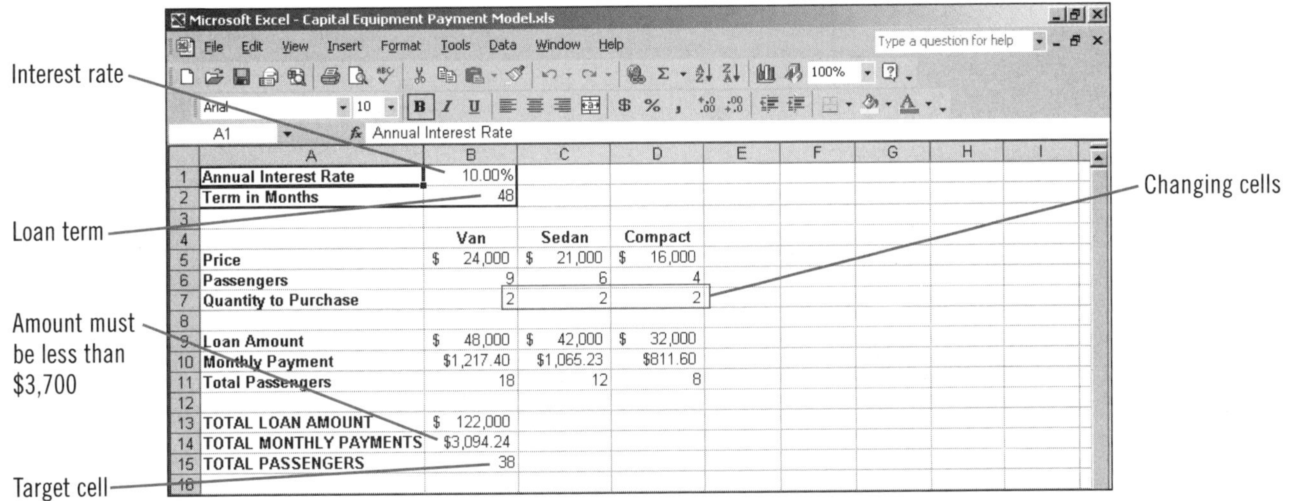

FIGURE K-18: Adding constraints

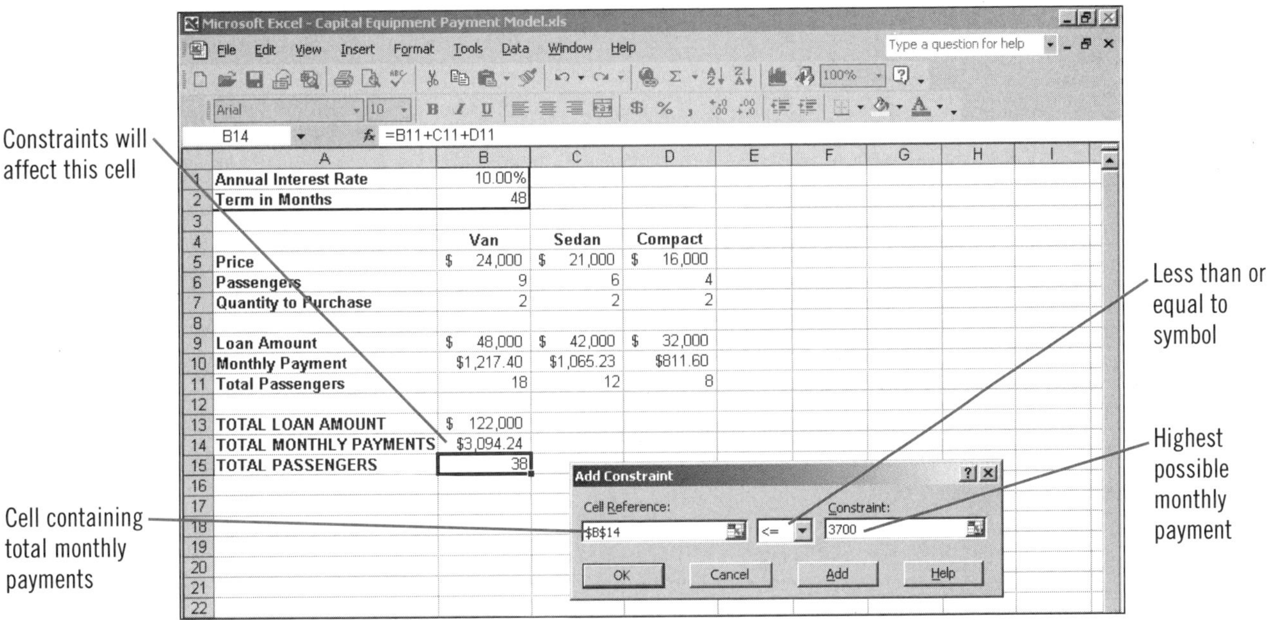

FIGURE K-19: Completed Solver Parameters dialog box

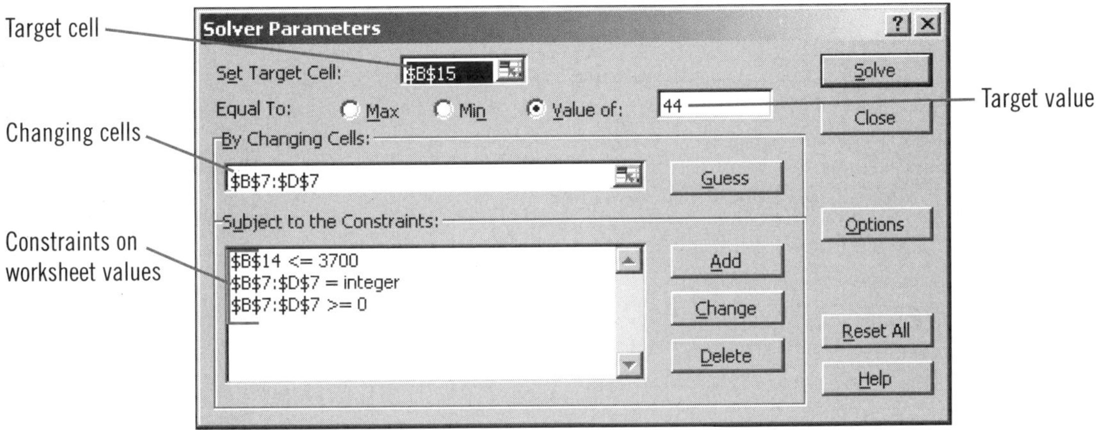

Excel 2002

Running Solver and Generating an Answer Report

After entering all the parameters in the Solver Parameters dialog box, you can run Solver to find a solution. In some cases, Solver may not be able to find a solution that meets all of your constraints; then you would need to enter new constraints and try again. Once Solver finds a solution, you can choose to create a special report displaying the solution. You have finished entering the parameters in the Solver Parameters dialog box. Jim wants you to run Solver and create an answer report.

1. Make sure your Solver Parameter dialog box matches Figure K-19 in the previous lesson
2. Click **Solve**
   After a moment, the Solver Results dialog box opens, indicating that Solver has found a solution. See Figure K-20. The solution values appear in the worksheet, but you decide to move them to a special Answer Report and display the original values in the worksheet.
3. Click the **Restore Original Values option button**, click **Answer** in the Reports list box, then click **OK**
   The Solver Results dialog box closes, and the original values appear in the worksheet. The Answer Report appears on a separate sheet.
4. Click the **Answer Report 1 sheet tab**
   The Answer Report displays the solution to the vehicle-purchasing problem, as shown in Figure K-21. To accommodate 44 passengers and keep the monthly payments under $3,700, you need to purchase two vans, three sedans, and two compact cars. Solver's solution includes two long decimals, in cells E8 and E14, that are so small as to be insignificant. Additionally, the Original Value column in the Answer Report doesn't contain any useful information.
5. Click cell **E8**, press **[Ctrl]**, click cell **E14**, click the **Decrease Decimal button** on the Formatting toolbar until the cells display no decimal places, right-click the **column D header**, then click **Delete** in the shortcut menu
   The Answer Report displays the Final Values for the number of vehicles as integers. See Figure K-22.
6. Press **[Ctrl][Home]**, enter your name in the worksheet footer, save the workbook, then preview and print the worksheet
   You've successfully found the best combination of vehicles using Solver. The settings you specified in the Solver Parameters for the Multiple Loans worksheet are saved along with the workbook.
7. Close the workbook and exit Excel

FIGURE K-20: Solver Results dialog box

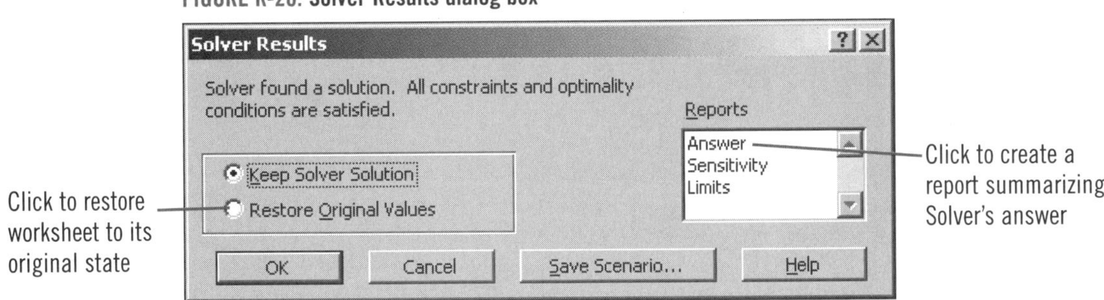

FIGURE K-21: Answer Report

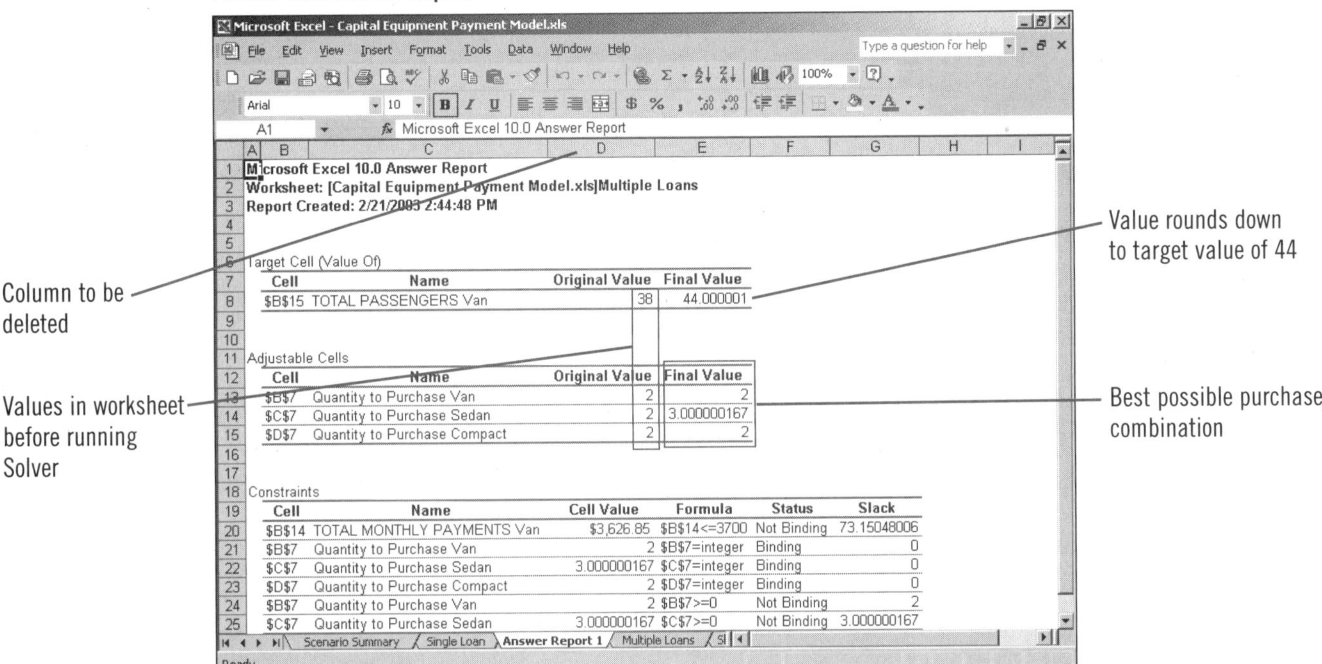

FIGURE K-22: Completed Answer Report

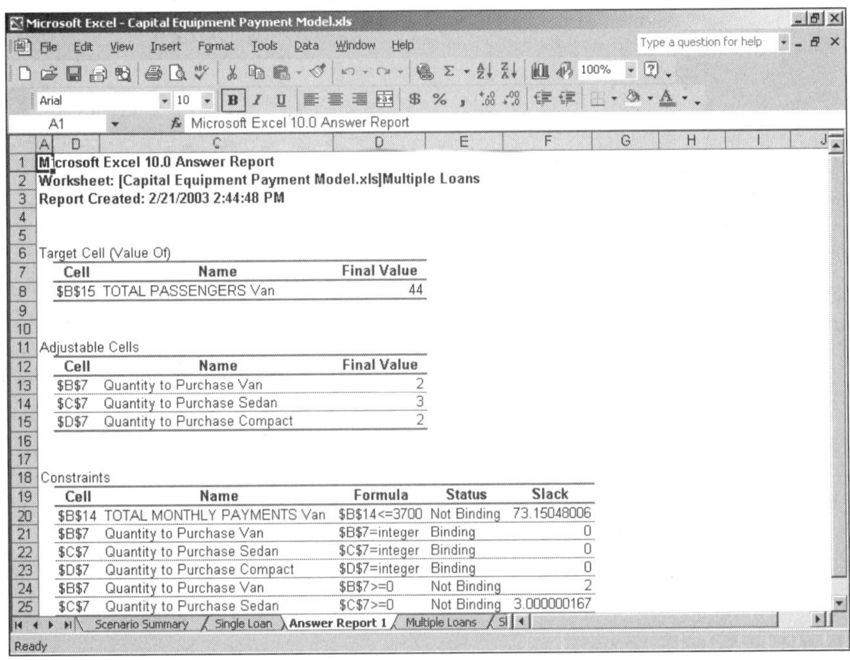

Excel 2002

Practice

▶ Concepts Review

Label each element of the Excel screen shown in Figure K-23.

FIGURE K-23

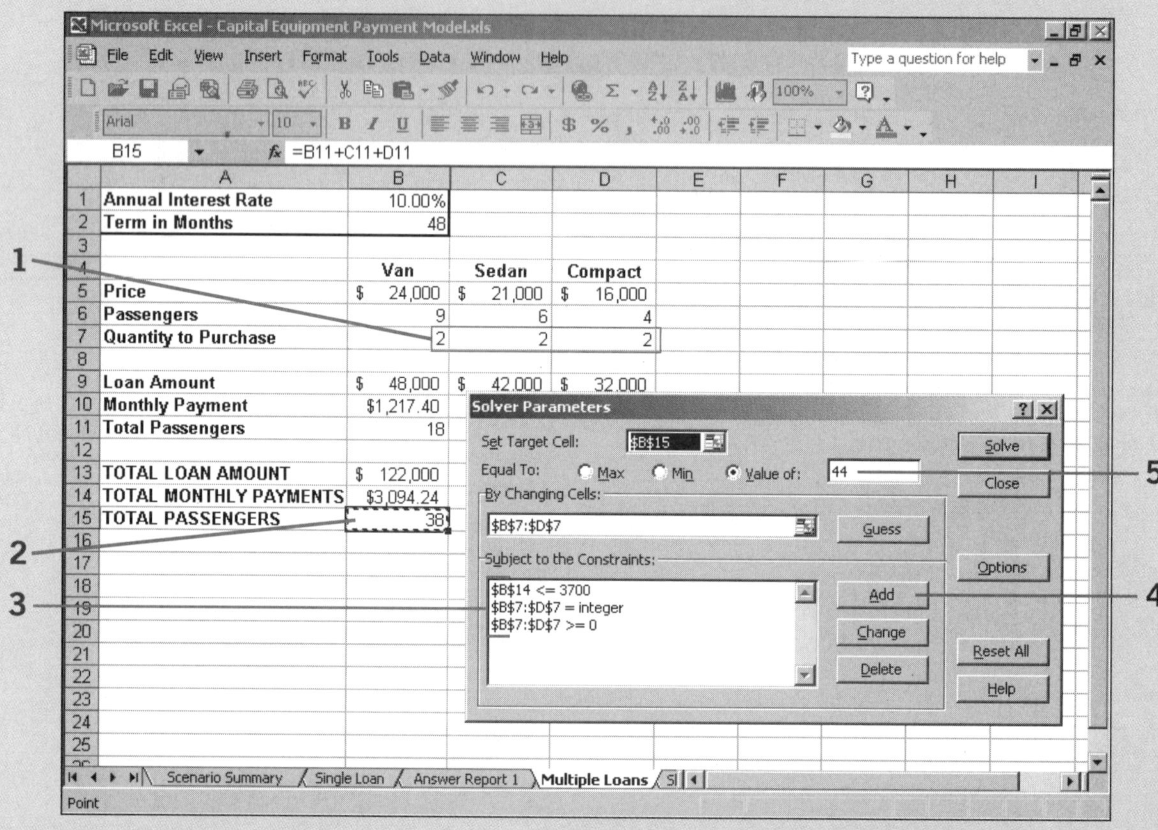

Match each term with the statement that describes it.

6. Two-input data table
7. Scenario summary
8. Goal Seek
9. One-input data table
10. Solver

a. Add-in that helps you solve complex what-if scenarios with multiple input values
b. Separate sheet with results from the worksheet's scenarios
c. Generates values resulting from varying two sets of changing values in a formula
d. Helps you backsolve what-if scenarios
e. Generates values resulting from varying one set of changing values in a formula

Select the best answer from the list of choices.

11. To hide the contents of a cell from view, you can use the custom number format:

a. ;;
b. ""
c. —
d. Blank

12. The integer constraint can be added to cells in the Solver Parameters dialog box by choosing:

a. **.00
b. **.**
c. **
d. Int

13. **When you use Goal Seek, you specify a ______________, then find the values that produce it.**
   a. Changing value
   b. Solution
   c. Row input cell
   d. Column input cell
14. **In Solver, the cell containing the formula is called the:**
   a. Changing cell.
   b. Input cell.
   c. Output cell.
   d. Target cell.

Skills Review

1. **Define a what-if analysis.**
   a. Start Excel, open the Project File EX K-2 from the drive and folder where your Project Files are stored, then save it as **Capital Equipment Repair Models**. Display the Cappuccino Machine Repair worksheet.
   b. State the purpose of the worksheet model.
   c. Locate the data input cells.
   d. Locate any dependent cells.
   e. Write three questions that this what-if analysis model could answer.
2. **Track a what-if analysis with Scenario Manager.**
   a. Set up the most likely scenario with the current data input values: Select the range B3:B5, then create a scenario called Most Likely.
   b. Add a scenario called Best Case using the same changing cells, but change the Labor cost per hr. in the $B$3 text box to **60**, change the Parts cost per job in the $B$4 text box to **55**, then change the Hrs. per job value in cell $B$5 to **1**. Add the scenario to the list.
   c. Add a scenario called Worst Case. For this scenario, change the Labor cost per hr. in the $B$3 text box to **80**, change the Parts cost per job in the $B$4 text box **80**, then change the Hrs. per job in the $B$5 text box to 3.
   d. If necessary, drag the Scenario Manager dialog box to the right until columns A and B are visible.
   e. Show the Worst Case scenario results.
   f. Show the Best Case scenario results. Finally, display the Most Likely scenario results.
   g. Close the Scenario Manager dialog box.
   h. Save the workbook.
3. **Generate a scenario summary.**
   a. Create names for the input value cells and the dependent cell in the range A3:B7 (based on the left column).
   b. Verify that the names were created.
   c. Create a Scenario Summary report using the Cost to complete job value in cell B7 as the result cell.
   d. Edit the title of the Summary report in cell B2 to read **Scenario Summary for Cappuccino Machine Repair**.
   e. Delete the Current Values column.
   f. Delete the notes beginning in cell B11.
   g. Return to cell A1, enter your name in the sheet footer, save the workbook, then preview and print the Scenario Summary report in landscape orientation.
4. **Project figures using a data table.**
   a. Click the Cappuccino Machine Repair sheet tab.
   b. Enter the label **Labor $** in cell D3.
   c. Format the label so that it is boldfaced and right-aligned.
   d. In cell D4, enter **60**; then in cell D5, enter **65**.
   e. Select range D4:D5, then use the fill handle to extend the series to cell D9.
   f. Reference the job cost formula in the upper-right corner of the table structure: In cell E3, enter **=B7**.
   g. Format the contents of cell E3 as hidden, using the ;; Custom formatting type on the Number tab of the Format Cells dialog box.

h. Generate the new job costs based on the varying labor costs: Select range D3:E9 and create a data table. In the Table dialog box, make cell B3 the Column input cell.
i. Format range E4:E9 as currency.
j. Enter your name in the worksheet footer, save the workbook, preview the worksheet, then print it in portrait orientation.

5. **Create a two-input data table.**
   a. Move the contents of cell D3 to cell C6.
   b. Delete the contents of range E4:E9 but do not clear the formatting.
   c. Format cell E3 using the General category on the Number tab of the Format Cells dialog box, then move the contents of cell E3 to cell D3.
   d. Format the contents of cell D3 as hidden, using the ;; Custom formatting type on the Number tab of the Format Cells dialog box.
   e. Enter **Hrs. per job** in cell F2, and format it so it is boldfaced.
   f. Enter **1.5** in cell E3, enter **2** in cell F3, then enter **2.5** in cell G3.
   g. Select range D3:G9 and create a data table, making cell B5 the row input cell and cell B3 the column input cell.
   h. Format the range F4:G9 as currency.
   i. Save the workbook, preview the worksheet, then print it in portrait orientation.
6. **Use Goal Seek.**
   a. Determine what the parts would have to cost so that the cost to complete the job is $150. Click cell B7, and open the Goal Seek dialog box.
   b. Enter a job cost of **150** as the To value, and **B4** (the Parts cost) as the By changing cell; write down the parts cost that Goal Seek finds, and return to the worksheet.
   c. Use **[Ctrl][Z]** to reset the parts cost to its original value.
   d. Enter the cost of the parts in cell B14.
   e. Determine what the labor would have to cost so that the cost to complete the job is $125. Enter the result in cell B15.
   f. Save the workbook, preview the worksheet, then print it in portrait orientation.
7. **Perform a complex what-if analysis with Solver and generate an Answer Report.**
   a. Click the Vehicle Repair sheet tab to make it active, then open the Solver dialog box.
   b. Make B16 the target cell, with a target value of 160.
   c. Use cells B6:D6 as the changing cells.
   d. Specify that cell B14 must be greater than or equal to 5000.
   e. Specify that cell B15 must be greater than or equal to 6000.
   f. Use Solver to find a solution.
   g. Generate an Answer Report and restore the original values to the worksheet.
   h. Edit the Answer Report to delete the original values column.
   i. Enter your name in the report footer, save the workbook, preview then print the Answer Report in portrait orientation.
   j. Close the workbook then exit Excel.

► Independent Challenge 1

You are a sales representative for Ed-Toys, a toy company located in Minneapolis, Minnesota. Your sales territory includes five states in the Midwest. You submit a monthly expense report detailing car expenses calculated on a mileage basis. Your vehicle expenses have been increasing as your sales territory has gotten larger. Your sales manager has asked you to research the monthly cost of purchasing a company car to see if it is more economical than expensing vehicle costs on a mileage basis. You have created a preliminary worksheet model to determine the monthly payments for a $20,000 car, based on several different interest rates and loan terms using data from the company's bank. You will compare two-, three-, and four-year car loans. Using Scenario Manager, you will create the following three scenarios: a four-year loan at 8.97%; a three-year loan at 8%; and a two-year loan at 7.5%. You will create a Scenario Summary report for your manager showing the payment details.

a. Start Excel, open the Project File EX K-3 from the drive and folder where your Project Files are stored, then save it as **Car Loan Payment Model**.

b. Create cell names in column B based on the labels in column A by selecting the range A4:B11 and using the Name option on the Insert menu.

c. Using Scenario Manager and assuming a loan amount of $20,000, create the following three scenarios:

Scenario Name	Interest Rate	Term
8.97 percent	.0897	48
8 percent	.08	36
7.5 percent	.075	24

Use cells B5:B6 as the changing cells for each scenario. Enter the interest rate in the first Scenario values text box and the number of months in the second Scenario values text box.

d. Show each scenario to make sure it performs as intended, then display the 8.97 percent scenario.

e. Generate a scenario summary titled **Scenario Summary for $20,000 Car Purchase**. Use cells B9:B11 as the Result cells.

f. Delete the Current Values column. Delete the notes at the bottom of the report.

g. Enter your name in the Scenario Summary footer, save the workbook, preview the scenario summary, then print it in portrait orientation.

h. Close the workbook, then exit Excel.

Independent Challenge 2

You are a senior staff associate at Capital Adventures, a venture capital firm located in Albany, New York. One of the vice presidents has asked you to prepare a loan summary report for a software development company seeking capital for a business expansion. You need to develop a model to show what the monthly payments would be for a $700,000 loan, over 5- and 10-year terms, with interest rates ranging in 0.25% increments. You will first create a two-input data table that shows the results of varying loan term and interest rates, then you will use goal seek to specify a total payment amount for this loan application.

a. Start Excel, open the Project File EX K-4 from the drive and folder where your Project Files are stored, then save it as **Capital Loan Payment Model**.

b. Reference cell B9 in cell D4, and format the contents of cell D4 as hidden.(*Hint:* If the ;; custom type is not listed, enter it in the Type: text box.)

c. Using cells D4:F13, create a data table structure with varying interest rates for 5- and 10-year terms. Use cells D5:D13 for the interest rates, with 6% as the lowest possible rate and 8% the highest. Vary the rates in between by 0.25%. Use Figure K-24 as a guide.

FIGURE K-24

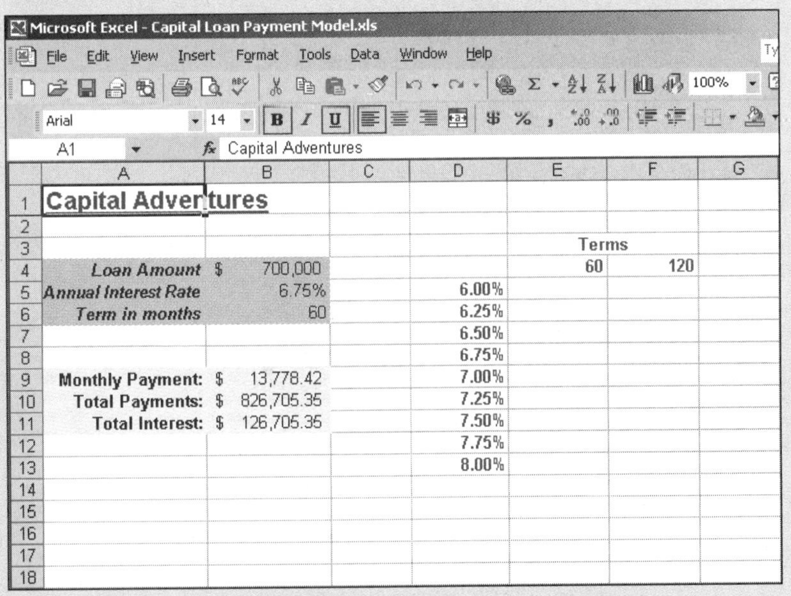

Microsoft Excel - Capital Loan Payment Model.xls

	A	B	C	D	E	F	G
1	Capital Adventures						
2							
3					Terms		
4	Loan Amount	$ 700,000			60	120	
5	Annual Interest Rate	6.75%		6.00%			
6	Term in months	60		6.25%			
7				6.50%			
8				6.75%			
9	Monthly Payment:	$ 13,778.42		7.00%			
10	Total Payments:	$ 826,705.35		7.25%			
11	Total Interest:	$ 126,705.35		7.50%			
12				7.75%			
13				8.00%			
14							
15							
16							
17							
18							

d. Generate the two-input data table that shows the effect of varying interest rates and loan terms on the monthly payments. Use cell B6, Term in Months, as the Row input cell, and cell B5, the Annual Interest Rate, as the Column input cell. Format cells E5:F13 as Currency with two decimal places.

e. Click cell **B10** and use Goal Seek to find the interest rate necessary for a total payment amount of $800,000. Use cell B5, the Annual Interest Rate, as the By changing cell.

f. Enter your name in the worksheet footer, save the workbook, then preview and print the worksheet.

g. Close the workbook, then exit Excel.

► Independent Challenge 3

You are the owner of Computer City, a small computer store, where you custom configure PCs to sell to the home and business markets. You have created a PC production financial model to determine the costs and profits associated with your three most popular configurations: PC-1, PC-2, and PC-3. You want to show how the hourly cost affects total profit for each PC model your company produces. To do this, you decide to use a one-input data table. You also want to do a what-if analysis regarding the effect of hours per unit on total profit. You decide to solve the problem by using Solver, where you can specify multiple constraints for the solution. Finally, you will produce an answer report summarizing your analysis.

a. Start Excel, open the Project File EX K-5 from the drive and folder where your Project Files are stored, then save it as **PC Production Model**.

b. Create a data table structure with varying hourly costs, in $5 increments, from $15 to $45 in cells C11:C17. Reference the profit formulas in cells H6:H8 across the top of the table in cells D10:F10. (*Hint:* Although this is a one-input data table, you will have multiple columns, one for each model's profit formula.) Use Figure K-25 as a guide.

c. Generate the one-input data table that shows the effect of varying hourly cost on the profitability of each computer configuration. Select cells C10:F17 for the data table and use Cell B2 as the Column input cell.

d. Format cells D10:F17 as Currency with two decimal places. Boldface the data table row that contains the same values as the total profit figures in cells H6:H8 (the current values).

e. Use Solver to set the total profit of all configurations to $22,000. Use the hours per unit, cells B6:B8, as the changing cells. Specify that cells B6:B8 must be greater than or equal to 0 and less than or equal to 5.

f. Generate an Answer Report and restore the original values in the worksheet.

g. Enter your name in the model footer and the Answer Report footer, save the workbook, preview then print both the model worksheet and the Answer Report in landscape orientation.

h. Close the workbook then exit Excel.

FIGURE K-25

Microsoft Excel - PC Production Model.xls

A1: PC Production Model for August 2003

	A	B	C	D	E	F	G	H
1	PC Production Model for August 2003							
2	Hourly cost	30						
3	Resource cost	67						
4								
5		Hrs per Unit	Resources per Unit	Cost to Produce	Retail Price	Unit Profit	Units Produced	Total Profit
6	PC-1	4.00	6	522	925	403	13	5239
7	PC-2	3.00	9	693	1200	507	15	7605
8	PC-3	5.00	12	954	1,600	646	12	7,752
9	TOTAL			PC-1 Profit	PC-2 Profit	PC-3 Profit		20,596
10				$5,239.00	$7,605.00	$ 7,752.00		
11			$ 15					
12			$ 20					
13		Hourly	$ 25					
14		Cost	$ 30					
15			$ 35					
16			$ 40					
17			$ 45					

Independent Challenge 4

You are the VP of marketing for E-Learn, a distance learning consulting firm. You will be relocating to Toronto, Ontario to set up the first Canadian office. Since you will be there for a minimum of two years, you are considering purchasing a home. You have $20,000 saved for a down payment, and you are looking for a home in the $220,000 range. You will research mortgage rates for Toronto banks on the Web, finding fixed and variable rates. You will then enter information about a bank and its rates in an Excel worksheet and use the data to estimate your monthly housing payments. You have created a preliminary worksheet model to determine monthly payments for fixed and variable rates. Since rates fluctuate, you need to investigate the effect of rate changes on your monthly payments.

Go to the AltaVista search engine at www.altavista.com then enter "Toronto AND Bank" in the Search box. You can also use Yahoo!, Excite, Infoseek, or another search engine of your choice. Some search engines use & or + in place of AND in the search text.

a. Use the search engine links to find the fixed and variable rate for a 25-year loan at a Toronto bank. (*Hint:* The Royal Bank in Toronto, Canada, at www.royalbank.com, has a link for rates.)

b. Start Excel, open the Project File EX K-6 from the drive and folder where your Project Files are stored, then save it as **Mortgage Research**.

c. Use the Fixed and Variable worksheets to enter the name of a bank in Toronto and its current fixed and variable rate for a 25-year mortgage.

d. Create a data table structure for each worksheet with varying interest rates for 25- and 30-year terms. Assume that the 30-year rate at the bank is the same as the 25-year rate. Begin with a rate 1% lower than the current rate, as the lowest possible rate. Make the highest possible interest rate 1% greater than the current rate, and vary the rates in between by 0.25%. Use Figure K-26 as a guide.

e. Reference the monthly payment cell in each table and format it as hidden.

f. Generate a two-input data table for each worksheet. Use cell B5 as the Column input cell and B6 as the Row input cell.

g. You decide to go with a variable rate mortgage, and you want to limit your housing payments to $1,200 per month. You can accomplish this by using some of your savings to increase your down payment. Find the loan amount for a variable rate mortgage that would result in monthly payments of $1,200. Use Goal seek to find the answer and note it on the Variable worksheet. Restore the Variable worksheet to its original values.

h. Enter your name in the footers of both worksheets, save the workbook, preview the worksheets, then print them in portrait orientation.

i. Close the workbook then exit Excel.

FIGURE K-26

Microsoft Excel - Mortgage Research.xls

A1 — Mortgage Loan Payment Model

	A	B	C	D	E	F	G
1	Mortgage Loan Payment Model						
2	BANK:	ROYAL BANK					
3					Terms		
4	Loan Amount	$ 200,000			300	360	
5	Annual Interest Rate	8.75%		7.75%			
6	Term in Months	300		8.00%			
7				8.25%			
8				8.50%			
9	Monthly Payment:	$ 1,644.29		8.75%			
10	Total Payments:	$ 493,286.18	Rates	9.00%			
11	Total Interest:	$ 293,286.18		9.25%			
12				9.50%			
13				9.75%			

FIXED / VARIABLE / Sheet3

Ready

Visual Workshop

Create the worksheet shown in Figure K-27. Make sure to generate all three tables as data tables. Save the workbook as **Notebook Payment Model**. Add your name to the footer, then preview and print the worksheet. Print the worksheet again with the formulas displayed.

FIGURE K-27

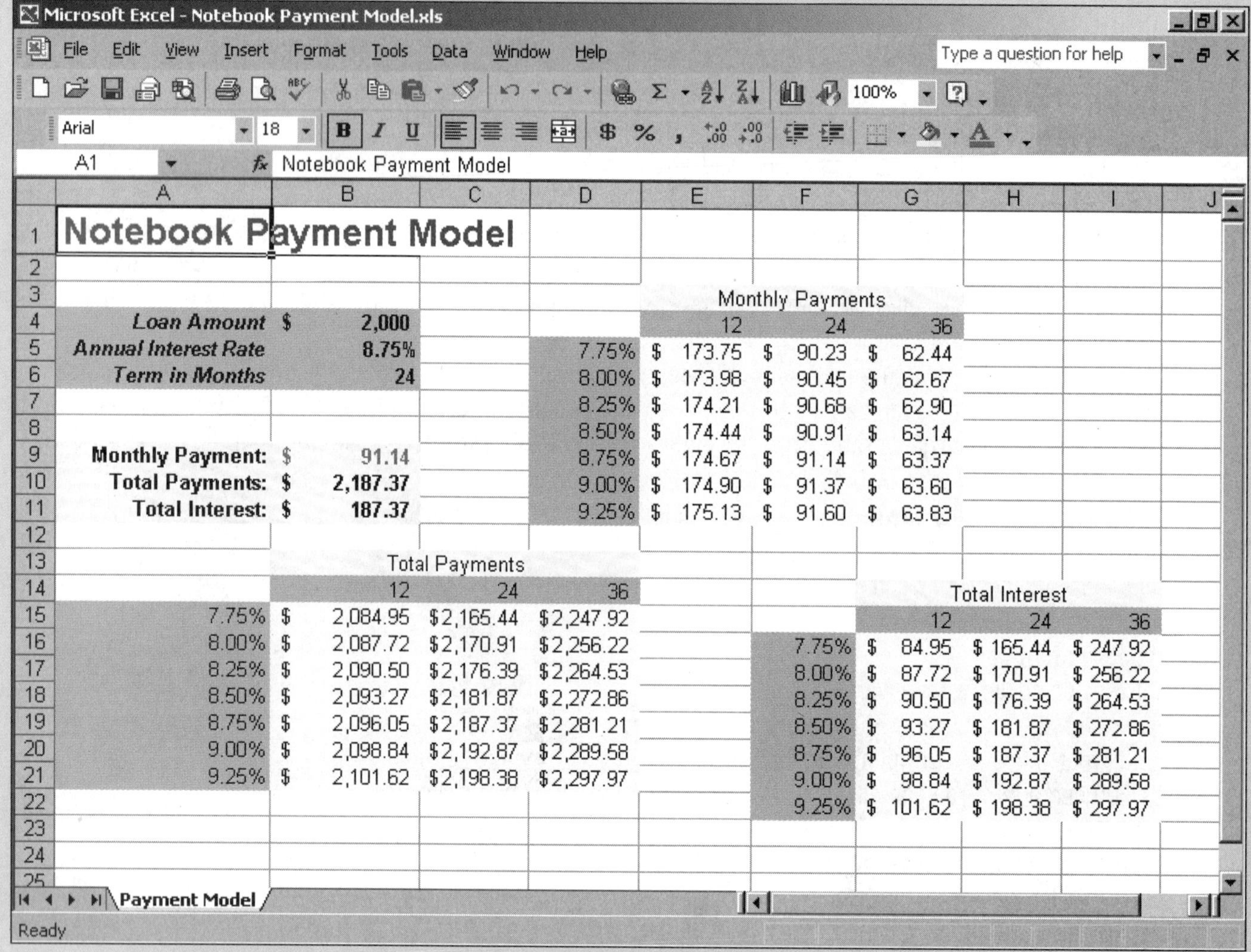

Microsoft Excel - Notebook Payment Model.xls

A1 — Notebook Payment Model

Notebook Payment Model

Loan Amount	$ 2,000
Annual Interest Rate	8.75%
Term in Months	24
Monthly Payment:	$ 91.14
Total Payments:	$ 2,187.37
Total Interest:	$ 187.37

Monthly Payments

	12	24	36
7.75%	$ 173.75	$ 90.23	$ 62.44
8.00%	$ 173.98	$ 90.45	$ 62.67
8.25%	$ 174.21	$ 90.68	$ 62.90
8.50%	$ 174.44	$ 90.91	$ 63.14
8.75%	$ 174.67	$ 91.14	$ 63.37
9.00%	$ 174.90	$ 91.37	$ 63.60
9.25%	$ 175.13	$ 91.60	$ 63.83

Total Payments

	12	24	36
7.75%	$ 2,084.95	$2,165.44	$2,247.92
8.00%	$ 2,087.72	$2,170.91	$2,256.22
8.25%	$ 2,090.50	$2,176.39	$2,264.53
8.50%	$ 2,093.27	$2,181.87	$2,272.86
8.75%	$ 2,096.05	$2,187.37	$2,281.21
9.00%	$ 2,098.84	$2,192.87	$2,289.58
9.25%	$ 2,101.62	$2,198.38	$2,297.97

Total Interest

	12	24	36
7.75%	$ 84.95	$ 165.44	$ 247.92
8.00%	$ 87.72	$ 170.91	$ 256.22
8.25%	$ 90.50	$ 176.39	$ 264.53
8.50%	$ 93.27	$ 181.87	$ 272.86
8.75%	$ 96.05	$ 187.37	$ 281.21
9.00%	$ 98.84	$ 192.87	$ 289.58
9.25%	$ 101.62	$ 198.38	$ 297.97

Payment Model

Ready

Excel 2002

Unit L

Analyzing Data with PivotTables

Objectives

- Plan and design a PivotTable report
- MOUS Create a PivotTable report
- Change the summary function of a PivotTable report
- Analyze three-dimensional data
- Update a PivotTable report
- Change the structure and format of a PivotTable report
- MOUS Create a PivotChart report
- Use the GETPIVOTDATA function

With the Excel **PivotTable** feature, you can summarize selected data in a worksheet, then list and display that data in a table format. The interactive quality of a PivotTable allows you to freely rearrange, or "pivot," parts of the table structure around the data and summarize any data values within the table. You also can designate a PivotTable page field that lets you view list items three-dimensionally, as if they were arranged in a stack of pages. There are two PivotTable features in Excel: PivotTable reports and PivotChart reports. In this unit, you will plan, design, create, update, and change the layout and format of a PivotTable report. You will also add a page field to a PivotTable report, then create a PivotChart report. The Sales Department is getting ready for its annual meeting and the eastern region sales manager has asked Jim Fernandez to develop an analysis of products sold in its Boston, New York, and Washington, DC stores over the past year. Jim asks you to create a PivotTable to summarize the 2002 sales data by quarter, product, and city.

Excel 2002

Planning and Designing a PivotTable Report

Creating a PivotTable report (often called a PivotTable) involves only a few steps. Before you begin, however, you need to review the data and consider how a PivotTable can best summarize it. Jim asks you to design his PivotTable using the following guidelines:

Details

- **Review the list information**
  Before you can effectively summarize list data in a PivotTable, you need to know what information each field contains and understand the list's scope. You are working with product sales information that Jim received from MediaLoft's eastern region sales manager. This list is shown in Figure L-1.

- **Determine the purpose of the PivotTable and write down the names of the fields you want to include**
  The purpose of your PivotTable is to summarize sales information by quarter across various cities. You will include the following fields in the PivotTable: Product ID, Item, City, Quarter, and Sales.

- **Determine which field contains the data you want to summarize and which summary function you want to use**
  You want to summarize sales information by summing the sales field for each product in a city by quarter. You'll do this by using the Excel Sum function.

- **Decide how you want to arrange the data**
  The layout of a PivotTable is crucial in delivering its intended message. You will define Product ID as a column field, City, and Quarter as row fields, and Sales as a data summary field. See Figure L-2.

- **Determine the location of the PivotTable**
  You can place a PivotTable in any worksheet of any workbook. Placing a PivotTable on a separate worksheet makes it easier to locate, however, and prevents you from accidentally overwriting parts of an existing sheet. You decide to create the PivotTable as a new worksheet in the current workbook.

FIGURE L-1: Sales worksheet

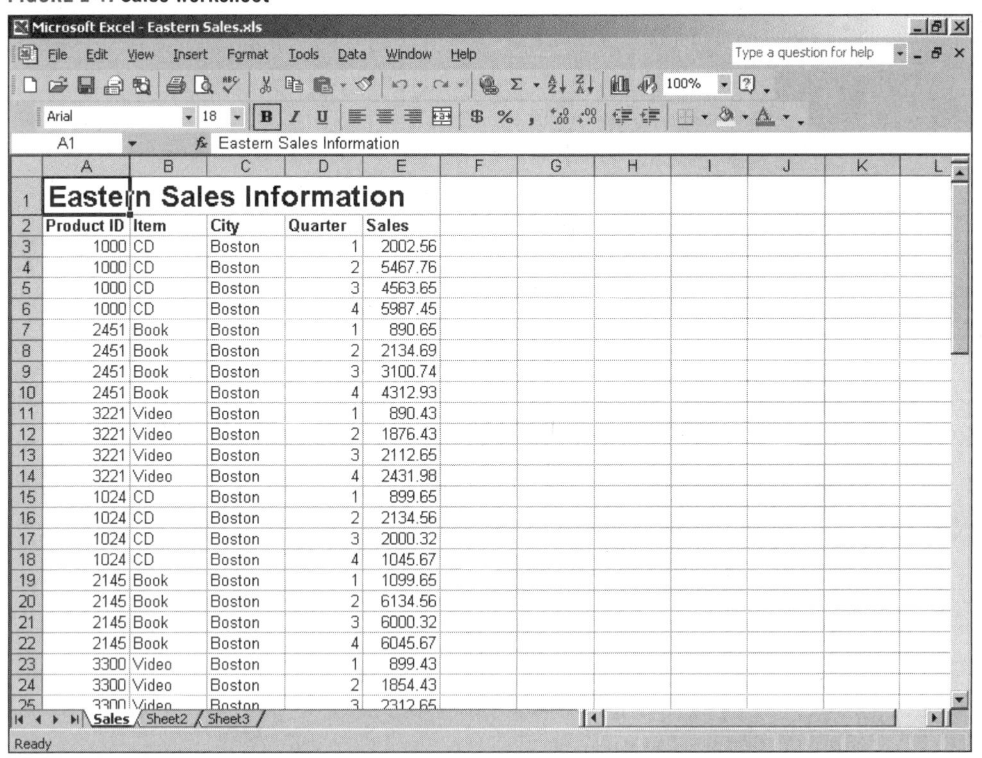

Excel 2002

FIGURE L-2: Example of a PivotTable report

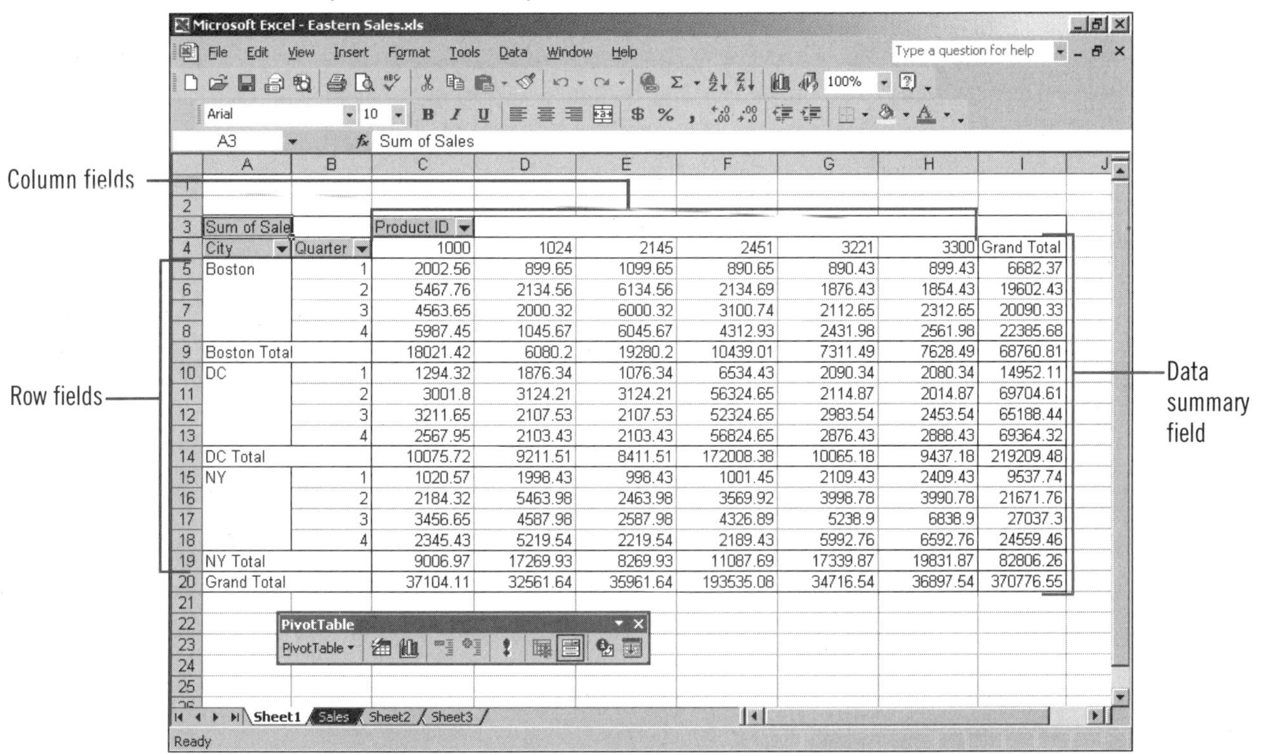

Excel 2002

Creating a PivotTable Report

Once you've planned and designed your PivotTable, you can create it. The PivotTable Wizard takes you through the process step by step. With the planning and design stage complete, you are ready to create a PivotTable that summarizes sales information. The sales managers in Boston, New York, and Washington, DC will use this information to develop a marketing plan for the coming year.

1. Start Excel if necessary, open the Project File **EX L-1** from the drive and folder where your Project Files are stored, then save it as **Eastern Sales**

   This worksheet contains the year's sales information for the MediaLoft's eastern region, including Product ID, Item, City, Quarter, and Sales. Notice that the records are sorted by city.

2. Select cell **A1** if necessary, click **Data** on the menu bar, then click **PivotTable and PivotChart Report**

   The first PivotTable and PivotChart Wizard dialog box opens, as shown in Figure L-3. This is where you specify the type of data source you want to use for your PivotTable: an Excel list or database, an external data source (for example, a Microsoft Access file), or multiple consolidation ranges (another term for worksheet ranges). You also have the option of choosing a PivotTable or PivotChart report.

QuickTip

If the Office Assistant opens, close it by clicking No, don't provide help now.

3. Make sure the **Microsoft Excel list or database option button** is selected, make sure **PivotTable** is selected, then click **Next**

   The second PivotTable and PivotChart Wizard dialog box opens. Because the cell pointer was located within the list before you opened the PivotTable Wizard, Excel automatically completes the Range box with the table range that includes the selected cell—in this case, $A$2:$E$74. You can either type a new range in the Range box or use the range Excel suggests.

4. Click **Next**

   The third PivotTable and PivotChart Wizard dialog box opens. You use this dialog box to specify the location of the PivotTable.

5. Make sure **New Worksheet** is selected, then click **Finish**

   A worksheet appears with an empty PivotTable, as shown in Figure L-4. The PivotTable toolbar also appears. It contains buttons that allow you to manipulate data. The list window contains field names that you can drag into various "drop areas" of the PivotTable to analyze your data.

Trouble?

To display the PivotTable toolbar, click View on the menu bar, point to Toolbars, then click PivotTable to select it.

6. If the PivotTable list is not on the right side of the screen, double-click its title bar, then drag its left border so your screen matches Figure L-4

7. Drag the **Product ID** field from the PivotTable Field List to the area marked **Drop Column Fields Here**, drag the **City** field to the **Drop Row Fields Here** area, then drag the **Quarter** field to the row fields area to the right of the City field

   As you drag a field into the PivotTable area, a miniature PivotTable layout appears attached to the pointer, with blue shading to indicate your location in the PivotTable. Releasing the mouse button will place the field in the area that is shaded in blue. You have created a PivotTable with the Product IDs as column headers and Cities and Quarters as row labels.

Trouble?

If the Quarter field did not appear as a row label, drag it from its position to the right of the City row label.

8. Drag the **Sales** field to the **Drop Data Items Here** area

   Because SUM is the Excel default function for data fields containing numbers, Excel automatically calculates the sum of the sales by product ID and by city and quarter. You can use more than one summary function in a PivotTable by dragging multiple field buttons to the data area. The PivotTable tells you that Product #1000 Boston sales were twice the New York sales level. Product 2451 was the best selling product overall, as you can see in the grand total row. See Figure L-5.

9. Save the workbook

FIGURE L-3: First PivotTable Wizard dialog box

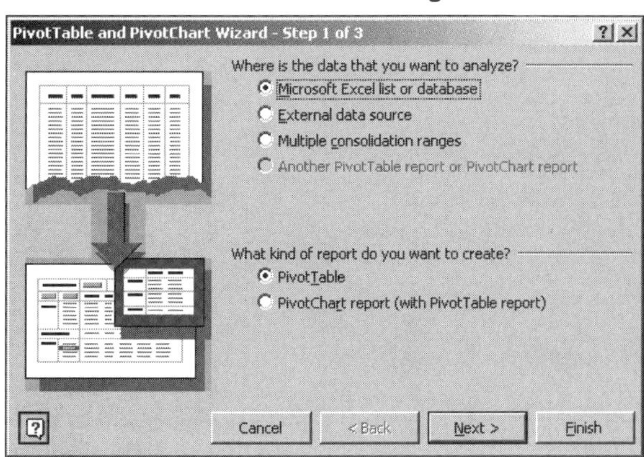

FIGURE L-4: New PivotTable ready to receive field data

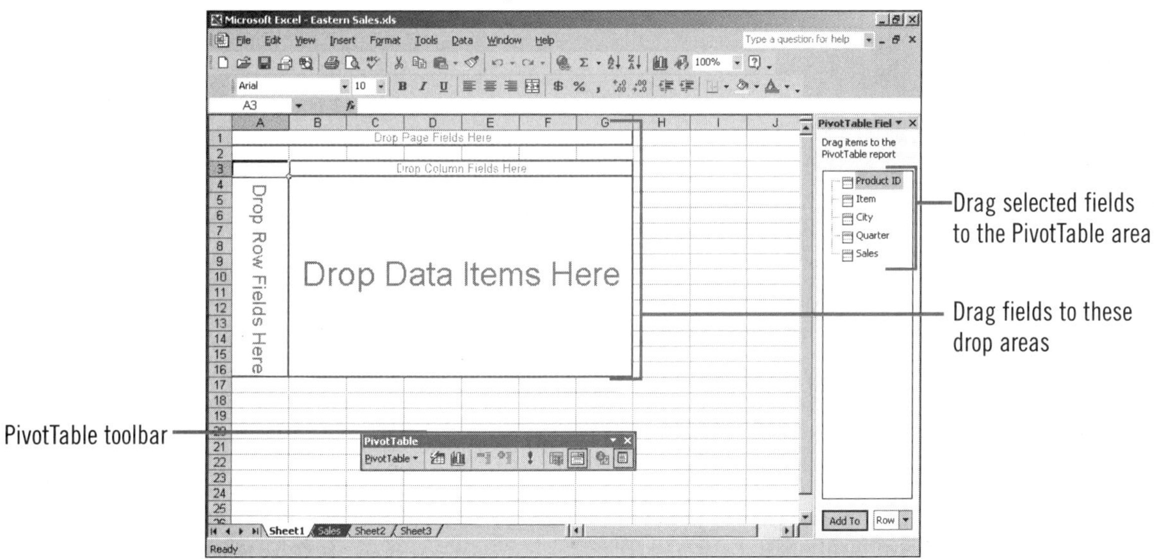

FIGURE L-5: New PivotTable with fields in place

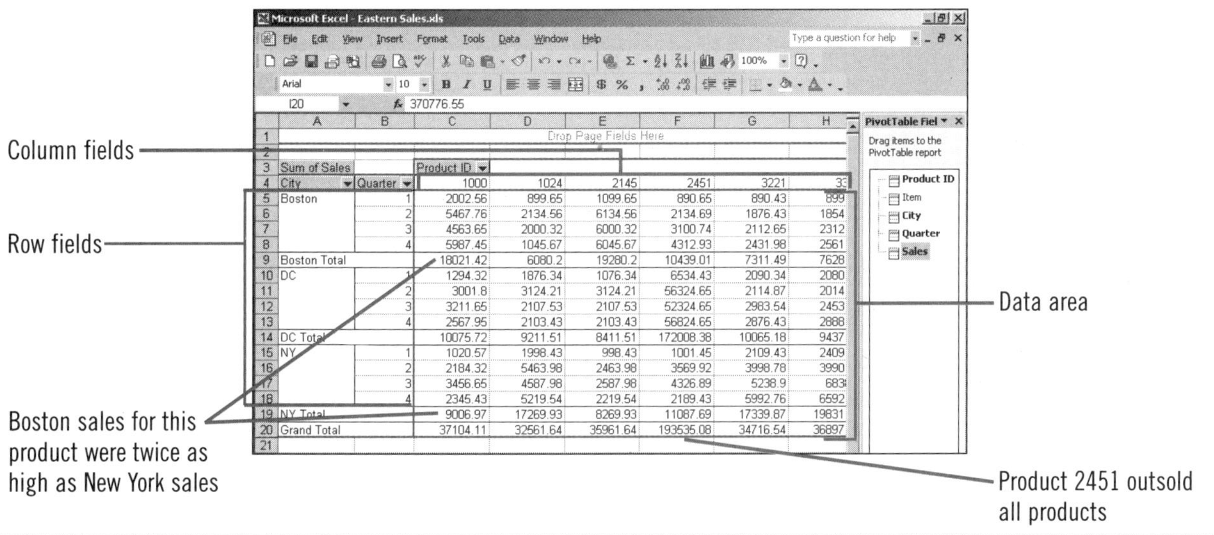

Excel 2002

Changing the Summary Function of a PivotTable Report

A PivotTable's **summary function** controls what type of calculation is applied to the table data. Unless you specify otherwise, Excel applies the SUM function to numeric data and the COUNT function to data fields containing text. However, you can easily change the SUM function to a different summary function, such as AVERAGE, which calculates the average of all values in the field. Jim wants you to calculate the average sales for the northeastern cities using the AVERAGE function.

Trouble?

If your PivotTable Field dialog box says "Subtotals" instead of "Summarize by" click Cancel, be sure you have clicked a cell in the data area, then click the Field Settings button.

1. **Click any cell in the data area (A3:I20), then click the Field Settings button on the PivotTable toolbar**
   The PivotTable Field dialog box opens. The selected function in the Summarize by list box determines how the data will be calculated. The PivotTable toolbar buttons are described in Table L-1.
2. **In the Summarize by list box, click Average, then click OK**
   The PivotTable Field dialog box closes. The data area of the PivotTable shows the average sales for each product by city and quarter. See Figure L-6. After reviewing the data, you decide that it would be more useful to sum the salary information than to average it.
3. **Click the Field Settings button on the PivotTable toolbar; in the Summarize by list box, click Sum, then click OK**
   The PivotTable Field dialog box closes and Excel recalculates the PivotTable—this time, summing the sales data instead of averaging it.
4. **Rename Sheet1 PivotTable, add your name to the worksheet footer, then save and print the workbook**

QuickTip

When you name a PivotTable sheet, it is best to avoid using spaces in the name. If a PivotTable name contains a space, you must put single quotes around the name when you refer to it in a function.

FIGURE L-6: PivotTable showing averages

Average for Product ID 1000 in Boston

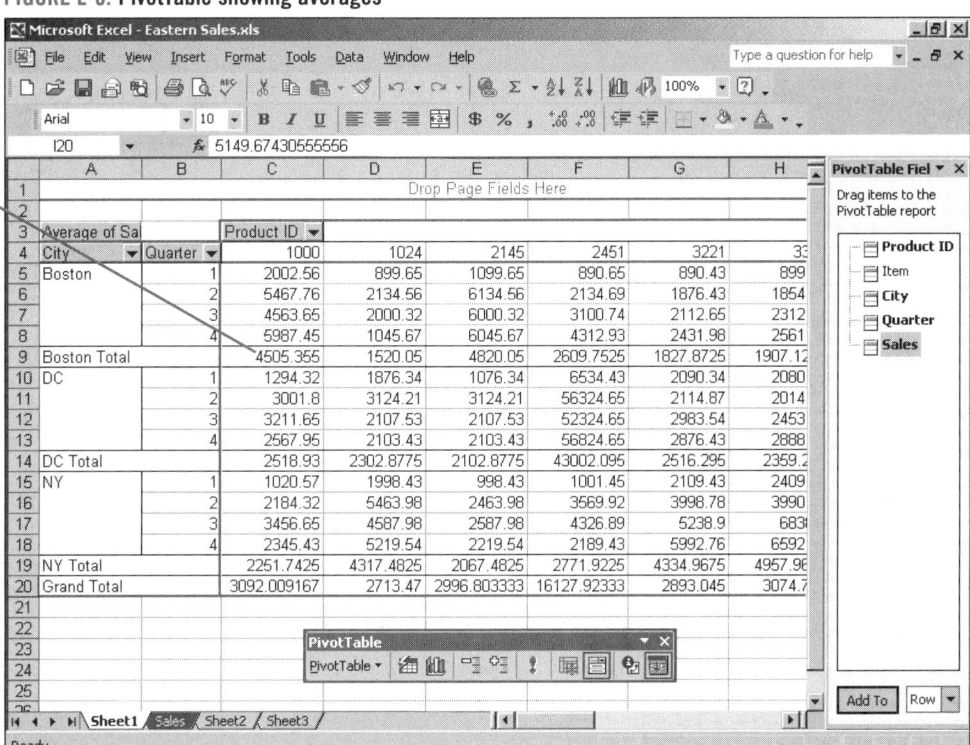

TABLE L-1: PivotTable toolbar buttons

button	name	description
PivotTable ▾	**PivotTable Menu**	Displays menu of PivotTable commands
	Format Report	Displays a list of PivotTable AutoFormats
	Chart Wizard	Creates a PivotChart report
	Hide Detail	Hides detail in table groupings
	Show Detail	Shows detail in table groupings
	Refresh Data	Updates list changes within the table
	Include Hidden Items In Totals	Includes values for all items in totals, including hidden items
	Always Display Items	Turns on drop down selections for PivotTable fields
	Field Settings	Displays a list of field settings
	Show/Hide Field List	Displays/hides PivotTable fields in the list window; in a chart, displays or hides outlines and labels

Excel 2002

Analyzing Three-Dimensional Data

When you place row and column fields to create a PivotTable, you are working with two-dimensional data. You can convert a PivotTable to a three-dimensional data analysis tool by adding a page field. A **page field** makes the data appear as if it is stacked in pages, thus adding a third dimension to the analysis. When using a page field, you are in effect filtering data through that field. You can add a page field by dragging a field to the Drop Page Fields Here area or by using the Add To button in the PivotTable Field List. Jim wants you to filter the PivotTable so that only one quarter's data is visible at one time.

Steps

1. Click the **Quarter field name** in the PivotTable Field List, click the list arrow in the lower-right corner of the list, select **Page Area**, click **Add To**
   The PivotTable is re-created with a page field showing data for all the quarters. See Figure L-7. You can easily view the data for each quarter.
2. In the PivotTable cell B1, click the **Quarter list arrow**
3. Click **1**, then click **OK**
   The PivotTable displays the sales data for the first quarter only, as shown in Figure L-8.
4. Click the **Quarter list arrow**, click **4**, then click **OK**
   The sales for the fourth quarter appear.
5. Save the workbook

QuickTip

To display each page of the page field on a separate worksheet, click PivotTable on the PivotTable toolbar, click Show Pages, then click OK.

FIGURE L-7: PivotTable with Quarter as a page field

Quarter is in the Page field area

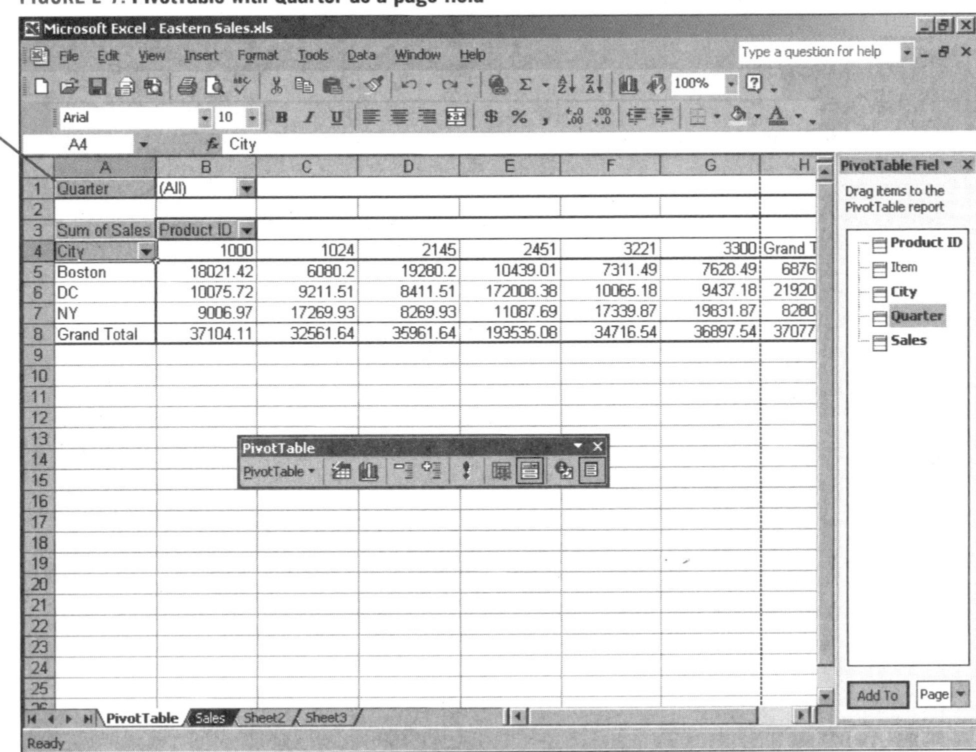

FIGURE L-8: PivotTable filtered to show only first quarter sales

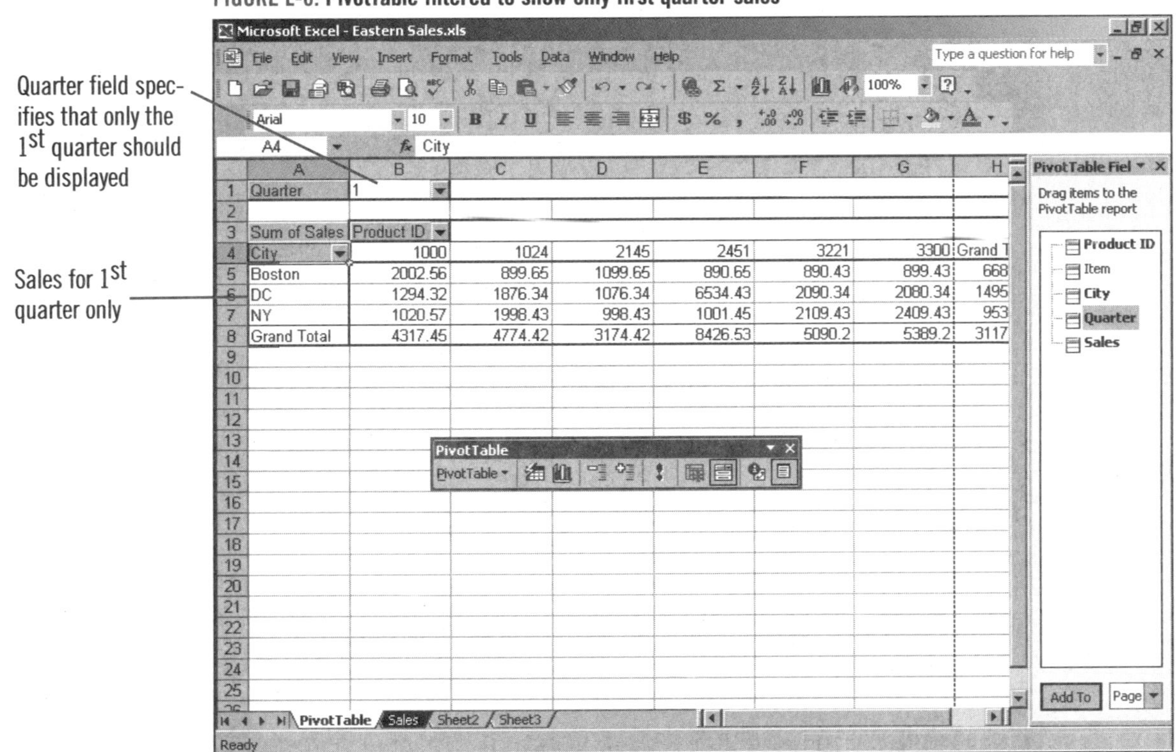

Excel 2002

Excel 2002

Updating a PivotTable Report

The data in a PivotTable Report looks like typical worksheet data. Because the PivotTable data is linked to a source list, however, the values and results in the PivotTable are read-only values. That means you cannot move or modify part of a PivotTable by inserting or deleting rows, editing results, or moving cells. To change PivotTable data, you must edit the items directly in the list you used to create the table, called the **source list**, and then update, or **refresh**, the PivotTable to reflect the changes. Jim just learned that sales information for a custom CD sold in Boston during the fourth quarter was never entered into the Sales worksheet. Jim asks you to add information about this CD to the current list; you start by inserting a row for the new information in the Sales worksheet.

Steps 1 2 3 4

1. Click the **Sales sheet tab**
   By inserting the new row in the correct position by city, you will not need to sort the list again. Also, by adding the new information within the list range, the new row data will be included automatically in the list range.

2. Right-click the **row 27 header**; then on the shortcut menu, click **Insert**
   A blank row appears as the new row 27, and the data in the old row 27 moves down to row 28. You'll enter the data on the CD in the new row 27.

3. Enter the data for the new CD using the following information

Product ID	1924
Item	CD
City	Boston
Quarter	4
Sales	2354.87

   The PivotTable does not yet reflect the additional data.

QuickTip

Scroll left and right as necessary to view PivotTable totals.

4. Click the **PivotTable sheet tab**, then make sure the **Quarter 4** page is displayed
   Notice that the fourth quarter list does not currently include this new CD information and that the grand total is $116309.46. Before you select the Refresh Data command to refresh the PivotTable, you need to make sure that the cell pointer is located within the current table range.

QuickTip

If you want Excel to refresh your PivotTable report automatically when you open the workbook it is contained in, click the PivotTable list arrow on the PivotTable toolbar, click Table Options, under Data Source options select Refresh on open, then click OK.

5. Click anywhere within the table range (A3:H8), then click the **Refresh Data button** on the PivotTable toolbar
   The PivotTable now includes the new CD information in column H, and the grand total has increased by the amount of the CD's sales (2354.87) to 118664.33. See Figure L-9.

6. Save the workbook

FIGURE L-9: **Updated PivotTable report**

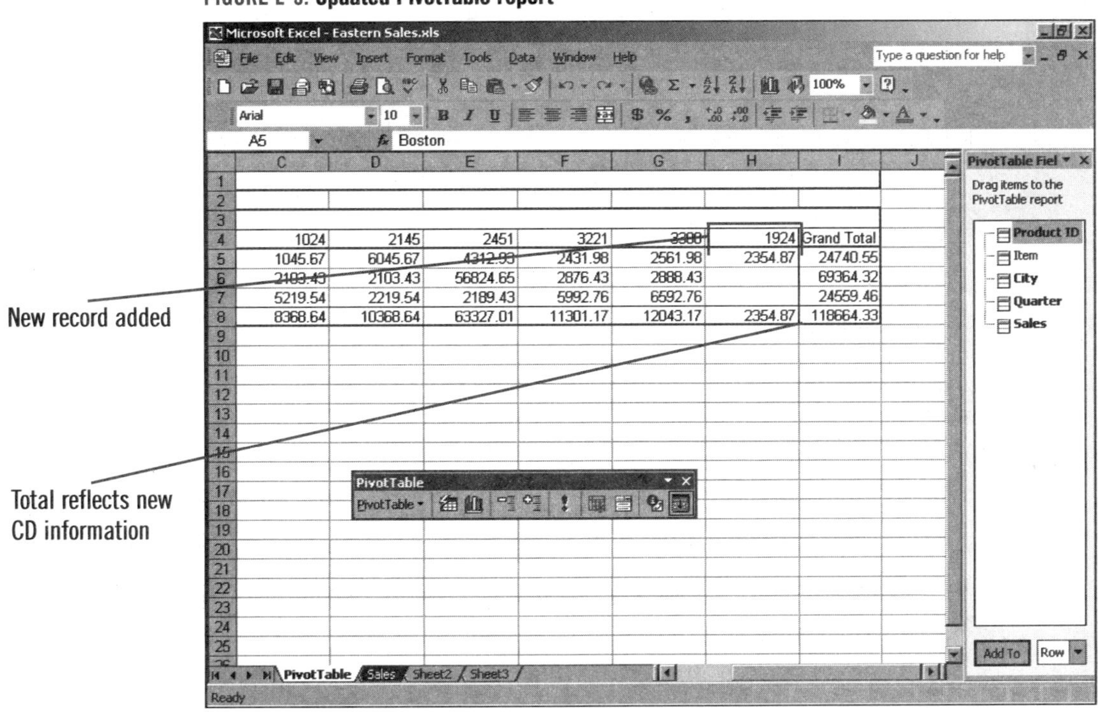

Maintaining original table data

Once you select the Refresh Data command, you cannot undo the operation. If you want the PivotTable to display the original source data, you must change the source data list, then reselect the Refresh Data command. If you're concerned about the effect refreshing the PivotTable might have on your work, save a second (working) copy of the workbook so that your original data remains intact.

Excel 2002

Changing the Structure and Format of a PivotTable Report

Although you cannot change the actual data in a PivotTable, you can alter its structure and appearance at any time. You might, for example, add a column field, or switch the positions of existing fields. You can quickly change the way data is displayed in a PivotTable by dragging field buttons in the worksheet from a row position to a column position, or vice versa. Alternately, you may want to enhance the appearance of a PivotTable by changing the way the text or values are formatted. It's a good idea to format a PivotTable using AutoFormat, because once you refresh a PivotTable, any formatting that has not been applied to the cells through AutoFormat is removed. The eastern sales manager has asked Jim to include item information in the sales report. Jim asks you to add item as a page field and then format the PivotTable.

Steps

1. **Make sure that the PivotTable sheet is active, that the cell pointer is located anywhere inside the PivotTable (the range A3:I8), and that the PivotTable Field List is visible**
   When you move fields in a PivotTable, you can drag them as you did when you first moved the fields into the PivotTable area.
2. **Click the Item field, drag it to the Page area, and drop it above the Quarter button**
   The Item field is added as a Page field to the PivotTable above the Quarter Page field. See Figure L-10. You will use the Item list arrow in the next lesson to display only the CD sales information. Now you are ready to format the PivotTable.
3. **Click any cell inside the PivotTable, click the Field Settings button on the PivotTable toolbar, then in the PivotTable Field dialog box, click Number**
4. **Under Category in the Format Cells dialog box, click Accounting, keep the Decimal Places as 2, click OK, then click OK again**
   The PivotTable Field dialog box closes, and the sales amounts are formatted with commas and dollar signs.
5. **Click the Format Report button on the PivotTable toolbar bar; in the AutoFormat dialog box, scroll down and click Table 2, click OK, then click outside the range to deselect it**
   You need to provide the eastern sales manager with sales information for all four quarters.
6. **Click the Quarter list arrow, click All, then click OK**
   The completed PivotTable appears as shown in Figure L-11. The AutoFormat is applied to all pages of the PivotTable, and the PivotTable Field List closes.
7. **Save the workbook, preview the PivotTable, then print it in landscape orientation**

QuickTip

Report formats 1–10 are indented formats, like a banded database report. Tables 1–10 are not indented. Indented reports contain only row fields, not column fields.

FIGURE L-10: Revised PivotTable structure

Item field is now in the Page area

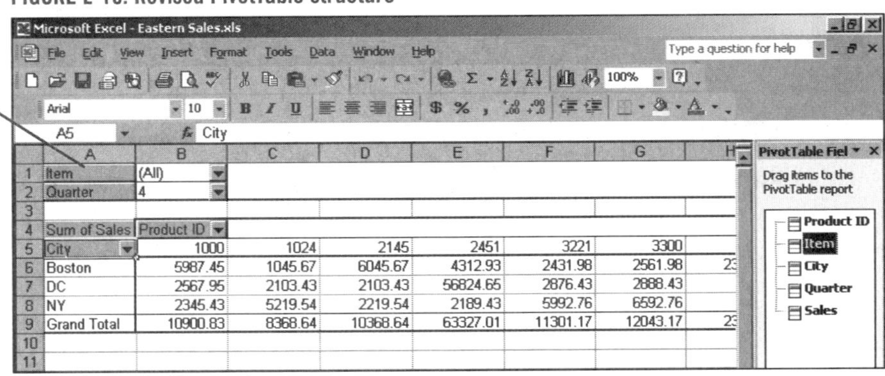

FIGURE L-11: Completed Pivot Table report

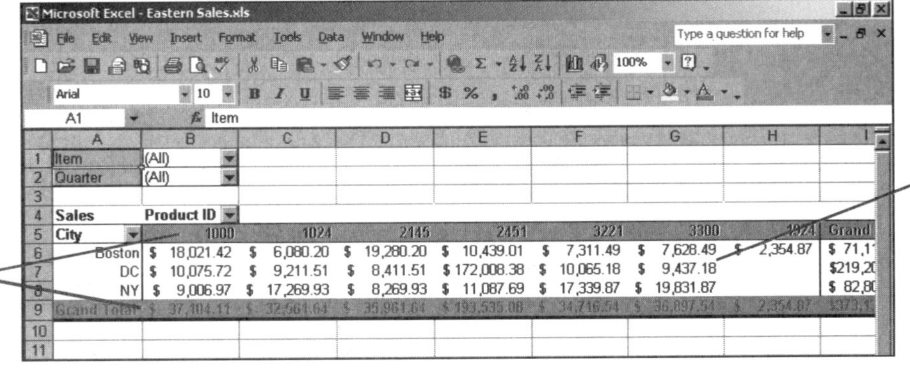

AutoFormat has applied shading and blue headings and totals

Numbers appear in Accounting format

CLUES TO USE

Customizing PivotTables

You can customize the default Excel PivotTable to show information in a format that is appropriate for your particular audience. If your audience requires more descriptive field names in order to understand the PivotTable information, you can rename a field by clicking the field name in the PivotTable, clicking the Field Settings button on the PivotTable toolbar, then entering a new name in the Name text box. To modify the order of items in the table, right-click a cell, then use the commands on the Order submenu to reorder the selected item(s). To add or hide detail, right-click a cell, then use the commands on the Group and Show Detail submenu to expand, display or hide more detail. When you show details of a selected area, Excel creates a new worksheet containing the detail you requested.

Excel 2002

Creating a PivotChart Report

A **PivotChart report** is a chart that you create from data or from a PivotTable report. Like a PivotTable report, a PivotChart report has fields that you can drag to explore new data relationships. Table L-2 describes how the elements in a PivotTable report correspond to the elements in a PivotChart report. When you create a PivotChart directly from data, Excel automatically creates a corresponding PivotTable report. When you change a PivotChart report by dragging fields, Excel updates the corresponding PivotTable report to show the new layout. You can create a PivotChart report from any PivotTable report to reflect that view of your data, but if you use an indented PivotTable report format, your chart will not have series fields; indented PivotTable report formats do not include column fields. Jim wants you to chart the fourth quarter CD sales and the yearly CD sales average for the eastern sales manager. You use the Chart Wizard to create a column chart from the PivotTable data.

QuickTip

If your PivotTable report is an indented format, move at least one field to the column area before you create a PivotChart report to display a series field on the chart.

1. Click the **Item list arrow**, click **CD**, click **OK**, click the **Quarter list arrow**, click **4**, then click **OK**

   The fourth quarter CD sales information appears in the PivotTable. See Figure L-12. You will create the PivotChart from the displayed PivotTable information.

2. Click any cell in the PivotTable, then click the **Chart Wizard button** on the PivotTable toolbar

   A new chart sheet opens with the 4th quarter CD sales displayed as a bar chart, as shown in Figure L-13. Jim wants you to change the chart to show the average sales for all quarters.

3. Click the **Quarter list arrow** on the chart sheet, click **All**, then click **OK**

   The chart now represents the sum of CD sales for the year. You will change the summary function to display average sales.

4. Click **Sum of Sales** on the PivotChart, click the **Field Settings button** on the PivotTable toolbar, click **Average** in the PivotTable Field dialog box, then click **OK**

   You can also click the Sales label in the PivotTable before opening the Field Settings dialog box to change the Sum of Sales Function. The PivotChart report is recalculated to display averages.

5. Rename the chart sheet **PivotChart**, place your name in the chart sheet footer, save the workbook, then preview and print the PivotChart report

   The final PivotChart report displaying the average CD sales for the year is shown in Figure L-14.

TABLE L-2: PivotTable and PivotChart elements

PivotTable items	PivotChart items
row fields	category fields
column fields	series fields
page fields	page fields

4th Quarter CD Sales selected

FIGURE L-12: PivotTable displaying 4th quarter CD sales

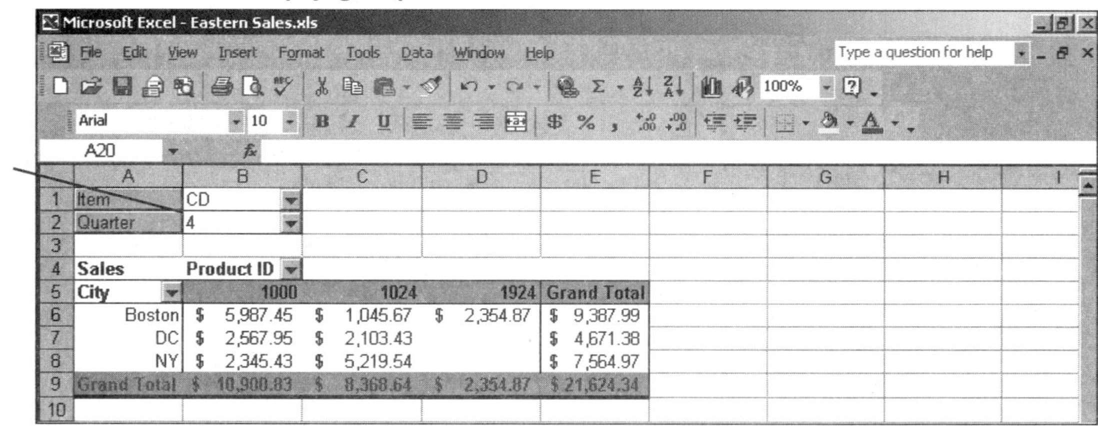

Microsoft Excel - Eastern Sales.xls

	A	B	C	D	E
1	Item	CD			
2	Quarter	4			
3					
4	Sales	Product ID			
5	City	1000	1024	1924	Grand Total
6	Boston	$ 5,987.45	$ 1,045.67	$ 2,354.87	$ 9,387.99
7	DC	$ 2,567.95	$ 2,103.43		$ 4,671.38
8	NY	$ 2,345.43	$ 5,219.54		$ 7,564.97
9	Grand Total	$ 10,900.83	$ 8,368.64	$ 2,354.87	$ 21,624.34

FIGURE L-13: New chart sheet displaying 4th quarter CD sales

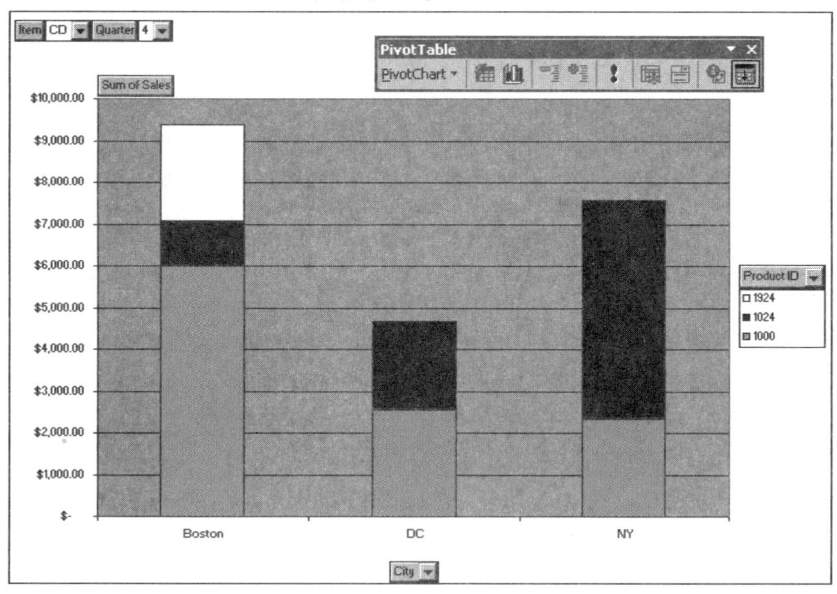

FIGURE L-14: Completed PivotChart report

Chart now shows average sales for the year

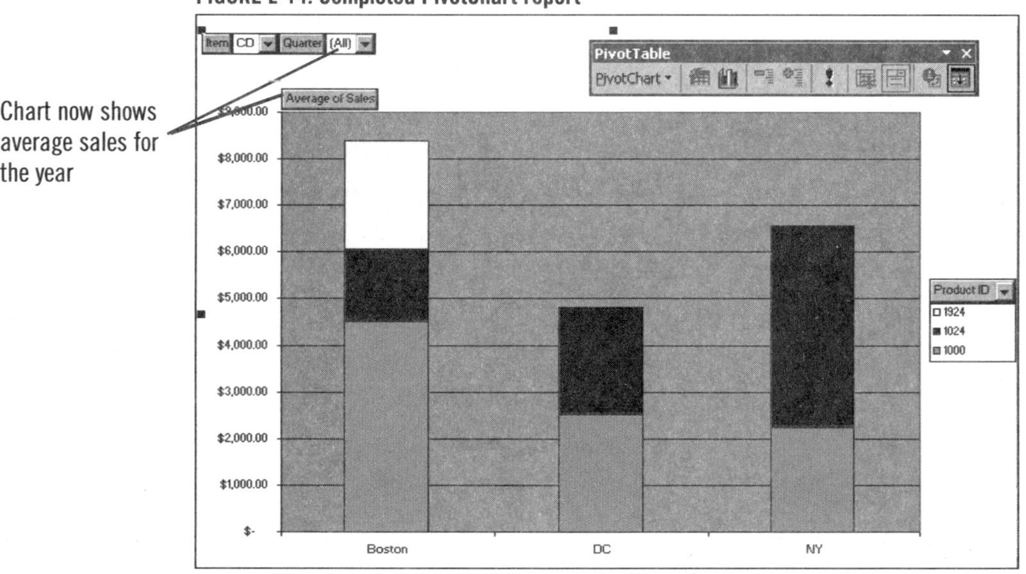

Excel 2002

Excel 2002

Using the GETPIVOTDATA Function

Because you can rearrange a PivotTable so easily, you can't use an ordinary cell reference when you want to reference a PivotTable cell in another worksheet. If you change the way data is displayed in a PivotTable, the data moves, rendering an ordinary cell reference incorrect. Instead, to retrieve summary data from a PivotTable, you need to use the Excel GETPIVOTDATA function. Its syntax is displayed in Figure L-15. In preparing for the Boston sales meeting, the eastern sales manager asks Jim to include the yearly sales total for the Boston store in the Sales sheet. Jim asks you to retrieve this information from the PivotTable and place it in the Sales sheet. You use the GETPIVOTDATA function to retrieve this information.

1. Click the **PivotTable sheet tab**
   The sales figures in the PivotTable are average values for CDs. You need to show sales information for all items and change the summary information back to Sum.
2. Click the Item list arrow, click **All**, then click **OK**
   The PivotChart report displays sales information for all items.
3. Click **Average of Sales** on the PivotTable, click the **Field Settings button** on the PivotTable toolbar, click **Sum** in the Summarize by list, then click **OK**
   The PivotChart report is recalculated to display sales totals. Next, you will include the total for sales for the Boston store in the Sales sheet by retrieving it from the PivotTable.
4. Click the **Sales sheet tab**, click cell **G1**, type **Total Boston Sales:**, click the **Enter button** on the Formula bar, click the **Align Right button** on the Formatting toolbar, then click the **Bold button** on the Formatting toolbar
   The GETPIVOTDATA function will retrieve the total Boston sales from the PivotTable.
5. Click cell **H1**, type **=GETPIVOTDATA(PivotTable!A4,"Boston")** then click
   The function's first argument, PivotTable!A4, references cell A4 within the PivotTable range (A4 could be replaced by any cell in the PivotTable). The second argument, "Boston", describes the label for the summary information you want.
6. Click the **Currency Style button** on the Formatting toolbar
   The current sales total for Boston store is $71,115.68, as shown in Figure L-16. This is the same value displayed in cell I6 of the PivotTable. The GETPIVOTDATA function will work correctly only when the sales figures for all quarters are displayed in the PivotTable. You can verify this by displaying a single quarter in the PivotTable and viewing the effect on the Sales worksheet.
7. Click the **PivotTable sheet tab**, click the **Quarter list arrow**, click **1**, click **OK**, then click the **Sales sheet tab**
   The total in cell H1 is incorrect. It will be corrected when you redisplay all quarters.
8. Click the **PivotTable sheet tab**, click the **Quarter list arrow**, click **(All)**, click **OK**, then click the **Sales sheet tab**
   The correct value—$71,115.68—is once again displayed in cell H1.
9. Enter your name in the Sales sheet footer, save the workbook, then preview and print the Sales worksheet
10. Close the file and exit Excel

QuickTip

If a PivotTable's sheet name contains a space, put single quotes around the PivotTable name in the first argument of the GETPIVOTDATA function.

FIGURE L-15: Syntax of GETPIVOTDATA function

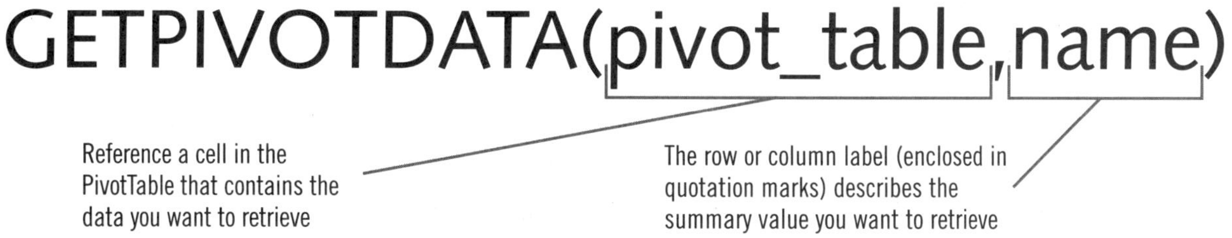

GETPIVOTDATA(pivot_table,name)

Reference a cell in the PivotTable that contains the data you want to retrieve

The row or column label (enclosed in quotation marks) describes the summary value you want to retrieve

FIGURE L-16: Completed Sales worksheet showing total Boston sales

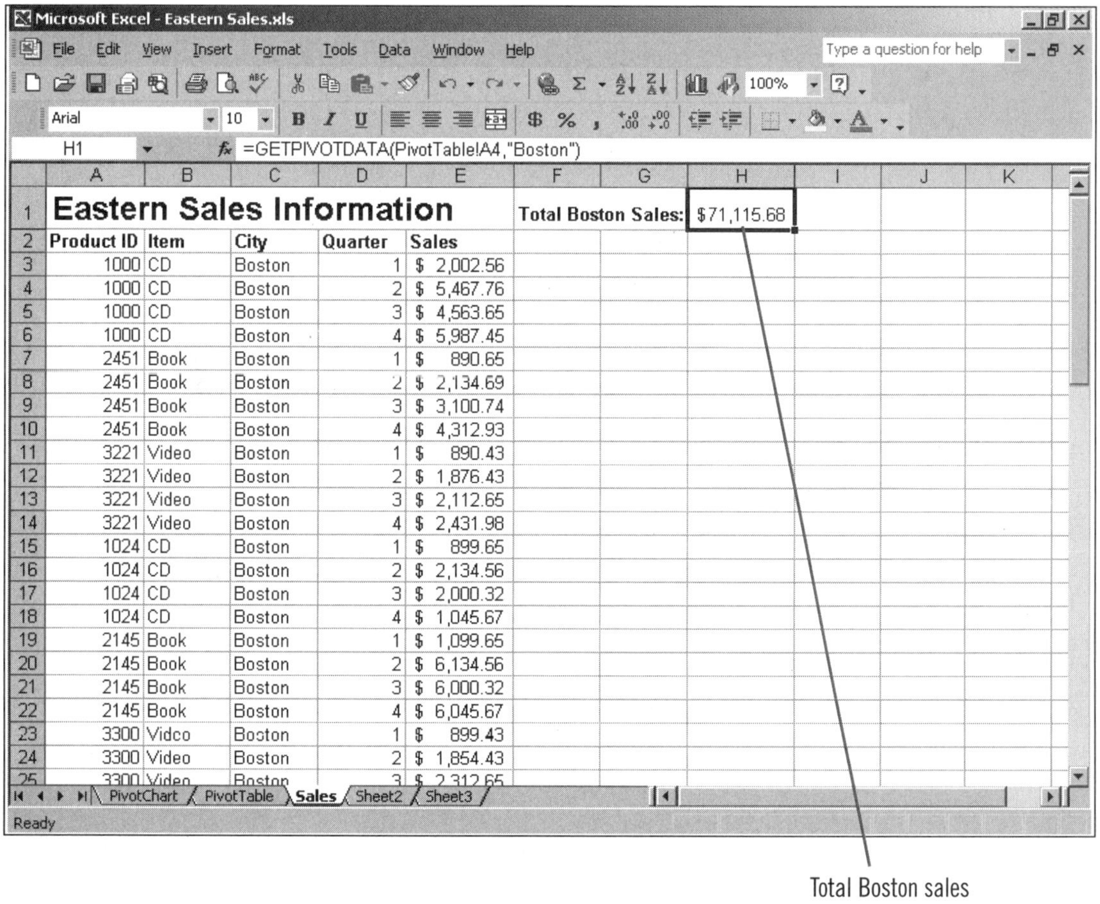

Microsoft Excel - Eastern Sales.xls

File Edit View Insert Format Tools Data Window Help

H1 =GETPIVOTDATA(PivotTable!A4,"Boston")

	A	B	C	D	E	F	G	H
1	Eastern Sales Information					Total Boston Sales:		$71,115.68
2	Product ID	Item	City	Quarter	Sales			
3	1000	CD	Boston	1	$ 2,002.56			
4	1000	CD	Boston	2	$ 5,467.76			
5	1000	CD	Boston	3	$ 4,563.65			
6	1000	CD	Boston	4	$ 5,987.45			
7	2451	Book	Boston	1	$ 890.65			
8	2451	Book	Boston	2	$ 2,134.69			
9	2451	Book	Boston	3	$ 3,100.74			
10	2451	Book	Boston	4	$ 4,312.93			
11	3221	Video	Boston	1	$ 890.43			
12	3221	Video	Boston	2	$ 1,876.43			
13	3221	Video	Boston	3	$ 2,112.65			
14	3221	Video	Boston	4	$ 2,431.98			
15	1024	CD	Boston	1	$ 899.65			
16	1024	CD	Boston	2	$ 2,134.56			
17	1024	CD	Boston	3	$ 2,000.32			
18	1024	CD	Boston	4	$ 1,045.67			
19	2145	Book	Boston	1	$ 1,099.65			
20	2145	Book	Boston	2	$ 6,134.56			
21	2145	Book	Boston	3	$ 6,000.32			
22	2145	Book	Boston	4	$ 6,045.67			
23	3300	Video	Boston	1	$ 899.43			
24	3300	Video	Boston	2	$ 1,854.43			
25	3300	Video	Boston	3	$ 2,312.65			

PivotChart / PivotTable / Sales / Sheet2 / Sheet3

Ready

Total Boston sales

Practice

► Concepts Review

Label each element of the Excel screen shown in Figure L-17.

FIGURE L-17

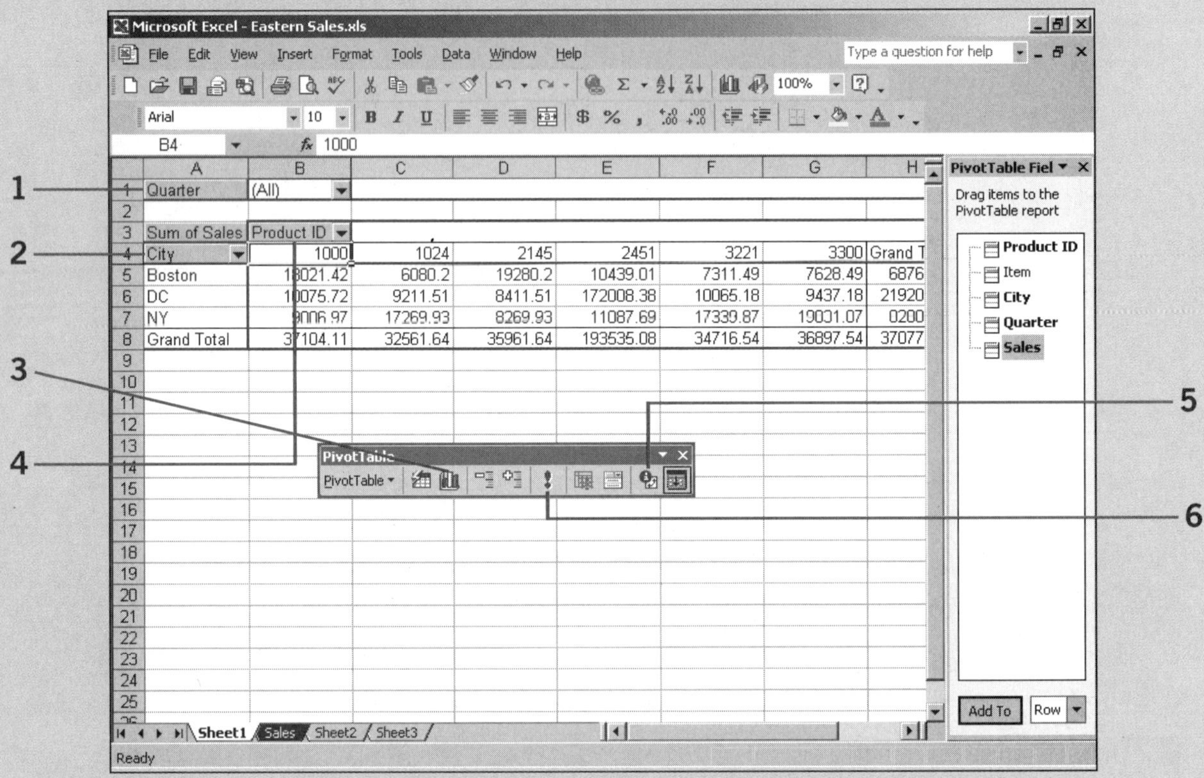

Match each term with the statement that describes it.

7. **COLUMN area**
8. **GETPIVOTDATA function**
9. **DATA area**
10. **PivotTable page**
11. **Summary function**

a. Retrieves information from a PivotTable.
b. Displays fields as column labels.
c. Shows data for one item at a time in a table.
d. Displays values.
e. Determines if data will be summed or averaged.

Select the best answer from the list of choices.

12. A PivotTable report is best described as an Excel feature that
- **a.** Requires a source list.
- **b.** "Stacks" pages of data.
- **c.** Allows you to display, summarize, and analyze list data.
- **d.** Displays columns and rows of data.

13. Which PivotTable report field allows you to average values?
- **a.** Row field
- **b.** Page field
- **c.** Data field
- **d.** Column field

14. To make changes to PivotTable data, you must
- **a.** Edit cells in the source list and then refresh the PivotTable.
- **b.** Create a page field.
- **c.** Edit cells in the PivotTable and then refresh the source list.
- **d.** Drag a column header to the column area.

Skills Review

1. Plan and design a PivotTable.
- **a.** Start Excel, open the Project File titled EX L-2 from the drive and folder where your Project Files are stored, then save it as **July CDs**.
- **b.** You'll create a PivotTable to show the sum of sales across products and regions. Study the list, then write down the field names you think should be included in the PivotTable. Determine which fields you think should be column fields, row fields, and data fields, then sketch a draft PivotTable.

2. Create a PivotTable report.
- **a.** Using the data on the Sales List sheet, generate a PivotTable report on a new worksheet, and arrange the data fields as follows (*Hint:* In the Row area, place the Store field to the left of the Sales Rep field.):

Field	Area
Store	Row
Sales Rep	Row
Product	Column
Sales $	Data

3. Change the summary function of a PivotTable report.
- **a.** Change the PivotTable summary function to Average using the Field settings button.
- **b.** Rename the new sheet **July PivotTable**.
- **c.** Enter your name in the PivotTable report footer, save the workbook, then print the PivotTable report in landscape orientation.
- **d.** Change the Summary function back to Sum.

4. Analyze three-dimensional data.
- **a.** Place the Region field in the page field area.
- **b.** Display sales for only the East region.
- **c.** Save the workbook, then print the worksheet.

5. Update a PivotTable.

- **a.** With the July PivotTable sheet active, note the NY total for The Sunset Trio.
- **b.** Activate the Sales List sheet and create a new blank row 8.
- **c.** Enter the following data in row 8:

Product	The Sunset Trio
Region	East
Store	NY
Sales $	3900
Sales Rep	L. Smith

- **d.** Refresh the PivotTable so it reflects the new data item.
- **e.** Note the NY total for The Sunset Trio in the East and verify that it increased by 3900.
- **f.** Save the workbook, preview then print the PivotTable.

6. Change the structure and format of a PivotTable.

- **a.** With the July PivotTable active, redisplay data for all regions.
- **b.** Drag fields so that the following areas contain only the following fields: (*Hint:* To remove fields from an area, drag them back over to the field area in the PivotTable Field list window.)

Field	**Area**
Product	Row
Sales Rep	Column
Store	Page
Sales $	Data

- **c.** Use the Field Settings button on the PivotTable toolbar to change the numbers to Currency format with 0 decimal places.
- **d.** Use the Format Report button on the PivotTable toolbar to apply the Table 4 AutoFormat, save the workbook, then print the PivotTable, fit to one page.

7. Create a PivotChart report.

- **a.** Use the existing PivotTable data to create a PivotChart report on a new worksheet.
- **b.** Rename the chart sheet PivotChart.
- **c.** Change the chart to display average sales.
- **d.** Change the chart to display average sales for the NY store only.
- **e.** Add your name to the chart sheet footer.
- **f.** Save the workbook, preview then print the chart.
- **g.** Change the summary function on the PivotChart sheet back to Sum.

8. Use the GETPIVOTDATA function.

- **a.** Change the store field on the July PivotTable to show information for all stores.
- **b.** In cell D27 of the Sales List sheet, enter the function **=GETPIVOTDATA('July PivotTable'!A4,"S. Jones")** to retrieve the grand total for S. Jones from the July PivotTable.
- **c.** Format the value in cell D27 as currency with no decimal places.
- **d.** Enter your name in the Sales List sheet footer, save the workbook, then preview and print the worksheet.
- **e.** Close the workbook and exit Excel.

Independent Challenge 1

You are the bookkeeper for the small accounting firm called Chavez, Long, and Doyle. Until recently, the partners had been tracking their hours manually in a log. You have created an Excel list to track basic information: billing date, partner name, client name, nature of work, and billable hours. It is your responsibility to generate a table summarizing this billing information by client. You will create a PivotTable that sums the hours by accountant and date for each project. Once the table is completed, you will create a column chart representing the billing information.

a. Start Excel, open the Project File titled EX L-3 from the drive and folder where your Project Files are stored, then save it as **Partner Billing Report**.

b. Create a PivotTable on a separate worksheet that sums hours by partner and dates according to client. Use Figure L-18 as a guide.

c. Name the new sheet **PivotTable** and apply the Table 3 AutoFormat to the table.

d. On a separate sheet, create a PivotChart showing the PivotTable Information.

e. Change the summary function in the chart to **Average**.

f. Add your name to the three worksheet footers, save the workbook, then preview and print both the PivotTable and the PivotChart in landscape orientation.

g. Close the workbook and exit Excel.

FIGURE L-18

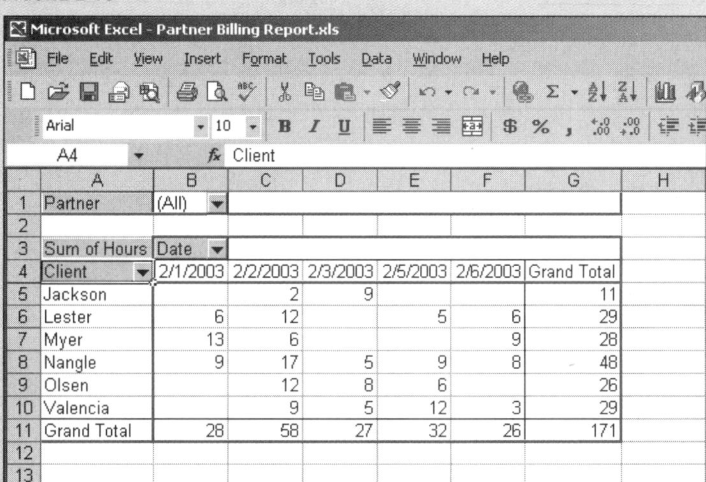

Microsoft Excel - Partner Billing Report.xls

	A	B	C	D	E	F	G
1	Partner	(All)					
2							
3	Sum of Hours	Date					
4	Client	2/1/2003	2/2/2003	2/3/2003	2/5/2003	2/6/2003	Grand Total
5	Jackson		2	9			11
6	Lester	6	12		5	6	29
7	Myer	13	6			9	28
8	Nangle	9	17	5	9	8	48
9	Olsen		12	8	6		26
10	Valencia		9	5	12	3	29
11	Grand Total	28	58	27	32	26	171

Independent Challenge 2

You are the owner of three midsized computer stores called PC Assist. One is located downtown, one is in the Plaza Mall, and one is in the Sun Center shopping center. You have been using Excel to maintain a sales summary list for the second quarter sales in the following three areas: hardware, software, and miscellaneous items. You want to create a PivotTable to analyze and graph the sales in each category by month and store. Use Figure L-19 as a guide.

a. Start Excel, open the Project File titled EX L-4 from the drive and folder where your Project Files are stored, then save it as **Second Qtr Sales**.

b. Rename the worksheet **Sales**.

c. Create a PivotTable on a new worksheet that sums the sales amount for each store across the rows and each category of sales down the columns. Add a page field for month.

d. Change the summary function in the PivotTable to **Average**.

e. Format the PivotTable using the Table 6 AutoFormat.

FIGURE L-19

Microsoft Excel - Second Qtr Sales.xls

	A	B	C	D	E
1	Month	May			
2					
3	Average of Amount	Category			
4	Store	Hardware	Misc	Software	Grand Total
5	Downtown	$46,557	$2,242	$26,452	$25,084
6	Plaza Mall	$41,445	$8,911	$12,999	$21,118
7	Sun Center	$29,458	$4,556	$11,222	$15,079
8	Grand Total	$39,153	$5,236	$16,891	$20,427

Excel 2002

- **f.** Format the amounts as Currency with no decimal places.
- **g.** Name the sheet **PivotTable**.
- **h.** On a separate sheet, create a PivotChart report for the May sales data in all three stores. (*Hint:* Create the PivotChart then use the Page field list arrow to select May.)
- **i.** Add a descriptive title to your chart, using the Chart Options dialog box.
- **j.** Add your name to the worksheet footers, save the workbook, then print the PivotTable and the PivotChart.
- **k.** Close the workbook and exit Excel.

► Independent Challenge 3

You manage a group of sales offices in the Western region for a cellular phone company called Digital West. Management has asked you to provide a summary table showing information on your sales staff, their locations, and their titles. You have been using Excel to keep track of the staff in the San Francisco, Phoenix, and Portland offices. Now you will create a PivotTable and PivotChart summarizing this information.

- **a.** Start Excel, open the Project File titled EX L-5 from the drive and folder where your Project Files are stored, then save it as **Western Sales Employees**.
- **b.** Create a PivotTable on a new worksheet that lists the number of employees in each city, with the names of the cities listed across the columns and the titles listed down the rows. (*Hint*: Remember that the default summary function for cells containing text is Count.) Use Figure L-20 as a guide.

FIGURE L-20

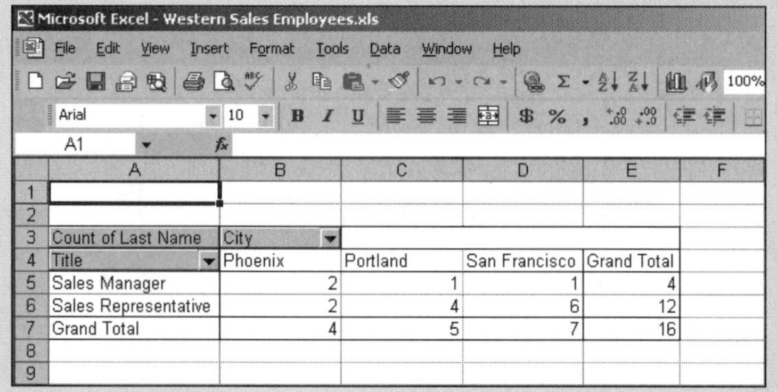

Microsoft Excel - Western Sales Employees.xls

	A	B	C	D	E	F
1						
2						
3	Count of Last Name	City				
4	Title	Phoenix	Portland	San Francisco	Grand Total	
5	Sales Manager	2	1	1	4	
6	Sales Representative	2	4	6	12	
7	Grand Total	4	5	7	16	
8						
9						

- **c.** Name the new sheet **PivotTable**.
- **d.** Add the label **Total Portland Staff:** in cell C19 of the Employee List sheet. Right-align and boldface the label in cell C19.
- **e.** Create a formula in cell D19 that retrieves the total number of employees located in Portland from the PivotTable.
- **f.** Create a PivotChart using the PivotTable information that shows the number of employees in each store by position.
- **g.** Add a chart title of **Western Sales Staff**.
- **h.** Add your name to the three worksheet footers, save the workbook, then print the PivotTable, the Employee List, and the PivotChart.
- **i.** Close the workbook and exit Excel.

Independent Challenge 4

You are a member of an investment group that meets weekly on Thursday evenings. The group is focusing on the NYSE and NASDAQ exchanges this month. You need to prepare a report for this week's meeting showing the performance of three NASDAQ and three NYSE stocks over the past five business days. You decide to use a PivotTable and a PivotChart to represent the market trends for the stocks you are researching. You will begin by researching stock prices on the Web and charting each stock for the past five business days. Then you will use a PivotTable function to display each stock's weekly high. Last, you will use a PivotChart to represent each stock's five-day performance.

Go to the AltaVista search engine at www.altavista.com and enter **stock AND price** in the Search box. Follow the links to stock quotes. You can also use Yahoo!, Excite, Infoseek, or another search engine of your choice. Find prices for the past five days for three NASDAQ and three NYSE stocks. (Some search engines use & or + in place of AND in the search text.)

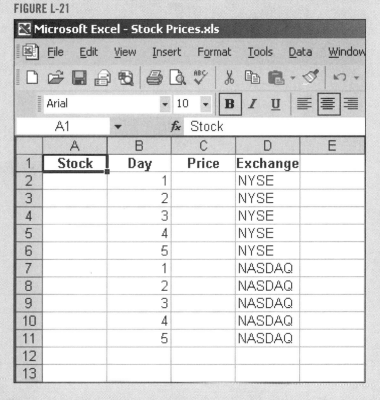

a. Start Excel, create a new workbook, then save it as **Stock Prices** in the drive and folder where your Project Files are stored.
b. Create a list that contains your stock research data. Name the list worksheet Price. Use Figure L-21 as a guide.
c. Create a PivotTable on a new worksheet that sums the stock prices for each stock across the rows and each day down the columns. Add a page field for Exchange. Name the PivotTable sheet **PivotTable**.
d. Format the sales figures appropriately and apply the Table 6 AutoFormat.
e. Change the summary function in the PivotTable to **MAX** to show the highest stock price.
f. Create a PivotChart report from your data on a separate sheet. Change the Column chart to a Bar chart. (*Hint:* Use the Chart Type dialog box). Rename the sheet **Chart**.
g. Enter the label **Highest Price** in cell F1 of the Price sheet. Left-align and boldface the label in cell F1.
h. Create a formula in cell I1 that retrieves the highest price for one of your stocks over the past five days from the PivotTable. Add the stock name to the label in cell F1.
i. Add your name to the worksheet footers, save the workbook, then print the PivotTable, the Price sheet, and the PivotChart.
j. Close the workbook and exit Excel.

FIGURE L-21

Microsoft Excel - Stock Prices.xls

File Edit View Insert Format Tools Data Window

Arial 10 B I U

A1 fx Stock

	A	B	C	D	E
1	**Stock**	**Day**	**Price**	**Exchange**	
2		1		NYSE	
3		2		NYSE	
4		3		NYSE	
5		4		NYSE	
6		5		NYSE	
7		1		NASDAQ	
8		2		NASDAQ	
9		3		NASDAQ	
10		4		NASDAQ	
11		5		NASDAQ	
12					
13					

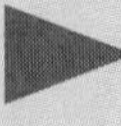

▶ Visual Workshop

Open the workbook titled EX L-6 from the drive and folder where your Project Files are stored, then save it as Photo Store. Using the data in the workbook provided, create the PivotTable shown in Figure L-22. (*Hint:* There are two data summary fields and the table has been formatted using the Table 4 AutoFormat.) Add your name to the PivotTable sheet footer, then preview and print the PivotTable. Save the worksheet, then close the workbook.

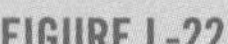

FIGURE L-22

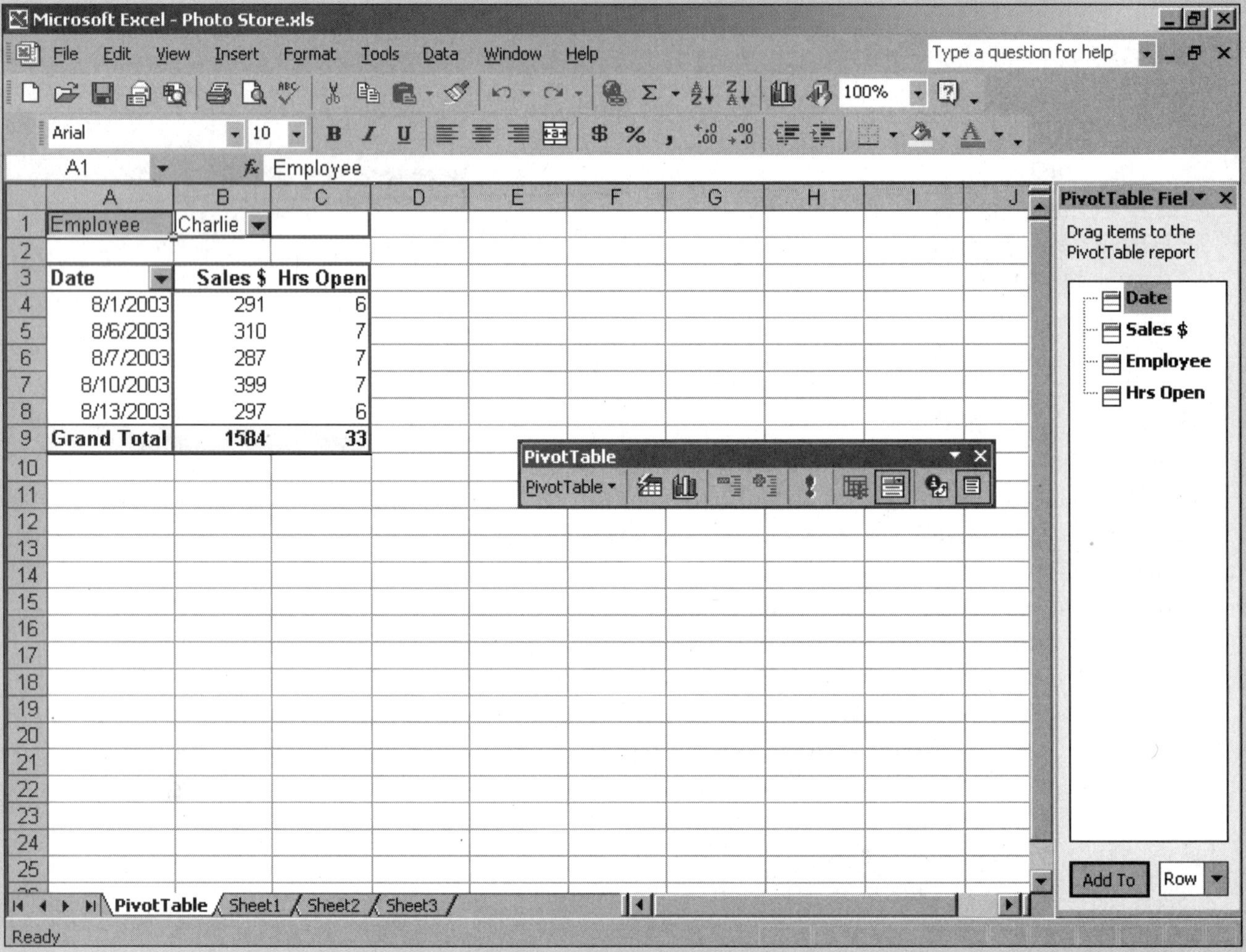

Microsoft Excel - Photo Store.xls
File Edit View Insert Format Tools Data Window Help
Type a question for help
100%
Arial
10
A1
Employee
Employee
Charlie
Date
Sales $
Hrs Open
8/1/2003 291 6
8/6/2003 310 7
8/7/2003 287 7
8/10/2003 399 7
8/13/2003 297 6
Grand Total 1584 33
PivotTable
PivotTable ▾
PivotTable Fiel
Drag items to the PivotTable report
Date
Sales $
Employee
Hrs Open
Add To
Row
PivotTable
Sheet1
Sheet2
Sheet3
Ready

Exchanging

Data with Other Programs

Objectives

- Plan a data exchange
- MOUS Import a text file
- MOUS Import a database table
- MOUS Insert a graphic file in a worksheet
- Embed a worksheet
- Link a worksheet to another program
- Embed an Excel chart into a PowerPoint slide
- MOUS Import a list into an Access table

In a Windows environment, you can freely exchange data between Excel and most other Windows programs, a process known as integration. In this unit, you will plan a data exchange between Excel and other Microsoft Office programs. MediaLoft's upper management has asked office manager Jim Fernandez to research the possible purchase of CafeCorp, a small company that operates cafés in large businesses, hospitals, and, more recently, drug stores. Jim is reviewing the broker's paper documents and electronic files and developing a presentation on the feasibility of acquiring this company. To complete this project, Jim asks you to help set up the exchange of data between Excel and other programs.

Excel 2002

Planning a Data Exchange

Because the tools available in Windows and Windows-compatible programs are so flexible, exchanging data between Excel and other programs is easy. The first step involves planning what you want to accomplish with each data exchange. Jim asks you to use the following guidelines to plan data exchanges between Excel and other programs in order to complete the business analysis project.

1. **Identify the data you want to exchange, its file type, and, if possible, the program used to create it**
   Whether the data you want to exchange is a graphics file, a database file, a worksheet, or consists only of text, it is important to identify the data's **source program** (the program used to create it) and the file type. Once you identify the source program, you can determine options for exchanging that data with Excel. Jim has been asked to analyze a text file containing the CafeCorp product data. Although he does not know the source program, Jim knows that the file contains unformatted text. A file that consists of text but no formatting is sometimes called an **ASCII** or **text** file. Because ASCII is a universally accepted file format, Jim can easily import an ASCII file into Excel. See Table M-1 for a partial list of other file formats that Excel can import. For more information on importable file formats, see the Help topic "File format converters supplied with Excel".

2. **Determine the program with which you want to exchange data**
   Besides knowing which program created the data you want to exchange, you must also identify which program will receive the data, the **destination program**, which determines the procedure you will use to perform the exchange. You might want to insert a graphic object into an Excel worksheet or add a spreadsheet to a Word document. Jim received a database table of CafeCorp's corporate customers created with Access. After determining that Excel can import Access tables and reviewing the import procedure, he will import that database file into Excel so he can analyze it using Excel tools.

3. **Determine the goal of your data exchange**
   Although it is convenient to use the Office Clipboard to cut, copy, and paste data within and between programs, you cannot retain a connection with the source program or document when using these methods. However, there are two ways to transfer data within and between programs that allow you to retain some connection with the source document and/or the source program. These data transfer methods use a Windows feature known as **object linking and embedding**, or **OLE**. The data to be exchanged, called an **object**, may consist of text, a worksheet, or any other type of data. You use **embedding** to insert a copy of the original object in the destination document and, if necessary, to subsequently edit this data separately from the source document. This process is illustrated in Figure M-1. You use **linking** when you want the information you inserted to be updated automatically when the data in the source document changes. This process is illustrated in Figure M-2. Embedding and linking are discussed in more detail later in this unit. Jim has determined that he needs to use both object embedding and object linking for his analysis and presentation project.

4. **Set up the data exchange**
   When you exchange data between two programs, it is often best to start both programs prior to starting the exchange. You might also want to tile the program windows on the screen either horizontally or vertically so that you can see both during the exchange. You will work with Excel, Word, Access, and PowerPoint when exchanging data for this project.

5. **Execute the data exchange**
   The steps you use will vary, depending on the type of data you want to exchange. Jim is ready to have you start the data exchanges for the business analysis of CafeCorp.

FIGURE M-1: **Embedded object**

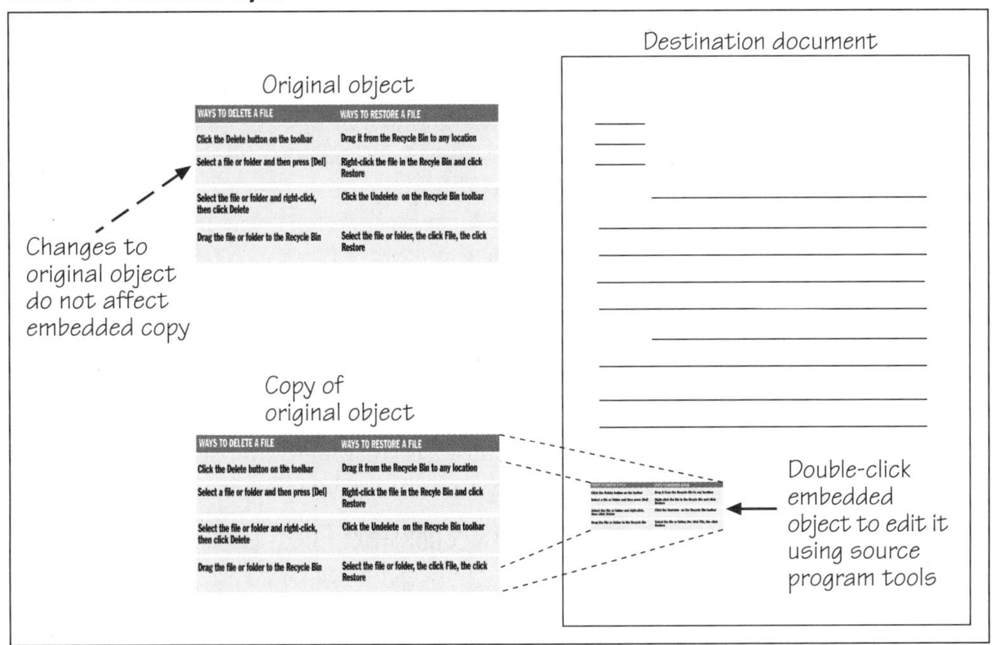

FIGURE M-2: **Linked object**

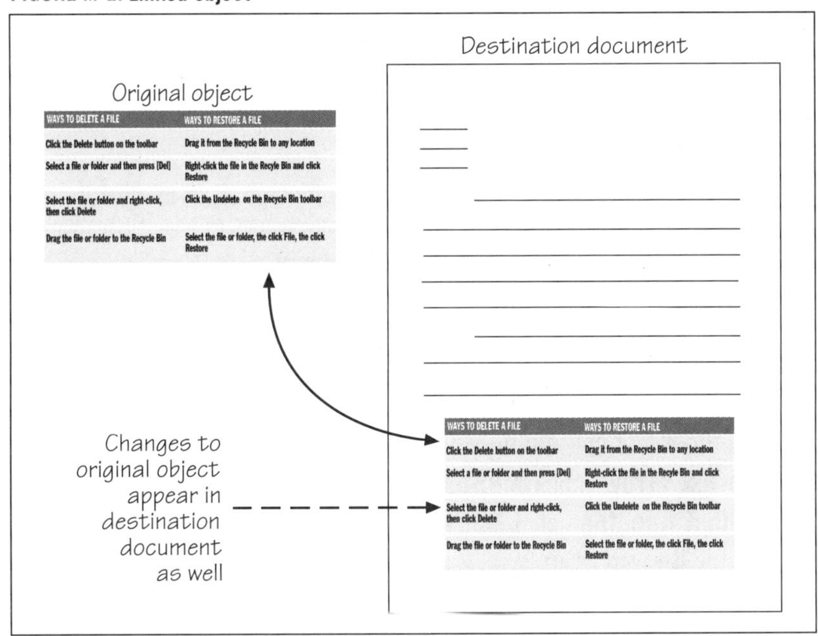

TABLE M-1: **Importable file formats and extensions**

file format	file extension(s)	file format	file extensions
dBASE 2,3,4	dbf	**CSV (Comma Separated Values)**	csv
Excel 97-XP	xls, xlt (template), xlw (workspace)	**DIF (Data Interchange Format)**	dif
Quattro/Quattro Pro	wq1, wb1, wb3	**Formatted Text (Space or column delimited)**	txt, prn
Lotus 1-2-3	wks, wk1, wk3, wk4	**Text (Tab delimited)**	txt
HTML	htm	**XML Spreadsheet**	xml
Web Archive	mht	**SYLK (Symbolic Link)**	slk
Microsoft Works	wks		

Excel 2002

Importing a Text File

You can import data created in other programs into Excel by opening the file, as long as Excel can read the file type. After importing the file, use the Save As command on the File menu to save the data in Excel format. Text files use a tab or space as the **delimiter**, or column separator, to separate columns of data. When you import a text file into Excel, the Text Import Wizard automatically opens and describes how text is separated in the imported file. Now that Jim has planned the data exchange, he wants you to import a tab-delimited text file containing product cost and pricing data from CafeCorp.

1. Start Excel if necessary, click the **Open button** on the Standard toolbar, click the Look in list arrow, then navigate to the folder containing your Project Files
   The Open dialog box shows only those files that match the file types listed in the Files of type box—usually Microsoft Excel files. In this case, however, you're importing a text file.

Trouble?

In the Preview window, a small square separates each field. If the Preview window contains odd-looking characters, make sure you selected the correct original data type.

2. Click the **Files of type list arrow**, click **Text Files**, click **EX M-1**, then click **Open**
   The first Text Import Wizard dialog box opens. See Figure M-3. Under Original data type, the Delimited option button is selected. In the Preview of file box, line 1 indicates that the file contains three columns of data: Item, Cost, and Price. No changes are necessary in this dialog box.
3. Click **Next**
   The second Text Import Wizard dialog box opens. Under Delimiters, the tab character is selected as the delimiter, and the Data preview box contains lines showing where the delimiters divide the data into columns.
4. Click **Next**
   The third Text Import Wizard dialog box opens with options for formatting the three columns of data. Under Column data format, the General option button is selected. This is the best formatting option for text mixed with numbers.
5. Click **Finish**
   Excel imports the text file into the blank worksheet as three columns of data: Item, Cost, and Price.

QuickTip

If you do not specify Excel as the file tupe, the program will ask you if you want to proceed. Click No, then choose Excel in the Save As type list box.

6. Maximize the Excel window if necessary, click **File** on the menu bar, click **Save As**, make sure the folder containing your Project Files appears in the Save in box, click the **Save as type list arrow**, click **Microsoft Excel Workbook**, change the filename to **CafeCorp - Product Info**, then click **Save**
   The file is saved as an Excel workbook, and the new name appears in the title bar. The sheet tab automatically changes to the name of the imported file, EX M-1. The worksheet information would be easier to read if it were formatted and if it showed the profit for each item.
7. Double-click the border between the headers in **Columns A** and **B**, click cell **D1**, type **Profit**, click cell **D2**, type =, click cell **C2**, type -, click cell **B2**, click the **Enter button** on the Formula bar, then copy the formula in cell D2 to the range **D3:D18**
8. Center the column labels, apply bold formatting to them, format the data in columns B, C, and D using the Number style with two decimal places, then click cell **A1**
   Figure M-4 shows the completed worksheet, which analyzes the text file data you imported into Excel.
9. Add your name to the worksheet footer, save the workbook, preview and print the list in portrait orientation, then close the workbook

FIGURE M-3: First Text Import Wizard dialog box

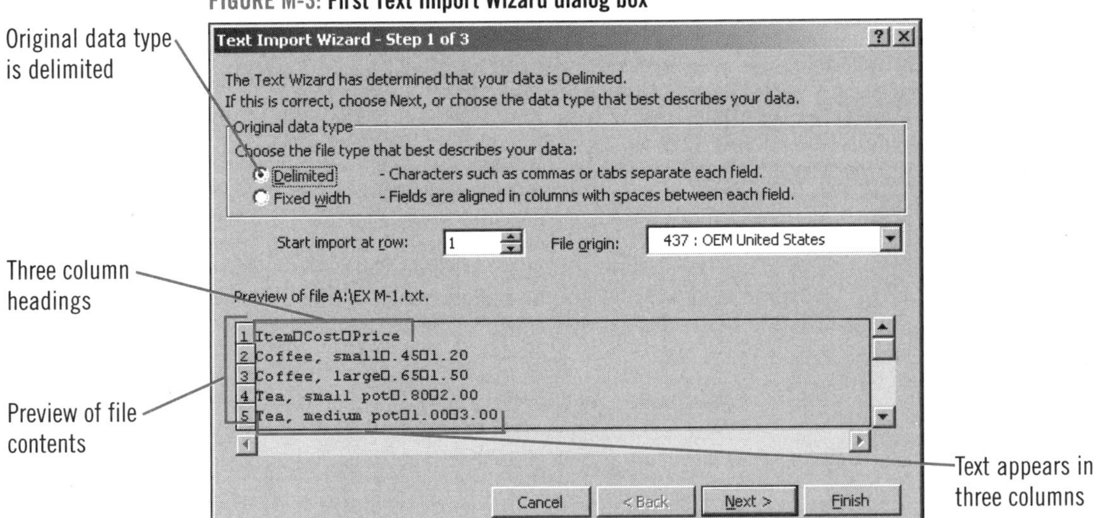

FIGURE M-4: Completed worksheet with imported text file

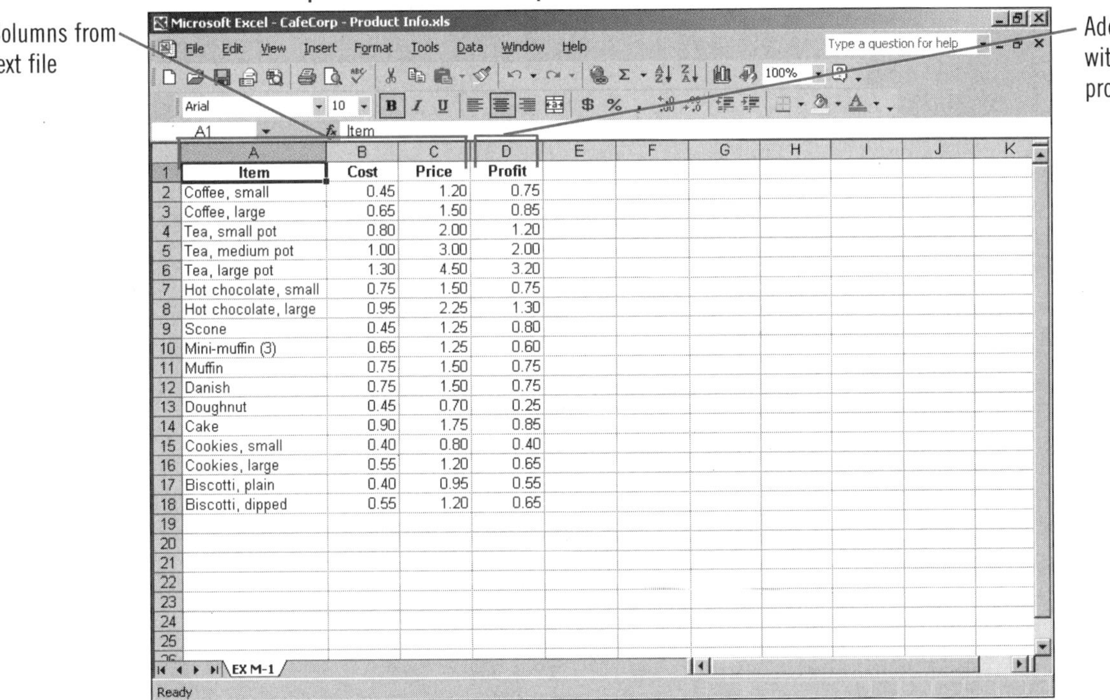

	A	B	C	D
1	Item	Cost	Price	Profit
2	Coffee, small	0.45	1.20	0.75
3	Coffee, large	0.65	1.50	0.85
4	Tea, small pot	0.80	2.00	1.20
5	Tea, medium pot	1.00	3.00	2.00
6	Tea, large pot	1.30	4.50	3.20
7	Hot chocolate, small	0.75	1.50	0.75
8	Hot chocolate, large	0.95	2.25	1.30
9	Scone	0.45	1.25	0.80
10	Mini-muffin (3)	0.65	1.25	0.60
11	Muffin	0.75	1.50	0.75
12	Danish	0.75	1.50	0.75
13	Doughnut	0.45	0.70	0.25
14	Cake	0.90	1.75	0.85
15	Cookies, small	0.40	0.80	0.40
16	Cookies, large	0.55	1.20	0.65
17	Biscotti, plain	0.40	0.95	0.55
18	Biscotti, dipped	0.55	1.20	0.65

Excel 2002

Other ways to import files

Another way to open the Text Import Wizard is by pointing to Import External Data on the Data menu, clicking Import Data, then selecting a data source. Although the Text Import Wizard gives you the most flexibility, there are other ways to import text files.

On the Windows desktop you can drag a text file to the Excel program icon (not the shortcut). On the Windows desktop, you can also drag a text file into a blank worksheet. In a later lesson you will import files using the Object option of the Insert menu.

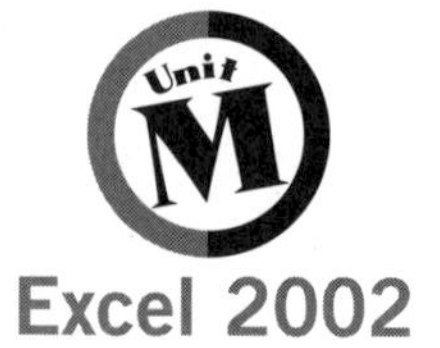

Excel 2002

Importing a Database Table

In addition to importing text files, you can also use Excel to import files from other programs or from database tables. To import files that contain supported file formats, open the file in Excel, then work with the data and save it as an Excel workbook. Jim received a database table of CafeCorp's corporate customers, which was created with Access. He asks you to import this table into Excel, then format, sort, and total the data.

Steps

QuickTip

You can also import information from a database using the Excel Query Wizard. Click Data on the menu bar, point to Import External Data, then click New Database Query. You must first install the optional Microsoft Query. See the Excel help topic "About importing data."

1. Click the **Open button** on the Standard toolbar, then make sure the folder or disk containing your Project Files appears in the Look in box
2. Click the **Files of type list arrow**, scroll down and click **Access Databases**, click **EX M-2**, then click **Open**
   Excel opens the database table and names the sheet tab EX M-2. The External Data toolbar appears on the screen. See Figure M-5. Once you save the table as an Excel workbook, you can analyze the data using Excel tools.
3. Click **File** on the menu bar, click **Save As**, make sure the folder containing your Project Files appears in the Save in box, then make sure Microsoft Excel workbook appears in the Save as type box
4. Change the file name to **CafeCorp - Corporate Customer Info**, then click **Save**
5. Rename the sheet tab **Corporate Customer Info**, then format the data in **columns F** and **G** with the Number format, using commas and zero decimal places
   You are ready to sort the data in columns F and G.
6. Click cell **G2**, then click the **Sort Descending button** on the Standard toolbar
   The records are reorganized in descending order according to the amount of the 2002 orders.
7. Select the range **F19:G19**, click the **AutoSum button** on the Standard toolbar
8. Add a border around the range **F19:G19**, then return to cell A1
   Your completed worksheet should match Figure M-6.
9. Add your name to the worksheet footer, save the workbook, then print the list in landscape orientation

QuickTip

The purple triangle in the corner of cell B1 is a smart tag.

Using Smart Tags

When Excel recognizes certain data types, it marks the cell with a smart tag, a small purple triangle that appears when the program recognizes cell data. For example, if you type a name that matches a name in an Excel address book, you can use the smart tag to send an e-mail to that person from within Excel. To see a list of what actions you can take, point to the smart tag, then click the Smart Tag Actions button that appears. To turn smart tags on or off, click Tools on the menu bar, click AutoCorrect Options, then select or deselect "Label data with smart tags" on the Smart Tags tab.

FIGURE M-5: Imported Access table

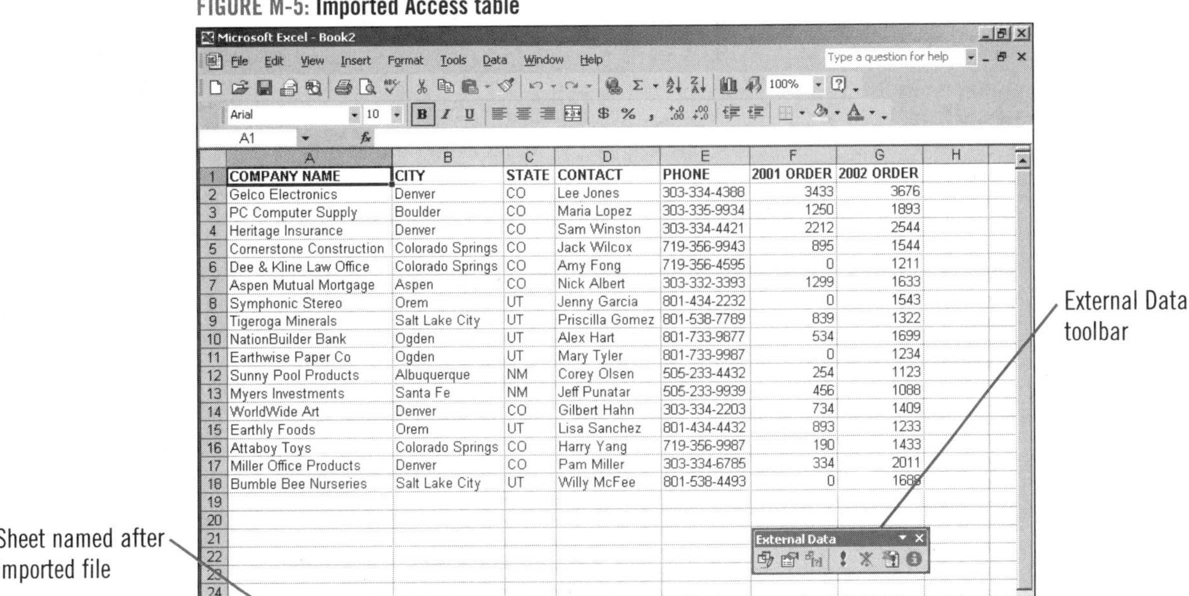

	A	B	C	D	E	F	G
1	COMPANY NAME	CITY	STATE	CONTACT	PHONE	2001 ORDER	2002 ORDER
2	Gelco Electronics	Denver	CO	Lee Jones	303-334-4388	3433	3676
3	PC Computer Supply	Boulder	CO	Maria Lopez	303-335-9934	1250	1893
4	Heritage Insurance	Denver	CO	Sam Winston	303-334-4421	2212	2544
5	Cornerstone Construction	Colorado Springs	CO	Jack Wilcox	719-356-9943	895	1544
6	Dee & Kline Law Office	Colorado Springs	CO	Amy Fong	719-356-4595	0	1211
7	Aspen Mutual Mortgage	Aspen	CO	Nick Albert	303-332-3393	1299	1633
8	Symphonic Stereo	Orem	UT	Jenny Garcia	801-434-2232	0	1543
9	Tigeroga Minerals	Salt Lake City	UT	Priscilla Gomez	801-538-7789	839	1322
10	NationBuilder Bank	Ogden	UT	Alex Hart	801-733-9877	534	1699
11	Earthwise Paper Co	Ogden	UT	Mary Tyler	801-733-9987	0	1234
12	Sunny Pool Products	Albuquerque	NM	Corey Olsen	505-233-4432	254	1123
13	Myers Investments	Santa Fe	NM	Jeff Punatar	505-233-9939	456	1088
14	WorldWide Art	Denver	CO	Gilbert Hahn	303-334-2203	734	1409
15	Earthly Foods	Orem	UT	Lisa Sanchez	801-434-4432	893	1233
16	Attaboy Toys	Colorado Springs	CO	Harry Yang	719-356-9987	190	1433
17	Miller Office Products	Denver	CO	Pam Miller	303-334-6785	334	2011
18	Bumble Bee Nurseries	Salt Lake City	UT	Willy McFee	801-538-4493	0	1688

FIGURE M-6: Completed worksheet containing imported data

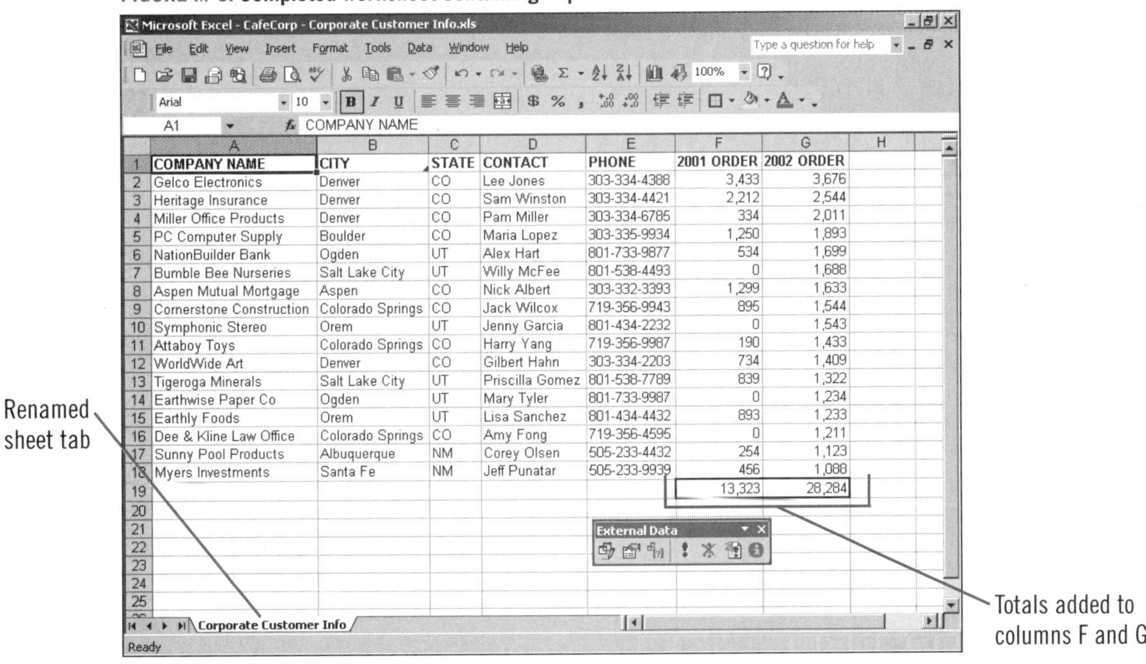

	A	B	C	D	E	F	G
1	COMPANY NAME	CITY	STATE	CONTACT	PHONE	2001 ORDER	2002 ORDER
2	Gelco Electronics	Denver	CO	Lee Jones	303-334-4388	3,433	3,676
3	Heritage Insurance	Denver	CO	Sam Winston	303-334-4421	2,212	2,544
4	Miller Office Products	Denver	CO	Pam Miller	303-334-6785	334	2,011
5	PC Computer Supply	Boulder	CO	Maria Lopez	303-335-9934	1,250	1,893
6	NationBuilder Bank	Ogden	UT	Alex Hart	801-733-9877	534	1,699
7	Bumble Bee Nurseries	Salt Lake City	UT	Willy McFee	801-538-4493	0	1,688
8	Aspen Mutual Mortgage	Aspen	CO	Nick Albert	303-332-3393	1,299	1,633
9	Cornerstone Construction	Colorado Springs	CO	Jack Wilcox	719-356-9943	895	1,544
10	Symphonic Stereo	Orem	UT	Jenny Garcia	801-434-2232	0	1,543
11	Attaboy Toys	Colorado Springs	CO	Harry Yang	719-356-9987	190	1,433
12	WorldWide Art	Denver	CO	Gilbert Hahn	303-334-2203	734	1,409
13	Tigeroga Minerals	Salt Lake City	UT	Priscilla Gomez	801-538-7789	839	1,322
14	Earthwise Paper Co	Ogden	UT	Mary Tyler	801-733-9987	0	1,234
15	Earthly Foods	Orem	UT	Lisa Sanchez	801-434-4432	893	1,233
16	Dee & Kline Law Office	Colorado Springs	CO	Amy Fong	719-356-4595	0	1,211
17	Sunny Pool Products	Albuquerque	NM	Corey Olsen	505-233-4432	254	1,123
18	Myers Investments	Santa Fe	NM	Jeff Punatar	505-233-9939	456	1,088
19						13,323	28,284

Exporting cell data

Most of the file types that Excel can import (listed in Table M-1) are also the file types to which Excel can export, or deliver data. Excel can also export HTML and XML formats for the Web. To export an Excel worksheet, use the Save As command on the File menu, click the Save as type list arrow, then select the desired format. Saving in a non-Excel format might result in the loss of formatting that is unique to Excel.

Excel 2002

Inserting a Graphic File in a Worksheet

A graphic object (such as a drawing, logo, or photograph) can greatly enhance a worksheet's visual impact. The Picture options on the Insert menu make it easy to insert graphics into an Excel worksheet. Once you've inserted a picture, you can edit it using the tools on the Picture toolbar. Jim wants you to insert a copy of the MediaLoft logo at the top of the corporate customer list. A copy of the logo, previously created by the company's Marketing department, is saved as a graphics file in .jpg format on a disk. You start by creating a space for the logo on the worksheet.

Steps

1. Select **rows 1** through **5**, click **Insert** on the menu bar, then click **Rows**
   Five blank rows appear above the header row. To insert a picture, you use the Insert menu.
2. Click cell **A1**, click **Insert** on the menu bar, then point to **Picture**
   The Picture submenu opens. See Figure M-7. This menu offers several options for inserting graphics. You will insert a picture that you already have in a file.
3. Click **From File**, make sure the folder containing your Project Files appears in the Look in box, then click **EX M-3**
   The file has a .jpg file extension. JPEG files can be viewed in a Web browser. The selected graphic appears in the Insert Picture dialog box along with other picture files in your Project Files folder. See Figure M-8.

Trouble?

If your dialog box does not show previews, click the Views list arrow, then click Thumbnails.

4 Click **Insert**
   Excel inserts the graphic and opens the Picture toolbar.

5. Position the pointer over the small circle in the logo's lower right corner, drag the corner up and to the left so that the logo's outline fits within rows 1–5
   The logo would look more prominent if it had a border.
6. With the graphic still selected, click the **Line Style button** here on the Picture toolbar, click the **1-1/2 pt** line style, then press **[Esc]** to deselect the graphic and close the Picture toolbar
   The Picture toolbar closes, and the graphic is displayed with a border.
7. If the graphic overlaps row six, select the image, drag its lower-right corner to resize it, then deselect the graphic
8. Save the workbook
   See Figure M-9.
9. Preview then print the worksheet in landscape orientation, close the workbook, then exit Excel

QuickTip

You can insert shapes, clip art, scanned pictures, and special text effects into your worksheet. You can also use a graphic as a hyperlink to another file or as a way to run a macro. For more information on inserting graphics see the Help topic "About drawing objects and pictures."

FIGURE M-7: Picture menu

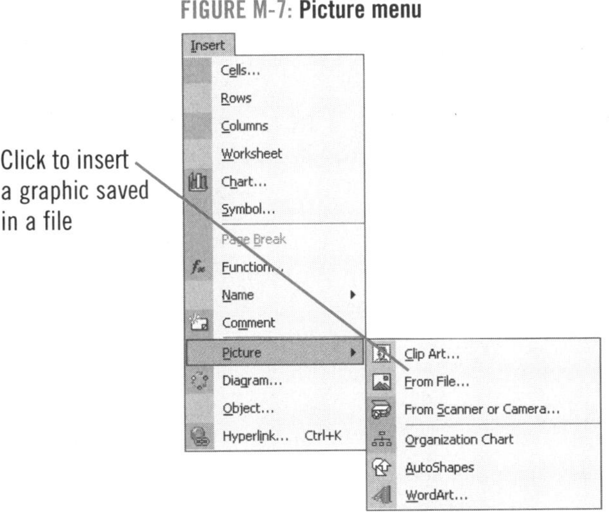

FIGURE M-8: Insert Picture dialog box

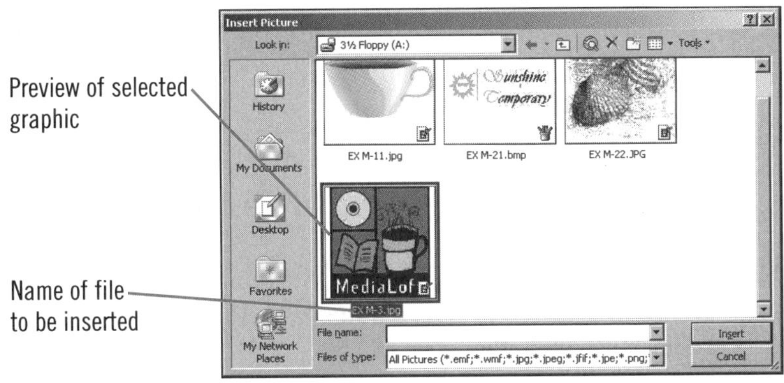

FIGURE M-9: Worksheet with inserted picture

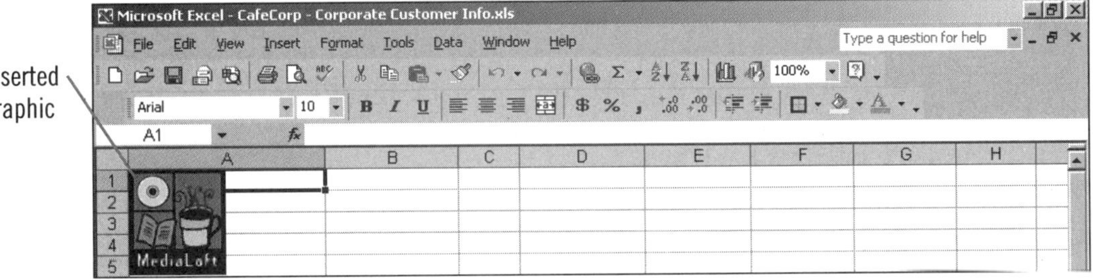

CLUES TO USE

Importing data from HTML files

You can easily import information from HTML files and Web pages into Excel by using drag and drop or the Insert Object command. To use drag and drop, open Internet Explorer, then open the HTML file or Web page that contains the data you want to import. Resize the Explorer window so it covers only half of the screen. Open the Excel file to which you want to import the data, then resize the Excel window so it covers the other half of the screen. In the Explorer window, highlight the table or information you want to import, then drag it over to the Excel window. When the pointer changes to a white arrow with a plus sign, release the mouse button. The table will appear in your Excel document, ready for analysis. You can also open an HTML file from your intranet or a Web site in Excel and modify it. To retrieve data from a particular Web page on a regular basis, use a Web query, which you'll learn about in the next unit.

Excel 2002

Embedding a Worksheet

Microsoft Office programs work together to make it easy to copy an object (such as text, data, or a graphic) in a source program and then insert it into a document in a different program (the destination program). If you insert the object using a simple Paste command, however, you retain no connection to the source program. That's why it is often more useful to embed objects rather than simply paste them. Embedding allows you to edit an Excel workbook from within a different program using Excel commands and tools. If you send a Word document with an embedded worksheet to another person, you do not need to send a separate Excel file with it. All the necessary information is embedded in the Word document. When you embed information, you can either display the data itself, or an icon representing the data; users double-click the icon to view the embedded data. Jim decides to update Maria on the project status. He asks you to prepare a Word memo, including the projected sales worksheet embedded as an icon. You begin by starting the Word program and opening the memo.

1. Click the **Start button** on the taskbar, point to **Programs**, then click **Microsoft Word**
   The Word program opens, with a blank document displayed in the Word window.
2. Click the **More documents button** in the New Document task pane, make sure the folder containing your Project Files appears in the Look in box, click **EX M-4**, then click **Open**
   The memo opens in Word.
3. Click **File** on the menu bar, click **Save As**, make sure the folder containing your Project Files appears in the Save in box, change the file name to **CafeCorp - Sales Projection Memo**, then click **Save**
   You want to embed the worksheet below the last line of the document.
4. Press **[Ctrl][End]**, click **Insert** on the menu bar, click **Object,** then Click the **Create from File tab** in the Object dialog box
5. Click **Browse**, make sure the folder containing your Project Files appears in the Look in box, click **EX M-5**, click **Insert**, then select the **Display as Icon check box**
   The Object dialog box now shows the file to be embedded. See Figure M-10. You are now ready to embed the object.
6. Click **OK**
   The memo now contains an embedded copy of the sales projection worksheet, displayed as an icon. See Figure M-11.
7. Double-click the **Microsoft Excel Worksheet icon**, then maximize the Excel window and the worksheet window
   The Excel program starts and displays the embedded worksheet. See Figure M-12. Any changes you make to the embedded object using Excel tools will not be reflected in the source document. Similarly, if you open the source document in the source program, changes you make will not be reflected in the embedded copy.
8. Click **File** on the Excel menu bar, click **Close & Return to A:\CafeCorp - Sales Projection Memo.doc**, click the Word document on the task bar to activate it, if necessary, then click the **Save button** on the Word toolbar to save the memo

QuickTip

You can also use the Object dialog box to embed an HTML file in an Excel worksheet.

FIGURE M-10: **Object dialog box**

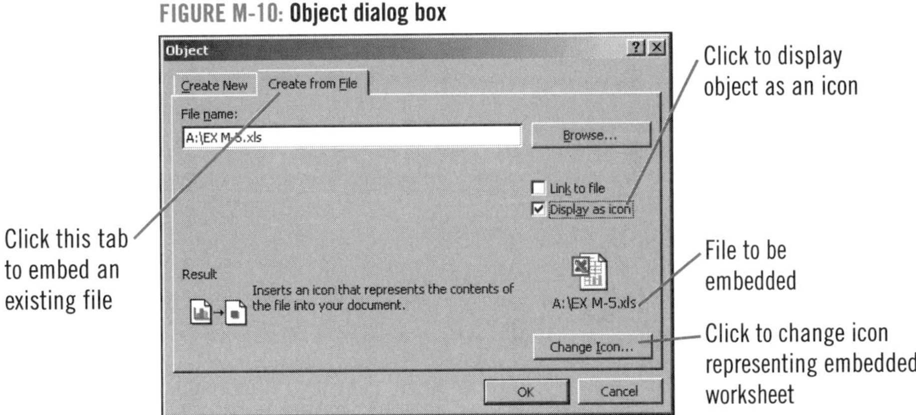

FIGURE M-11: **Memo with embedded worksheet**

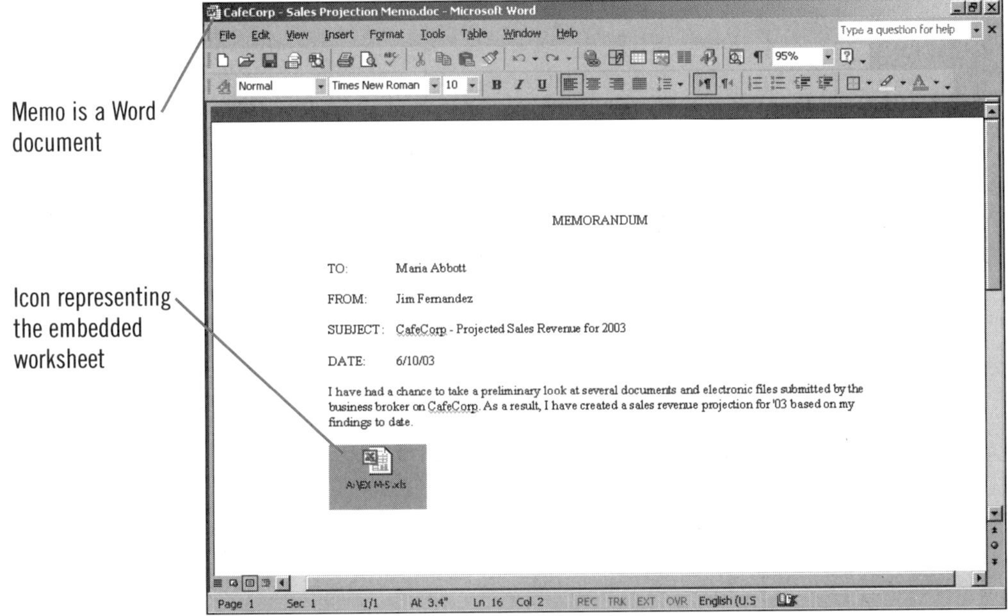

FIGURE M-12: **Embedded worksheet opened in Excel**

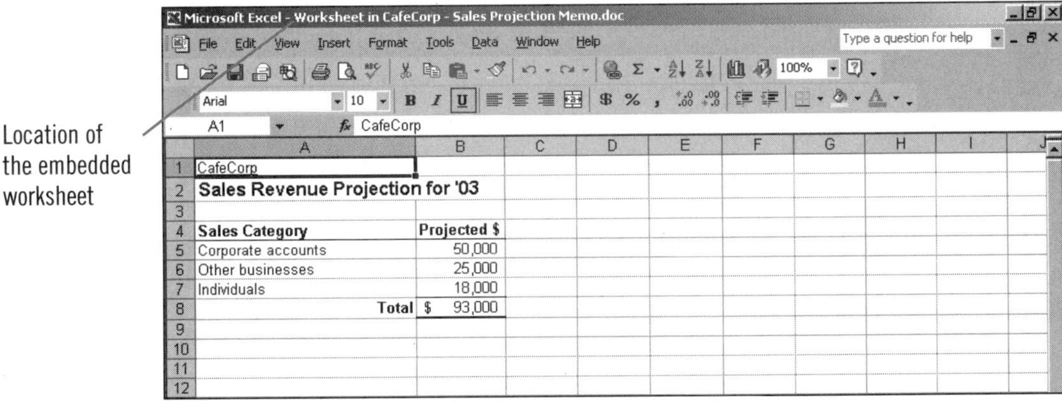

Excel 2002

Excel 2002

Linking a Worksheet to Another Program

Linking a worksheet into another program retains a connection with the original document as well as the original program. When you link a worksheet to another program, the link contains a connection to the source document so that, when you double-click it, the source document opens for editing. Once you link a worksheet to another program, any changes you make to the original worksheet (the source document) are reflected in the linked object. Jim realizes he may be making some changes to the workbook he embedded in the memo to Maria. To ensure that these changes will be reflected in the memo, he feels you should use linking instead of embedding. He asks you to delete the embedded worksheet icon and replace it with a linked version of the same worksheet.

Steps

1. With the Word memo still open, click the Microsoft Excel Worksheet icon to select it if necessary, then press **[Delete]**
   The embedded worksheet is removed. The linking process is similar to embedding.
2. Make sure the insertion point is below the last line of the memo, click **Insert** on the Word menu bar, click **Object**, then click the **Create from File tab** in the Object dialog box
3. Click **Browse**, make sure the folder containing your Project Files appears in the Look in box, click **EX M-5**, click **Insert**, select the **Link to file check box,** then click **OK**
   The memo now displays a linked copy of the sales projection worksheet. See Figure M-13. In the future, any changes made to the source file, EX M-5, will also be made to the linked copy in the Word memo. In the next step, you'll verify this by making a change to the source file and viewing its effect on the Word memo.
4. Click the **Save button** on the Standard toolbar, then close the Word memo and exit Word
   You will test the link by opening the worksheet and changing the sales projection for other businesses to $20,000.
5. Start Excel if necessary, open the file **EX M-5** from the drive and folder where your Project Files are stored, click cell **B6**, type **20,000**, then press **[Enter]**
   Now you will open the Word memo to verify that the same change was made automatically to the linked copy of the worksheet.
6. Start Word, open **CafeCorp - Sales Projection Memo** from the drive and folder where your Project Files are stored
   A message about updating the link may appear briefly. The memo reappears on your screen with the new amount automatically inserted. See Figure M-14.
7. Click **View** on the menu bar, click **Header and Footer**, type your name in the header box, click **Close** on the Header and Footer toolbar, save, preview and print, and close the memo, then exit Word
8. Close the Excel worksheet without saving it, then exit Excel

FIGURE M-13: **Memo with linked worksheet**

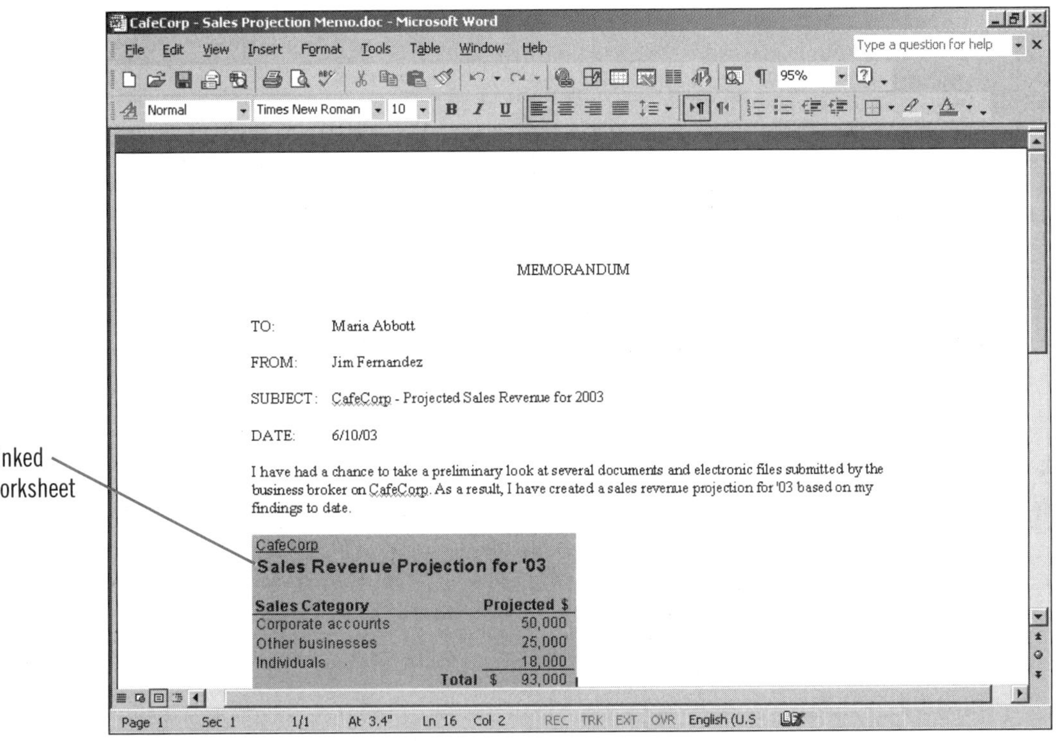

FIGURE M-14: **Memo with link updated**

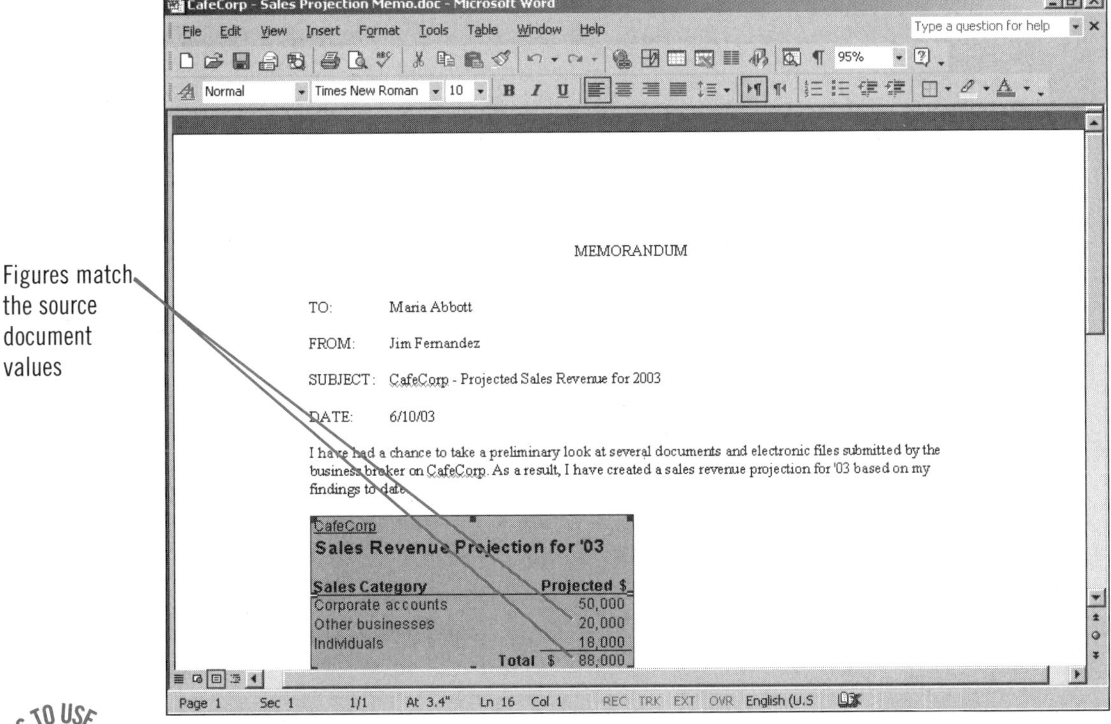

CLUES TO USE

Managing links

When you make changes to a source file, the link is updated automatically each time you open the destination document. You can manage linked objects further by choosing Links on the Edit menu. This opens the Links dialog box, which allows you to update a link or to change the source file of a link. You can also break a link by selecting the source file in the Links dialog box and clicking Break Link.

Excel 2002

Embedding an Excel Chart into a PowerPoint Slide

Microsoft PowerPoint is a presentation graphics program that you can use to create slide show presentations. For example, you could create a slide show to present a sales plan to management or to inform potential clients about a new service. PowerPoint slides can include a mix of text, data, and graphics. Adding an Excel chart to a slide can help to illustrate data and give your presentation more visual appeal. Upper management asks Jim to brief the Marketing department on the possible acquisition of CafeCorp, based on his analysis so far. Jim will make his presentation using PowerPoint slides. He decides to add an Excel chart to one of the presentation slides, illustrating the 2004 sales projection data. He begins by starting PowerPoint.

Steps

1. Click the **Start button** on the task bar, point to **Programs**, then click **Microsoft PowerPoint**
   A new PowerPoint presentation window opens.
2. Click the **Open button** on the Standard toolbar, make sure the folder containing your Project Files appears in the Look in box, click **EX M-6**, click **Open**, then save the presentation as **Marketing Department Presentation**
   The presentation appears in Normal view and contains three panes and the Drawing toolbar, as shown in Figure M-15. The outline of the presentation in the Outline pane on the left shows the title and text for each slide. You will add an Excel chart to slide 2, "2004 Sales Projections". To add the chart, you first need to select the slide on which it will appear.
3. Click the **Slide 2 icon** in the Outline pane
   The slide appears in the Slide pane on the right.
4. Click **Insert** on the menu bar, then click **Object**
   The Insert Object dialog box opens. You want to insert an object (the Excel chart) that has already been saved as a file.
5. Click the **Create from file option button**, click **Browse**, make sure the folder containing your Project Files appears in the Look in box, click **EX M-7**, click **OK**, in the Insert Object dialog box click **OK** again, then press **[Esc]** to deselect the object
   After a moment, a pie chart illustrating the 2004 sales projections appears in the slide. You'll switch from Normal view to Slide Show view to display the slide on the full screen the way the audience will see it.
6. Click **View** on the PowerPoint menu bar, then click **Slide Show**
   After a pause, the first slide appears on the screen. You need to display slide 2, which contains your graphic.
7. Press **[Enter]**
   The finished sales projection slide appears, as shown in Figure M-16. The presentation for the Marketing Department is complete.
8. Press **[Esc]**, in the Outline pane click at the end of the slide 2 text: "2004 Sales Projections"; press **[Spacebar]**, type **by** followed by your name, then click the **Save button** on the PowerPoint Standard toolbar
9. Click **File** on the menu bar, click **Print**, under Print Range select the **Current slide** option, click **OK**, close the presentation, then exit PowerPoint

FIGURE M-15: Presentation in Normal view

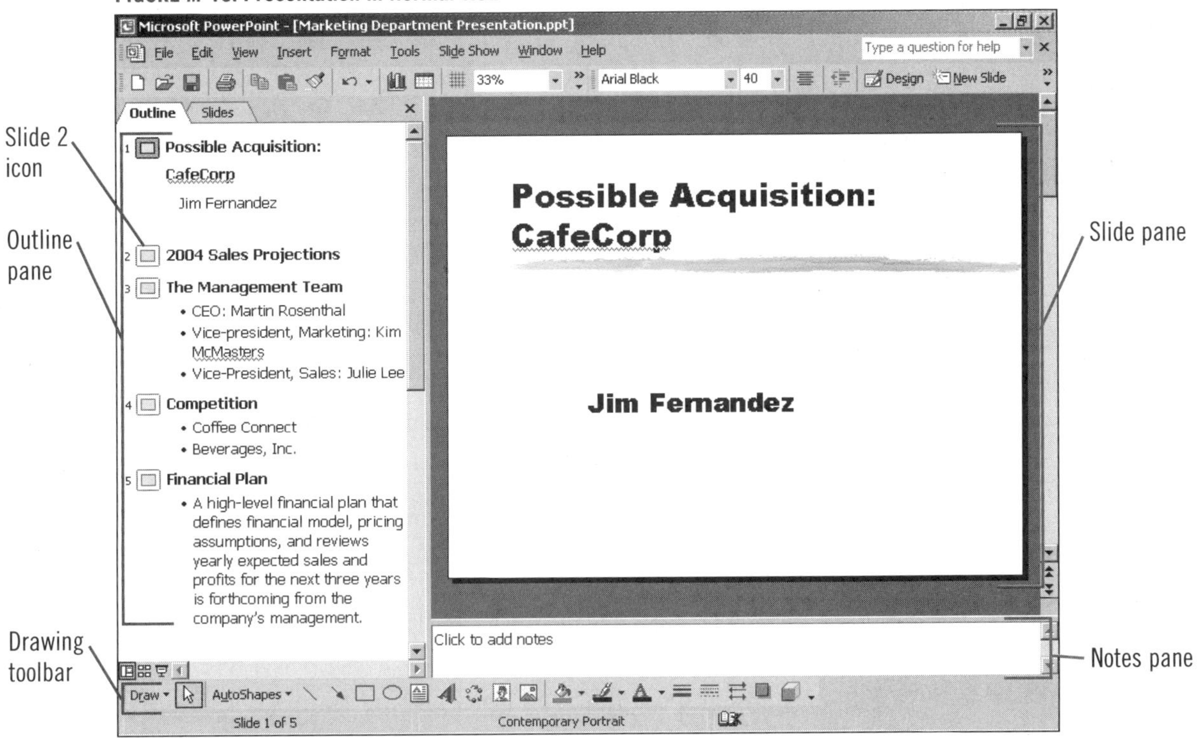

FIGURE M-16: Completed Sales Projections slide in Slide Show view

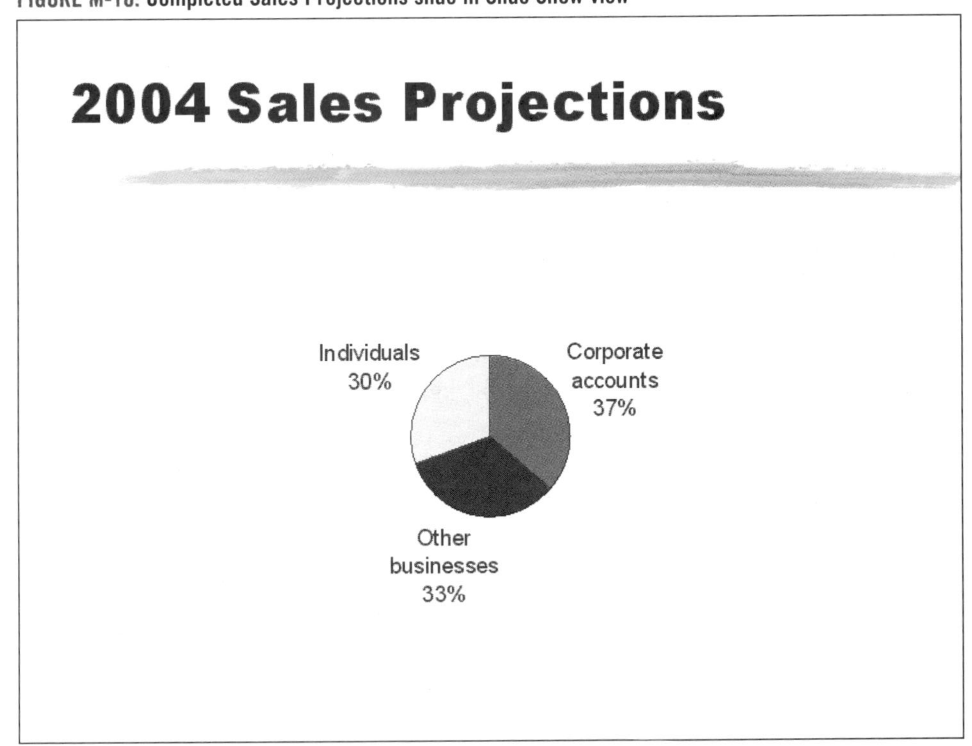

Excel 2002

Excel 2002

Importing a List into an Access Table

An Excel list can be easily imported into Microsoft Access, a database program. Column labels in Excel become field names in Access. Once converted to Access format, a data list is called a **table**. In the process of importing an Excel list, Access will specify a primary key for the new table. A **primary key** is the field that contains unique information for each record (row) of information. Jim has just received a workbook containing salary information for the managers at CafeCorp. He asks you to convert the list to a Microsoft Access table.

Steps

1. Click the **Start button**, point to **Programs**, then click **Microsoft Access**
   The Microsoft Access window opens.
2. Click the **Blank database button** in the task pane, make sure the folder containing your Project Files appears in the Save in box, change the filename to **CafeCorp Management**, then click **Create**
   The database window for the CaféCorp Management database opens. You are ready to import the Excel list.
3. Click **File** on the menu bar, point to **Get External Data**, click **Import**, make sure the folder containing your Project Files appears in the Look in box, select **Microsoft Excel** in the Files of type box, click **EX M-8**, then click **Import**
   The First Import Spreadsheet Wizard dialog box opens. See Figure M-17. In the next dialog box, you'll indicate that you want to use the column headings in the Excel list as the field names in the Access database.
4. Click **Next**, select the **First Row Contains Column Headings check box**, click **OK**, then click **Next**
   Your first row column headings contain spaces, and the Import Spreadsheet Wizard informs you that these will be converted to valid Access field names. You want to store the Excel data in a new table.
5. Make sure the **In a New Table option button** is selected, then click **Next**
   The Wizard has converted the column headings from the Excel list into field names. You can also indicate which columns from the Excel list you do not want to import.
6. Scroll right until the **Annual Salary column** is in view, click anywhere in the column to select it, then select the **Do not import field (Skip) check box** under Field Options; repeat this procedure for each of the five empty columns to the right of the Annual Salary field
   Your completed Import Spreadsheet Wizard dialog box should match Figure M-18. In the next dialog box you will you specify the table's **primary key**, the field containing unique information for each record. The Social Security field is unique for each person in the list.
7. Click **Next**, select the **Choose my own primary key option**, make sure Social Security appears in the list box next to the selected option button, click **Next,** click **Finish**, then click **OK**
   The icon and name of the new Access table ("Compensation") appears in the database window.
8. Make sure that **Compensation** is selected, click **Open** In the Database toolbar, then maximize the table window
   The data from the Excel worksheet is displayed in a new Access table. See Figure M-19.
9. Enter your name in the Social Security column in the bottom row of the table, click the **Save button** on the Access toolbar, click the **Print button** on the Access toolbar to print the table, close the table, then exit Access

QuickTip

You can also use the Microsoft AccessLinks Add-in program, available on the Web, to convert an Excel list to an Access table from within Excel.

QuickTip

Access does not permit certain characters in field names. If your list's field names contain spaces between words or any of the following special characters: a period (.), an exclamation point (!), an accent mark (`), or brackets ([ ]), Access will convert them to valid Access field names.

QuickTip

Specifying a primary key allows you to retrieve data more quickly in the future.

FIGURE M-17: **First Import Spreadsheet Wizard dialog box**

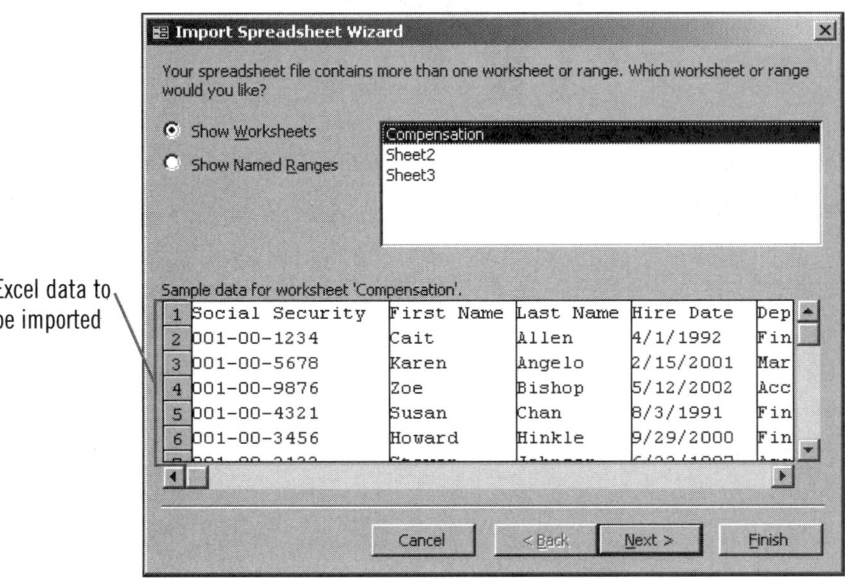

FIGURE M-18: **Completed Import Spreadsheet Wizard dialog box**

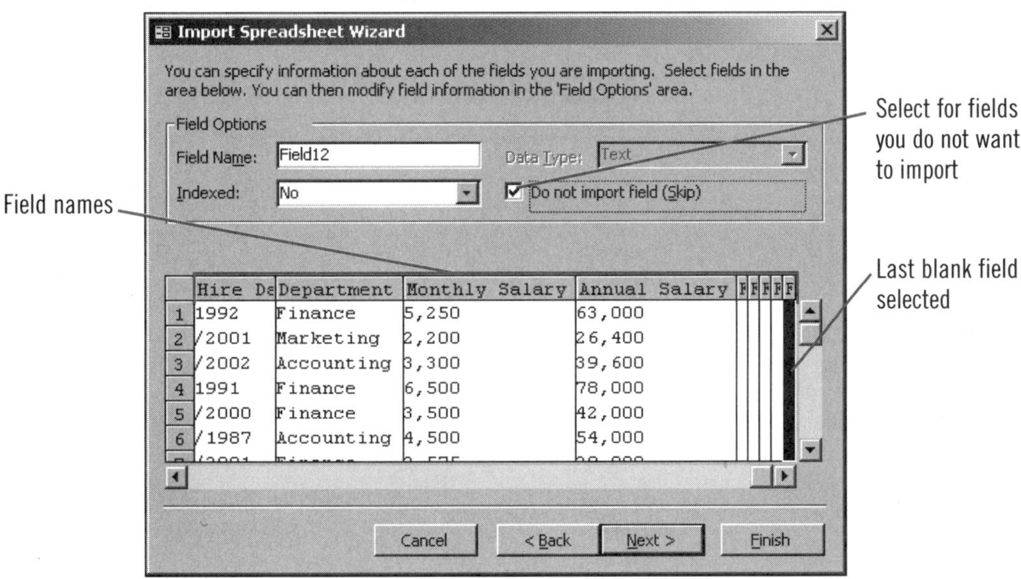

FIGURE M-19: **Completed Access table**

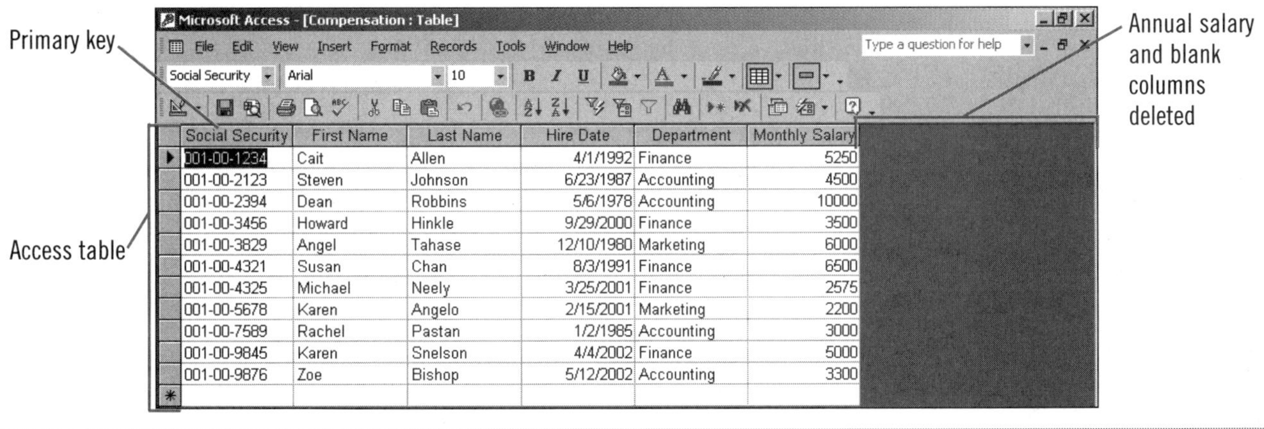

Social Security	First Name	Last Name	Hire Date	Department	Monthly Salary
001-00-1234	Cait	Allen	4/1/1992	Finance	5250
001-00-2123	Steven	Johnson	6/23/1987	Accounting	4500
001-00-2394	Dean	Robbins	5/6/1978	Accounting	10000
001-00-3456	Howard	Hinkle	9/29/2000	Finance	3500
001-00-3829	Angel	Tahase	12/10/1980	Marketing	6000
001-00-4321	Susan	Chan	8/3/1991	Finance	6500
001-00-4325	Michael	Neely	3/25/2001	Finance	2575
001-00-5678	Karen	Angelo	2/15/2001	Marketing	2200
001-00-7589	Rachel	Pastan	1/2/1985	Accounting	3000
001-00-9845	Karen	Snelson	4/4/2002	Finance	5000
001-00-9876	Zoe	Bishop	5/12/2002	Accounting	3300

Practice

► Concepts Review

Label each element of the Excel screen shown in Figure M-20.

FIGURE M-20

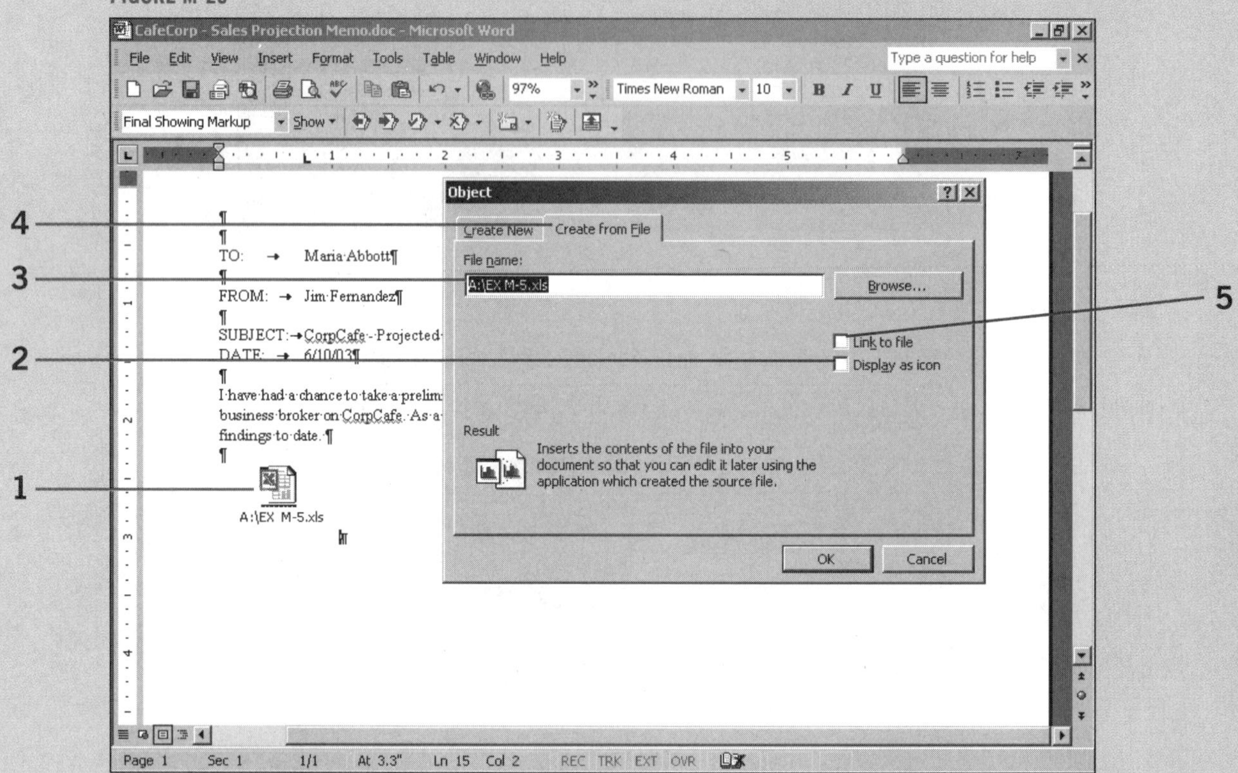

Match each term with the statement that describes it.

6. **Source document**
7. **Linking**
8. **Destination document**
9. **Embedding**
10. **Presentation program**
11. **Table**

a. File from which the object to be embedded or linked originates
b. Copies an object and retains a connection with the source program and source document
c. Document receiving the object to be embedded or linked
d. An Excel list converted to Access format
e. Copies an object and retains a connection with the source program
f. Used to create slide shows

Select the best answer from the list of choices.

12. An ASCII file:
- **a.** Contains formatting but no text.
- **b.** Contains an unformatted worksheet.
- **c.** Contains a PowerPoint presentation.
- **d.** Contains text but no formatting.

13. An object consists of:
- **a.** Text only.
- **b.** Text, a worksheet, or any other type of data.
- **c.** A worksheet only.
- **d.** Database data only.

14. Which of the following is true about converting an Excel list to an Access table?
- **a.** Access field names do not permit spaces.
- **b.** You must convert all the columns in the list to an Access table.
- **c.** The column headings cannot be used as the table's field names.
- **d.** All of the above.

15. To view a worksheet that has been embedded as an icon in a Word document, you need to:
- **a.** Click View, then click Worksheet.
- **b.** Drag the icon.
- **c.** Click File, then click Open.
- **d.** Double-click the worksheet icon.

16. To display numbers with a dollar sign, you can use the following format:
- **a.** Accounting.
- **b.** Currency.
- **c.** Both a and b.
- **d.** Number.

Skills Review

1. Import a text file.
- **a.** Start Excel, open the tab-delimited text Project File titled EX M-9 from the drive and folder where your Project Files are stored, then save it as an Excel workbook with the name **CafeCorp New Products**.
- **b.** Widen the columns as necessary so that all the data is visible.
- **c.** Format the data in columns B and C using the Accounting style with two decimal places.
- **d.** Center the column labels and apply bold formatting.
- **e.** Add your name to the worksheet footer, save the workbook, print the list in portrait orientation, then close the workbook.

2. Import a database table.
- **a.** In the Excel program, open the Access Project File EX M-10 from the drive and folder where your Project Files are stored, then save it as an Excel workbook named **CafeCorp January Budget**.
- **b.** Rename the sheet tab **Budget**.
- **c.** Change the column labels so they read as follows: **Budget Category**, **Budget Item**, **Month**, and **Amount Budgeted**.
- **e.** Use AutoSum to calculate a total in cell D26, then add a border around the cell.
- **f.** Format range D2:D26 using the Accounting style with no decimal places.
- **g.** Center the column labels and adjust the column widths as necessary.
- **h.** Save the workbook.

3. **Insert a graphic file in a worksheet.**
   a. Add four rows above row 1 to create space for a graphic.
   b. Insert the picture file EX M-11 from the drive and folder where your Project Files are stored in rows 1–4.
   c. Resize and reposition it as necessary so it doesn't cover up any column headings.
   d. Open the Picture toolbar if necessary and use the Line style button to add a 1-point border around the graphic, then deselect it.
   e. Add your name to the worksheet footer, save the workbook, then print the worksheet in portrait orientation.
4. **Embed a worksheet.**
   a. In cell A33, enter **For details on CafeCorp salaries, click this icon:**.
   b. In cell D33, use the Object dialog box to embed the worksheet object EX M-12 from the drive and folder where your Project Files are stored displaying it as an icon.
   c. Reposition the icon as necessary, double-click it to verify that the worksheet opens, then close it.
   d. Save the workbook, then print the Budget worksheet in portrait orientation.
5. **Link a worksheet to another program.**
   a. Delete the embedded object icon and the label in cell A33.
   b. Use the Object dialog box to link the spreadsheet object EX M-12 to cell A33, displaying the worksheet, not an icon.
   c. Save the workbook, note that John Kelly's salary is $6,500, then close the workbook.
   d. Open the EX M-12 workbook, then change the John Kelley's salary to 6,000.
   e. Open the **CafeCorp January Budget** workbook, click **Update** when you are asked if you want to update links, then verify that John Kelly's salary has changed to 6,000 and that the new total salaries is $46,740.
   f. Save the CafeCorp January Budget workbook, then print the Budget worksheet in portrait orientation.
   g. Close both workbooks without saving changes to the EX M-12 workbook, then exit Excel.
6. **Embed an Excel chart into a PowerPoint slide.**
   a. Start PowerPoint.
   b. Open the PowerPoint Project File EX M-13 from the drive and folder where your Project Files are stored, then save it as **Monthly Budget Meeting**.
   c. Display Slide 2, January Expenditures.
   d. Insert the Excel file EX M-14 from the drive and folder where your Project Files are located in the slide.
   e. View the slide with the chart in Slide Show view.
   f. Press [Esc] to return to Normal view, save the presentation, print the slide, then exit PowerPoint.
7. **Import a list into an Access table.**
   a. Start Access.
   b. Create a blank database named **Budget List** on the drive and folder where your Project Files are stored.
   c. Import the Excel list EX M-15 from the drive and folder where your Project Files are stored. Use the first row as column headings, store the data in a new table, do not import the month column, let Access add the primary key, and use the default table name January Budget.
   d. Open the January Budget table in Access and widen the column borders as necessary to fully display the field names.
   e. Enter your name in the Budget category of row 25 in the January budget table, save the database file, print the table, then exit Access.

► Independent Challenge 1

You are opening a new store, Bridge Blades, that rents in-line skates in San Francisco, California. The owner of Gateway In-line, a similar store in San Francisco, is retiring and has agreed to sell you a text file containing his list of supplier information. You need to import this text file into Excel so that you can manipulate the data. Later you will convert the Excel file to an Access table, so that you can give it to your partner who is building a supplier database.

a. Start Excel, open the Project File titled EX M-16 from the drive and folder where your Project Files are stored, then save it as **Skate Supplier List**. (*Hint:* This is a tab delimited text file)

b. Adjust the column widths as necessary. Rename the worksheet **Supplier List**.

c. Center the column labels and apply bold formatting.

d. Sort the list in ascending order, first by ITEM PURCHASED, then by SUPPLIER. Your worksheet should look like Figure M-21.

e. Add your name to the worksheet footer, save the workbook, print the worksheet in landscape orientation, close the workbook, then exit Excel.

FIGURE M-21

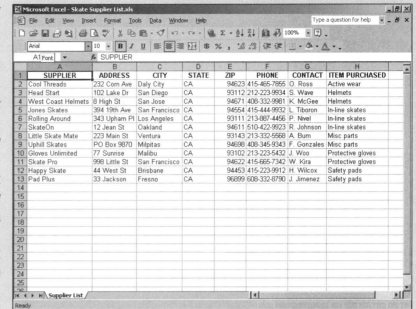

	A	B	C	D	E	F	G	H
1	SUPPLIER	ADDRESS	CITY	STATE	ZIP	PHONE	CONTACT	ITEM PURCHASED
2	Cool Threads	232 Corn Ave	Daly City	CA	94623	415-465-7855	O. Ross	Active wear
3	Head Start	102 Lake Dr	San Diego	CA	93112	212-223-9934	S. Wave	Helmets
4	West Coast Helmets	8 High St	San Jose	CA	94671	408-332-9981	K. McGee	Helmets
5	Jones Skates	394 19th Ave	San Francisco	CA	94554	415-444-9932	L. Tiboron	In-line skates
6	Rolling Around	343 Upham Pl	Los Angeles	CA	93111	213-887-4456	P. Nivel	In-line skates
7	SkateOn	12 Jean St	Oakland	CA	94611	510-422-9923	R. Johnson	In-line skates
8	Little Skate Mate	223 Main St	Ventura	CA	93143	213-332-5568	A. Bum	Misc parts
9	Uphill Skates	PO Box 9870	Milpitas	CA	94698	408-345-9343	F. Gonzales	Misc parts
10	Gloves Unlimited	77 Sunrise	Malibu	CA	93102	213-223-5432	J. Woo	Protective gloves
11	Skate Pro	998 Little St	San Francisco	CA	94622	415-665-7342	W. Kira	Protective gloves
12	Happy Skate	44 West St	Brisbane	CA	94453	415-223-9912	H. Wilcox	Safety pads
13	Pad Plus	33 Jackson	Fresno	CA	96899	608-332-8790	J. Jimenez	Safety pads

f. Start Access, click the Blank database button in the New File task pane to create a new database on the drive and folder where your Project Files are stored. Name the new database **Supplier List**.

g. Import the Excel file, **Skate Supplier List**, from the drive and folder where your Project Files are stored. (*Hint*: Use the Get External Data option on the File menu to import the list.)

h. Use the column labels as the field names, store the data in a new table, import all columns in the list, then let Access add the primary key.

i. Open the Access table Supplier List and AutoFit the columns.

j. Enter your name in the Supplier column in Row 14, save the table, print the table in landscape orientation, close the table, then exit Access.

Independent Challenge 2

You are the newly hired manager at ReadIt, an independent bookstore in your town. A past employee, Roberta Carlson, has filed a grievance that she was underpaid in January 1996. The files containing the payroll information for early 1996 are in Lotus 1-2-3 (WK1) format. In June 1996, the owner switched the business records to Microsoft Excel. You have located the files containing the payroll information you need. You will import the Lotus 1-2-3 file, convert it to an Excel workbook, and correct the formatting in order to verify the values and formulas, especially those for Roberta Carlson, to determine if she was indeed underpaid. The yearly payroll information for 1996 is in an Excel file, and you will link it to the converted Lotus file.

a. Start Excel, open the Lotus 1-2-3 file titled EX M-17 from the drive and folder where your Project Files are stored, then save it as an Excel workbook titled **Payroll Info**.

b. Add gridlines to the worksheet. (*Hint:* Click Tools on the menu bar, click Options, click the View tab, then select the Gridlines check box.)

c. Determine if Roberta was indeed underpaid by examining the worksheet formulas. Correct any formula errors that you find. (*Hint:* The FICA column contains an incorrect formula based on the FICA rate in cell B18.)

d. Delete the dashes in rows 5, 15, and 17. Change the font color of cell C6 from blue to automatic color.

e. Format all dollar values in columns E, F, and G using the Accounting style with two decimal places. Widen the columns as necessary.

f. Center the column labels and apply bold formatting. Rename the sheet tab Payroll. Apply the Classic 2 AutoFormat to cells A4:G16.

g. In cell A21, enter **Click here for yearly payroll information:**.

h. Embed the worksheet object EX M-18 in cell A22 from the drive and folder where your Project Files are stored as an icon, then double-click the icon to verify that the worksheet opens.

i. Delete the icon for EX M-18 and the text in cell A21. Link the spreadsheet object EX M-18 to cell A21, displaying the worksheet, not an icon. Save and close the Payroll Info workbook. Change Joy Yee's salary to 7000 in the source file (the EX M-18 workbook) and make sure the link in the Payroll Info workbook is updated.

j. Add your name to the Payroll Info worksheet footer, save the Payroll Info workbook, then print the worksheet in landscape orientation.

k. Close EX M-18 without saving the change to Joy Yee's salary.

► Independent Challenge 3

You are a loan officer for the Naples, Florida branch of EastWest bank. You have been asked to give a presentation to a group of bank vice presidents about the types and number of loan applications your branch has received in the past year. To illustrate your loan data, you will add an Excel chart to one of your slides, showing the most popular loan types and the number of applications received this year for each.

a. Start Excel, create a new workbook, then save it as **Consumer Loans** in the drive and folder where your Project Files are stored.

b. Enter the loans and the corresponding number of applications shown in Table M-2 into the Consumer Loans workbook. Name the sheet with the loan data **Loans**.

c. Create a pie chart from the loan data on a new sheet. Add a title of **Loan Applications by Type** to your chart. Increase the font size to 24 in the chart title, and to 20 in the legend. Your chart should look like Figure M-22.

d. Save the workbook, then close the workbook with the chart sheet the active sheet.

e. Start PowerPoint, open the PowerPoint Project File EX M-19 from the drive and folder where your Project Files are stored, then save it as **Loan Presentation**.

f. Insert the Excel chart from the Consumer Loans workbook into slide 2.

g. View the slide in Slide Show view, then press [Esc] to end the show.

h. Edit slide 1 to include your name. (*Hint:* Click the first slide in the Outline pane, select the name **Allen Oles**, then type your name.) Save the presentation. Use the File menu to open the Print dialog box. Specify that you want to print slides 1 and 2 using the slides radio button.

i. Close the presentation, then exit PowerPoint and Excel.

TABLE M-2

Loan type	Number of applications
Fixed home loans	1556
New car loans	6400
Used car loans	4452
Adjustable home loans	860
Boat loans	350

FIGURE M-22

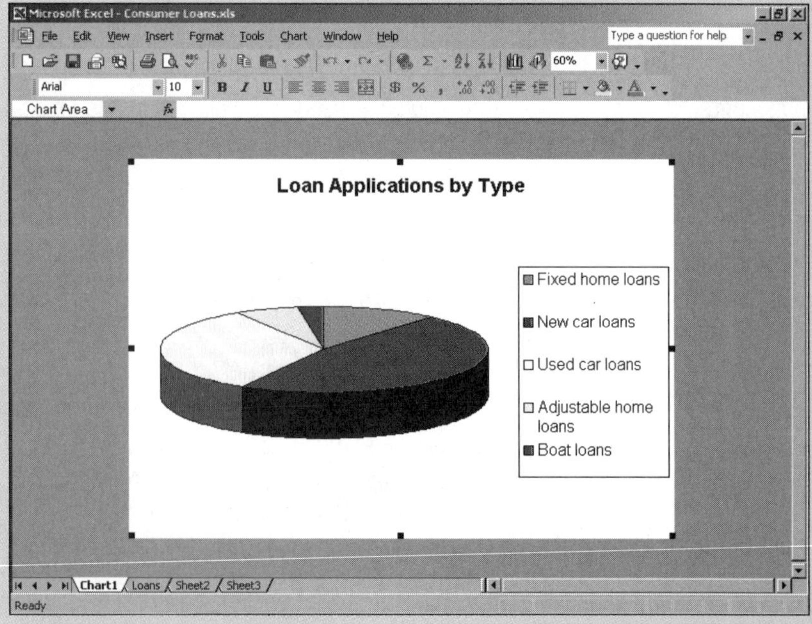

Independent Challenge 4

You are an assistant to the vice president of Sunshine Temporary, a temporary agency located in Winnipeg, Manitoba. Presently, Sunshine Temporary contracts with local companies to staff temporary secretarial and data entry positions. Management is considering adding permanent and temporary technical positions to the job titles it currently helps its clients fill. The vice president has asked you to prepare an Excel workbook showing the current open positions in the Sunshine Temporary database; she also wants you to include salary information for professional positions for which companies in the United States and Canada are recruiting. You will import a database list of current openings at Sunshine Temporary into an Excel workbook. Then you will use the Web to research professional salaries in the U.S. and Canada and enter that information in the workbook.

a. Start Excel, open the Access file titled EX M-20 from the drive and folder where your Project Files are stored, then save it as an Excel workbook titled **Temp Jobs**.

b. Rename the sheet tab **Open Positions**.

c. Sort the list in ascending order by Position.

d. Enter **Average Hourly Rate** in cell B14, then enter a function in cell C14 to find the average of all Hourly Rates in column C.

e. Format the data in column C using the Accounting style with 2 decimal places.

f. Add four rows above row 1 to create space for a graphics file, and insert the picture file EX M-21 from the drive and folder where your Project Files are stored. Resize the graphic as necessary.

g. Apply the List 1 AutoFormat to the range A5:C16. Compare your worksheet to Figure M-23.

h. Open your Web browser and go to the search engine of your choice and search for job postings for technical positions. You can use AltaVista, Yahoo!, Excite, Infoseek, or another search engine. Find postings for six technical positions in the U.S. and Canada. Note the following information from the job postings: job title, state or province, country, and the salary range. Some salaries may be listed as hourly rates.

FIGURE M-23

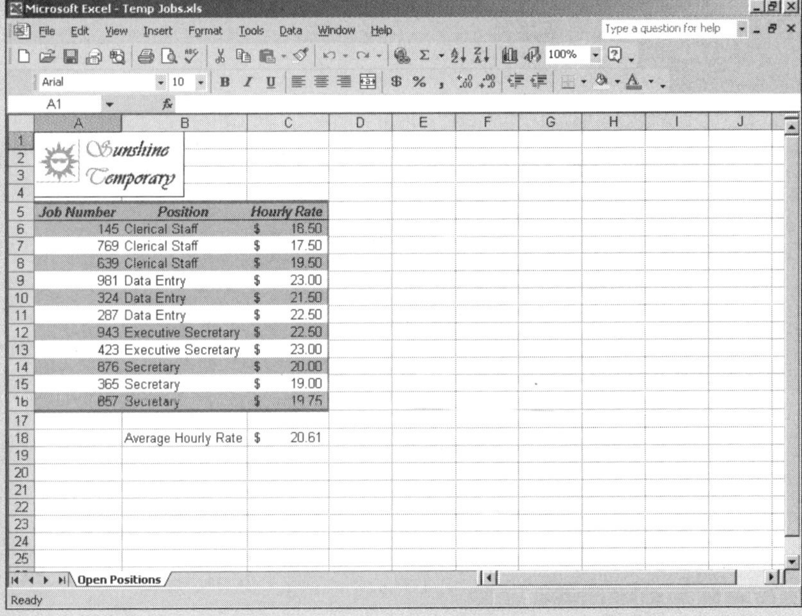

i. Add a worksheet named Technical Positions to the right of the Open Positions worksheet, in the workbook. Enter the label **Position** in cell A1, **State/Province** in cell B1, **Country** in cell C1, and **Salary Range** in cell D1. Resize the columns as necessary. Use the information from your Web search to enter six records.

j. Enter your name in the footers of both sheets, save the workbook, then print both worksheets.

k. Close the workbook, then exit Excel.

▶ Visual Workshop

Create the worksheet shown in Figure M-24. Insert the graphic file EX M-22 and embed the workbook file EX M-23 as an icon. Both files are located in your Project Files folder. Resize both objects as necessary. Enter your name in the worksheet footer, save the workbook as **Atlantic Price List**, then print the worksheet.

FIGURE M-24

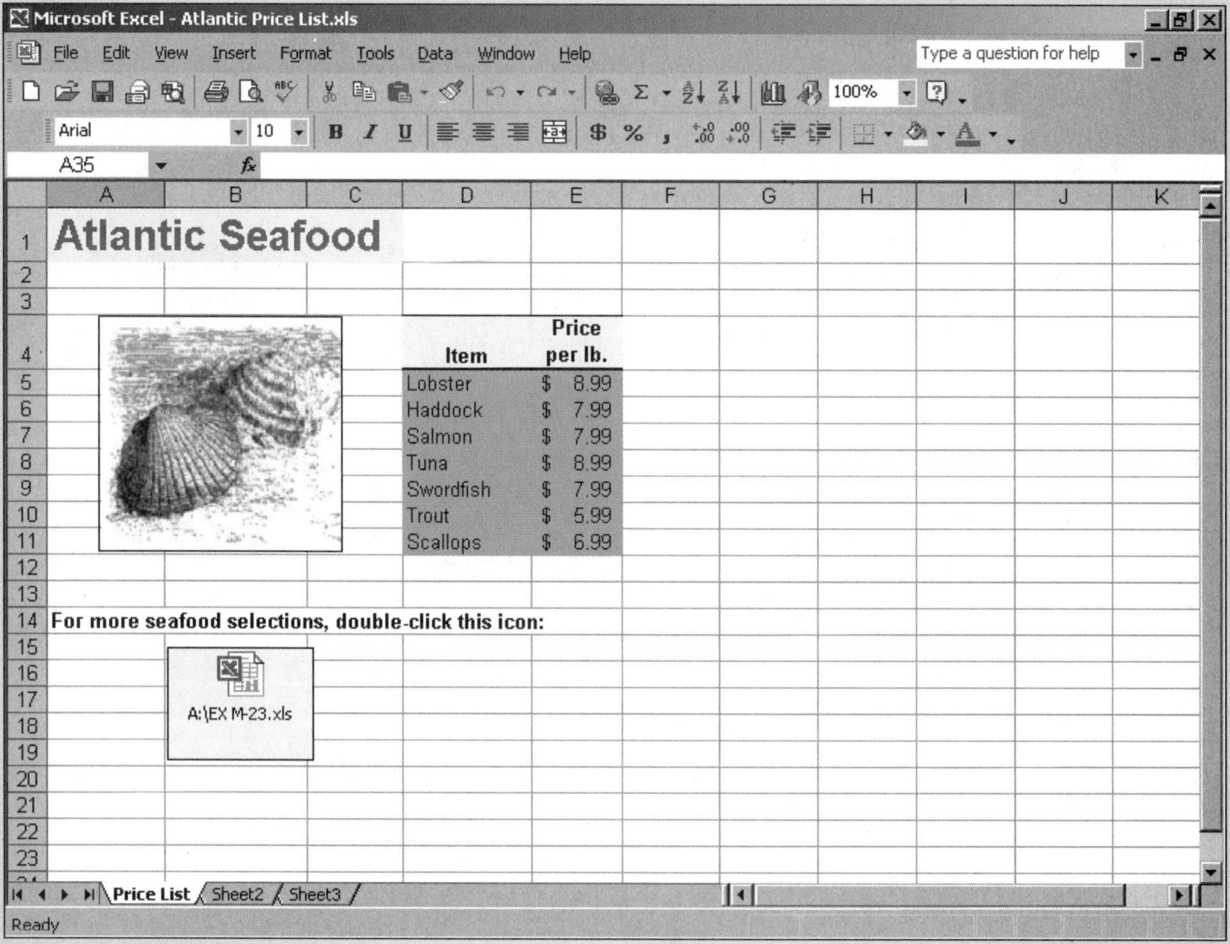
Microsoft Excel - Atlantic Price List.xls
File Edit View Insert Format Tools Data Window Help
Type a question for help
100%
Arial
10
A35
Atlantic Seafood
Item
Price per lb.
Lobster $ 8.99
Haddock $ 7.99
Salmon $ 7.99
Tuna $ 8.99
Swordfish $ 7.99
Trout $ 5.99
Scallops $ 6.99
For more seafood selections, double-click this icon:
A:\EX M-23.xls
Price List
Sheet2
Sheet3
Ready

Excel 2002

Unit N

Sharing

Excel Files and Incorporating Web Information

Objectives

- MOUS ► Share Excel files
- MOUS ► Set up a shared workbook for multiple users
- MOUS ► Track revisions in a shared workbook
- MOUS ► Apply and modify passwords
- MOUS ► Create an interactive worksheet for the Web
- MOUS ► Create a PivotTable list for the Web
- MOUS ► Add Web hyperlinks to an Excel file
- MOUS ► Run Web queries to retrieve external data

With the recent growth of networks, company intranets, and the World Wide Web, people are increasingly sharing electronic spreadsheet files with others for review, revision, and feedback. They are also incorporating information from intranets and the Web into their worksheets. Jim Fernandez has some MediaLoft corporate information he wants to share with corporate office employees and store managers. He also wants to track information about MediaLoft's competitors.

Excel 2002

Sharing Excel Files

Microsoft Excel provides many different ways to share spreadsheets electronically with people in your office, in your company, or anywhere on the Web. You can post workbooks, worksheets, or other parts of workbooks for users to interact with on a company intranet or on the Web. Users can retrieve and review them. When you share workbooks, however, you have to consider how you will protect information that you don't want everyone to see. You can also use Excel workbooks to run queries to retrieve data from the Web. Jim considers the best way to share his Excel workbooks with corporate employees and store managers. He also thinks about how to obtain Web data to use in his workbooks. He considers the following issues:

- **Allowing others to use a workbook**
  When you share Excel files with others, you need to set up your workbooks so that several users can simultaneously open them from a network server, modify them electronically, and return their revisions to you for incorporation with others' changes. You can view each user's name and the date each change was made. Jim wants to obtain feedback on selected store sales and customer information from MediaLoft corporate staff and store managers.

- **Controlling access to workbooks on a server**
  When you set up a workbook on a network server, you may want to control who can open and change it. You can do this easily with Excel passwords. Jim assigns a password to his workbook and gives it to the corporate staff and store managers, so only they will be able to open the workbook and revise it.

- **Distributing workbooks to others**
  There are several ways of making workbook information available to others. You can send it to recipients simultaneously as an e-mail attachment or as the body of an e-mail message; you can **route** it, or send it sequentially to each user, who then forwards it on to the next recipient using a **routing slip**, or list of recipients. You can also save the file in HTML format and post it on a company intranet server or on the Web, where people can view it with their Web browsers. Jim decides to make an Excel workbook available to others by putting it on a company server.

- **Publishing a worksheet for use on an intranet or the World Wide Web**
  When you save a workbook as a Web page, you can save the entire workbook or a single worksheet. You can specify that you want to make it **interactive**, meaning that users can make changes to it when they view it in their browsers. They do not need to have the Excel program on their computer. See Figure N-1. The changes remain in effect until users close their browsers. Jim decides to publish the worksheet with the MediaLoft café pastry sales information.

- **Interactive PivotTables**
  You can save a PivotTable in HTML format so people can only view it, but the data is much more useful if people can interact with it using their browsers, just as they would in Excel. To make an Excel PivotTable interactive, you need to save it as a PivotTable list. Jim wants corporate staff to explore sales data using their browsers just as he would with Excel.

- **Creating hyperlinks to the Web**
  You can make Web information available to workbook users by creating hyperlinks to any site on the Web. Jim decides to include a hyperlink to a competitor's Web site so the sales managers can view competitive information.

- **Using an Excel query to retrieve data from the Web**
  You can use Microsoft Query to import data from the Web into an Excel workbook. Then you can organize and manipulate the information using Excel spreadsheet and graphics tools. Jim decides to use a query to get stock information about one of MediaLoft's competitors. See Figure N-2.

FIGURE N-1: **Interactive worksheet in Web browser**

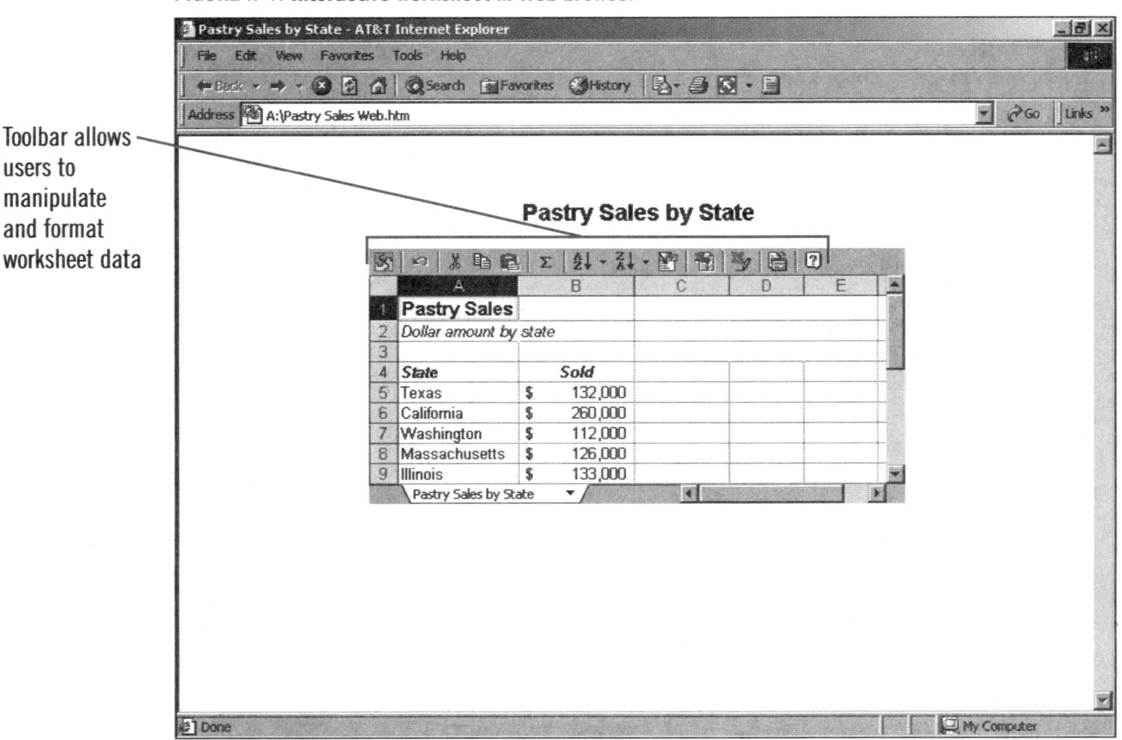

Toolbar allows users to manipulate and format worksheet data

FIGURE N-2: **Data retrieved from the Web using a Web query**

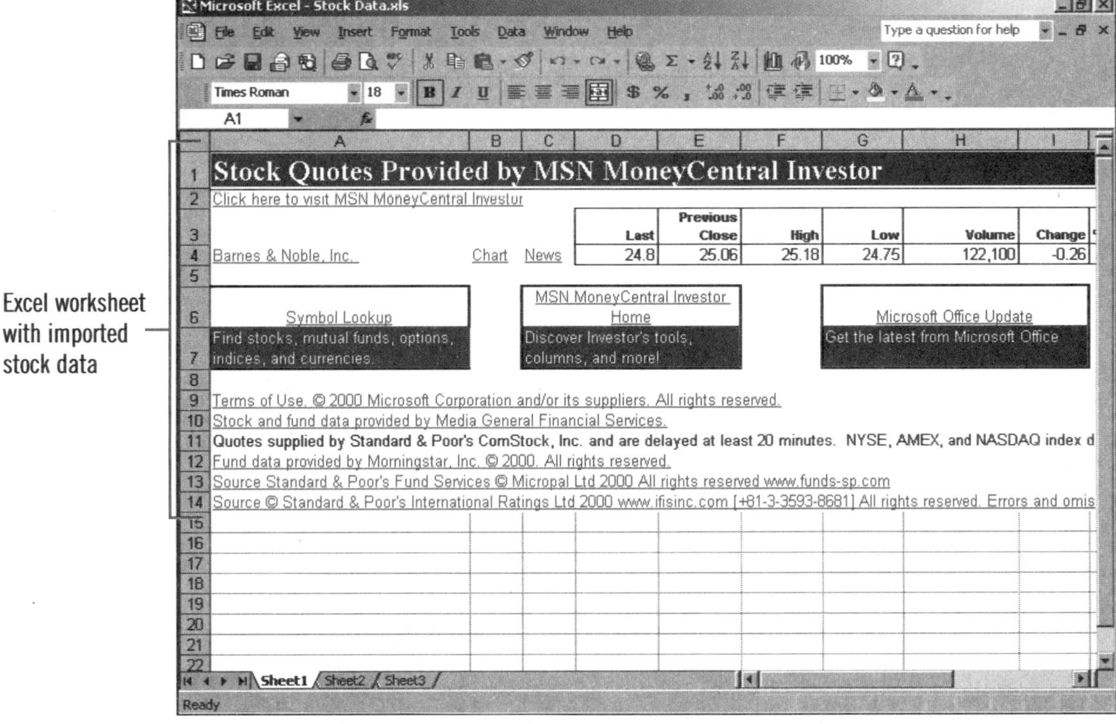

Excel worksheet with imported stock data

Excel 2002

Setting up a Shared Workbook for Multiple Users

You can make an Excel file a **shared workbook** so that several users can open and modify it at the same time. This is very useful for workbooks that you want others to review on a network server. The workbook is equally accessible to all network users. When you share a workbook, you can have Excel keep a list of all changes to the workbook, which you can view and print at any time. Jim asks you to help him put a shared workbook containing customer and sales data on the company's network. He wants to get feedback from selected corporate staff and store managers before using the information in a presentation at the next corporate staff meeting. You begin by making his workbook containing customer and sales data a shared workbook.

Steps

1. **Start Excel, open the Project File EX N-1 from the drive and folder where your Project Files are stored, then save it as Sales Info**
   The workbook with the sales information opens, displaying three worksheets. The first is the chart of MediaLoft pastry sales for the first quarter, the second contains data about pastry sales by state, and the third contains a listing of sales for selected stores and sales representatives for the last four quarters.

2. **Click Tools on the menu bar, then click Share Workbook**
   The Share Workbook dialog box opens. See Figure N-3.

3. **Click the Editing tab, if necessary**
   The dialog box lists the names of people who are currently using the workbook. You are the only user, so your name, or the name of the person entered as the computer user, appears, along with the date and time.

4. **Click to select the check box next to Allow changes by more than one user at the same time, then click OK**
   A dialog box appears, asking if you want to save the workbook. This will resave it as a shared workbook.

5. **Click OK**
   Excel saves the file as a shared workbook. The Title bar now reads Sales Info.xls [Shared]. See Figure N-4. This version replaces the unshared version.

QuickTip

You can remove users from the list by clicking their names and clicking Remove User.

QuickTip

You can return the workbook to unshared status. To do so, click Tools, click Share Workbook, then deselect the "Allow changes by more than one user at the same time" option on the Editing tab.

FIGURE N-3: **Share Workbook dialog box**

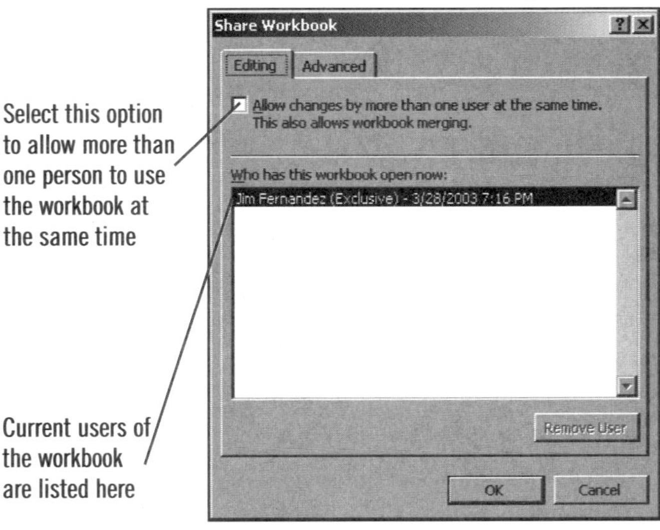

FIGURE N-4: **Shared workbook**

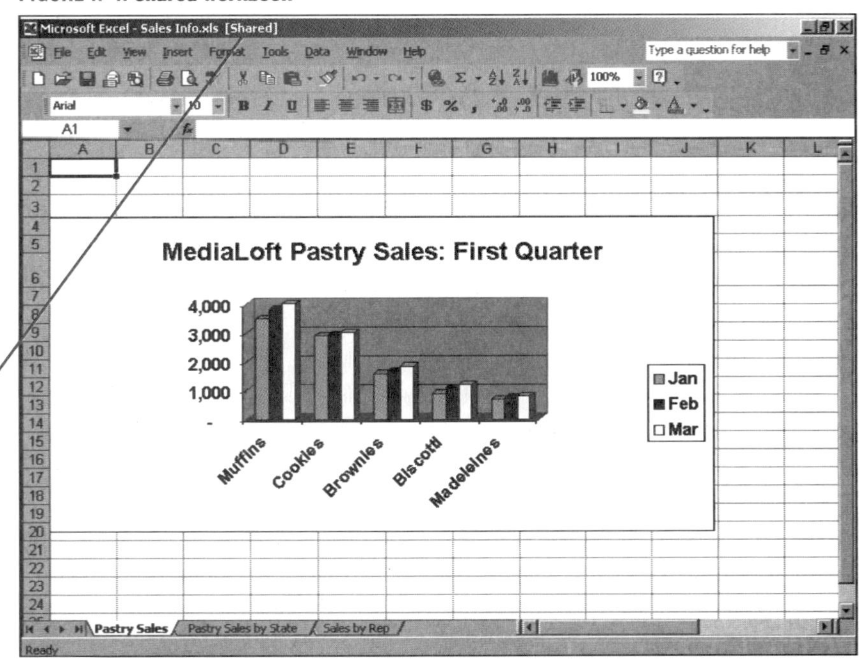

Excel 2002

Excel 2002

Tracking Revisions in a Shared Workbook

When you share workbooks, it is often helpful to **track** modifications, or identify who made which changes. If you disagree with any of the changes, you can reject them. When you activate the Excel change tracking feature, changes appear in a different color for each user. Each change is identified with the username and date. In addition to highlighting changes, Excel keeps track of all changes in a **change history**, a list of all changes that you can place on a separate worksheet so you can review them all at once. Jim asks you to set up the shared Sales Info workbook so that all future changes will be tracked. You will then open a workbook that has been on the server and review the changes and the change history.

1. **Click Tools on the menu bar, point to Track Changes, click Highlight Changes**
   The Highlight Changes dialog box opens, allowing you to turn on change tracking. You can also specify which changes to highlight and whether you want to display changes on the screen or save the change history in a separate worksheet. See Figure N-5.

2. **Click to select Track changes while editing check box if necessary, remove check marks from all other boxes except for Highlight changes on screen, click OK, then click OK in the dialog box that informs you that you have yet to make changes**
   Leaving the When, Who, and Where check boxes blank allows you to track all changes.

3. **Click the Pastry Sales by State tab, change the sales figure for Texas to 133,000, press [Enter], then move the mouse pointer over the cell you just changed**
   A border with a small triangle in the upper-left corner appears around the cell you changed, and a ScreenTip appears with your name, the date, the time, and details about the change. See Figure N-6. Cells that other users change will appear in different colors.

4. **Save and close the workbook**

5. **Open the Project File EX N-2 from the drive and folder where your Project Files are stored, then save it as Sales Info Edits**
   Jim Fernandez and Jose Mendel have made changes to a version of this workbook. You want to view the details of these changes.

6. **Click Tools on the menu bar, point to Track Changes, click Highlight Changes, click the When check box in the Highlight Changes dialog box to deselect it, click to select the List changes on a new sheet check box, then click OK**
   The History tab appears, as shown in Figure N-7, with a record of each change in the form of a filtered list. You could click the Who list arrow in row 1 to show a list of Jose Mendel's changes only.

7. **Click each sheet tab and examine the changes on each one by holding the pointer over each change and viewing the ScreenTip, then click the History sheet tab**

8. **Enter your name in the History sheet footer, print the History sheet in landscape orientation on one page, save the workbook, observe that the History sheet closes automatically, then close the workbook**
   The change history printout shows who made which changes to the workbook.

QuickTip

Once the "Track changes while editing" feature is selected, you can review all changes made to a shared workbook by clicking Tools on the menu bar, pointing to Track Changes, then clicking Accept or Reject Changes. To review all changes, you need to clear the check boxes in the "Select Changes to Accept or Reject" dialog box, then click OK. The Accept or Reject Changes dialog box opens and allows you to review each change to the workbook and accept or reject it.

QuickTip

Because saving the file closes the History sheet, you need to print it before saving the workbook.

FIGURE N-5: **Highlight Changes dialog box**

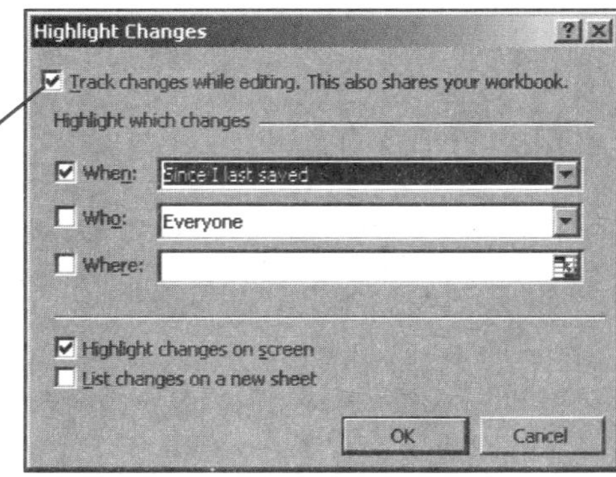

FIGURE N-6: **Tracked change**

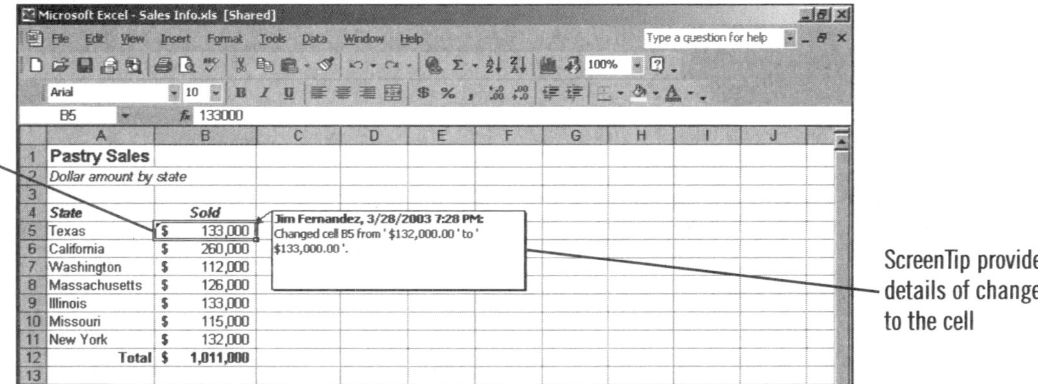

	A	B
1	Pastry Sales	
2	Dollar amount by state	
3		
4	State	Sold
5	Texas	$ 133,000
6	California	$ 260,000
7	Washington	$ 112,000
8	Massachusetts	$ 126,000
9	Illinois	$ 133,000
10	Missouri	$ 115,000
11	New York	$ 132,000
12	Total	$ 1,011,000

FIGURE N-7: **History sheet tab with change history**

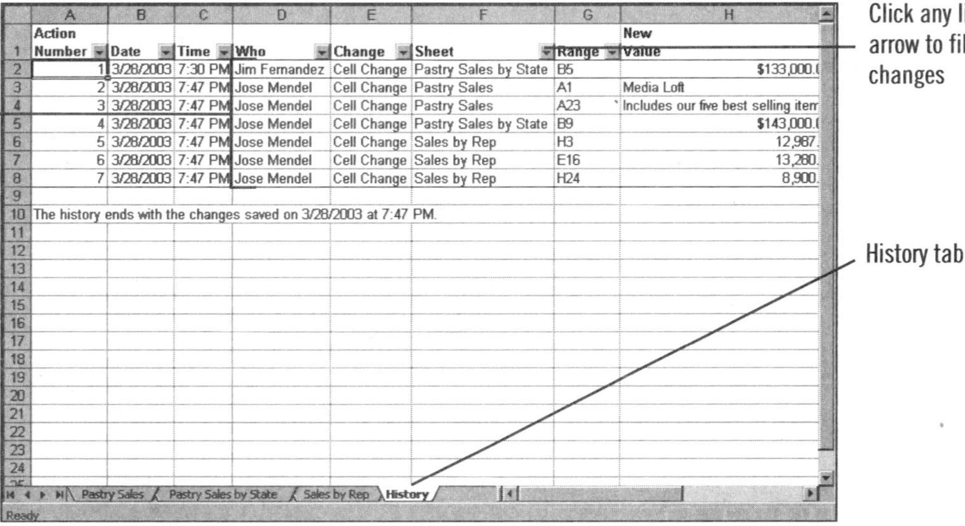

Action Number	Date	Time	Who	Change	Sheet	Range	New Value
1	3/28/2003	7:30 PM	Jim Fernandez	Cell Change	Pastry Sales by State	B5	$133,000.(
2	3/28/2003	7:47 PM	Jose Mendel	Cell Change	Pastry Sales	A1	Media Loft
3	3/28/2003	7:47 PM	Jose Mendel	Cell Change	Pastry Sales	A23	Includes our five best selling iten
4	3/28/2003	7:47 PM	Jose Mendel	Cell Change	Pastry Sales by State	B9	$143,000.(
5	3/28/2003	7:47 PM	Jose Mendel	Cell Change	Sales by Rep	H3	12,987.
6	3/28/2003	7:47 PM	Jose Mendel	Cell Change	Sales by Rep	E16	13,280.
7	3/28/2003	7:47 PM	Jose Mendel	Cell Change	Sales by Rep	H24	8,900.

The history ends with the changes saved on 3/28/2003 at 7:47 PM.

Merging workbooks

Instead of putting the shared workbook on a server, you may want to distribute copies to your reviewers via e-mail. Once everyone has entered their changes, you can merge the changed copies into one master workbook that will contain all the changes. Each copy you distribute must be designated as shared, and the Change History feature, on the Advanced tab of the Share Workbook dialog box, must be activated. Once you get the changed copies back, open the master copy of the workbook, click Tools on the menu bar, then click Compare and Merge Workbooks. The Select Files to Merge Into Current Workbook dialog box opens. Select the workbooks you want to merge, then click OK.

Excel 2002

Applying and Modifying Passwords

When you place a shared workbook on a server, you may want to use a password so that only authorized people will be able to open it or make changes to it. *If you lose your password, you will not be able to open or change the workbook.* Passwords are case sensitive, so you must type them exactly as you want users to type them, with the same spacing and using the same case. Jim wants you to put the workbook with sales information on one of the company's servers. You decide to save a copy of the workbook with two passwords: one that users will need to open it, and another that they will use to make changes to it.

1. Open the Project File **EX N-1** from the drive and folder where your Project Files are stored, click **File** on the menu bar, click **Save As**, click **the Tools list arrow** in the Save As dialog box, then click **General Options**
   The Save Options dialog box opens, with two password boxes: one to open the workbook, and one to allow changes to the workbook. See Figure N-8.
2. In the "Password to open" text box, type **Saturn**
   Be sure to type the S uppercase and the rest of the letters lowercase. This is the password that users will have to type to open the workbook. When you enter passwords, the characters you type are masked with asterisks (***) for security purposes.
3. Press **[Tab]** twice, in the Password to modify text box type **Atlas**, then click **OK**
   This is the password that users will have to type to make changes to the workbook. A dialog box asks you to verify the first password by reentering it.
4. Enter **Saturn** in the first Confirm Password dialog box, click **OK,** enter **Atlas** in the second Confirm Password dialog box, then click **OK**
5. Edit the filename so it reads **Sales Info PW**, click **Save,** then close the workbook
6. Reopen the workbook **Sales Info PW**, enter the password **Saturn** when prompted for a password, click **OK**, then enter **Atlas** to obtain write access
   The Password dialog box is shown in Figure N-9. Obtaining write access for a workbook allows you to modify it.
7. Click **OK,** click the **Pastry Sales by State Sheet tab**, click cell **A-14** then enter **One-year totals**
   You were able to make this change because you obtained write access privileges using the password "Atlas."
8. Save and close the workbook

QuickTip

You can press [Enter] rather than clicking OK after entering a password. This allows you to keep your hands on the keyboard.

QuickTip

You can protect ranges of cells in a worksheet with a password by clicking Tools, pointing to Protection, then clicking Allow Users to Edit Ranges.

Removing passwords

You must know a workbook's password in order to change or delete it. Open the workbook, click File on the menu bar, then click Save As. In the Save As dialog box, click the Tools list arrow, then click General Options. If necessary, double-click to highlight the symbols for the existing passwords in the Password to open or Password to modify boxes, press [Delete], click OK, change the filename if desired, then click Save.

FIGURE N-8: Save Options dialog box

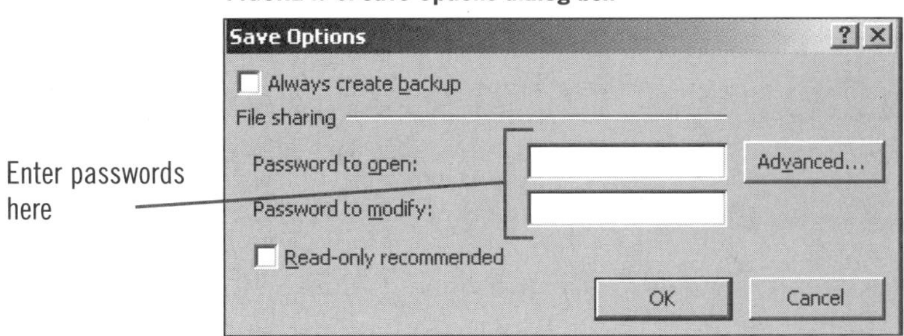

FIGURE N-9: Password entry prompt

Excel 2002

What is XML?

XML, or **Extensible Markup Language**, isn't really a language but rather a system for defining other languages. XML provides a way to express structure in data. Structured data is **tagged**, or marked up, for its content, meaning, or use. For example, an XML data marker (tag) that contains an item's cost might be named, COST. With XML you can create structured information related to services, products, or business transactions and easily share that information. This data exchange can take place over the Web or other networks. Since XML lets you customize data for specific groups and organizations, it is becoming a universal format for business and industry information sharing. A tool for reading XML documents is called an **XML parser**. Although Netscape 6 and IE 5.5 include XML parsers in their browsers, XML is not just used for the Web. XML is used to store any kind of structured information, and pass it between different computers either within an organization or in business to business transactions, thereby allowing groups of people and organizations to easily exchange information.

Excel 2002

Creating an Interactive Worksheet for the Web

You can save entire workbooks or individual worksheets in HTML format. When you publish a worksheet with **interactivity**, users can modify, format, sort, and analyze data using their Web browsers. To work with interactive data, users must have installed Internet Explorer version 4.01 or later as well as the Office Web Components. Users do not need to have Excel installed on their computers. Jim asks you to save the Pastry Sales by State sheet as an interactive Web page.

Steps

1. Open the Project File **EX N-1** from the drive and folder where your Project Files are stored, then save it as **Sales Info 2**
2. Click the **Pastry Sales by State sheet tab**, click **File** on the menu bar, click **Save as Web Page**
   The Save As dialog box opens. See Figure N-10. This dialog box allows you to specify what workbook components you want to publish, the title of the published file, and whether you want users to be able to modify the published document.
3. Click the **Selection: Sheet option button**, select the **Add interactivity check box**, click **Change Title**, enter **Pastry Sales by State**, click **OK**, then click **Publish**
4. In the Publish as section, click **Browse**, make sure the folder with your Project Files appears as the Save in location, type the filename **pastry**, then click **OK**
5. Click to select the **Open published web page in browser check box** if necessary, click **Publish**, then maximize your browser window
   The HTML version of your worksheet opens in your browser. See Figure N-11. You can make changes to the worksheet using Internet Explorer.
6. Change the Sold number for Washington in cell B7 to **115,000**, then press **[Enter]**
   The total updates automatically to 1,013,000. Changes you make using your browser remain in effect until you close your browser.
7. Select the range **A5:B11**, click the **Sort Ascending button** on the toolbar above the worksheet
   The data is sorted according to state name. You can also remove the total.
8. Select the range **A4:B11**, click the **AutoFilter button** on the toolbar above the worksheet, click the **State list arrow**, click the **Total check mark** to remove it, then click **OK**
9. With the range A4:B11 selected, click the **Commands and Options button** on the toolbar above the worksheet, click the **Fill Color list arrow**, click any light color, click outside the range, then close the dialog box
10. Enter your name in cell A15 of the worksheet, click **File** on the menu bar, click **Print**, click **OK**, then close your browser

QuickTip

If you select the "AutoRepublish every time this workbook is saved" check box, the Web page will be updated automatically every time you save the Excel file.

QuickTip

When you close your browser you will lose all changes made to your published worksheet unless you first click the Export to Microsoft Excel button at the top of the worksheet.

QuickTip

If the Commands and Options button is not available to you, click View on the menu bar, then click Refresh.

FIGURE N-10: Save As dialog box

Select to publish entire workbook

Select to add interactivity

Select to publish selected worksheet

Click to publish as a Web page

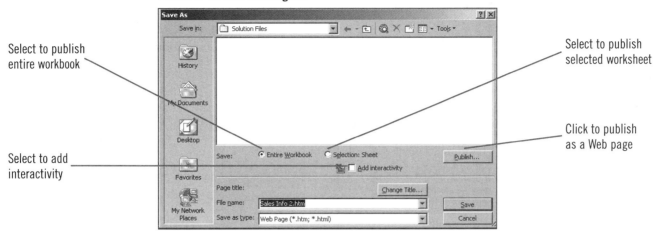

FIGURE N-11: Pastry Sales by State worksheet as Web page in Internet Explorer

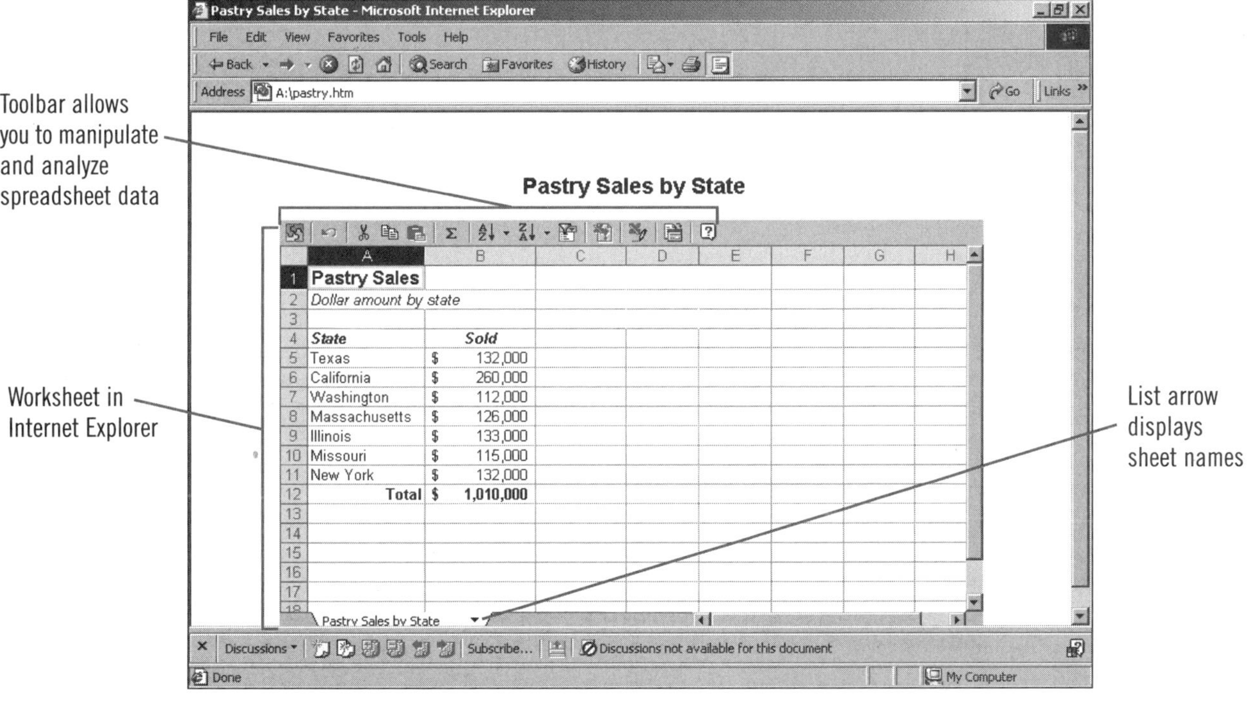

Creating XML queries

You can create and save Web queries to XML files on the Web the same way you create Web queries to HTML files. Click Data on the menu bar, point to Import External Data, then click New Web Query. In the New Web Query dialog box, enter the address of the XML data on the Web or a local network. When using a Web query to import data from XML files, you should select Full HTML formatting in the Web Query options. You can specify parts of an XML document to import or import the entire file.

Excel 2002

Creating a PivotTable List for the Web

Not only can you create interactive worksheets that users can modify in their Web browsers, but you can also create interactive PivotTables that users can analyze by dragging fields to get different views of the data. An interactive PivotTable for the Web is called a **PivotTable list**. Users cannot enter new values to the list, but they can filter and sort data, add calculations, and rearrange data to get a different perspective on the information. As the PivotTable list creator, you have complete control over what information is included from the source data, which could be an Excel worksheet, a PivotTable, or external data (for example, an Access database). You can include only selected columns of information if you wish. You can also include charts with your PivotTable data. As with spreadsheets you publish in HTML format, users view PivotTable lists in their browsers, and changes they make to them are retained only for that browser session. The HTML file remains in its original form. Jim has compiled some sales information about sales representatives at selected stores for the last four quarters. He asks you to save it as a PivotTable list so he and selected corporate staff and store managers can review the information using their Web browsers.

1. Click the **Sales by Rep tab** in the **Sales Info 2** workbook
   You will create the PivotTable list directly from the data, rather than creating an Excel PivotTable first.
2. Click **File** on the menu bar, click **Save as Web Page**, click the **Selection: Sheet option button**, click the **Add interactivity check box** to select it, then click **Publish**
3. Make sure **Items on Sales by Rep** is displayed in the Choose text box and that **Sheet - All contents of Sales by Rep** appears in the Choose list
   All items on the Sales by Rep sheet will be displayed in the PivotTable list.
4. Click the **Add interactivity with list arrow**, then select **PivotTable functionality**
   PivotTable functionality allows users to manipulate items on the PivotTable list in the same way they would on a PivotTable in Excel.
5. Click **Browse**, edit the filename to read **repinfo.htm** make sure the folder containing your Project Files appears in the Save in text box, click **OK**, then make sure **Open published web page in browser** is checked
   You are ready to publish the PivotTable list. See Figure N-12.
6. Click **Publish**, then maximize the Internet Explorer window if necessary
   The new PivotTable list opens in Internet Explorer. Its layout looks similar to a PivotTable report in Excel, with row and column fields and field drop-down arrows. As with an Excel PivotTable, you can change the layout to view the data in different ways. In the browser, however, there is no PivotTable toolbar so you need to drag the field headings to the desired drop areas.
7. Drag the **Store field** to the Row area, then drag the **Department field** to the Column area
   The layout of the PivotTable list has changed. Now, the data is organized by department and store. This rearrangement of data allows you to see, for example, that Barnard sold the most books in the Boston store, while Haile sold the most books in the Seattle store. See Figure N-13.
8. Click **File** on the menu bar, click **Print**, click **OK**, then close your browser

QuickTip

To return the PivotTable to its original state, click the Address box containing the URL and press [Enter].

QuickTip

Depending on your browser and printer, your Print dialog box may have a Print button instead of an OK button.

FIGURE N-12: Publish as Web Page dialog box

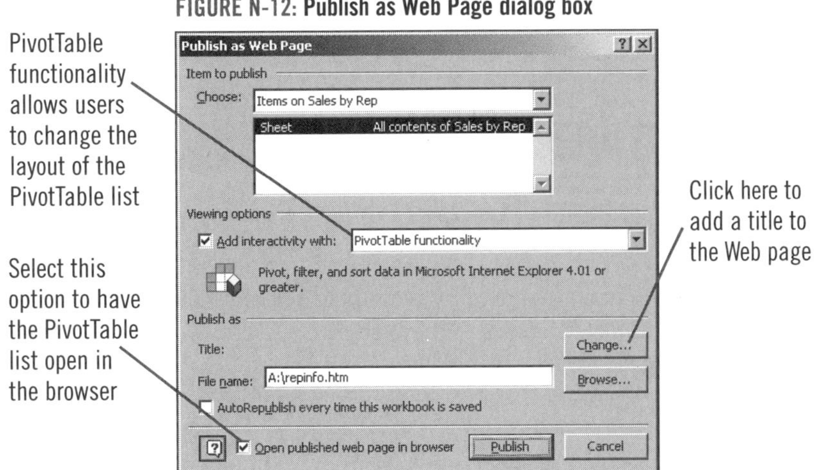

FIGURE N-13: PivotTable list with new layout in Internet Explorer

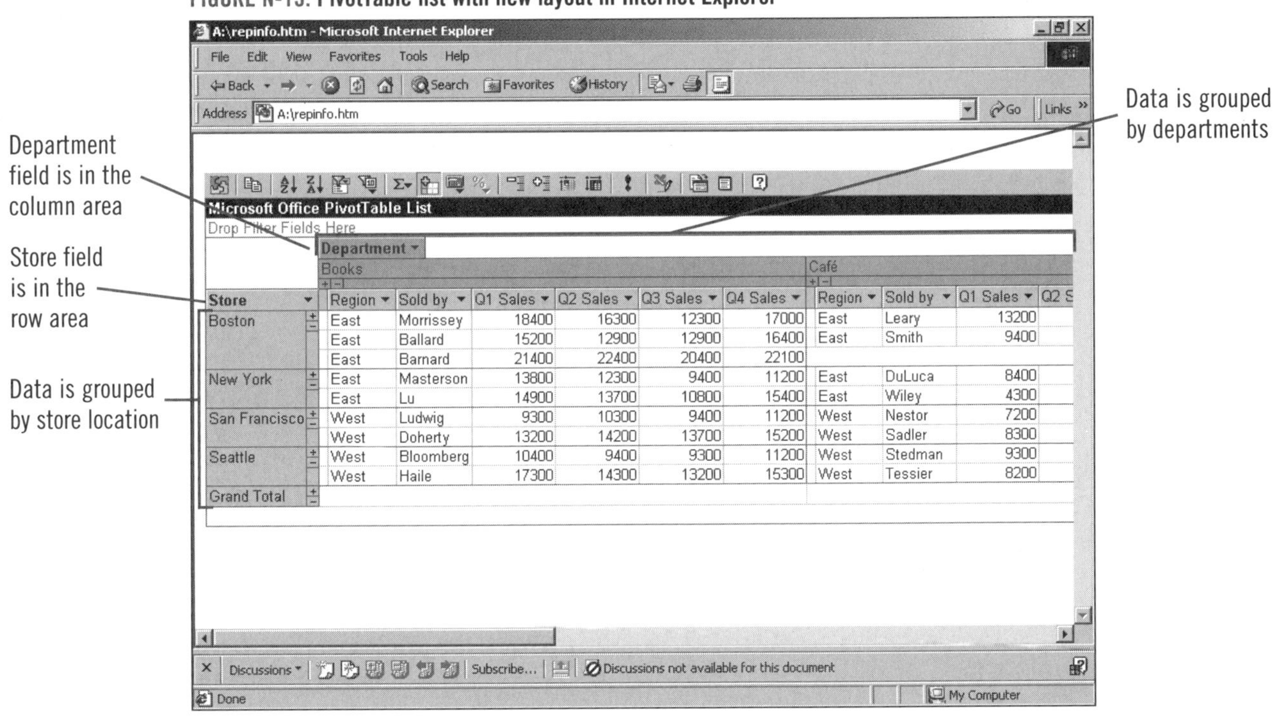

Store	Region	Sold by	Q1 Sales	Q2 Sales	Q3 Sales	Q4 Sales	Region	Sold by	Q1 Sales
Boston	East	Morrissey	18400	16300	12300	17000	East	Leary	13200
	East	Ballard	15200	12900	12900	16400	East	Smith	9400
	East	Barnard	21400	22400	20400	22100			
New York	East	Masterson	13800	12300	9400	11200	East	DuLuca	8400
	East	Lu	14900	13700	10800	15400	East	Wiley	4300
San Francisco	West	Ludwig	9300	10300	9400	11200	West	Nestor	7200
	West	Doherty	13200	14200	13700	15200	West	Sadler	8300
Seattle	West	Bloomberg	10400	9400	9300	11200	West	Stedman	9300
	West	Haile	17300	14300	13200	15300	West	Tessier	8200
Grand Total									

Adding fields to a PivotTable list using the Web browser

You can add fields to a PivotTable list by clicking the Field List button on the toolbar above the PivotTable to open the PivotTable Field List dialog box. Click the field that you want to add, click the area list arrow in the lower-right corner of the box, click the section where you want to add the field: Row Area, Column Area, Filter Area, Data Area, or Detail Data, then click Add to. If Add to is not available, the PivotTable creator may have restricted access to it.

Excel 2002

Adding Web Hyperlinks to an Excel File

In addition to using hyperlinks to connect related Excel files, you can also create hyperlinks in Excel files to information on the Web. Every Web page is identified by a unique Web address called a **Uniform Resource Locator (URL)**. You create a hyperlink to a Web page in an Excel file by specifying its URL in the Insert Hyperlink dialog box. Jim decides that users of the Pastry Sales worksheet would find it helpful to view competitive information. He asks you to include a hyperlink to one of MediaLoft's competitors, Barnes and Noble, which is also a café bookstore.

Steps

1. In the Sales Info 2 workbook, click the **Pastry Sales worksheet**, click cell **A2**, type **Barnes and Noble**, then click the **Enter button** on the Formula bar
2. Click the **Insert Hyperlink button** on the Standard toolbar
   The Insert Hyperlink dialog box opens. This is where you specify the target for the hyperlink, the Barnes and Noble Web site, by entering its URL, http://www.bn.com.
3. Under Link to, click **Existing File or Web Page** if necessary to select it, type **http://www.bn.com** in the Address text box
   See Figure N-14.
4. Click **OK**
   The Barnes and Noble text changes to blue, underlined text, indicating that it is a hyperlink. You should always test new hyperlinks to make sure they link to the correct destination. To test this hyperlink, you must have an Internet connection and a Web browser installed on your computer.
5. Click the **Barnes and Noble** hyperlink in cell A2
   Your Web browser opens and displays the Barnes and Noble Web page.
6. Click **File** on the menu bar, click **Print**, click **OK**, then click the **Back button** on the Web toolbar
   You return to the Sales Info 2 worksheet.
7. Save the workbook, close it, then close your browser

Trouble?

If you have a dial-up connection to your Internet service provider, you may need to connect first.

Trouble?

If the Back button is not available on the Web toolbar, click the taskbar button with the Excel icon to return to Excel. Depending on your browser and printer, your Print dialog box may have a Print button instead of an OK button.

Click to link to a Web page or an existing file

Address for Barnes and Noble

FIGURE N-14: Insert Hyperlink dialog box

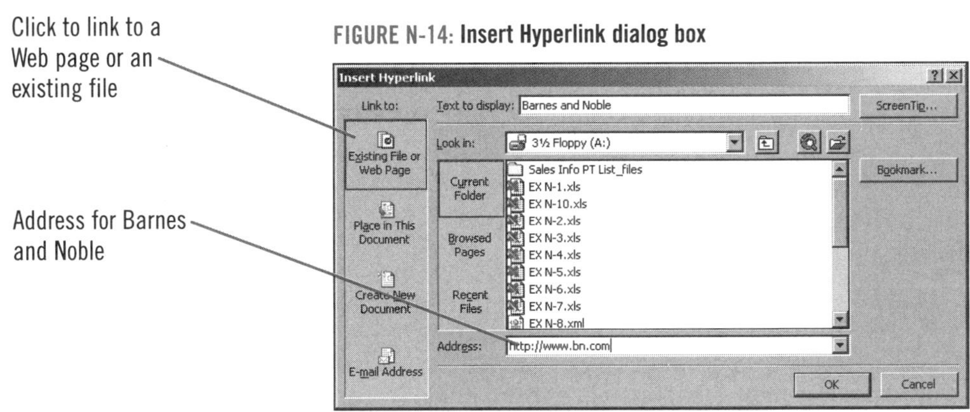

FIGURE N-15: Barnes and Noble Web site in Internet Explorer

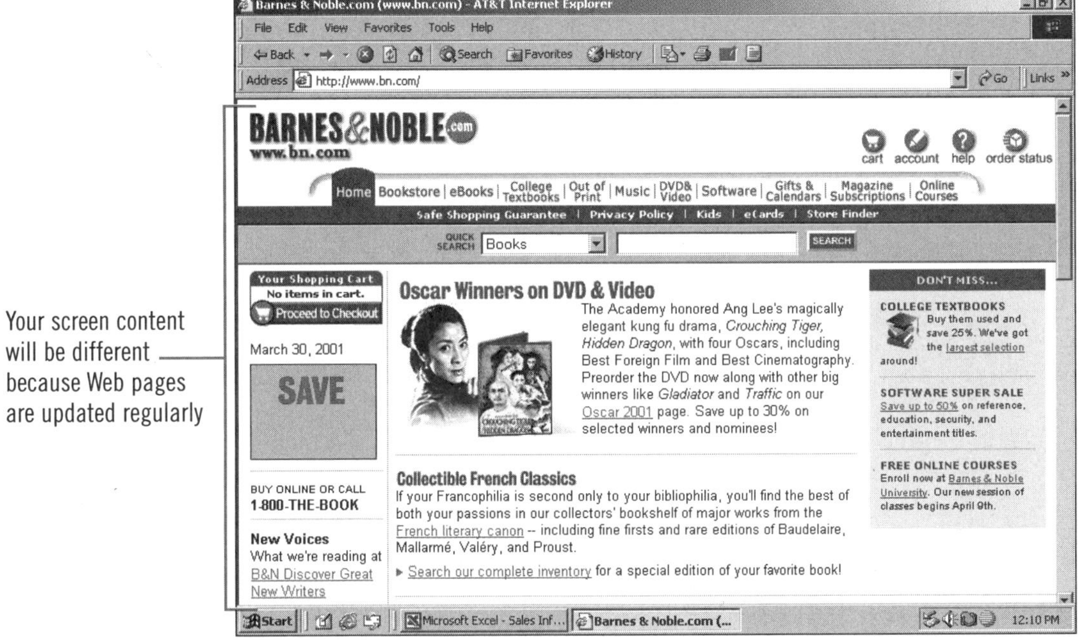

Your screen content will be different because Web pages are updated regularly

Creating Web queries

To retrieve data from a particular Web page on a regular basis, it's easiest to create a customized Web query. Click Data on the menu bar, point to Import External Data, then click New Web Query. In the New Web Query dialog box, type the address of the Web page from which you want to retrieve data, then click Go. Click the arrows [icon] next to the information you want to bring into a worksheet or click the upper-left arrow to import the entire page, then click Import. The Import Data dialog box opens and allows you to specify where you want the imported data placed in the worksheet. You can save a query for future use by clicking the Save Query button [icon] in the New Web Query dialog box after you go to the site. The query is saved as a file with an .iqy file extension. To use the query, follow the steps in the next lesson.

Excel 2002

Running Web Queries to Retrieve External Data

Often you'll want to access information on the Web to incorporate into an Excel worksheet. Using Excel, you can obtain data from a Web site by running a **Web query**, then you can save the information in an existing or new Excel workbook. Web queries are saved with the .iqy file extension. Several Web query files come with Excel. As part of a special project, Jim needs to obtain stock information on MediaLoft's competitors. He asks you to run a Web query to obtain the most current stock information from the Web.

Steps

QuickTip

You can use Excel smart tags to insert refreshable stock quotes in a workbook. Enter the stock symbol in uppercase letters, and then click outside the cell. Click the cell's Smart Tag Actions list arrow and select Insert refreshable stock price.

1. Create a new workbook, then save it as **Stock Data** on the drive and folder where your Project Files are stored
2. Click **Data** on the menu bar, point to **Import External Data**, then click **Import Data**
   The Select Data Source dialog box opens. See Figure N-16. This is where you select the Web query you want to run.
3. Click **MSN MoneyCentral Investor Stock Quotes**, then click **Open**
   The Import Data dialog box opens. Here you can specify the worksheet location where you want the imported data to appear.
4. Make sure the **Existing worksheet option button** is selected, click cell **A1** If necessary to place $A$1 in the Existing worksheet text box, then click **OK**
   The Enter Parameter Value dialog box opens, prompting you to enter a stock symbol. The stock symbol for Barnes and Noble is BKS.
5. Enter **BKS** in the Enter Parameter Value dialog box, then click **OK**
   The MSN MoneyCentral Investor stock quote for Barnes and Noble appears on the screen. See Figure N-17. Jim wants you to obtain more information on Barnes and Noble's financial status.
6. Click the **Barnes & Noble, Inc. link** on the stock quote page
   A Web page opens in your browser, with quote details. See Figure N-18.
7. Click **File** on the menu bar, click **Print**, click **OK**, close the browser, save and close the workbook, then exit Excel

FIGURE N-16: Select Data Source dialog box

Predefined Web queries from Microsoft

FIGURE N-17: Stock quote in Stock Data worksheet

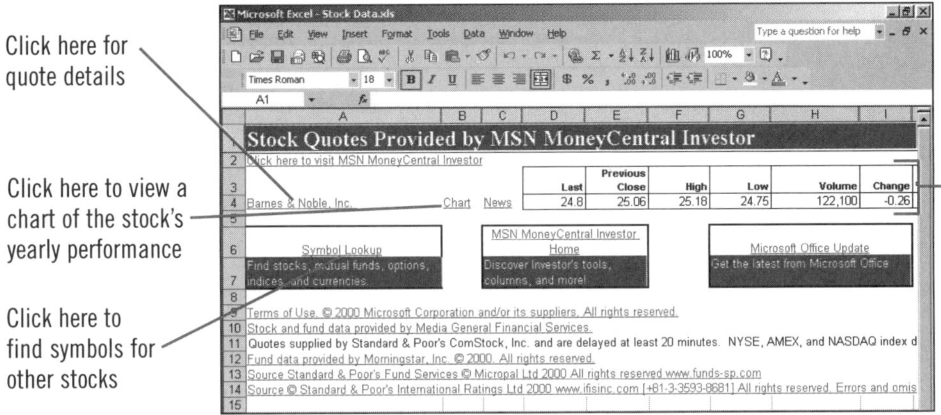

FIGURE N-18: Quote details for Barnes and Noble

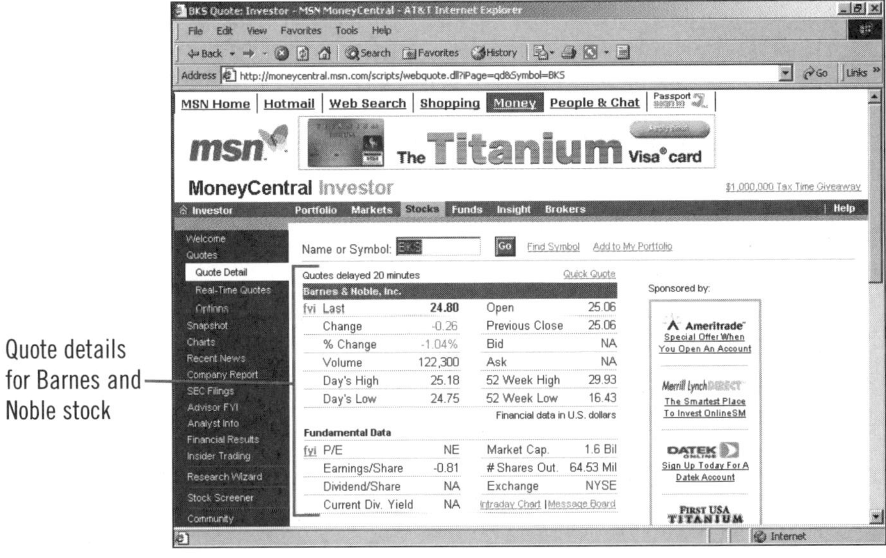

Exporting XML structured data from Excel

You can save an Excel workbook as XML spreadsheet data by clicking File on the menu bar, clicking Save As, and then selecting XML Spreadsheet in the Save as type text box. When you save an Excel spreadsheet in XML spreadsheet format, some Excel features such as charts, custom views, outlining, scenarios, shared workbook information, and graphic objects are lost.

Excel 2002

Practice

▶ Concepts Review

Label each of the elements shown in Figure N-19.

FIGURE N-19

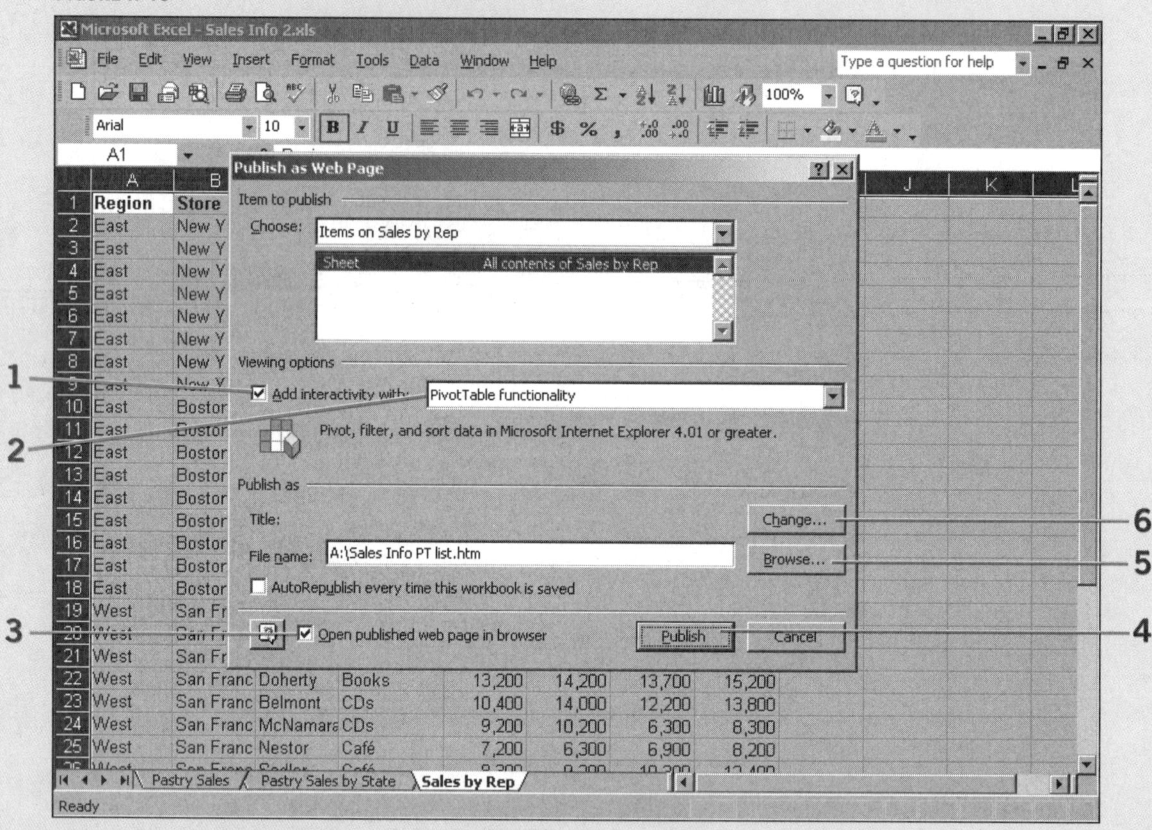

Match each item with the statement that describes it.

7. Change history
8. Web query
9. Shared workbook
10. PivotTable list
11. URL

a. A unique address on the Web
b. Used by many people on a network
c. An interactive PivotTable
d. Used to access information from the Web
e. A record of edits others have made to a worksheet

Select the best answer from the list of choices.

12. A list of recipients to whom you are sending a workbook sequentially is called a:
- **a.** PivotTable.
- **b.** Routing slip.
- **c.** Hypertext document.
- **d.** Shared workbook.

13. Which of the following can be saved in HTML format and then manipulated on the Web?
- **a.** A worksheet
- **b.** A PivotTable
- **c.** A workbook
- **d.** All of the above

14. Which of the following allows you to obtain data from a Web?

a. Web Wizard
b. PivotTable
c. Data query
d. Web query

15. A shared workbook is a workbook that:

a. Has hyperlinks to the Web.
b. Several people can use at the same time.
c. Is published on the Web.
d. Requires a password to open.

16. Working with a PivotTable list, you can:

a. Add fields by clicking the Field List button.
b. Drag fields to the Row area.
c. Drag fields to the Column area.
d. All of the above.

Skills Review

1. Set up a shared workbook for multiple users.

a. Start Excel, open the Project File EX N-3 from the drive and folder where your Project Files are stored, then save it as **Ad Campaigns**.
b. Use the Share Workbook option on the Tools menu to set up the workbook so that more than one person can use it at one time.
c. Use the Advanced tab in the Share Workbook dialog box to specify that the change history should be maintained for 1,000 days.

2. Track revisions in a shared workbook.

a. Specify that all changes should be highlighted using the Track Changes option on the Tools menu. Specify that changes should be both highlighted on the screen and listed in a new sheet.
b. In the Ads Q1 All Stores worksheet, change the Billboards totals to $34,000 for each month.
c. Save the file.
d. Display the History sheet by reopening the Highlight Changes dialog box, clicking the When check box to deselect it, then reselecting the option for List changes on a new sheet.
e. Enter your name in the History sheet footer, print the History sheet, then save and close the workbook.

3. Apply and modify passwords.

a. Open the Project File EX N-3 from the drive and folder where your Project Files are stored, open the Save As dialog box, then open the General Options dialog box.
b. Set the password to open the workbook as **Ads** and the password to modify it as **Spring**.
c. Save the password-protected file as **Ad Campaigns PW**.
d. Close the workbook.
e. Reopen the workbook and verify that you can change it, using passwords where necessary.

4. Create an interactive worksheet for the Web.

a. Save the Ads Q1 All Stores worksheet as an interactive Web page, with spreadsheet functionality. Set the title bar to read **Ad Campaign Forecast** and save it to the folder containing your Project Files with the filename **campaign**. Open the Web page in Internet Explorer. (*Hint:* If Internet Explorer is your default browser, you can use the 'Open published web page in browser' option in the Publish as Web Page dialog box.)
b. Using Internet Explorer, add totals for each month in B11:D11, then add a grand total to cell E11.
c. Use the Commands and Options dialog box to fill the range B11:E11 with yellow.
d. Sort the list in ascending order by ad type. (*Hint:* Select the range A3:E10 before clicking the **Sort Ascending** button.)
e. Add your name to cell A13, print the worksheet from Internet Explorer, then close Internet Explorer.

5. **Create a PivotTable list for the Web.**
   a. In the Ad Campaigns PW workbook, save the worksheet Ad Detail as an interactive Web page with PivotTable functionality. Add a title of **Ad Forecast**, and save it as **storeads** in the folder containing your Project Files.
   b. Open the file in your Web browser and drag the Region field to the Row Field area. Drag the Department Field to the Column Field area.
   c. Print the Web page from Internet Explorer, showing the changed data orientation.
6. **Add Web Hyperlinks to an Excel file.**
   a. In the Ad Campaigns PW workbook, display the Ads Q1 All Stores worksheet, then in cell A13 enter the text **American Advertising Federation**. Make cell A13 a hyperlink to the American Advertising Federation at **http://www.aaf.org** with a ScreenTip of **Click to go to American Advertising Federation**.
   b. Test the hyperlink.
   c. Enter your name in the Ads Q1 All Stores worksheet footer, save the workbook, print the worksheet, then close the workbook.
7. **Run queries to retrieve external data.**
   a. Create a new workbook, then save it as **Stock Quotes** in the drive and folder where your Project Files are stored.
   b. Use the Select Data Source dialog box to select the Web query **MSN Money Central Investor Major Indices**.
   c. Specify that you want to place the data to cell A1 of the current worksheet.
   d. Place your name in the worksheet footer, save the workbook, then preview and print the worksheet in landscape orientation on one page.
   e. Save the Stock Quotes workbook in XML spreadsheet format. (*Hint:* Click File, click Save As, make sure the folder containing your Project Files appears in the Save in text box, select XML Spreadsheet in the Save as type text box, then click Save.)
   f. Close the workbook, then exit Excel.

► Independent Challenge 1

Blantyre Consulting helps small businesses attain profitability by monitoring their sales and expense information. The consultants in the organization share information via the company intranet. As a Blantyre consultant, you are setting up information for a new client, Boston Touring Company, which specializes in giving trolley and bus tours in Boston, Massachusetts, and the surrounding area. You are preparing a shared workbook for the three consultants working on the first quarter data for this project. They will each make changes to the first quarter figures, then you will merge all three workbooks into one master workbook, where you will accept or reject their changes.

a. Start Excel, open the Project File EX N-4 from the drive and folder where your Project Files are stored, then save it as **Boston Touring**. The workbook has been shared so the other consultants can modify it. Notice the current figures for each month.
b. Merge the files EX N-5, EX N-6, and EX N-7 into the Boston Touring Workbook. (*Hint:* Click Tools, click Compare and Merge Workbooks, make sure the folder containing your Project Files appears in the Look in text box, click the file EX N-5, press and hold [Ctrl], select the files EX N-6 and EX N-7, then click OK.) Notice that the totals changed.
c. Review each change made by the consultants and accept each one individually. (*Hint:* Click Tools, point to Track Changes, Click Accept or Reject Changes, clear all check boxes from the Select Changes to Accept or Reject dialog box, click OK, then review each selection, clicking Accept after each change.) Compare your merged values with Figure N-20.

FIGURE N-20

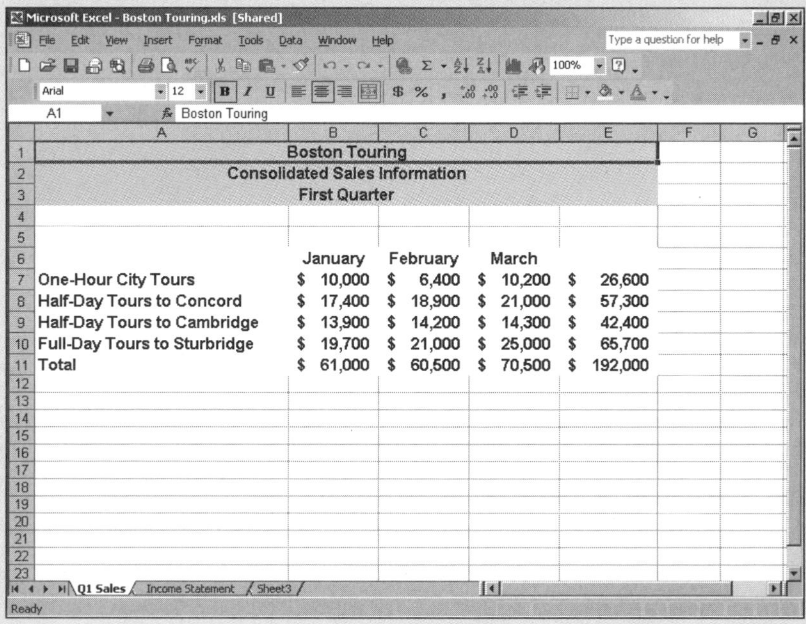

	A	B	C	D	E
1	Boston Touring				
2	Consolidated Sales Information				
3	First Quarter				
6		January	February	March	
7	One-Hour City Tours	$ 10,000	$ 6,400	$ 10,200	$ 26,600
8	Half-Day Tours to Concord	$ 17,400	$ 18,900	$ 21,000	$ 57,300
9	Half-Day Tours to Cambridge	$ 13,900	$ 14,200	$ 14,300	$ 42,400
10	Full-Day Tours to Sturbridge	$ 19,700	$ 21,000	$ 25,000	$ 65,700
11	Total	$ 61,000	$ 60,500	$ 70,500	$ 192,000

d. Enter your name in the Q1 Sales worksheet footer, then save the workbook.

e. Print the merged Q1 Sales worksheet on one page, close the workbook, then exit Excel.

► Independent Challenge 2

The First North Bank has a Web page containing information about its current rates and procedures for opening an account. John Barnes, the customer service manager, has asked you to set up an Excel worksheet for the Web site that will allow customers to enter various mortgage amounts and interest rates, and automatically see what their monthly payments, total payments, and total interest would be. A loan payment model with the current interest rate for a 30-year loan is on the bank's intranet as an XML document. You will import the XML data into an Excel worksheet, format it, then publish it as an interactive spreadsheet.

a. Start Excel, create a new workbook, then save it as **Mortgage Calculator** on the drive and folder where your Project Files are stored.

b. Import the XML file EX N-8 into the Mortgage Calculator worksheet. (*Hint:* Click Data, point to Import External Data, click Import Data, make sure the folder containing your Project Files appears in the Look in text box, click EX N-8, click Open, then click OK to place the data starting in cell A1.)

c. Format the imported data using Figure N-21 as a guide, then save the workbook. (*Note:* Cell D6 should be formatted as a Percentage with two decimal places.)

FIGURE N-21

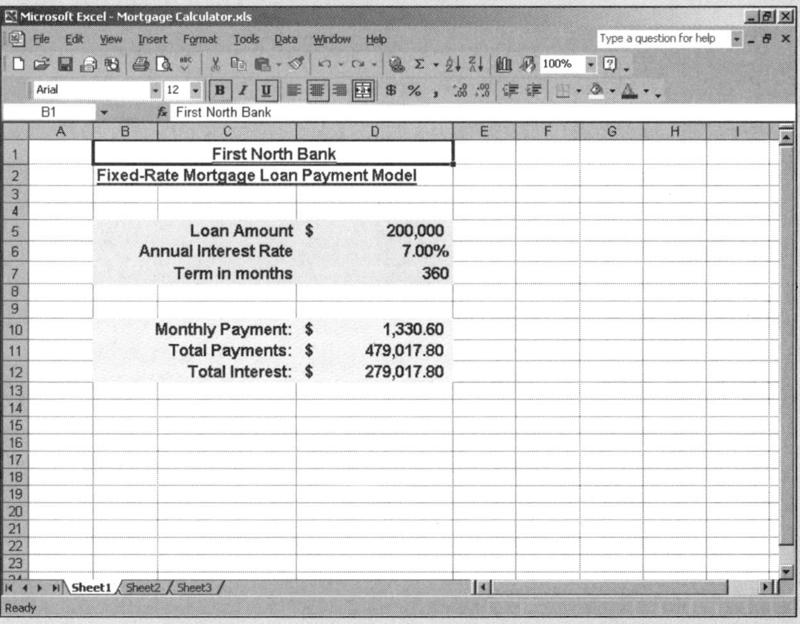

	B	C	D
1	First North Bank		
2	Fixed-Rate Mortgage Loan Payment Model		
5		Loan Amount $	200,000
6		Annual Interest Rate	7.00%
7		Term in months	360
10		Monthly Payment: $	1,330.60
11		Total Payments: $	479,017.80
12		Total Interest: $	279,017.80

d. Rename Sheet1 **Calculator** and delete the labels in rows 1 and 2.. Save the worksheet in HTML format with interactive spreadsheet functionality. Add the title **Loan Calculator** to the title bar. Save the file with the name **calc**.

e. Open the HTML file in your browser, then test the calculator. Enter various mortgage amounts, interest rates, and term lengths to make sure the payment information changes appropriately.

f. Print the payment Information for a $175,000 loan at 7.5% for 360 months.

g. Close Internet Explorer and the Mortgage Calculator workbook, then exit Excel.

Independent Challenge 3

Tuckerman Teas is an import and export firm with offices in Tokyo and London. They distribute specialty teas to shops in the United States and Canada. Tuckerman wants the employees in both offices to be able to analyze sales data, but because of incompatible software, they must rely on their Web browsers. The current sales information is stored in an XML file on Tuckerman's intranet site. You have been asked to help them set up a file that all employees will be able to access on the intranet site using their browsers. You will begin by creating a Web query to the XML data and placing the information in an Excel spreadsheet. You will format the spreadsheet and then publish it as a PivotTable list that all employees can use to analyze the data using their Web browsers.

a. Start Excel, create a new workbook, then save it as **Tuckerman Teas** on the drive and folder where your Project Files are stored.

b. Create an XML query to import data from file EX N-9 on the drive and folder where your Project Files are stored into the Tuckerman Teas workbook. (*Hint:* Click Data, point to Import External Data, then click New Web Query. In the Address text box, enter the path to your Project Files followed by the filename EX N-9.xml. For example, if your files are stored on a floppy disk, you should enter a:\EX N-9.xml. Click Go. You should see the XML code. Click Import, then click OK to place the data starting in cell A1.)

c. Format the imported worksheet data using fonts and colors to make it more attractive. Format the range D2:F45 as Accounting format with zero decimal places. Rename Sheet 1 **First Quarter** and add a pink color to the tab. Use Figures N-22A and N-22B as a guide. Save the workbook.

FIGURE N-22A

	Category	Type	Variety	January	February	March
2	Blends	Breakfast	Red Label Pfannings	$ 21,000	$ 25,000	$ 16,000
3	Blends	Breakfast	Irish Blend	$ 1,500	$ 14,000	$ 21,000
4	Blends	Breakfast	Windsor Blend	$ 4,000	$ 14,000	$ 10,000
5	Blends	Breakfast	King's Breakfast	$ 25,000	$ 17,000	$ 20,000
6	Blends	Afternoon	Sumatra Blend	$ 17,000	$ 16,000	$ 22,000
7	Blends	Afternoon	Java Darjeeling	$ 15,000	$ 14,000	$ 11,000
8	Blends	Afternoon	Fleet St. Yunan	$ 3,000	$ 4,000	$ 10,000
9	Blends	Afternoon	Chinese Blend	$ 15,000	$ 18,000	$ 21,000
10	Blends	Afternoon	Bergamot Treat	$ 19,000	$ 22,000	$ 14,000
11	Blends	Afternoon	Finest Earl Gray	$ 11,000	$ 12,000	$ 11,000
12	Flavored	Breakfast	Peach Surprise	$ 9,000	$ 4,000	$ 16,000
13	Flavored	Breakfast	Raspberry Choice	$ 10,000	$ 13,000	$ 12,000
14	Flavored	Breakfast	Orange Spice	$ 12,000	$ 12,000	$ 13,000
15	Flavored	Breakfast	Christmas Blend	$ 11,000	$ 14,000	$ 11,000
16	Flavored	Breakfast	Citrus Bergamot	$ 8,000	$ 30,000	$ 2,000
17	Flavored	Afternoon	Yunan Orange	$ 12,000	$ 9,000	$ 10,000
18	Flavored	Afternoon	Strawberry Blend	$ 22,000	$ 19,000	$ 10,000
19	Flavored	Afternoon	Lemon Grass	$ 26,000	$ 22,000	$ 24,000
20	Flavored	Afternoon	Mint Tisane	$ 15,000	$ 12,000	$ 29,000
21	Flavored	Afternoon	Apricot Raspberry	$ 2,000	$ 14,000	$ 11,000
22	Flavored	Afternoon	Chamomile Spice	$ 15,000	$ 25,000	$ 15,000
23	Flavored	Afternoon	Almond Spice	$ 22,000	$ 14,000	$ 11,000
24	Japanese	Breakfast	Sencha Green	$ 3,000	$ 4,000	$ 20,000
25	Japanese	Breakfast	Japanese Cherry	$ 15,000	$ 17,000	$ 20,000

FIGURE N-22B

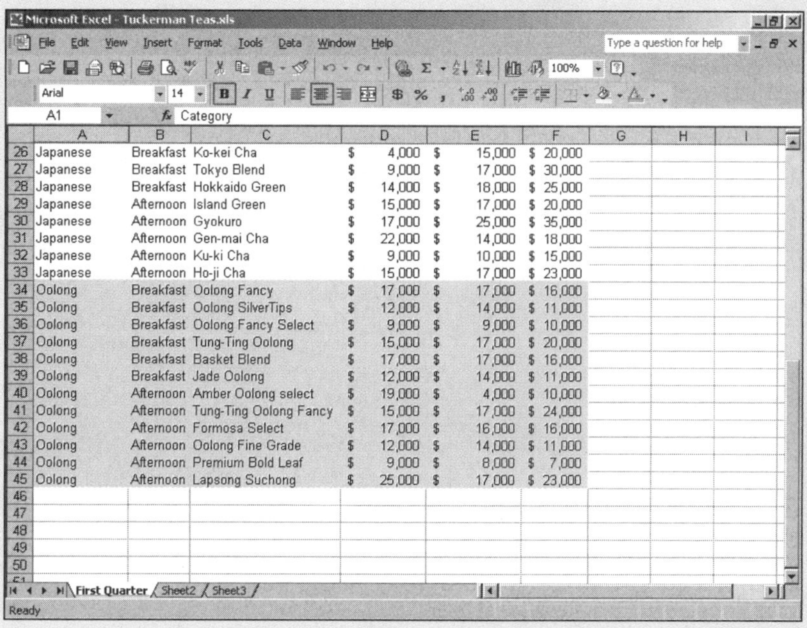

Microsoft Excel - Tuckerman Teas.xls

	A	B	C	D	E	F
26	Japanese	Breakfast	Ko-kei Cha	$ 4,000	$ 15,000	$ 20,000
27	Japanese	Breakfast	Tokyo Blend	$ 9,000	$ 17,000	$ 30,000
28	Japanese	Breakfast	Hokkaido Green	$ 14,000	$ 18,000	$ 25,000
29	Japanese	Afternoon	Island Green	$ 15,000	$ 17,000	$ 20,000
30	Japanese	Afternoon	Gyokuro	$ 17,000	$ 25,000	$ 35,000
31	Japanese	Afternoon	Gen-mai Cha	$ 22,000	$ 14,000	$ 18,000
32	Japanese	Afternoon	Ku-ki Cha	$ 9,000	$ 10,000	$ 15,000
33	Japanese	Afternoon	Ho-ji Cha	$ 15,000	$ 17,000	$ 23,000
34	Oolong	Breakfast	Oolong Fancy	$ 17,000	$ 17,000	$ 16,000
35	Oolong	Breakfast	Oolong SilverTips	$ 12,000	$ 14,000	$ 11,000
36	Oolong	Breakfast	Oolong Fancy Select	$ 9,000	$ 9,000	$ 10,000
37	Oolong	Breakfast	Tung-Ting Oolong	$ 15,000	$ 17,000	$ 20,000
38	Oolong	Breakfast	Basket Blend	$ 17,000	$ 17,000	$ 16,000
39	Oolong	Breakfast	Jade Oolong	$ 12,000	$ 14,000	$ 11,000
40	Oolong	Afternoon	Amber Oolong select	$ 19,000	$ 4,000	$ 10,000
41	Oolong	Afternoon	Tung-Ting Oolong Fancy	$ 15,000	$ 17,000	$ 24,000
42	Oolong	Afternoon	Formosa Select	$ 17,000	$ 16,000	$ 16,000
43	Oolong	Afternoon	Oolong Fine Grade	$ 12,000	$ 14,000	$ 11,000
44	Oolong	Afternoon	Premium Bold Leaf	$ 9,000	$ 8,000	$ 7,000
45	Oolong	Afternoon	Lapsong Suchong	$ 25,000	$ 17,000	$ 23,000

d. Save the First Quarter worksheet as a Web page with PivotTable functionality. Have **Sales** appear in the title bar and as a title, and save the HTML file as **teasales**. Use the 'Open published web page in browser' option to view the Web page in Internet Explorer.

e. Use the AutoFilter arrows to display only the Japanese and Oolong categories of tea.

f. Drag the Category field to the Row Field area and the Type field to the Column Field area.

g. Click the upper-left cell in the worksheet. Use the Captions tab of the Commands and Options dialog box to enter your name in the Filter drop area of the PivotTable. (*Hint:* In the Select caption text box, choose Filter drop area, then enter your name in the Caption text box.)

h. Print the PivotTable list in Internet Explorer.

i. Close Internet Explorer, close the Tuckerman Teas workbook, then exit Excel.

Independent Challenge 4

You belong to an investment group that meets regularly to discuss investment topics and manage a small stock portfolio. The group is focusing on NASDAQ stocks, and you are preparing a presentation on the company Amazon.com. You will use the MSN MoneyCentral Investor Stock Quotes Web query to track the stock history of Amazon.com. Then you will produce a chart that shows the stock price history for the year. To give the group a perspective on how Amazon has performed relative to the NASDAQ index, you will plot the overall performance of the NASDAQ index for the same time period on the chart containing the Amazon stock history.

a. Start Excel, create a new workbook, then save it as **Trend Analysis** on the drive and folder where your Project Files are stored.

b. Run the Web Query **MSN MoneyCentral Investor Stock Quotes** to obtain a stock quote for Amazon.com. The stock symbol is AMZN.

c. Display the chart of this data by clicking the **Chart** link on the worksheet.

d. Use the Customize Chart section to add a comparison chart for the NASDAQ index. (*Hint:* You need to click Refresh chart after clicking the NASDAQ check box.)

e. Print the Chart page comparing the Amazon history with the NASDAQ history.

f. Close Internet Explorer, save the Trend Analysis workbook, close the workbook, then exit Excel.

▶ Visual Workshop

Start Excel, open the Project File EX N-10 from the drive and folder where your Project Files are stored, then save it as **Percussion**. Save the worksheet in interactive HTML format, using the title bar text shown in Figure N-23. Save the Web file with the name **percsale**. Use Internet Explorer to obtain totals for each quarter and to apply formatting to totals, column headings, and the company name as shown in Figure N-23. Adjust column widths as shown. Enter your name in cell A9, then print the Web page from Internet Explorer with your modifications and calculations applied.

FIGURE N-23

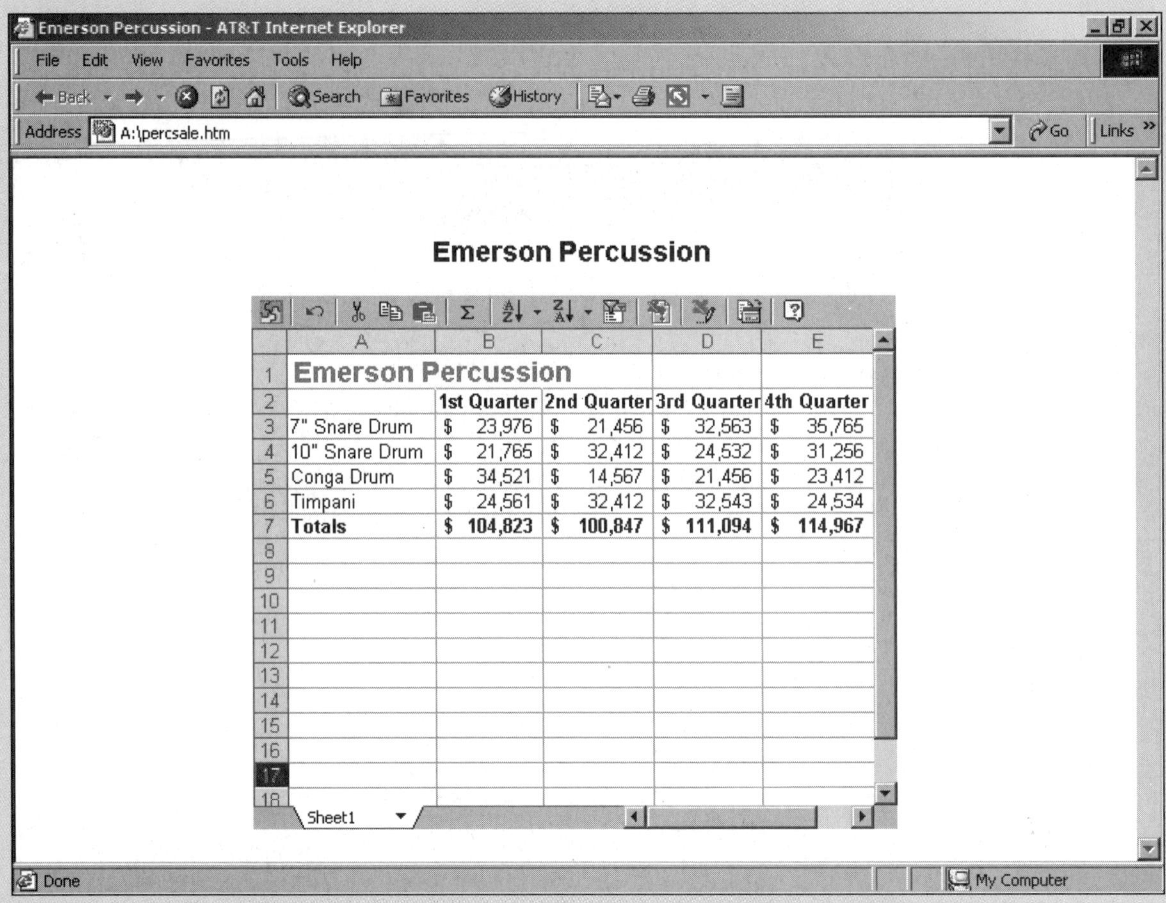

	A	B	C	D	E
1	**Emerson Percussion**				
2		**1st Quarter**	**2nd Quarter**	**3rd Quarter**	**4th Quarter**
3	7" Snare Drum	$ 23,976	$ 21,456	$ 32,563	$ 35,765
4	10" Snare Drum	$ 21,765	$ 32,412	$ 24,532	$ 31,256
5	Conga Drum	$ 34,521	$ 14,567	$ 21,456	$ 23,412
6	Timpani	$ 24,561	$ 32,412	$ 32,543	$ 24,534
7	**Totals**	**$ 104,823**	**$ 100,847**	**$ 111,094**	**$ 114,967**
8					
9					
10					
11					
12					
13					
14					
15					
16					
17					
18					

Customizing

Excel and Advanced Worksheet Management

Objectives

- MOUS ► Find files
- MOUS ► Audit a worksheet
- MOUS ► Outline a worksheet
- MOUS ► Control worksheet calculations
- ► Create custom AutoFill lists
- MOUS ► Customize Excel
- MOUS ► Add a comment to a cell
- MOUS ► Create a template

Excel includes numerous tools and options designed to help you work as efficiently as possible. In this unit, you will learn how to use some of these elements to find errors and hide unnecessary detail. You'll also find out how to eliminate repetitive typing chores, save calculation time when using a large worksheet, and customize basic Excel features. Finally, you'll learn how to document your workbook and save it in a format that makes it easy to reuse. MediaLoft's assistant controller, Lisa Wong, routinely asks Jim Fernandez to help with a variety of spreadsheet-related tasks. You will use the numerous tools and options available in Excel to help Jim perform his work quickly and efficiently.

Excel 2002

Finding Files

The Search task pane in Excel contains powerful searching tools that make it easy for you to find files. You can search for a file in several ways, such as by name or according to specific text located within a particular file. When searching for a file, you must specify one or more **criteria**, or conditions that must be met, to find your file. For example, you can specify that Excel should find only files that have the word "Inventory" in the filename and/or that were created after 6/15/2003. Recently, Jim created a workbook that tracks the number of overtime hours worked in each MediaLoft store. He can't remember the exact name of the file, so he asks you to search for it by the first few letters of the filename.

Steps

1. Start Excel if necessary, then click the Search button on the Standard toolbar
   The Search task pane offers both basic and advanced search features. You can switch between the Basic and Advanced panes by using the first link at the bottom of the pane.

QuickTip

You can also search for text within Excel files. For example, if you know that your worksheet contains the text "Overtime hours", you can specify this in the "Search text:" text box of the Basic Search task pane.

2. In the Search pane, if Basic Search appears in the title bar, click the **Advanced Search** link; if there are search criteria listed in the Value text box above the Search button, click **Remove All**
   All previous search conditions are cleared. Jim thinks the filename he needs starts with the prefix EX O but he's not sure of the remaining filename characters.

3. Click the **Property list arrow**, click **File name**, make sure the Condition text box displays **includes**, click in the Value text box, then type **EX O***
   Be sure you type the letter "O" and not a zero. You'll use the wildcard symbol * (an asterisk) to substitute for the remaining unknown characters. You need to specify where you want Excel to search for the file.

4. Under Other Search Options, click the **Search in list arrow**, click the "Everywhere" check box to clear it if necessary, select the check box next to the drive and folder that contains your Project Files, then click any cell in the worksheet

5. Click the **Results should be list arrow**, select Excel Files, if it's not already selected, deselect any other files types, then click any cell in the worksheet
   Compare your Search pane to Figure O-1.

QuickTip

If the AdvancedSearch doesn't locate your file, try changing the Search in location to My Computer.

6. Click **Search**, then click **Yes** to add the property "File name" to the search criteria
   Five files are displayed that begin with "EX O". See Figure O-2. Once you have found the file you want, you can open and edit the file in its application, create a new document based on the file, copy a link to the file to the Office Clipboard, or view the file's properties.

7. Move the pointer over the EX O-1 filename, then click its list arrow
   The options for file EX O-1 are listed, including an option to open the Properties dialog box.

8. Click the file **EX O-1** in the Search pane
   The EX O-1 workbook opens.

9. Close the Search Results pane, then save the workbook as **Overtime Hours** in the drive and folder where your Project Files are stored

FIGURE O-1: Advanced Search pane

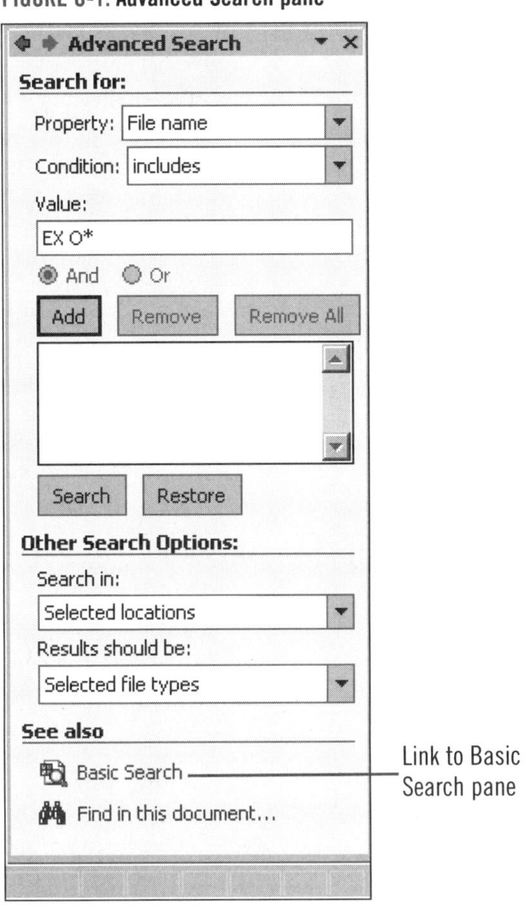

FIGURE O-2: Search results

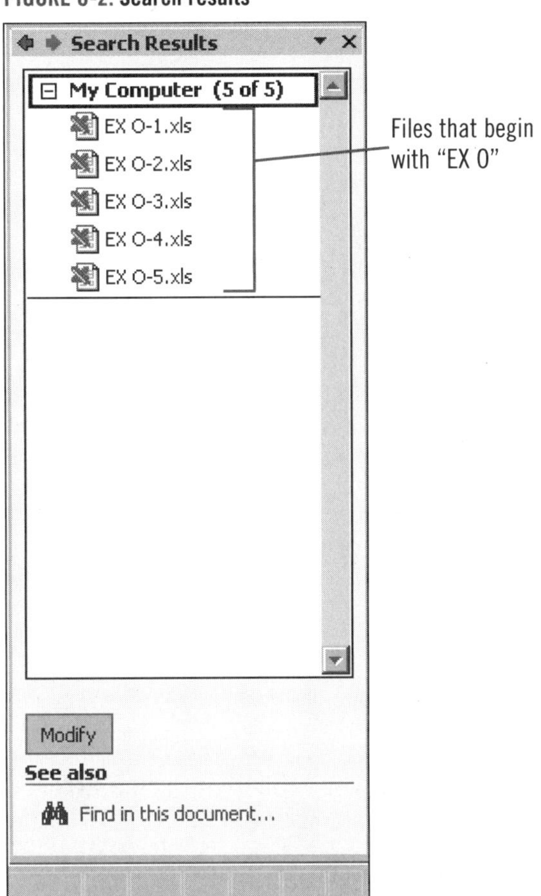

Excel 2002

Using file properties

Excel automatically tracks specific file properties, such as author name, file size, and file type, and displays them when you display file properties. You can also enter additional file properties, such as a descriptive title or a subject. In the [Filename] Properties dialog box, click the Summary tab, then add any information you want. See Figure 0-3. A button appears at the bottom of the summary information labeled Advanced>> or Simple>>. (If you are using Windows 98, the Advanced and Simple options are not available.) You can see a detailed summary of file properties by clicking the Advanced>> button. Clicking the Simple>> button opens a more concise summary. To search for a file by a specific property, in the Advanced Search pane, select Text or property in the Property list, then enter the property text in the Value box.

FIGURE O-3: EX O-1 Properties dialog box

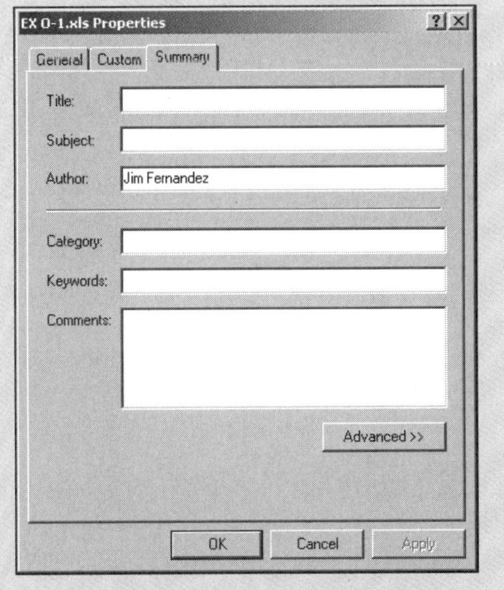

Excel 2002

Auditing a Worksheet

The Excel **auditing** feature helps you track errors and check worksheet logic. Because errors can occur at any stage of worksheet development, it is important to include auditing as part of your workbook-building process. Jim asks you to help audit the worksheet that tracks the number of overtime hours at each store to verify the accuracy of the year-end totals.

Steps

1. **Drag the vertical split box (the small box to the right of the horizontal scroll arrow) to the left until the vertical window pane divider is located between columns A and B, then scroll the right pane until columns P through S are visible**
   Green triangles appear in the upper left corner of cells that Excel detects as having possible errors. See Figure O-4. When you click a cell containing an error, the Trace Error button appears next to the cell.

2. **Click cell S6, click the arrow next to the Trace Error button, then click Show Formula Auditing Toolbar**
   You use the buttons on the Formula Auditing toolbar, shown in Figure O-5, to identify any errors in your worksheet. Cell S6 contains an entry #DIV/0!. This indicates a **divide-by-zero error**, which occurs when you attempt to divide a value by zero. The Trace Error button on the Auditing toolbar helps locate the source of this problem.

3. **Click the Trace Error button on the Formula Auditing toolbar**
   The formula bar reads =R6/$R$16, indicating that the value in cell R6 will be divided by the value in cell R16. Tracer arrows, or **tracers**, point from cells that might have caused the error to the active cell containing the error, as shown in Figure O-5. The tracers extend from cells R6 and R16 to cell S6. Note that cell R6 contains a value, whereas cell R16 is blank. In Excel formulas, blank cells have a value of zero. That means the value in cell R6 cannot be divided by the value in cell R16 (zero) because division by zero is impossible. To correct the error, you must edit the formula so that it references cell R15, the grand total of overtime hours, not R16.

4. **Press [F2] to switch to Edit mode, edit the formula to read =R6/$R$15, then click the Enter button on the formula bar**
   The error message and tracer arrows disappear, and the formula produces the correct result, 8%, in cell S6. Next, notice that the total for the Boston store in cell R5 is unusually high compared with the totals of the other stores. You can investigate this value by tracing the cell's precedents—the cells on which cell R5 depends.

5. **Click cell R5, click the Trace Precedents button on the Auditing toolbar, then scroll left until you see the tracer's starting point**
   The tracer arrow runs between cells B5 and R5, indicating that the formula in cell R5 reflects the quarterly *and* monthly totals of overtime hours. Only the quarterly totals should be reflected in cell R5.

6. **Click the Remove Precedent Arrows button, in cell R5 click the AutoSum button on the Standard toolbar, then press [Enter]**
   The tracer arrow disappears, the formula changes to sum only the quarterly totals, and the correct result, 490, appears in cell R5. Correcting the formula in cell R5 also adjusts the Grand Total percentage in cell S5 to 14%. Now that all the errors in the worksheet have been identified and corrected, you are finished auditing. The remaining triangles do not represent actual errors.

7. **Click Window on the menu bar, click Remove Split, then close the Auditing toolbar and save the workbook**

QuickTip

To find cells with formulas that refer to a specific cell, click the cell, then click the Trace Dependents button on the Formula Auditing toolbar. You can remove the Dependent tracer arrows by clicking Remove Dependent Arrows button on the Formula Auditing toolbar.

QuickTip

You can also double-click the split to remove it.

FIGURE O-4: Worksheet ready for auditing

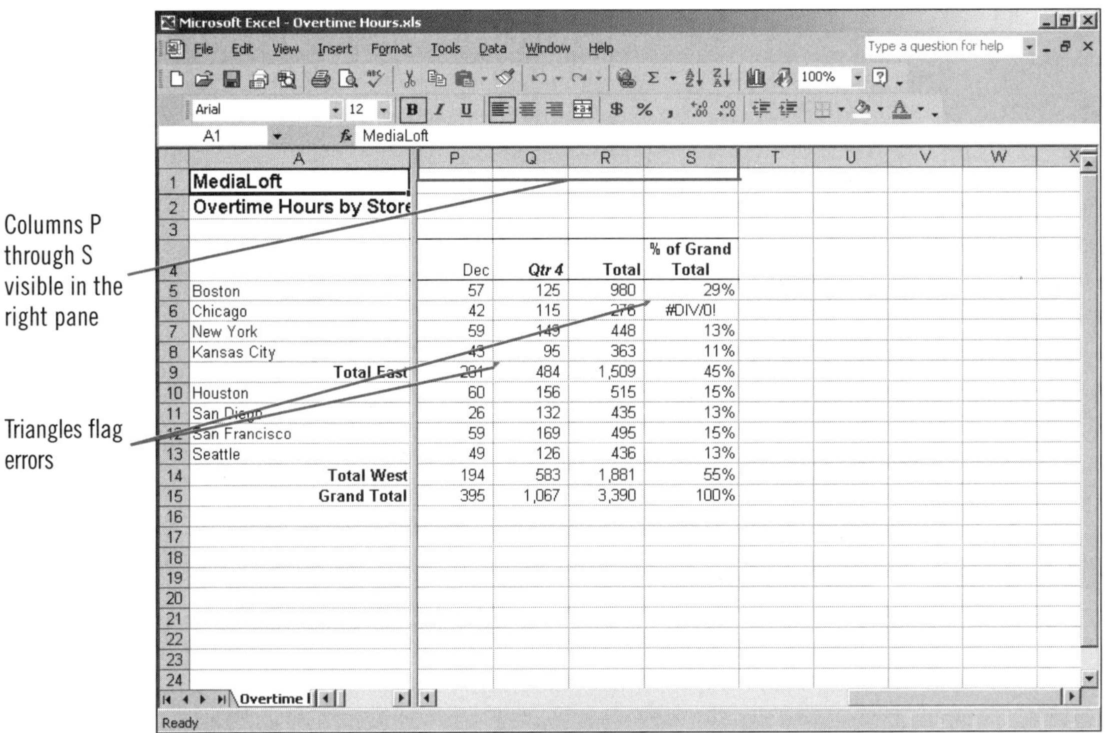

FIGURE O-5: Worksheet with traced error

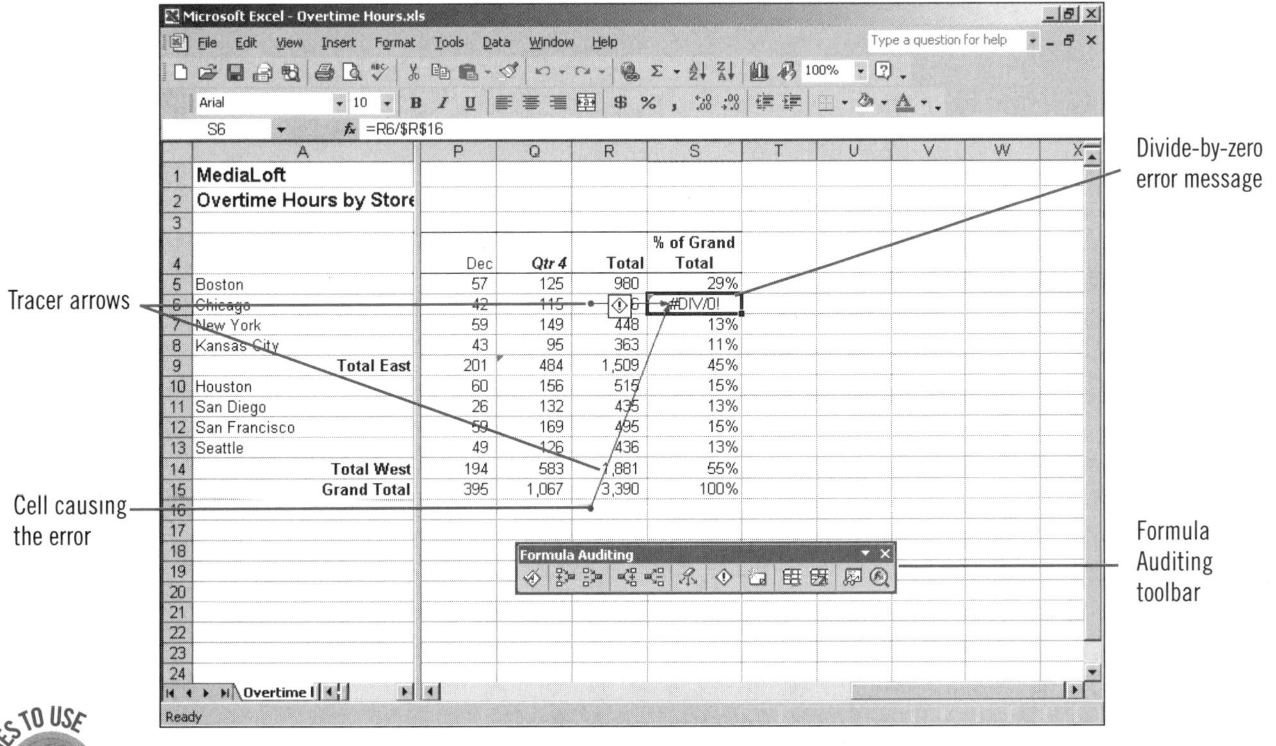

Excel 2002

Clues to Use: Correcting circular references

A cell with a circular reference contains a formula that refers to its own cell location. If you accidentally enter a formula with a circular reference, a warning box will open alerting you to the problem. Click OK to display the Circular Reference toolbar or click Help to open a Help window explaining how to find the circular reference. In simple formulas, a circular reference is easy to spot. To correct it, edit the formula to remove any reference to the cell where the formula is located.

Excel 2002

Outlining a Worksheet

The Excel Outline command displays a worksheet with buttons that allow you to adjust the worksheet display to show only the critical rows and columns. For outlining to function with the default, worksheet formulas must point consistently in the same direction: Summary rows, such as subtotal rows, must be located below related data, and summary columns, such as grand total columns, must be located to the right of related data. (If you're not sure which way your formulas point, click the Trace Precedents button on the Auditing toolbar.) You can outline an entire worksheet or a range of cells in a worksheet. Jim needs to give Lisa Wong, the MediaLoft assistant controller, the first and second quarter totals. He asks you to outline the first and second quarter information on the worksheet and to emphasize the subtotals for the East and West regions.

Steps

1. Press **[Ctrl][Home]**, then select the cell range A1:I15
   The first and second quarter information is selected.

2. Click **Data** on the menu bar, point to **Group and Outline**, then click **Auto Outline**
   The range is displayed in Outline view, as shown in Figure O-6. There are several ways to change the amount of detail in an outlined worksheet, but the easiest is by using the Column Level and Row Level buttons, which hide varying amounts of detail. The Row Level 1 button hides everything in the worksheet except the most important row or rows—in this case, the Grand Total row.

3. Click the **Row Level 1 button** 1
   This selection doesn't display enough information, so you'll try the Row Level 2 button, which hides everything except the second most important rows—in this case, the subtotal rows and the Grand Total row.

4. Click the **Row Level 2 button** 2
   Now you can see the rows you want. Next, you'll display only the columns you choose—in this case, the Qtr 1 and Qtr 2 columns.

5. Click the **Column Level 1 button** 1
   The first and second quarter totals appear, and the monthly figures are no longer visible. You need a printed copy of the worksheet.

6. Place your name in the worksheet footer, then preview and print the outlined range of cells on the worksheet
   The preview should look like Figure O-7. You're finished using the outlining feature.

7. Click the **Row Level 3 button** 3, then click the **Column Level 2 button** 2
   The first and second quarterly monthly figures for each store reappear.

8. Click **Data** on the menu bar, point to **Group and Outline**, then click **Clear Outline**
   The Outline view closes, and the column and row level buttons are no longer visible. The worksheet returns to Normal view.

QuickTip

You can group or ungroup a range of cells if the Auto Outline feature doesn't organize the worksheet data the way your want. Select the rows or columns you want to group, click Data on the menu bar, point to Group and Outline, then click Group or Ungroup.

QuickTip

If your summary information appears above your detail rows or to the left of your detail columns, you need to change the outline settings. Click Data on the menu bar, point to Group and Outline, then click Settings. The Settings dialog box will let you change the outline criteria.

FIGURE O-6: Range in Outline view

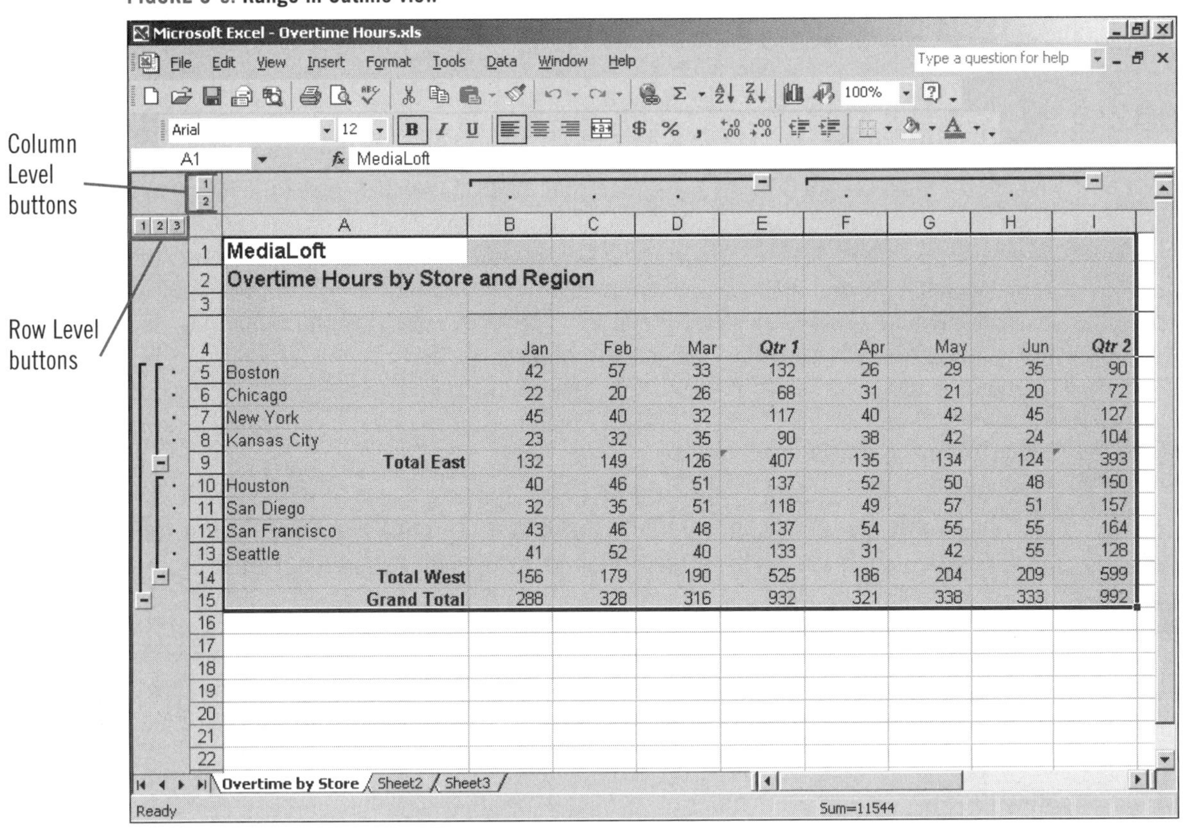

FIGURE O-7: Printed Range outline

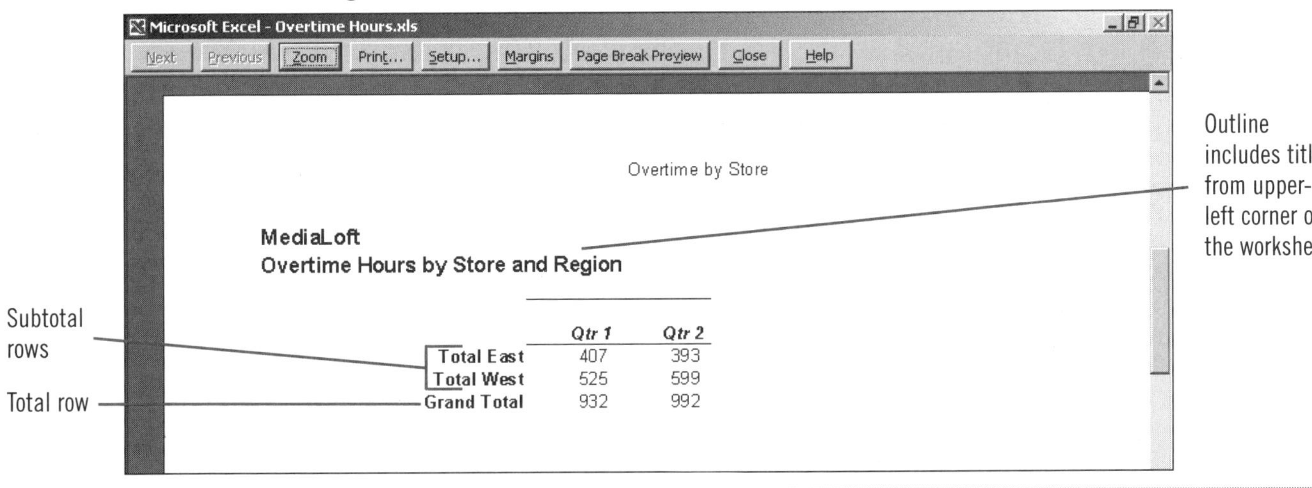

Excel 2002

Excel 2002

Controlling Worksheet Calculations

Whenever you change a value in a cell, Excel automatically recalculates all the formulas in the worksheet based on that cell. This automatic calculation is efficient until you create a worksheet so large that the recalculation process slows down data entry and screen updating. Worksheets with many formulas, data tables, or functions may also recalculate slowly. In these cases, you might want to selectively determine if and when you want Excel to perform calculations automatically. You do this by applying the manual calculation option. Once you change the calculation mode to manual, the manual mode is applied to all open worksheets. Because Jim knows that using specific Excel calculation options can help make worksheet building more efficient, he asks you to change from automatic to manual calculation.

Steps

1. **Click Tools on the menu bar, click Options, then click the Calculation tab**
   The Calculation tab of the Options dialog box opens, as shown in Figure O-8.

2. **Under Calculation, click to select the Manual option button**
   When you select the Manual option, the "Recalculate before save" box automatically becomes active and contains a check mark. Because the workbook will not recalculate until you save or close and reopen the workbook, you must make sure to recalculate your worksheet before you print it and after you make changes.

> **QuickTip**
> To automatically recalculate all worksheet formulas except one- and two-input data tables, under Calculation, click Automatic except tables.

3. **Click OK**
   Jim informs you that the December total for the San Francisco store is incorrect. You'll freeze the worksheet panes and adjust the entry in cell P12 accordingly.

4. **Click cell B5, click Window on the menu bar, click Freeze Panes, then scroll right to bring columns P through S into view**

5. **Click cell P12, type 96, then click the Enter button on the formula bar**
   See Figure O-9. The total formulas are *not* updated, and the percentage in cell S12 is still 15%. The word "Calculate" appears in the status bar to indicate that a specific value in the worksheet did indeed change and must be recalculated. You can press [F9] at any time to calculate all the open worksheets manually or [Shift][F9] to calculate just the active worksheet.

6. **Press [Shift][F9], then save the workbook**
   See Figure O-10. The percentage in cell S12 is now 16% instead of 15%. The other formulas in the worksheet affected by the value in cell P12 changed as well. Because this is a relatively small worksheet that recalculates quickly, you will return to automatic calculation.

> **QuickTip**
> If a worksheet formula is linked to a worksheet that you have not recalculated and you update that link, you will see a message informing you of the situation. To update the link using the current value, click OK. To use the previous value, click Cancel.

7. **Click Tools on the menu bar, click Options, click the Calculation tab if necessary, under Calculation click the Automatic option button, then click OK**
   Now any additional changes you make to the worksheet will be recalculated automatically.

FIGURE O-8: Calculation tab of the Options dialog box

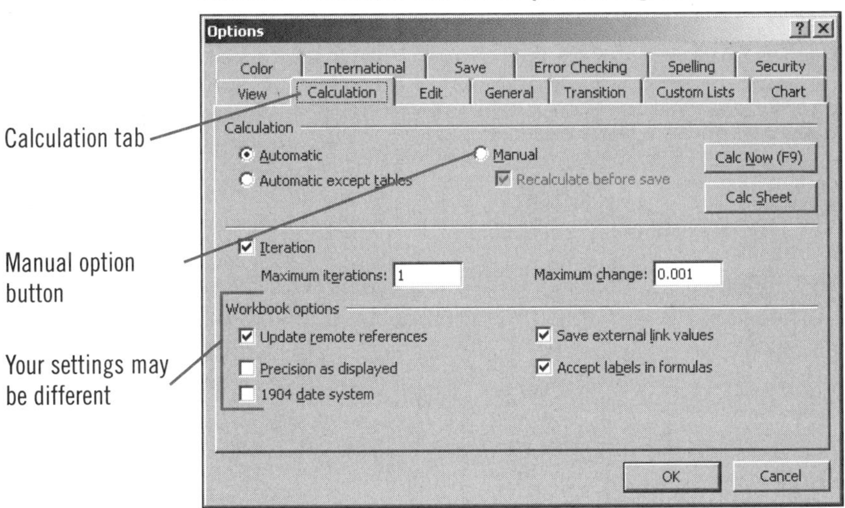

FIGURE O-9: Worksheet in manual calculation mode

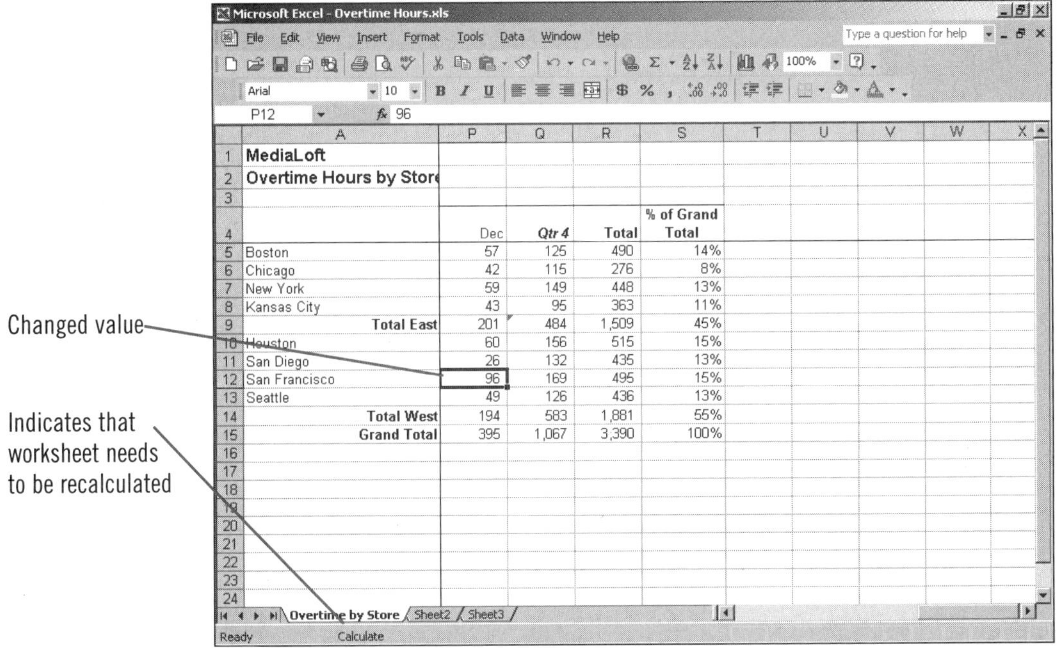

	A	P	Q	R	S
1	MediaLoft				
2	Overtime Hours by Store				
3					
4		Dec	Qtr 4	Total	% of Grand Total
5	Boston	57	125	490	14%
6	Chicago	42	115	276	8%
7	New York	59	149	448	13%
8	Kansas City	43	95	363	11%
9	Total East	201	484	1,509	45%
10	Houston	60	156	515	15%
11	San Diego	26	132	435	13%
12	San Francisco	96	169	495	15%
13	Seattle	49	126	436	13%
14	Total West	194	583	1,881	55%
15	Grand Total	395	1,067	3,390	100%

FIGURE O-10: Worksheet with updated values

	A	P	Q	R	S
1	MediaLoft				
2	Overtime Hours by Store				
3					
4		Dec	Qtr 4	Total	% of Grand Total
5	Boston	57	125	490	14%
6	Chicago	42	115	276	8%
7	New York	59	149	448	13%
8	Kansas City	43	95	363	11%
9	Total East	201	484	1,509	44%
10	Houston	60	156	515	15%
11	San Diego	26	132	435	13%
12	San Francisco	96	206	532	16%
13	Seattle	49	126	436	13%
14	Total West	231	620	1,918	56%
15	Grand Total	432	1,104	3,427	100%

Excel 2002

Creating Custom AutoFill Lists

Whenever you need to type a list of words regularly, you can save time by creating a custom AutoFill list. Then you need only to enter the first value in a blank cell and drag the AutoFill handle. Excel will enter the rest of the information for you. Figure O-11 shows some examples of AutoFill lists. Jim often has to repeatedly enter MediaLoft store names and regional total labels in various worksheets. He asks you to create an AutoFill list to save time in performing this task. You begin by selecting the names and total labels in the worksheet.

Steps

1. Select the range **A5:A15**
2. Click **Tools** on the menu bar, click **Options**, then click the **Custom Lists tab**
   See Figure O-12. The Custom Lists tab shows the existing AutoFill lists. The Import list from cells box contains the range you selected in Step 1.
3. Click **Import**
   The list of names is highlighted in the Custom lists box and appears in the List entries box. You will test the custom AutoFill list by placing it in a blank worksheet.
4. Click **OK**, click the **Sheet2 tab**, then enter **Boston** in cell A1
5. Position the pointer over the AutoFill handle in the lower-right corner of cell A1
   Notice that the pointer changes to +, as shown in Figure O-13.
6. Click and drag the pointer down to cell **A11**, then release the mouse button
   The highlighted range now contains the custom list of store names and total rows you created. You've finished creating and applying your custom AutoFill list, and you will delete it from the Options dialog box in case others will be using your computer.
7. Click **Tools** on the menu bar, click **Options**, click the **Custom Lists tab** if necessary, click the list of store and region names in the Custom lists box, click **Delete**, click **OK** to confirm the deletion, then click **OK** again
8. Save the workbook

QuickTip

If a list of store names already appears in the Custom lists box, the person using the computer before you forgot to delete it. Click the list, click Delete, then proceed with Step 3. It isn't possible to delete the four default lists for days and months.

QuickTip

You can also drag the AutoFill handle to the right to enter a custom list.

FIGURE O-11: Sample AutoFill lists

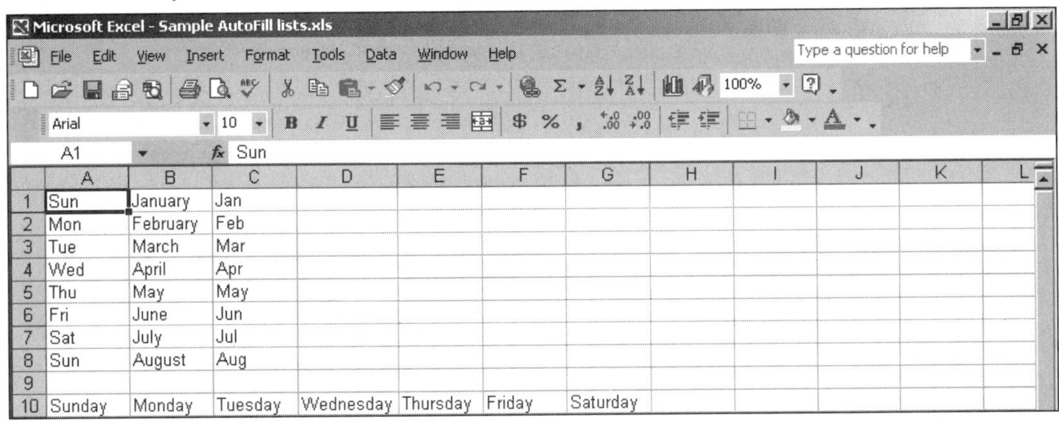

FIGURE O-12: Custom Lists tab

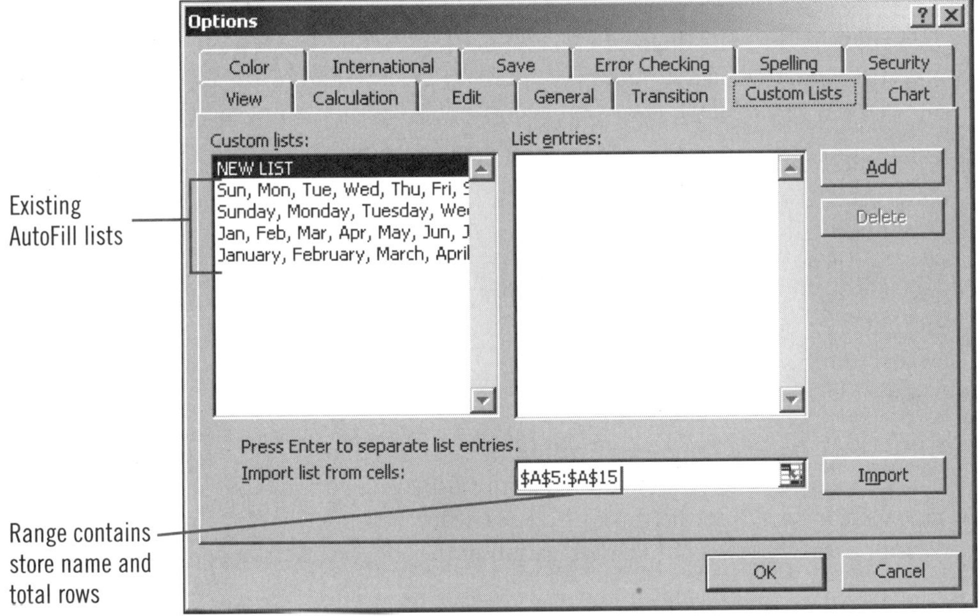

FIGURE O-13: Applying a custom AutoFill list

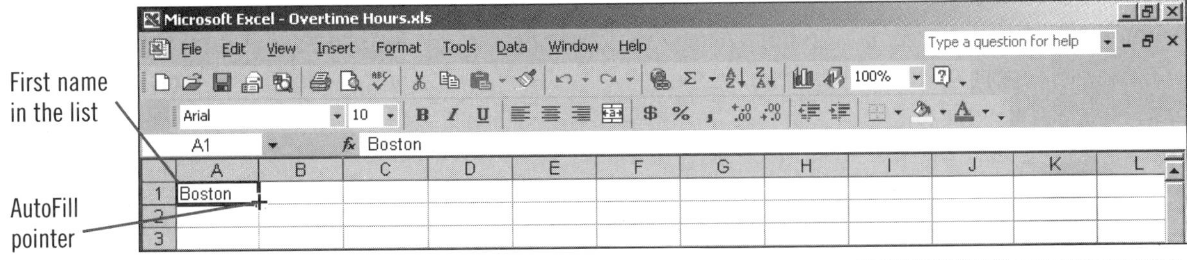

Excel 2002

Customizing Excel

The Excel default settings for editing and viewing a worksheet are designed with user convenience in mind. You may find, however, that a particular setting doesn't always fit your needs (for example, the location where the cell selector moves after you press [Enter]). The thirteen tabs of the Options dialog box allow you to customize Excel to suit your work habits and needs. You've already used the Calculation tab to switch to manual calculation and the Custom Lists tab to create your own AutoFill list. The most commonly used Options dialog box tabs are explained in more detail in Table O-1. Jim is curious about how he might customize Excel to allow him to work more efficiently. He asks you to use a blank workbook to explore some of the features of Excel available in the Options dialog box.

Steps

1. Click the **New button** on the Standard toolbar, click **Tools** on the menu bar, click **Options**, then click the **Edit tab**
   In some worksheets, it's more convenient to have the cell selector automatically move right one cell, rather than down one cell, after you press [Enter].
2. Click the **Direction list arrow**, then click **Right**
   See Figure O-14. You can enter detailed information (or properties) to document your workbook in the Properties dialog box. This documentation may be useful to co-workers because it allows them to read a summary of your workbook without actually having to open it; they can right-click the file in the Open dialog box, then click Properties.
3. Click the **General tab**, then click the **Prompt for workbook properties check box**
   Now, when you save a workbook, a dialog box will open asking you to enter file properties. Jim thinks the workbook would look better without gridlines.
4. Click the **View tab**, then under Window options, click the **Gridlines check box** to deselect it
   This setting, as well as the others under "Window options," affects only the active worksheet. Next, you'll check the results of your new workbook settings.
5. Click **OK**, type **Accounts Receivable** in cell A1, then press **[Enter]**
   The information in your new worksheet is displayed without any gridlines. In addition, the cell selector moved to the right of cell A1 when you pressed [Enter]. Next, as you save the workbook, you'll enter some information in the Properties dialog box.
6. Save the workbook as **Accounts** in the drive and folder where your Project Files are stored; in the Accounts Properties dialog box click the **Summary tab** if necessary, then in the Comments text box, type **Sample workbook used to practice customizing Excel**
   See Figure O-15.
7. Click **OK**
   Now that you've finished exploring the Options dialog box, you need to reestablish the original Excel settings. You don't need to adjust the Gridlines setting because that change applied only to the active worksheet.
8. Click **Tools** on the menu bar, click **Options**, click the **Edit tab**, click the **Direction list arrow**, click **Down**, click the **General tab**, click the **Prompt for workbook properties check box** to deselect it, click **OK**, then close the workbook
   The Overtime Hours workbook is still open.

FIGURE O-14: Edit tab in the Options dialog box

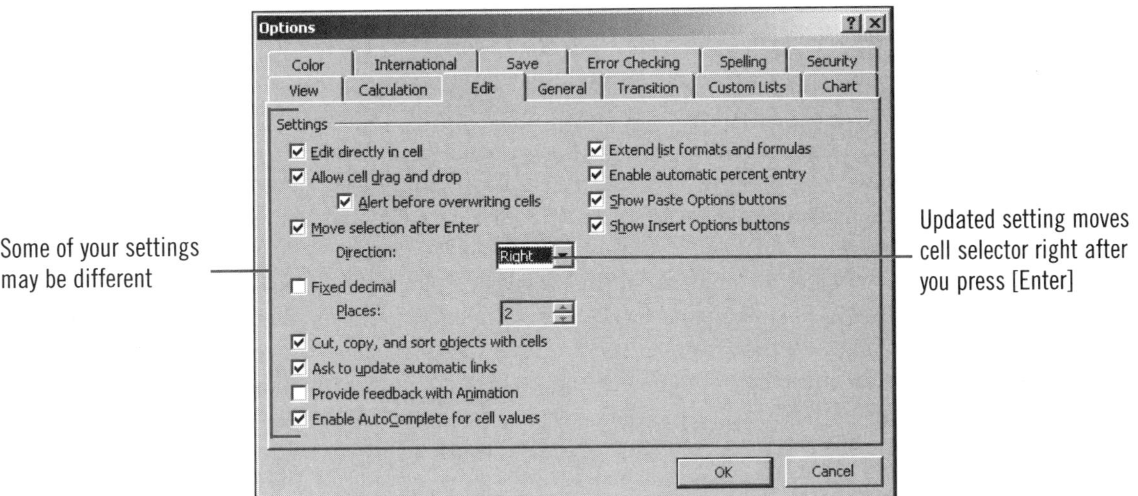

FIGURE O-15: Properties dialog box

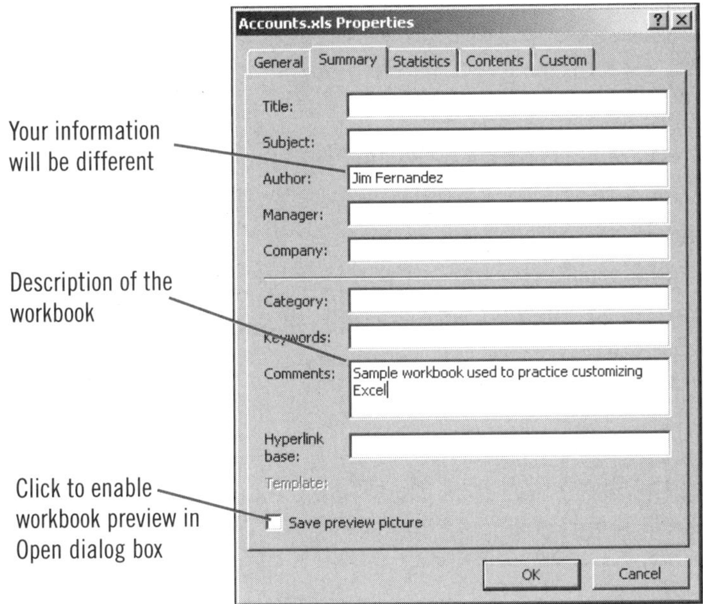

TABLE O-1: Selected Options dialog box tabs

tab	description
Calculation	Controls how the worksheet is calculated; choices include automatic and manual
Chart	Controls how empty cells are treated in a chart and whether chart tips are displayed
Color	Allows you to copy a customized color palette from one workbook to another
Custom Lists	Allows you to add or delete custom AutoFill lists
Edit	Controls the direction in which the cell selector moves after you press [Enter]; also contains other editing features
General	Controls the option to display the Properties dialog box when saving a workbook, the number of sheets in a new workbook, and the drive and folder used in the Save dialog box by default; user name is also listed here
Transition	Provides options useful for users familiar with Lotus 1-2-3 and sets the default file type for saved worksheets
View	Controls the visibility of the Formula bar, startup task pane, windows in taskbar, status bar, gridlines, row and column headers, and scroll bars; also controls the option to display formulas in a worksheet

Excel 2002

Adding a Comment to a Cell

If you plan to share a workbook with others, it's a good idea to **document**, or make notes about, basic assumptions, complex formulas, or questionable data. Reading your documentation, a co-worker can quickly become familiar with your workbook. The easiest way to document a workbook is to use **cell comments**, which are notes about your workbook that appear when you place the pointer over a cell. When you sort or copy and paste cells, any comments attached to them will move to the new location. In PivotTable reports, however, the comments stay attached to the cell where they are entered. If the layout of the PivotTable changes, the comments do not move with the worksheet data. Jim thinks one of the figures in the worksheet may be incorrect. He asks you to add a comment for Lisa, pointing out the possible error.

Steps

1. Click the **Overtime by Store sheet tab**, then right-click cell **P11**
2. Click **Insert Comment** on the shortcut menu
   The Comment box opens, as shown in Figure O-16. Notice that Excel automatically includes the username at the beginning of the comment. The username is the name that appears on the General tab of the Options dialog box. Notice the white sizing handles on the border of the Comment box. You can drag these handles to change the size of the box.
3. Type **Is this figure correct? It looks low to me.**
   The text automatically wraps to the next line as necessary.
4. Click outside the Comment box
   A red triangle appears in the upper-right corner of cell P11, indicating that a comment is attached to the cell. People who use your worksheet can easily display comments.
5. Place the pointer over cell P11
   The comment appears next to the cell. When you move the pointer outside of cell P11, the comment disappears. The worksheet is now finished and ready for printing.
6. Click **File** on the menu bar, click **Page Setup**, click the **Page tab** if necessary, specify landscape orientation and fit the worksheet to one page
   On a second printed page, you'll print only the cell comment along with its associated cell reference.
7. Click the **Sheet tab**, under Print click the **Comments list arrow**, click **At end of sheet**, click the **Row and column headings check box** to select it, click **Print**, then click **OK**
   Your comment is printed on a separate page after the worksheet.
8. Save the workbook

QuickTip

You can also insert a comment by clicking the Comment option on the Insert menu or by clicking the New Comment button on the Reviewing or the Formula Auditing toolbar.

QuickTip

To display both the comment indicators and the comments in all worksheet cells, click Tools, click Options, click the View tab, then select the Comment & indicator option button in the Comments section. See Figure O-17.

FIGURE O-16: Comment box

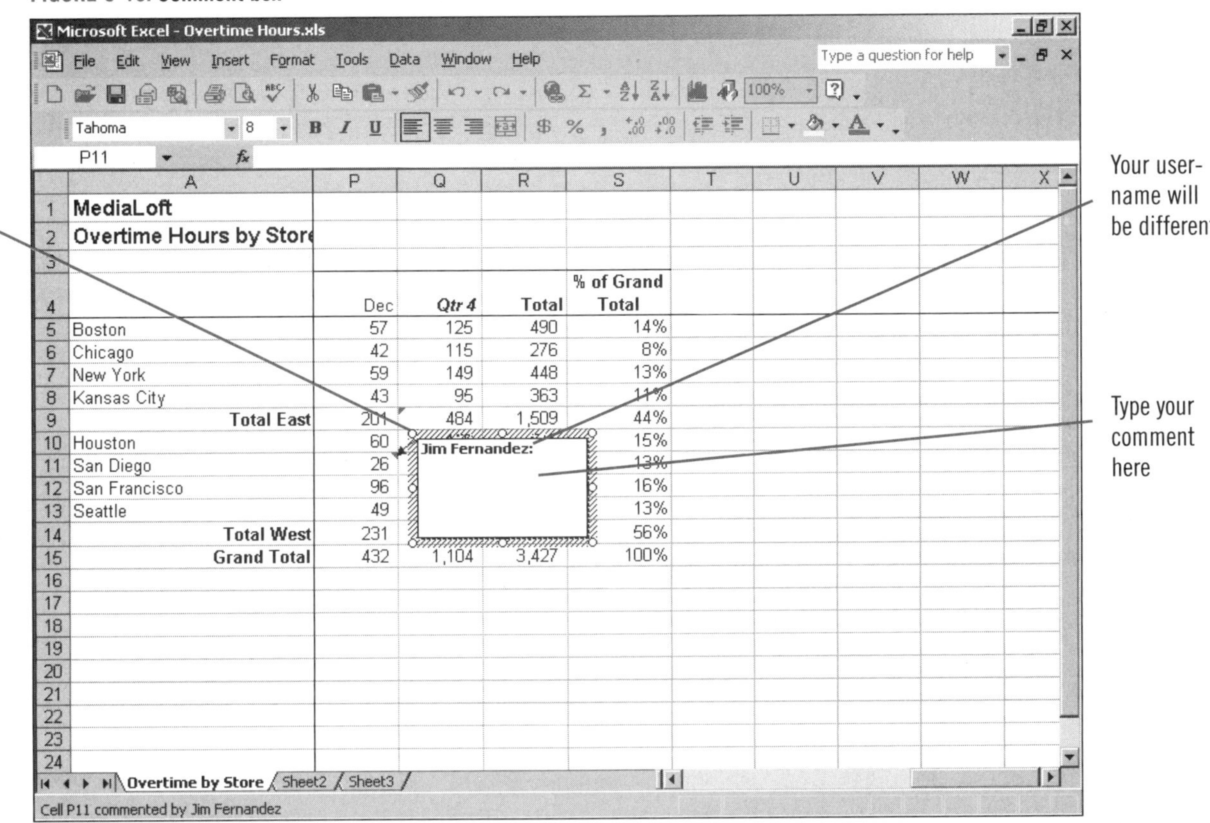

FIGURE O-17: View tab in the Options dialog box

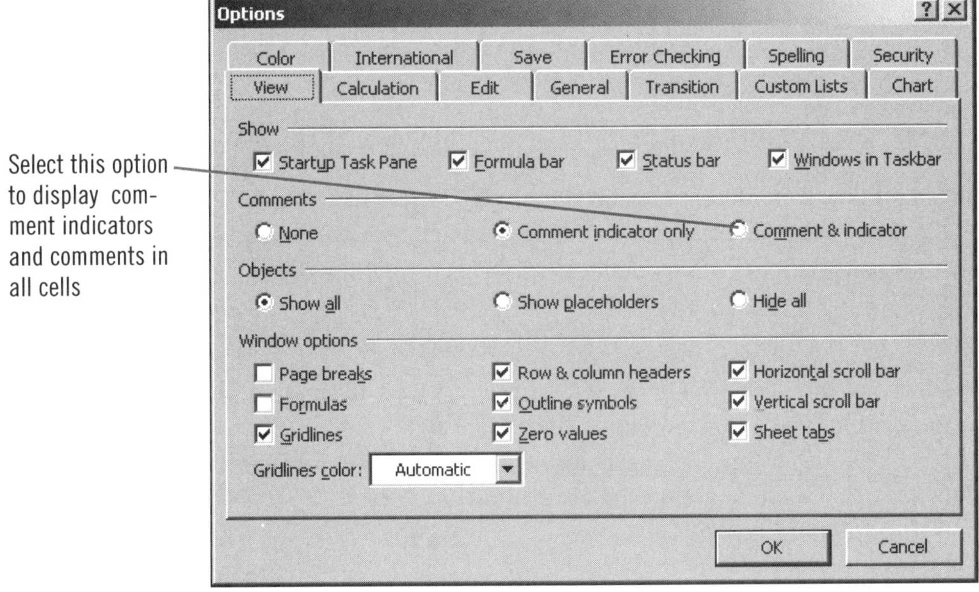

Editing, copying, and deleting comments

To edit an existing comment, select the cell to which the comment is attached, click Insert on the menu bar, then click Edit Comment. You can also right click a cell with a comment and select Edit Comment from the shortcut menu. To copy only comments, copy the cell contents, right-click the destination cell, select Paste Special, click Comments, then click OK. You can delete a comment by right-clicking the cell it is attached to, then selecting Delete Comment.

Excel 2002

Creating a Template

A **template** is a workbook that contains text (such as column and row labels), formulas, macros, and formatting you use repeatedly. Once you save a workbook as a template, it provides a model for creating a new workbook without your having to reenter standard data. Excel provides several templates on the Spreadsheet Solutions tab of the New dialog box. In most cases, though, you'll probably want to create your own template from a worksheet you use regularly. When you save a file as a template, the original workbook remains unchanged. Jim plans to use the same formulas, titles, frozen panes, and row and column labels from the Overtime Hours worksheet for subsequent yearly worksheets. He asks you to delete the extra sheets, the comments, and the data for each month, and then save the workbook as a template.

Steps

1. **Click the Sheet2 tab, press [Ctrl], click the Sheet3 tab, right-click the Sheet3 tab, click Delete, then click Delete again**

2. **Right-click cell P11, then click Delete Comment**

   Now that you've removed the extra sheets and the comment, you'll delete the data on overtime hours. You'll leave the formulas in rows 9, 14, and 15, and in columns E, I, M, Q, R, and S, however, so that another user can simply begin entering data without having to re-create the formulas.

3. **Press [Ctrl], select the ranges B5:D8, B10:D13, F5:H8, F10:H13, J5:L8, J10:L13, N5:P8, and N10:P13, press [Delete], then click anywhere to deselect the ranges**

   See Figure O-18. The hyphens in the subtotal and total rows and columns indicate that the current value of these cells is zero. The divide by zero error messages in column S are only temporary and will disappear as soon as you open the template, save it as a workbook, and begin to enter next year's data. To make the template easier to use, it's best to have the first data entry cell selected when you save it.

4. **Scroll left to bring columns B through G into view, then click cell B5**

5. **Click File, click Save As, click the Save as type list arrow, then click Template**

   Excel adds the .xlt extension to the filename and automatically switches to the Templates folder, as shown in Figure O-19. If you are using a computer on a network, you may not have permission to save to the Templates folder. You'll save your template to the drive and folder where your Project Files are stored instead.

6. **Click the Save in list arrow, click the drive and folder containing your Project Files, click Save, close the workbook, then exit Excel**

   Next year, when Jim needs to compile the information for overtime hours, he can simply open a document based on the Overtime Hours template or apply the template to a new document and begin entering data.

FIGURE O-18: Preparing the template

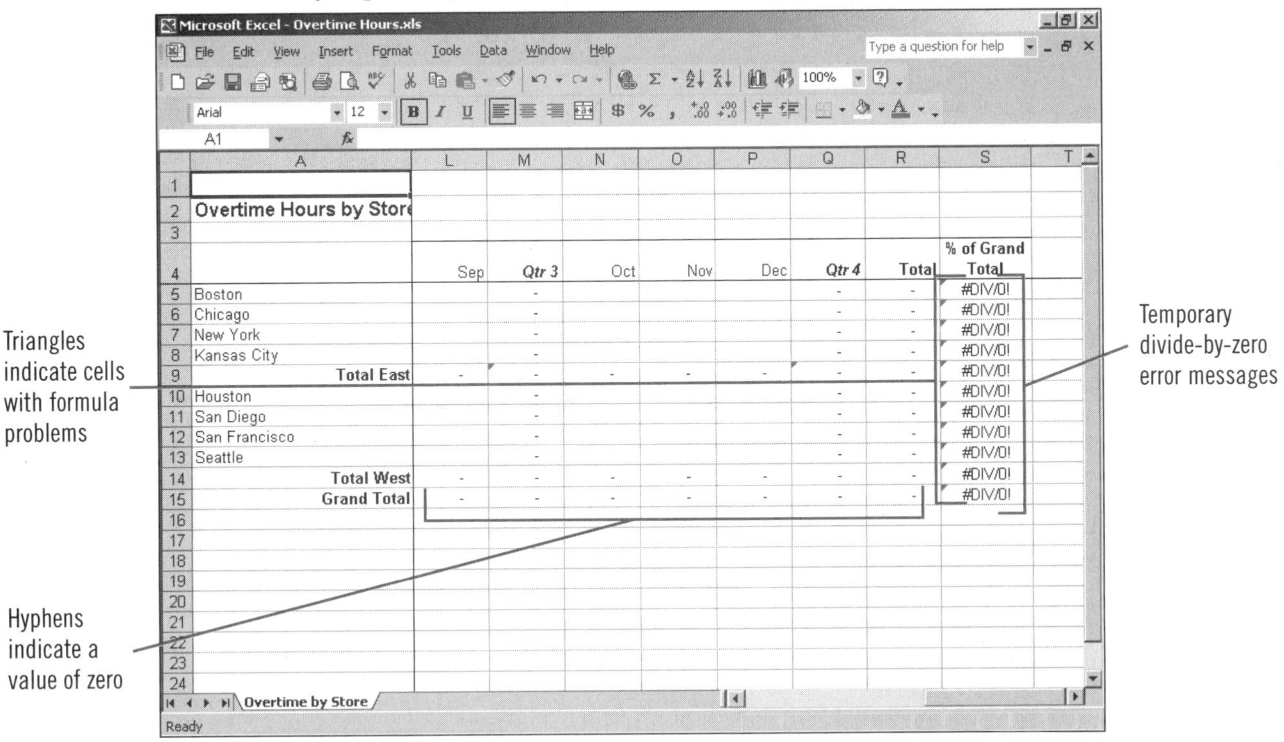

FIGURE O-19: Saving a template

Excel 2002

CLUES TO USE

Editing and applying templates

You can open a document based on your template (that is, apply a template to a document) by clicking File, clicking New, clicking Choose workbook under "New from existing workbook" in the task pane, navigating to the location where the template is stored then double-clicking the template name. The New Workbook task pane also contains a section "New from template". If you click General Templates, then click the Spreadsheet Solutions tab, you have access to several ready-made templates designed for business-related tasks. The "New from template" section also contains links to templates you might have previously stored on the Web or on a network drive, and to templates on the Microsoft.com Web site. To edit a template, you must open the template itself (the .xlt file), change it, then save it under the same name. The changes will be applied only to new documents you create; it does not change documents you've already created using the template.

Excel 2002

Practice

► Concepts Review

Label each element of the Excel screen shown in Figure O-20.

FIGURE O-20

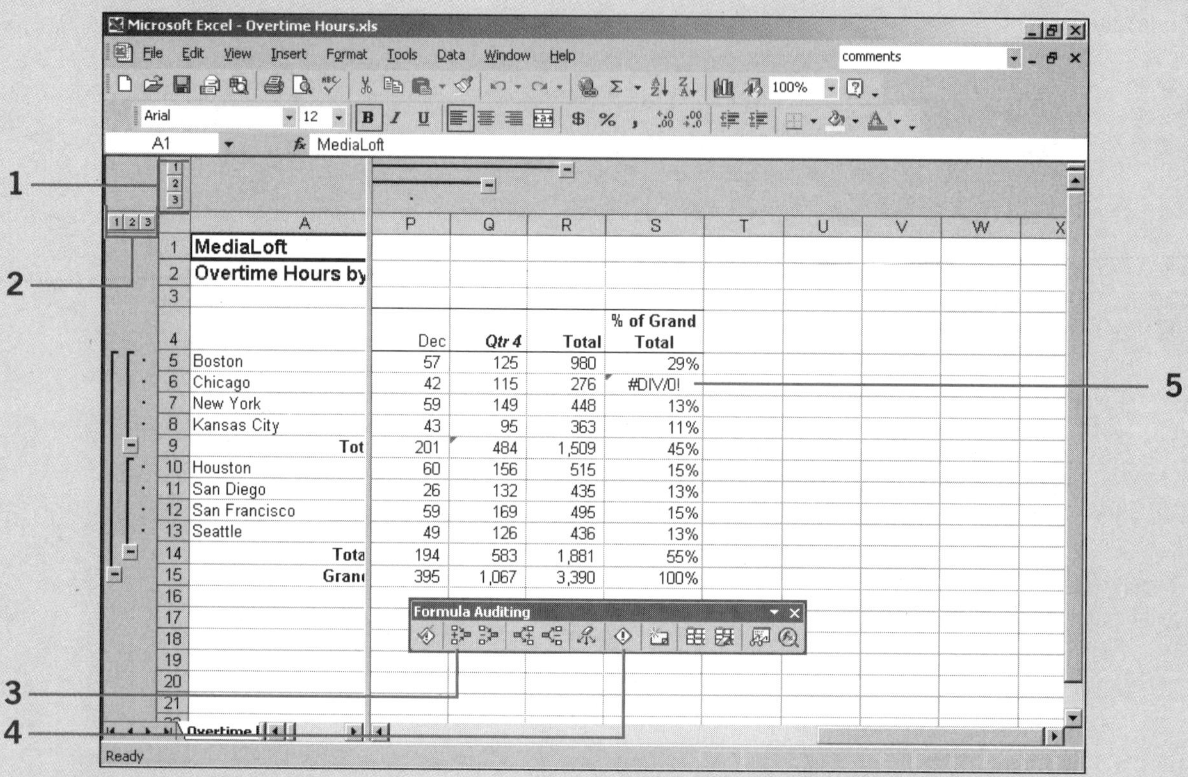

Match each term with the statement that describes it.

6. Note that appears when you place the pointer over a cell
7. Contains settings for customizing Excel
8. Calculates the worksheet manually
9. Occurs in a formula that refers to its own cell location
10. Automatically enters a list in a worksheet
11. Used to track errors and determine worksheet logic
12. Used to locate files
13. Allows you to display the most important columns and rows

a. Search task pane
b. Options dialog box
c. Auditing toolbar
d. Outlining a worksheet
e. Circular reference
f. [Shift][F9]
g. AutoFill
h. Comment

Select the best answer from the list of choices.

14. When searching for a file, which of these characters can substitute for unknown characters in a filename?
- **a.** #
- **b.** &
- **c.** !
- **d.** *

15. You can search for a file by:
- **a.** Name.
- **b.** Text within the file.
- **c.** Property.
- **d.** All of the above

16. The __________ button locates the cells used in the active cell's formula.
- **a.** Trace Antecedents
- **b.** Trace Precedents
- **c.** Function
- **d.** Validation Circle

17. The __________automatically hides everything in the worksheet except the most important row or rows.
- **a.** Trace Dependents button
- **b.** Row Level 1 button
- **c.** Trace Precedents button
- **d.** Trace Error button

18. To apply a custom AutoFill list you:
- **a.** Press [Shift][F9].
- **b.** Click the AutoFill tab in the Edit dialog box.
- **c.** Type the first cell entry and drag the AutoFill handle.
- **d.** Select the list in the worksheet.

19. The __________ tab in the Options dialog box controls whether the Properties dialog box is displayed when you save a workbook.
- **a.** General
- **b.** Edit
- **c.** Properties
- **d.** View

Skills Review

1. Find files.

- **a.** Start Excel, open the Advanced Search pane, then use the wildcard character * to enter the search criterion for all files that include EX O. Search in the drive and folder containing your Project Files. Limit the search to Excel files only. (*Hint*: Remember to clear previous search criteria.)
- **b.** Display the properties for file EX O-2.
- **c.** Open the workbook EX O-2 from the Search Results task pane.
- **d.** Close the Search Results task pane, then save the workbook as **Cafe Budget**.

2. Audit a worksheet.

- **a.** Display the Formula Auditing toolbar and drag it to the bottom of the worksheet.
- **b.** Select cell B10, then use the Trace Dependents button to locate all the cells that depend on this cell. (*Hint*: Click the button three times.)
- **c.** Clear the arrows from the worksheet using the Remove All Arrows button on the Formula Auditing toolbar.
- **d.** Select cell B19, use the Trace Precedents button on the Auditing toolbar to find the cells on which that figure is based, then correct the formula in cell B19. (*Hint*: It should be B7-B18.)
- **e.** Select cell G6, trace the error it contains, then correct the formula. (*Hint*: It should be F6/F7.)
- **f.** Remove any arrows from the worksheet, close the Auditing toolbar, then save the workbook.

3. Outline a worksheet.

- **a.** Group the income information in rows 5 through 7. (*Hint*: Select rows 5 through 7, click Data on the menu bar, point to Group and Outline, then click Group.)
- **b.** Hide the income information in rows 5 through 7 by clicking - to the left of the income rows.
- **c.** Enter your name in the worksheet header, then print the Budget worksheet; fit it to one page, with the income information hidden.
- **d.** Redisplay the income rows by clicking the +.

e. Remove the row grouping. (*Hint*: With the grouped rows selected, click Data on the menu bar, point to Group and Outline, then click Ungroup.)
f. Click cell A1, then display the worksheet in Outline view.
g. Use the Row Level buttons to display only the Net Profit values in the budget.
h. Print the outlined worksheet.
i. Use the Row Level buttons to display all the rows in the budget.
j. Clear the outline from the worksheet.

4. Control worksheet calculations.
a. Open the Options dialog box and switch to manual calculation.
b. Change the figure in cell B6 to 30,200.
c. Recalculate the worksheet manually, using the appropriate key combination.
d. Turn off manual calculation and save the workbook.

5. Create custom AutoFill lists.
a. Select the range A4:A19.
b. Open the Custom Lists tab in the Options dialog box. Delete any custom lists except the four default day and month lists.
c. Import the selected text into the dialog box.
d. Close the dialog box.
e. On Sheet2, enter **Income** in cell A1.
f. Drag the fill handle to cell A15.
g. Select cell A1, and drag its fill handle to cell O1.
h. Open the Options dialog box again, and delete the custom list you just created.
i. Save the workbook.

6. Customize Excel.
a. With Sheet2 still selected, open the Options dialog box.
b. On the Edit tab, change the direction of the cell selector to **Up**.
c. On the General tab, indicate that you want the Properties dialog box to appear when you save a workbook.
d. On the View tab, turn off the worksheet gridlines.
e. Close the dialog box and return to Sheet2, which is now displayed without gridlines.
f. Click the Budget tab, and notice that this worksheet is displayed with gridlines.
g. Open a new workbook.
h. Type your name in cell C5, then press Enter. Check to make sure that the cell selector moves up to cell C4.
i. Save the workbook, to the drive and folder where your Project Files are stored, as **Customizing Excel**. Add your name, if necessary, and the comment **Sample workbook** to the Properties dialog box, then close the workbook.
j. Open the Options dialog box, change the cell selector direction back to **Down**, then turn off the Prompt for workbook properties option. Close the Options dialog box.

7. Add a comment to a cell.
a. In the Budget sheet, select cell E12.
b. Open a Comment box by using the Comment command on the Insert menu.
c. Type **Does this include TV and radio spots, or only newspaper and magazine advertising? It is very important to include these.**
d. Drag the resize handles on the borders of the Comment box until you can see the entire comment.
e. Click anywhere outside the Comment box to close it.
f. Display the comment, then check it for errors.
g. Edit the comment in cell E12 so it ends after the word "spots", with a question mark at the end.
h. Print the worksheet and your comment, with the comment appearing at the end of the sheet.
i. Enter your name in the Sheet 2 footer, change the orientation to landscape, fit it to one page, then print it.
j. Save the workbook.

8. Create a template.

a. Delete Sheet2 and Sheet3.

b. Delete the comment in cell E12.

c. Delete the budget data for all four quarters. Leave the worksheet formulas intact.

d. Select cell B5, then save the workbook as a template, in the folder containing your Project Files. Use the filename **Budget Template**.

e. Close the template.

f. Open a document based on the template using the New Workbook task pane.(*Hint:* Use the Choose workbook option under New from existing workbook.)

g. Enter your own data for all four quarters and in every budget category.

h. Save the workbook as Cafe Budget 2 to the drive and folder where your Project Files are stored.

i. Print the Budget worksheet, then close the workbook and exit Excel.

Independent Challenge 1

You are a manager at Life Skills, a nonprofit agency devoted to helping people with severe learning disabilities become proficient computer users. Your department specializes in hands-on instruction for software programs. During the month of October, you created a check register in Excel for department expenses. Before you begin generating a November register, however, you want to check the October register for errors. In your worksheet audit, you will look for missing check numbers, miscalculated totals, and formula errors. You will also add comments to document the worksheet.

a. Start Excel, open the Project File titled EX O-3 from the drive and folder where your Project Files are stored, then save it as **2003 Monthly Check Register**.

b. Select cell F16 and use the Trace Error button to open the Formula Auditing toolbar.

c. The balance in cell F16 does not reflect the RAM upgrade on 10/15/03. Use the Trace Precedents button to show the logic of the formula in F16. Once you identify the error in cell F16, edit the formula to subtract the RAM expense from the previous balance. (*Hint*: The formula should be F15-E16.)

d. Because of illness, your Excel instructor taught only two hours of a six-hour course. Create a comment indicating this in cell C19 to remind you that he owes you four hours.

e. Use the Trace Error button to determine the source of the problem in cell E24. Edit the formula to solve the problem, then format the cell to display a percentage with no decimal places. (*Hint*: The formula should be E23/F3.)

f. Add your name to the worksheet footer, then save the workbook. Preview the worksheet, then use Page Setup to specify that the worksheet should be printed on one page and the comment on another page.

g. Close the Formula Auditing toolbar, print the worksheet, save and close the workbook, then exit Excel.

Independent Challenge 2

You are a manager at EarthSchool, a nonprofit agency located in Toronto, Ontario. Your agency's mission is to educate elementary-school-aged students about environmental issues. One of your responsibilities is to keep track of your department's regular monthly expenses. Your assistant has compiled a list of fixed expenses in an Excel workbook but can't remember the filename. Once you find the file by using the Search tools in the Search pane, you want to create a custom AutoFill list including each expense item to save time in preparing similar worksheets in the future. Finally, you will temporarily switch to manual formula calculation, then turn off the worksheet gridlines to make the expense data easier to read.

a. Start Excel, then use the Search pane to find a file, in the drive and folder where you Project Files are stored, with the text "EarthSchool" in the workbook. (*Hint*: Use the Search text box in the Basic Search pane.) Open the workbook.

b. Save the workbook as **Monthly Budget** in the drive and folder where your Project Files are stored, then close the Search Results task pane.

c. Select the cells containing the list of expense items, then open the Options dialog box and import the list into the Custom Lists tab.
d. Close the Options dialog box and use the AutoFill handle to insert your list in column C in Sheet2. Compare your Sheet2 to Figure O-21.
e. Add your name to the Sheet2 footer, save the workbook, then preview and print Sheet2.
f. Return to the Fixed Expenses sheet and delete your custom list from the Options dialog box.
g. Use the Options dialog box to switch to manual calculation and to turn off the gridlines in the Fixed Expenses sheet.
h. Change the expense for Printer paper to 37.00. Calculate the worksheet formulas manually.
i. Turn on automatic calculation again; add your name to the footer, save the workbook, then print the Fixed Expenses worksheet.
j. Close the workbook and exit Excel.

FIGURE O-21

	A	B	C	D	E	F
1			Rent			
2			Paper clips			
3			Printer paper			
4			Binders			
5			Copying			
6			Overhead transparencies			
7			Phone bill			
8			Disk labels			
9			Misc. books			
10			Earth Sciences contract instructor			
11			Marine Biology contract instructor			
12			Small Business Loan			
13						
14						

► Independent Challenge 3

Your business, Kidcare, helps parents find high-quality in-home childcare. In exchange for a one-time fee, you recruit and interview potential nannies, confirm references, and conduct thorough background checks. In addition, once a nanny has been hired, you provide training in child development and infant CPR. Currently, you are preparing your budget for the next four quarters. After you enter the data for each expense and income category, you will create a condensed version of the worksheet using Excel outlining tools.

a. Start Excel, create a new workbook, then save it as **Kidcare** in the drive and folder where your Project Files are stored.
b. Enter a title of **Yearly Budget**, then enter the following column labels: **Description, 1st Qtr, 2nd Qtr, 3rd Qtr, 4th Qtr**, and **Total**.
c. Enter labels for the following income items: **Nanny Fee, Child Development Course, CPR Course**, and **Income subtotal**. Enter labels for at least six office expense items and the Expenses subtotal. Create a row for Net cash flow calculations. Format the worksheet appropriately.
d. Enter expenses and income data for each quarter. Subtotal the income items and the expenses. Create formulas for the total column and the cash flow row (income - expenses).

FIGURE O-22

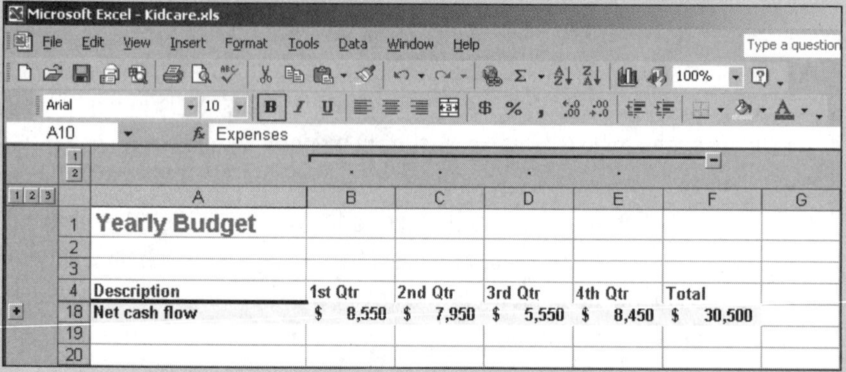

Microsoft Excel - Kidcare.xls

File Edit View Insert Format Tools Data Window Help

A10 | Expenses

	A	B	C	D	E	F	G
1	Yearly Budget						
2							
3							
4	Description	1st Qtr	2nd Qtr	3rd Qtr	4th Qtr	Total	
18	Net cash flow	$ 8,550	$ 7,950	$ 5,550	$ 8,450	$ 30,500	
19							
20							

e. Check the outline settings to make sure the summary rows are below the detail rows and the summary columns are to the right of the detail columns. (*Hint:* Click Data, point to Group and Outline, then click Settings.) Display the worksheet in Outline view.

f. Use the Row level 1 button on the outline to display only the Net cash flow row. Compare your outline structure to Figure O-22. Your Net cash flow data will be different.

g. Add your name to the footer, save the workbook, then print the outlined worksheet.

h. Redisplay all the rows, then use the outline again to hide the data for each quarter, showing only the Total column. Save the workbook then print the outlined worksheet.

i. Clear the outline, then print the entire worksheet. Close the workbook and exit Excel.

Independent Challenge 4

As the Marketing Manager of products at NewSite, a Web development firm, you frequently travel to customer sites. After every trip, you submit an expense report for reimbursement of your travel expenditures. A template containing the input fields and formulas would speed up the process of preparing this report. You decide to research the templates available in the Microsoft Office template gallery to see if any are suitable for recording your travel expenses.

a. Start Excel, then use the link for Templates on Microsoft.com. in the New from template section of the task pane to connect to the Microsoft Office Template Gallery. After you reach the Microsoft Office Update page, click the appropriate country if necessary.

b. Find an expense statement template in the Microsoft Office template gallery. (*Hint*: Click the link for Business Forms, click the link for Expense Reports, then click the Expense statement link.) Accept any licensing agreements, and if you get a Security Warning dialog box asking you to install and run Microsoft Office tools, click Yes. (*Hint:* If the Web site has changed since this book was printed, search on "templates" on the Microsoft Office page)

FIGURE O-23

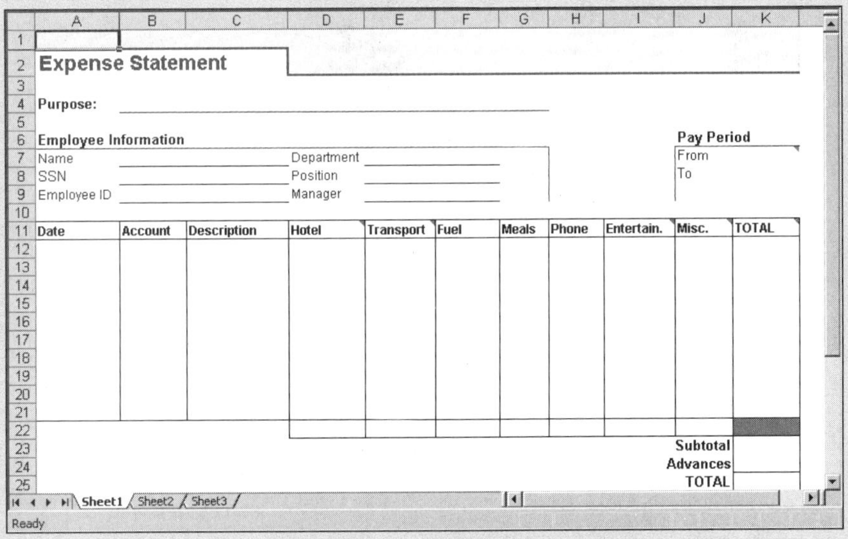

c. When you can see the template preview, click **Edit in Microsoft Excel** to open a new workbook based on the template.

d. Save the new workbook as a template to the folder containing your Project Files and name it **Expense Statement**.

e. Edit the template to: Change the font color of the text in cell A3 to blue, and delete row 1. Compare your template to Figure O-23

f. Save and close the Expense Statement template. Open a workbook based on the Expense Statement template and save it in the drive and folder where your Project Files are stored as **My Expense Statement**.

g. Enter two lines of your own expense data for a business trip. Enter your name in the Name field. Widen columns as necessary.

h. Edit the comment in cell D11 to add a statement "Includes all taxes".

i. Outline the worksheet and use the Row Level buttons to display only the total information.

j. Print the outlined worksheet showing the total information.

k. Save and close the workbook and exit Excel.

► Visual Workshop

Open the workbook titled EX O-5, then click Cancel to close the dialog box warning you of a circular reference. Save the workbook as **Zoo Count** in the drive and folder where your Project Files are stored. Use the auditing and formatting techniques you have learned so far to correct any errors so that the worksheet entries and formulas match Figure O-24. Make sure to include the comment in cell E21. Add your name to the footer, then preview and print the worksheet and comment, showing row and column headings.

FIGURE O-24

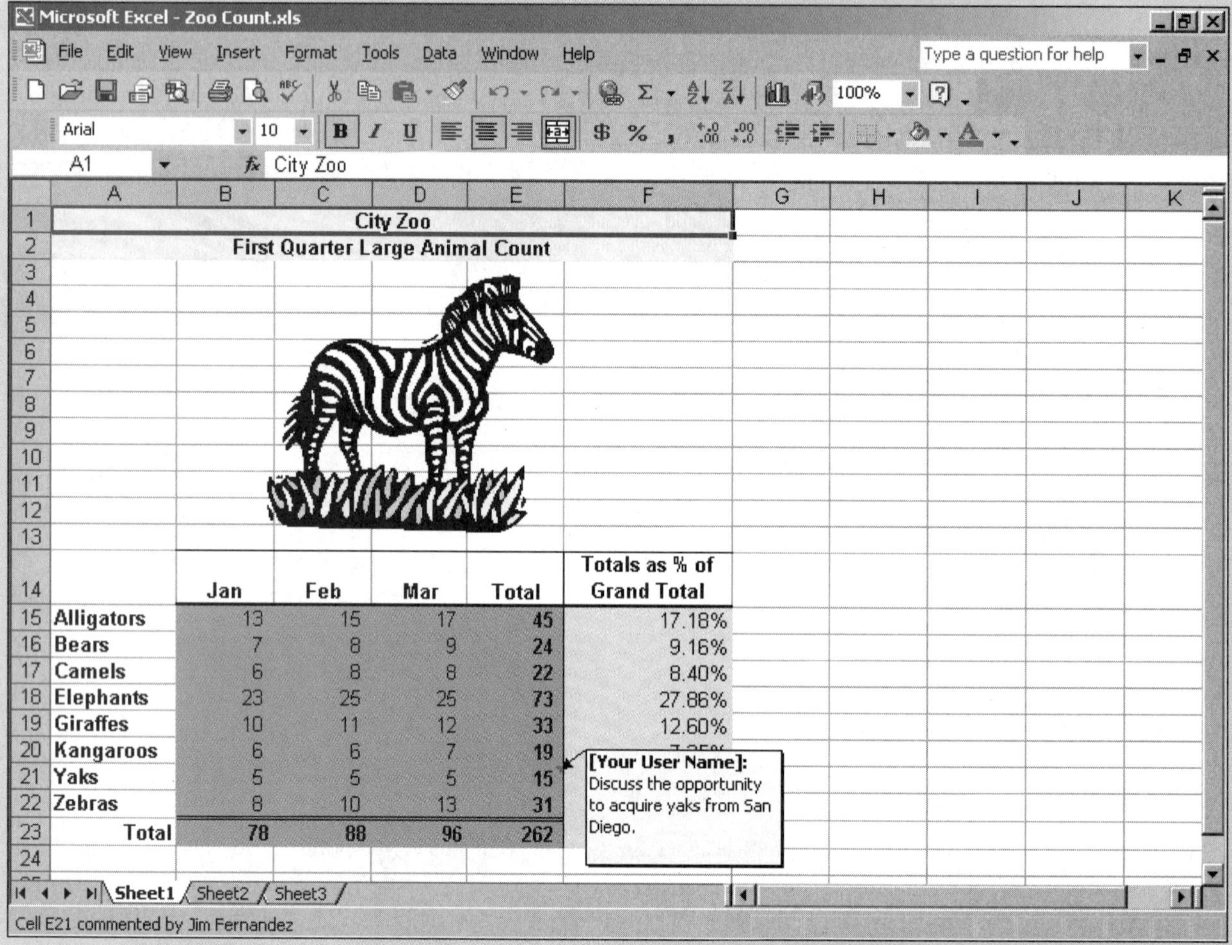

Microsoft Excel - Zoo Count.xls

A1 City Zoo

	A	B	C	D	E	F
1	City Zoo					
2	First Quarter Large Animal Count					
14		Jan	Feb	Mar	Total	Totals as % of Grand Total
15	Alligators	13	15	17	45	17.18%
16	Bears	7	8	9	24	9.16%
17	Camels	6	8	8	22	8.40%
18	Elephants	23	25	25	73	27.86%
19	Giraffes	10	11	12	33	12.60%
20	Kangaroos	6	6	7	19	[illegible]
21	Yaks	5	5	5	15	
22	Zebras	8	10	13	31	
23	Total	78	88	96	262	

[Your User Name]: Discuss the opportunity to acquire yaks from San Diego.

Sheet1 / Sheet2 / Sheet3

Cell E21 commented by Jim Fernandez

Programming with Excel

Objectives

- View VBA code
- Analyze VBA code
- Write VBA code
- Add a conditional statement
- Prompt the user for data
- Debug a macro
- Create a main procedure
- Run a main procedure

All Excel macros are written in a programming language called Visual Basic for Applications, or simply, **VBA**. When you create a macro with the Excel macro recorder, the recorder writes the VBA instructions for you. You can also create an Excel macro by entering VBA instructions manually. The sequence of VBA statements contained in a macro is called a **procedure**. In this unit, you will view and analyze existing VBA code, then you will write VBA code on your own. You will learn how to add a conditional statement to a procedure, as well as how to prompt the user for information while the macro is running. You will also find out how to locate any errors, or bugs, in a macro. Finally, you will combine several macros into one main procedure. Alice Wegman, MediaLoft's marketing manager, has asked Jim Fernandez to automate some of the division's time-consuming tasks. You will help Jim by creating five Excel macros for the Marketing Department.

Excel 2002

Viewing VBA Code

Before you can write Excel macro procedures, you must become familiar with the VBA (Visual Basic for Applications) programming language. A common method of learning any programming language is to view existing code. To view VBA code, you open the Visual Basic Editor, which contains a Project window, a Properties window, and a Code window. The VBA code for macro procedures appears in the Code window. The first line of a procedure, called the **procedure header**, defines the procedure's type, name, and arguments. Items displayed in blue are **keywords**, which are words recognized as part of the VBA programming language. **Comments**, which are notes explaining the code, are shown in green, and the remaining code is shown in black. You use the Visual Basic Editor to view or edit an existing macro as well as to create new macros. Each week, MediaLoft receives a text file from the KHOT radio station, containing information about weekly radio ads. Alice has already imported the text file into a worksheet but it still needs to be formatted. Jim asks you to work on a macro to automate the process of formatting this imported text file.

Steps

Trouble?

If you get a security error message when attempting to run your macro, the security level may be set too high in the workbook. You can enable macros for the Workbook by pointing to the Macro Option on the Tools menu and selecting Security. Set the security level to Medium or Low, then close and reopen the workbook.

1. Start Excel, if necessary, then open the Project File titled **EX P-1** from the drive and folder where your Project Files are stored, click **Enable Macros**, then save it as **KHOT Procedures**

   The virus warning, shown in Figure P-1, alerts you that the worksheet contains macros. The KHOT Procedures workbook displays a blank worksheet. This is the workbook that you will use to create and store all the procedures for this lesson.

2. Click **Tools** on the menu bar, point to **Macro**, then click **Macros**

   The Macro dialog box opens with the FormatFile macro procedure in the list box. If you have any macros saved in your Personal Macro workbook they will also be listed in the Macro dialog box.

3. If it is not already selected, click **FormatFile**, click **Edit**, then in the Project Explorer window, click **Format** if it is not already selected

   The Visual Basic Editor displays the FormatFile procedure in the Code window. See Figure P-2. See Table P-1 to make sure your screen matches those in the unit.

4. Make sure both the Visual Basic window and the Code window are maximized to match Figure P-2

5. Examine the top three lines of code, which contain comments, and the first line of code beginning with Sub FormatFile ( )

   Notice that the different parts of the procedure appear in various colors. The third line of comments explains that the keyboard shortcut for this macro procedure is Ctrl+F. The keyword *Sub* in the procedure header indicates that this is a **Sub procedure**, or a series of Visual Basic statements that perform an action but do not return a value. In the next lesson, you will analyze the procedure code to see what each line does.

TABLE P-1: Matching your screen to the unit figures

If...	Do this...
The Properties or Project Explorer window is not displayed	Click the Properties Window button then click the Project Explorer button on the toolbar
You see only the code window	Click Tools on the menu bar, click Options, click the Docking tab, then make sure the Project Explorer and Properties Window options are selected
You do not see folders in the Project Explorer window	Click the Toggle Folders button on the Project Explorer window toolbar

FIGURE P-1: Virus warning dialog box

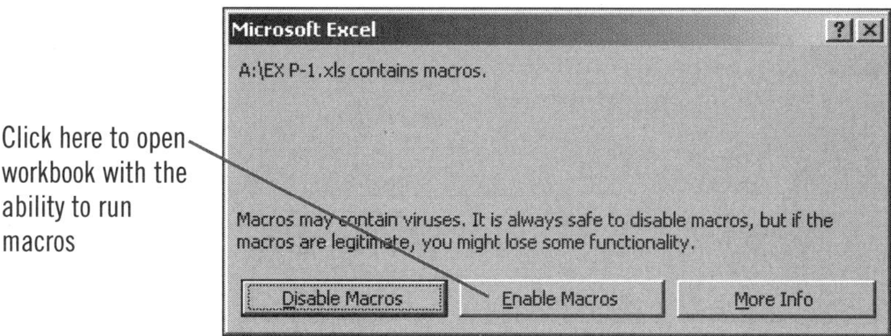
Click here to open workbook with the ability to run macros
Microsoft Excel
A:\EX P-1.xls contains macros.
Macros may contain viruses. It is always safe to disable macros, but if the macros are legitimate, you might lose some functionality.
Disable Macros
Enable Macros
More Info

FIGURE P-2: Procedure displayed in the Visual Basic Editor

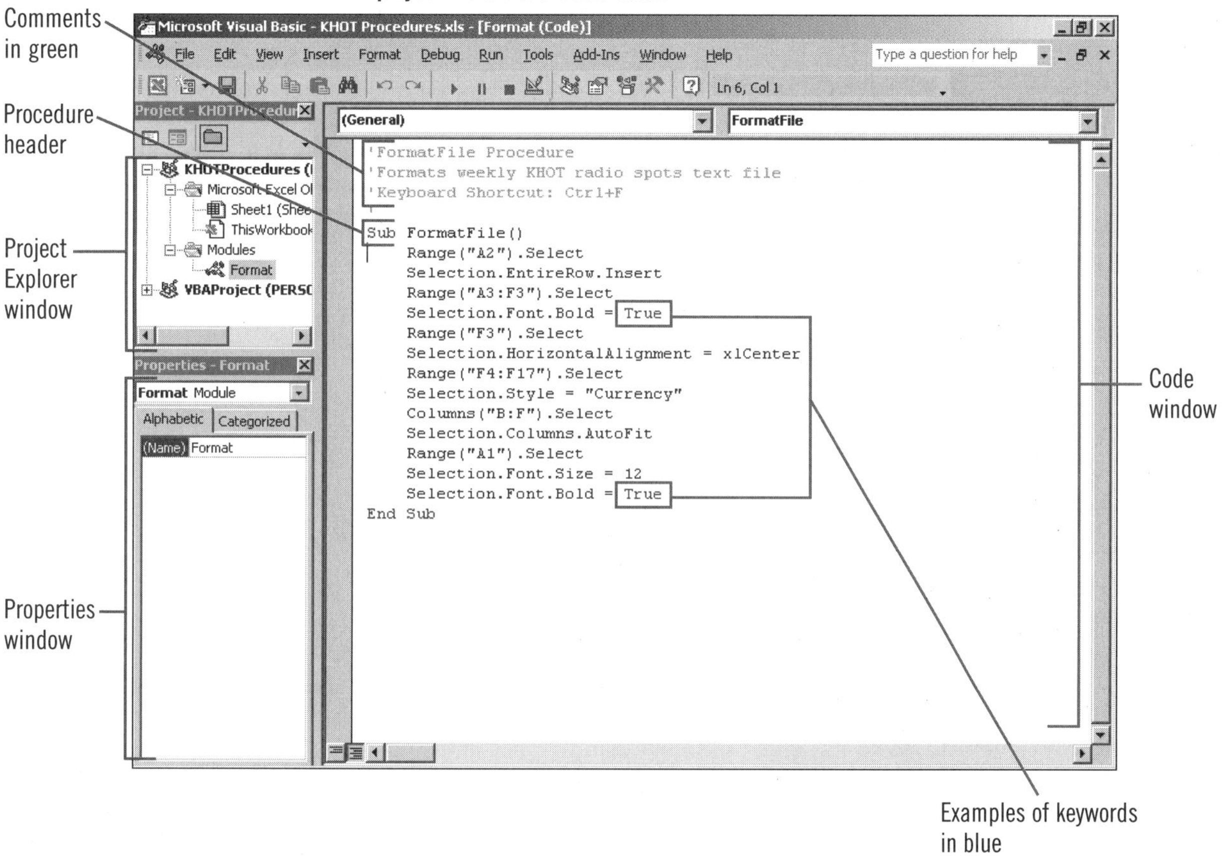
Comments in green
Procedure header
Project Explorer window
Properties window
Code window
Examples of keywords in blue
Microsoft Visual Basic - KHOT Procedures.xls - [Format (Code)]
(General)
FormatFile
'FormatFile Procedure
'Formats weekly KHOT radio spots text file
'Keyboard Shortcut: Ctrl+F
Sub FormatFile()
Range("A2").Select
Selection.EntireRow.Insert
Range("A3:F3").Select
Selection.Font.Bold = True
Range("F3").Select
Selection.HorizontalAlignment = xlCenter
Range("F4:F17").Select
Selection.Style = "Currency"
Columns("B:F").Select
Selection.Columns.AutoFit
Range("A1").Select
Selection.Font.Size = 12
Selection.Font.Bold = True
End Sub

CLUES TO USE

Understanding the Visual Basic Editor

A **module** is the Visual Basic equivalent of a worksheet. In it, you store macro procedures, just as you store data in worksheets. Modules, in turn, are stored in workbooks (or **projects**), along with worksheets. You view and edit modules in the Visual Basic Editor, which is made up of three windows, Project Explorer (also called the Project window), the Code window, and the Properties window. **Project Explorer** displays a list of all open projects (or workbooks) and the worksheets and modules they contain. To view the procedures stored in a module, you must first select the module in Project Explorer (just as you would select a file in Windows Explorer). The **Code window** then displays the selected module's procedures. The **Properties window** displays a list of characteristics (or properties) associated with the module. A newly inserted module has only one property, its name.

Excel 2002

Analyzing VBA Code

You can learn a lot about the VBA language simply by analyzing the code generated by the Excel macro recorder. The more VBA code you analyze, the easier it will be for you to write your own programming code. Before writing any new procedures, you will analyze a previously written one that applies formatting to a worksheet, then you will open a worksheet that you want to format and run the macro.

Steps 1 2 3 4

1. **With the FormatFile procedure still displayed in the Code window, examine the next four lines of code, beginning with `Range("A2").Select`**
   See Figure P-3. Every element of Excel, including a range, is considered an **object**. A **range object** represents a cell or a range of cells. The statement *Range("A2").Select* selects the range object cell A2. Notice that several times in the procedure a line of code (or **statement**) selects a range, and then subsequent lines act on that selection. The next statement, *Selection.EntireRow.Insert*, inserts a row above the selection, which is currently cell A2. The next two lines of code select range A3:F3 and apply bold formatting to that selection. In VBA terminology, bold formatting is a value of an object's Bold property. A **property** is an attribute of an object that defines one of the object's characteristics (such as size) or an aspect of its behavior (such as whether it is enabled). The properties of an object are listed in the Properties window. To change the characteristics of an object, you change the values of its properties. For example, to apply bold formatting to a selected range, you assign the value True to the range's Bold property. To remove bold formatting, assign the value False.
2. **Examine the remaining lines of code, beginning with `Range ("F3").Select`**
   The next two statements select the range object cell F3 and center its contents, then the following two statements select the F4:F17 range object and format it as currency. Column objects B through F are then selected and their widths set to AutoFit. Finally, the range object cell A1 is selected, its font size is changed to 12, and its Bold property is set to True. The last line, *End Sub*, indicates the end of the Sub procedure and is also referred to as the **procedure footer**.
3. **Click the View Microsoft Excel button on the Visual Basic Editor Standard toolbar to return to Excel**
   The macro is stored in the KHOT Procedures workbook. This way Jim can use it repeatedly each week after he receives that week's data. He wants you to open the workbook containing data for January 1–7 and run the macro to format that data. You must leave the KHOT Procedures workbook open to use the macro stored there.
4. **Open the workbook titled EX P-2, maximize the window if necessary, then save it as KHOT Advertising**
   This is the workbook containing data you want to format.
5. **Press [Ctrl][F] to run the procedure**
   The FormatFile procedure formats the text, as shown in Figure P-4.
6. **Place your name in the Jan 1-7 sheet footer, save the workbook, then print the worksheet**
   Now that you've successfully viewed and analyzed VBA code and run the macro, you will learn how to write your own code.

FIGURE P-3: VBA code for the FormatFile procedure

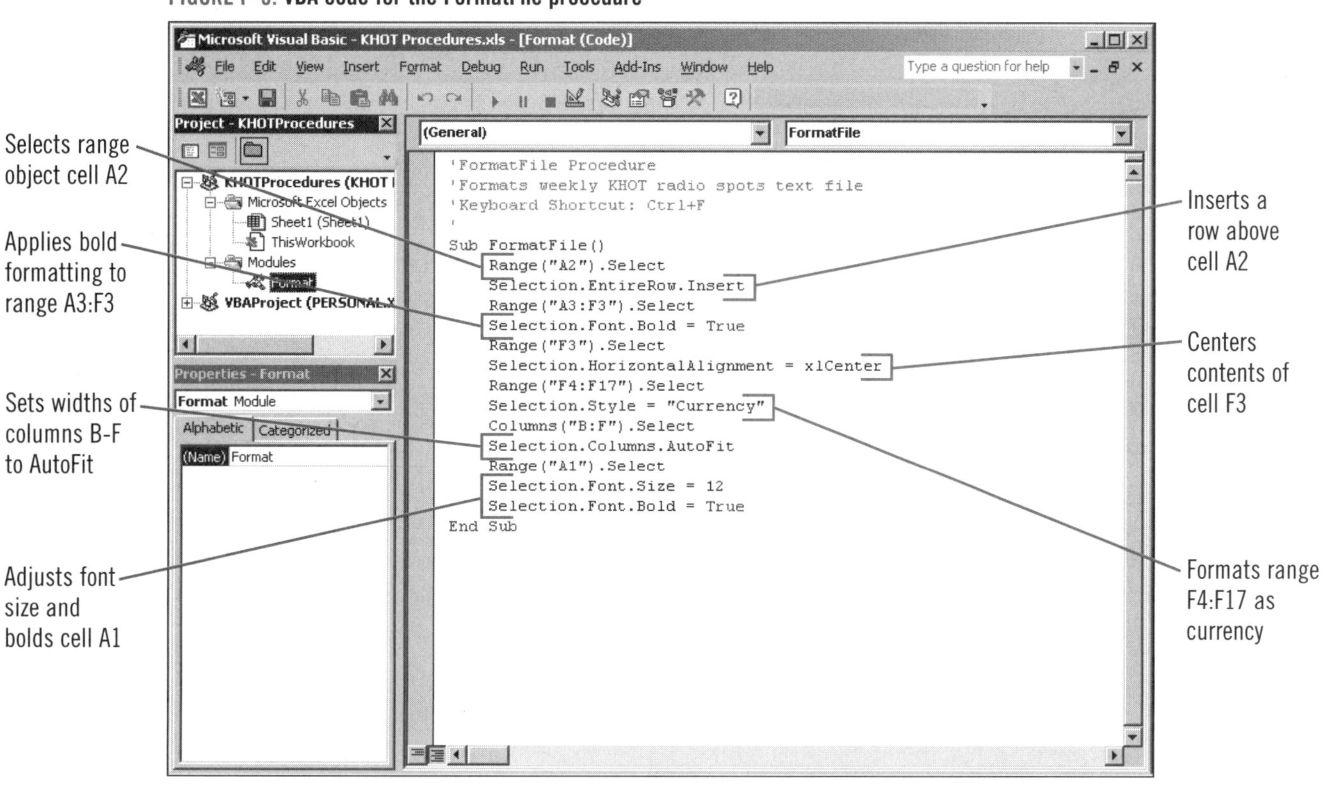
Microsoft Visual Basic - KHOT Procedures.xls - [Format (Code)]
Project - KHOTProcedures
Properties - Format
(General)
FormatFile
'FormatFile Procedure
'Formats weekly KHOT radio spots text file
'Keyboard Shortcut: Ctrl+F
Sub FormatFile()
Range("A2").Select
Selection.EntireRow.Insert
Range("A3:F3").Select
Selection.Font.Bold = True
Range("F3").Select
Selection.HorizontalAlignment = xlCenter
Range("F4:F17").Select
Selection.Style = "Currency"
Columns("B:F").Select
Selection.Columns.AutoFit
Range("A1").Select
Selection.Font.Size = 12
Selection.Font.Bold = True
End Sub
Selects range object cell A2
Applies bold formatting to range A3:F3
Sets widths of columns B-F to AutoFit
Adjusts font size and bolds cell A1
Inserts a row above cell A2
Centers contents of cell F3
Formats range F4:F17 as currency

FIGURE P-4: Worksheet formatted using the FormatFile procedure

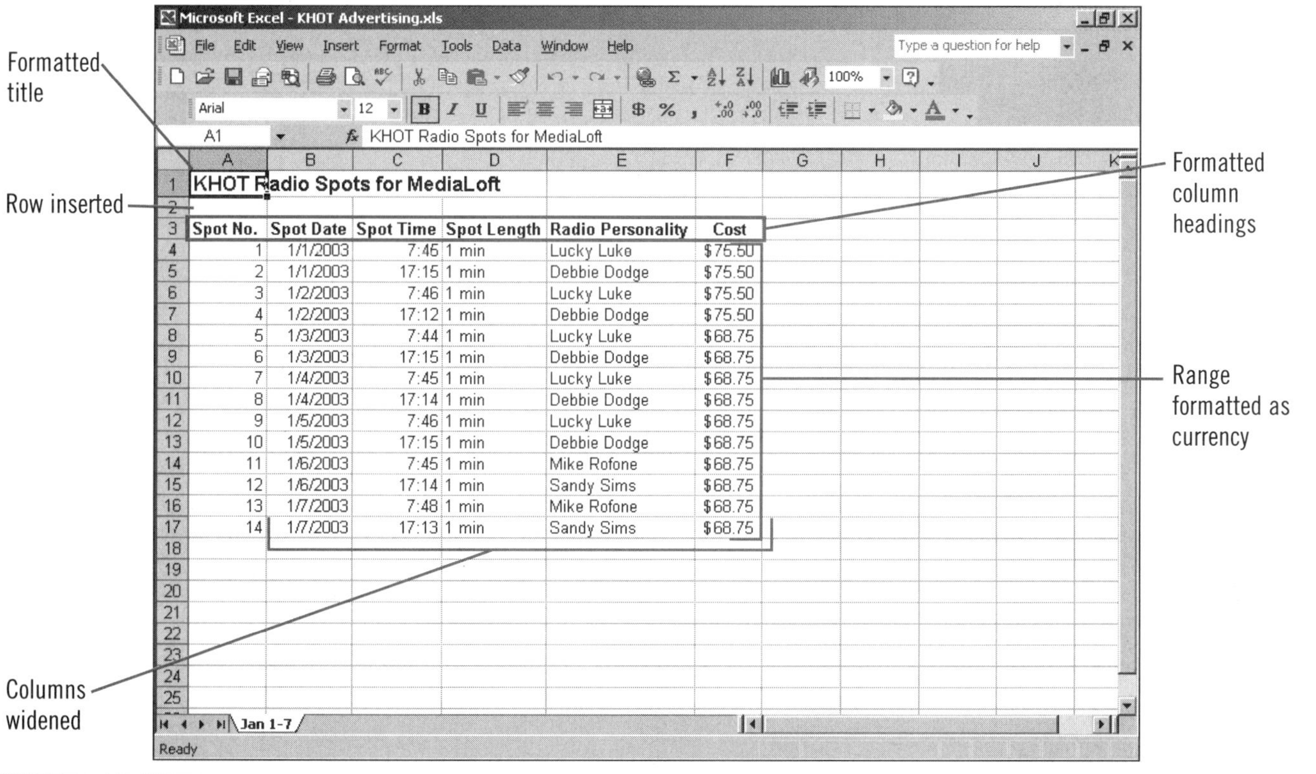
Microsoft Excel - KHOT Advertising.xls
KHOT Radio Spots for MediaLoft
Formatted title
Row inserted
Columns widened
Formatted column headings
Range formatted as currency
Jan 1-7
Ready

Spot No.	Spot Date	Spot Time	Spot Length	Radio Personality	Cost
1	1/1/2003	7:45	1 min	Lucky Luke	$75.50
2	1/1/2003	17:15	1 min	Debbie Dodge	$75.50
3	1/2/2003	7:46	1 min	Lucky Luke	$75.50
4	1/2/2003	17:12	1 min	Debbie Dodge	$75.50
5	1/3/2003	7:44	1 min	Lucky Luke	$68.75
6	1/3/2003	17:15	1 min	Debbie Dodge	$68.75
7	1/4/2003	7:45	1 min	Lucky Luke	$68.75
8	1/4/2003	17:14	1 min	Debbie Dodge	$68.75
9	1/5/2003	7:46	1 min	Lucky Luke	$68.75
10	1/5/2003	17:15	1 min	Debbie Dodge	$68.75
11	1/6/2003	7:45	1 min	Mike Rofone	$68.75
12	1/6/2003	17:14	1 min	Sandy Sims	$68.75
13	1/7/2003	7:48	1 min	Mike Rofone	$68.75
14	1/7/2003	17:13	1 min	Sandy Sims	$68.75

Excel 2002

Writing VBA Code

To write your own code, you first need to open the Visual Basic Editor and add a module to the workbook. You can then begin entering the procedure code. In the first few lines of a procedure, you typically include comments indicating the name of the procedure, a brief description of the procedure, and shortcut keys, if applicable. When writing Visual Basic code for Excel, you must follow the formatting rules, or **syntax**, of the VBA programming language exactly. A misspelled keyword or variable name will cause a procedure to fail. Each week, Alice asks Jim to total the cost of the radio ads. You will help him by writing a procedure that will automate this routine task.

Steps

Trouble?

If the Code window is empty, verify that the workbook that contains your procedures (KHOT Procedures) is open.

1. With the Jan 1-7 worksheet still displayed, click **Tools** on the menu bar, point to **Macro**, then click **Visual Basic Editor**
   Two projects are displayed in the Project Explorer window, KHOT Procedures (which contains the Format macro) and KHOT Advertising Jan 1-7 (which contains the weekly data). The FormatFile procedure is again displayed in the Visual Basic Editor.
2. Click the **Modules folder** in the KHOT Procedures project
   You will store all of the procedures in the KHOT Procedures project. The property name could be more descriptive.
3. Click **Insert** on the Visual Basic Editor menu bar, then click **Module**
   A new, blank module, with the default name Module1, is inserted in the KHOT Procedures workbook.

QuickTip

As you type, you may see words in drop-down lists. This optional feature is explained in the "Entering Code" Clues to Use section on the next page. For now, just continue to type.

4. Click **(Name)** in the Properties window, then type **Total**
   The module name ("Total") should not be the same as the procedure name (which will be "AddTotal"). In the Figure P-5 code, comments begin with an apostrophe and the lines of code under "Sub AddTotal ( )" have been indented using the Tab key. When you enter the code in the next step, after you type *Sub AddTotal( )* (the procedure header) and press [Enter], the Visual Basic Editor will automatically enter *End Sub* (the procedure footer) in the Code window.
5. Click in the **Code window**, then type the procedure code exactly as shown in Figure P-5
   The lines that begin with *ActiveCell.Formula* insert the information enclosed in quotation marks into the active cell. For example, *ActiveCell.Formula = "Weekly Total:"* inserts the words "Weekly Total:" into cell E18, the active cell. The *With* clause near the bottom of the procedure is used to repeat several operations on the same object.
6. Compare the procedure code you entered in the Code window with Figure P-5; if necessary, make any corrections, then click the **Save KHOT Procedures.xls button** on the Visual Basic Editor Standard toolbar
7. Click the **View Microsoft Excel button** on the toolbar, if necessary, click KHOT Advertising.xls on the taskbar to display the worksheet; with the Jan 1-7 worksheet displayed, click **Tools** on the Excel menu bar, point to **Macro**, then click **Macros**
   Macro names have two parts. The first part ('KHOT Procedures.xls'!) indicates the workbook where the macro is stored. The second part (AddTotal or FormatFile) is the name of the procedure, taken from the procedure header.

QuickTip

If an error message appears, click Debug. Click the Reset button on the toolbar, correct the error, then repeat Steps 6–8.

8. Click **'KHOT Procedures.xls'!AddTotal** to select it, if necessary, then click **Run**
   The AddTotal procedure inserts and formats the ad expenditure total in cell F18, as shown in Figure P-6.
9. Save the workbook

FIGURE P-5: **VBA code for the AddTotal procedure**

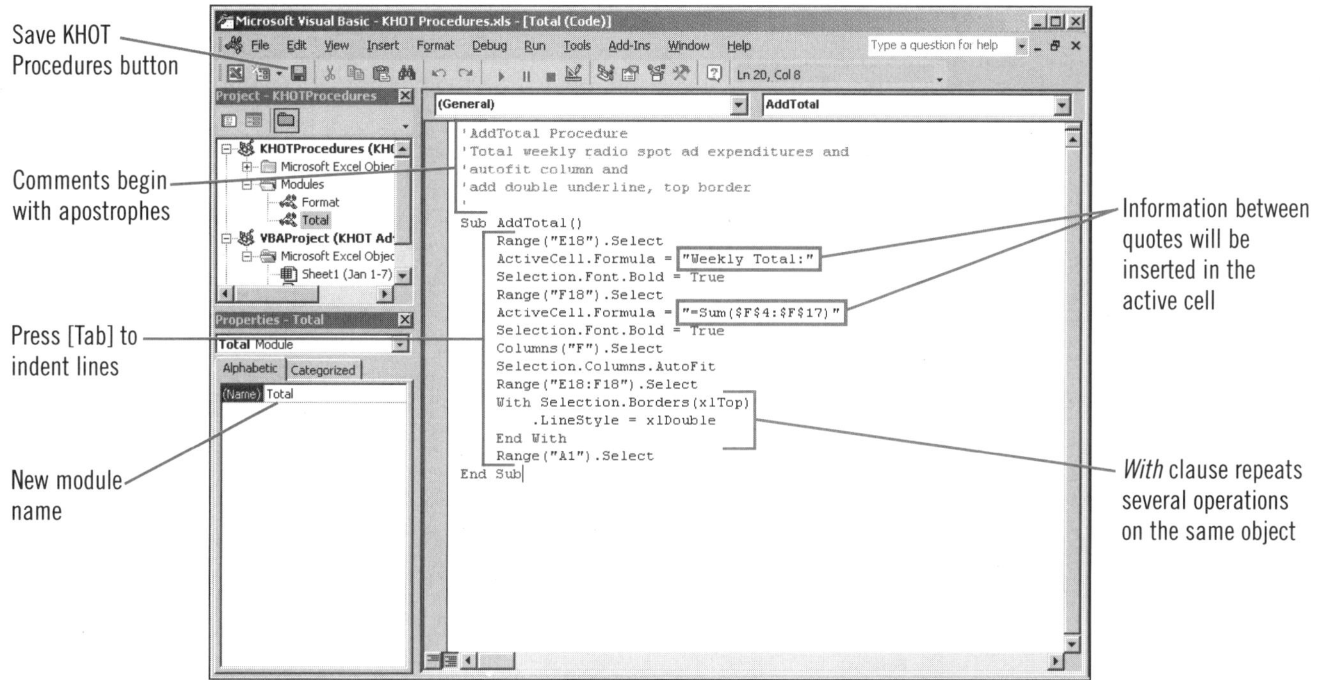

FIGURE P-6: **Worksheet after running the AddTotal procedure**

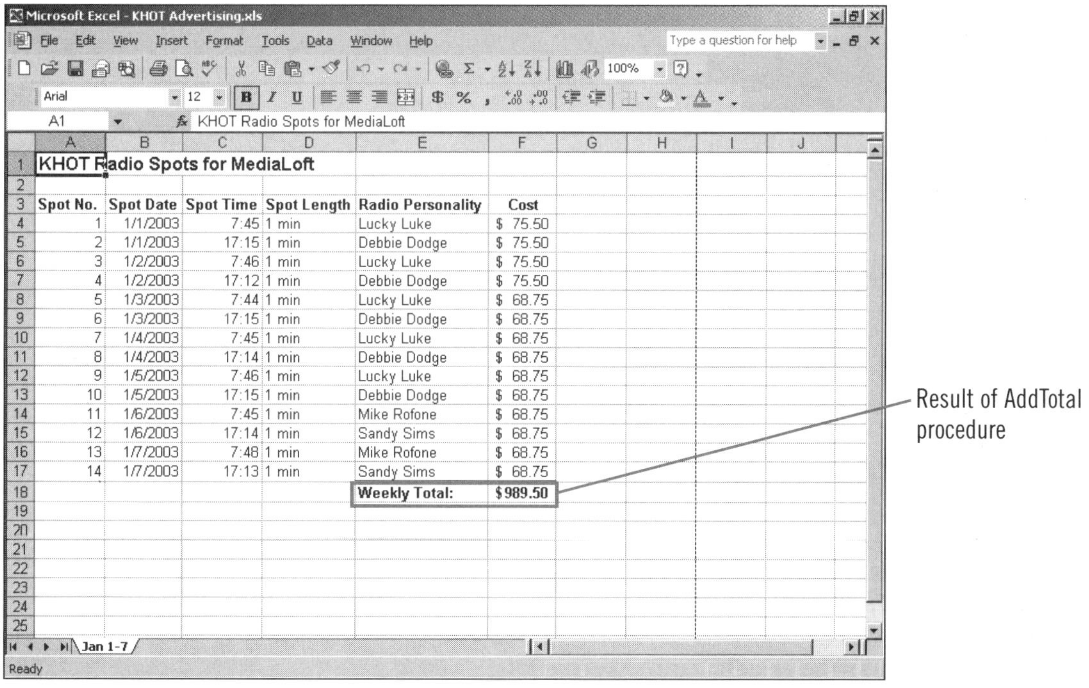

	A	B	C	D	E	F
1	KHOT Radio Spots for MediaLoft					
2						
3	Spot No.	Spot Date	Spot Time	Spot Length	Radio Personality	Cost
4	1	1/1/2003	7:45	1 min	Lucky Luke	$ 75.50
5	2	1/1/2003	17:15	1 min	Debbie Dodge	$ 75.50
6	3	1/2/2003	7:46	1 min	Lucky Luke	$ 75.50
7	4	1/2/2003	17:12	1 min	Debbie Dodge	$ 75.50
8	5	1/3/2003	7:44	1 min	Lucky Luke	$ 68.75
9	6	1/3/2003	17:15	1 min	Debbie Dodge	$ 68.75
10	7	1/4/2003	7:45	1 min	Lucky Luke	$ 68.75
11	8	1/4/2003	17:14	1 min	Debbie Dodge	$ 68.75
12	9	1/5/2003	7:46	1 min	Lucky Luke	$ 68.75
13	10	1/5/2003	17:15	1 min	Debbie Dodge	$ 68.75
14	11	1/6/2003	7:45	1 min	Mike Rofone	$ 68.75
15	12	1/6/2003	17:14	1 min	Sandy Sims	$ 68.75
16	13	1/7/2003	7:48	1 min	Mike Rofone	$ 68.75
17	14	1/7/2003	17:13	1 min	Sandy Sims	$ 68.75
18					Weekly Total:	$989.50

Entering code using the scrollable word list

To assist you in entering the VBA code, the Editor often displays a list of words that can be used in the macro statement. Typically, the list appears after you press [.] (period). To include a word from the list in the macro statement, select the word in the list, then double click it or press [Tab]. For example, to enter the *Range("E12").Select* instruction, type *Range(" E12")*, then press [.] (period). Type *s* to bring up the words beginning with s, select the Select command in the list, then press [Tab] to enter the word "Select" in the macro statement.

Excel 2002

Adding a Conditional Statement

Sometimes, you may want a procedure to take an action based on a certain condition or set of conditions. For example, *if* a salesperson's performance rating is a 5 (top rating), *then* calculate a 10% bonus; otherwise (*else*), there is no bonus. One way of adding this type of conditional statement in Visual Basic is by using an **If...Then...Else statement**. The syntax for this statement is: "If *condition* Then *statements* Else [*else statements*]." The brackets indicate that the Else part of the statement is optional. Alice wants the worksheet to point out if the amount spent on radio ads stays within or exceeds the $1,000 budgeted amount. You will use Excel to add a conditional statement that indicates this information. You start by returning to the Visual Basic Editor and inserting a new module in the KHOT Procedures project.

Steps

QuickTip

You can also return to the Visual Basic Editor by clicking its button on the taskbar.

1. With the Jan 1-7 worksheet still displayed, click **Tools** on the menu bar, point to **Macro**, click **Visual Basic Editor**, verify that KHOT Procedures is the active project in the Project Explorer window, click **Insert** on the Visual Basic Editor menu bar, then click **Module**
   A new, blank module named Module1 is inserted in the KHOT Procedures workbook.
2. In the Properties window click **(Name)**, then type **Budget**
3. Click in the Code window, then type the code exactly as shown in Figure P-7
   Notice the comment lines (in green) in the middle of the code. These lines help explain the procedure.

QuickTip

The If...Then...Else statement is similar to the Excel IF function.

4. Compare the procedure you entered with Figure P-7; if necessary, make any corrections, click the **Save KHOT Procedures.xls button** on the Visual Basic Editor Standard toolbar, then click the **View Microsoft Excel button**
5. If necessary, click **KHOT Advertising.xls** in the taskbar to display it; with the Jan 1-7 worksheet displayed, click **Tools** on the menu bar, point to **Macro**, click **Macros**, in the Macro dialog box, click **'KHOT Procedures.xls'!BudgetStatus**, then click **Run**
   The BudgetStatus procedure indicates the status—within budget—as shown in Figure P-8.
6. Save your work

FIGURE P-7: VBA code for the BudgetStatus procedure

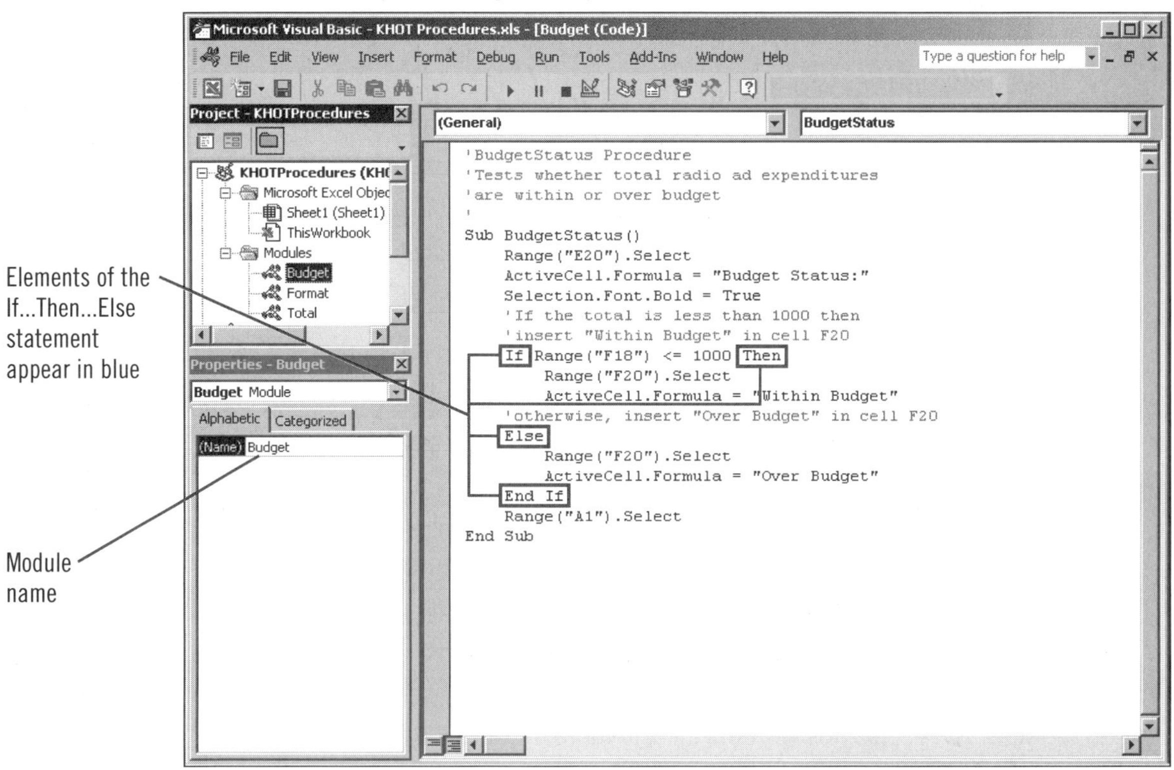

FIGURE P-8: Result of running BudgetStatus procedure

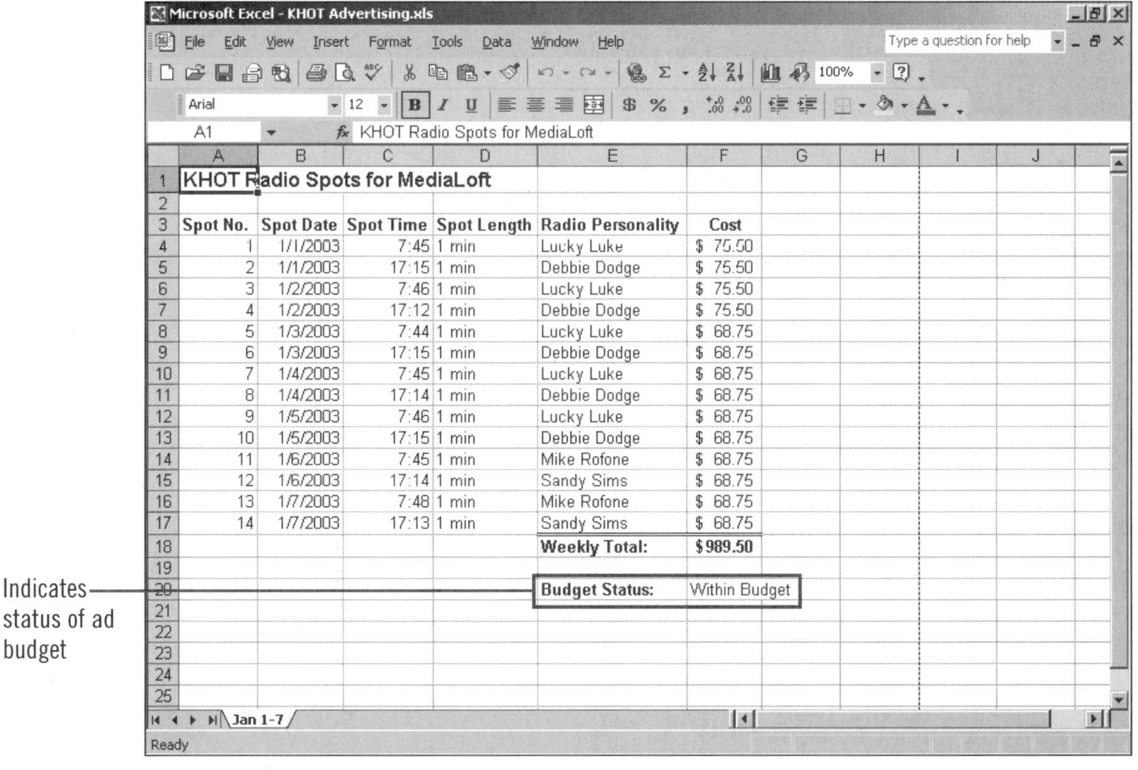

KHOT Radio Spots for MediaLoft

Spot No.	Spot Date	Spot Time	Spot Length	Radio Personality	Cost
1	1/1/2003	7:45	1 min	Lucky Luke	$ 75.50
2	1/1/2003	17:15	1 min	Debbie Dodge	$ 75.50
3	1/2/2003	7:46	1 min	Lucky Luke	$ 75.50
4	1/2/2003	17:12	1 min	Debbie Dodge	$ 75.50
5	1/3/2003	7:44	1 min	Lucky Luke	$ 68.75
6	1/3/2003	17:15	1 min	Debbie Dodge	$ 68.75
7	1/4/2003	7:45	1 min	Lucky Luke	$ 68.75
8	1/4/2003	17:14	1 min	Debbie Dodge	$ 68.75
9	1/5/2003	7:46	1 min	Lucky Luke	$ 68.75
10	1/5/2003	17:15	1 min	Debbie Dodge	$ 68.75
11	1/6/2003	7:45	1 min	Mike Rofone	$ 68.75
12	1/6/2003	17:14	1 min	Sandy Sims	$ 68.75
13	1/7/2003	7:48	1 min	Mike Rofone	$ 68.75
14	1/7/2003	17:13	1 min	Sandy Sims	$ 68.75
				Weekly Total:	**$989.50**
				Budget Status:	Within Budget

Excel 2002

Prompting the User for Data

When automating routine tasks, you sometimes need to pause a macro to allow user input. You use the VBA InputBox function to display a dialog box that prompts the user for information. A **function** is a predefined procedure that returns (creates and displays) a value; in this case the value returned is the information the user enters. The required elements of an InputBox function are as follows: *object*.InputBox("*prompt*"), where "*prompt*" is the message that appears in the dialog box. For a detailed description of the InputBox function, use the Visual Basic Editor's Help menu. You decide to create a procedure that will insert the user's name in the left footer area of the workbook. You'll use the InputBox function to display a dialog box in which the user can enter his or her name. You will also type an error into the procedure code, which you will correct in the next lesson.

Steps

1. With the Jan 1-7 worksheet displayed, click **Tools** on the menu bar, point to **Macro**, click **Visual Basic Editor**, verify that KHOT Procedures is the active project, click **Insert** on the Visual Basic Editor menu bar, then click **Module**
   A new, blank module is inserted in the KHOT Procedures workbook.
2. In the Properties window, click **(Name)**, then type **Footer**
3. Click in the Code window, then type the procedure code exactly as shown in Figure P-9
   Like the Budget procedure, this procedure also contains comments that explain the code. The first part of the code, *Dim LeftFooterText As String*, **declares**, or defines, *LeftFooterText* as a text string variable. In Visual Basic, a **variable** is a location in memory in which you can temporarily store one item of information. Dim statements are used to declare variables and must be entered in the following format: Dim *variablename* As *datatype*. The datatype here is "string." In this case, you plan to store the information received from the input box in the temporary memory location called LeftFooterText. Then you can place this text in the left footer area. The remaining statements in the procedure are explained in the comment line directly above each statement. Notice the comment pointing out the error in the procedure code. You will correct this in the next lesson.
4. Review your code, make any necessary changes, click the **Save KHOT Procedures.xls button** on the Visual Basic Editor Standard toolbar, then click the **View Microsoft Excel button**
5. With the Jan 1-7 worksheet displayed, click **Tools** on the menu bar, point to **Macro**, click **Macros**, in the Macro dialog box click **'KHOT Procedures.xls'!FooterInput**, then click **Run**
   The procedure begins, and a dialog box generated by the InputBox function appears, prompting you to enter your name. See Figure P-10.
6. With the cursor in the text box, type your name, then click **OK**
7. Click the **Print Preview button** on the Standard toolbar
   Although the customized footer with the date is inserted on the sheet, because of the error, your name does *not* appear in the left section of the footer. In the next lesson, you will learn how to step through a procedure's code line by line. This will help you locate the error in the FooterInput procedure.
8. Click **Close**
   You return to the Jan 1-7 worksheet.

QuickTip

To enlarge your Code window, place the mouse pointer on the left border of the Code window until it turns into ↔, then drag the border to the left until the Code window is the desired size.

Trouble?

If your macro doesn't prompt you for your name, it may contain a spelling or syntax error. Return to the Visual Basic Editor, click the Reset button, correct your error by referring to Figure P-9, then repeat Steps 4 and 5. You'll learn more about how to correct such macro errors in the next lesson.

FIGURE P-9: VBA code for the FooterInput procedure

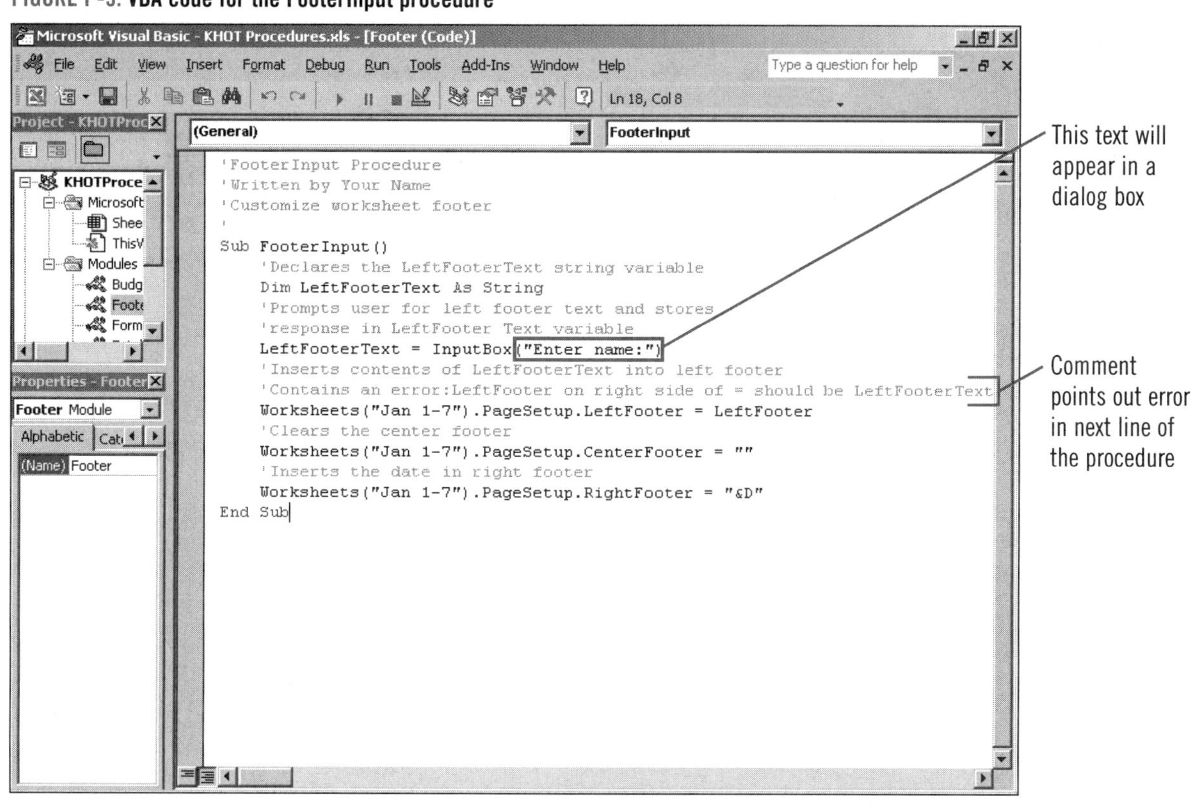

FIGURE P-10: InputBox function's dialog box

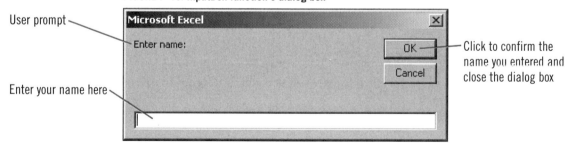

Excel 2002

Steps

Debugging a Macro

When a macro procedure does not run properly, it can be due to an error, referred to as a **bug**, in the code. To assist you in finding the bug(s) in a procedure, the Visual Basic Editor helps you step through the procedure's code, one line at a time. When you locate the error, you can then correct, or **debug**, it. You decide to debug the macro procedure to find out why it failed to insert your name in the worksheet's footer.

1. With the KHOT Advertising Jan 1-7 worksheet still displayed, click **Tools** on the menu bar, point to **Macro**, click **Macros**, in the Macro dialog box, click **'KHOT Procedures.xls'!FooterInput**, then click **Step Into**
   The Visual Basic Editor appears with the statement selector positioned on the first statement of the procedure. See Figure P-11.
2. Press **[F8]** to step through the code
   The statement selector skips over the comments and the line of code beginning with Dim. The Dim statement indicates that the procedure will store your name in a variable named LeftFooterText. Because Dim is a declaration of a variable and not a procedure statement, the statement selector skips it and moves to the line containing the InputBox function.
3. Press **[F8]** again; with the cursor in the text box in the InputBox function dialog box, type your name, then click **OK**
   The Visual Basic Editor reappears. The statement selector is now positioned on the statement that reads *Worksheets ("Jan 1-7").PageSetup.LeftFooter = LeftFooter*. This statement inserts your name (which you just typed in the Input Box) in the left section of the footer. This is the instruction that does not appear to be working correctly.
4. If necessary, scroll right until the end of the LeftFooter instruction is visible, then place the mouse pointer on **LeftFooter**, as shown in Figure P-12
   The last part of the InputBox function should be the variable (LeftFooterText), where the procedure stored your name. Rather than containing your name, however, the variable at the end of the procedure(LeftFooter) is empty. That's because the InputBox function assigned your name to the LeftFooterText variable, not to the LeftFooter variable. Before you can correct this bug, you need to turn off the Step Into feature.
5. Click the **Reset button** on the Visual Basic Editor Standard toolbar to turn off the Step Into feature, click at the end of the statement containing the error, then replace the variable LeftFooter with **LeftFooterText**
   The revised statement now reads *Worksheets("Jan 1-7").PageSetup.LeftFooter = LeftFooterText.*
6. Delete the comment line pointing out the error
7. Click the **Save KHOT Procedures.xls button** on the Visual Basic Editor Standard toolbar, then click the **View Microsoft Excel button** on the Visual Basic Editor toolbar
8. With the Jan 1-7 worksheet displayed, click **Tools** on the menu bar, point to **Macro**, click **Macros**; in the Macro dialog box, click **'KHOT Procedures.xls'!FooterInput**, click **Run** to rerun the procedure, when prompted, type your name, then click **OK**
9. Click the **Print Preview button** on the Standard toolbar
   Your name now appears in the left section of the footer.
10. Click **Close**, save the workbook, then print the worksheet

FIGURE P-11: Statement selector positioned on first procedure statement

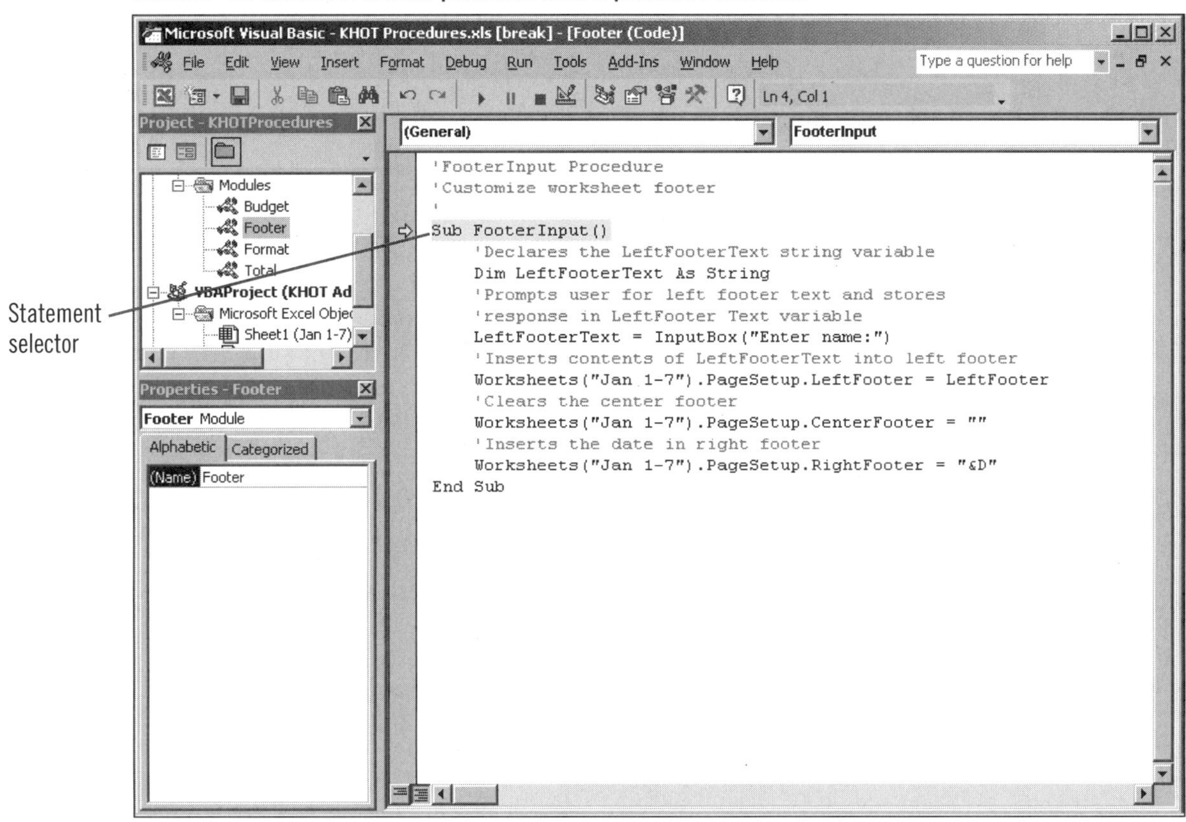

FIGURE P-12: Value contained in LeftFooter variable

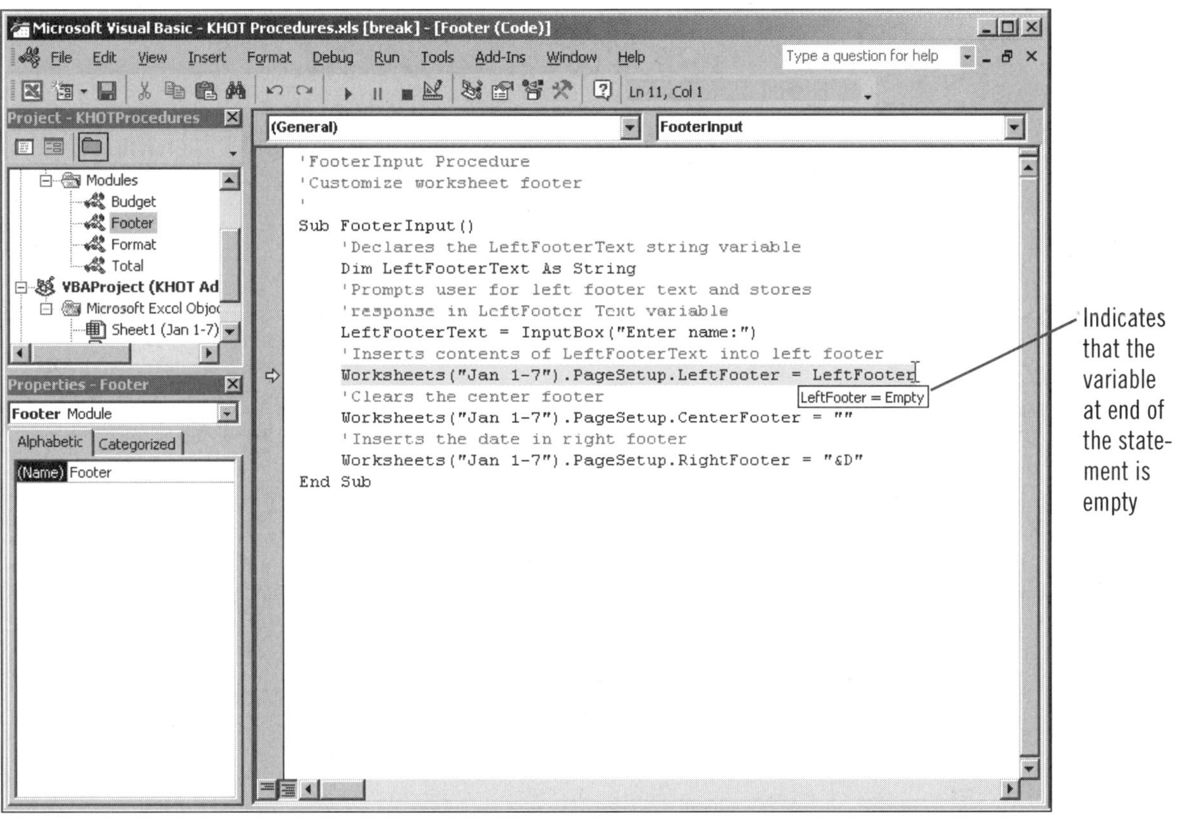

Excel 2002

Creating a Main Procedure

When you routinely need to run several macros one after another, you can save time by combining them into one procedure. The resulting procedure, which processes (or runs) multiple procedures in sequence, is referred to as the **main procedure**. To create a main procedure, you type a Call statement for each procedure you want to run. The syntax of the Call statement is Call *procedurename*, where *procedurename* is the name of the procedure you want to run. To avoid having to run his macros one after another every month, Jim asks you to create a main procedure that will run (or call) each of the procedures in the KHOT Procedures workbook in sequence.

Steps

1. With the Jan 1-7 worksheet displayed, click **Tools** on the menu bar, point to **Macro**, then click **Visual Basic Editor**
2. Verify that KHOT Procedures is the active project, click **Insert** on the menu bar, then click **Module**
   A new, blank module is inserted in the KHOT Procedures workbook.
3. In the Properties window, click **(Name)**, then type **MainProc**
4. In the Code window, enter the procedure code exactly as shown in Figure P-13
5. Compare your main procedure code with Figure P-13, correct any errors, if necessary, then click the **Save KHOT Procedures.xls button** on the Visual Basic Editor Standard toolbar
   To test the new main procedure you need an unformatted version of the KHOT radio spot workbook.
6. Click the **View Microsoft Excel button** on the Visual Basic Editor Standard toolbar, then close the KHOT Advertising workbook
   The KHOT Procedures workbook remains open.
7. Open the Project File titled EX P-2 from the drive and folder where your Project Files are stored, then save it as **KHOT Advertising Version 2**
   In the next lesson, you'll run the main procedure.

FIGURE P-13: **VBA code for the MainProcedure procedure**

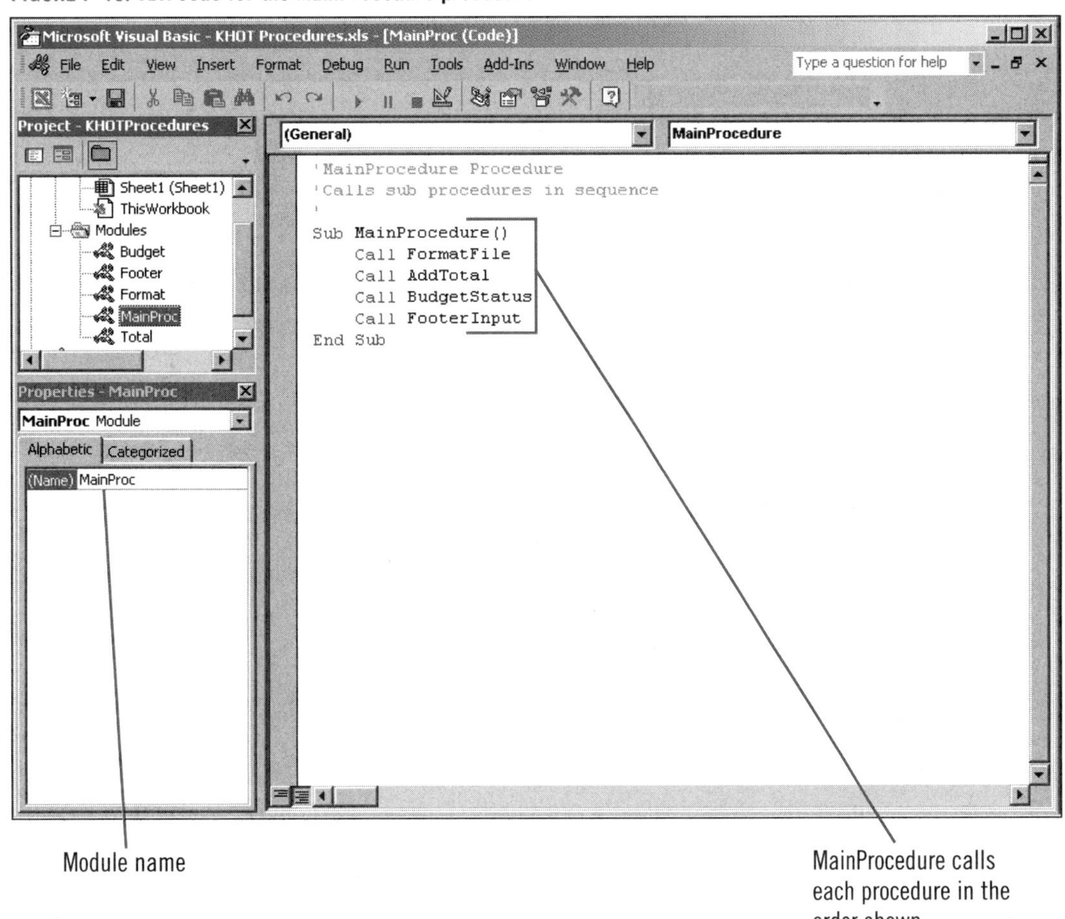

Excel 2002

Excel 2002

Running a Main Procedure

Running a main procedure allows you to run several macros in sequence. You can run a main procedure just as you would any other macro procedure—by selecting it in the Macro dialog box, then clicking Run. You have finished creating Jim's main procedure, and you are ready to run it. If the main procedure works correctly, it should format the worksheet, insert the ad expenditure total, insert a budget status message, and add your name to the worksheet footer.

Steps

1. With the Jan 1-7 worksheet displayed, click **Tools** on the menu bar, point to **Macro**, then click **Macros**; in the Macro dialog box, click **'KHOT Procedures.xls'! MainProcedure**, click **Run**, when prompted, type your name, then click **OK**
   The MainProcedure runs the FormatFile, AddTotal, BudgetStatus, and FooterInput procedures in sequence. You can see the results of the FormatFile, AddTotal, and BudgetStatus procedures in the worksheet window. See Figure P-14. To view the results of the FooterInput procedure, you need to switch to the Preview window.
2. Click the **Print Preview button** on the Standard toolbar, verify that your name appears in the left footer area, then click **Close**
   You could print each procedure separately, but it's faster to print all the procedures in the workbook at one time.
3. Click **Tools** on the menu bar, point to **Macro**, then click **Visual Basic Editor**
4. In the Project Explorer window, double-click each procedure and add a comment line after the procedure name that reads **'Written by [your name]**, then click the **Save KHOT Procedures.xls button** on the Visual Basic Editor Standard toolbar
5. Click **File** on the Visual Basic Editor menu bar, then click **Print**
   The Print - KHOTProcedures dialog box opens, as shown in Figure P-15. Collectively, all procedures in a workbook are known as a project.
6. In the Print - KHOTProcedures dialog box, click the **Current Project option button**, then click **OK**
   Each procedure prints on a separate page.
7. Click the **View Microsoft Excel button** on the Visual Basic Editor Standard toolbar
8. Save the KHOT Advertising Version 2 workbook and close it; close the KHOT Procedures workbook, then exit Excel

FIGURE P-14: Result of running MainProcedure procedure

Microsoft Excel - KHOT Advertising Version 2.xls

A1 — KHOT Radio Spots for MediaLoft

	A	B	C	D	E	F
1	KHOT Radio Spots for MediaLoft					
2						
3	Spot No.	Spot Date	Spot Time	Spot Length	Radio Personality	Cost
4	1	1/1/2003	7:45	1 min	Lucky Luke	$ 75.50
5	2	1/1/2003	17:15	1 min	Debbie Dodge	$ 75.50
6	3	1/2/2003	7:46	1 min	Lucky Luke	$ 75.50
7	4	1/2/2003	17:12	1 min	Debbie Dodge	$ 75.50
8	5	1/3/2003	7:44	1 min	Lucky Luke	$ 68.75
9	6	1/3/2003	17:15	1 min	Debbie Dodge	$ 68.75
10	7	1/4/2003	7:45	1 min	Lucky Luke	$ 68.75
11	8	1/4/2003	17:14	1 min	Debbie Dodge	$ 68.75
12	9	1/5/2003	7:46	1 min	Lucky Luke	$ 68.75
13	10	1/5/2003	17:15	1 min	Debbie Dodge	$ 68.75
14	11	1/6/2003	7:45	1 min	Mike Rofone	$ 68.75
15	12	1/6/2003	17:14	1 min	Sandy Sims	$ 68.75
16	13	1/7/2003	7:48	1 min	Mike Rofone	$ 68.75
17	14	1/7/2003	17:13	1 min	Sandy Sims	$ 68.75
18					Weekly Total:	$989.50
19						
20					Budget Status:	Within Budget

Jan 1-7

Ready

Formatting added to worksheet

Total cost calculated

Budget Status message inserted

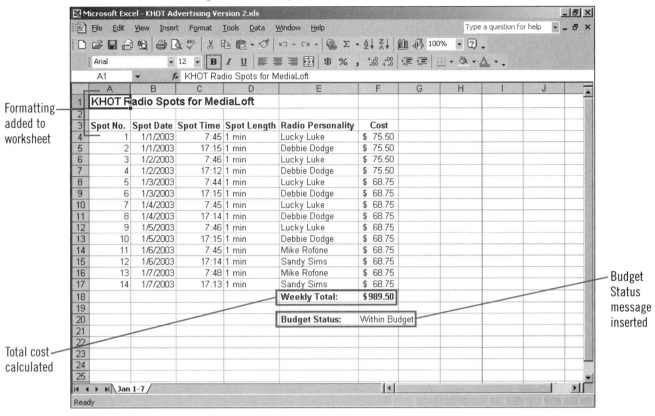

FIGURE P-15: Printing the macro procedures

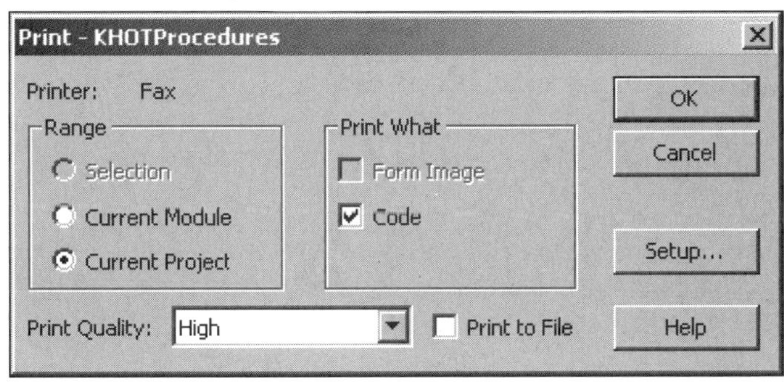

Excel 2002

Practice

► Concepts Review

Label each element of the Visual Basic Editor screen shown in Figure P-16.

FIGURE P-16

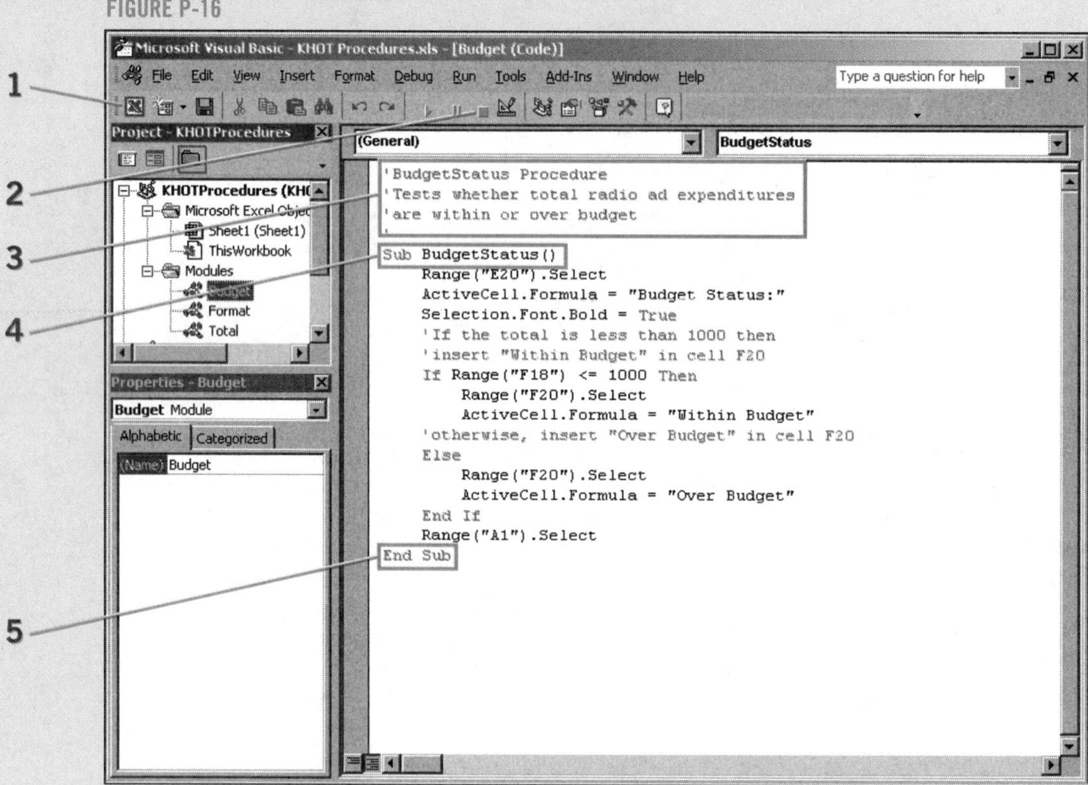

Match each term with the statement that describes it.

6. Procedure
7. Sub procedure
8. Keywords
9. Comments
10. Function

a. Another term for a macro in Visual Basic for Applications (VBA)
b. A procedure that returns a value
c. Words that are recognized as part of the programming language
d. A series of statements that perform an action but don't return a value
e. Descriptive text used to explain parts of a procedure

Select the best answer from the list of choices.

11. What must you keep in mind when typing VBA code?
- a. Typographical errors can cause your procedures to fail.
- b. You can edit your code just as you would text in a word processor.
- c. The different parts of the code will appear in different colors.
- d. All of the above.

12. You enter the statements of a macro in:
- a. The Macro dialog box.
- b. Any blank worksheet.
- c. The Properties window of the Visual Basic Editor.
- d. The Code window of the Visual Basic Editor.

13. If your macro doesn't run correctly, you should:
- a. Create an If . . . Then . . . Else statement.
- b. Select the macro in the Macro dialog box, click Step Into, and then debug the macro.
- c. Click the Reset button.
- d. Close the workbook and start over with a new macro.

14. Comments are displayed in ___________ in VBA code.
- a. Red
- b. Blue
- c. Green
- d. Black

15. Keywords are displayed in ___________ in VBA code.
- a. Red
- b. Blue
- c. Green
- d. Black

16. The keyword Sub in a procedure header indicates a:
- a. Sub procedure.
- b. Sub function.
- c. Sub module.
- d. Sub workbook.

17. Which window in the Visual Basic Editor displays a list of all open projects?
- a. Code
- b. Properties
- c. Project Explorer
- d. Open Projects

18. Which window in the Visual Basic Editor displays the code for the selected module's procedures?
- a. Code
- b. Properties
- c. Project Explorer
- d. Open Projects

19. Which window in the Visual Basic Editor displays a list of characteristics associated with a module?
- a. Code
- b. Properties
- c. Project Explorer
- d. Open Projects

▶ Skills Review

1. **View and analyze VBA code.**
   a. Start Excel, open the Project File titled EX P-3 from the drive and folder where your Project Files are stored, enable macros, then save it as **Northeast Sales**.
   b. Review the unformatted January 2003 worksheet.
   c. Open the Visual Basic Editor.
   d. Select the ListFormat module and review the FormatList procedure.
   e. Insert comments in the procedure code describing what action you think each line of code will perform. (*Hint*: One of the statements will sort the list alphabetically by city.)
   f. Save the macro, return to the worksheet, then run the FormatList macro.
   g. Compare the results with the code and your comments.
   h. Save the workbook.
2. **Write VBA code.**
   a. Open the Visual Basic Editor and insert a new module named **Total** in the Northeast Sales project.
   b. Enter the code for the SalesTotal procedure exactly as shown in Figure P-17.
   c. Save the macro, then return to the January 2003 worksheet and run the SalesTotal macro. Save the workbook.
3. **Add a conditional statement.**
   a. Open the Visual Basic Editor and insert a new module named **Goal** in the Northeast Sales project.
   b. Enter the SalesGoal procedure exactly as shown in Figure P-18.
   c. Save the macro, then return to the January 2003 worksheet and run the SalesGoal macro. The procedure should enter the message "Missed goal" in cell E18. Save the workbook.
4. **Prompt the user for data.**
   a. Open the Visual Basic Editor and insert a new module named **Header** in the Northeast Sales project.
   b. Enter the HeaderFooter procedure exactly as shown in Figure P-19. You will be entering errors in the procedure that will be corrected in Step #5.
   c. Return to the January 2003 worksheet and run the HeaderFooter macro. When you encounter a runtime error, click End.
   d. Save the workbook.
5. **Debug a macro.**
   a. Run the HeaderFooter macro again. When you encounter a runtime error, click Debug.

FIGURE P-17

```
'SalesTotal Procedure
'Totals January sales
Sub SalesTotal()
    Range("E17").Select
    ActiveCell.Formula = "=SUM($E$3:$E$16)"
    Selection.Font.Bold = True
    With Selection.Borders(xlTop)
        .LineStyle = xlSingle
    End With
    Range("A1").Select
End Sub
```

FIGURE P-18

```
'SalesGoal Procedure
'Tests whether sales goal was met
'
Sub SalesGoal()
    'If the total is >=185000, then insert "Met Goal"
    'in cell E18
    If Range("E17") >= 185000 Then
       Range("E18").Select
       ActiveCell.Formula = "Met goal"
    'otherwise, insert "Missed goal" in cell E18
    Else
       Range("E18").Select
       ActiveCell.Formula = "Missed goal"
    End If
End Sub
```

FIGURE P-19

```
'HeaderFooter Procedure
'Procedure to customize the header and footer
'
Sub HeaderFooter()
    'Inserts the filename in the header
    Worksheets("January 2003").PageSetup.CenterHeader = "&F"
    'Declares the variable LeftFooterText as a string
    Dim LeftFooterText As String
    'Prompts user for left footer text
    LeftFooter = InputBox("Enter your full name:")
    'Inserts response into left footer
    Workbooks("January 2003").PageSetup.LeftFooter = LeftFooterText
    Workbooks("January 2003").PageSetup.CenterFooter = ""
    'Inserts the date into right footer
    Workbooks("January 2003").PageSetup.RightFooter = "&D"
End Sub
```

b. The statement selector is positioned on the following incorrect procedure statement: *Workbooks("January 2003").PageSetup.LeftFooter = LeftFooterText.*
(*Hint*: Note that Workbooks, instead of Worksheets, was incorrectly entered in the statement.)
c. Change *Workbooks* in the incorrect line of code to **Worksheets**. Do the same for the two occurrences of Workbooks that follow this line.
d. Exit debug mode by clicking the Reset button, then return to the January 2003 worksheet and run the HeaderFooter macro again.
e. Check the header and footer. Notice that the procedure did not display your name in the left section of the footer.
f. Use the Step Into feature to find the error in the code, and then correct it. Make sure you exit debug mode by clicking the Reset button. (*Hint*: The variable containing your name is LeftFooter.)
g. Return to the January 2003 worksheet and run the HeaderFooter macro again.
h. Verify that your name now appears in the left section of the footer.
i. Save the workbook.

6. **Create and run a main procedure.**
a. Return to the Visual Basic Editor, insert a new module, then name it **MainProc**.
b. Begin the main procedure by entering comments in the code window that provide the procedure's name (MainProcedure) and explain that its purpose is to run the FormatList, SalesTotal, SalesGoal, and HeaderFooter procedures.
c. Enter the procedure header: **Sub MainProcedure()**.
d. Enter four Call statements that will run the FormatList, SalesTotal, SalesGoal, and HeaderFooter procedures in sequence.
e. Save the procedure and return to Excel.
f. Open the EX P-3 workbook, then save it as **Northeast Sales Version 2**.
g. Run the MainProcedure macro, entering your name when prompted. (*Hint*: In the Macro dialog box, the macro procedures you created will now have *'Northeast Sales.xls'!* as part of their names. That's because the macros are stored in the Northeast Sales workbook, not in the Northeast Sales Version 2 workbook.)
h. Save the Northeast Sales Version 2 workbook, print the January 2003 worksheet, then close the Northeast Sales Version 2 workbook.
i. Return to the Visual Basic Editor, enter your name in a comment line in each procedure, print the current project's code, then close the Visual Basic Editor.
j. Return to Excel, close the Northeast Sales workbook, then exit Excel.

► Independent Challenge 1

You work at Art Place, an art supply store located in Portland, Maine. Your co-worker Audrey is on vacation for two weeks, and you have taken over her projects. The information systems manager, Monique, asks you to document and test the Excel procedure Qtr1, which Audrey wrote for the company's accountant. You will run the macro procedure first to see what it does, then you will add comments to the VBA code to document it. Lastly, you will enter data to verify that the formulas in the macro work correctly.

a. Start Excel, open the Project File titled EX P-4 from the drive and folder where your Project Files are stored, enable macros, then save it as **First Quarter Income**.
b. Run the Qtr1 macro, noting anything you think should be mentioned in your documentation.
c. Review the Qtr1 procedure in the Visual Basic Editor. It is stored in the Quarter 1 module.
d. Document the procedure by annotating the printed code, indicating the actions the procedure performs and the objects (ranges) that are affected. (*Hint*: The month names are entered into cells B1, C1, and D1. The income row headers are entered into cells A2, A4, A5, and A6. The Total Income header is entered into cell A8. The column

headers are bolded. The row headers are bolded. Columns A through E are AutoFitted. Totals are entered into cells B8, C8, and D8.)

e. Enter your name in a comment line.
f. Save the procedure, then print the procedure code.
g. Return to the First Quarter Income workbook and use Figure P-20 as a guide to enter data in cells B4:D6 of Sheet1.
h. Check the total income calculations in row 8 to verify that the macro is working correctly.
i. Enter your name in the Sheet1 footer, save the worksheet, then print the worksheet.
j. Close the workbook, then exit Excel.

FIGURE P-20

	A	B	C	D	E
1		January	Feburary	March	
2	Income				
3					
4	Supplies	400	500	450	
5	Classes	700	600	500	
6	Consulting	200	800	750	
7					
8	Total Income				

▶ Independent Challenge 2

You work in the sales office of an automobile dealership called Team Motors. Each month you are required to produce a report stating whether sales quotas were met for the following three vehicle categories: compacts, sedans, and sports/utility. This quarter, the sales quotas for each month are as follows: compacts 60, sedans 45, and sports/utility 60. The results this month were 40, 55, and 70, respectively. You decide to create a procedure to automate your monthly task of determining the sales quota status for the vehicle categories. You would like your assistant to take this task over when you go on vacation next month. Because he has no previous experience with Excel, you decide to create a second procedure that prompts a user with input boxes to enter the actual sales results for the month.

a. Start Excel, open the Project File titled EX P-5 from the drive and folder where your Project Files are stored, then save it as **Sales Quota Status**.
b. Use the Visual Basic Editor to insert a new module named **Quotas** in the Sales Quota Status workbook. Create a procedure in the new module named **SalesQuota**, that determines the sales quota status for each vehicle category and enters Yes or No in the Status column. The VBA code is shown in Figure P-21.
c. Add comments to document the SalesQuota procedure, including your name, then save it.
d. Insert a new module named **MonthlySales**. Create a second procedure named **Sales** that prompts a user for sales data for each vehicle category, enters the input data in the appropriate cells, then calls the SalesQuota procedure. The VBA code is shown in Figure P-22. Save the Sales procedure.
e. Use the Macro dialog box to assign a shortcut of [Ctrl] + [w] to the Sales macro. (*Hint*: In the Macro dialog box select the Sales macro and click **Options**.) Insert a line on the worksheet that tells the user to press [Ctrl] + [w] to enter sales data.
f. Run the Sales macro using the shortcut key combination and enter 40 for compact sales, 55 for sedan sales, and 70 for Sports/Utility sales. Correct any errors in the VBA code.
g. Insert your name in a "Created by" comment below the procedure name. Enter comments to document the macro actions. Save the procedure.

FIGURE P-21

```
Sub SalesQuota()
    If Range("C4") >= 60 Then
        Range("D4").Select
        ActiveCell.Formula = "Yes"
    Else
        Range("D4").Select
        ActiveCell.Formula = "No"
    End If
    If Range("C5") >= 45 Then
        Range("D5").Select
        ActiveCell.Formula = "Yes"
    Else
        Range("D5").Select
        ActiveCell.Formula = "No"
    End If
    If Range("C6") >= 60 Then
        Range("D6").Select
        ActiveCell.Formula = "Yes"
    Else
        Range("D6").Select
        ActiveCell.Formula = "No"
    End If

End Sub
```

FIGURE P-22

```
Sub Sales()

    Dim Compact As String
    Compact = InputBox("Enter Compact Sales")
    Range("C4").Select
    Selection = Compact

    Dim Sedans As String
    Sedans = InputBox("Enter Sedan Sales")
    Range("C5").Select
    Selection = Sedans

    Dim SportsUtility As String
    SportsUtility = InputBox("Enter Sports/Utility Sales")
    Range("C6").Select
    Selection = SportsUtility

    Call SalesQuota

End Sub
```

h. Print the current project's code, then close the Visual Basic Editor.
i. Return to the workbook, enter your name in the Quotas sheet footer, then print the worksheet.
j. Close the workbook, then exit Excel.

▶ Independent Challenge 3

You own a flower store named Tulips located in Naples, Florida. You have started to advertise your business using a local magazine, billboards, cable TV, radio, and local newspapers. Every month you prepare a report with the advertising expenses detailed by source. You decide to create a macro that will format the monthly reports in a consistent way. Since you add the same footers on every report you create, you will create another macro that will add a footer to a document. Finally, you will create a main procedure that will call the macros to format the report and add a footer. You begin by creating a workbook with data you can use to test the macros. You will save the macros you create in this workbook.

a. Use Figure P-23 as a guide to create a workbook containing the January advertising expenses. Save the workbook as **Tulip Ads** in the drive and folder where your Project Files are stored.
b. Insert a module named **Format**, then create a procedure named Formatting that:
   - Selects a cell in row 3 and inserts a row in the worksheet above it
   - Selects the cost data in column C and formats it as currency. (*Hint*: After the row is inserted, this range is C5:C9.)
   - Selects cell A1 before ending

FIGURE P-23

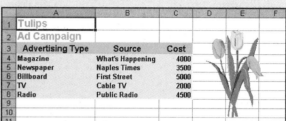

	A	B	C	D	E	F
1	Tulips					
2	Ad Campaign					
3	Advertising Type	Source	Cost			
4	Magazine	What's Happening	4000			
5	Newspaper	Naples Times	3500			
6	Billboard	First Street	5000			
7	TV	Cable TV	2000			
8	Radio	Public Radio	4500			
9						
10						
11						

c. Save the Formatting procedure.
d. Insert a module named **Foot**, then create a procedure named Footer that:
   - Declares a string variable for text that will be placed in the left footer
   - Uses an input box to prompt the user for his or her name and places the name in the left footer
   - Places the filename in the center footer
   - Places the date in the right footer
e. Save the Footer procedure.
f. Insert a module named **Main**, then create a procedure named MainProc that calls the new Footer procedure and the Formatting procedure.
g. Save your work, then run the MainProc procedure. Debug each procedure as necessary.
h. Insert your name in a comment line under each procedure name, then print the code for the current project.
i. Return to the January worksheet, save the workbook, then print the worksheet.
j. Close the workbook, then exit Excel.

Independent Challenge 4

You are working as an assistant currency trader for an international bank based in London. To keep on top of the fluctuating world currencies, you create a daily report using data imported from the Web to an Excel spreadsheet. Since you perform the same formatting and place the same header and footer on each report, you decide to write a macro that will do this automatically.

a. Start Excel, create a new workbook, then save it as **Currency Rates** in the drive and folder where your Project Files are stored.

b. Go to the AltaVista search engine at www.altavista.com and enter **currency AND rates** in the Search box. Follow the links to find the world currency rates for the day. You can also use Yahoo!, Excite, Infoseek, or another search engine of your choice. (*Hint:* www.bloomberg.com/uk lists the world currency rates. In the currencies section there is a link to More Currencies.)

c. Drag the currency rate information from the Web page into Sheet1 of your Currency Rates workbook.

d. Use the Visual Basic Editor to create a procedure, named formatting that does the following:

- Inserts a blank row after the column headers
- Changes the font size of the column and row headers to 12
- Bolds the currency data
- Adds a center header of "Currency Exchange Rates"
- Adds a footer with your name in the left section and the date in the right section

e. Enter your name as a comment in the procedure.

f. Save your work then return to the worksheet and test the new macro.

g. Debug the macro as necessary, print the module, then close the Visual Basic Editor.

h. Save the workbook, then print the workbook in landscape orientation.

i. Close the workbook, then exit Excel.

► Visual Workshop

Open the Project File titled EX P-6 and save it as **Strings** in the drive and folder where your Project Files are stored. Create a macro procedure that will format the worksheet as shown in Figure P-24. Insert your name in a comment line under the procedure name, then print the procedure code.

FIGURE P-24

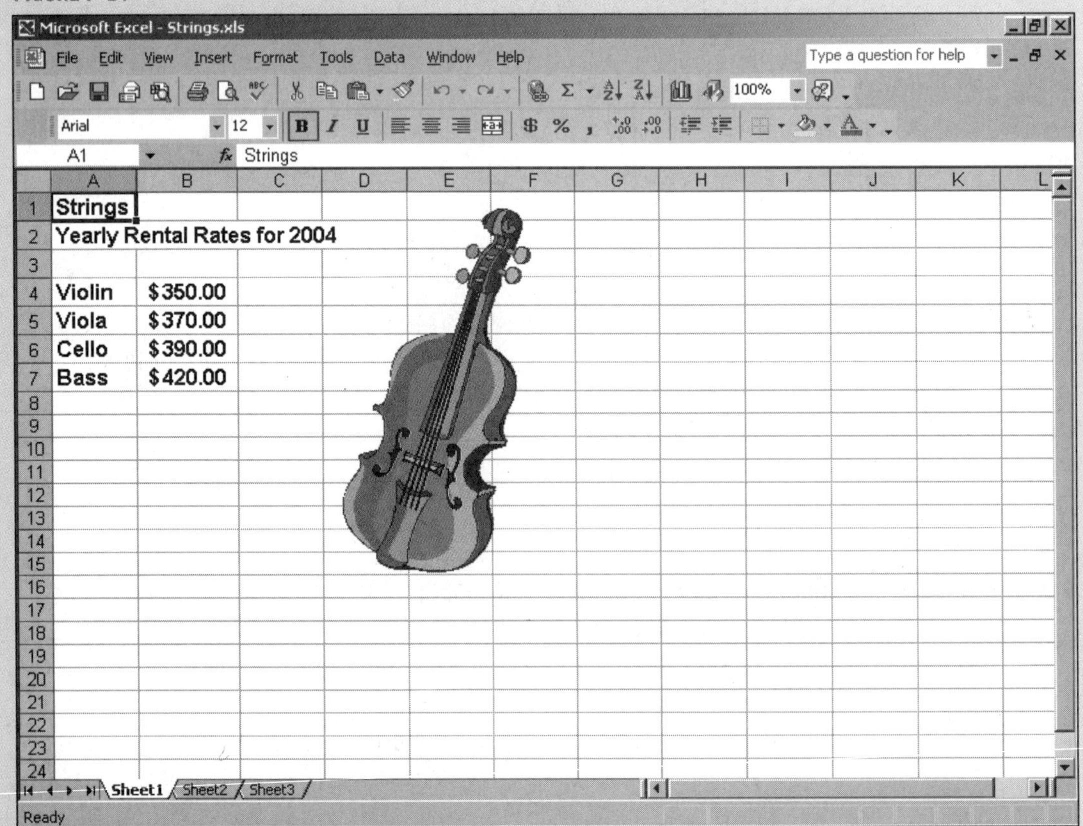

Formatting
a Disk

A **disk** is a device on which you can store electronic data. Disks come in a variety of sizes and have varying storage capacities. Your computer's **hard disk**, one of its internal devices, can store large amounts of data. **Floppy disks**, on the other hand, are smaller, inexpensive, and portable. Most floppy disks that you buy today are 3½" (the diameter of the inside, circular part of the disk). Disks are sometimes called **drives**, but this term really refers to the name by which the operating system recognizes the disk (or a portion of the disk). The operating system typically assigns a drive letter to a drive (which you can reassign if you want). For example, on most computers the hard disk is identified by the drive letter "C" and the floppy drive by the drive letter "A." The amount of information a disk can hold is called its **capacity**, usually measured in megabytes (Mb). The most common floppy disk capacity is 1.44 Mb. Newer computers come with other disk drives, such as a **Zip drive**, a kind of disk drive made to handle **Zip disks**. These disks are portable like floppy disks, but they can contain 100 Mb, far more than regular floppy disks. In this appendix, you will prepare a floppy disk for use.

Windows 2000

Formatting a Disk

In order for an operating system to be able to store data on a disk, the disk must be formatted. **Formatting** prepares a disk so it can store information. Usually, floppy disks are formatted when you buy them, but if not, you can perform this function yourself using Windows 2000. To complete the following steps, you need a blank floppy disk or a disk containing data you no longer need. Do not use your Project Disk for this lesson, as all information on the disk will be erased.

Steps

Trouble?

This unit assumes that the drive that will contain your floppy disks is drive A. If not, substitute the correct drive any time you are instructed to use the 3½ Floppy (A:) drive.

1. Start Windows if necessary, then place a 3½" floppy disk in drive A
2. Double-click the **My Computer icon** on the desktop
   My Computer opens, as shown in Figure AP-1. This window lists all the drives and printers that you can use on your computer. Because computers have different drives, printers, programs, and other devices installed, your window will probably look different.
3. Right-click the **3½ Floppy (A:) icon**
   When you click with the right mouse button, a pop-up menu of commands that apply to the item you right-clicked appears. Because you right-clicked a drive, the Format command is available.

Trouble?

Windows cannot format a disk if it is write-protected; therefore, you may need to slide the write-protect tab over until it clicks to continue. See Figure AP-3 to locate the write-protect tab on your disk.

4. Click **Format** on the pop-up menu
   The Format dialog box opens, as shown in Figure AP-2. In this dialog box, you specify the capacity of the disk you are formatting, the File system, the Allocation unit size, the kind of formatting you want to do, and if you want, a volume label. You are doing a standard format so you will accept the default settings.
5. Click **Start**, then, when you are warned that formatting will erase all data on the disk, click **OK** to continue
   Windows formats your disk. After the formatting is complete, you will probably see a summary about the size of the disk; it's okay if you don't.
6. Click **OK** when the message telling you that the format is complete appears, then click **Close** in the Format dialog box

QuickTip

Once a disk is formatted, you do not need to format it again. However, some people use the Quick Format option to erase the contents of a disk quickly, rather than having to select the files and then delete them.

7. Click the **Close button** in the My Computer window
   My Computer closes and you return to the desktop.

FIGURE AP-1: My Computer window

Drive containing your disk

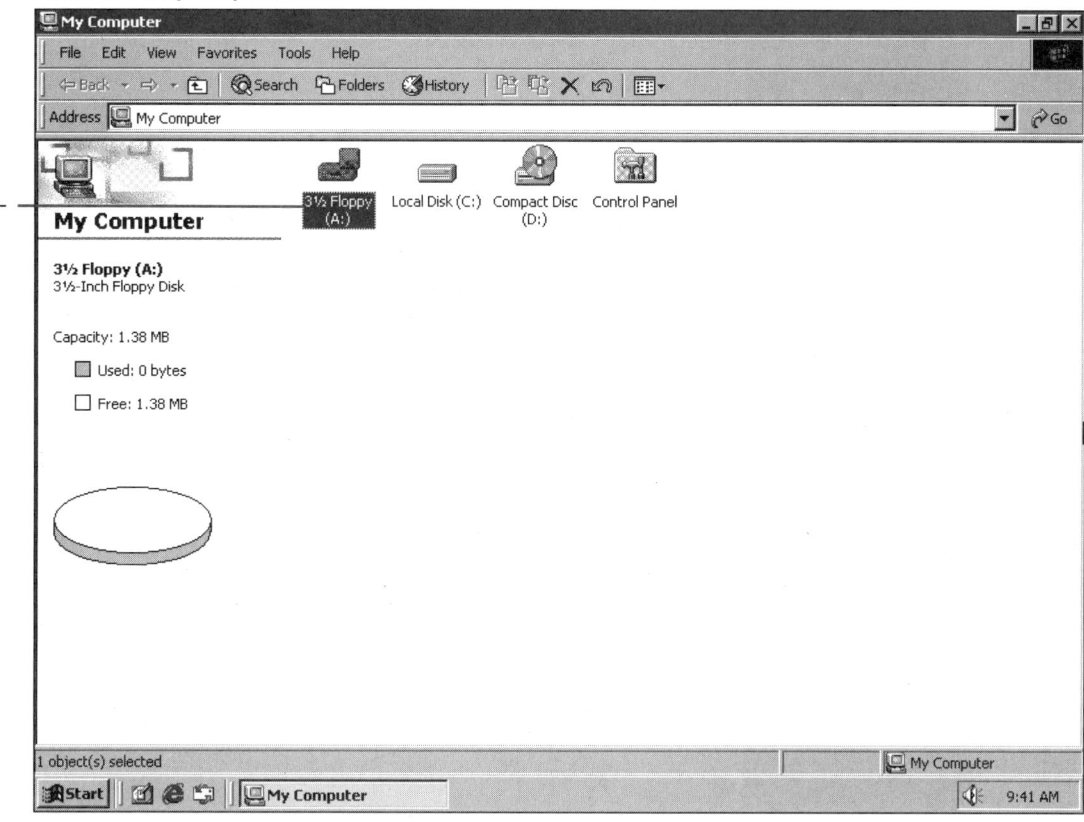

FIGURE AP-2: Format dialog box

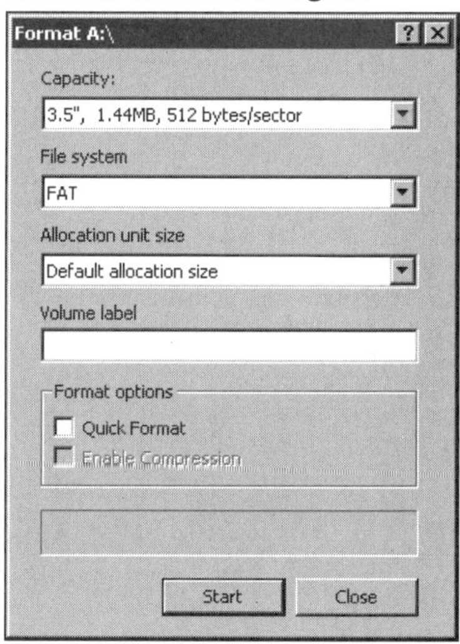

FIGURE AP-3: Write-protect tab

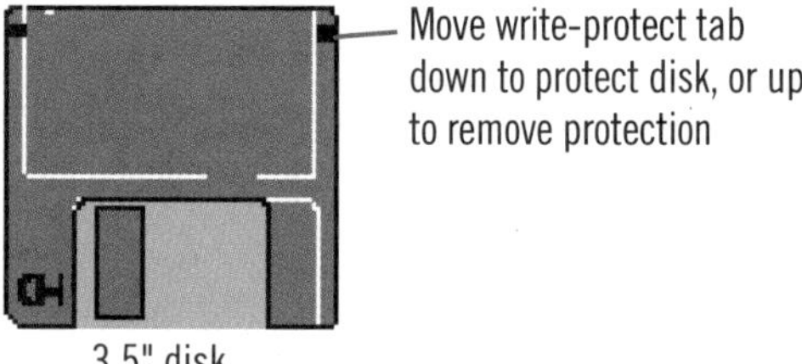

Project Files List

Read the following information carefully!

It is very important to organize and keep track of the files you need for this book.

1. Find out from your instructor the location of the Project Files you need and the location where you will store your files.

- To complete many of the units in this book, you need to use Project Files. Your instructor will either provide you with a copy of the Project Files or ask you to make your own copy.
- If you need to make a copy of the Project Files, you will need to copy a set of files from a file server, stand-alone computer, or the Web to the drive and folder where you will be storing your Project Files.
- Your instructor will tell you which computer, drive letter, and folders contain the files you need, and where you will store your files.
- You can also download the files by going to www.course.com. See the inside back cover of the book for instructions on how to download your files.

2. Copy and organize your Project Files.

Floppy disk users

- If you are using floppy disks to store your Project Files, the list on the following pages shows which files you'll need to copy onto your disk(s).
- Unless noted in the Project Files List, you will need one formatted, high-density disk for each unit. For each unit you are assigned, copy the files listed in the **Project File Supplied column** onto one disk.
- Make sure you label each disk clearly with the unit name (e.g., Excel Unit A).
- When working through the unit, save all your files to this disk.

Users storing files in other locations

- If you are using a zip drive, network folder, hard drive, or other storage device, use the Project Files List to organize your files.
- Create a subfolder for each unit in the location where you are storing your files, and name it according to the unit title (e.g., Excel Unit A).
- For each unit you are assigned, copy the files listed in the **Project File Supplied column** into that unit's folder.
- Store the files you modify or create for each unit in the unit folder.

3. Find and keep track of your Project Files and completed files.

- Use the **Project File Supplied column** to make sure you have the files you need before starting the unit or exercise indicated in the **Unit and Location column**.
- Use the **Student Saves File As column** to find out the filename you use when saving your changes to a Project File that was provided.
- Use the **Student Creates File column** to find out the filename you use when saving a file you create new for the exercise.

Unit and Location	Project File Supplied	Student Saves File As	Student Creates File
Windows 2000 Unit A	(No files provided or created)		
Windows 2000 Unit B			
DISK 1			
Lessons	Win_B-1.bmp		
DISK 2			
Skills Review	Win_B-2.bmp		
Excel Unit A			
Lessons	EX A-1.xls	MediaLoft Cafe Budget.xls	
Skills Review	EX A-2.xls	MediaLoft Toronto Cafe.xls	MediaLoft Balance Sheet.xls
Independent Challenge 1	(No files provided or created)		
Independent Challenge 2			Sample Payroll.xls
Independent Challenge 3			Training Workbook.xls
			Template Sample.xls
Independent Challenge 4			New Computer Data.xls
Visual Workshop			Carrie's Camera and Darkroom.xls
Excel Unit B			
Lessons	EX B-1.xls	Author Events Forecast.xls	
Skills Review	EX B-2.xls	Office Furnishings.xls	
Independent Challenge 1			Young Brazilians.xls
Independent Challenge 2	EX B-3.xls	Beautiful You Finances.xls	
Independent Challenge 3			Learn-it-All.xls
Independent Challenge 4			Temperature Conversions.xls
Visual Workshop			Annual Budget.xls
Excel Unit C			
Lessons	EX C-1.xls	Ad Expenses.xls	
Skills Review			MediaLoft GB Inventory.xls
	EX C-2.xls	Monthly Operating Expenses.xls	
Independent Challenge 1	EX C-3.xls	BY Inventory.xls	
Independent Challenge 2	EX C-4.xls	Community Action.xls	
Independent Challenge 3			Classic Instruments.xls
Independent Challenge 4			Currency Conversions.xls
Visual Workshop	EX C-5.xls	Projected March Advertising Invoices.xls	
Excel Unit D			
Lessons	EX D-1.xls	MediaLoft Sales - Eastern Division.xls	
Skills Review			MediaLoft Vancouver Software Usage.xls

Unit and Location	Project File Supplied	Student Saves File As	Student Creates File
Independent Challenge 1	EX D-2.xls	Springfield Theater Group.xls	
Independent Challenge 2	EX D-3.xls	BY Expense Charts.xls	
Independent Challenge 3	EX D-4.xls	Bright Light.xls	
Independent Challenge 4			New Location Analysis.xls
Visual Workshop	EX D-5.xls	Quarterly Advertising Budget.xls	
Excel Unit E			
Lessons	EX E-1.xls	Company Data.xls	
Skills Review	EX E-2.xls	Manager Bonuses.xls	
Independent Challenge 1	EX E-3.xls	Mike's Sales.xls	
Independent Challenge 2	EX E-4.xls	Fly Away Sales.xls	
Independent Challenge 3			Custom Fit Loan Options.xls
Independent Challenge 4			IRA Rates.xls
Visual Workshop			Car Payment Calculator.xls
Excel Unit F			
Lessons	EX F-1.xls	Timecard Summary.xls	
Lessons	Pay Rate Classifications.xls		Student creates hyperlink to this file from Timecard Summary file
Lessons		timesum.htm	Student creates from Timecard Summary file
Skills Review	EX F-2.xls	San Francisco Budget.xls	
Skills Review	Expense Details.xls		Student creates hyperlink to this file from San Francisco Budget file
Skills Review		sfbudget.htm	Student creates from San Francisco Budget file
Independent Challenge 1			Software Sales Summary.xls
Independent Challenge 2	EX F-3.xls	Update to Check Register.xls	
Independent Challenge 3			Monthly Long Distance.xls
Independent Challenge 3			Next Door.xls
Independent Challenge 3			Phonebill.xlw (Workspace file student creates from the Monthly Long Distance and Next Door files.)
Independent Challenge 3			Monthly Long Distance -5.xls
Independent Challenge 4			Camera Research file
Independent Challenge 4		camera.htm	Student creates from Camera Research file
Visual Workshop		Martinez.xls	
Visual Workshop			martinez.htm
Excel Unit G			
Lessons			My Excel Macros.xls
Skills Review			Macros.xls

Unit and Location	Project File Supplied	Student Saves File As	Student Creates File
Independent Challenge 1			Excel Utility Macros.xls
Independent Challenge 2			Header and Footer Stamp.xls
Independent Challenge 3			Computers Inc Macro.xls
Independent Challenge 4	EX G-1.xls		Office Supplies.xls
Visual Workshop			File Utility Macros.xls
Excel Unit H			
Lessons	EX H-1.xls	New Customer List.xls	
Skills Review			MediaLoft New York Employee List.xls
Independent Challenge 1			Personalize IT.xls
Independent Challenge 2	EX H-2.xls	Television Shows of the Past.xls	
Independent Challenge 3	EX H-3.xls	Best Films.xls	
Independent Challenge 4			MP3 Titles.xls
Visual Workshop			Famous Jazz Performers.xls
Excel Unit I			
Lessons	EX I-1.xls	Survey Data.xls	
	EX I-1.xls	Survey Data 2.xls	
	EX I-1.xls	Survey Data 3.xls	
Skills Review	EX I-2.xls	Compensation Summary.xls	
	EX I-2.xls	Compensation Summary 2.xls	
Independent Challenge 1	EX I-3.xls	Olive Oil.xls	
Independent Challenge 2	EX I-4.xls	Custom Books - Invoice DB.xls	
	EX I-4.xls	Custom Books - Lookup.xls	
Independent Challenge 3	EX I-5.xls	Bestsellers.xls	
	EX I-5.xls	Bestsellers 2.xls	
Independent Challenge 4	EX I-6.xls	Hotels.xls	
Visual Workshop			Commission Lookup.xls
Excel Unit J			
Lessons	EX J-1.xls	Pastry Sales.xls	
Skills Review	EX J-2.xls	MediaLoft Coffee Sales.xls	
Independent Challenge 1	EX J-3.xls	Cheese Order Tracking.xls	
Independent Challenge 2	EX J-4.xls	Customer Survey.xls	
Independent Challenge 3			September Sales.xls
Independent Challenge 4	EX J-5.xls	Tea Sales.xls	
Visual Workshop			The Dutch Garden.xls
Excel Unit K			
Lessons	EX K-1.xls	Capital Equipment Payment Model.xls	
Skills Review	EX K-2.xls	Capital Equipment Repair Models.xls	

Unit and Location	Project File Supplied	Student Saves File As	Student Creates File
Independent Challenge 1	EX K-3.xls	Car Loan Payment Model.xls	
Independent Challenge 2	EX K-4.xls	Capital Loan Payment Model.xls	
Independent Challenge 3	EX K-5.xls	PC Production Model.xls	
Independent Challenge 4	EX K-6.xls	Mortgage Research.xls	
Visual Workshop			Notebook Payment Model.xls
Excel Unit L			
Lessons	EX L-1.xls	Eastern Sales.xls	
Skills Review	EX L-2.xls	July CDs.xls	
Independent Challenge 1	EX L-3.xls	Partner Billing Report.xls	
Independent Challenge 2	EX L-4.xls	Second Qtr Sales.xls	
Independent Challenge 3	EX L-5.xls	Western Sales Employees.xls	
Independent Challenge 4			Stock Prices.xls
Visual Workshop	EX L-6.xls	Photo Store.xls	
Excel Unit M			
Lessons	EX M-1.txt	CafeCorp – Product Info.xls	
	EX M-2.mdb	CafeCorp - Corporate Customer Info.xls	
	EX M-3.jpg	(Graphic file inserted into CafeCorp - Corporate Customer Info)	
	EX M-4.doc	CafeCorp – Sales Projection Memo.doc	
	EX M-5.xls	(Worksheet embedded and linked into Sales Projection Memo)	
	EX M-6.ppt	Marketing Department Presentation.ppt	
	EX M-7.xls	(Excel chart embedded into Marketing Department Presentation)	
			CafeCorp Management.mdb
	EX M-8.xls	(Spreadsheet imported into Cafe Corp Management)	
Skills Review	EX M-9.txt	CafeCorp New Products.xls	
	EX M-10.mdb	CafeCorp January Budget.xls	
	EX M-11.jpg	(Picture embedded in CafeCorp January Budget file)	
	EX M-12.xls	(Worksheet embedded and then linked into CafeCorp January Budget)	
	EX M-13.ppt	Monthly Budget Meeting.ppt	
	EX M-14.xls	(Excel chart embedded into Monthly Budget Meeting)	
Skills Review			Budget List.mdb
	EX M-15.xls	(Excel list imported into Budget List)	
Independent Challenge 1	EX M-16.txt		Skate Supplier List.xls Supplier List.mdb (Skate Supplier List converted to Access)

Unit and Location	Project File Supplied	Student Saves File As	Student Creates File
Independent Challenge 2	EX M-17.wk1	Payroll Info.xls	
	EX M-18.xls	(Worksheet embedded and linked into Payroll Info)	
Independent Challenge 3			Consumer Loans.xls
	EX M-19.ppt	Loan Presentation.ppt	
Independent Challenge 4	EX M-20.mdb	Temp Jobs.xls	
	EX M-21.bmp	(Graphic inserted into Temp Jobs)	
Visual Workshop			Atlantic Price List.xls
	EX M-22.jpg	(Graphic inserted into Atlantic Price list)	
	EX M-23.xls	(Workbook embedded into Atlantic Price List)	
Excel Unit N			
Lessons	EX N-1.xls	Sales Info.xls	
	EX N-2.xls	Sales Info Edits.xls	
	EX N-1.xls	Sales Info PW.xls	
	EX N-1.xls	Sales Info 2.xls	
		pastry.htm (created from Sales Info 2)	
		repinfo.htm (created from Sales Info 2)	
			Stock Data.xls
Skills Review	EX N-3.xls	Ad Campaigns.xls	
	EX N-3.xls	Ad Campaigns PW.xls	
		campaign.htm (created from Ad Campaigns PW)	
		Storeads.htm (created from Ad Campaigns PW)	
			Stock Quotes.xls
			Stock Quotes.xml
Independent Challenge 1	EX N-4.xls	Boston Touring.xls	
	EX N-5.xls	(Merged into Boston Touring)	
	EX N-6.xls	(Merged into Boston Touring)	
	EX N-7.xls	(Merged into Boston Touring)	
Independent Challenge 2			Mortgage Calculator.xls
	EX N-8.xml	(Imported into Mortgage Calculator)	
		calc.htm (created from Mortgage Calculator)	
Independent Challenge 3			Tuckerman Teas.xls
	EX N-9.xml	(Imported into Tuckerman Teas)	
		teasales.htm (created from Tuckerman Teas)	
Independent Challenge 4			Trend Analysis.xls

Unit and Location	Project File Supplied	Student Saves File As	Student Creates File
Visual Workshop	EX N-10.xls		Percussion.xls
		percsale.htm (created from Percussion)	
Excel Unit O			
Lessons	EX O-1.xls	Overtime Hours.xls	
			Accounts.xls
		Overtime Hours.xlt (template created from Overtime Hours)	
Skills Review	EX O-2.xls	Cafe Budget.xls	
		Customizing Excel (created from Café Budget)	
		Budget Template.xlt (created from Café Budget)	
Independent Challenge 1	EX O-3.xls	2003 Monthly Check Register.xls	
Independent Challenge 2	EX O-4.xls	Monthly Budget.xls	
Independent Challenge 3			Kidcare.xls
Independent Challenge 4			Expense Statement.xlt
		My Expense Statement.xls (created from Expense Statement template)	
Visual Workshop	EX O-5.xls	Zoo Count.xls	
Excel Unit P			
Lessons	EX P-1.xls	KHOT Procedures.xls	
	EX P-2.xls	KHOT Advertising.xls	
	EX P-2.xls	KHOT Advertising Version 2.xls	
Skills Review	EX P-3.xls	Northeast Sales.xls	
	EX P-3.xls	Northeast Sales Version 2.xls	
Independent Challenge 1	EX P-4.xls	First Quarter Income.xls	
Independent Challenge 2	EX P-5.xls	Sales Quota Status.xls	
Independent Challenge 3			Tulip Ads.xls
Independent Challenge 4			Currency Rates.xls
Visual Workshop	EX P-6.xls	Strings.xls	

Microsoft Excel 2002 Core MOUS Certification Objectives

Below is a list of the Microsoft Office User Specialist program objectives for the Core Excel 2002 skills, showing where each MOUS objective is covered in the Lessons and Practice. For more information on which Illustrated titles meet MOUS certification, please see the inside front cover.

MOUS standardized coding number	Activity	Lesson page where skill is covered	Location in lesson where skill is covered	Practice
Ex2002-1	**Working with Cells and Cell Data**			
Ex2002-1-1	Insert, delete and move cells	EXCEL B-12 EXCEL B-19 EXCEL C-6	Step 7 Clues to Use Step 6	Skills Review Skills Review Skills Review, Independent Challenge 4
Ex2002-1-2	Enter and edit cell data including text, numbers, and formulas	EXCEL A-10 EXCEL B-4 EXCEL B-6 EXCEL B-8 EXCEL B-10 EXCEL C-2 EXCEL C-3 EXCEL E-2 EXCEL E-8	Steps 1–7 Step 2 Tip Steps 2–9 Steps 1–6 Steps 1–5 Clues to Use Steps 2–9 Steps 2–7 Clues to Use Steps 3–5 Steps 1–3	Skills Review, Independent Challenges 2–4 Skills Review Skills Review, Independent Challenges 1–4 Skills Review, Independent Challenges 1–4 Skills Review, Independent Challenge 2 Skills Review, Independent Challenges 1–4 Skills Review, Independent Challenges 1–4 Skills Review, Independent Challenges 1, 3, 4 Skills Review, Independent Challenges 1, 3
Ex2002-1-3	Check spelling	EXCEL C-16	Steps 1–5	Skills Review, Independent Challenges 1–4
Ex2002-1-4	Find and replace cell data and formats	EXCEL E-2 EXCEL F-15	Step 2 Clues to Use	Skills Review Independent Challenge 2
Ex2002-1-5	Work with a subset of data by filtering lists	EXCEL H-5	Clues to Use	Independent Challenge 4
Ex2002-2	**Managing Workbooks**			
Ex2002-2-1	Manage workbook files and folders	EXCEL A-8	Steps 1–3 Step 4 Tip	Skills Review
Ex2002-2-2	Create workbooks using templates	EXCEL A-9	Clues to Use	Independent Challenge 3
Ex2002-2-3	Save workbooks using different names and file formats	EXCEL A-8 EXCEL F-16	Steps 4–5 Steps 1–5; Step 1 Tip	Skills Review, Independent Challenges 1–4 Skills Review, Independent Challenges 3–4

MOUS standardized coding number	Activity	Lesson page where skill is covered	Location in lesson where skill is covered	Practice
Ex2002-3	**Formatting and Printing Worksheets**			
Ex2002-3-1	Apply and modify cell formats	EXCEL C-2	Steps 2–7	Skills Review, Independent Challenges 1–4
		EXCEL C-3	Clues to Use	Skills Review
		EXCEL C-4	Steps 2–5	Skills Review, Independent Challenge 2, Visual Workshop
		EXCEL C-6	Steps 1–7	Skills Review, Independent Challenges 1–4, Visual Workshop
		EXCEL C-12	Steps 1–8	Skills Review, Independent Challenges 1, 4, Visual Workshop
		EXCEL C-14	Steps 2–5	Skills Review, Independent Challenges 1, 2, 4, Visual Workshop
Ex2002-3-2	Modify row and column settings	EXCEL C-10	Steps 1–6	Skills Review, Independent Challenges 1, 2
		EXCEL F-2	Steps 1–6	Skills Review
		EXCEL F-8	Steps 1–4	Skills Review
		EXCEL F-9	Table	Skills Review
Ex2002-3-3	Modify row and column formats	EXCEL C-6	Steps 6–7	Skills Review, Independent Challenges 2-4
		EXCEL C-7	Table	Skills Review
		EXCEL C-8	Steps 1–7	Skills Review, Independent Challenges 1–3
		EXCEL C-9	Clues to Use	Independent Challenge 3
Ex2002-3-4	Apply styles	EXCEL E-4	Step 4	Skills Review, Independent Challenge 2
Ex2002-3-5	Use automated tools to format worksheets	EXCEL C-7	Clues to Use	Independent Challenges 3, 4
Ex2002-3-6	Modify Page Setup options for worksheets	EXCEL C-16	Step 8	Independent Challenge 2
		EXCEL D-16	Step 4	Skills Review
		EXCEL E-16	Intro, Step 5 Tip, Step 6	Skills Review, Independent Challenges 1, 3, 4
		EXCEL E-17	Clues to Use	Independent Challenge 2
		EXCEL F-5	Clues to Use	Skills Review, Independent Challenges 1–4, Visual Workshop
		EXCEL H-16	Step 2	Independent Challenge 2
		EXCEL H-17	Clues to Use	Independent Challenge 4
Ex2002-3-7	Preview and print worksheets and workbooks	EXCEL H-16	Step 2 Tip	Independent Challenge 2
		EXCEL H-17	Clues to Use	Skills Review, Independent Challenge 2

MOUS standardized coding number	Activity	Lesson page where skill is covered	Location in lesson where skill is covered	Practice
Ex2002-4	**Modifying Workbooks**			
Ex2002-4-1	Insert and delete worksheets	EXCEL F-4	Steps 1, 3	Skills Review, Independent Challenges 2, 3
Ex2002-4-2	Modify worksheet names and positions	EXCEL A-12	Step 3 Tip, Steps 5–6	Skills Review, Independent Challenge 3
Ex2002-4-3	Use 3-D references	EXCEL F-6	Steps 3–5	Skills Review, Independent Challenges 1–3
Ex2002-5	**Creating and Revising Formulas**			
Ex2002-5-1	Create and revise formulas	EXCEL B-6	Steps 1–6	Skills Review, Independent Challenges 1, 2, 4, Visual Workshop
		EXCEL B-8	Steps 1–5, Clues to Use	Skills Review, Independent Challenges 1, 2, 4, Visual Workshop
		EXCEL B-10	Steps 4–6	Skills Review, Independent Challenge 2
		EXCEL B-14	All	Skills Review, Independent Challenges 1, 4
		EXCEL B-16	Steps 1–6	Skills Review, Independent Challenges 1, 4, Visual Workshop
		EXCEL B-18	Steps 4–7	Skills Review, Independent Challenges 1, 4, Visual Workshop
		EXCEL E-2	Steps 3–5	Skills Review, Independent Challenges 1,2
		EXCEL E-12	Steps 1–3	Skills Review
Ex2002-5-2	Use statistical, date and time, financial, and logical functions in formulas	EXCEL B-10	Steps 1–4, 6	Independent Challenge 2
		EXCEL B-11	Clues to Use	Skills Review
		EXCEL E-2	Steps 3–5	Skills Review
		EXCEL E-8	Steps 1–2	Skills Review, Independent Challenge 1
		EXCEL E-10	Steps 1–4	Skills Review
		EXCEL E-12	Steps 1–8	Skills Review, Independent Challenge 4
		EXCEL E-14	Steps 1–3	Skills Review, Independent Challenge 3, Visual Workshop
		EXCEL E-15	Clues to Use	Independent Challenge 4
Ex2002-6	**Creating and Modifying Graphics**			
Ex2002-6-1	Create, modify, position and print charts	EXCEL D-4	Steps 2–7	Skills Review, Independent Challenges 1–4
		EXCEL D-6	Steps 3–8	Skills Review, Visual Workshop
		EXCEL D-8	Steps 3–6	Skills Review, Independent Challenges 1–4
		EXCEL D-10	Steps 1–6	Skills Review, Independent Challenges 1–4
		EXCEL D-12	Steps 1–8	Skills Review, Independent Challenges 1, 3
		EXCEL D-14	Steps 1–8	Skills Review, Independent Challenges 2, 3, Visual Workshop
		EXCEL D-16	Steps 2–7	Skills Review, Independent Challenges 1–4, Visual Workshop
		EXCEL D-17	Clues to Use	

MOUS standardized coding number	Activity	Lesson page where skill is covered	Location in lesson where skill is covered	Practice
Ex2002-6-2	Create, modify and position graphics	EXCEL C-5 EXCEL D-14	Clues to Use Steps 1–8	Independent Challenge 3 Skills Review, Independent Challenges 2, 3, Visual Workshop
Ex2002-7	**Workgroup Collaboration**			
Ex2002-7-1	Convert worksheets into Web pages	EXCEL F-16	Steps 1–8	Skills Review, Independent Challenge 4, Visual Workshop
Ex2002-7-2	Create hyperlinks	EXCEL F-14	Steps 3–7 Clues to Use	Skills Review, Independent Challenges 3, 4, Visual Workshop
Ex2002-7-3	View and edit comments	EXCEL C-11 EXCEL F-17	Clues to Use Clues to Use	Skills Review Skills Review

Microsoft Excel 2002 Expert MOUS Certification Objectives

Below is a list of the Microsoft Office User Specialist program objectives for the Expert Excel 2002 skills showing where each MOUS objective is covered in the Lessons and Practice. This table lists the Expert MOUS certification skills covered in the units in this book. For more information on which Illustrated titles meet MOUS certification, please see the inside cover of this book.

MOUS standardized coding number	Activity	Lesson page where skill is covered	Location in lesson where skill is covered	Practice
Ex2002e-1	**Importing and Exporting Data**			
Ex2002e-1-1	Import data to Excel	EXCEL M-4 EXCEL M-6 EXCEL N-16	Steps 1–6 Steps 1–4 Steps 2–6	Skills Review, Independent Challenge 1 Skills Review, Independent Challenge 4 Skills Review, Independent Challenge 4
Ex2002e-1-2	Export data from Excel	EXCEL N-11	Clues to Use	Skills Review
Ex2002e-1-3	Publish worksheets and workbooks to the Web	EXCEL F-16	Steps 1–6	Skills Review, Independent Challenge 4, Visual Workshop
Ex2002e-2	**Managing Workbooks**			
Ex2002e-2-1	Create, edit, and apply templates	EXCEL O-16 EXCEL O-17	Steps 1–6 Clues to Use	Skills Review, Independent Challenge 4
Ex2002e-2-2	Create workspaces	EXCEL F-11	Clues to Use	Independent Challenge 3
Ex2002e-2-3	Use Data Consolidation	EXCEL F-6	Steps 3–5	Skills Review, Independent Challenges 1, 2, 3
Ex2002e-3	**Formatting Numbers**			
Ex2002e-3-1	Create and apply custom number formats	EXCEL E-9	Clues to Use	Independent Challenge 1
Ex2002e-3-2	Use conditional formats	EXCEL C-14 EXCEL C-15	Steps 2–5 Clues to Use	Skills Review, Independent Challenges 1, 2, 4, Visual Workshop Skills Review
Ex2002e-4	**Working with Ranges**			
Ex2002e-4-1	Use named ranges in formulas	EXCEL E-4	Steps 1–3, Step 1 Tip	Skills Review, Independent Challenge 2
Ex2002e-4-2	Use Lookup and Reference functions	EXCEL I-12 EXCEL I-13	Steps 4–9 Clues to Use	Skills Review, Independent Challenges 2, 4, Visual Workshop
Ex2002e-5	**Customizing Excel**			
Ex2002e-5-1	Customize toolbars and menus	EXCEL G-14 EXCEL G-16	Steps 1–5 Steps 3–7	Skills Review, Independent Challenges 2, 3 Skills Review, Independent Challenges 1, 2
Ex2002e-5-2	Create, edit, and run macros	EXCEL G-2 EXCEL G-4 EXCEL G-6 EXCEL G-8 EXCEL G-9	Bullets Steps 2–10 Steps 2–6 Steps 1–5 Clues to Use	Skills Review, Independent Challenges 1, 2, 3, 4, Visual Workshop

MOUS standardized coding number	Activity	Lesson page where skill is covered	Location in lesson where skill is covered	Practice
Ex2002e-6	**Auditing Worksheets**			
Ex2002e-6-1	Audit formulas	EXCEL O-4	Step 5, Tip	Skills Review, Visual Workshop
Ex2002e-6-2	Locate and resolve errors	EXCEL O-4	Steps 2–4	Skills Review, Independent Challenge 1, Visual Workshop
Ex2002e-6-3	Identify dependencies in formulas	EXCEL O-4	Step 5, 6, Tip	Skills Review, Visual Workshop
Ex2002e-7	**Summarizing Data**			
Ex2002e-7-1	Use subtotals with lists and ranges	EXCEL I-10	Steps 2–7	Skills Review, Independent Challenges 1, 2, 3
Ex2002e-7-2	Define and apply filters	EXCEL I-4	Steps 1–3	Skills Review, Independent Challenge 4
Ex2002e-7-3	Add group and outline criteria to ranges	EXCEL I-11 EXCEL O-6	Clues to Use Steps 2–7	Skills Review, Independent Challenges 1, 3 Skills Review, Independent Challenge 3
Ex2002e-7-4	Use data validation	EXCEL I-16	Steps 3–8	Skills Review, Independent Challenges 1, 2, 3, 4
Ex2002e-7-5	Retrieve external data and create queries	EXCEL N-15	Clues to Use	Independent Challenge 4
Ex2002e-7-6	Create Extensible Markup Language (XML) Web queries	EXCEL N-17	Clues to Use	Skills Review, Independent Challenges 2, 3
Ex2002e-8	**Analyzing Data**			
Ex2002e-8-1	Create PivotTables, PivotCharts, and Pivot Table/PivotChart reports	EXCEL L-2 EXCEL L-4 EXCEL L-14 EXCEL N-12	Bullets Steps 2–8 Steps 2–4 Steps 2–7	Skills Review Skills Review, Independent Challenges 1, 2, 3, 4, Visual Workshop Skills Review, Independent Challenges 1, 2, 3, 4 Skills Review, Independent Challenge 3
Ex2002e-8-2	Forecast values with what-if analysis	EXCEL J-8	Clues to Use	Independent Challenge 4, Visual Workshop
Ex2002e-8-3	Create and display scenarios	EXCEL K-4	Steps 2–8, Clues to Use	Skills Review, Independent Challenge 1
Ex2002e-9	**Workgroup Collaboration**			
Ex2002e-9-1	Modify passwords, protections, and properties	EXCEL F-8 EXCEL F-9 EXCEL F-9	Steps 1–5 Table Clues to Use	Skills Review Skills Review Independent Challenge 3
Ex2002e-9-2	Create a shared workbook	EXCEL N-2 EXCEL N-4	Bullets Steps 2–5	Skills Review Skills Review
Ex2002e-9-3	Track, accept and reject changes to workbooks	EXCEL N-6	Steps 1–7, Tip	Skills Review, Independent Challenge 1
Ex2002e-9-5	Merge workbooks	EXCEL N-7	Clues to Use	Independent Challenge 1

Glossary

Accessories Built-in programs that come with Windows 2000.

Active Desktop The screen that appears when you first start Windows 2000, providing access to your computer's programs and files and to the Internet. See also Desktop.

Active program The program that you are using, differentiated from other open programs by a highlighted program button on the taskbar and a differently colored title bar.

Active window The window that you are currently using, differentiated from other open windows by a differently colored title bar.

Address Bar The area below the toolbar in My Computer and Windows Explorer that you use to open and display a drive, folder, or Web page.

Back up To save files to another location in case you have computer trouble and lose files.

Browser A program, such as Microsoft Internet Explorer, designed to access the Internet.

Bullet mark A solid circle that indicates that an option is enabled.

Capacity The amount of information a disk can hold, usually measured in megabytes (Mb).

Cascading menu A list of commands from a menu item with an arrow next to it; pointing at the arrow displays a submenu from which you can choose additional commands.

Check box A square box in a dialog box that you click to turn an option on or off.

Check mark A mark that indicates that a feature is enabled.

Classic style A Windows 2000 setting in which you single-click to select items and double-click to open them.

Click To press and release the left mouse button once.

Clipboard Temporary storage space on your computer's hard disk containing information that has been cut or copied.

Close To quit a program or remove a window from the desktop. The Close button is usually located in the upper-right corner of a window.

Command A directive that provides access to a program's features.

Command button In a dialog box, a button that carries out an action. A command button usually has a label that describes its action, such as Cancel or Help. If the label is followed by an ellipses (...), clicking the button displays another dialog box.

Context-sensitive help Help that is specifically related to what you are doing.

Control Panel Used to change computer settings such as desktop colors or mouse settings.

Copy To place information onto the Clipboard in order to paste it in another location, but also leaving it in the original location.

Cut To remove information from a file and place it on the Clipboard, usually to be pasted into another location.

Default Settings preset by the operating system or program.

Delete To place a file or folder in the Recycle Bin, where you can either remove it from the disk permanently or restore it to its original location.

Desktop The screen that appears when you first start Windows 2000, providing access to your computer's programs and files and to the Internet. See also Active Desktop.

Dialog box A window that opens when more information is needed to carry out a command.

Document A file that you create using a program such as WordPad.

Double-click To press and release the left mouse button twice quickly.

Drag To move an item to a new location using the mouse.

Drive A device that reads and saves files on a disk and is also used to store files; floppy drives read and save files on floppy disks, whereas hard drives read and save files on your computer's built-in hard disk.

Edit To change the content or format of an existing file.

Explorer Bar The pane on the left side of the screen in Windows Explorer that lists all drives and folders on the computer.

File An electronic collection of information that has a unique name, distinguishing it from other files.

File hierarchy A logical structure for folders and files that mimics how you would organize files and folders in a filing cabinet.

File management The process of organizing and keeping track of files and folders.

Floppy disk A disk that you insert into a disk drive of your computer (usually drive A or B) to store files.

Folder A collection of files and/or other folders that helps you organize your disks.

Font The design of a set of characters (for example, Times New Roman).

Format To enhance the appearance of a document by, for example, changing the font or font size, adding borders and shading to a document.

Graphical user interface (GUI) An environment made up of meaningful symbols, words, and windows in which you can control the basic operation of a computer and the programs that run on it.

Hard disk A disk that is built into the computer (usually drive C) on which you store files and programs.

Highlighting When an icon is shaded differently, indicating it is selected. See also Select.

Icon Graphical representation of computer elements such as files and programs.

Inactive Refers to a window or program that is open but not currently in use.

Input device An item, such as a mouse or keyboard, that you use to interact with your computer.

Insertion point A blinking vertical line that indicates where text will appear when you type.

Internet A worldwide collection of over 40 million computers linked together to share information.

Internet style A Windows 2000 setting in which you point to select items and single-click to open them. See also Web style.

Keyboard shortcut A keyboard alternative for executing a menu command (for example, [Ctrl][X] for Cut).

List box A box in a dialog box containing a list of items; to choose an item, click the list arrow, then click the desired item.

Maximize To enlarge a window so it fills the entire screen. The Maximize button is usually located in the upper-right corner of a window.

Menu A list of related commands in a program (for example, the File menu).

Menu bar A bar near the top of the program window that provides access to most of a program's features through categories of related commands.

Minimize To reduce the size of a window. The Minimize button is usually located in the upper-right corner of a window.

Mouse A hand-held input device that you roll on your desk to position the mouse pointer on the Windows desktop. See also Mouse pointer.

Mouse buttons The two buttons on the mouse (right and left) that you use to make selections and issue commands.

Mouse pointer The arrow-shaped cursor on the screen that follows the movement of the mouse. The shape of the mouse pointer changes depending on the program and the task being executed. See also Mouse.

Multi-tasking Working with more than one window or program at a time.

My Computer A program that you use to manage the drives, folders, and files on your computer.

Open To start a program or open a window; also used to describe a program that is running but not active.

Operating system A computer program that controls the basic operation of your computer and the programs you run on it. Windows 2000 is an example of an operating system.

Option button A small circle in a dialog box that you click to select an option.

Paint A drawing program that comes with Windows 2000.

Pane A section of a divided window.

Point To position the mouse pointer over an item on your computer screen; also a unit of measurement (1/72nd inch) used to specify the size of text.

Pointer trail A shadow of the mouse pointer that appears when you move the mouse; helps you locate the pointer on your screen.

Pop-up menu A menu that appears when you right-click an item on the desktop.

Program Task-oriented software that you use for a particular kind of work, such as word processing or database management. Microsoft Access, Microsoft Excel, and Microsoft Word are all programs.

Program button A button on the taskbar that represents an open program or window.

Properties Characteristics of a specific computer element (such as the mouse, keyboard, or desktop display) that you can customize.

Quick Launch toolbar A toolbar located next to the Start button on the taskbar that contains buttons to start Internet-related programs and show the desktop.

Random access memory (RAM) The memory that programs use to perform necessary tasks while the computer is on. When you turn the computer off, all information in RAM is lost.

Recycle Bin An icon that appears on the desktop that represents a temporary storage area on your computer's hard disk for deleted files, which remain in the Recycle Bin until you empty it.

Restore To reduce the window to its previous size before it was maximized. The Restore button is usually located in the upper-right corner of a window.

Right-click To press and release the right mouse button once.

ScreenTip A description of a toolbar button that appears when you position the mouse pointer over the button.

Scroll bar A bar that appears at the bottom and/or right edge of a window whose contents are not entirely visible; you click the arrows or drag the box in the direction you want to move. See also Scroll box.

Scroll box A rectangle located in the vertical and horizontal scroll bars that indicates your relative position in a window. See also Scroll bar.

Select To click and highlight an item in order to perform some action on it. See also Highlighting.

Shortcut A link that you can place in any location that gives you instant access to a particular file, folder, or program on your hard disk or on a network.

Shut down The action you perform when you have finished working with Windows 2000; after you shut down it is safe to turn off your computer.

Slider An item in a dialog box that you drag to set the degree to which an option is in effect.

Spin box A box with two arrows and a text box; allows you to scroll in numerical increments or type a number.

Start button A button on the taskbar that you use to start programs, find and open files, access Windows Help and more.

Tab A place in a dialog box where related commands and options are organized.

Taskbar A strip at the bottom of the screen that contains the Start button, Quick Launch toolbar, and shows which programs are running.

Text box A rectangular area in a dialog box in which you type text.

Title bar The area along the top of the window that indicates the filename and program used to create it.

Toolbar A strip with buttons that allow you to activate a command quickly.

Web page A document that contains highlighted words, phrases, and graphics that link to other documents on the Internet.

Web site A computer on the Internet that contains Web pages.

Web style A Windows 2000 setting in which you point to select items and single-click to open them. See also Internet style.

Window A rectangular frame on a screen that can contain icons, the contents of a file, or other usable data.

Windows Explorer A program that you use to manage files, folders, and shortcuts; allows you to work with more than one computer, folder, or file at once.

Windows Help An online "book" stored on your computer, complete with an index and a table of contents, that contains information about Windows 2000.

WordPad A word processing program that comes with Windows 2000.

World Wide Web Part of the Internet that consists of Web sites located on different computers around the world.

Zip disk A portable disk that can contain 100 Mb, far more than a regular floppy disk.

Zip drive A drive that can handle Zip disks.

Glossary

3-D references A reference that uses values on other sheets or workbooks, effectively creating another dimension to a workbook.

Absolute reference A cell reference that contains a dollar sign before the column letter and/or row number to indicate the absolute, or fixed, contents of specific cells. For example, the formula $A$1+$B$1 calculates only the sum of these specific cells no matter where the formula is copied in the workbook.

Active cell The current location of the cell pointer.

Address The location of a specific cell or range expressed by the coordinates of column and row; for example, A1. See *Cell address*.

Alignment The horizontal placement of cell contents; for example, left, center, or right.

Analyze To manipulate data, such as a list, with Excel or another tool.

Anchors Cells listed in a range address. For example, in the formula =SUM(A1:A15), A1 and A15 are anchors.

Apply To open a document based on an Excel template.

Area chart A line chart in which each area is given a solid color or pattern to emphasize the relationship between the pieces of charted information.

Arguments Information a function needs to create the answer. In an expression, multiple arguments are separated by commas. All of the arguments are enclosed in parentheses; for example, =IF(RATING=5, SALARY*.10,0).

Argument ToolTip A yellow box that appears as you build a function; shows function elements, which you can click to display online help for each one.

Arithmetic operator A symbol used in a formula, such as + or -, /, or *, to perform mathematical operations.

ASCII file A text file that contains data but no formatting; instead of being divided into columns, ASCII file data are separated, or delimited, by tabs or commas.

Attribute The styling features such as bold, italics, and underlining that can be applied to cell contents.

Auditing An Excel feature that helps track errors and check worksheet logic.

AutoComplete A feature that automatically completes labels entered in adjoining cells in a column.

AutoFill A feature that creates a series of text or numbers when a range is selected using the fill handle.

AutoFit A feature that automatically adjusts the width of a column to accommodate its widest entry when the boundary to the right of the column selector is double-clicked.

AutoFormat Preset layouts that can be applied to format a range or worksheet instantly. Excel comes with 16 AutoFormats that include colors, fonts, and numeric formatting.

AutoSum A button that automatically creates totals by applying the SUM function.

Background color The color applied to the background of a cell.

Backsolving A problem-solving method in which you specify a solution and then find the input value that produces the answer you want; sometimes described as a what-if analysis in reverse.

Bar chart A chart that shows information as a series of (horizontal) bars.

Border The edge of a selected area of a worksheet. Lines and color can be applied to borders.

Bug In programming, an error that causes a procedure to run incorrectly.

Cancel button The X in the formula bar; it removes information from the formula bar and restores the previous cell entry.

Cell The intersection of a column and row in a worksheet.

Cell address The unique location identified by intersecting column and row coordinates.

Cell comments Notes you've written about a workbook that appear when you place the pointer over a cell.

Cell pointer A highlighted rectangle around a cell that indicates the active cell.

Cell reference The address or name that identifies a cell's position in a worksheet; it consists of a letter that identifies the cell's column and a number that identifies its row; for example, cell B3. Cell references in worksheets can be used in formulas and are relative or absolute.

Change history A worksheet containing a list of changes made to a shared workbook.

Changing cells In what-if analysis, cells that contain the values that change in order to produce multiple sets of results.

Chart A graphic representation of information from a worksheet. Types include 2-D and 3-D column, bar, pie, area, and line charts.

Chart sheet A separate sheet that contains a chart linked to worksheet data.

Chart title The name assigned to a chart.

Chart Wizard A series of dialog boxes that helps create or modify a chart.

Check box A square box in a dialog box that can be clicked to turn an option on or off.

Circular reference A formula that refers to its own cell location.

Clear A command on the Edit menu used to erase a cell's contents, formatting, or both.

Clipboard A temporary storage area for cut or copied items that are available for pasting. See *Office Clipboard*.

Clipboard task pane A task pane that shows the contents of the Office Clipboard; contains options for copying and pasting items.

Clipboard toolbar A toolbar that shows the contents of the Office Clipboard; contains buttons for copying and pasting items to and from the Office Clipboard.

Close A command that closes the file so you can no longer work with it, but keeps Excel open so that you can continue to work on other workbooks.

Code window In the Visual Basic Editor, the window that displays the selected module's procedures, written in the Visual Basic programming language.

Column chart The default chart type in Excel that displays information as a series of (vertical) columns.

Column heading The gray box containing the letter above the column.

Column label Words at the top of a column that describe the data in that column.

Comments In a Visual Basic procedure, notes that explain the purpose of the macro or procedure; they are preceded by a single apostrophe and appear in green on a color monitor. See *cell comments.*

Complex formula An equation that uses more than one type of arithmetic operator.

Conditional format The format of a cell based on its value or the outcome of a formula.

Conditional formula A formula that makes calculations based on stated conditions, such as calculating a rebate based on a purchase amount.

Consolidate To add together values on multiple worksheets and display the result on another worksheet.

Control menu box A box in the upper-left corner of a window used to resize or close a window.

Copy A command that copies the content of selected cells and places it on the Clipboard.

Criteria Conditions that must be met when searching for files.

Criteria range A cell range containing one row of labels (usually a copy of column labels) and at least one additional row underneath it that contains the criteria you want to match.

Custom chart type A specially formatted Excel chart.

Cut A command that removes the cell contents from the selected area of a worksheet and places them on the Clipboard.

Data entry area The unlocked portion of a worksheet where users are able to enter and change data.

Data form In an Excel list (or database), a dialog box that displays one record at a time.

Data label Descriptive text that appears above a data marker in a chart.

Data marker A graphical representation of a data point, such as a bar or column.

Data point Individual piece of data plotted in a chart.

Data series The selected range in a worksheet that Excel converts into a graphic and displays as a chart.

Data table A range of cells that shows the resulting values when one or more input values are varied in a formula; when one input value is changed, the table is called a one-input data table, and when two input values are changed, it is called a two-input data table. In a chart it is a grid containing the chart data.

Database An organized collection of related information. In Excel, a database is called a list.

Debug In programming, to correct an error in code.

Declare In the Visual Basic programming language, to define a text string as a variable.

Delete A command that removes cell contents from a worksheet.

Delimiter A tab or space used in text files to separate columns of data.

Dependent cell A cell, usually containing a formula, whose value changes depending on the values in the input cells. For example, a payment formula or function that depends on an input cell containing changing interest rates is a dependent cell.

Destination program In a data exchange, the program that will receive the data.

Dialog box A window that opens when more information is needed to carry out a command.

Divide-by-zero error An Excel worksheet error that occurs when a formula attempts to divide a value by zero.

Document To make notes about basic worksheet assumptions, complex formulas, or questionable data.

Dynamic page breaks In a larger workbook, horizontal or vertical dashed lines that represent the place where pages print separately. They also adjust automatically when you insert or delete rows or columns, or change column widths or row heights.

Edit A change made to the contents of a cell or worksheet.

Electronic spreadsheet A computer program that performs calculations on data and organizes information into worksheets. A worksheet is divided into columns and rows, which form individual cells.

Embedding Inserting a copy of data into a destination document; you can double-click the embedded object to modify it using the tools of the source program.

Enter button The check mark in the formula bar used to confirm an entry.

Exploding pie slice A slice of a pie chart that has been pulled away from the whole pie to add emphasis.

Extensible Markup Language (XML) A system for defining languages using tags to structure data.

External reference indicator The exclamation point (!) used in a formula to indicate that a referenced cell is outside the active sheet.

Extract To place a copy of a filtered list in a range you specify in the Advanced Filter dialog box.

Field In a list (an Excel database), a column that describes a characteristic about records, such as first name or city.

Field name A column label that describes a field.

File properties Attributes of a file, such as author name, file size, and file type.

Fill color Cell background color.

Fill Down A command that duplicates the contents of the selected cells in the range selected below the cell pointer.

Fill handle A small square in the lower-right corner of the active cell used to copy cell contents.

Fill Right A command that duplicates the contents of the selected cells in the range selected to the right of the cell pointer.

Filter To hide data in an Excel list that does not meet specified criteria.

Find A command used to locate information the user specifies.

Floating toolbar A toolbar within its own window that is not anchored along an edge of the worksheet.

Font The typeface or design of a set of characters (letters, numbers, symbols, and punctuation marks).

Font size The size of characters, measured in units called points (pts).

Footer Information that prints at the bottom of each printed page; on screen, a footer is visible only in Print Preview. To add a footer, use the Header and Footer command on the View menu.

Format The appearance of text and numbers, including color, font, attributes, borders, and shading. See also *Number format*.

Format Painter A feature used to copy the formatting applied to one set of text or in one cell to another.

Formatting toolbar A toolbar that contains buttons for frequently used formatting commands.

Formula A set of instructions used to perform numeric calculations (adding, multiplying, averaging, etc.).

Formula bar The area below the menu bar and above the Excel workspace where you enter and edit data in a worksheet cell. The formula bar becomes active when you start typing or editing cell data. It includes the Enter button, the Cancel button, and the Insert Function button.

Formula prefix An arithmetic symbol, such as the equal sign (=), used to start a formula.

Freeze To hold in place selected columns or rows when scrolling in a worksheet that is divided in panes. See also *panes*.

Function A special, predefined formula that provides a shortcut for a commonly used calculation; for example, AVERAGE. In the Visual Basic programming language, a predefined procedure that returns a value.

Function Wizard A feature that provides assistance in entering the arguments for a selected function.

Goal cell In backsolving, a cell containing a formula in which you can substitute values to find a specific value, or goal.

Goal Seek A problem-solving method in which you specify a solution and then find the input value that produces the answer you want; sometimes described as a what-if analysis in reverse.

Gridlines Horizontal and/or vertical lines within a chart that make the chart easier to read. Also refers to the horizontal and vertical lines on a worksheet.

Header Information that prints at the top of each printed page; on screen, a header is visible only in Print Preview. To add a header, use the Header and Footer command on the View menu.

Help system A utility that gives you immediate access to definitions, steps, explanations, and useful tips.

Hide To make rows, columns, formulas, or sheets invisible to workbook users.

HTML Hypertext Markup Language, the format of pages that a Web browser such as Internet Explorer or Netscape Navigator can read.

Hyperlink An object (a filename, a word, a phrase, or a graphic) in a worksheet that, when you click it, will display another worksheet, called the target.

Hypertext Markup Language (HTML) The language used to describe the content and format of Web pages.

If...Then...Else statement In the Visual Basic programming language, a conditional statement that directs Excel to perform specified actions under certain conditions; its syntax is "If *condition* Then *statements* Else [*elsestatements*].

Input Information that produces desired results in a worksheet.

Input cells Spreadsheet cells that contain data instead of formulas and that act as input to a what-if analysis; input values often change to produce different results. Examples include interest rates, prices, or other data.

Insertion point Blinking I-beam that appears in the formula bar during entry and editing.

Interactivity A feature of a worksheet saved as an HTML document and posted to an intranet or Web site that allows users to manipulate data using their browsers.

Internet A large computer network made up of smaller networks and computers.

Intranet An internal network site used by a particular group of people who work together.

Keywords In a macro procedure, words that are recognized as part of the Visual Basic programming language.

Label Descriptive text or other information that identifies the rows and columns of a worksheet. Labels are not included in calculations.

Label prefix A character that identifies an entry as a label and controls the way it appears in the cell.

Landscape orientation A print setting that positions the worksheet on the page so the page is wider than it is tall.

Legend A key explaining how information is represented by colors or patterns in a chart.

Line chart A graph of data that is mapped by a series of lines. Line charts show changes in data or categories of data over time and can be used to document trends.

Linking The dynamic referencing of data in other workbooks, so that when data in the other workbooks is changed, the references in the current workbook are automatically updated.

List The Excel term for a database, an organized collection of related information.

Lock To secure a row, column, or sheet so that data there cannot be changed.

Logical test The first part of an IF function; if the logical test is true, then the second part of the function is applied, and if it is false, then the third part of the function is applied. In the function IF(Balance>1,000,Rate*0.05,0), the 5% rate is applied to balances over $1,000.

Macro A set of instructions, or code, that performs tasks in the order you specify.

Main procedure A procedure containing several macros that run sequentially.

Mixed reference Formula containing both a relative and an absolute reference.

Mode indicator A box located at the lower-left corner of the status bar that informs you of the program's status. For example, when Excel is performing a task, the word "Wait" appears.

Model A worksheet used to produce a what-if analysis that acts as the basis for multiple outcomes.

Module In Visual Basic, a module is stored in a workbook and contains macro procedures.

More Buttons button A button you click on a toolbar to view toolbar buttons that are not currently visible.

Mouse pointer A symbol that indicates the current location of the mouse on the desktop. The mouse pointer changes its shape at times; for example, when you insert data, select a range, position a chart, change the size of a window, or select a topic in Help.

Moving border The dashed line that appears around a cell or range that is copied to the Clipboard.

Name box The left-most area in the formula bar that shows the cell reference or name of the active cell. For example, A1 refers to cell A1 of the active worksheet. You can also get a list of names in a workbook using the Name list arrow.

Named range A range of cells given a meaningful name; it retains its name when moved and can be referenced in a formula.

Number format A format applied to values to express numeric concepts, such as currency, date, and percentage.

Object A chart or graphic image that can be moved and resized and contains handles when selected. In object linking and embedding (OLE), the data to be exchanged between another document or program.

Object In Visual Basic, every Excel element, including ranges.

Object Linking and Embedding (OLE) A Microsoft Windows technology that allows you to transfer data from one document and program to another using embedding or linking.

Office Assistant An animated character that appears to offer tips, answer questions, and provide access to the program's Help system.

Office Clipboard A temporary storage area shared by all Office programs that can be used to cut, copy, and paste multiple items within and between Office programs. The Office Clipboard can hold up to 24 items collected from any Office program. See also *Clipboard toolbar*.

One-input data table A range of cells that shows resulting values when one input value in a formula is changed.

Open A command that retrieves a workbook from a disk and displays it on the screen.

Order of precedence The order in which Excel calculates parts of a formula: (1) exponents, (2) multiplication and division, and (3) addition and subtraction.

Output The end result of a worksheet.

Page field In a PivotTable or a PivotChart report, a field area that lets you view data as if it is stacked in pages, effectively adding a third dimension to the data analysis.

Panes Sections into which you can divide a worksheet when you want to work on separate parts of the worksheet at the same time; one pane freezes, or remains in place, while you scroll in another pane until you see the desired information.

Paste A command that moves information on the Clipboard to a new location. Excel pastes the formula, rather than the result, unless the Paste Special command is used.

Paste Function A series of dialog boxes that lists and describes all Excel functions and assists the user in function creation.

Pie chart A circular chart that represents data as slices of pie. A pie chart is useful for showing the relationship of parts to a whole; pie slices can be extracted for emphasis. See also *Exploding pie slice*.

PivotChart report An Excel feature that lets you summarize worksheet data in the form of a chart in which you can rearrange, or "pivot," parts of the chart structure to explore new data relationships.

PivotTable Field List A window containing fields that can be dragged to creae or modify a PivotTable.

PivotTable list An interactive PivotTable on a Web or intranet site that lets users explore data relationships using their browsers.

PivotTable report An Excel feature that allows you to summarize worksheet data in the form of a table in which you can rearrange, or "pivot," parts of the table structure to explore new data relationships; also called a PivotTable.

PivotTable toolbar Contains buttons that allow you to manipulate data in a PivotTable.

Plot area The area of a chart that contains the chart itself, its axes, and the legend.

Point A unit of measure used for fonts and row height. One inch equals 72 points.

Pointing method Specifying formula cell references by selecting the desired cell with your mouse instead of typing its cell reference; this eliminates typing errors.

Portrait orientation A print setting that positions the worksheet on the page so the page is taller than it is wide.

Precedence Algebraic rules that Excel uses to determine the order of calculations in a formula with more than one operator.

Procedure A sequence of Visual Basic statements contained in a macro that accomplishes a specific task.

Procedure footer In Visual Basic, the last line of a Sub procedure.

Procedure header The first line in a Visual Basic procedure.

Primary Key The field in a database that contains unique information for each record.

Print Preview A command you can use to view the worksheet as it will look when printed.

Print title In a list that spans more than one page, the field names that print at the top of every printed page.

Program Task-oriented software (such as Excel or Word) that enables you to perform a certain type of task, such as data calculation or word processing.

Programs menu The Windows Start menu selection that lists all available programs on your computer.

Project In the Visual Basic Editor, the equivalent of a workbook; a project contains Visual Basic modules.

Project Explorer In the Visual Basic Editor, a window that lists all open projects (or workbooks) and the worksheets and modules they contain.

Property In Visual Basic, an attribute of an object that describes its character or behavior.

Properties window In the Visual Basic Editor, the window that displays a list of characteristics, or properties, associated with a module.

Range A selected group of adjacent cells.

Range format A format applied to a selected range in a worksheet.

Range object In Visual Basic, an object that represents a cell or a range of cells.

Record In a list (an Excel database), data about an object or a person.

Refresh To update a PivotTable so it reflects changes to the underlying data.

Relative cell reference A type of cell reference used to indicate a relative position in the worksheet. It allows you to copy and move formulas from one area to another of the same dimensions. Excel automatically changes the column and row numbers to reflect the new position.

Replace A command used to find one set of criteria and replace it with new information.

Reset usage data An option that returns personalized toolbars and menus to their default settings.

Retrieve An action of the Autofilter to search for and list records.

Route To send an e-mail attachment sequentially to each user in a list, who then forwards it to the next user on the list.

Routing slip A list of e-mail users who are to receive an e-mail attachment.

Row height The vertical dimension of a cell.

Row heading The gray box containing the number to the left of the row.

Row label Words at the left of a row that describe the data in that row.

Save A command used to permanently store your workbook and any changes you make to a file on a disk. The first time you save a workbook you must give it a filename.

Save As A command used to create a duplicate of the current workbook with a new filename. Used the first time you save a workbook.

Scenario A set of values you use to forecast results; the Excel Scenario Manager lets you store different scenarios.

Scenario summary An Excel table that compiles data from various scenarios so that you can view the scenario results next to each other for easy comparison.

Search criterion The specification for data that you want to find in an Excel list, such as "Brisbane" or "is greater than 1000."

Selection handles Small boxes appearing along the corners and sides of charts and graphic images that are used for moving and resizing.

Series of labels Pre-programmed series, such as days of the week and months of the year. They are formed by typing the first word of the series, then dragging the fill handle to the desired cell.

Shared workbook An Excel workbook that several users can open and modify.

Sheet Another term used for a *worksheet*.

Sheet tab A description at the bottom of each worksheet that identifies it in a workbook. In an open workbook, move to a worksheet by clicking its sheet tab. Also known as *Worksheet tab*.

Sheet tab scrolling buttons Buttons that enable you to move among sheets within a workbook.

Sizing handles Another name for selection handles.

Sort keys Criteria on which a sort, or a reordering of data, is based.

Source list The list on which a PivotTable is based.

Source program In a data exchange, the program used to create the data you are embedding or linking.

Spell check A command that attempts to match all text in a worksheet with the words in the dictionary and then flags words that don't match as possible errors.

Standard chart type A commonly used column, bar, pie, or area chart in the Excel program; each type has several variations. For example, a column chart variation is the Columns with Depth.

Start To open a software program so you can use it.

Statement In Visual Basic, a line of code.

Status bar The bar at the bottom of the Excel window that provides information about various keys, commands, and processes.

Sub procedure A series of Visual Basic statements that perform an action but do not return a value.

Summary function In a PivotTable, a function that determines the type of calculation applied to the PivotTable data, such as SUM or COUNT.

Syntax In the Visual Basic programming language, the formatting rules that must be followed so that the macro will run correctly.

Table In an Access database, a list of data. In Excel, a special list containing worksheet data that can be searched using Excel features.

Target The location that a hyperlink displays after you click it.

Target cell In what-if analysis (specifically, in Excel Solver), the cell containing the formula.

Task pane A window on the right side of the Excel screen that lets you access templates, search for and open files, insert clip art, and copy items to the clipboard.

Template A workbook containing text, formulas, macros, and formatting you use repeatedly; when you create a new document, you can open a document based on the template workbook. The new document will automatically contain the formatting, text, formulas, and macros in the template.

Text annotations Labels added to a chart to draw attention to a particular area.

Text color The color applied to the text within a cell.

Tick marks Notations of a scale of measure on a chart axis.

Title bar The bar at the top of the window that indicates the program name and the name of the current worksheet.

Toggle button A button that turns a feature on and off.

Toolbar A bar that contains buttons that give you quick access to the most frequently used commands.

Tracers In Excel worksheet auditing, arrows that point from cells that might have caused an error to the active cell containing an error.

Track To identify and keep a record of who makes which changes to a workbook.

Truncate To shorten the display of cell contents.

Two-input data table A range of cells that shows resulting values when two input values in a formula are changed.

Type a question for help box The list box at the right end of the menu bar where you can type or select questions for the Help system.

Uniform Resource Locator (URL) A unique address for a location on the World Wide Web; www.course.com is an example.

Values Numbers, formulas, or functions used in calculations.

Variable In the Visual Basic programming language, a slot in memory in which you can temporarily store an item of information; variables are often declared in Dim statements such as *DimNameAsString*.

View A set of display or print settings that you can name and save for access at another time. You can save multiple views of a worksheet.

Visual Basic for Applications (VBA) A programming language used to create macros in Excel.

Web query An Excel feature that lets you obtain data from a Web, Internet, or intranet site and places it in an Excel workbook for analysis.

What-if analysis A decision-making feature in which data is changed and automatically recalculated.

Wildcard A special symbol you use in defining search criteria in the data form or Replace dialog box. The most common types of wildcards are the question mark (?), which stands for any single character, and the asterisk (*), which represents any group of characters.

Window A rectangular area of a screen where you view and work on a worksheet.

Workbook A collection of related worksheets contained within a single file.

Worksheet An electronic spreadsheet containing 256 columns by 65,536 rows.

Worksheet tab See *Sheet tab*.

Worksheet window The worksheet area in which data is entered.

World Wide Web A structure of documents, called pages, connected over a large computer network called the Internet.

X-axis The horizontal line in a chart.

X-axis label A label describing the x-axis of a chart.

XML (Extensible Markup Language) A system for defining languages using tags to structure data.

XML Parser A tool for reading XML documents.

Y-axis The vertical line in a chart.

Y-axis label A label describing the y-axis of a chart.

Zoom A feature that enables you to focus on a larger or smaller part of the worksheet in Print Preview.

Index

Index

▶D

▶E

▶F

Index

Index

Index